Lecture Notes in Computer Science 5036

Commenced Publication in 1973
Founding and Former Series Editors:
Gerhard Goos, Juris Hartmanis, and Jan van Leeuwen

Editorial Board

David Hutchison
 Lancaster University, UK
Takeo Kanade
 Carnegie Mellon University, Pittsburgh, PA, USA
Josef Kittler
 University of Surrey, Guildford, UK
Jon M. Kleinberg
 Cornell University, Ithaca, NY, USA
Alfred Kobsa
 University of California, Irvine, CA, USA
Friedemann Mattern
 ETH Zurich, Switzerland
John C. Mitchell
 Stanford University, CA, USA
Moni Naor
 Weizmann Institute of Science, Rehovot, Israel
Oscar Nierstrasz
 University of Bern, Switzerland
C. Pandu Rangan
 Indian Institute of Technology, Madras, India
Bernhard Steffen
 University of Dortmund, Germany
Madhu Sudan
 Massachusetts Institute of Technology, MA, USA
Demetri Terzopoulos
 University of California, Los Angeles, CA, USA
Doug Tygar
 University of California, Berkeley, CA, USA
Gerhard Weikum
 Max-Planck Institute of Computer Science, Saarbruecken, Germany

Song Wu Laurence T. Yang Tony Li Xu (Eds.)

Advances in Grid and Pervasive Computing

Third International Conference, GPC 2008
Kunming, China, May 25-28, 2008
Proceedings

Springer

Volume Editors

Song Wu
Huazhong University of Science and Technology
School of Computer Science
Wuhan, Hubei, China, 430074
E-mail:wusong@hust.edu.cn

Laurence T. Yang
Tony Li Xu
St. Francis Xavier University
Department of Computer Science
Antigonish, NS, B2G 2W5, Canada
E-mail: {ltyang,txu}@stfx.ca

Library of Congress Control Number: 2008926600

CR Subject Classification (1998): F.1, F.2, D.1, D.2, D.4, C.2, C.4, H.4, K.6

LNCS Sublibrary: SL 1 – Theoretical Computer Science and General Issues

ISSN   0302-9743
ISBN-10   3-540-68081-0 Springer Berlin Heidelberg New York
ISBN-13   978-3-540-68081-9 Springer Berlin Heidelberg New York

This work is subject to copyright. All rights are reserved, whether the whole or part of the material is concerned, specifically the rights of translation, reprinting, re-use of illustrations, recitation, broadcasting, reproduction on microfilms or in any other way, and storage in data banks. Duplication of this publication or parts thereof is permitted only under the provisions of the German Copyright Law of September 9, 1965, in its current version, and permission for use must always be obtained from Springer. Violations are liable to prosecution under the German Copyright Law.

Springer is a part of Springer Science+Business Media

springer.com

© Springer-Verlag Berlin Heidelberg 2008
Printed in Germany

Typesetting: Camera-ready by author, data conversion by Scientific Publishing Services, Chennai, India
Printed on acid-free paper   SPIN: 12270415   06/3180   5 4 3 2 1 0

Preface

Welcome to the proceedings of the 2008 International Conference on Grid and Pervasive Computing (GPC 2008) which was held in Kunming, Yunnan, China, May 25–28, 2008.

Grid computing presents a new trend in distributed computing for coordinating large-scale heterogeneous resource sharing and problem solving in dynamic, multi-institutional virtual organizations. Grid computing not only can be used for distributed supercomputing massive data processing, but can also be a common platform and way for utility and service computing. It covers mainframes or supercomputers as well as more powerful personal computers and even small and smart devices, ranging from personal digital assistants to unseen chips in our cars, appliances and telephones. Projecting this trend into the future, we envision an explosion of interconnected high-performance computers and smart devices that can make our research and daily lives easier and more productive. Grid and Pervasive Computing (GPC) is an annual international conference on the emerging areas of merging grid computing and pervasive computing. GPC provides a high-profile, leading-edge forum for researchers and engineers alike to present their latest research in the field of grid computing and pervasive computing.

This year there were 184 paper submissions from all across the world. All the papers were reviewed by at least two referees from the conference's Technical Program Committee or by external reviewers. In order to allocate as many papers as possible and keep the high quality of the conference, we finally decided to accept 45 papers, representing an acceptance rate of 24%. We believe that all of these papers and topics not only provided novel ideas, new results, work in progress and state-of-the-art techniques in this field, but also stimulated future research activities in the area of grid and pervasive computing. This conference was a result of the hard work of very many people such as external reviewers, Program and Technical Committee members. We would like to express our sincere thanks to everyone involved. Ultimately, however, the success of the conference will be judged by how well the delegates participated, learnt, interacted and established contacts with other researchers. The committees provided the venue and created the environment to allow these objectives to be achieved, ensuring that the conference was an outstanding success.

March 2008

Song Wu
Laurence T. Yang
Tony Li Xu

Organization

GPC 2008 was organized by Huazhong University of Science and Technology (HUST) and Yunnan University. It was held in cooperation with the IEEE Computer Society, and *Lecture Notes in Computer Science (LNCS)* of Springer.

Executive Committee

Steering Chairs	Hai Jin, Huazhong University of Science and Technology, China
Steering Members	Christophe Cérin, University of Paris XIII, France
	Sajal K. Das, University of Texas at Arlington, USA
	Jean-Luc Gaudiot, The University of California - Irvine, USA
	Kuan-Ching Li, Providence University, Taiwan
	Cho-Li Wang, University of Hong Kong, China
	Chao-Tung Yang, Tunghai University, Taiwan
	Albert Y. Zomaya, University of Sydney, Australia
General Chairs	Ian Foster, University of Chicago, USA
	Lionel Ni, Hong Kong University of Science and Technology, China
Program Chairs	Laurence T. Yang, St. Francis Xavier University, Canada
	Song Wu, Huazhong University of Science and Technology, China
Workshop Chairs	Ching-Hsien Hsu, Chung Hua University, Taiwan
	Deqin Zou, Huazhong University of Science and Technology, China
Publicity Chairs	Rodrigo F. de Mello, University of Sao Paulo, Brazil
	Wenbin Jiang, Huazhong University of Science and Technology, China

Publication Chair	Tony Li Xu, St. Francis Xavier University, Canada
Finance and Registration Chair	Xia Xie, Huazhong University of Science and Technology, China
Web Chair	Ke Fan, Huazhong University of Science and Technology, China
Local Chair	Hao Li, Yunnan University, China

Program Committee

Jemal Abawajy	Deakin University, Australia
Nabil Abdennadher	University of Applied Sciences, Switzerland
Mark Baker	University of Reading, UK
Ken Barker	University of Calgary, Canada
Jiannong Cao	Hong Kong Polytechnic University, China
Jerry Hsi-Ya Chang	NCHC, Taiwan
Ruay-Shiung Chang	National Dong Hwa University, Taiwan
Wenguang Chen	Tsinghua University, China
Xiaowu Chen	Beihang University, China
Yeh-Ching Chung	National Tsing Hua University, Taiwan
Toni Cortes	Universitat Politecnica de Catalunya, Spain
Mieso Denko	University of Guelph, Canada
Luiz DeRose	Cray Research, USA
Rudolf Eigenmann	Purdue University, USA
Ke Fan	Huazhong University of Science and Technology, China
Noria Foukia	University of Otago, New Zealand
Wolfgang Gentzsch	Microelectronics Center of North Carolina, USA
Dan Grigoras	University College Cork, Ireland
Xiangjian He	University of Technology Sydney, Australia
Xubin He	Tennessee Technological University, USA
Michael Hobbs	Deakin University, Australia
Hung-Chang Hsiao	National Cheng Kung University, Taiwan
Hui-Huang Hsu	Tamkang University, Taiwan
Bin Hu	Birmingham City University, UK
Kuo-Chan Huang	National Taichung University, Taiwan
Sajid Hussain	Acadia University, Canada
Mohamed Jemni	ESSTT, Tunisia
Stephen Jenks	University of California, USA
Young-Sik Jeong	Wonkwang University, Korea
Weijia Jia	City University of Hong Kong, China
Hai Jiang	Arkansas State University, USA

Wenbin Jiang	Huazhong University of Science and Technology, China
Hai Jin	Huazhong University of Science and Technology, China
Yong-Kee Jun	Gyeongsang National University, Korea
Daniel S. Katz	Louisiana State University, USA
Moon J. Kim	IBM, USA
Domenico Laforenza	CNR, Italy
Francis C.M. Lau	University of Hong Kong, China
Jenq Kuen Lee	National Tsing Hua University, Taiwan
Ruilin Li	Huazhong University of Science and Technology, China
Ming-Lu Li	Shanghai Jiao Tong University, China
Damon Shing-Min Liu	National Chung Chen University, Taiwan
Hai Liu	University of Ottawa, Canada
Pangfeng Liu	National Taiwan University, Taiwan
Victor Malyshkin	Russian Academy of Sciences, Russia
Beniamino Di Martino	Second University of Naples, Italy
Pedro Medeiros	New University of Lisbon, Portugal
Rodrigo F. de Mello	University of Sao Paulo, Brazil
Dan Meng	Institute of Computing Technology, CAS, China
Philippe Navaux	Federal University of Rio Grande do Sul, Brazil
Daniel Olmedilla	Hannover University, Germany
Mohamed Ould-Khaoua	University of Glasgow, UK
Jong Hyuk Park	Kyungnam University, Korea
Jean-Louis Pazat	IRISA, France
Cynthia A. Phillips	Sandia National Laboratories, USA
Wasim Raad	King Fahd University of Petroleum and Minerals, Saudi Arabia
Omer F. Rana	Cardiff University, UK
Sanjay Ranka	University of Florida, USA
Won-Woo Ro	Yonsei University, Korea
David De Roure	University of Southampton, UK
Masoud Sadjadi	Florida International University, USA
Mitsuhisa Sato	Tsukuba University, Japan
Xuanhua Shi	Huazhong University of Science and Technology, China
Pradip K. Srimani	Clemson University, USA
Ruppa K. Thulasiram	University of Manitoba, Canada
Chien-Min Wang	Academia Sinica, Taiwan
Cho-Li Wang	University of Hong Kong, China
Xingang Wang	University of Plymouth, UK
Song Wu	Huazhong University of Science and Technology, China
Jan-Jan Wu	Academia Sinica, Taiwan

Nong Xiao   National University of Defense Technology, China
Naixue Xiong   Japan Advanced Institute of Science and Technology, Japan
Tony Li Xu   St. Francis Xavier University, Canada
Jingling Xue   University of New South Wales, Australia
Laurence T. Yang   St. Francis Xavier University, Canada
Chao-Tung Yang   Tunghai University, Taiwan
Shaowen Yao   Yunnan University, China
Zhiwen Yu   Kyoto University, Japan
Sherali Zeadally   University of the District of Columbia, USA
Xuejie Zhang   Yunnan University, China
Yuezhi Zhou   Tsinghua University, China
Yanmin Zhu   Imperial College London, UK

Additional Reviewers

Hsi-Ya Chang
Patrizio Dazzi
Ahmed Eleuch
Adel Essafi
Hazem Fkaier
Henrique Freitas
Dan Grigoras
Selim Kalayci

Moon Kim
Nicolas Maillard
Juan Martinez
Franco Maria Nardini
Antonio Panciatici
Monica Py
Rodrigo Righi
Khalid Saleem

Roberto Souto
Hailong Sun
Gabriele Tolomei
Nicola Tonellotto
Gianni Valenti
David Villegas
Zhiyong Yu

Table of Contents

Keynote Speeches (Abstracts)

Massively Distributed Systems: From Grids and P2P to Clouds 1
  Kai Hwang

Building Distributed, Wide-Area Applications with WheelFS 2
  M. Frans Kaashoek

Virtualization Technology: Past, Present, and Future 3
  Wen-Hann Wang

Track 1: Cluster Computing

Domino-Effect Free Crash Recovery for Concurrent Failures in Cluster
Federation 4
  Bidyut Gupta, Shahram Rahimi, Vineel Allam, and Vamshi Jupally

Tidset-Based Parallel FP-tree Algorithm for the Frequent Pattern
Mining Problem on PC Clusters 18
  Jiayi Zhou and Kun-Ming Yu

Optimizing Communications of Data Parallel Programs in Scalable
Cluster Systems 29
  Chun-Ching Wang, Shih-Chang Chen, Ching-Hsien Hsu, and Chao-Tung Yang

Track 2: Grid Computing

The Development of a Drug Discovery Virtual Screening Application
on Taiwan Unigrid 38
  Li-Yung Ho, Pangfeng Liu, Chien-Min Wang, and Jan-Jan Wu

PGWFT: A Petri Net Based Grid Workflow Verification and
Optimization Toolkit 48
  Haijun Cao, Hai Jin, Song Wu, and Yongcai Tao

A Probability-Based Framework for Dynamic Resource Scheduling in
Grid Environment... 59
  San-Yih Hwang, Jian Tang, and Hong-Yang Lin

A Mobile Agent-Based Statistic Execution Model for Grid
Computing 71
  Wenyu Qu, Keqiu Li, and Yong Zhang

An Optimization of Resource Replication Access in Grid Cache 83
Fangai Liu and Fenglong Song

ADVE: Adaptive and Dependable Virtual Environments for Grid
Computing 93
Xuanhua Shi, Hai Jin, Wei Zhu, and Li Qi

An Incentive Approach for Computational Resource Sharing in the
Autonomous Environment 104
Chuliang Weng, Minglu Li, and Xinda Lu

Using Moldability to Improve Scheduling Performance of Parallel Jobs
on Computational Grid 116
Kuo-Chan Huang, Po-Chi Shih, and Yeh-Ching Chung

A Fuzzy Grid-QoS Framework for Obtaining Higher Grid Resources
Availability 128
David Allenotor and Ruppa K. Thulasiram

Guarantee the Victorious Probability of Grid Resources in the
Competition for Finite Tasks 140
Lei Yao, Guanzhong Dai, Huixiang Zhang, and Shuai Ren

Co-allocation in Data Grids: A Global, Multi-User Perspective 152
Adam H. Villa and Elizabeth Varki

Scheduling for Atomic Broadcast Operation in Heterogeneous Networks
with One Port Model 166
Ching-Hsien Hsu, Tai-Lung Chen, Bing-Ru Tsai, and Kuan-Ching Li

A Resource Discovery Algorithm with Probe Feedback Mechanism in
Multi-domain Grid Environment 178
*Libing Wu, Yanxiang He, Jianqun Cui, Simeng Wang,
Laurence T. Yang, and Naixue Xiong*

Middleware Integration and Deployment Strategies for
Cyberinfrastructures 187
*Sebastien Goasguen, Krishna Madhavan, David Wolinsky,
Renato Figueiredo, Jaime Frey, Alain Roy, Paul Ruth, and
Dongyan Xu*

A Multi-site Resource Allocation Strategy in Computational Grids 199
Chao-Tung Yang and Sung-Yi Chen

Track 3: High Performance Computing

A Clustering Model for Multicast on Hypercube Network 211
Song Lu and XiaoDong Yang

Performance Evaluation of End-to-End Path Capacity Measurement
Tools in a Controlled Environment 222
  Wenwei Li, Bin Zeng, Dafang Zhang, and Jinmin Yang

Protein Sequence Motif Discovery on Distributed Supercomputer 232
  Santan Challa and Parimala Thulasiraman

Parallel and Distributed Particle Collision Simulation with
Decentralized Control 244
  Ruipeng Li, Hai Jiang, Hung-Chi Su, Bin Zhang, and Jeff Jenness

Track 4: Network Storage

Modeling and Simulation of Self-similar Storage I/O 256
  Zhaobin Liu, Bo Jiang, Zixiang Zhao, and Yunhan Jiang

PCOW: Pipelining-Based COW Snapshot Method to Decrease First
Write Penalty 266
  Zhikun Wang, Dan Feng, Ke Zhou, and Fang Wang

A Component-Based Analytical Performance Model of IP-Based
SAN 275
  Min Wang, Wei Xu, and Lu Xu

Track 5: Peer-to-Peer Computing

QCast: A QoS-Aware Peer-to-Peer Streaming System with DHT-Based
Multicast 287
  Zhinuan Cai and Xiaola Lin

A Construction of Peer-to-Peer Streaming System Based on Flexible
Locality-Aware Overlay Networks 296
  Chih-Han Lai, Yu-Wei Chan, and Yeh-Ching Chung

Managing Data for Evaluating Trust in Unstructured Peer-to-Peer
Networks 308
  Zhitang Li, Huaiqing Lin, Chuiwei Lu, and Yejiang Zhang

A Gossip-Based Protocol to Reach Consensus Via Uninorm Aggregation
Operator 319
  Qiaoli Huang, Shiqun Yin, and Zhixing Huang

HilbertChord: A P2P Framework for Service Resources Management ... 331
  Derong Shen, Yichuan Shao, Tiezheng Nie, Yue Kou,
  Zhenhua Wang, and Ge Yu

A Peer-to-Peer Assisting Scheme for Live Streaming Services 343
  Jian Wan, Liangjin Lu, Xianghua Xu, and Xueping Ren

A Novel Ownership Scheme to Maintain Web Content Consistency 352
    Chi-Hung Chi, Choon-Keng Chua, and Weihong Song

Together: A Hybrid Overlay for Application-Layer Multicast in
Heterogeneous Environment 364
    Zuo Ke, Dong-min Hu, Huai-min Wang, and Quan-yuan Wu

Track 6: Pervasive Computing

Node Placement of Linear Wireless Multimedia Sensor Networks for
Maximum Network Lifetime 373
    Ming Cao, Laurence T. Yang, Xinmeng Chen, and Naixue Xiong

The Weighted Shortest Path Search in Mobile GIS Services 384
    Min Peng, Naixue Xiong, Gang Xie, and Laurence T. Yang

On Maximizing the Throughput of Convergecast in Wireless Sensor
Networks 396
    Nai-Luen Lai, Chung-Ta King, and Chun-Han Lin

A Self-organizing Communication Architecture for ZigBee 409
    Seong Hoon Kim, Jeong Seok Kang, and Hong Seong Park

Track 7: Semantic Web and Semantic Grid

A Semantic Service Matching Middleware for Mobile Devices
Discovering Grid Services 422
    Tao Guan, Ed Zaluska, and David De Roure

A Pragmatic Approach for the Semantic Description and Matching of
Pervasive Resources 434
    *Ayomi Bandara, Terry Payne, David De Roure,
    Nicholas Gibbins, and Tim Lewis*

An Efficient Method to Measure the Semantic Similarity of
Ontologies 447
    James Z. Wang, Farha Ali, and Pradip K. Srimani

A Dynamic Awareness Model for Service-Based Collaborative Grid
Application in Access Grid 459
    Xiaowu Chen, Xiangyu Ji, and Qinping Zhao

Track 8: Service-Oriented Computing

A Suggested Framework for Exploring Contextual Information to
Evaluate and Recommend Services 471
    Hao Wu, Fei Luo, Xiaomin Ning, and Hai Jin

A Model of Service Scheduling Based on Market Mechanism and
Semantic.. 483
   Gang Wang, Yuhui Qiu, and Guolin Pu

Flexible and Semantics-Based Support for Web Services Transaction
Protocols 492
   Trieu Minh, Nhut Le, and Jinli Cao

EX_QoS Driven Approach for Finding Replacement Services in
Distributed Service Composition 504
   Lei Yang, Yu Dai, and Bin Zhang

Author Index 517

Massively Distributed Systems : From Grids and P2P to Clouds

Kai Hwang

University of Southern California, Los Angeles

Abstract. This keynote describes the evolution of massively distributed computing systems and their key techniques. Clusters of computers now prevail, expand, and become the core components in large-scale computational/ information/data Grids. The Open Grid Service Architecture, specifying the Grid software, protocol, and service standards, are only partially implemented in Globus and other Grid toolkits. Grid security demand globalization among various PKI authorities and interoperability between wired and wireless networks. Very little progress being made in special networks, hardware, languages, and operating systems for Grid/Cloud computing. Business Grids/ Clouds are under development by Google, IBM, Sun, Microsoft, etc., and widespread acceptance is hindered by selfish behavior and security concerns. Briefly, the keynote includes rise and fall of computing technologies and hot paradigms in the last 35 Years, and presents the implication that computing clouds over the Internet will be the next battlefield among competitors.

Building Distributed, Wide-Area Applications with WheelFS

M. Frans Kaashoek

Massachusetts Institute of Technology, Massachusetts

Abstract. It is a challenge to build applications that need to share data and are distributed across hundreds or thousands of computers in a wide-area network (e.g., PlanetLab or on a Grid). In order to cope with high latency, throughput bottlenecks, and temporary failures, such applications typically implement their own storage plan or use special-purpose storage solutions (e.g., DISC, Globus, Carbonite, etc.). Inspired by the success of the Google File System for cluster applications, this proposal investigates whether a general-purpose wide-area file system could simplify building distributed applications. In particular, this talk presents a preliminary design, called WheelFS. WheelFS's goal is to ease the development of distributed applications such as cooperative Web caches, data-intensive Grid applications, and PlanetLab measurements, perhaps reducing the storage management code to a simple script around the application's core logic. Towards this goal, WheelFS adopts many features from existing file systems, and adds two new ones: semantic cues, and write-locally-read-globally. This talk will also discuss several specific applications that can potentially benefit from using WheelFS.

Joint work with: Jeremy Stribling (MIT), Emil Sit (MIT), Jinyang Li (NYU), and Robert Morris (MIT).

Virtualization Technology: Past, Present, and Future

Wen-Hann Wang

Software and Solutions Group
Intel Asia-Pacific Research and Development Ltd.
Software and Solutions and Product Development, China

Abstract. Effective sharing and utilization of machine resources have been an active research area since the early days of computing. Virtualization technology was a popular way toward effective resource sharing some four decades ago. It was later replaced by time-sharing systems which incur lower computing overhead. Recent advances in computing platform performance brought virtualization technology back to the main stage. Furthermore, innovations in architecture support for virtualization made many exciting usage models possible. In this presentation I will examine what the field had accomplished in the past. I will then briefly review the wide array of current virtualization technologies and how they are being deployed. I will conclude by projecting where future virtualization technologies might take us.

Domino-Effect Free Crash Recovery for Concurrent Failures in Cluster Federation

Bidyut Gupta, Shahram Rahimi, Vineel Allam, and Vamshi Jupally

Computer Science Department
Southern Illinois University
Carbondale, IL 62901 USA
{bidyut,rahimi,vallam,vjupally}@cs.siu.edu

Abstract. In this paper, we have addressed the complex problem of recovery for concurrent failures in cluster computing environment. We have proposed a new approach in which we have dealt with both inter cluster orphan and lost messages unlike the existing works. The proposed recovery approach is free from the domino-effect and hence guarantees the least amount of re-computation after recovery. Besides, a process needs to save only its recent local checkpoint, which is also the case for a cluster. So number of trips to stable storage per process is always one during recovery. The proposed common check pointing interval is such that it enables a process to log the minimum number of messages it has sent. These features make our approach superior to the existing works.

1 Introduction

Cluster federation is a union of clusters, where each cluster contains a certain number of processes. Cluster computing environments have provided a cost-effective solution to many distributed computing problems by investing inexpensive hardware [1], [2], [9]. With the growing importance of cluster computing, its fault-tolerant aspect deserves significant attention. It is known that checkpointing and rollback recovery are widely used techniques that allows a system to progress in spite of a failure [4]-[8], [10]-[12].

In cluster computing, considering the characteristics of cluster federation architecture, different checkpointing mechanisms may be used within and between clusters. For example, a cluster may employ either coordinated checkpointing scheme or independent (asynchronous) checkpointing scheme for its processes to take their local checkpoints. Note that in cluster computing failure of a cluster means failure of its one or more processes. It is the responsibility of each cluster to determine its consistent local checkpoint set that consists of one checkpoint from each process present in it. Note that in such a consistent set, there does not exist any orphan message between any pair of the checkpoints of the set [1],[2],[4],[5]. But this consistent local checkpoint set, also known as cluster level checkpoint (CLC) of the cluster, may not be consistent with the other clusters' consistent local checkpoint sets, because clusters interact through messages (inter cluster messages) which result in dependencies between the clusters. Therefore, a collection of consistent local checkpoint sets, one from each cluster in the cluster federation, does not necessarily produce a consistent federation level checkpoint (also known as federation level recovery line). Consequently, rollback of one failed cluster may force some other clusters to rollback in order to maintain consistency of operation by the cluster federation. In the worst case, consistency requirement may force the system to rollback to the initial state of the system, losing all the work performed before a failure. This uncontrolled propagation of rollback is known as domino-effect [10]. Thus, there is a need to have a second level of checkpointing so that after recovery from a failure the individual clusters in the federation can restart their computation from their respective cluster level checkpoints, which are all mutually consistent with each other. All such mutually consistent checkpoints form a recovery line for the cluster federation.

The above discussion is all about determining a recovery line such that there is no orphan message in the cluster federation [1], [2], [13]. In this work we consider recovery in cluster federation which, in addition to the inter cluster orphan messages, will also take care of any inter cluster lost and delayed messages.

Before we go further, we have stated briefly what we mean by the above mentioned three kinds of messages and why we need to consider these messages. In this paper unless otherwise mentioned, by 'a cluster C^i sends a message m to cluster C^j', we mean that some process in cluster C^i sends a message m to some process in cluster C^j. Similarly, by 'a cluster C^i receives a message m from Cluster C^j', we mean that some process in cluster C^i receives a message m from some process in cluster C^j. Also the mth cluster level checkpoint of the ith cluster C^i is denoted as CLC^i_m. It also means that the mth local checkpoints of all processes of cluster C^i form the mth cluster level checkpoint CLC^i_m of cluster C^i.

We now explain the effect of the three kinds of the messages using a simple example of a cluster federation that consists of only two clusters. Consider Fig. 1 (a). Now we observe that Cluster C^1 after taking its cluster level checkpoint CLC^1_1 sends an inter cluster message m to cluster C^2. The receiving process in C^2 processes the message and then takes its local checkpoint that belongs to CLC^2_1 and continues. Now assume that a failure f has occurred at cluster C^1. After the system recovers from the failure, assume that processes in both C^1 and C^2 will restart from their respective local checkpoints belonging to CLC^1_1 and CLC^2_1. However, the sender of the message m in C^1 will resend the message m again since it did not have the chance to record the sending event of the message. Thus some process in cluster C^2 will receive it again and process it again, even though it did process it once before it took its checkpoint belonging to CLC^2_1. This duplicate processing of the message will result in wrong computation. This message is called an orphan because the receiving event of the message is recorded by the receiving process in its recent local checkpoint belonging to CLC^2_1, where as the sending event is not recorded. Unless proper care is taken, if the processes / clusters indeed restart from these two checkpoints, the distributed application will result in wrong computation due to the presence of the orphan message.

Now consider Fig. 1(b). Assume that after recovery the clusters restart from their respective checkpoints CLC^1_1 and CLC^2_1. That is, processes in the clusters C^1 and C^2 restart from their respective local checkpoints that form the cluster level checkpoints

CLC^1_1 and CLC^2_1. Note that the sending event of the message m has already been recorded by the sending process in its recent local checkpoint belonging to CLC^1_1 and so C^1 will not resend it, because it knows that it has already sent the message to C^2. However, the receiving event of the message m has not been recorded by C^2, since it occurred after C^2 took its checkpoint. As a result, C^2 will not get the message again, even though for correct operation it needs the message. In this situation message m is called a lost message. Therefore, for correct operation any such inter cluster lost message needs to be logged and resent when the system restarts after recovery.

Next consider Fig. 1(c). It is seen that because of some reason the message m has been delayed and C^2 did not even receive it before the failure occurred. Now as in the case of the lost message, if the clusters restart from their respective checkpoints as shown, cluster C^1 will not resend it and as a result, cluster C^2 will not get the message again, even though for correct operation it needs the message. In this situation message m is called a delayed message. Therefore, for correct operation any such inter cluster delayed message needs to be logged and resent when the system restarts after recovery.

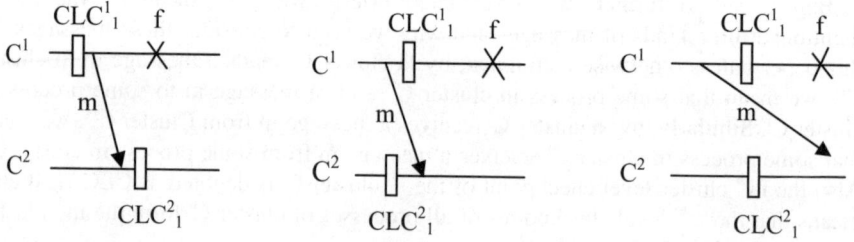

Fig. 1(a). Orphan message   **Fig. 1(b).** Lost message   **Fig. 1(c).** Delayed message

Problem formulation: In this work we address the following problem: given the recent consistent local checkpoint set of each cluster (i.e. a CLC per cluster) in an n cluster system, after the system recovers from failures how to handle properly any inter cluster orphan, lost, or delayed message so that all clusters (and hence all processes belonging to all clusters) can restart from their respective recent (latest) cluster level checkpoints. In other words, it means that recovery will be domino-effect free and there is no need to have a second level of check pointing algorithm unlike some existing works [2], [13] to determine a consistent federation level checkpoint. Finally, we handle concurrent cluster failures, i.e. when two or more clusters fail concurrently. Note that the existing works have considered only single failures.

To fulfill our objective, we assume that in each cluster, cluster level checkpoints are taken following the scheme proposed in [3], because in that scheme there does not exist any orphan message between any pair of the recent local checkpoints belonging to a cluster level checkpoint of any cluster. We also assume that the value of the common check pointing interval, say T is same for all clusters and is just larger than the maximum message passing time between any two processes of the cluster federation. The reason for choosing such a value for T has been stated in Section 2.3.

One important feature of our approach is that the recent cluster level checkpoints may not be consistent from the viewpoint of the existence of inter cluster orphan messages unlike the existing works; but we have tackled this problem easily by just defining process behavior as mentioned in Sections 3.2 and 3.3.

In this context, it may be noted that even though our main focus in this work is on inter cluster lost, delayed, and orphan messages, still our proposed idea can easily be extended to handle intra cluster lost and delayed messages. We have briefly stated in Section 4.3 how it can be done.

2 Relevant Data Structures and System Model

2.1 System Model

The distributed system has the following characteristics [4], [14], [15]:

1. Processes do not share memory and they communicate via messages sent through channels.
2. Channels can lose messages. However, they are made effectively lossless and order of the messages is preserved by some end-to-end transmission protocol.
3. Processes are deterministic.
4. Processors are fail stop. When a process fails, all other processes are notified of the failure in finite time. We also assume that no further processor (process) failures occur during the execution of the recovery algorithm. The algorithm is restarted if there are further failures.

2.2 Relevant Data Structures

Before we state the relevant data structures and their use in our proposed algorithm we need to define the following. The ith cluster level checkpoint (CLC) of a cluster is defined as a set of the ith local checkpoints, one from each process belonging to the cluster. The set of the events occurring between two consecutive cluster level checkpoints of a cluster is termed a checkpoint interval. A message between clusters is termed as inter cluster application message and a message between processes of the same cluster is termed as intra cluster message. The ith federation level checkpoint (i.e. a federation level recovery line) is a set of the ith CLCs, one from each cluster.

Let the cluster federation under consideration consist of n clusters, where each cluster consists of a number of processes. We denote the ith cluster as C^i. For cluster C^i consisting of r processes, its mth cluster level checkpoint is represented as $CLC^i_m = \{c^1_m, c^2_m, ..., c^j_m, ..., c^r_m\}$, where c^j_m is the mth local checkpoint taken by process p_j of cluster C^i.

We assume that each application message is piggybacked with the sender id and a sequence number assigned by the sender. If the message is intra cluster, the sender is just a process in the same cluster. Otherwise the sender is a process in a different cluster. These sequence numbers are used to preserve the order of the messages when a receiving process takes action on these messages.

Each process p_i in a cluster C^k maintains two vectors at its xth local checkpoint c^i_x ($\in CLC^i_x$). These are: one sent vector $V^i_{x(ksent)}$ and one received vector $V^i_{x(krecv)}$. These vectors are initialized to zero when the system starts, as well as restarts computation after a failure.

(i) $V^i_{x(ksent)} = [v^{i1}_{xk}, v^{i2}_{xk}, v^{i3}_{xk}, \ldots, v^{ij}_{xk}, \ldots, v^{i(k-1)}_{xk}, v^{i(k+1)}_{xk}, \ldots, v^{in}_{xk}]$, where n is the number of clusters and v^{ij}_{xk} represents the set of the inter cluster messages along with their respective sequence numbers sent by process p_i in cluster C^k to processes in cluster C^j in the check pointing interval between CLC^i_{x-1} and CLC^i_x. So, $V^i_{x(ksent)}$ represents the logged inter cluster messages sent by P_i in cluster C^k in the check pointing interval between CLC^i_{x-1} and CLC^i_x.

Now, v^{ij}_{xk} is further expressed in the following way.

$v^{ij}_{xk} = [s^{i1}_{xk}, s^{i2}_{xk}, s^{i3}_{xk}, \ldots, s^{ip}_{xk}, \ldots, s^{im}_{xk}]$, where m is the number of processes in cluster C^j and s^{ip}_{xk} represents the set of the inter cluster messages along with their respective sequence numbers sent by process p_i in C^k to process p_p in C^j in the check pointing interval between CLC^i_{x-1} and CLC^i_x.

Also $Sq^{ij}_{ksent,p} = \max\{s^{ip}_{xk}\}$ means that $Sq^{ij}_{ksent,p}$ represents the largest sequence number of all messages sent by process p_i in C^k to process p_p in C^j in the check pointing interval between CLC^i_{x-1} and CLC^i_x.

(ii) $V^i_{x(krecv)} = [r^{i1}_{xk}, r^{i2}_{xk}, r^{i3}_{xk}, \ldots, r^{ij}_{xk}, \ldots, r^{i(k-1)}_{xk}, r^{i(k+1)}_{xk}, \ldots, r^{in}_{xk}]$, where n is the number of clusters and r^{ij}_{xk} represents the set of the sequence numbers of the inter cluster messages along with their respective sender ids received by process p_i in cluster C^k from processes in cluster C^j in the check pointing interval between CLC^i_{x-1} and CLC^i_x. Note that $V^i_{x(krecv)}$ does not log the received messages.

Now, r^{ij}_{xk} is further expressed as follows.

$r^{ij}_{xk} = [s'^{i1}_{xk}, s'^{i2}_{xk}, s'^{i3}_{xk}, \ldots, s'^{ip}_{xk}, \ldots, s'^{im}_{xk}]$, where m is the number of processes in cluster C^j and s'^{ip}_{xk} represents the set of the sequence numbers of the inter cluster messages received by process p_i in C^k from process p_p in C^j in the check pointing interval between CLC^i_{x-1} and CLC^i_x.

Also $Sq^{ij}_{krecv,p} = \max\{s'^{ip}_{xk}\}$ means that $Sq^{ij}_{krecv,p}$ represents the largest sequence number of all messages received by process p_i in C^k from process p_p in C^j in the check pointing interval between CLC^i_{x-1} and CLC^i_x.

2.3 Delayed Message and Check Pointing Interval

We now state the reason for considering the value of the common check pointing interval T to be just larger than the maximum message passing time between any two processes of the clusters. It is known that to take care of the lost and delayed messages the existing idea is message logging. So naturally the question arises for how long a process will go on logging the messages it has sent. We have shown below that because of the above mentioned value of the common check pointing interval T, a process p_i needs to save in its recent local checkpoint c^i_x ($\in CLC^i_x$) only all the inter cluster messages it has sent in the recent check pointing interval between CLC^i_{x-1} and CLC^i_x. In other words, we are able to use as little information related to the lost and delayed messages as possible for consistent operation after the system restarts.

Consider the situation shown in Fig. 2. As before we will explain using a simple system of only two clusters and the observation is true for cluster environment of any size as well. Observe that because of our assumed value of T, the duration of the check pointing interval, any message m sent by cluster C^i before it takes its checkpoint CLC^i_{x-1} always arrives before the recent checkpoint CLC^j_x of cluster C^j. So such a message can not be either a lost or a delayed message. So any such message m does not need to be resent as it is always processed by the receiving cluster C^j before its recent checkpoint CLC^j_x. Therefore, there is no need to log such messages. However, messages, such as m' and m'', sent by cluster C^i in the check pointing interval between CLC^i_{x-1} and CLC^i_x may be lost or delayed. So in the event of a failure, say, f as shown in the figure, in order to avoid any inconsistency in the computation after the system restarts from the recent checkpoints, we need to log only such sent messages at the recent checkpoint CLC^i_x of the sender so that they can be resent after the clusters restart. Observe that in the event of a failure, any delayed message, such as message m'', is essentially a lost message as well. Hence, in our approach, we consider only the recent cluster level checkpoints of the clusters and the messages logged at these recent checkpoints are the ones sent only in the recent check pointing interval. From now on, by 'lost message' we will mean both lost and delayed message.

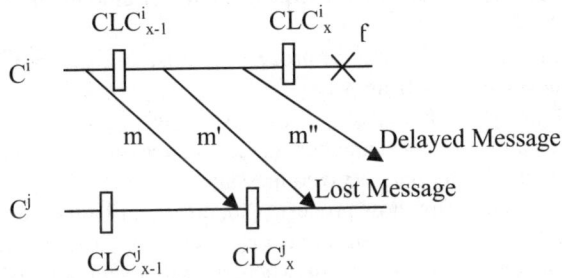

Fig. 2. Message m can not be a delayed message

3 Working Principle of the Recovery Scheme

In our proposed approach, we have assumed that the recent local checkpoints of every cluster form a consistent local checkpoint set, also known as the CLC of the cluster. We also have assumed that processes / clusters restart from their respective recent local checkpoints / cluster level checkpoints irrespective of the presence of any inter cluster lost and orphan messages among these checkpoints. That is, the recovery line consists of only the recent local checkpoints of all the processes of all the clusters. To maintain the correctness of the distributed computation after the system restarts, we need to have a mechanism to identify the inter cluster lost and orphan messages so that the lost messages can be resent and the duplicate messages caused by the orphan messages can be ignored. We first state how to identify inter cluster lost messages and then we state the mechanism to identify and ignore the duplicate inter cluster messages. We use two control messages, namely, a recovery message and a pseudo recovery message. The former one is issued only once by every failed process after its recovery and the later one is issued only once by every fault free process.

3.1 Lost Messages

For simplicity we explain the idea using a cluster federation consisting of two clusters only. This idea is true for any cluster federation of any number of clusters. Consider

Fig. 3 in which process $p_i \in C^k$ and $p_p \in C^j$. The recent local checkpoint of p_i is c^i_x ($\in$ CLC^k_x) and that of p_p is c^p_x ($\in CLC^j_x$). The sent and received vectors at the checkpoints are shown. To keep the discussion simple we assume that process p_i has not communicated so far to any other process in cluster C^j and similarly process p_p also has not communicated so far to any other process in cluster C^k. We now briefly explain the formation of the sent vector of process p_i which is shown here as $V^i_{x(ksent)}$ = [(6,7)] and the received vector of process p_p, which is $V^p_{x(jrecv)}$ = [(6)]. The other vectors can be similarly explained.

The sent vector at c^i_x is $V^i_{x(ksent)} = [v^{ij}_{xk}]$ and since p_i so far has communicated with p_p only, therefore $v^{ij}_{xk} = [0, 0, 0, ..., s^{ip}_{xk}, ..., 0]$.

Also $s^{ip}_{xk} = \{6,7\}$. This means that p_i has sent to p_p messages with sequence numbers 6 and 7.

Therefore $Sq^{ij}_{ksent,p} = \max\{s^{ip}_{xk}\} = \max \{6,7\} = 7$.

In words, at this time the maximum sequence number among all the messages sent by p_i to p_p is 7.

Now consider the received vector of process p_p. It is: $V^p_{x(jrecv)} = [r^{pk}_{xj}]$ and since p_p so far received messages only from p_i.

Therefore, $r^{pk}_{xj} = [0, 0, 0, ..., s'^{pi}_{xj}, ..., 0]$. Also $Sq^{pk}_{jrecv,i} = \max\{s'^{pi}_{xj}\} = \{6\} = 6$. That is, the maximum sequence number among all messages received is 6. In this case, eventually there is only one received message.

We now explain below first how process p_i identifies any inter cluster lost message it has sent to process p_p. Assume that process p_p has failed. After recovery it rolls back to its recent local checkpoint c^p_x from where it will eventually restart. However, before it restarts, it has to determine if it has sent any inter cluster message(s) to process p_i which eventually has become a lost message because of the failure. For this purpose, it sends the recovery message, denoted as M^p_r, and piggybacked with the highest sequence number of all messages it has received from process p_i during the last checkpoint interval (i.e. between c^p_{x-1} and C^p_x). As we have calculated above, this sequence number is $Sq^{pk}_{jrecv,i} = \max\{s'^{pi}_{xj}\} = \{6\} = 6$.

Now, process p_i after receiving the piggybacked recovery message $< M^p_r, Sq^{pk}_{jrecv,i} >$ checks to see if $Sq^{ij}_{ksent,p} > Sq^{pk}_{jrecv,i}$. If so, then p_i learns that it has already sent messages to process p_p having the sequence numbers starting with $Sq^{pk}_{jrecv,i} +1$ to $Sq^{ij}_{ksent,p}$ which eventually are now the lost messages. So, p_i will resend these messages to p_p preserving their order according to their sequence numbers after it restarts its computation from its recent checkpoint. In the example of Fig. 3, $Sq^{ij}_{ksent,p}$ = $\max\{s^{ip}_{xk}\} = \max \{6,7\} = 7$ and $Sq^{pk}_{jrecv,i} = \max\{s'^{pi}_{xj}\} = \{6\} = 6$.

So, there is one lost message from p_i to p_p. It is the message m_7. So, p_i will resend message m_7 to p_p after it restarts its computation.

Next we explain how process p_p identifies any lost message sent to process p_i.

Next, to identify the lost messages sent by p_p to p_i, we do the following. Process p_i after receiving the recovery message, will send a control message, termed as pseudo recovery message and denoted as M^i_{prec} to p_p piggybacked with $Sq^{ij}_{krecv,p} = \max\{s'^{ip}_{xk}\}$. After receiving $< M^i_{prec}, Sq^{ij}_{krecv,p}>$ process p_p checks to see if $Sq^{pk}_{jsent,i}> Sq^{ij}_{krecv,p}$, where $Sq^{pk}_{jsent,i} = \max\{s^{pi}_{xj}\}$ = the largest sequence number of all messages sent by process p_p to process p_i. If it is, the messages it sent to p_i with sequence numbers from $Sq^{ij}_{krecv,p} +1$ to $Sq^{pk}_{jsent,i}$ are the lost messages from p_p to p_i. So, p_p must

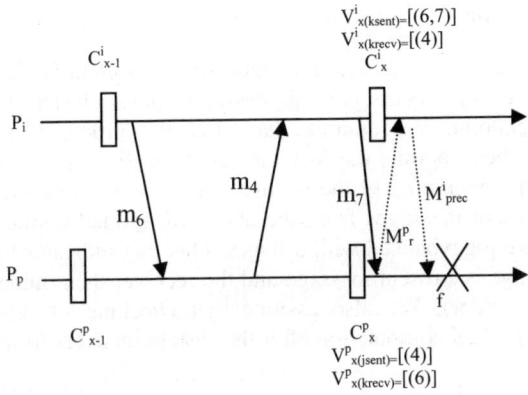

Fig. 3. Handling of lost message

resend these messages preserving their order according to their sequence numbers after it restarts its normal computation. Observe that for the example in Fig. 3, $Sq^{ij}_{krecv,p} = 4$ and $Sq^{pk}_{jsent,i} = 4$. So, there is no lost message from p_p to p_i.

In general, for any cluster federation, processes must follow the following two rules in order to identify inter cluster lost messages.

<u>*Rule 1*</u>: *Each faulty process first rolls back to its recent local checkpoint. Then it sends the recovery message only to those processes in other clusters from which it has received inter cluster messages in the recent check pointing interval. It never sends the pseudo recovery message.*

<u>*Rule 2*</u>: *Each fault-free process first rolls back to its recent local checkpoint. Next, when it receives for the first time a recovery message, it sends the pseudo recovery message only to those processes in other clusters from which it has received inter cluster messages in the recent check pointing interval. It never sends the recovery message.*

3.2 Orphan Messages

When the normal computation restarts, every process p_k does the following. Whenever process p_k receives any inter cluster piggybacked application message, < m, (sender id,*) > it checks if this piggybacked sequence number,'*' corresponding to the sender already exists in its recent received vector. If so, it ignores the message since it is a duplicate message. This means that message m has already been sent earlier by the sender before the occurrence of the failure and also it was sent after the sender took its recent checkpoint (the sender is now resending the message). Hence it was an orphan message. However, since the receiving process p_k has already processed the message once before taking its recent checkpoint and prior to the occurrence of the failure, therefore process p_k must ignore this message since it is a duplicate message; otherwise the underlying distributed computation will be incorrect.

3.3 Process Behavior

The objective of our proposed recovery algorithm is to identify the inter cluster lost messages sent by every process p_k to processes in other clusters with respect to its recent local checkpoint. We assume that after the processes restart from their respective recent check points, the lost messages are first resent to the appropriate receivers before the beginning of the normal computation preserving their order. To differentiate the resent messages from the above mentioned duplicate messages, the resent messages are piggybacked with a flag,$. This flag indicates to the receiver that the received message is a resent message and the receiver then immediately processes it (preserving the order). We also assume that checking of orphan messages is performed during normal computation after the system recovers from a failure.

4 Algorithm to Identify Lost Messages

The proposed algorithm identifies the inter cluster lost messages sent by every process p_i. For this purpose, it uses the Rules 1 and 2 mentioned in Section 3.1.

4.1 Algorithm Lost-Message-Recovery

Input: The recent cluster level checkpoint of each cluster is its consistent local checkpoint set.
Output: Lost messages sent by each process are identified.
Responsibility of every process p_i ($\in C^k$) that has participated in inter cluster communication in the recent check pointing interval is stated below:
When process p_i fails:

p_i sends recovery message $< M^i{}_r, Sq^{is}{}_{krecv,p} >$ to every process p_p, from which it has received inter cluster message; /* to help p_p ($\in C^s$) to identify its lost messages sent to p_i*/

/* for every recovery message received from a process from other clusters, process p_i does the following */
if process p_i receives a recovery message $< M^l{}_r, Sq^{lk}{}_{jrecv,i} >$ from p_l, where $p_l \in C^j$ and $k \neq j$
/* process p_l has also failed and inter cluster lost messages from p_i to p_l are to be identified*/
if $Sq^{ij}{}_{ksent,l} > Sq^{lk}{}_{jrecv,i}$
p_i records lost messages in R_i ; /* messages with sequence numbers starting with $Sq^{lk}{}_{jrecv,i} + 1$ to $Sq^{ij}{}_{ksent,l}$ are recorded as lost messages sent by p_i to p_l*/

/* for every pseudo recovery message received from a process from other clusters, process p_i does the following */
if process p_i receives pseudo recovery message $< M^l{}_{prec}, Sq^{lk}{}_{jrecv,i} >$ from p_l, $p_l \in C^j$, $k \neq j$
/* to identify lost messages from p_i to p_l */

if $Sq^{ij}{}_{ksent,l} > Sq^{lk}{}_{jrecv,i}$
p_i records lost messages in R_i ; /* messages with sequence numbers starting with $Sq^{lk}{}_{jrecv,i} + 1$ to $Sq^{ij}{}_{ksent,l}$ are recorded as lost messages sent by p_i to p_l*/

When p_i is not faulty

p_i receives recovery message $< M^l_r, Sq^{lk}_{jrecv,i} >$ from p_l, where $p_l \in C^l$ and $k \neq j$
/* process p_l has failed and inter cluster lost messages from p_i to p_l are to be identified*/

if it is the first recovery message it has received
  p_i sends pseudo recovery message $< M^i_{prec}, Sq^{is}_{krecv,p} >$ to every process p_p, from which it
  has received inter cluster message;   /* to help p_p ($\in C^s$) to identify its lost messages sent to p_i*/

  if $Sq^{ij}_{ksent,l} > Sq^{lk}_{jrecv,i}$
    p_i records lost messages in R_i;   /* messages with sequence numbers starting with
                                                $Sq^{lk}_{jrecv,i} +1$ to $Sq^{ij}_{ksent,l}$ are recorded as lost messages
                                                sent by p_i to p_l */
  else if $Sq^{ij}_{ksent,l} > Sq^{lk}_{jrecv,i}$
    p_i records lost messages in R_i;   /* messages with sequence numbers starting with
                                                $Sq^{lk}_{jrecv,i} +1$ to $Sq^{ij}_{ksent,l}$ are recorded as lost messages
                                                sent by p_i to p_l */

/* for every pseudo recovery message received from a process from other clusters, process p_i does the following */

if process p_i receives pseudo recovery message $< M^l_{prec}, Sq^{lk}_{jrecv,i} >$ from p_l, $p_l \in C^l$, $k \neq j$
                                    /* to identify lost messages from p_i to p_l */

  if $Sq^{ij}_{ksent,l} > Sq^{lk}_{jrecv,i}$
    p_i records lost messages in R_i;   /* messages with sequence numbers starting with
                                                $Sq^{lk}_{jrecv,i} +1$ to $Sq^{ij}_{ksent,l}$ are recorded as lost messages
                                                sent by p_i to p_l */

Theorem 1: Algorithm Lost-Message-Recovery together with the assumed process behavior results in correct computation of the underlying distributed application.

Proof: Let us start with the case when a process, say process p_i ($\in C^k$) fails. After it recovers, we observe that it receives the pseudo recovery message $< M^l_{prec}, Sq^{lk}_{jrecv,i} >$ from every fault free process p_l belonging to other cluster to which it has sent messages. By testing, if $Sq^{ij}_{ksent,l} > Sq^{lk}_{jrecv,i}$ it identifies and records the lost messages, if any, that it has sent to p_l. Also when it receives the recovery message $< M^l_r, Sq^{lk}_{jrecv,i} >$ from each faulty process p_l belonging to other cluster to which it has sent messages, then by testing $Sq^{ij}_{ksent,l} > Sq^{lk}_{jrecv,i}$ it identifies and records any lost messages, if any, that it has sent to the faulty process.

Now assume that p_i has not failed. When it receives the recovery message $< M^l_r, Sq^{lk}_{jrecv,i} >$ from each faulty process p_l belonging to other cluster to which it has sent messages, then by testing $Sq^{ij}_{ksent,l} > Sq^{lk}_{jrecv,i}$ it identifies and records any lost messages, if any, that it has sent to the faulty process. In a similar way, it finds the lost messages it has sent when it receives any pseudo recovery message from a fault free process. It also helps other processes to determine their lost messages by sending pseudo recovery message to them. Thus, when the algorithm terminates, every process has the knowledge about the lost messages it has sent to others.

Now considering the assumed process behavior, all lost messages are resent to the appropriate receivers when the processes restart their computation and no orphan message is processed twice. Therefore, the recovery algorithm together with the assumed process behavior ensures correct execution of any distributed application.

4.2 Performance

The salient features of the proposed recovery approach are as follows:

1) It is domino-effect free recovery and hence guarantees the least amount of re-computation after recovery. 2) A process / cluster needs to save only its recent local checkpoint / cluster level checkpoint. So number of trips to stable storage per process is always one during recovery. 3) Since the common check pointing interval is just larger than the maximum message passing time between any two processes of the cluster federation, therefore a process needs to log at its recent local checkpoint only those messages it has sent in the recent check pointing interval. 4) It takes care of all inter cluster lost, delayed, and orphan messages. 5) It takes care of concurrent failures and so obviously it takes care of all single failure as well.

For message complexity, let us consider the following scenario. Assume that the total number of processes in the cluster federation is N out of which N_1 processes have failed. Let N_2 be the number of the fault free processes. An approximate estimate is that there are $N_1 xN$ number of recovery messages and $N_2 xN$ is the number of the pseudo recovery messages. So total number of messages is ($N_1 xN + N_2 xN$), and therefore, the message complexity is $O(N^2)$. However, the calculated complexity is only an approximation since a faulty process after recovery never sends any recovery message to any other process, faulty or not, in its own cluster. Also it sends the recovery message only to those processes in other clusters from which it has received inter cluster messages in the recent check pointing interval. Same is true for pseudo recovery messages also. Therefore, in reality this number will be much less.

Comparisons. Below we have presented a detailed comparison of our approach with the existing approaches.

Comparison with the work in [1]: In [1] the assumed architecture is such that multiple coordinated check pointing subsystems are connected with a single independent check pointing subsystem. The architecture is a very restricted one in the sense that the above mentioned multiple coordinated subsystems can not communicate directly with each other; rather they do it via the independent subsystem. This assumed restricted architecture is one of the main short comings of this work.

Our proposed approach is independent of any particular architecture. Besides, the work in [1] does not consider inter cluster lost and delayed messages, unlike our proposed work. Also the work in [1] considers only single failure. Another important difference is that in our approach there is no domino-effect, which guarantees the least amount of re-computation after recovery and only one trip to the stable storage during recovery.

Comparison with the work in [2]: In the proposed recovery algorithm [2] a cluster takes two types of checkpoints; processes inside a cluster take checkpoints synchronously and a cluster takes a communication induced checkpoint whenever it receives an inter cluster application message. Thus it needs two levels of check pointing. Each cluster maintains a sequence number (SN) which is incremented each time a cluster level checkpoint is taken. Each cluster maintains a DDV (Direct dependency vector) with size equal to the number of clusters in the cluster federation. Whenever a cluster fails, after recovery it broadcasts an alert message piggybacked with the SN of the failed cluster. All other clusters receive this alert message and some of them may decide to roll back depending on certain condition involving their corresponding entries in the DDV vectors. Each time there is a rollback, the rolled back cluster further broadcasts the alert message with its SN triggering the next iteration of the algorithm. The algorithm terminates when there is no more any alert message. Observe that both this algorithm and ours are architecture independent unlike in [1].

One main drawback of the algorithm in [2] is that if all clusters have to roll back except the failed cluster, then it becomes an all to all broadcasting of the alert message. This may result in a message storm.

Other important drawbacks that are absent in our approach are as follows. This algorithm needs two levels of check pointing and several iterations may be needed for its completion. Besides it considers only inter cluster orphan message. It suffers from the domino effect and hence it may need considerable amount of re-computation after recovery Also, since each process/ cluster may have to save several checkpoints, therefore during recovery a process may have to make several trips to the stable storage in order to determine which checkpoint(s) need to be skipped (i.e. which checkpoints can not belong to the recovery line of the cluster federation). It may be noted that larger the number of such trips, larger will be the execution time of the algorithm. It delays the execution of the recovery algorithm further. Finally, it can handle only single failures.

Moreover, in [2], whenever a cluster of size n has to take a consistent local checkpoint set, it requires 3*(n-1) control messages as it follows a three phase synchronous approach [10]. In our approach, processes in every cluster takes local checkpoints following the single phase non-blocking check pointing algorithm of [3]; hence the number of the control messages is drastically reduced to only (n-1).

Comparison with the work in [13]: The recovery algorithm in [13] uses communication induced check pointing scheme as in [2]. Both this algorithm and our proposed algorithm have the following main advantage: simultaneous execution of the algorithm by all participating clusters contributes to the speed of execution and both are architecture independent.

However, the work in [13] has the following shortcomings when compared to our approach. These are: it considers only inter cluster orphan message. It suffers from the domino effect. Also, since each process/cluster may have to save several checkpoints, therefore during recovery a process may have to make several trips to the stable storage in order to determine which checkpoint(s) need to be skipped. It delays the execution of the recovery algorithm further. Another limitation is that it can handle only single failures. In Table 1 we have summarized the main differences of all these approaches.

Table 1. Comparison Summary

Criteria	Our Approach	Alg [1]	Alg [2]	Alg [13]
Architecture Dependent	No	Yes	No	No
Domino –Effect Free	Yes	No	No	No
Concurrent Failures	Yes	No	No	No
Inter Cluster Lost Message	Yes	No	No	No
No. of checkpoints/process	1	>>1	>>1	>>1

4.3 Consideration of Intra Cluster Lost Messages

Our proposed idea can easily be extended to handle intra cluster lost and delayed messages in the following way. Each process p_i ($\in C^k$) needs to maintain another sent vector and another received vector. This sent vector is similar to the one used for inter cluster messages except that it logs only the intra cluster messages sent by p_i to other processes in the same cluster C^k during its recent check pointing interval. Similarly the received vector will represent the set of the sequence numbers of the messages received by p_i from every other process p_j of the same cluster C^k during the recent check pointing interval. To identify intra cluster lost messages, our proposed algorithm can be easily modified so that communication via the recovery and pseudo recovery messages will take place only among processes in the same cluster C^k. Observe that since the local checkpoints in a cluster are taken following the scheme in [3], so there will be no intra cluster orphan messages among the local checkpoints of the processes in a cluster. So there will be no duplicate intra cluster messages.

5 Conclusion

In this work, we have presented a recovery scheme for cluster computing environment. We have dealt with both inter cluster orphan and lost messages as well as concurrent failures. None of the existing works in this area have dealt with either inter cluster lost messages, or concurrent failures. The other important feature is that a process needs to log only the messages it has sent during its recent check pointing interval. This puts a limit on the amount of the logged messages. Besides, each process restarts from its recent local checkpoint; the meaning is two fold: there is minimum re-computation per process after recovery and each process needs to save only one checkpoint, ensuring efficient memory utilization. Finally, observe that in our approach, we have not made any attempt to make the recent cluster level checkpoints consistent from the viewpoint of the existence of inter cluster orphan messages unlike the existing works, but we have tackled this problem easily by just defining process behavior as mentioned in Section 3.

However, the work in [13] has the following shortcomings when compared to our approach. These are: it considers only inter cluster orphan message. It suffers from the domino effect. Also, since each process/ cluster may have to save several checkpoints, therefore during recovery a process may have to make several trips to the stable storage in order to determine which checkpoint(s) need to be skipped. It delays the execution of the recovery algorithm further. Another limitation is that it can handle only single failures. In Table 1 we have summarized the main differences of all these approaches.

References

1. Cao, J., Chen, Y., Zhang, K., He, Y.: Checkpointing in Hybrid Distributed Systems. In: Proceedings of the 7th International Symposium on Parallel Architectures, Algorithms and Networks (ISPAN 2004), Hong Kong, China, pp. 136–141 (2004)
2. Monnet, S., Morin, C., Badrinath, R.: Hybrid Checkpointing for Parallel Applications in Cluster Federations. In: Proceedings of the 4th IEEE/ACM International Symposium on Cluster Computing and the Grid, Chicago, USA, pp. 773–782 (2004)
3. Gupta, B., Rahimi, S., Rias, R.A., Bangalore, G.: A Low-Overhead Non-Blocking Checkpointing Algorithm for Mobile Computing Environment. In: Chung, Y.-C., Moreira, J.E. (eds.) GPC 2006. LNCS, vol. 3947, pp. 597–608. Springer, Heidelberg (2006)
4. Koo, R., Toueg, S.: Checkpointing and Rollback-Recovery for Distributed Systems. IEEE Transactions on Software Engineering SE-13(1), 23–31 (1987)
5. Wang, Y.: Consistent Global Checkpoints That Contain a Given Set of Local Checkpoints. IEEE Transactions on Computers 46(4), 456–468 (1997)
6. Tsai, J., Kuo, S.-Y., Wang, Y.-M.: Theoretical Analysis for Communication-Induced Checkpointing Protocols with Rollback Dependency Trackability. IEEE Transactions on Parallel and Distributed Systems 9(10), 963–971 (1998)
7. Gupta, B., Banerjee, S.K., Liu, B.: Design of New Roll-Forward Recovery Approach for Distributed Systems. IEE Proceedings-Computers and Digital Techniques 149(3), 105–112 (2002)
8. Manivannan, D., Singhal, M.: Asynchronous Recovery Without using Vector Timestamps. Journal of Parallel and Distributed Computing 62(2), 1695–1728 (2002)
9. Qi, X., Parmer, G., West, R.: An Efficient End-Host Architecture for Cluster Communication. In: Proceedings of the 2004 IEEE Intl. Conf. on Cluster Computing, San Diego, USA, pp. 83–92 (2004)
10. Singhal, M., Shivaratri, N.G.: Advanced Concepts in Operating Systems. McGraw-Hill Inc., New York (1994)
11. Elnozahy, E.N., Johnson, D.B., Zwaenepoel, W.: The Performance of Consistent Check Pointing. In: Proceedings of the 11th Symp. on Reliable Distributed Systems, pp. 86–95 (1992)
12. Cao, G., Singhal, M.: On Coordinated Checkpointing in Distributed Systems. IEEE Transactions on Parallel and Distributed Systems 9(12), 1213–1225 (1998)
13. Gupta, B., Rahimi, S., Ahmad, R., Chirra, R.: A Novel Recovery Approach for Cluster Federations. In: Cérin, C., Li, K.-C. (eds.) GPC 2007. LNCS, vol. 4459, pp. 519–530. Springer, Heidelberg (2007)
14. Venkatesan, S., Juang, T., Alagar, S.: Optimistic Crash Recovery Without Changing Application Messages. IEEE Transactions on Parallel and Distributed Systems 8(3), 263–271 (1997)
15. Jalote, P.: Fault Tolerance in Distributed Systems. PTR Prentice Hall, New Jersey (1994)

Tidset-Based Parallel FP-tree Algorithm for the Frequent Pattern Mining Problem on PC Clusters

Jiayi Zhou[1] and Kun-Ming Yu[2]

[1] Institute of Engineering Science, Chung Hua University
jyzhou@pdlab.csie.chu.edu.tw
[2] Department of Computer Science and Information Engineering, Chung Hua University
Hsinchu 300, Taiwan
yu@chu.edu.tw

Abstract. Mining association rules from a transaction-oriented database is a problem in data mining. Frequent patterns are essential for generating association rules, time series analysis, classification, etc. There are two categories of algorithms for data mining, the generate-and-test approach (Apriori-like) and the pattern growth approach (*FP-tree*). Recently, many methods have been proposed for solving this problem based on an *FP-tree* as a replacement for Apriori-like algorithms, because these need to scan the database many times. However, even for the pattern growth method, the execution time takes long when the database is large or the given support is low. Parallel- distributed computing is good strategy for solving this problem. Some parallel algorithms have been proposed, however, the execution time increases rapidly when the database increases or when the given minimum threshold is small. In this study, an efficient parallel- distributed mining algorithm based on an *FP-tree* structure – the Tidset-based Parallel FP-tree (*TPFP-tree*) – is proposed. In order to exchange transactions efficiently, transaction identification set (*Tidset*) was used to directly choose transactions without scanning databases. The algorithm was verified on a Linux cluster with 16 computing nodes. It was also compared with a *PFP-tree* algorithm. The dataset generated by IBM's Quest Synthetic Data Generator to verify the performance of algorithms was used. The experimental results showed that this algorithm can reduce the execution time when the database grows. Moreover, it was also observed that this algorithm had better scalability than the *PFP-tree*.

Keywords: frequent pattern mining, parallel processing, association rule, data mining, tidset.

1 Introduction

The extraction of frequent patterns in a transaction-oriented database can be a problem in research in terms of mining association rules [1,11], time series analysis, classification [4], etc. The basic concept of frequent pattern in a database implies many transactions, and each transaction is a set of items. A pattern that occurs frequently in a data set is found by using frequent pattern mining. Most research

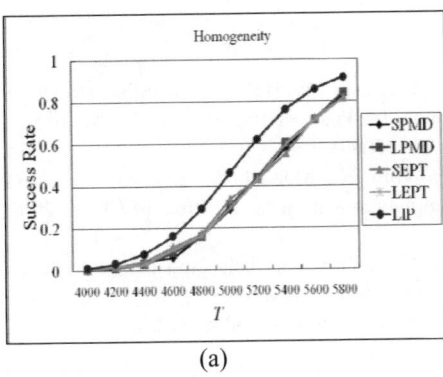 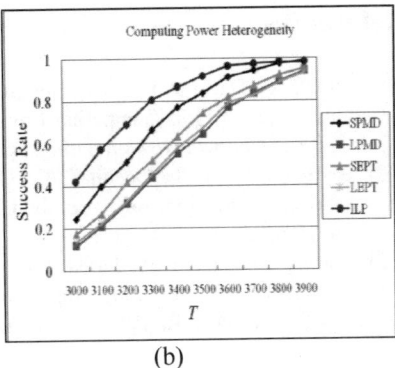

Fig. 4. Success rates of the five strategies in (a) a homogeneous environment and (b) a heterogeneous environment

tasks. The computation-costly strategy, ILP, as expected, has the best performance. However, the enormous computing time spent in resource scheduling for ILP makes it impractical in the complex grid environment.

Figure 4(b) shows the success rates of the various strategies under heterogeneous environment. It reveals that SPMD is a better strategy than LPMD, SEPT and LEPT under such a setting because it tends to give priority to tasks located in critical paths. However, this observation may not hold under other circumstances, which are not shown here for brevity. Nevertheless, we observe that SPMD is indeed the best heuristic in an overwhelming number of cases.

6 Conclusion

We have proposed a probabilistic framework for resource scheduling on a grid environment in which the task response time is estimated as a random variable with probability distribution function. We have proposed a systematic integer linear programming as well as two heuristic strategies, namely LPMD and SPMD, for dynamically scheduling resources. We also performed experiments using synthetic data from a protein annotation workflow. The preliminary experimental results demonstrate that considering the uncertain factors of task response time in task scheduling does yield better performance, especially in a heterogeneous environment. Of the two proposed heuristics, SPMD generally yields better performance.

In the future, we plan to conduct more experiments to comprehensively compare the various scheduling strategies. In addition, while this work focuses on computation-intensive workflows, there exist a large number of grid applications that are data-intensive. We are in the process of extending our work to deal with data-intensive grid applications.

Acknowledgement

This work was supported in part by the National Science Council of Taiwan under Grant NSC 96-2752-H-110-005–PAE.

References

[1] Afzal, A., Darlington, J., McGough, A.S.: Stochastic Workflow Scheduling with QoS Guarantees in Grid Computing Environments. In: Proc. of International Conference on Grid and Cooperative Computing, pp. 185–194 (2006)
[2] Blythe, J., Jain, S., Deelman, E., Gil, Y., Vahi, K., Mandal, A., Kennedy, K.: Task scheduling strategies for workflow-based applications in grids. In: Proc. of CCGri 2005, pp. 759–767 (2005)
[3] Cao, J., Spooner, D.P., Jarvis, S.A., Nudd, G.R.: Grid load balancing using intelligent agents. Future Generation Comput. Syst. 21(1), 135–149 (2005)
[4] Duan, R., Prodan, R., Fahringer, T.: Run-time optimisation of grid workflow applications, pp. 33–40 (2006)
[5] Mandal, A., Kennedy, K., Koelbel, C., Marin, G., Mellor-Crummey, J., Liu, B., Johnsson, L.: Scheduling strategies for mapping application workflows onto the grid. In: Proc. of HPDC 2005, pp. 125–134 (2005)
[6] Nino-Mora, J.: Stochastic scheduling. In: Floudas, C.A., Pardalos, P.M. (eds.) Encyclopedia of Optimization, pp. 367–372 (2005) [Updated version]
[7] O'Brien, A., Newhouse, S., Darlington, J.: Mapping of scientific workflow within the e-protein project to distributed resources. In: Proc. of UK e-Science all Hands Meeting, pp. 404–409 (2004)
[8] Paranhos da Silva, D., Cirne, W., Vilar Brasileiro, F.: Trading cycles for information: Using replication to schedule bag-of-tasks applications on computational grids. In: Proc. of the Euro-Par, pp. 169–180 (2003)
[9] Patel, Y., Mcgough, A.S., Darlington, J.: QoS support for workflows in A volatile grid. In: Proc. of Gri 2006, pp. 64–71 (2006)
[10] Spooner, D.P., Cao, J., Jarvis, S.A., He, L., Nudd, G.R.: Performance-Aware Workflow Management for Grid Computing. The Computer Journal 48, 347–357 (2005)
[11] Vanderster, D.C., Dimopoulos, N.J., Sobie, R.J.: Metascheduling multiple resource types using the MMKP. In: Proc. of Grid 2006, pp. 231–237 (2006)
[12] Weiss, G., Pinedo, M.: Scheduling Tasks with Exponential Service Times on Non-Identical Processors to Minimize Various Cost Functions. Journal of Applied Probability, 187–202 (1980)
[13] Yu, J., Buyya, R., Chen, K.T.: Cost-based scheduling of scientific workflow applications on utility grids. In: Proc. of 2005.First International Conference on E-Science and Grid Computing, pp. 8–16 (2005)

A Mobile Agent-Based Statistic Execution Model for Grid Computing

Wenyu Qu[1], Keqiu Li[2], and Yong Zhang[3]

[1] School of Computer Science and Technology, Dalian Maritime University
1 Linghai Road, Dalian, 116026, China
eunice.qu@gmail.com
[2] Department of Computer Science and Engineering, Dalian University of Technology
1 Linggong Road, Dalian, 116024, China
keqiu@dlut.edu.cn
[3] Department of Computer, Liaoning Normal University
850 Huanghe Road, Dalian, 116029, China

Abstract. This paper employs mobile agents in grid computing systems. We propose a hierarchical routing model by using mobile agents to collect and update the dynamic changes of routing information in grid systems. User tasks are sent from the source node to the destination in a statistic manner, which has been proved to be the only optimal solution that makes inference on the known traffic information and approximates to a unbiased distribution. Our method is fault tolerant, scalable, and relies completely on local information. Extensive simulations shows the prior of our algorithm to state-of-art algorithms. ...

1 Introduction

Grid computing is an innovative approach that leverages existing IT infrastructure to optimize compute resources and manage data and computing workloads. According to Gartner, "a grid is a collection of resources owned by multiple organizations that is coordinated to allow them to solve a common problem." Grid computing is originated in the early 1990s as a metaphor for making computer power as easy to access an electric grid [10]. It is not a new concept but one that has gained recent renewed interest and activity for a couple of main reasons: Grid computing can be a cost effective way to resolve IT issues in the areas of data, computing and collaboration; especially if they require enormous amounts of compute power, complex computer processing cycles or access to large data sources. Grid computing can be a coordinated sharing of heterogeneous computing resources across a networked environment that allows users to get their answers faster.

A key challenge of grid computing is creating large-scale, end-to-end scientific applications that draw from pools of specialized scientific components to derive elaborate new results [11]. Currently, Grid allows to segment a job workload into independent units of work to be processed in parallel across any number of heterogeneous computers within a network and is being extended to include support for piping to allow dependent processes to overlap their execution and eliminate the need to write intermediate results to disk. Due to the lack of central control over the hardware, there is no way to guarantee that nodes will not drop out of the network at random times. Some nodes (like laptops or dialup Internet customers) may also be available for computation but not network communications for unpredictable periods. To enhance the dynamicity, automatism, as well as the interoperability of Grid system, and to decentralize the core components to optimize the throughput, mobile agent technology is expected to be a promising solution to these demands.

Mobile agent technology has been proposed for about one decade and has been successfully deployed for collecting and processing network information over the Internet, telecommunication networks and other types of networks. Mobile agents are programs that can freely migrate from node to node in a network, at times and to places of their own choosing, acting on behalf of their users to perform intelligent decision-making tasks. Created in one execution environment, it can transport its state and code with it to another execution environment in the network, where it resumes execution. This ability allows it to move to a system containing an object with which it wants to interact and then to take advantage of being in the same host or network as the object, which expresses the core idea behind mobile agents, that is, bring the computation to the data rather than the data to the computation. In [17], Lange summarized seven good reasons for mobile agents. Although none of these merits are unique to mobile agents, no competing technique shares all seven. Mobile agents provide a single, general framework in which distributed, information-oriented applications can be implemented efficiently and easily, with the programming burden spread evenly across information, middleware, and client providers.

This paper employs mobile agents in grid computing systems. We propose a hierarchical routing model, using routing agents to collect and update the dynamic changes of routing information in grid systems. Routing agents are classified into short-distant agents and long-distant agents, each with a specified life limit/number of hops and routing scope. Another kind of agents, execution agents, carrying user tasks, move from the source node to the destination node in a statistic manner to avoid the possible traffic congest caused by a too much popular route. Extensive simulations shows the prior of our algorithm comparing to state-of-art algorithms.

The remainder of this paper is organized as follows. Section 2 defined the function of agents in our model. Section 2.3 proposes our algorithm. Section 3 gives a clear view on the performance of our schemes through comparison with other existing schemes and Section 4 summarizes our work and concludes this paper.

2 Agents

To meet the demands of dynamicity, automatism, interoperability, and throughput optimization, we design an agent-based grid computing model in which agents are divided into two kinds to cover the demands, namely, routing agents vs. execution agents.

The majority of foragers exploit the food sources in the closer vicinity of their hive while a minority among them visit food sites faraway from their hive. We transformed this observation into an agent model that has two types of agents: short-distance agents and long-distance agents. Short-distance agents collect and disseminate routing information in the neighborhood (up to a specific number of hops) of their source node while long-distance agents collect and disseminate routing information to all nodes of a grid system.

2.1 Routing Agents

The network is organized into geographical partitions called groups. A partition results from particularities of the network topology. Each group has one representative node. Currently the lowest IP address node in a group is elected as the representative node. If this node crashes then the next higher IP address node takes over the job. Routing agents roam in the system, both inside groups or among groups, collecting and disseminating routing information. Generally, a close destination to the source node is much desirable compared to a remote one.

Short-distance agents. Each node in a group has a routing scope which consists of all nodes that can be reached in a small given number of hops (short distance). Each non-representative node periodically sends a short-distance agent (SDA), by broadcasting replicas of it to each neighbor node. When a replica of a particular SDA arrives at a node it updates routing information there, and the replica will be flooded again, however, it will not be sent to the neighbor from where it arrived. This process continues until the life time of the agent has expired. If another replica of this agent had been received already at a node, the newly arrived replica will be killed.

long-distance agents. Representative nodes only launch long-distance agents (LDA) that would be received by the neighbors and propagated as in 2.1. However, their life time (number of hops) is limited by the long-distance limit. Each LDA caries and collects path information while traveling and updates those information at each visited node, including the journey time for its source node to the current node along the searched route. Thus each node maintains current routing information for reaching nodes within its group and for reaching the representative nodes of groups.

Denote the itinerary of a LDA as a set of nodes $0, 1, 2, \cdots, i, \cdots$ where 0 is the source node, the journey time of a LDA from 0 to i, denoted by J_i, can be expressed by a recurrence fomular as follows:

$$J_i = J_{i-1} + t_{i-1,i} \tag{1}$$

where $t_{i-1,i}$ is the time that the LDA used from the $(i-1)$-th node to the i-th node. Let $b_{i-1,i}$, $t_{i-1,i}$, $p_{i-1,i}$ denote the bandwidth, transmission delay, and propagation delay of link $\{(i-1) \to i\}$, respectively, which can be approximated achieved by transmitting hello packets, we have

$$t_{i-1} \doteq q_{i-1,i}/b_{i-1,i} + t_{i-1,i} + p_{i-1,i}. \qquad (2)$$

where $q_{i-1,i}$ is the size of queue (in bits)on node $(i-1)$ to be send to node i. Here, we don't take the protocol processing delays into account.

2.2 Execution Agents

The user tasks (whose destination is beyond the group of the given node) are carried by execution agents (EA) to the representative node of the group containing the destination node. The next hop for an EA is selected in a probabilistic manner according to the quality measure of the neighbors, as a result, not all EAs follow the best paths. This will help in maximizing the system performance though an EA may not follow the best path (In comparison OSPF always chooses a next hop on the shortest path). The probabilistic decision to be made for EAs' migration should satisfy

1. It makes inference on all the known traffic information.
2. It is unbiased. That is, the probability should mostly balance the traffic cost on each link.

which can be modeled as a multi-objective problem and resulted in the following solution:

$$\rho_{ij}(x) = \frac{\exp\{\theta f_{ij}(x)\}}{\sum_{l \in NB(i)} \exp\{\theta f_{il}(x)\}}, \quad j \in NB(i). \qquad (3)$$

where $NB(i)$ is the set of neighbor nodes of i and p_{ij} is the probability that the EA will move from i to j. $\theta \geq 0$ is a weigh coefficient, which is defined by the user, and f_{ij} indicates the overload (e.g., transmission load) between node i and j. Obviously, when θ is small, the gained probability distribution mainly reflects the requirement of unbiased distribution. With the increase of θ's value, the effect of the overload function increases. It has been proved that this probability distribution is the only optimal solution that makes inference on the known traffic information and approximates to a unbiased distribution.For detailed description please refer to our previous research [20].

2.3 Algorithm Design

In our model, each node i maintains three types of routing tables: Intro Group (IrG), Inter Group (IeG) and Group Membership (GM). IrG routing table IrG_i is organized as a vector of size $|G(i)| \times (|NB(i)|)$, where $G(i)$ is the set of groupmates in the group of node i and $NB(i)$ is the set of neighbor nodes of i. Each entry $IrG_i(j,k)$ is a pair of queuing delay and propagation delay (Q_{jk}, Pd_{jk}) that a packet will experience in reaching destination k via neighbor

Table 1. An Example of IrG Routing Table

IrG_i	k_1	$\cdots$	$k_{|G(i)|}$
j_1	$\left(Q_{(j_1,k_1)}, Pd_{(j_1,k_1)}\right)$	$\cdots$	$\left(Q_{(j_1,k_{|G(i)|})}, Pd_{(j_1,k_{|G(i)|})}\right)$
$\vdots$	$\vdots$	$\ddots$	$\vdots$
$j_{|NB(i)|}$	$\left(Q_{(j_{|NB(i)|},k_1)}, Pd_{(j_{|NB(i)|},k_1)}\right)$	$\cdots$	$\left(Q_{(j_{|NB(i)|},k_{|G(i)|})}, Pd_{(j_{|NB(i)|},k_{|G(i)|})}\right)$

j for $k = k_1, k_2, \cdots, k_{|G(i)|}$ and $j = j_1, j_2, \cdots, j_{|NB(i)|}$. Table 1 shows an example of IrG_i. In the IeG routing table, the queuing delay and propagation delay values for reaching the representative nodes are stored. The structure of the IeG routing table is similar to the IrG routing table. The GM routing table provides the mapping of known destinations to a group. Below provides the pseudo code of our algorithms.

Algorithm 1. - routing agents

foreach i
   while $(t \leq T)$
      if $(t \bmod = 0)$
         if $(i \in RN)$
            $h_i := LL; \ b_i := LDA$
         else
            $h_i := SL; \ b_i := SDA$
         endif
         send b_i to all $j \in NB(i)$
      endif
   endwhile
endfor

Algorithm 2. - hello packets

foreach i
   while $(t \leq T)$
      if $(t \bmod = 0)$
         send a HP to all $j \in NB(i)$
         if (time out before a response from neighbor)
            the neighbor is down;
            update the routing table and send agents to inform others
         endif
      endif
   endwhile
endfor

Algorithm 3. - routing table

foreach i
  while $(t \leq T)$
    foreach agent b_s arrives at i from $j \in NB(i)$
      if$(i \in G(s))$
        $\alpha := \alpha + \frac{q_{ij}}{b_{ij}}$ and $\beta := \beta + p_{ij}$;
        update IrG_i routing table entries $Q_{js} = \alpha$ and $P_{js} = \beta$;
        update $\alpha(\alpha := \sum_{k \in N(i)}(q_{ks} \times \rho_{ks}))$ and $\beta(\beta := \sum_{k \in N(i)}(p_{ks} \times \rho_{ks}))$
      else
        $\alpha := \alpha + \frac{q_{ij}}{b_{ij}}$ and $\beta := \beta + p_{ij}$;
        update IeG routing table entries $Q_{jz} = \alpha$ and $Pd_{jz} = \beta$;
        update $\alpha(\alpha := \sum_{k \in N(i)}(q_{kz \times \rho_{kz}}))$ and $\beta(\beta := \sum_{k \in N(i)} p_{kz \times \rho_{kz}})$
      endif
      if(b_s already visited node i)
        kill b_s
      else
        use priority queues to forward b_s to all $k \in NB(i)$」
      endif
    endfor
  endwhile
endfor

Algorithm 4. - execution agents

foreach i
  while $(t \leq T)$
    foreach execution agent EA_{sd} received at i from j
      if (destination d $\in G(i)$)
        consult IrG_i to find delays to d;
        calculate $\rho_{ik}, k \in NB(i)$ for reaching d
      else
        consult GM_i to find node w;
        consult IeG_i to find delays to node w;
        calculate $\rho_{ik}, k \in NB(i)$ for reaching w
      endif
    endfor
  endwhile
endfor

3 Experimental Studies

The goal of our experimental studies was to gain a better understanding of the working mechanisms and performance of our algorithm. The Japanese Internet Backbone (NTTNET) We use the Japanese Internet Backbone (NTTNET) as the simulation framework (see Figure 1).

Table 2. Notations used in the algorithms

n	the number of nodes in the system
t	the current time
Δt	time interval for agent generation
T	the time limit of the simulation
RN	the set of representative nodes
LDA	long-distant agent
Δh	time interval for HP generation
SDA	short-distant agent
q_{ij}	the size of queue on link ij (in bits)
LL	life limit of LDA
α	the average queue delay between s and the current node
SL	life limit of SDA
β	the average propagation delay between s and the current node
HP	hello packet
P_{js}	the transmission delay between s and i through j
G(s)	the set of group mates of s
Q_{js}	the queue delay between s and i through j
b_{ij}	the bandwidth of link ij
NB(i)	the set of neighbor nodes of i
p_{ij}	the propagation delay on link ij

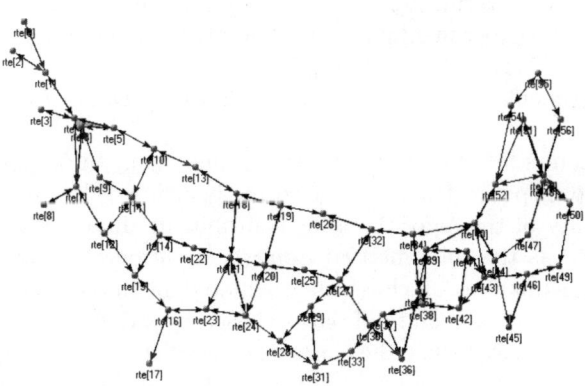

Fig. 1. The Japanese Backbone (NTTNET)

It is a 57 node, 162 bidirectional links network. The link bandwidth is 6 Mbits/sec and the propagation delay is from 2 to 5 milliseconds. The size of data packet is 512 bytes and the size of an agent is 48 bytes. Traffic is defined in terms of open sessions. A session is defined between two nodes and it remains active until a certain amount of data are transferred at a given rate. Each session is characterized completely by session size, the generation rate of sessions (GRS), and the sending rate of the packets (SRP). In the simulation, session size is set to be 2 Mbits.

We implemented our algorithm (OA) together with OSPF [7] and AntNet [2] to evaluate and compare the efficiency of these three algorithms. OSPF is a routing protocol used in Internet. It is based on the shortest path routing by using the Dijkstra algorithm. It uses only the best path towards the destination to forward the data packets and this best path is computed with the costs of edges, normally the distances of links. As OSPF ignores the queuing delays, it cannot work well during heavy traffic loads. AntNet is a dynamic routing algorithm proposed by Di Caro and Dorigo [2]. It is inspired from the foraging activity of real ants. In contrast with OSPF, AntNet measures the queuing delay and tries to find a globally optimal solution that satisfies the dynamic constraints. However, AntNet has to store all possible solutions for its statistical method. Because the heuristic measuring has a relation with a percentage of the data flow, the correctness of heuristic measuring would be worse under the condition of a low load on the network. In addition, when the queuing delay is low, a stochastic process is no more sensible. Our algorithm utilizes inner agents to disseminate the state of the network to the routers in real-time. It does not need any global information such as the structure of the topology and cost of links among routers, which not only balances the local traffic flow but also enhances fault tolerance. Compared to AntNet, this enhancement in performance is achieved with a little more routing overhead which is defined as the ratio between the bandwidth occupied by the routing packets and the total network bandwidth, but this overhead remains constant for a given topology.

Firstly, we play experiments on the effects of number of hops of SDA to the routing table. The experimental results show that the increasing of the number of hops after 10 does not bring significant performance improvements. In the following experiments, we set the number of hops of SDA to 7 and that of LDA to 40.

Two parameters are introduced for our comparison, throughput and packet delay. The throughput is defined as the correctly delivered bits per second, which shows the ability of the algorithms for transmitting data streams. The packet delay is defined as the time interval from the creation of a data packet to its arrival at the destination, which is only calculated for the correctly received data packets. It indicates the quality of paths chosen by a data packet.

Figure 2 and Figure 3 show the comparison results of the average throughput and the average packet delay between OSPF, AntNet, and our algorithm.

Originally, there is a normal load of GRS=2.7 seconds and SRP=0.3 second. From 500 seconds to 1000 seconds, all nodes sent data to node 4 with SRP=0.05 seconds. It can be seen that both our algorithm and AntNet are able to cope with the transient overload. OSPF shows the poorest performance. It can also be seen that the average packet delay for our algorithm is less than 0.1 second as compared to 0.5 second for AntNet. Again, OSPF shows the poorest performance.

We also compared the deliver rate among these three algorithms which states the proportion of packets correctly delivered. Table 3 shows the results of the deliver rate which is defined as the quotient of the amount of received packets

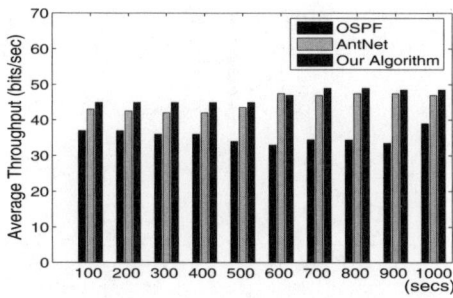

Fig. 2. The average throughput when all nodes sent data to node 4 from 500 seconds to 1000 seconds

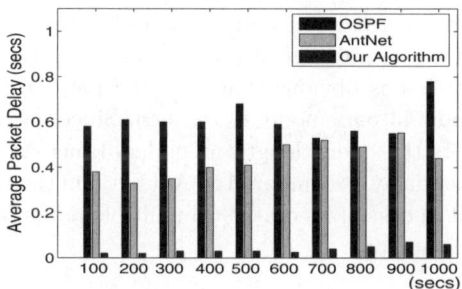

Fig. 3. The average packet delay when all nodes sent data to node 4 from 500 seconds to 1000 seconds

Table 3. The Comparison of Deliver Rate

Parameters (Sec)		Deliver Rate (%)		
GRS(Sec)	SRP(Sec)	OSPF	AntNet	Our Algorithm
4.5	0.5	83.21	96.85	99.99
2.5	0.5	82.46	97.31	99.99
1.5	0.5	80.13	97.24	99.99
2.5	0.05	83.94	95.94	99.68

to the amount of sent packets. From the simulation results, we can see that our algorithm achieves a similar performance to AntNet, which is much better than OSPF.

Figure 4 shows the results of the comparison between our algorithm and AntNet in which node 21 crashed at 300 seconds, node 40 crashed at 500 seconds, and both of them were repaired at 800 seconds.

Here, GRS=4.7 seconds and SRP=0.05. The purpose of this experiment was to analyze the fault tolerant behavior of our algorithm. The GRS and SRP is selected to ensure that no packets are dropped because of the congestion. Based on our experimental results, our algorithm is able to deliver 97% of deliverable

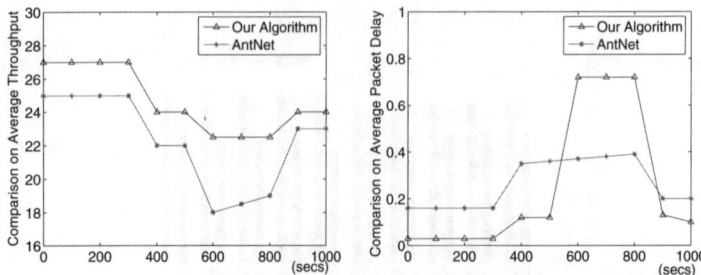

Fig. 4. Node 21 is down at 300 and node 40 is down at 500 and both repaired at 800

packets as compared to 89% by AntNet. From the figure we can see that our algorithm has a superior throughput and lesser packet delay. But once node 40 crashes, the packet delay of our algorithm increases because of higher load at node 43. From Figure 1 it is obvious that the only path to the upper part of the network is via node 43 once node 40 crashed. Since our algorithm is able to deliver more packets the queue length at node 43 increased and this led to relatively poorer packet delay as compared to AntNet. On the contrary, although node 21 is critical, but in case of its crash still multiple paths exist to the middle and upper part of the topology.

4 Conclusion

Grid computing is an innovative approach that leverages existing IT infrastructure to optimize compute resources and manage data and computing workloads. A key challenge of grid computing is creating large-scale, end-to-end scientific applications that draw from pools of specialized scientific components to derive elaborate new results. In this paper, we addressed this problem by introducing mobile agent technology into grid computing. Two kinds of agents, namely, routing agents and execution agents, were employed. An exceptional routing mechanism was proposed for routing in different scopes, by further dividing routing agents into short-distant agents and long-distant agents. User tasks were carried by execution agents from the source node to the destination, following a statistic route. Extensive simulations compared our algorithm to state-of-art algorithms and showed that our method was fault tolerant, scalable, and relies completely on local information.

References

1. Balakrishnan, H., Kaashoek, M.F., Karger, D., Morris, R., Stoica, I.: Looking Up Data in P2P Systems. Commu. of the ACM 46, 43–48 (2003)
2. Caro, G., Dorigo, M.: AntNet: Distributed Stigmergetic Control for Communications Networks. Jour. of Arti. Intel. Research 9, 317–365 (1998)

3. Chawathe, Y., Ratnasamy, S., Breslau, L., Lanham, N., Shenker, S.: Making Gnutella-like P2P Systems Scalable. In: ACM SIGCOMM Conf. Proc., pp. 407–418 (2003)
4. Cohen, E., Shenker, S.: Replication Strategies in Unstructured Peer-to-Peer Networks. ACM SIGCOMM Comp. Commu. Review 32, 177–190 (2002)
5. Crespo, A., Garcia-Molina, H.: Routing Indices for Peer-to-Peer Systems. In: ICDCS Conf. Proc., pp. 23–32 (2002)
6. Dasgupta, P.: Intelligent Agent Enabled Genetic Ant Algorithm for P2P Resource Discovery. In: Moro, G., Bergamaschi, S., Aberer, K. (eds.) AP2PC 2004. LNCS (LNAI), vol. 3601, pp. 213–220. Springer, Heidelberg (2005)
7. Dijkstra, E.: A Note on Two Problems in Connection with Graphs. Numer. Math., 269–271 (1959)
8. Dunne, C.: TUsing Mobile Agents for Network Resource Discovery in Peer-to-Peer Networks. SIGecom Exchanges, Newsletter of the ACM Special Interest Group on E-Commerce 2, 1–9 (2001)
9. Ferreira, R., Ramanathan, M., Awan, A., Grama, A., Jagannathan, S.: Search with Probabilistic Guarantees in Unstructured Peer-to-Peer Networks. In: P2P Conf. Proc., pp. 165–172 (2005)
10. Foster, I., Kesselman, C.: Computational Grids, ch.2. In: The Grid: Blueprint for a New Computing Infrastructure, Morgan Kaufmann, San Francisco (1999)
11. Gil, B., Deelman, W., Blythe, J., Kesselman, C., Tangmunarunkit, H.: Artificial Intelligence and Grids: Workflow Planning and Beyond. IEEE Intel. Systems 19, 26–33 (2004)
12. Gkantsidis, C., Mihail, M., Saberi, A.: Random Walks in Peer-to-Peer Networks. In: IEEE INFOCOM Conf. Proc. (2004)
13. Iamnitchi, A., Ripeanu, M., Foster, I.: Small-World File-Sharing Communities. In: IEEE INFOCOM Conf. Proc. (2004)
14. Jagadish, H., Ooi, B., Vu, Q., Zhang, R., Zhou, A.: Vbi-Tree: A Peer-to-Peer Framework for Supporting Multi-Dimensional Indexing Schemes. In: ICDE Conf. Proc., vol. 34 (2006)
15. Joynes, E.: Information Theory and Statistical Mechanics. The Phys. Review 108, 171–190 (1957)
16. Koloniari, G., Pitoura, E.: Peer-to-Peer Management of XML Data: Issues and Research Challenges. ACM SIGMOD Record 34, 6–17 (2005)
17. Lange, D., Oshima, M.: Seven Good Reason for Mobile Agents. Commu. of the ACM 42, 88–89 (1999)
18. Leontiadis, E., Dimakopoulos, V., Pitoura, E.: Cache Updates in a Peer-to-Peer Network of Mobile Agents. In: P2P Conf. Proc., pp. 10–17 (2004)
19. Lv, Q., Cao, P., Cohen, E., Li, K., Shenker, S.: Search and Replication in Unstructured Peer-to-Peer Networks. In: ICS Conf. Proc., pp. 84–95 (2002)
20. Qu, W., Shen, H., Jin, Y.: Theoretical Analysis on A Traffic-Based Routing Algorithm of Mobile Agents. In: IAT Conf. Proc., pp. 520–526 (2005)
21. Sahin, O., Gupta, A., Agrawal, D., El Abbadi, A.: A Peer-to-Peer Framework for Caching Range Queries. In: ICDE Conf. Proc., pp. 165–176 (2004)
22. Shannon, C.: A Mathematical Theory of Communication. Bell System Tech. Jour. 27, 379–428 (1948)
23. Srivatsa, M., Gedik, B., Liu, L.: Large Scaling Unstructured Peer-to-Peer Networks with Heterogeneity-Aware Topology and Routing. IEEE Trans. on Paral.and Distr. Syst. 17, 1277–1293 (2006)

24. Tewari, S., Kleinrock, L.: Analysis of Search and Replication in Unstructured Peer-to-Peer Networks. In: SIGMETRICS Conf. Proc., pp. 404–405 (2005)
25. Yang, B., Garcia-Molina, H.: Designing a Super-Peer Network. In: ICDE Conf. Proc., pp. 49–60 (2003)
26. Yang, K., Wu, C., Ho, J.: AntSearch: An Ant Search Algorithm in Unstructured Peer-to-Peer Networks. IEICE Trans. on Commu. E89-B, 2300–2308 (2006)

An Optimization of Resource Replication Access in Grid Cache*

Fangai Liu[1] and Fenglong Song[2]

[1] Department of Computer Science, ShanDong Normal University
JiNan China, 250014
Liufangai@yahoo.com.cn
[2] The Institute of Computing Technology, China Academy of Science
Beijing China,100080
songfenglong@ict.ac.cn

Abstract. In a grid system, resources are located in different nodes and a grid member can obtain its resources from different positions. But the disproportion between the resource distributions and its property of heterogeneity cause communication bottlenecks, which can decrease the grid performance. To solve this problem, cache techniques have been proposed. However, in a grid, how to access the resources in an economic way and how to decide whether one resource replica should be cached, are the two long standing problem. In this paper, an economic model is proposed to optimize the cache management policy. A parallel algorithm of accessing data from m resource sites is improved, where we propose a strataties on how to select the m resource sites to access the data in parallel. By this means, the single site failure problem can be solved. The test results show that the strategies we propose are efficient.

1 Introduction

The goal of grid system is to realize resource sharing among the dynamic and distributed virtual organizations [1]. The sharing we are concerned with is not primarily file exchange but rather direct access to computers, software, data, and other resources, which is a transparent environment of resource sharing and cooperation. But many factors can cause high latency, such as the network transmission latency, bottlenecks caused by the disproportions between the capabilities of the resources in the grid and its property of heterogeneity, etc [2]. Therefore, the network latency becomes the bottleneck of the grid performance. In this paper, we adopt cache techniques [2] to buffer the resources used frequently, thus reducing the latency caused by the network transmission and improving the grid performance.

Using cache can reduce the repeating transmission when several tasks want to access the same resource, which not only saves the limited network bandwidth and relaxes the load of some central server, but also reduces the cost caused by the transmission among

---

* The paper is supported by National Science Foundation of China(90612002) and The Shandong Science and Technology Plan(2005GG3201114).

the heterogeneous systems. The grid cache is a significant technique and plays an important role in solving the communication bottleneck. Using an appropriate grid cache strategy can effectively reduce the communication latency.

As to the grid cache, much researches are focused on the strategy of grid cache replacement, for instance, the research done by Ekow Otoo, Arie Shoshani, etc [3]. It is supposed that the resource needed has been transferred to the local storage, and it should be cached. Since the cache capacity is limited, so it causes the replacement. However, in a grid, how to access the resource in a cost way and how to decide whether one resource replica should be cached, are the two long standing problem.

In this paper, an economic model is introduced into grid cache strategies. Based on economic strategies, we have given an optimal admission policy to minimize the cost in grids, and the precondition is the reduction of the latency. Further more, on the behalf of the data-accessing algorithm which discusses the resource accessing policy in [5], a parallel algorithm of accessing data from m resource sites is given [5]. But how to select the m resource sites to access the data in parallel is not discussed in [5]. Here we give an answer. By this means, the single site failure problem can be solved.

2 The Reason for Economic Model

To compute the value of resources in grid, researchers have introduced economic model into grid, such as William H.Bell and David G.Cameron who solve the file replication in data grid [7],and Mark Carman who have optimized the file access and replication based on economic model [4]. In addition, the introduction of economic model in grid is a step that must steps out from theoretical research to practical application.

Introducing economy has the following advantages [8]:

(1) Distributing resources dynamically, having stronger self-adoption, and application can request resources according to the actual conditions .

(2) Making decision decentralized. The resource owner and user reach identical opinion through negotiation, thus can cancel the omniscience, and the user-centered system is highly scalable.

(3) Distributing resources based on value, adopting identical measurement as to all resources, providing a fair foundation of depositing and withdrawing grid resources on any user. And users can trade all kinds of resources.

(4) Encouraging the resource owner to contribute its own resources and make profit through introducing the economic principle, thus benefiting to set up extensive grid system.

(5) Resource requester and provider can make decision following its own actual conditions, so that maximize its own utility and interests。

After listing the reasons of introducing economic models, now we turn to discuss the policy of accessing resource replica.

3 Policy of Accessing the Resource Replica

When a grid system can not get the resource requested, it should access one of its replica by a most effective way, and we can adopt the parallel optimal data-accessing algorithm which introduced in [5], where a parallel algorithm of accessing data from m resource sites is given. But how to select the m resource sites is not discussed in [5], and it is a programming problem, so we will discuss it by evolution algorithm, which utilizes the special advantage in planning and search of the algorithm of EA [9].

3.1 Storage Resource Manager

In the agent-based grid resource management system[6], it makes up of three layers, that is, resource layer, agent layer and application layer. Where, the resource layer is a set that contains the real physical resources, and the application layer is a set that contains the users and organizations that request the grid resources, and the agent layer is a tie that contacts the two former layers. The agent layer contains three sorts of agents, i.e., resource agent, application agent and information server agent.

There is an exclusive resource agent for every sort of resource in grid, whose main function is to adjust the price of the resources according to the supply and demand situation dynamic, and to negotiate with the application agent about the resource accessing scheme. The application agent is to be correspondent to each user, and the main function is to explain the user's request, and get the concrete description of the requested resource, so that the resource agent can understand it. In addition, it sends the resource request to the information service agent(ISA), which is responsible for information exchange and service of the grid.

Storage Resource Manager(SRM) can be the storage resource agent, and its main function is to manage its storage resources, and provide a united interface for sorts of different storage system, and optimize its utility efficiency [4].

SRM is a middleware in grid system, which can make resource-sharing more flexible [3]. If there is not some resource, SRM should access one of the resource replica by the most effective way.

3.2 Selection of the Data-Accessing Sites

Cache is a sort of grid resource, and its resource agent is SRM, and SRM makes as best profit as possible through interacts with other resource agents.

3.2.1 Mathematical Model

SRM assesses the possible value of the resource accessing policy on the basis of the resource prices and the web availability at the moment, so that it can get a resource replica at a most effective way.

The price of the one sort of resources is different according to the different market in which the site locates. That is, the price is changed via the real need. The price is higher when the demand is higher, and otherwise it is lower. The goal of SRM is to get some resource via lowest cost, so it will select the sites that have the lowest price. But maybe it causes the web congestion and the site failure, so we introduce the current status of the net to assess the validity. On the whole, we introduce the following parameters:

Suppose the requested resource by SRM is labeled as ri, and there are n sites which own its replica, and the price vector is defined as P= (p1,p2,......,pn). Define the n dimension vector S=(s1,s2,...,sn), where sj=1,if access the resource from the site j, otherwise sj=0,(j=1,2,...,n). The goal of the SRM is the lowest cost, that is:

$$\min f1(S) = \sum_{j=1}^{n} sj * pj \quad , s.t. \quad pj > 0 \qquad ①$$

Considering the real status of the net where the site locates, we define the net status vector B=(b1,b2,...,bn), where the larger of the value bi are, the better of the service that can get from the site i. So the other goal of the SRM is to get the resource as quickly as possible, that is, the net service available is as larger as possible, so plus the goal to ①,we get the equation:

$$\min f2(S) = \sum_{j=1}^{n} sj * pj - \sum_{j=1}^{n} sj * bj \quad s.t. \quad pj > 0, bj > 0 \qquad ②$$

In addition, we should give the user the right to decide the more significant facet of the two former mentioned above according to their real request, so we improve the equation ② as follows:

$$\min f3(S) = \sum_{j=1}^{n} sj(\alpha * pj - \beta * bj) \quad , s.t. \quad pj > 0, bj > 0 , \alpha + \beta = 1 \qquad ③$$

Where, α defines the ratio that the user want to cost in the whole, i.e., the larger the value of α, the lower the cost should be; and β defines the ratio of the accessing speed in the whole.

We introduce the restrict function to vanish the subject as follows:

$$\min f(S) = \sum_{j=1}^{n} sj(\alpha * pj - \beta * bj) + Mj[\min(0, pj)] + Mj[\min(0, bj)] \quad , s.t. \quad , \alpha + \beta = 1 \qquad ④$$

where Mj is a positive number as large as possible.

3.2.2 Criterion of Assessing the Access Scheme

It is not the fact that the more sites we choose, the better performance we can obtain when we access a resource in parallel. The effect of the access scheme is not sharp equal to the number of the sites which will provide its resource replica to the user. On the model above mentioned, the 0-1 vector S is defined by SRM random, and it gives one possible access scheme. To every random vector S, the number of the source sites is different, thus the scheme that make the equation □ lowest is the current best resource-accessing scheme.

3.3 Policy of SRM Accessing Resource Replica

The goal of the SRM is to select a scheme in which the price on every site is as low as possible, and at the same time the net service available is as great as possible. To solve the programming problem, we adopt the EA [9].

3.3.1 Principle of EA

As the GA adopts the stable ratio of the crossover and mutation, so for the complicated multi-optimizing problem, its efficiency is lower. EA, as a development of GA, is random search algorithm based on the natural selection and evolvement. The procedure of the concrete problem as follows:

(1) design the concrete chromosome;
(2) define the Fitness Function ;
(3) assess the individual fitness of the current population;
(4) re-list the individual in the selected set so as to generate the next population;
(5) judge if the algorithm reaches the end condition. If so, the optimum individual is the optimum solution; else to (3).

3.3.2 Resource Accessing Policy Based on GA

When SRM requests some resource, firstly, it sends a resource-requested information to ISA, then waits for the return from ISA with the vector describing the sites that have the resource, and corresponding vector of the price, and the vector of the current net status. Suppose these vectors are all n dimension. SRM define a n dimension 0-1 vector random, i.e., $S=(s1,s2,...,sn)$.

SRM defines a range that describes the maximum cost and the minimum cost according to the vector of price returned from ISA, and then assesses the individual fitness with it, and then defines the set of selection. The ending condition of the algorithm is the number N that describes the layer of iteration. N is defined by SRM. The algorithm as follows:

(1) send (ri) to the ISA;
(2) Wait for ISA(),
   assume $\alpha(0 \leq \alpha \leq 1)$, $\beta=1-\alpha$,
   initialize number N,
   assume Mj (j=1,2,...,n) as the positive number as large as possible;
(3) define the n dimension vector of 0 and 1 as chromosome, such as Si, (i=0, 1, ...,m),and the corresponding transform scheme is the initial solution:
   $S1=(s11, s12,..., s1n)$
   $S2=(s21, s22,..., s2n)$
   ......
   $Sm=(sm1, sm2,..., smn)$

So we can get the m fitness value, that is the result of equation ④,such as:F1, F2,......, Fn;

(4) assessing F1,F2,......,Fn, and select the individual that accord with the range of assessing to make up the selection set, such as S1,S2,......;

(5) as to the vector S that in the selection set, we modify the element from 0 to 1 or from 1 to 0 random, so that we get the next population;

(6) judge the ending condition, if so, get the optimum solution; else to (4);

Then select the corresponding vector S of 0 and 1 as the accessing scheme, which is solved by [5].

4 Cache Admission Policy Based on Economy

SRM decides whether to use its storage as cache, then assesses whether caches a resource object. The goal is to get as great profit as possible [4]. Now we introduce the economic model into the cache policy. Before we design the cache admission policy with most profit, we should give the definition of the resource value.

4.1 Deduction of the Resource Value

Now we discuss the cache admission policy.

4.1.1 Value of the Cached Resource

To the cache admission policy based on the economy, grid resources are the same as the goods in the market. They are purchased by the agents which need them. If one resource object has been cached (i.e.,F), then when SRM uses the resource next time, it need not to buy it again, so the value of one resource at one moment tk is defined as the cost saved in a time interval. In addition, if we consider the real physical position of the resource, that is, considering the special cost, then the value of the resource should be direct proportion to it. Suppose the price of resource F is pi at ti, and Tavg is the average caching time of all sorts of resources, and U as the special cost, then the value of F at time tk is defined as: from then on, the cost saved for using F in a time interval Tavg. Then the value of the resource cached can be given as the following equation:

$$V(F, tk) = (1-\alpha) \sum_{i=k+1}^{k+n} pi\delta(F, Fi) + \alpha U \qquad (5)$$

Where, δ is a comparable function, and it returns 1 if the two parameter are identical, else returns 0; and tk+n≤tk+Tavg<tk+n+1; 0≤α≤1, α describes how significant of the special cost of the resource requested.

4.1.2 Predict the Value of a New Resource

To a new resource that a local application requests, SRM forecast the value of caching it.

According to the real investigation of Ekow Otoo[3], the job that requests the resource F1 is independent to each other, so the request for F1 obeys Possion distribution. Suppose that at time tk SRM caches F1 and at time t F1 is replaced by another resource object, then F1 has been cached for time $\Delta t = t - t_k$, ($t > t_k$). And during the caching of F1, the probability requesting it is as follows:

$$\text{Prob}(F1) = e^{-\Delta t / T_{avg}}$$

As the number of requesting a new resource is not known at first, so we adopt the way that the least past forecast the future. Suppose that during interval T_{avg} the requesting number of the resource that is being replaced is $g(t)$, then during the interval $[t_k, t_k + T_{avg}]$, the times requested of F1 can be assessed as:

$$\text{Prob}(F1) * g(t)$$

Suppose that at time t_k, the cost that buys F1 is $C(F1, t_k)$, then the value of F1 can be assessed as:

$$V(F1, t_k) = \alpha [C(F1, t_k) + \sum_{i=k+1}^{k+n} C(F1, t_i) * \text{Prob}(F1) g(t)] + \beta U \qquad (6)$$

Where, $t_k + n \leq t_k + T_{avg} < t_k + n + 1$; $0 \leq \alpha, \beta \leq 1$, and $\alpha + \beta = 1$, α describes the significance of the current price of the resource, and β describes the significance of the special cost of the resource.

4.2 Cache Admission Policy Based on Economy

4.2.1 Profit Difference of the Investment

If the resource requested (such as F1) is not cached, then SRM should buy it from remote site. The local agent decides whether to cache it or not.

On the other hand, the cache capacity is limited, so caching a new resource object maybe mean the replacement of another resource object that has cached (such as F). Then at time t, the profit difference of caching F1 is as follows:

$$\Delta P(t) = \frac{\Delta t}{T_{avg}} * \Delta V - C(F1, t_k) \quad \text{Where} \quad \Delta V = V(F1, t_k) - V(F, t_k) \qquad (7)$$

Only when $\Delta P(t) > 0$, SRM would cache it, and only the profit difference is positive can it be invested by the cache capacity.

4.2.2 Probability of the Positive Profit

To the equation ⑦, plus the $\Delta P(t) > 0$, we can induce the equation:

$$\frac{\Delta t}{T_{avg}} > \frac{C}{\Delta V} \qquad (8)$$

In addition, according to the real investigation of Mark Carman[4], we know that the resource requirement is independent to each other in grid, so the time that local agents invest the cache capacity to some resource objects obeys the Possion distribution. On the other hand, once the resource requested is cached, then the cost can be saved, so the probability of the positive profit is in direct proportion to the time in which it is stored in cache. So the positive profit difference that invest the cache capacity to one resource is as following equation:

$$\text{Prob} = e^{-\Delta t / T_{avg}} \qquad (9)$$

Integrate the equation ⑧ and ⑨, we can get the following equation:

$$\text{Prob} < e^{-C/\Delta V} \qquad (10)$$

Equation ⑩ describes that the positive profit difference that invest the cache capacity to one resource is less the value $e^{-C/\Delta V}$.

4.2.3 Cache Admission Policy Based on Economy

The local agent defines a threshold value for the positive profit difference according to the real status, such as P0. The local agent assesses the value $e^{-C/\Delta V}$ for the new resource requested, if the result satisfies the inequation $e^{-C/\Delta V} \geq P0$, then caches it; otherwise, if $e^{-C/\Delta V} < P0$, then does not cache it.

5 Analysis and Evaluation

We simulate the algorithm and policy mentioned above by the simulator of the economic grid, i.e., GridSim[10]. To test our own algorithm, we modify the Java program Broker in the directory %gridsim%\ application\gridbroker\source\ gridbroker and create the simulation environment by Visual Modeler.

Since the limit of pages, we do not give the simulation results of the resource accessing policy and only give the simulation results of cache admission policy. We have defined 5 resources with resource-2 and resource-3 already cached and their prices are zero. The prices of other resources are variable random. If we adopt the LRU cache replacement policy, and simulate 10 times, we obtain the comparison statistic results with traditional cache admission policy as follows.

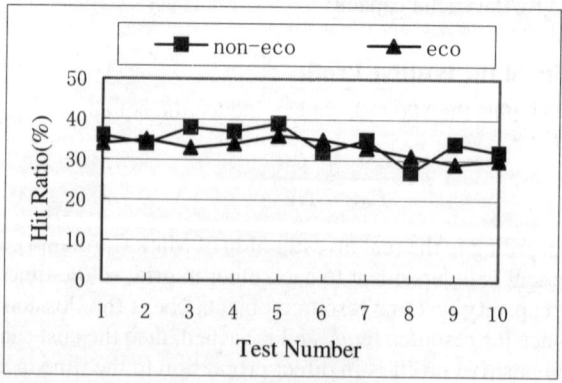

Fig. 1. Comparison of Hit Ratio

From figure 1, we know that the average hit ratio has no obviously variable, but in sharp comparison, the cost has been significantly reduced, as shown in figure 2.

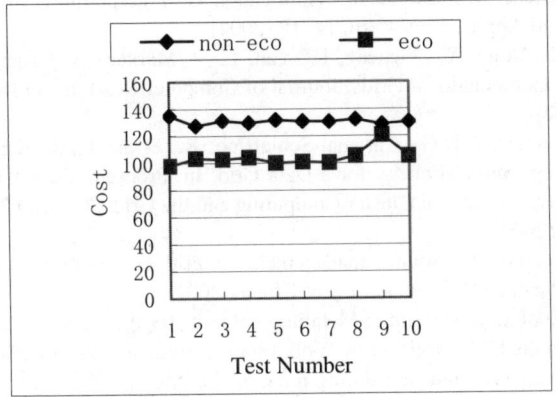

Fig. 2. Comparison of Cost

From the simulation, we know that the optimization based on economy to the grid cache admission policy can reduce the access cost and at the same time, the average hit ration has no obviously change.

6 Conclusion

In this paper, we have analyzed the current status of the research on grid cache and its relative questions, especially on the economic model of grid cache. Based on how to access the resources in an economic way and how to decide whether one resource replica should be cached, an economic model is proposed to optimize the cache management policy, which introduce the price mechanism to grid cache management and optimizes it on the point of profit. A parallel algorithm of accessing data from m resource sites is improved, where we propose a strataties on how to select the m resource sites to access the data in parallel. Next we want to improve the economic model further and enlarge it into resoure discovery algorithms.

References

1. Foster, I., Kesselman, C., Tuecke, S.: The Anatomy of the Grid:Enabling Scable Virtual Organizations. International Journal of Supercomputer Applications 15(3), 1–10 (2001)
2. Mei, C., Zhihui, D.: An Analysis of Some Problems in Grid Cache. Computer Science 31(5), 15–17 (2004)
3. Otoo, E., Shoshani, A.: Accurate Modeling of Cache Replacement Policies in a Data Grid. In: Proceedings of the 20th IEEE/11th NASA Goddard Conference on Mass Storage Systems and Technologies(MSS 2003), IEEE Press, San Diego, California (2003)

4. Carman, M., Zini, F., Serafini, L.: Towards an Economy-based Optimisation of File Access and Replication on a Data Grid. In: Proceedings of the 2nd IEEE/ACM International Symposium on Cluster and the Grid(CCGRID 2002), IEEE Press, Berlin, Germany (2002)
5. Quan, G., Xicheng, W., Guiyan, L.: Application Grid Techniques Analyzing. Computer Engineering and Applications 40(6), 14–17 (2004)
6. Hongqiang, C., Nong, X., Xicheng, L., Yan, L.: A Market-based Approach to Allocate Resources for Computational Grids. Journal of Computer Resarch and Develepment 39(8), 913–916 (2002)
7. Bell, W.H., Gameron, D.G., Carvajal-Schiaffino, R., et al.: Evaluation of an Economy-Based File Replication Strategy for a Data Grid. In: Proceedings of the 3rd IEEE/ACM International Symposium on Cluster Computing and the Grid(CCGRID 2003), IEEE Press, Tokyo, Japan (2003)
8. Jing, D.: Research of resource management in grid environment. In: Doctor Thesis, University of Science and Technology of China (2002)
9. Qingxia, Y.: Evolution Algorithm. Metallurgical Industry Press, Beijing (2000)
10. Buyya, R., Murshed, M.: GridSim: A Toolkit for the Modeling and Simulaton of Distributed Resource Management and Scheduling for Grid Computing. The Journal of Concurrency and Computation: Practice and Experience 14(13), 1175–1220 (2002)

ADVE: Adaptive and Dependable Virtual Environments for Grid Computing*

Xuanhua Shi, Hai Jin, Wei Zhu, and Li Qi

Services Computing Technology and System Lab,
Cluster and Grid Computing Lab,
Huazhong University of Science and Technology, Wuhan, 430074, China
{xhshi,hjin}@hust.edu.cn, {zw283927,quick.qi}@gmail.com

Abstract. Due to its potential, the use of virtual machines in grid computing is attracting increasing attention. Most of the researches focus on how to create or destroy a virtual execution environments for different kinds of applications, the policy of managing the virtual environments isn't widely discussed. This paper proposes an adaptive and dependable virtual execution environment for grid computing called ADVE, which focuses on the policy of managing dependable virtual execution environments, such as when to create and destroy a new virtual execution execution environment, when to migrate applications from one virtual workspace to a new virtual workspace. We conduct experiments over a cluster to evaluate the performance of ADVE, and the experimental results show that ADVE can improve the throughput and the reliability of Grid resources with the adaptive management of virtual machines.

1 Introduction

Nowadays, grid computing attracts more and more attentions in high performance computing area. By defining standardized protocols for discovering, accessing, monitoring, and managing remote computers, storage systems, networks, and other resources, grid technologies make it possible to allocate resources to applications dynamically, in an on-demand fashion [11]. However, while grids offer users access to many diverse and powerful resources, they do little to ensure that once a resource is accessed, it fulfills user expectations for quality of service. The problem is that most grid platforms today do not support performance isolation: activities associated with one user or virtual organization (VO) [13] can influence the performance seen by other processes executing on the same platform in an uncontrolled way. Another serious issue is that while grids provide access to many resources with diverse software configurations, a users application will typically run only in a specific, customized software environment. Variations in operating systems, middleware versions, library environments, and filesystem layouts all pose barriers to application portability.

---

* This work is partly funded by the National Science Foundation of China under grant No. 60603058 and National 973 Basic Research Program of China under grant No. 2007CB310900.

Due to its potential, virtual machine is attractive to high performance computers. Virtual machines present the image of a dedicated raw machine to each user [19]. This abstraction is very powerful for grid computing because users then become strongly decoupled from the system software of the underlying resource, and other users sharing the resource. In terms of administration, virtual machines allow the configuration of an entire operating system to be independent from that of the computational resource; it is possible to completely represent a VM guest machine by its virtual state (e.g. stored in a conventional file) and instantiate it in any VM host, independently of the location or the software configuration of the host. Furthermore, we can migrate running VMs to appropriate resources. Upon the above reasons, the merge of virtual machine and grid computing is promising.

The use of virtual machines in grid computing has been proposed before [12] [17]. In this paper, we present an adaptive and dependable virtual environment for grid computing called ADVE, which allows a grid client to define an environment in terms of its requirements (such as resource requirements or software configuration), manage it, and then deploy the environment in the grid. Moreover, ADVE can change its configuration during the runtime. For example, ADVE can handle the problem when and where to create a virtual execution environment, when to change the number of the virtual execution environments, and what kind of situation to migrate one application to another virtual execution environment. ADVE is implemented with virtual machine technology and the adaptive component [2]. The virtual machine technology supports the definition, deployment and destroying of the virtual execution environment, and the adaptive component handles the dynamic management of the virtual execution environment.

The paper is organized as follows. Section 2 discusses the related work, and section 3 describes the architecture of ADVE. In section 4, the performance evaluations are presented. We conclude in section 5 with a brief look at future work.

2 Related Work

For the flexibility of resource management and user management, the use of virtual machine is very popular in grid computing. Reference [12] proposes an overview of merge virtual machine and grid computing. The In-Vigo project [1] [18] made substantial progress in this direction while the Virtuoso [21] and VIOLIN [16] projects explored networking issues arising from use of VMs in this setting. Globus virtual workspace proposes the virtual workspace (VW) abstraction to describe such environments and showed how this abstraction can be implemented by using virtual machines for grid computing [17]. Attempts to capture requirements of an execution environment to some extent and automate their deployment have also been made before: for example, the virtual appliance project [20] uses virtual machines configured based on descriptions in a configuration language to ease administrative burden, and the Cluster on Demand (COD) project [7] allows a user to choose from a database of configurations to configure a partition of a cluster. The Xenoserver project [22] is building an infrastructure for wide-area distributed computing based on virtual machines similar to Globus virtual workspace. We differ from these projects by our focus on the dynamic features of managing virtual execution environment for grid applications during the application runtime.

The adaptive computing is not a new concept, for example, an adaptive scheduling method is presented in [5], while this method doesn't give full control of applications to the developers. In [10], a Program Control Language is proposed, which provides a novel means of specifying adaptations in distributed applications. Gorender et. al presented an adaptive programming model for fault-tolerant distributed computing, which provides upper-layer applications with process state information according to the QoS [14]. In [3], a component-based autonomous repair management in distributed systems is presented, which provides the adaptive replication ability to manage the subsystems. The related work has the similar concepts to ADVE, whereas, ADVE focuses on providing an adaptive execution environment for grid applications which targets fault-tolerance and load balancing for grid computing with adaptive technology. DRIC framework proposed an policy-based fault-tolerance architecture for grid applications [15]. DRIC has the similar concept to make a dependable grid computing environment for grid applications as ADVE, while DRIC focus on provide fault-tolerance technique for applications themselves with the help of the grid middleware, such as checkpointing the application, re-submitting the application, while ADVE focuses on creating adaptive execution environments for grid applications. An adaptive replication middle-ware is presented by MEAD research group [9]. Just like DRIC, MEAD also targets the fault-tolerance of the applications themselves, not the environments.

3 Architecture of ADVE

In this section, the architecture of ADVE is presented first, and the adaptive model in ADVE is discussed, which makes dynamic actions according to the dynamic changes of the grid environments and users' requests. Later, the situations for adaptation is discussed, and the policies and plans are also presented in this section.

3.1 Components of ADVE

As illustrated in section 1, ADVE is implemented with virtual machines and adaptive components. The adaptive capability of ADVE is fulfilled by the Dynaco component [8]. Dynaco is a component which provides the capability for developers to make adaptive decisions with policies and plans. The components of ADVE is shown in Fig. 1. ADVE is composed by three parts, the adaptive component, the virtual execution adaptor (VEA), and the virtual execution environment (VEE).

- **Adaptive components.** Adaptive components are implemented with Dynaco. In ADVE, the Dynaco gets the system information of the grid environment from *Monitor* with pull or push method, the *Monitor* collects the

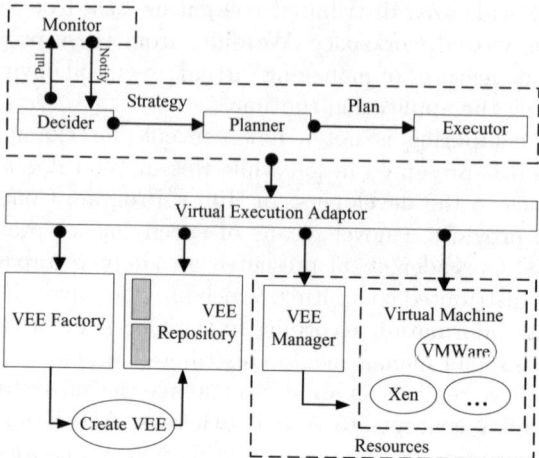

Fig. 1. Components of ADVE

information of the grid environment and job status, such as the network traffic, cpu load, and job requests. The Dynaco make adaptive decisions with the internal components of *Decider* and *Planner*. Decider makes *strategies* to guide the planner to make an adaptive *plan* for *executor*. The *Decider* makes the strategy based on the *policy*, which describes component-specific information required to make the decisions. The *Planner* is a program that modifies the components. The planner makes an adaptation plan that makes the component adopt a given strategy by the decider, and the plan-making is based on the *guide*. The *executor* take the adaptive action to the outsider. The *Executor* is a virtual machine to interpret the plan provided by the planner by means of *actions*. For example *creating a virtual execution environment* is an action. Dynaco has implemented the dynamic framework, we only add adaptive policies and guides to guide the adaptation, for example, *upon system overload, create an new virtual execution environment* is a policy, and *transfer new image and deploy the new image* can be the guide for the strategy of creating a new virtual execution.

- **Virtual execution adaptor.** The virtual execution adaptor is a bridge between the Dynaco and the virtual execution environment. Because Dynaco only handles the adaptive policy, the VEE creation and management should be handled by the grid middleware, and interaction between the virtual machine and the grid also needs a bridge to fix the gap, for example, creating a virtual execution environment and executing grid application on it should handles the interaction between grid middlewares and virtual machines. The VEA have the following functions: passing the request of a grid user to VEA and transferring the responses back from the VEEs to the grid user; pulling and pushing the monitoring information of the VEEs to the monitor; passing

the deployment and suspending action from Dynaco to VEEs; starting the applications on the virtual environment; and migrating one application from one VEE to another environment.
- **Virtual execution environment.** The VEE is based on Globus virtual workspation [17]. The VEE refines the execution environment layer in grid architecture: rather than mapping jobs directly onto hardware resources, VEE maps jobs to preconfigured execution environments which can then be mapped to grid resources. Since a VEE may exist beyond its deployment, and may in fact be deployed many times on different resources during its lifetime, two new services are introduced: VEE Repository which provides a management interface to execution environment, and VEE Manager which orchestrates their deployment. In order to create a VEE instance, VEA contacts the VEE Factory with a VEE description by XML schema. A negotiation process may take place to ensure that the VEE is created in a policy controlled way. The newly created VEE is registered with a VEE Repository, which provides a grid service interface allowing for inspection and management of VEE and keeps track of resources implementing VEE such as virtual machine images. As a result of creation the client is returned a WSRF [6] end-point reference (EPR) to the workspace. To deploy a VEE on a specific resource, VEA contacts a VEE Manager grid service on that resource and presents it the VEEs EPR. The VEE Manager allows a client to deploy/undeploy, start/stop, and also pause/unpause execution environment. Based on such functions, the adaptive components can make adaptive actions to improve the execution performance.

3.2 Model of Adaptive Virtual Environment

As mentioned above, ADVE tries to provide a flexible and dependable environment for grid applications. The targets of ADVE system is to improve the ratio of the grid resources' usage and to enhance the application reliability. These targets are fulfilled by the adaptive model in ADVE system. To illustrate the adaptive model, some definitions are presented first.

Definition 1. Throughput (T): Throughput of a grid resource (R) is defined as the number of requests that R can handle in a specific time interval (t).

Definition 2. Reliability (r): Reliability of a grid application is defined as the possibility that no application failure has occurred in a specific time interval (t).

Definition 3. Adaptive Overhead (AO): The adaptive overhead is defined as the sum of the Dynaco starting time and passing adaptive instruction to actions. The time for passing adaptive instruction to actions refers to the time that the instruction passing from *decider* to *VEA*.

Definition 4. Virtual Machine Overhead (VMO): The virtual machine overhead is defined as the execution time for starting/stopping, pausing/unpausing, and deploying/undeploying of the virtual machine.

To improve the throughput of the grid resources, ADVE creates a new VEE dynamically according to user requests and resources usage. To enhance the reliability of an application, ADVE creates a new VEE to migrate the application or to create an replica of the application. ADVE uses a decision-making method to make adaptive actions to improve the system performance. The target equation for decision making is shown in Eq. 1.

$$\begin{cases} Maxmum(T); \\ Maxmum(r); \\ Minmum(AO*i + VMO*j). \end{cases} \quad (1)$$

where i in Eq. 1 refers to the number of actions that Dynaco takes, and j refers to the number of virtual machine management. According to Eq. 1, the adaptive model in ADVE is a multi-objective decision making problem, and ADVE takes *Analytic Hierarchy Process Method* (AHP) to make decisions [23].

3.3 Situations for Adaptation

To illustrate the adaptive model, we first present the situations for adaptation. Generally, there are three situations that ADVE will make adaptive actions to improve the performance, they are as follows:

- Number of request changes. When there are new users' requests arrive, the load for each VEE changes, and ADVE will compute the decision-making target function to decide whether to create a new VEE or not. At the other side, when the number of users' request decrease, ADVE will compute the decision-making target function to decide whether to stop a VEE to decrease the management overhead and execution management of a virtual machine.
- computational load changes. When one computational resources is overload, for example CPU is overload, ADVE will create a new VEE to handle this. When some computational load decrease, ADVE will undeploy a VEE to reduce the management overhead.
- Resources down. In grid environment, it is very common that some resources are down during job execution. When some resources down, ADVE will create new VEEs on new available resources to take over the request on failed resources.

3.4 Adaptive Policies and Plans

Based on the situation analysis above, we can present the adaptive policies and the plans in ADVE, the policies and the plans are defined with Java language which can be recognized and interpreted by Dynaco system. To illustrate policies and plans simply, we take a natural language to present them. The policy for the change of request numbers can be given as Table 1.

In Table 1, there are two actions that need plans to guide, and they are *create a new VEE* and *undeploy a VEE*. Fig. 2 shows the plan template for creating a VEE. As shown in Fig. 2, to create a new VEE, ADVE need to take the following

Table 1. Policies for the change of user request numbers

Situation	Stategy
{upon request increase over a threshold}	create a new VEE
{upon request decrease than a threshhold}	undeploy a VEE

> **Algorithm**: *Create a new VEE*
>
> *Preparing a virtual machine image;*
>
> *Searching available resources for deploying;*
>
> *Transferring virtual machine image;*
>
> *Deploying virtual machine as grid services;*
>
> *Returning VEEID;*

Fig. 2. Plan template for creating a new VEE

actions: preparing a virtual machine image for the VEE; searching available resources to deploy the virtual machine; transferring the virtual machine to the selected resources; deploying the virtual machine as grid services; and returning the ID of VEE to the VEE manager.

4 Performance Evaluation

As mentioned above, ADVE is implemented with Globus virtual workspace. ADVE uses Xen (version 3.0) as the implementation of virtual machine. The Grid services and infrastructure were implemented by using GT4 (Version 4.0.5). The VM image is Debian (version 3.1) with the size of about 1 GB. To stage a VEE, the VEE Manager transfers the virtual machine image (including description metadata and the implementation-specific image) from the VEE Repository to the host node by using GridFTP. All experiments were run on a 2.33 GHz with 4GB memory Xeon server configured to run single-CPU guest VMs. Once the transferring of VM image is complete, the VEE Manager waits for the VEA to start the VEE, which includes creating a VEE resource, loading the VM image into memory, and booting the VM.

The performance impact of virtual machines on applications has been shown to be small (typically under 5% of slowdown) for different application classes [4]. In our evaluation, we first explored the throughput of the adaptive implementation. In our preliminary evaluation, we explored the performance impact of different ways of using VMs as part of Grid infrastructure. We also conducted a preliminary evaluation of VM usage with applications. The application service is an image grey transformation algorithm, and the request of a user is a call to rend a image on specific grid resources. The throughput between ADVE and the grid system without adaptive VMs is shown in Fig. 3.

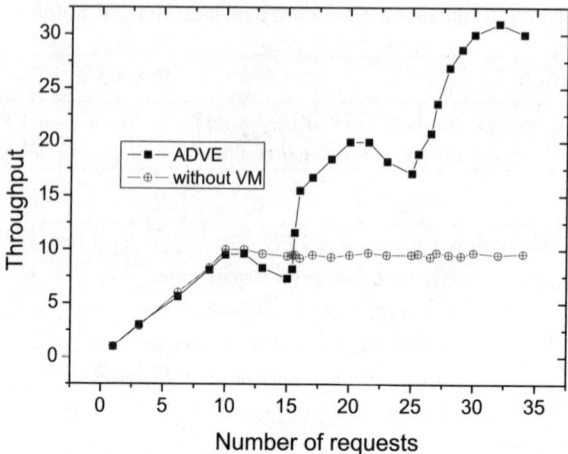

Fig. 3. Throughput of ADVE

In Fig. 3, the x-axis shows the numbers of request in one minute, the y-axis shows the throughput in one minute. From Fig. 3, we can see the follows:

1) If the number of requests in one minute is less than 10, the throughputs of ADVE and the grid system without adaptive VMs are almost the same, and the throughput grows linearly. This shows that when the pressure for user requests is not so high, ADVE and the grid system without VMs perform almost the same. Also, we can see that the throughput of ADVE is a little lower than the system without VMs, this throughput difference comes from the small overhead of VMs.

2) If the number of requests in one minute is more than 10 and less than 17, the throughput of ADVE is lower than the system without VMs. The reason for this is that ADVE will create new VEEs to improve the throughput, while the deployment of VEE will create new overhead, and the throughput will decrease.

3) If the number of requests in one minute is more than 17, the throughput of ADVE is much higher than the system without adaptive VMs. The reason for this is that there are more VEEs to handle the request, and the throughput grows.

4) There are three decreasing arcs in the line describes the throughput of ADVE in Fig. 3. The reason for these decreasing is that ADVE is creating new VEEs, and the deployment of a new VEE brings extra overhead, while the numbers of VEEs doesn't change during the deployment process.

The second evaluation explored the reliability of applications on ADVE. We ran image grey transformation program, the failure-free execution time is about 60 seconds. We set the checkpoint interval of the application is about 6 seconds, and the checkpoint overhead and the recovery time from the checkpoint image are about 0.5 second. We set the down time of the grid middleware and the VEE as 60 seconds. The evaluation results are shown in Fig 4. We experiment one thousand jobs for each mean time to failure (MTTF) testing, and the execution time in Fig. 4 is the mean time of these executions. Fig. 4 shows the relationship between the execution time and the mean time to failure. In Fig. 4, the x-axis shows the MTTF, the y-axis shows the the mean time of these executions. From Fig. 4, we can see the follows:

1) When the MTTF is less than 60 seconds, the execution time over ADVE is much less than the system without adaptive VMs. This shows that ADVE is suitable for long-duration jobs over unreliable grid environments.

2) If the MTTF is longer than 120 seconds, the execution time difference between the ADVE and the non-adaptive system is very small. The difference decreasing can be explain as this: an application runs over a reliable environment can get a good reliability, so the improvement will not be so obvious. Fig. 4 also shows that the execution time over ADVE is a little smaller than over non-adaptive systems, this shows that an application can more reliability of the applications even over reliable environments with ADVE than with non-adaptive system, despite of the extra overhead of ADVE.

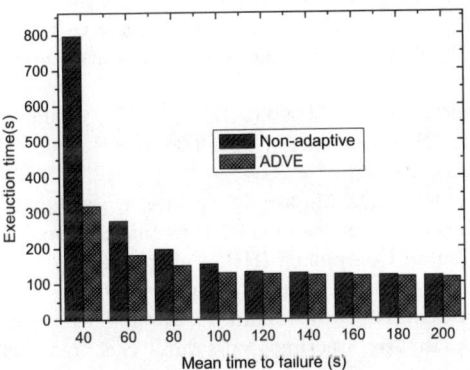

Fig. 4. Throughput of ADVE

5 Conclusions and Future Work

In this paper, an adaptive and dependable virtual execution environment called ADVE is presented. ADVE merges the idea of adaptive computing and virtual machine technology to provide a virtual dynamic execution environment for Grid applications. ADVE creates or undeploys virtual machines over physical Grid resources based on Grid environment changes and Grid users' requests changes, such as number of service requests changes, resource load changes. The experiment conducted in this paper shows that ADVE can improve the throughput of the Grid resources and the reliability of Grid applications with the adaptive virtual machine technology. In the near future, we will improve ADVE with more dynamic policies to enhance the reliability of Grid applications and to improve the flexibility of management of virtual machines. Moreover, we will improve the performance of virtual machine image transferring with I/O scheduling technology.

References

1. Adabala, S., Chadha, V., Chawla, P., Figueiredo, R., Fortes, J., Krsul, I., Matsunaga, A., Tsugawa, M., Zhang, J., Zhao, M., Zhu, L., Zhu, X.: From Virtualized Resources to Virtual Computing Grids: The In-VIGO System. Future Generation Computer Systems (2004)
2. Buisson, J., André, F., Pazat, J.: A Framework for Dynamic Adaptation of Parallel Components. In: Proceeds of ParCo 2005 (September 2005)
3. Bouchenak, S., Boyer, F., Hagimont, D., et al.: Architecture-Based Autonomous Repair Management: An Application to J2EE Clusters. In: Proceedings of the IEEE Symposium on Reliable Distributed Systems (2005)
4. Barham, P., Dragovic, B., Fraser, K., Hand, S., Harris, T., Ho, A., Neugebar, R., Pratt, I., Warfield, A.: Xen and the Art of Virtualization. In: ACM Symposium on Operating Systems Principles (SOSP) (2003)
5. Berman, F., Wolski, R., Casanova, H., et al.: Adaptive Computing on the Grid using AppLes. IEEE Trans. on Parallel and Distributed Systems (TPDS) 14(4), 369–382 (2003)
6. Czajkowski, K., Ferguson, D., Foster, I., Frey, J., Graham, S., Sedukhin, I., Snelling, D., Tuecke, S., Vambenepe, W.: The WS-Resource Framework (2004), http://www.globus.org/wsrf
7. Chase, J., Grit, L., Irwin, D., Moore, J., Sprenkle, S.: Dynamic Virtual Clusters in a Grid Site Manager. In: Proceedings of 12th International Symposium on High Performance Distributed Computing (HPDC-12) (2003)
8. Dynaco, http://gforge.inria.fr/projects/dynaco
9. Dumitras, T., Srivastava, D., Narasimhan, P.: Architecting and Implementing Versatile Dependability. In: Architecting Dependable Systems, vol. III (2005)
10. Ensink, B., Stanley, J., Adve, V.: Program Control Language: a Programming Language for Adaptive Distributed Applications. Journal of Parallel and Distributed Computing 62(11), 1082–1104 (2003)
11. Foster, I.: The Grid: A New Infrasture for 21st Century Science. Physics Today 55(22), 42–47 (2002)
12. Figueiredo, R., Dinda, P., Fortes, J.: A Case for Grid Computing on Virtual Machines. In: 23rd International Conference on Distributed Computing Systems (2003)
13. Foster, I., Kesselman, C., Tuecke, S.: The Anatomy of the Grid: Enabling Scalable Virtual Organizations. International Journal of Supercomputer Applications 15(3), 200–222 (2001)
14. Gorender, S., de Araújo Macêdo, R.J., Raynal, M.: An Adaptive Programming Model for Fault-Tolerant Distributed Computing. IEEE Transactions on Dependable and Secure Computing 4(1), 18–31 (2007)
15. Jin, H., Shi, X., Qiang, W., Zou, D.: DRIC: Dependable Grid Computing Framework. IEICE Transactions on Information and Systems E89-D(2), 612–623 (2006)
16. Jiang, X., Xu, D.: VIOLIN: Virtual Internetworking on OverLay INfrastructure. Department of Computer Sciences Technical Report CSD TR 03-027, Purdue University (2003)

17. Keahey, K., Foster, I., Freeman, T., Zhang, X., Galron, D.: Virtual Workspaces in the Grid. In: Proceedings of Europar 2005, Lisbon, Portugal (September 2005)
18. Krsul, I., Ganguly, A., Zhang, J., Fortes, J., Figueiredo, R.: VMPlants: Providing and Managing Virtual Machine Execution Environments for Grid Computing. In: SC 2004, Pittsburgh, PA (2004)
19. Meyer, R.A., Seawright, L.H.: A virtual machine time sharing system. IBM System Journal 9(3), 199–218 (1970)
20. Sapuntzakis, C., Brumley, D., Chandra, R., Zeldovich, N., Chow, J., Lam, M.S., Rosenblum, M.: Virtual Appliances for Deploying and Maintaining Software. In: Proceedings of the 17th Large Installation Systems Administration Conference (LISA 2003) (2003)
21. Sundararaj, A., Dinda, P.: Towards Virtual Networks for Virtual Machine Grid Computing. In: 3rd USENIX Conference on Virtual Machine Technology (2004)
22. xenoserver project, http://www.xenoservers.net/
23. Zahedi, F.: The analytic hierachy process - a survey of the method and its applications. Interfaces 16(4), 96–108 (1986)

An Incentive Approach for Computational Resource Sharing in the Autonomous Environment

Chuliang Weng, Minglu Li, and Xinda Lu

Department of Computer Science and Engineering,
Shanghai Jiao Tong University, Shanghai 200240, China
weng-cl@cs.sjtu.edu.cn

Abstract. Advances in computer technology and network technology provide a chance that multiple distributed computational resources can be shared by Internet to solve large-scale computing problems. In this paper, we focus on computational resources, and present an incentive sharing approach for this kind of resources in the autonomous environment. Firstly, we describe the sharing scenario, in which the barter auction mechanism is adopted and the deed is used to keep the trace of trades between different resource control domains. Then we discuss the evaluation methodology for testing the proposed approach. Thirdly, the auction schema is described, and the calling strategy and the responding strategy of auction are introduced. The simulation is performed based on the synthetic workloads to evaluate the performance of the auction strategies, and experimental results indicate that the barter auction method can allow computational resource domains to provide better computing service to their users.

1 Introduction

Internet-based computing [1] such as grid computing and peer-to-peer computing is a new occurring computing scenario with the development of network technology and computer technology. With these technologies, multiple independent domains can share computer resources with each other, such as storage resources and computational resources.

However, one more important characteristic of general Internet-based computing is that computational resources don't belong to one organization and correspondingly are not controlled under one administrator. Traditional client-server models and scheduling strategies will be not suitable for the new occurring computing mode.

On the other hand, the economic incentive mechanism is an effective means, and some research efforts are focusing on introducing economic mechanisms such as tânonment and auction into resource management for Internet-based computing [2], which usually is based on the assumption of using economic currency. However, this mode needs the specified organization to manage currency and price resources, which will become a burden and attenuate the advantage of the economic mechanism.

How to apply appropriate economic mechanisms and business models to the Internet-based computing, is still a major challenge. In this paper, we propose an incentive approach for Internet-based resource sharing, wherein there is no centralized auctioneer responsible for pricing resources, and resources are shared by the barter auction mechanism. A barter auction is an auction where the auctioneer is willing to accept barter offers from bidders, rather than currency.

In this paper, we focus on one kind of resource sharing, i.e., computational resources, and the rigid job model is adopted [3][4], where rigid jobs are jobs that specify the number of processors they need, and run for a certain time using this number of processors. Our main goal is to study the resource sharing by the barter auction among different resource control domains, and analyze the benefit from the peer-to-peer resource sharing with the barter auction and the tradeoff among different auction strategies.

Specifically, we have the following contributions in this paper. We present a resource sharing mechanism by which different autonomous resource domains can exploit computational resources in the other domains with considering the economic interest of individuals; we examine two different bidding strategies that domains can use for determining how to organize the auction and how to respond to it; we implement the presented mechanism and strategies with simulation, and give the simulation results to analyze the performance.

The rest of this paper is organized as follows. Related work is briefly discussed in Section 2, and the resource sharing scenario is described in Section 3. Evaluation methodology is described in Section 4, and Section 5 describes the auction strategies, and the experiment is performed in Section 6. At last, Section 7 concludes this paper.

2 Related Works

There are some research efforts on the resource management for the Internet-based computing based on economic mechanism.

Spawn [5] is a market-based computational system that utilizes idle computational resources in a heterogeneous network of workstations. Spawn adopts the sealed-bid, second-price auction to achieve resource allocation fairly. In GRACE [6][2], a significant research is performed on applying economic mechanisms to resource management for grid computing, however, the work is at high level and no implementation or performance has been put forward, and how to apply economic models to grid computing properly is still an open problem. In G-commerce [7], there are resource consumers and resource producers in the system. Commodities market and auction are adopted to analyze the efficiency of resource allocation respectively, and the two market strategies are compared in terms of price stability, market equilibrium, consumer efficiency and producer efficiency. GridIS [8] is a P2P decentralized scheduling framework, wherein there are two kinds of partes: resource consumers and resource providers, and the price mechanism is adopted to realize the incentive-based scheduling objectives.

One work focusing on storage resources sharing is [9], where the first-price, sealed bid auction is adopted, and it is a barter system rather than trading by money. The barter model for resource sharing in data grids is presented in [10].

Differing from these existed works, in this paper, the barter method is used to achieve the computational resource sharing among different resource control domains, where not only the economic interest is considered but also the pricing difficulty in the dynamic Internet-based computing environment can be avoided. Compared to the previous work, the presented method is more realistic and can be applied more flexibly to the practical scenario.

3 Sharing Scenario and Deed

In the Internet-based computing environment, computational resources are autonomous, that is to say, the owner of computational resources has the ultimate control right on the resources and has its own self-interest of its resources, which differs from the existed centralized and voluntary computing environment, where a scheduler can control the utilization of computational resources and assign computational jobs on all computational resources.

3.1 Sharing Scenario

In this paper, the term "domain" is used to denote an individual administrative domain of computational resources, and the organization of domains in the Internet-based computing environment is illustrated as Fig. 1.

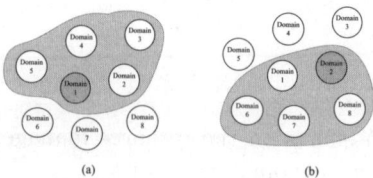

Fig. 1. A sharing scenario

As Fig. 1 shows, sometime domain 1 employed the computing resources in domain 2, 3, 4, and 5, illustrated as Fig. 1(a). At the other time, domain 2 employed the computing resources in domain 1, 6, 7 and 8, illustrated as Fig. 1(b). For domain 1 and 2, they achieve the goal of employing more resources than they owned when its load is larger than its capacity, through trading away idle resources at the other time.

3.2 Deed

As the resource sharing is not free, and the economic factor should be considered. For keeping the trace of resource trades, the concept of the deed is adopted in this paper, which acts as a bookkeeping mechanism among domains that trust each other.

The *deed* is a contract among domains that trust each other and is the warrant of one domain to employ computational resources in another domain. The domain requesting the remote computational resources is called as *debtor*, and the domain providing resources to the outside is called as *debtee*. Considering the rigid job model adopted in this paper, the number of CPU and the runtime with this number of CPU should be defined in a deed. Therefore, a deed between two domains is a quadruple: $deed_i = <debtee_i, debtor_i, num\_proc_i, runtime_i>$.

Where, the *debtor* and the *debtee* are different autonomous domains, and *debtor* has used computational resources in the *debtee*, which is described by num_proc processors for the time $runtime$. The runtime is the execution time based on the CPU speed of the debtor.

When trading with an existed deed, the trading job should have the same number of processors as in the existed deed, and the completion of the trade is achieved by modifying the existed deed. Otherwise, a new deed is created. It should be noted that the two domains maybe have multiple deeds, and these deeds should have different values of num_proc.

4 Evaluation Methodology

4.1 Resource Model

Corresponding to the sharing scenario (see section 3), we describe the resource in terms of domain. Formally, D_i denotes domain i, and the Internet-based computing environment can be denoted by $\Theta = \{D_1, D_2, ..., D_n\}$, where the number of domains in the environment is n.

One domain is considered as a supercomputer, and can process parallel jobs. We assume that it consists of a certain number of processors with a certain speed. Formally, there are p_i homogeneous processors in domain i, and p_i is equal to the power of 2, and the speed of processors is u_i.

In addition, one submitted job can be executed in all domains in the computing environment. Although computers in different domains maybe have different architectures or different operating systems. However, some technologies can be used to overcome the obstacle. For example, the application programmed with the Java language can run on multiple operating systems, or applications running on Linux can run on AIX operating system in IBM pSeries just after being recompiled [11].

The computing job studied in this paper is computation-intensive rather than communication-intensive, and the runtime of a computing job is far greater than the time of transferring the executable file and the data file. For simplicity, we will do not consider the communication time between different domains.

4.2 Workload Modelling

In this paper, we generate the synthetic workloads according to the Feitelson Model [3]. There is one job sequence on each domain, respectively. For each job arriving at one domain, it requires a certain number of processors, and has an arrival time, and has a runtime on the domain with the specified number of processors in a dedicated setting.

Formally, there is a job sequence C_i on domain i, which is submitted to this domain, and consists of job $jb_1^i, jb_2^i, ..., jb_{m_i}^i$, where, m_i is the total number of jobs in domain i. And each job jb_k^i submitted to domain i has the follow properties: $num\_proc(jb_k^i)$ is the required number of processors, $arr\_time(jb_k^i)$ is the arrival time, $run\_time_i(jb_k^i)$ is the runtime with the required number of processors on domain i.

The rigid job model is adopted [3][4]. Rigid jobs are jobs that specify the number of processors they require, and run for a certain time using this number of processors. If one domain is overloading, the new arrival jobs will be considered to be scheduled to the other domains after the domain bartering with other domains. As the CPU speed in one domain i usually differing from the CPU speed in the other domain j, we assume that the runtime of one job has the relation as Equation (1).

$$run\_time_j = run\_time_i \times \frac{u_i}{u_j} \qquad (1)$$

For avoiding the thrashing phenomenon that one job is scheduled on two domains in the come-and-go fashion before being executed, we assume that one job can not be rescheduled after it had been assigned to one domain.

4.3 Performance Metrics

The traditional performance metrics include two aspects, one is from the user's perspective, and the other is from the system's perspective. Besides the two performance metrics, we will consider one new metric referred to the barter auction.

Firstly, we define following parameters: $sta\_time(jb_k^i)$ denotes the start time of job jb_k^i, $fin\_time(jb_k^i)$ denotes the completed time of job jb_k^i, $res\_time(jb_k^i)$ denotes the response time of job jb_k^i, and $res\_time(jb_k^i) = fin\_time(jb_k^i) - arr\_time(jb_k^i)$.

From the perspective of users, we adopt the average job *slowdown* and average job wait time. *slowdown* is defined as follows: $sd(jb_k^i) = \frac{\max(res\_time(jb_k^i), \delta)}{\max(run\_time(jb_k^i), \delta)}$, where, for reducing the statistical impact of very short jobs, we adopt a minimum runtime according to [12], which is denoted by δ, we set $\delta = 10$ seconds in this paper.

The *wait time* of job jb_k^i is defined as follows: $wai\_time(jb_k^i) = sta\_time(jb_k^i) - arr\_time(jb_k^i)$.

The other performance metric is from the system's perspective. We adopt the resource *utilization* of each domain to evaluate the system performance, that is, the fraction of computational resources that are actually utilized in a certain duration. We define the utilization of domain i as follows: $U_i = \frac{\sum_{k=1}^{m_i^a} n_k^a \times run\_time_i(jba_k^i)}{p_i \times fin\_time(jba_{m_i^a}^i)}$, where, $\{jba_1^i, jba_2^i, ..., jba_{m_i^a}^i\}$ is the job sequence, which actually runs on domain i, and the total is m_i^a. n_k^a is the required number of processors corresponding to the job jba_k^i.

We define *uncleared deed ratio* to reflect the trade unbalance of one domain for a period of time T. It is defined as follows for domain D_k.

$$Unc\_ratio(D_k) = (\sum_{debtor_i=k} num\_proc_i \times runtime_i \\ - \sum_{debtee_i=k} num\_proc_i \times runtime_i)/(p_k \times T) \qquad (2)$$

5 Auction and Bidding Strategies

5.1 Auction Schema

In the Internet-based computing environment, one domain should consider the following issues: when to call auction if it is overload and how to organize one auction, and how to respond to the auction request from the other domains if it is underload.

Firstly, we pay attention to when to launch a barter auction. We adopt *auction event* to denote the time that an auction is launched. We assume that there is one launching domain in each auction event. When multiple domains are overload, a choosing algorithm is required to determine this domain. In this paper, the launching domain in each auction event is the domain with the maximal overload among all overloading domains at the auction event.

Then, we propose an auction schema for each domain in the Internet-based computing context, which is described with the following pseudo-code shown as Table 1. And the bidding strategies will be introduced in the next subsection.

In Table 1, T_q denotes the execution time of the queue of the uncompleted jobs and the arriving jobs on domain i before the next auction event. We adopt the jobs arrived in the interval between this auction event and the last auction event to forecast the arriving jobs before the next auction event. We assume that the domain is overloading if T_q is larger than a threshold Γ_{over}, and the domain is underloading if T_q is less than a threshold Γ_{under}. In addition, we adopt status $S_{autarkic}$ to describe the status that the domain only receives the jobs submitted from the local, and schedules the submitted jobs in the local context.

When an auction occurring, the calling or launching parter and the responding parters can use existed deeds or create new deeds if auctioning successfully, otherwise, the auction terminates without any trading.

5.2 Trading Procedure

After auctioning successfully, the next procedure is how to complete the trade. Specifically, the trading procedure is described as Table 2.

In Table 2, $runtime'$ equals the sum of $runtime$ and the bid B (that is, the length of time for running jobs on num_proc processors, provided by domain i to domain j as a response for this trade in the future, which is determined by domain j according to its bidding strategy).

Table 1. The auction schema

For domain i at each auction event:

step 1
  Estimate the current load according to the queue of the uncompleted jobs and arriving jobs on domain i.
  if $T_q > \Gamma_{over}$
  then domain i is overloading and goto **step 2**.
  else if $T_q < \Gamma_{under}$
  then domain i is underloading and goto **step 3**.
  else domain i will keep status $S_{autarkic}$ before the next auction event.

step 2
  1) Participate in the choosing procedure of the launching domain.
  2) **If** the domain is chosen as the launching domain, **then**:
    a) Determine the job set $C_{auction}$ for the forthcoming auction, and call auctions for the job set.
    b) If auctioning successfully, the local jobs are assigned to the remote domains and the corresponding deeds are exchanged.
  3) Domain i will keep status $S_{autarkic}$ before the next auction event.

step 3
  1) Wait for the bid request, and adopt the auction strategies to respond to the remote auction request if a bid is solicited.
  2) If auctioning successfully while the domain is not overloading, the remote jobs are received and scheduled as the same as the local jobs, in the meanwhile, the deeds are exchanged with the remote domains.
  3) Domain i will keep status $S_{autarkic}$ before the next auction event.

There are two situations for $runtime''$: If $runtime > B \times \frac{u_i}{u_j}$, $runtime'' = runtime - B \times \frac{u_i}{u_j}$, and the deed is $< i, j, num\_proc, runtime'' >$. Otherwise, $runtime'' = B - runtime \times \frac{u_j}{u_i}$, and the deed is $< j, i, num\_proc, runtime'' >$.

If $runtime''$ equals to zero, it indicates that the two domains have no debt in the situation that the number of processors required by the job is num_proc, then the two domains will destroy the deed with the specific num_proc, whose debtee and debtor are the two domains.

5.3 Bidding Strategies

According to the auction schema (See Table 1), the auction strategies consist of the strategy for the calling parter and the strategy for the responding parter.

The *calling strategy* of an auction focuses on when and how to launch an auction. We define the time for auctioning as *auction event*, and assume that *auction event* occurs in a fixed interval T_a, at which one domain will estimate the load status. The load status is estimated based on the queue of uncompleted

Table 2. The trading procedure

---

step 1
  if the debtor domain i and the debtee domain j has no deed with
    num_proc, which equals the number of processors required by the
    job in the trade to be completed.
  then goto **step 2**.
  else goto **step 3**.
step 2
  The debtor domain i and the debtee domain j create a new deed with
    the following format: $< j, i, num\_proc, runtime >$.
step 3
  if the debtor domain i had owed the debtee domain j according to
    the existed deed:
    $< j, i, num\_proc, runtime >$.
  then update the existed deed by:
    $< j, i, num\_proc, runtime' >$.
  else
    The formant of the existed deed is
    $< i, j, num\_proc, runtime >$,
    Correspondingly, update the existed deed by:
    $< debtee, debtor, num\_proc, runtime'' >$.

---

jobs and arriving jobs on the domain. If $T_q > \Gamma_{over}$ (See 5.1), the domain will participate in the choosing procedure of the calling or launching domain and act as a calling parter if success.

The job set $C_{auction}$ on the calling domain is the trading jobs, which is one part of the queue of the submitted and uncompleted jobs on the domain. As first come first serve (FCFS) is adopted as the queuing policy, so we define that $C_{auction}$ consists of the minimum set of the jobs in the tail of the job queue, which will be scheduled to remote domains so that the system load is expected to be less than the overload threshold.

The calling domain will solicit bids for each job in $C_{auction}$ from all other domains. In a bid, it is a time value, that is the time that the remote domain will use the corresponding number of processors in the calling domain in the near future, which is a barter for the specific job executed on the remote domain. If at least one bid is submitted, the calling domain will choose a winner, whose bid is the minimum of all bids, and a new deed or an existed deed with a modification is assigned to the remote domain. If two equal bids occur, the calling domain will choose one winner randomly. If no bid is submitted for a job in $C_{auction}$, the auction for this job will terminate, and the calling domain maybe launch another auction for the job in next auction event.

On the other hand, the *responding strategy* of an auction focuses on how to calculate the bid B for running a remote job on the local domain. We propose two responding or bidding strategies shown as follows in this paper.

One bidding strategy is that, the responding domain can use the *num_proc* processors in the calling domain for the time length B as a barter of running the auctioning job in itself, and the runtime of this job executed on the responding domain is $run\_time_{res}(trading\_job)$. Then, they have the following relation:

$$B = run\_time_{res}(trading\_job) \times \frac{u_{res}}{u_{cal}} \qquad (3)$$

which is in response to equation (1), and u_{res} and u_{cal} are the CPU speed of the responding domain and the calling domain, respectively. We call this strategy as the *EqualTimeBid* strategy.

The more flexible bidding strategy is that, the relation is

$$B = F(run\_time_{res}(trading\_job) \times \frac{u_{res}}{u_{cal}}) \qquad (4)$$

The responding domain can determine a bid based on some factors such as the load of its resources, how desirable to trade with the calling domain, and so on, which is captured by the function $F(\cdot)$. We call this strategy as the *AdaptiveBid* strategy.

In this paper, we define $F(x) = \frac{T_q}{T_a} \cdot x$, although there maybe exist more complicated fashions adopted for $F(\cdot)$. The rationale behind the defined $F(x)$ is that the underloading domain with the less load can make a cheaper price (a smaller bid) for the execution of the overloading jobs, which conforms to the economic principle in the practical society.

6 Experiment and Results

We had developed a discrete event-driven simulator with C programming language to study the performance of the presented approach. There are mainly two drives for the advance of simulation time, that is, one is the network delay of communication, and the other is the execution of jobs. As we assume that the computing job is computation-intensive rather than communication-intensive in this paper, correspondingly the network delay barely takes effect in the simulation time. Therefore, the communication overhead is not considered in the simulation, and we focus on implementing the auction and bidding strategies. The main purpose of the simulation is to evaluate the performance of the auction strategies used to share resources among different resource control domains.

For expressing the different speed of CPU in different domains, we assume that the speed of CPU in some domains is twice as the speed of CPU in the other domains, while there are 512 homogeneous CPU in each domain. More complicated situations can be easily extended.

In this paper, we adopt backfilling technology to schedule jobs, which attempts to schedule jobs that are behind in the priority queue of waiting jobs to unutilized nodes, rather than keep them idle. To prevent starvation of larger jobs, it requires that the execution of a job selected out of order will not delay the start of jobs that are ahead of it in the priority queue. This method is based on the estimation of jobs' execution time. As for queuing policy, first come first serve (FCFS) is adopted as the rule that prioritizes the order with which jobs are selected for execution. That is, jobs are ordered according to their arrival time. In short, the FCFS priority policy together with backfilling is adopted to schedule jobs in each domain.

The interval of auction events is 2 hours, that is, $T_a = 7200$ seconds. At each auction event, there is one calling parter, which is overloading, and the overload value in this domain is the maximum among all overloading domains at this time. At one auction event, one or more domains will act as responding parters on the condition that the domain is underloading. The calling pater will choose one appropriate parter for each job if the trade is successful, and schedule the overloading jobs to the corresponding domains. For determining the status of one domain, we set the threshold $\Gamma_{over} = \frac{4}{3}T_a$ and $\Gamma_{under} = \frac{1}{3}T_a$.

In the simulation, the synthetic workload is generated according to the Feitelson model [3]. The job sequence arrived in each domain includes 10000 jobs, in which the maximal number of processors required by jobs is 256.

For analyzing the performance of different strategies, the mean of interarrival time distribution varies from 300 seconds to 900 seconds with a step of 100 seconds, corresponding to the reduction of the system load. For testing average slowdown and uncleared deed ratio, we perform 500 runs for each simulation situation. As the standard deviation of our measurements is less than 10%, then the average value can capture the characteristic of the performance. And the characteristic of each measurement in different domains is similar, so we will only give the measurement in domain 1 and 2 because the space is limited in this article.

The average slowdown of the arrival 10000 jobs in domain 1, 2 is illustrated as Fig. 2. Fig. 2 shows that the resource sharing with the barter auction outperforms the scenario that each domain just processes its local jobs independently. In addition, the performance of the AdaptiveBid strategy is also better than the performance of the EqualTimeBid strategy.

Now we turn our attention to the trade balance of each resource domain with the two auction strategies (more specifically, they are responding strategies in

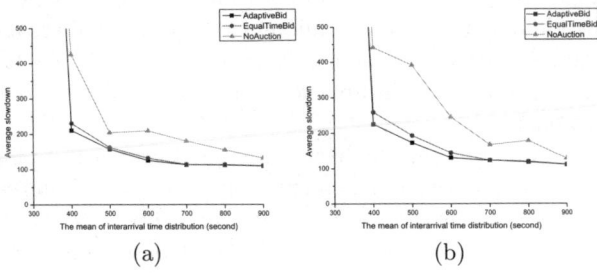

Fig. 2. The average slowdown of jobs arriving on each domain: (a) domain 1, (b) domain 2

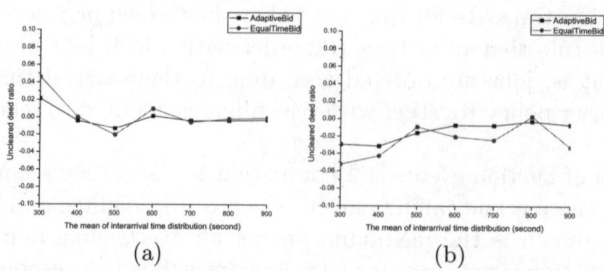

Fig. 3. The uncleared deed ratio of jobs arriving on each domain: (a) domain 1, (b) domain 2

the auction strategy). Uncleared deed ratio is adopted to evaluate the trade balance in each domain, which is defined as Equation (2).

The *uncleared deed ratio*s during the execution of the arrival 10000 jobs in domain 1, 2 are illustrated as Fig. 3. For each domain, the absolute value of the uncleared deed ratio is not larger than 10%, and the value is not larger than 6% for the majority of domains. The result indicates that the barter auction method proposed in this paper can achieve a good balance.

7 Conclusion

In this paper, we challenge the issue of sharing computational resources in the autonomous environment with considering the essential economic interest. Differing from the traditional method that one scheduler is responsible for scheduling jobs on multiple resource domains, the presented approach adopts the peer-to-peer mode to reflect approximately the nature of the autonomous environment. Differing from the existed economic approach used to resource management in the Internet-based computing context, the barter auction method is proposed to implement the paid resource sharing while avoiding the requirement of the concept of "money" and pricing resources.

Experimental results indicate that the presented approach can improve the performance of the computational resources from the end-users' perspective, and obtain a good trade balance between different computational resource domains, which is necessary for a barter system. So we can conclude that the presented incentive sharing approach is suitable for computational resources in the autonomous environment.

We have focused on applying the barter auction mechanism to implement the paid resource sharing between independent computational resource control domains. There is still much work worthy of further study, ongoing works include studying how to implement the deed in the Internet-based autonomous environment, and studying more bidding strategies and calling strategies corresponding to the different application scenarios.

Acknowledgment

This research was supported by the National Natural Science Foundation of China (No.90715030 and No.60503043).

References

1. Rosenberg, A., Yurkewych, M.: Guidelines for scheduling some common computation-dags for internet-based computing. IEEE Transactions on Computers 54, 428–438 (2005)
2. Buyya, R., Abramson, D., Venugopal, S.: The grid economy. Proceedings of the IEEE 93, 698–714 (2005)
3. Feitelson, D.: Experimental analysis of the root causes of performance evaluation results: A backfilling case study. IEEE Transactions on Parallel and Distributed Systems 16, 175–182 (2005)
4. Cirne, W., Berman, F.: A model for moldable supercomputer jobs. In: Proceedings of 15th International conference on Parallel and Distributed Processing Symposium (IPDPS 2001), pp. 59–79. IEEE Computer Society, Los Alamitos (2001)
5. Waldspurger, C., Hogg, T., Huberman, B., Kephart, J., Stornetta, S.: Spawn: A distributed computational economy. IEEE Transactions on Software Engineering 18, 103–117 (1992)
6. Buyya, R.: Economic-based Distributed Resource Management and Scheduling for Grid Computing. PhD thesis, Monash University, Australia (2002)
7. Wolski, R., Plank, J., Brevik, J., Bryan, T.: Analyzing market-based resource allocation strategies for the computational grid. The International Journal of High Performance Computing Applications 15, 258–281 (2001)
8. Xiao, L., Zhu, Y., Ni, L.M., Xu, Z.: Gridis: an incentive-based grid scheduling. In: Proceedings of the 19th IEEE International Parallel and Distributed Processing Symposium, pp. 65b – 65b. IEEE Computer Society Press, Los Alamitos (2005)
9. Cooper, B., Garcia-Molina, H.: Peer-to-peer data preservation through storage auctions. IEEE Transactions on Parallel and Distributed Systems 16, 246 257 (2005)
10. Ozturan, C.: Resource bartering in data grids. Scientific Programming 12, 155–168 (2004)
11. Aix affinity with linux: Technology paper (Technical report), http://www-03.ibm.com/servers/aix/products/aixos/linux/affinity_linux.pdf
12. Feitelson, D., Rudolph, L., Schwiegelshohn, U., Sevcik, K., Won, P.: Theory and practice in parallel job scheduling. In: Feitelson, D.G., Rudolph, L. (eds.) IPPS-WS 1997 and JSSPP 1997. LNCS, vol. 1291, pp. 1–34. Springer, Heidelberg (1997)

Using Moldability to Improve Scheduling Performance of Parallel Jobs on Computational Grid

Kuo-Chan Huang[1], Po-Chi Shih[2], and Yeh-Ching Chung[2]

[1] Department of Computer and Information Science
National Taichung University
No. 140, Min-Shen Road, Taichung, Taiwan
kchuang@mail.ntcu.edu.tw
[2] Department of Computer Science
National Tsing Hua University
101, Section 2, Kuang-Fu Road, Hsinchu, Taiwan
shedoh@sslab.cs.nthu.edu.tw, ychung@cs.nthu.edu.tw

Abstract. In a computational grid environment, a common practice is try to allocate an entire parallel job onto a single participating site. Sometimes a parallel job, upon its submission, cannot fit in any single site due to the occupation of some resources by running jobs. How the job scheduler handles such situations is an important issue which has the potential to further improve the utilization of grid resources as well as the performance of parallel jobs. This paper develops adaptive processor allocation methods based on the moldable property of parallel jobs to deal with such situations in a heterogeneous computational grid environment. The proposed methods are evaluated through a series of simulations using real workload traces. The results indicate that adaptive processor allocation methods can further improve the system performance of a load sharing computational grid.

1 Introduction

This paper deals with scheduling and allocating independent parallel jobs in a heterogeneous computational grid. Without grid computing local users can only run jobs on the local site. The owners or administrators of different sites are interested in the consequences of participating in a computational grid, whether such participation will result in better service for their local users by improving the job turnaround time. A common load-sharing practice is allocating an entire parallel job to a single site which is selected from all sites in the grid based on some criteria. However, sometimes a parallel job, upon its submission, cannot fit in any single site due to the occupation of some resources by running jobs. How the job scheduler handles such situations is an important issue which has the potential to further improve the utilization of grid resources as well as the performance of parallel jobs.

Multi-site parallel execution [7~12] is a possible approach to this issue. Previous research on homogeneous and heterogeneous grids has shown significant performance improvement. However, multi-site parallel execution in heterogeneous grid environments might lead to inefficient resource usage because the portion of computation on faster sites would finish earlier than those on slower sites but the faster sites' resources wouldn't be released until the entire parallel computation comes to the end. This inefficiency could in turn degrade the overall system performance. This paper develops adaptive processor allocation methods based on the moldable property of parallel jobs. The proposed methods are evaluated through a series of simulations using real workload traces. The results indicate that the adaptive processor allocation method outperforms the multi-site parallel execution approach and can further improve the system performance of a heterogeneous computational grid.

2 Related Work

Job scheduling for parallel computers has been subject to research for a long time. As for grid computing, previous works discussed several strategies for a grid scheduler. One approach is the modification of traditional list scheduling strategies for usage on grid [1~4].

England and Weissman in [5] analyzed the costs and benefits of load sharing of parallel jobs in the computational grid. Experiments were performed for both homogeneous and heterogeneous grids. However, in their works simulations of a heterogeneous grid only captured the differences in capacities and workload characteristics. The computing speeds of nodes on different sites are assumed to be identical. In this paper we deal with load sharing issues regarding heterogeneous grids in which nodes on different sites may have different computing speeds.

For load sharing there are several methods possible for selecting which site to allocate a job. Earlier simulation studies in the literature [1, 6] showed the best results for a selection policy called *best-fit*. In this policy a particular site is chosen on which a job will leave the least number of free processors if it is allocated to that site. However, these simulation studies are performed based on a computational grid model in which nodes on different sites all run at the same speed. In this paper we explore possible site selection policies for a heterogeneous computational grid. In such a heterogeneous environment nodes on different sites may run at different speeds.

In [7] the authors addressed the scheduling of parallel jobs in a heterogeneous multi-site environment. They also evaluated a scheduling strategy that uses multiple simultaneous requests. However, although dealing with a multi-site environment, the parallel jobs in their studies were not allowed for multi-site parallel execution. Each job was allocated to run within a single site.

The support of multi-site parallel execution [8~12] on a computational grid has been examined in previous works, concerning the execution of a job in parallel at different sites. Under the condition of a limited communication overhead, the results from [1, 3, 4, and 6] all showed that multi-site parallel execution can improve the overall average response time. The overhead for multi-site parallel execution mainly results from the slower communication between different sites compared to the intra-site communication. This overhead has been modeled by extending the execution time of a job by a certain percentage [2, 3, and 6].

In [2] the authors further examined the multi-site scheduling behavior by applying constraints for the job fragmentation during the multi-site scheduling. Two parameters were introduced for the scheduling process. The first parameter *lower bound* restricted the jobs that can be fragmented during the multi-site scheduling by a minimal number of necessary requested processors. The second parameter was implemented as a vector describing the maximal number of job fragments for certain intervals of processor numbers.

However, the simulation studies in the previous works are performed based on a homogeneous computational grid model in which nodes on different sites all run at the same speed. In this paper we explore possible multi-site selection policies for a heterogeneous computational grid. In [13] the authors proposed job scheduling algorithms which allow multi-site parallel execution, and are adaptive and scalable in a heterogeneous computational grid. However, the introduced algorithms require predicted execution time for the submitted jobs. In this paper, we deal with the site selection problem for multi-site parallel execution, requiring no knowledge of predicted job execution time.

In the literature [19~25] several strategies for scheduling moldable jobs have been introduced. Most of the previous works either assume the job execution time is a known function of the number of processors allocated to it or require users to provide estimated job execution time. In [18] without the requirement of known job execution time three adaptive processor allocation policies for moldable jobs were evaluated and shown to be able to improve the overall system performance in terms of average job turnaround time. In this paper adaptive processor allocation is viewed as an alternative to multi-site parallel execution for improving system utilization as well as shortening waiting time for user jobs.

3 Computational Grid Model and Experimental Setting

In the computational grid model, there are several independent computing sites with their own local workload and management system. The computational grid integrates the sites and shares their incoming jobs. Each participating site is a homogeneous parallel computer system. The nodes within each site run at the same speed and are linked with a fast interconnection network that does not favor any specific communication pattern [14]. The parallel computer system uses space-sharing and run the jobs in an exclusive fashion.

The system deals with an on-line scheduling problem without any knowledge of future job submissions. For the sake of simplicity, in this paper we assume a global grid scheduler which handles all job scheduling and resource allocation activities. The local schedulers are only responsible for starting the jobs after their allocation by the global scheduler. Theoretically a single central scheduler could be a critical limitation concerning efficiency and reliability. However, practical distributed implementations are possible, in which site-autonomy is still maintained but the resulting schedule would be the same as created by a central scheduler [15].

The grid is heterogeneous in the sense that nodes on different sites may differ in computing speed and different sites may have different numbers of nodes. The local site which a job is submitted from will be called the *home site* of the job henceforward in this paper. We assume the ability of jobs to run in multi-site mode. That means a job can run in parallel on a node set distributed over different sites when no single site can provide enough free processors for it due to a portion of resources are occupied by some running jobs. In addition, we assume all jobs have the moldable property. It means the programs are written in a way so that at runtime they can exploit different parallelisms for execution according to specific needs or available resource. Parallelism here means the number of processors a job uses for its execution. In our model we associated each job with several attributes. The following five attributes are provided before a simulation starts. The first four attributes are directly gotten from the SDSC SP2's workload log. The *slowdown* attribute is generated by the simulation program according to a specified statistical distribution.

- **Site number.** This indicates the home site of a job which it belongs to.
- **Number of processors.** It is the number of processors a job uses according to the data recorded in the workload log.
- **Submission time.** This provides the information about when a job is submitted to its home site.
- **Runtime.** It indicates the required execution time for a job using the specified number of processors on its home site. This information for runtime is required for driving the simulation to proceed. However, in our job scheduling methods the job scheduler does not know the job runtime prior to a job's execution. Therefore, they do not use this information to guide the determination process of job scheduling and allocation.
- **Slowdown.** It is a value indicating how much longer a job will take to finish its execution if it conducts multi-site parallel execution, compared to the runtime required when running in its home site. The runtime for multi-site parallel execution is equal to the runtime within its home site multiplied by the slowdown value.

Our simulation studies were based on publicly downloadable workload traces [16]. We used the SDSC's SP2 workload logs[1] and LANL's CM5 workload logs[2] on [16] as the input workload in the simulations. The detailed workload characteristics are shown in Tables 1 and 2.

In the SDSC's SP2 and LANL's CM5 systems the jobs in the logs are put into different queues and all these queues share the same pool of processors on the system. The SDSC's SP2 system has 128 processors and the LANL's CM5 has 1024 processors. In the following simulations these workload logs will be used to model the workload on a computational grid consisting of several different sites whose workloads correspond to the jobs submitted to the different queues respectively. Tables 3 and 4 show the corresponding configurations of the computational grid according to the respective workload logs under study. The number of processors on each site is determined according to the maximum number of required processors of the jobs belonged to the corresponding queue for that site.

---

[1] The JOBLOG data is Copyright 2000 The Regents of the University of California All Rights Reserved.
[2] The workload log from the LANL CM-5 was graciously provided by Curt Canada, who also helped with background information and interpretation.

To simulate the speed difference among participating sites we define a speed vector, e.g. speed=(sp1,sp2,sp3,sp4,sp5), to describe the relative computing speeds of all the five sites in the grid, in which the value 1 represents the computing speed resulting in the job execution time in the original workload log. We also define a load vector, e.g. load=(ld1,ld2,ld3,ld4,ld5), which is used to derive different loading levels from the original workload data by multiplying the load value ld_i to the execution times of all jobs at site i.

Table 1. Characteristics of the workload log on SDSC's SP2

	Number of jobs	Maximum execution time (sec.)	Average execution time (sec.)	Maximum number of processors per job	Average number of processors per job
Queue 1	4053	21922	267.13	8	3
Queue 2	6795	64411	6746.27	128	16
Queue 3	26067	118561	5657.81	128	12
Queue 4	19398	64817	5935.92	128	6
Queue 5	177	42262	462.46	50	4
Total	56490				

Table 2. Characteristics of the workload log on LANL's CM5

	Number of jobs	Maximum execution time (sec.)	Average execution time (sec.)	Maximum number of processors per job	Average number of processors per job
Group 1	79076	66164	158.90	1024	57
Group 2	85358	239892	2027.81	128	55
Group 3	22515	170380	3625.65	1024	210
Group 4	14394	239470	3815.42	1024	238
Total	201343				

Table 3. Configuration of the computational grid according to SDSC's SP2 workload

	total	site 1	site 2	site 3	site 4	site 5
Number of processors	442	8	128	128	128	50

Table 4. Configuration of the computational grid according to LANL's CM5 workload.

	total	site 1	site 2	site 3	site 4
Number of processors	3200	1024	128	1024	1024

4 Multi-site Parallel Execution

In this paper we use the average turnaround time of all jobs as the comparison criterion in all simulations, which is defined as:

$$\text{Average Turnaround Time} = \frac{\sum_{j \in \text{All Jobs}} (endTime_j - submitTime_j)}{TotalNumber ofJobs} \quad (1)$$

Multi-site parallel execution is traditionally regarded as a mechanism to enable the execution of such jobs requiring large parallelisms that exceed the capacity of any single site. This is a major application area in grid computing called distributed supercomputing [17]. However, multi-site parallel execution could be also beneficial for another application area in grid computing: high throughput computing [17]. In our high throughput computing model in this paper, each job's parallelism is bound by the total capacity of its home site. That means multi-site parallel execution is not inherently necessary for these jobs. However, for high throughput computing a computational grid is used in the space-sharing manner. It is therefore not unusual that upon a job's submission its requested number of processors is not available from any single site due to the occupation of a portion of system resources by some concurrently running jobs. In such a situation, splitting the job up into multi-site parallel execution is promising in shortening the turnaround time of the job through reducing its waiting time. However, in multi-site parallel execution the impact of bandwidth and latency has to be considered as wide area networks are involved. In this paper we summarize the overhead caused by communication and data migration as an increase of the job's runtime [2, 6]. The magnitude of this overhead greatly influences the achievable turnaround time reduction for a job which is allowed to perform multi-site parallel execution.

If a job is performing multi-site parallel execution, the runtime of the job is extended by the overhead which is specified by a parameter p [2]. Therefore the new runtime r^* is:

$$r^* = (1 + p) \times r \quad (2)$$

Where r is the runtime for the job running on a single site. As for the site selection issue in multi-site parallel execution, previous works in [1, 6] suggested the *larger-first* policy for a homogeneous grid environment, which repeatedly picks up a site with the largest number of free processors until all the selected sites together can fulfill the requirement of the job to be allocated. As a heterogeneous grid being considered, the speed difference among participating sites should be taken into account. An intuitive heuristic is called the *faster-first* policy, which each time picks up the site with the fastest computing speed instead of the site having the most amount of free processors. In [26] we developed an *adaptive* site selection policy which dynamically changes between the *larger-first* and the *faster-first* policies based on a calculation of which policy can further accommodate more jobs for immediate single-site execution.

Figure 1 is an example under the SDSC's SP2 workload, which demonstrates that supporting multi-site parallel execution can further improve the performance of a heterogeneous load sharing computational grid with the multi-site overhead $p=2$. Moreover, our proposed *adaptive* site selection policy outperforms the *larger-first* and the *faster-first* policies significantly. Actually in all the 120 simulations we performed for different speed configurations the *adaptive* policy performs better than the other two policies for each case.

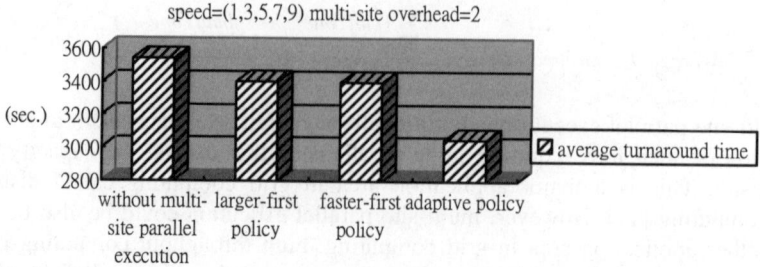

Fig. 1. Performance evaluation of adaptive site selection in multi-site parallel execution

5 Adaptive Processor Allocation Using Moldability

When a job can not fit in any single site in a computational grid, in addition to multi-site parallel execution, adaptive processor allocation is another choice which allocates a smaller number of processors than specified upon submission to a job, allowing it to fit in a single site for immediate execution. This would improve system utilization and shorten the waiting times for user jobs at the cost of enlarged job execution time. The combined effects of enlarged execution time and reduced waiting time for adaptive processor allocation on a homogeneous single-site parallel computer have been evaluated in previous work [18] and shown to be promising in improving average turnaround time for user jobs. In this section an adaptive processor allocation policy for a heterogeneous grid environment is developed. The major difference between the adaptive processors allocation procedures for a single-site parallel computer and for a heterogeneous grid environment is the site selection process regarding the calculation and comparison of computing power of different sites. A site's free computing power is defined as the number of free processors on it multiplied by the computing speed of a single processor. Similarly, the required computing power of a job is defined as the number of required processors specified upon job submission multiplied by the computing speed of a single processor on its home site. A configurable threshold parameter, *power*, with its value ranging from zero to one is defined in the adaptive processor allocation procedure. A site will be selected to allocate the job only when the site's free computing power is equal to or larger than the job's required computing power multiplied by the predefined threshold value and it provides the largest available computing power among all sites in the grid. Figure 2 is an example under the SDSC's SP2 workload, which demonstrates adaptive processor allocation can further improve system performance in a heterogeneous grid.

Figures 3 and 4 show that the value of the *power* parameter greatly affects the performance of the adaptive processor allocation method. Therefore, selection of an appropriate value for the *power* parameter becomes a critical issue when applying the adaptive processor allocation method to a heterogeneous grid. We conducted a series of 120-case simulations corresponding to all possible permutations of the site speed vector (1,3,5,7,9) and found that 0.5 is the best value for the *power* parameter under the SDSC's SP2 workload. Another series of 24-case simulations for all possible

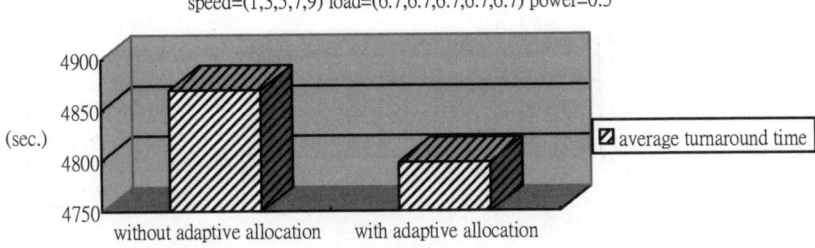

Fig. 2. Performance comparison of loading sharing with/without adaptive processor allocation

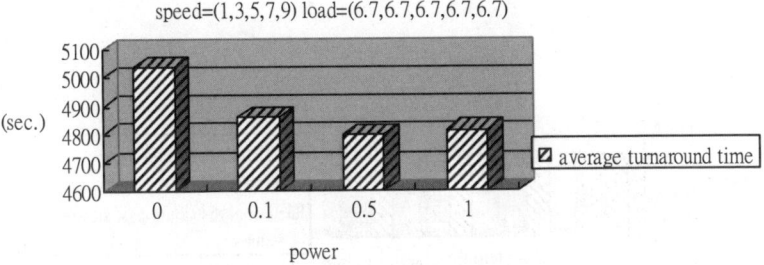

Fig. 3. Adaptive processor allocation with different power values under SDSC SP2 workload

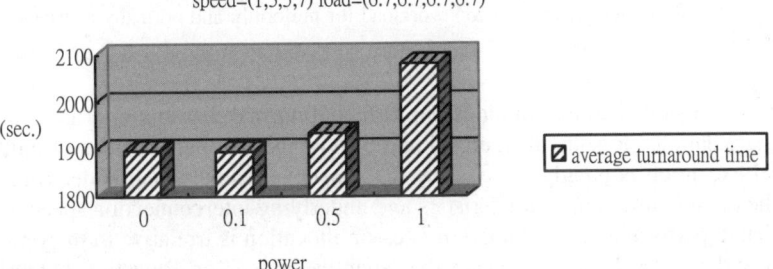

Fig. 4. Adaptive processor allocation with different power values under LANL CM5 workload

permutations of the four-site speed vector (1,3,5,7) indicate that 0.1 is the best value for *power* under the LANL's workload. 0.5 and 0.1 are then used for *power* throughput the following simulation studies in this section for the SDSC's SP2 and LANL's CM5 workloads, respectively.

Figures 5 and 6 compare multi-site parallel execution and adaptive processor allocation under the two different workloads. In our job model, each job is associated with an attribute, *slowdown*, which indicates how long its runtime would be extended to when performing multi-site parallel execution in the grid. In the simulations, the *slowdown* values for these jobs are generated according to specified statistical distributions and upper limits. The upper limits are denoted by p in figures 5 and 6.

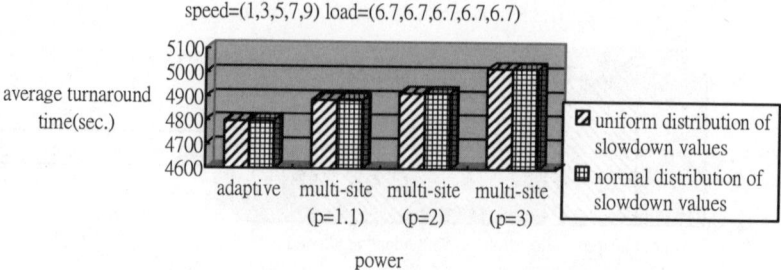

Fig. 5. Comparison under SDSC's SP2 workload for uniformly and normally distributed slowdown values

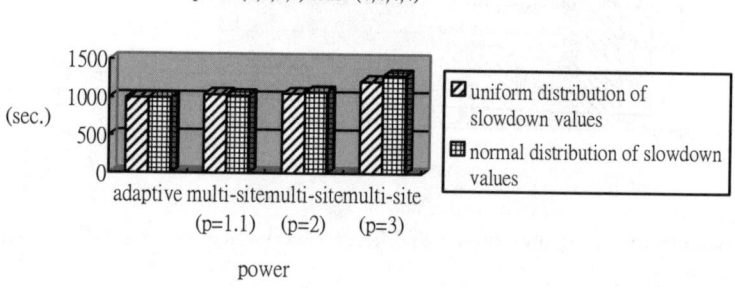

Fig. 6. Comparison under LANL's CM5 workload for uniformly and normally distributed slowdown values

Two types of statistical distributions, uniform and normal distributions, are evaluated in the simulations. Results in figures 5 and 6 show that the performance of multi-site parallel execution is greatly affected by the *slowdown* value which is determined by both the parallel program characteristics and underlying interconnection speed. On the other hand, performance of adaptive processor allocation is irrelative to the *slowdown* values and the results also indicate that adaptive processor allocation outperforms multi-site parallel execution in the simulations.

To further compare these two approaches for all possible permutations of speed vectors, we conducted a series of 120-case simulations under the SDSC's SP2 workload. The results are shown in figure 7. Adaptive processor allocation outperforms multi-site parallel execution in all cases and in average produces more than five times of performance improvement. Although, for a single job, multi-site parallel execution might outperform adaptive processor allocation, *e.g.* reducing the number of processors from 5 to 3 in adaptive processor allocation and the slowdown value being just 1.1 for multi-site parallel execution. The simulation results indicate that adaptive processor allocation is better considering overall performance. This might be because multi-site parallel execution would enlarge the total occupied time period of processor resources, *i.e.* execution time multiplied by the number of processors, while adaptive processor allocation would not. These results shed some light on how to handle the situation where a parallel job can not fit in any single site in a heterogeneous computational grid. Adaptive processor allocation might be a more promising solution than multi-site parallel execution when the parallel jobs have the moldable property.

Figure 8 is an example demonstrating how much performance improvement a load-sharing computational grid with adaptive processor allocation can bring under the SDSC's SP2 workload. Compared with the non-grid architecture, five independent clusters, the load-sharing grid with adaptive processor allocation leads to more than 4 times of performance improvement.

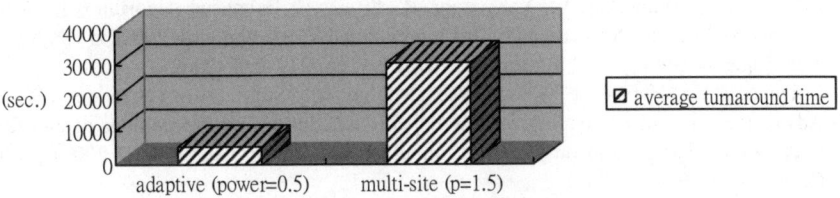

Fig. 7. Thorough comparison under SDSC's SP2 workload

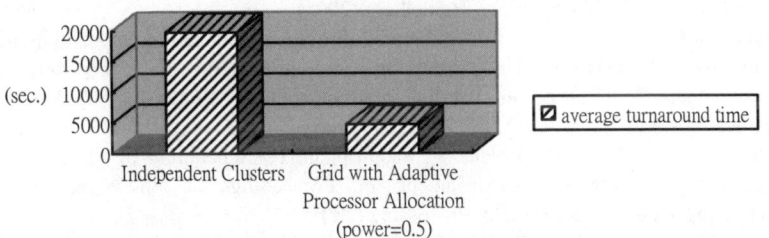

Fig. 8. Performance improvement with load-sharing grid using adaptive processor allocation

6 Conclusion

A grid environment is usually heterogeneous in nature in the real world at least for the different computing speeds at different participating sites. The heterogeneity presents a challenge for effectively arranging load sharing activities in a computational grid. This paper explores the job scheduling and allocation issue in heterogeneous computational grids when a parallel job, during the scheduling activities, cannot fit in any single site in the grid. Multi-site parallel execution is a possible approach to this issue. However, in heterogeneous grid environments it might lead to inefficient resource usage. This inefficiency could in turn degrade the overall system performance. This paper develops adaptive processor allocation methods based on the moldable property of parallel jobs. The proposed method is evaluated through a series of simulations using real workload traces. The results indicate that the adaptive processor allocation method outperforms the multi-site parallel execution approach and can further improve the system performance of a heterogeneous computational grid when parallel jobs have the moldable property.

References

1. Hamscher, V., Schwiegelshohn, U., Streit, A., Yahyapour, R.: Evaluation of Job-Scheduling Strategies for Grid Computing. In: Proceedings of the 7th International Conference on High Performance Computing, HiPC 2000, Bangalore, India, pp. 191–202 (2000)
2. Ernemann, C., Hamscher, V., Yahyapour, R., Streit, A.: Enhanced Algorithms for Multi-Site Scheduling. In: Proceedings of 3rd International Workshop Grid 2002, in conjunction with Supercomputing 2002, Baltimore, MD, USA, pp. 219–231 (2002)
3. Ernemann, C., Hamscher, V., Schwiegelshohn, U., Streit, A., Yahyapour, R.: On Advantages of Grid Computing for Parallel Job Scheduling. In: Proceedings of 2nd IEEE International Symposium on Cluster Computing and the Grid (CC-GRID 2002), Berlin, Germany, pp. 39–46 (2002)
4. Ernemann, C., Hamscher, V., Streit, A., Yahyapour, R.: On Effects of Machine Configurations on Parallel Job Scheduling in Computational Grids. In: Proceedings of International Conference on Architecture of Computing Systems, pp. 169–179 (2002)
5. England, D., Weissman, J.B.: Costs and Benefits of Load Sharing in the Computational Grid. In: Feitelson, D.G., Rudolph, L., Schwiegelshohn, U. (eds.) JSSPP 2004. LNCS, vol. 3277, pp. 160–175. Springer, Heidelberg (2005)
6. Huang, K.C., Chang, H.Y.: An Integrated Processor Allocation and Job Scheduling Approach to Workload Management on Computing Grid. In: Proceedings of the International Conference on Parallel and Distributed Processing Techniques and Applications, Las Vegas, USA, pp. 703–709 (2006)
7. Sabin, G., Kettimuthu, R., Rajan, A., Sadayappan, P.: Scheduling of Parallel Jobs in a Heterogeneous Multi-Site Environment. In: Proceedings of 9th Workshop on Job Scheduling Strategies for Parallel Processing (2003)
8. Brune, M., Gehring, J., Keller, A., Reinefeld, A.: Managing Clusters of Geographically Distributed High-Performance Computers. Concurrency – Practice and Experience 11, 887–911 (1999)
9. Bucur, A.I.D., Epema, D.H.J.: The Performance of Processor Co-Allocation in Multicluster Systems. In: Proceedings of the Third IEEE International Symposium on Cluster Computing and the Grid (2003)
10. Bucur, A.I.D., Epema, D.H.J.: The Influence of Communication on the Performance of Co-allocation. In: Feitelson, D.G., Rudolph, L. (eds.) JSSPP 2001. LNCS, vol. 2221, pp. 66–86. Springer, Heidelberg (2001)
11. Bucur, A.I.D., Epema, D.H.J.: Local versus Global Schedulers with Processor Co-Allocation in Multicluster Systems. In: Feitelson, D.G., Rudolph, L., Schwiegelshohn, U. (eds.) JSSPP 2002. LNCS, vol. 2537, pp. 184–204. Springer, Heidelberg (2002)
12. Banen, S., Bucur, A.I.D., Epema, D.H.J.: A Measurement-Based Simulation Study of Processor Co-allocation in Multicluster Systems. In: Feitelson, D.G., Rudolph, L., Schwiegelshohn, U. (eds.) JSSPP 2003. LNCS, vol. 2862, pp. 105–128. Springer, Heidelberg (2003)

13. Zhang, W., Cheng, A.M.K., Hu, M.: Multisite Co-allocation Algorithms for Computational Grid. In: Proceedings of the 20th International Parallel and Distributed Processing Symposium (2006)
14. Feitelson, D., Rudolph, L.: Parallel Job Scheduling: Issues and Approaches. In: Proceedings of IPPS 1995 Workshop: Job Scheduling Strategies for Parallel Processing, pp. 1–18 (1995)
15. Ernemann, C., Hamscher, V., Yahyapour, R.: Benefits of Global Grid Computing for Job Scheduling. In: Proceedings of the Fifth IEEE/ACM International Workshop on Grid Computing, pp. 374–379 (2004)
16. Parallel Workloads Archive (2008), http://www.cs.huji.ac.il/labs/parallel/workload/
17. Foster, I., Kesselman, C.: The Grid: Blueprint for a New Computing Infrastructure. Morgan Kaufmann Publishers, Inc., San Francisco (1999)
18. Huang, K.C.: Performance Evaluation of Adaptive Processor Allocation Policies for Moldable Parallel Batch Jobs. In: Proceedings of the Third Workshop on Grid Technologies and Applications, Hsinchu, Taiwan (2006)
19. Srinivasan, S., Krishnamoorthy, S., Sadayappan, P.: A Robust Scheduling Strategy for Moldable Scheduling of Parallel Jobs. In: Proceedings of the Fifth IEEE International Conference on Cluster Computing (2003)
20. Cirne, W., Berman, F.: Using Moldability to Improve the Performance of Supercomputer Jobs. Journal of Parallel and Distributed Computing 62(10), 1571–1601 (2002)
21. Srinivasan, S., Subramani, V., Kettimuthu, R., Holenarsipur, P., Sadayappan, P.: Effective Selection of Partition Sizes for Moldable Scheduling of Parallel Jobs. In: Sahni, S.K., Prasanna, V.K., Shukla, U. (eds.) HiPC 2002. LNCS, vol. 2552, pp. 174–183. Springer, Heidelberg (2002)
22. Cirne, W., Berman, F.: Adaptive Selection of Partition Size for Supercomputer Requests. In: Feitelson, D.G., Rudolph, L. (eds.) IPDPS-WS 2000 and JSSPP 2000. LNCS, vol. 1911, pp. 187–208. Springer, Heidelberg (2000)
23. Sabin, G., Lang, M., Sadayappan, P.: Moldable Parallel Job Scheduling Using Job Efficiency: An Iterative Approach. In: Proceedings of the 12th Workshop on Job Scheduling Strategies for Parallel Processing (2006)
24. Barsanti, L., Sodan, A.C.: Adaptive Job Scheduling via Predictive Job Resource Allocation. In: Proceedings of the 12th Workshop on Job Scheduling Strategies for Parallel Processing (2006)
25. Turek, J., Ludwig, W., Wolf, J.L., Fleischer, L., Tiwari, P., Glasgow, J., Schwiegelshohn, U., Yu, P.S.: Scheduling Parallelizable Tasks to Minimize Average Response Time. In: Proceedings of the Sixth Annual ACM Symposium on Parallel Algorithms and Architectures, pp. 200–209 (1994)
26. Huang, K.C., Shih, P.C., Chung, Y.C.: Towards Feasible and Effective Load Sharing in a Heterogeneous Computational Grid. In: Proceedings of the Second International Conference on Grid and Pervasive Computing, France (2007)

A Fuzzy Grid-QoS Framework for Obtaining Higher Grid Resources Availability*

David Allenotor** and Ruppa K. Thulasiram

Department of Computer Science,
University of Manitoba
Winnipeg, MB R3T 2N2
Canada
{dallen,tulsi}@cs.umanitoba.ca

Abstract. A computational grid ensures the on-demand delivery of computing resources, in a security-aware, shared, scalable, and standards-based computing environment. A major concern is how to evolve a general and an encompassing framework that guarantees users' satisfaction for using grid computing resources measured as Quality of Services (QoS). To obtain a higher QoS, effective QoS perceived by subscribers (users) must conform to specified QoS agreements in the Service Level Agreements (SLAs) document – a legal contract between the Grid Services Provider (GSP) and users. Sometimes, the effective user QoS does not conform to the specifications in the SLA because of the vagueness in linguistic definitions in the SLA. Existing approaches overcommitted grid resources to satisfy QoS requirement in SLA. In this paper, we propose a fuzzy logic framework for calibrating a user QoS that addresses the vagueness in linguistic definitions of the SLA document without overcommitting grid resources.

1 Introduction

Over the years, computation have revolutionized through the phases of using mainframes, vector computers, parallel computers, distributed computers, and metacomputers. Consequently, the average computational requirement has steadily increased leading to insufficient computational resources needed to run applications on a standalone computer. The High Performance Computing (HPC) system was introduced to provide effective and efficient utilization of the distributed resources [8]. However, the high cost of acquiring an HPC machine limited its application to only a few research and industrial communities. Fortunately, improvements in wide-area networking have enabled the aggregation of distributed resources across various collaborating businesses and research institutions to form the computational grid. The grid is a hardware and software infrastructure that

---

* This research was done with partial financial support from the Natural Sciences and Engineering Research Council (NSERC) Canada through Discovery Grants and with the University Research Grants Program (URGP) of the University of Manitoba.
** Corresponding author.

provides dependable, consistent, pervasive, and inexpensive access to high-end computational capabilities [9]. The Grid Services Providers (GSPs) organizes the grid resources (applications, memory, storage, and CPU/computational power, disk) and makes them available to the subscribed customers[1] on a shared basis. Following the grid developments, the following concerns are pertinent: (*i*) How do researchers (in the academia and industries) solve the problem of the ever increasing need for users to access massive computational resources and a high grid-QoS expectation? (*ii*) Although the grid has made reasonable standardization, however, how would the grid guarantee standards that facilitates interoperability among users and among GSPs? In an earlier study, Allenotor and Thulasiram ([19] and [20]) foresee a future where grid resources will be offered for a price and guided service quality (expressed as Quality of Service (QoS)). QoS describes a user's perception of a service to a set of pre-defined service conditions contained in a Service Level Agreements (SLAs) that is necessary to achieve a user-desired service quality. An SLA [10] is a legal contract in which a resource provider (say a GSP) agrees to deliver an acceptable minimum level of QoS to the users.

The SLA document contains a set of GSP-user agreed rules established to monitor and preserve the QoS provided by the GSPs. An SLA document may specify accept a "High" QoS and reject a "Low QoS. A crisp definition of a high or low QoS results to ambiguities in the corresponding SLA document contract. Linguistic terms such as "High", "Mid", and "Low" cannot easily be described using Boolean notations. Hence, we apply fuzzy logic [1] approach to capture real value of the embedded vagueness in SLA document. The GSP attempts to provide an acceptable level of QoS for resources requested by the consumer, but the GSP may have no complete knowledge of the level of future uncertainty in resources availability because of the flexibility in the quantity, quality, and or volume of resources the consumer would request. Then the GSP is faced with the only choice; to provide excess resources to meet entire needs. Suppose one or some of the users decide to use the earlier requested resources at a later date, this means more resources available than needed. The reverse is fewer resources available than needed. Therefore, the GSP may only meet the needs of its subscribed users by approximating available resources in the grid.

The rest of this paper is organized as follows. Section 2 discusses the related work. In Section 3, we provide a fuzzified and graduated rating for QoS called Degree of QoS (DoQoS) for completely specifying QoS and for the definition of the SLA document. Section 4 provides a fuzzy logic selection of QoS. The results of our simulation is given in Section 5 and Section 6 concludes the paper.

2 Related Work

Several analytical schemes such as statistical inference and evolutionary-fuzzy prediction [15], asymptotic approach of statistics [18], mathematical approximation schemes [21], and fuzzy set theory [23] provide a framework for analyzing

---

[1] Customer and user is used interchangeably to mean a user of grid resources.

QoS in a network system. The results of these analytic schemes are characterized by unpredictable nature of request patterns associated with network users.

Other research efforts that shared the vision of a grid computing system include Condo [11]. Condor is a high-speed computing system that exploits the idle cycles on a community of workstations. Legion [12] and Oceano [13] are two other systems that have features similar to those of a gird. Oceano provides a highly, scalable, and manageable infrastructure for a grid. In addition, it provides its subscribed users with the necessary resources to balance a contracted level of service as specified in the SLA requirements. Oceano attempts to resolve the problems associated with non-shared dedicated resources for each user in a grid. These problems include over-resource provisioning and lack of rapid response associated with inflexibility in high cost of providing QoS in grid. Oceano provides a cost alternative solution to the QoS problems. Legion [12] has some similarities to Condor but differs in that its design is object-based and it provides for a more general metacomputing system.

2.1 Fuzzy Logic, QoS, and SLAs

Vasilakos et al. [15] model a multiple service system in a network inter-domain (a networking environment that exists between two or more networks). They apply evolutionary fuzzy prediction to inter-domain routing to determine traffic patterns in Asynchronous Transfer Mode (ATM) network. Using statistical inferences, Vasilakos et al. noted that a consumer's future request is based on the past request patterns and show that a limited buffer size will introduce a poor communication and hence a poor QoS in a network. This finding propelled Knightly and Sheriff [18] to apply an asymptotic approach of statistics to estimate QoS parameters in a network. The asymptotic approach is an approximation scheme that approximates the probability of resources request loss for a buffer-controlled queue of resources. In a buffer controlled scheduler system, request for resources occurs when the request in-flow to the network exceed the network capacity.

Diao et al. [17] improve the uncertainty concerns (such as error of estimation of QoS parameters, unpredictable failure times of network systems, and irregular user request for resources) in [18] and [21] by applying fuzzy logic. Diao et al. provide a natural way to handle stochastic data by normalizing fuzzy membership functions to optimize profit in their constructed service level management model. The approach of Diao et al. circumvents the limitations (imprecision and uncertainties) of Knightly and Sheriff [18]. In a related effort, Loukas et al. Lorenz and Orda [21] use a heuristic approach to model QoS concerns in a network. Although their model referenced uncertainty constraints, they consider analytic measures for QoS, which are characterized by error term of approximation of QoS parameters. Karl et al. in [16] also model grid QoS. However, they did not consider the adverse effects a vagueness in the linguistic variables associated with SLA definitions could have on the grid-QoS so obtained. In this paper, our approach to modeling QoS applies to the grid and we introduce a new novel fuzzy scheme that differ from [21]. We model a user-oriented multi-service environment and simulate the action of multiple grid resource users.

3 Grid-QoS Framework

Fuzzy set theory models uncertainty (impreciseness) resulting from vagueness in natural language [1]. A fuzzy set [7] belong to different degrees, called grades of membership and defined as:

$$A = (x, \mu(x)) | x \in A, \mu_A(x) \in [0,1] \quad (1)$$

where $\mu_A(x)$ is called the membership function of the fuzzy set A. A fuzzy system allows multiple membership functions from the range 0 and 1. That is, a membership function maps all elements in the universal set X to the interval $[0,1]$. Generally,

$$\mu_A(x) : X \rightarrow [0,1] \quad (2)$$

The membership function $\mu_A(x)$ specifies the grade or degree of membership to which x belongs to the fuzzy set A. The mapping in Equation (2) associates each element in the fuzzy set A to a real number. Thus, as the $\mu_A(x)$ tends to 1, the degree of membership function tends to 100%. The choice of membership function is application dependent [2], [6], and [22]. In this paper, we consider a trapezoidal membership function for analysis because of its simplicity [14]. The general form of the trapezoidal membership function μ_{trap} is given as:

$$\mu_{trap}(x) = \begin{cases} 1 & \text{for } x \in [b,c] \\ \frac{x-a}{b-a} & \text{for } a \leq x < b \\ \frac{d-x}{d-c} & \text{for } c < x \leq d \\ 0 & \text{otherwise i.e., for } x \notin [a,b] \end{cases} \quad (3)$$

Figure 1 shows a trapezoidal membership function. $[a,d]$ marks the universe of discourse, b and c are the values of X for which $\mu_{trap}(x) = 1$. Given a crisp set, the process of fuzzification (or rule firing) transforms a crisp set into a fuzzy set [5]. Dubois and Prade [6] identify fuzzy logic to include a rule base (a collection of fuzzy rules that forms conditional "If-Then" statements), membership functions, and an inference procedure. The reversed process of defuzzification transforms the fuzzy set into its corresponding crisp value using the Centre of

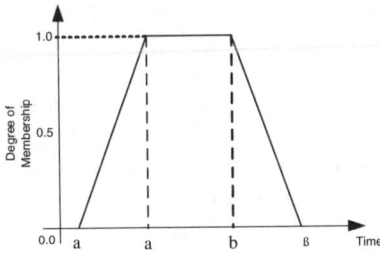

Fig. 1. Trapezoidal Membership Function

Area (COA) [3] and Mean of Maximum (MOM) [3]. Equation (4) describes an If-Then fuzzy condition.

$$IF\ anticedent\ 1\ \{AND\ anticedent\ 2\ AND\ \cdots\ \}\ THEN\ consequent \qquad (4)$$

The *antecedent proposition* takes the form of a fuzzy proposition such as "$\tilde{x}$ is P", where $\tilde{x}$ is called the linguistic variable [4] and P is called a linguistic constant. A linguistic variable [4] is characterized by a quintuple $(X, T(X), U, G, M)$ in which X is the name of the variable, $T(X)$ is the term set, U is a universe of discourse, G is the syntactic rule for generating the elements of $T(X)$, and M is the semantic rule for associating meaning with the linguistic values of X. The truth-value of the proposition is a real number $\mathcal{R}$ that lies between zero and one and depends on the match between $\tilde{x}$ and P. For example,

$$\begin{cases} Rule_1: IF\ X\ is\ A_1\ and\ Y\ is\ B_1\ THEN\ Level\ is\ High \\ Rule_2: IF\ X\ is\ A_2\ and\ Y\ is\ B_2\ THEN\ Level\ is\ Low \end{cases} \qquad (5)$$

Table 1 shows SLA contents specific to our simulation.

Table 1. Summary of SLA Contents

Constraints	Timing	Goal	Actual	Difference
Availability	8 AM-5 PM Monday–Friday	95%	100%	5%
Response	A % of response within 5 seconds	90%	95%	5%
Load	Transactions/minute during peak load (9 : 00 Am −11 : 00 AM) / Daily CPU hours	300/3.5	250/3.0	−50/ − 5
Accuracy	Errors due to Applications	0	0	0
Turnaround	% turnaround in 15 − 30 minutes	95% − 98%	85% − 100%	−10% − 2%

4 Quality of Service Selection

Our framework for grid-QoS, uses universe of discourse that ranges from Outstanding QoS (OQoS) to Unacceptable QoS (UQoS) (i.e., a fuzzy interval of $[0 \cdots 8]$). The various levels of user QoS satisfaction include (*a*) Outstanding QoS (OQoS): OQoS represents an Outstanding QoS and used to depict those values of user QoS that are not easily realizable by the GSP due to the overhead associated with their provision. A rating level of 8 is assigned to the OQoS variable. The OQoS is a rare user QoS expectation because it shows the extent of User satisfaction that are above what the user actually contracted in the SLA document; (*b*) High QoS (HQoS): The HQoS depicts the actual contracted QoS value. A rating level of 6 is assigned to all values of User's satisfaction that falls into this category; (*c*) Medium QoS (MQoS): MQoS represents the actual middle value that lies between the universe of discourse. The value is located between UQoS and OQoS and it has a level rating of 4. At a level of the MQoS the grid provides a 50% QoS to the user; (*d*) Low QoS (LQoS): The LQoS linguistic variable describes a low QoS value. The LQoS has a 2 level rating. Values at this level show that the grid fails to meet the user's QoS requirements, and (e) Unacceptable QoS (UQoS): The UQoS describes an unacceptable level of satisfaction in the value of QoS received by the user. The UQoS has a level rating value of 0 assigned to the UQoS. We give the linguistic variables as:

$$QoS = \{OQoS, HQoS, MQoS, LQoS, UQoS\} \quad (6)$$

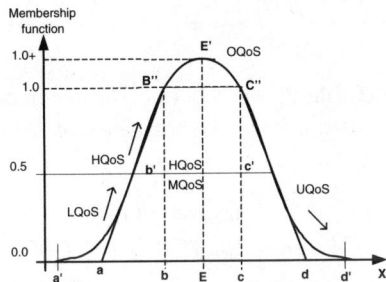

Fig. 2. QoS Linguistic Variables Expressed in Fuzzy Membership Functions

Consider Figure 2 which contains the three basic fuzzy membership functions such as: (i) parabola – $a'B''E'c''d'$, (ii) trapezoidal – $aB''c''d$, and (iii) triangle fuzzy membership functions $aB''b$ and $dC''c$. The following explains the relationship between the set of QoS linguistic variables. The OQoS is contained in the region of points of inflexion at E' given in Equation (7).

$$\frac{d(\mu_x(QoS))}{dX} = 0. \quad (7)$$

From Equation (7), the distance (membership function) is given as:

$$\mu_{x_1}(QoS) - \mu_{x_1^+}(QoS) = 0. \quad (8)$$

This relationship shows that although the region $(B''E'c'')$ may exist for theoretical analysis, such as the analysis of parabolic or bell shape membership functions it does not exist in practice since it may cause the SP to provide additional resources than the user actually require to meet the QoS demands. The region that guarantee a user QoS satisfactorily is located at line $B''c''$, where the membership function $\mu_x(QoS) = 1$. At line $b'c'$, the observed QoS membership function, $\mu_{QoS}(x) = 0.5$ (i.e., 50%) of the contracted value and below this margin, QoS is unacceptable. To formulate the trapezoidal membership function, Equation (6) are the associated rating levels are summarized in Table 2.

The general form of a trapezoidal membership function given in Equation (3) and adapted and redefined in Equation (9).

$$\mu_{QoS}(x) = \begin{cases} 1 & \text{for } x \in [b, c] \\ \frac{x-a}{b-a} & \text{for } a \leq x < b \\ \frac{d-x}{d-c} & \text{for } c < x \leq d \\ 0 & \text{otherwise i.e., for } x \notin [0.0, 8.0] \end{cases} \quad (9)$$

Table 2. The Rated QoS Levels

Linguistic Values	a	b	c	d	Crisp Value
UQoS	0.00	0.00	1.00	2.00	10%
LQoS	1.00	2.00	2.75	4.50	33%
MQoS	2.75	4.50	5.25	6.50	60%
HQoS	5.25	6.50	7.50	8.05	85%
OQoS	7.00	8.05_+	8.05_+	8.05_+	100_+%

Using Equation (9) and Table 2, we redefine the elements of QoS in terms of fuzzy logic in Equations (10 and 11). Other cases of MQoS, LQoS, and UQoS can be obtained in a similar manner.

$$\mu_{OQoS}(x) = \begin{cases} 1 & \text{for } x \in [8.0, 8.0_+] \\ \frac{x-7.5}{8.05_+ - 7.5} & \text{for } 7.50 \leq x \leq 8.05_+ \\ \frac{8.05_+ - x}{8.05_+ - 8.05_+} & \text{for } 8.0+ < x \leq 8.0+ \\ 0 & \text{otherwise i.e., for } x \notin [0.0, 8.0_+] \end{cases} \quad (10)$$

where 8.00+ is any value > 8.00.

$$\mu_{HQoS}(x) = \begin{cases} 1 & \text{for } x \in [6.50, 7.00] \\ \frac{x-5.25}{6.50-5.25} & \text{for } 5.25 \leq x \leq 6.50 \\ \frac{8.05_+ - x}{8.05_+ - 7.50} & \text{for } 7.50 < x \leq 8.05_+ \\ 0 & \text{otherwise i.e., for } x \notin [0.0, 8.0] \end{cases} \quad (11)$$

Table 2 shows the agreed values of the rated levels of grid-QoS. The boundary equations corresponding to these QoS rated levels are described by Equation ((10 and 11). For example, Line 1 of Table 2 describes the attributes of UQoS to include $a = 0, b = 0, c = 1.00, d = 2.00$. Using the COA defuzzifying scheme given as:

$$N_{Trap} = ((b-a) + (c-a) + (d-a))/4 + a \quad (12)$$

where a, b, c, and d follows from the definition of a trapezoidal fuzzy function. The defuzzified crisp value of UQoS corresponds to 10%. The rated QoS levels in Table 2 indicates the presence of QoS scaling in the range of 0 and 1. Figure 3 shows values of a, b, c, d for the formulated trapezoidal representation of the linguistic variables described in Table 2. The fuzzy inference engine consists of the five inputs and each has at least 3 fuzzy levels (thus, there are at least $5 * 3^5$ number of fuzzy rules in the inference engine). Figure 4 provides an overview of a graphic method of generating the fuzzy rule in the inference engine. Mapping each grid resources to the associated fuzzified values, we have: (*i*) Bandwidth with LRt, MRt, HRt, LErt, MErt, HErt, LSrv, MSrv, HSrv, LDqt, MDqt, and HDqt; (*ii*) Memory with LRt, MRt, HRt, LErt, MErt, HErt, LSrv, MSrv, HSrv, LDqt, MDqt, and HDqt; (*iii*) Hard disk storage with LRt, MRt, HRt, LErt, MErt, HErt, LSrv, MSrv, HSrv, LDqt, MDqt, and HDqt; (*iv*) CPU time with LRt, MRt, HRt, LErt, MErt, HErt, LSrv, MSrv, HSrv, LDqt, MDqt, and HDqt.

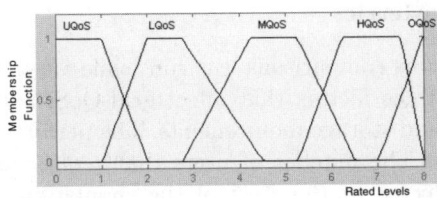

Fig. 3. Trapezoidal Representation of Fuzzy QoS

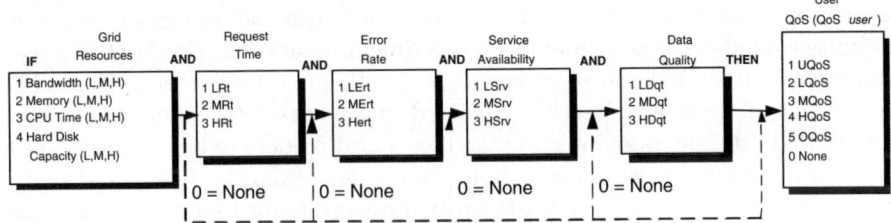

Fig. 4. Rule Generation for Fuzzy Inference Engine

Where LRt is Low Request time, MRt is Medium Request time, HRt is High Request time, LErt is Low Error rate, MErt is Medium Error rate, HErt is High Error rate, LSrv is Low Service availability, MSrv is Medium Service availability, HSrv is High Service availability, LDqt is Low Data quality, MDqt is Medium Data quality, and HDqt is High Data quality.

$$\text{IF (Bw is LBwd) AND (Er is LErt) THEN (User(QoS) is HQoS)(1).} \tag{13}$$

where in Equation (13), Bw is the bandwidth and Er is the error rate. The output of these mappings produces a user QoS which has a 5 fuzzy levels defined in Equation (6). The results obtained from the QoS simulation of a computational grid system contain a set of levels of QoS. These levels of QoS are verified for compliance with their contracted values in SLA document using fuzzy logic techniques. The fuzzy logic QoS SLAs that is adopted in this research uses the trapezoidal membership function given in Equation (3).

5 Experiments and Results

The following experiments were conducted on a quad-processor Intel Xeon running at 3.2 GHz with 1GB of RAM, 160 GB of hard disk. The operating system was Windows Vista. The simulator was written in the Java programming language and was compiled and run with Sun Microsystems's java distribution version 1.4.2 − 03.

5.1 Performance Metrics

To analyze data, various comparisons was run while varying SLA setup files to validate the effects of the factors that affect grid-QoS; bandwidth, CPU time, memory, processors, and storage requirements. The performance metrics include (a) Number of Users: The number of users that request for grid resources at any given time is selected at the start of the simulation. This metric is used to regulate the number of users in the grid. The number of grid users is not allowed to unduly increase without a bound. However, a maximum of 200 users could request for grid resources at any time. (b) Number of User's Requests: The number of requests per user is obtained by generating a set of random sequence of integer numbers. The bound of the maximum number of request that a user can have is 1000 and the minimum is 0. (c) Request Completion Time: The request completion time describes the average time taken for a user's request to be serviced (i.e., the time interval taken for a grid request to be acknowledged). In this simulation the request completion time ranges from $(1-3)$ seconds (ability to service a 98% user requests). (d) Error Rate and Error Limit: The error rate measures the deviation of expected QoS (i.e., the deviation observed when a perceived user QoS is measured against the contracted SLA values).

5.2 Simulation Configurations and Startup Specifications

The grid configuration file defines availability of grid resources and what the importance of those resources is in terms of QoS graded values. Table 3 describes the configuration setup for the grid simulation using memory, CPU, bandwidth, and disk as grid resources. A user is considered to have a "High" use of these resources if the grid offers a 256 MB of memory, 0.6 of CPU speed, 200 mbps of bandwidth, and 350 MB of free disk space. These values constitute the standard for the simulation carried out in this research. Memory is expressed in ratio for programming convenience $(256, 128, 32 : 8, 4, 1)$.

Table 3. Selected Grid Parameter Configuration

Resources	High	Medium	Low
Memory ($\times 1$ MB)	$128.00 - 256.00$	$32.00 - 127.99$	$0.00 - 31.99$
CPU ($\times 0.1$ GHz)	$3.00 - 6.00$	$1.00 - 2.99$	$0.00 - 0.99$
Bandwidth ($\times 0.1$ mbps)	$100.00 - 200.0$	$10.00 - 99.99$	$0.00 - 9.99$
Hard Disk ($\times 0.1$ GB)	$200.00 - 350.0$	$100.00 - 199.99$	$0.00 - 99.99$

5.3 Results

Table 4 shows the graded user's grid resources distribution to 10 users. For example, memory is considered "High" or "H" if it lies in the range of $128-256$ MB, "Medium" or "M" if the allocated value ranges between $32.00-127.99$ MB, and "Low" or "L" if a value in the range of $0.00-31.99$ MB is allocated. We obtain entries for CPU, Bandwidth, and Hard disk in a similar manner. The

Table 4. Simulated Grid Resources Usage

User	Memory	CPU	Bandwidth	Hard disk
User 0	$H, 255.99$	$H, 5.75$	$H, 189.83$	$M, 197.87$
User 1	$H, 250.63$	$H, 3.91$	$H, 197.17$	$H, 234.84$
User 2	$H, 255.00$	$L, 5.95$	$H, 190.76$	$L, 88.67$
User 3	$L, 122.80$	$H, 2.51$	$H, 194.75$	$H, 218.18$
User 4	$H, 219.46$	$H, 2.34$	$H, 157.24$	$M, 177.03$
User 5	$H, 200.97$	$H, 5.06$	$H, 199.37$	$M, 172.89$
User 6	$H, 204.45$	$L, 5.90$	$H, 140.27$	$H, 219.21$
User 7	$H, 253.66$	$H, 3.98$	$H, 157.53$	$M, 182.51$
User 8	$L, 103.95$	$H, 5.65$	$H, 186.07$	$M, 122.58$
User 9	$H, 249.55$	$H, 5.06$	$H, 185.92$	$M, 194.28$

Table 5. Corresponding Crisp Values Based on Crisp Values Obtained

Grid Resources	Trapezoidal Fuzzy Numbers [a, b, c, d]	Crisp QoS	Normalized QoS
Memory	[4.40, 5.60, 6.55, 7.34]	6.00	75%
CPU	[4.40, 5.60, 6.55, 7.34]	6.00	75%
Bandwidth	$[5.25, 6.50, 7.50, 8.08_+]$	7.0_+	$88_+\%$
Hard-disk	[3.33, 4.85, 5.67, 6.77]	5.16	64%

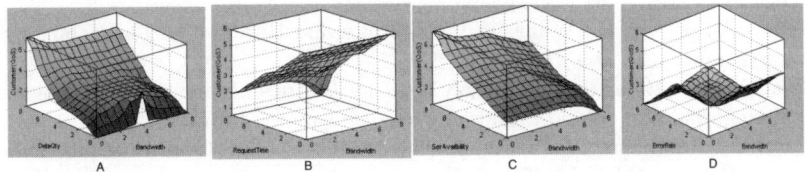

Fig. 5. The Effects of Bandwidth on User QoS

corresponding trapezoidal fuzzy boundaries of Table 5 are obtained using the COA method. This involves the average of grid resources usage. For example, in Table 4 memory has $5 * HQoS$ and $2 * MQoS$ averaged over 8 (the rating levels).

Figure 5 shows the effects of bandwidth on grid-QoS. The bandwidth effect on user QoS was simulated under the influence of data quality, request time, service availability, and error rates. A and C show that service availability and data quality are required to be high (100% each) to meet a corresponding 100% user QoS in the grid. However, In B, the bandwidth was maintained constantly at the contracted value of 200 mbps and this resulted to only a 25% rise in QoS.

6 Conclusions

We have studied the effects of various factors (grid resources specific) for modeling a user-acceptable grid-QoS. Using our framework, a user and a GSP does not necessarily have to spend extra money on getting a higher level of guarantee. However, depending of the contention among resources users requesting a certain level of QoS (such as OQoS) an additional premium may be required. Conversely, GSP may need to know fluctuation patterns and seasons of higher resources demand rather than best efforts service.

Future work include (on- going) simulation/experiments using a live grid scenario for a more in-depth analysis of how GSPs could dynamically restructure their resources using an SLA contract. This study opens up many challenging issues for further study in the computing market for providing flexibility in grid-QoS and in distributed computing. Hence our further plan will incorporate option and risk-hedging reservations and pricing techniques to facilitate user-grid-QoS flexibilities using a special case of real options.

References

1. Zadeh, L.A.: Fuzzy Sets. Information and Control 4, 338–353 (1965)
2. Zimmermann, H.J.: Fuzzy Set Theory and its Applications. Kluwer-Nijhoff, Dordrecht (1985)
3. Ross, T.J.: Fuzzy Logic with Engineering Applications, 2nd edn. Wiley, Chichester (2004)
4. Zadeh, L.: Fuzzy logic and its Application to Approximate Reasoning Sets. Information Processing, 591–594 (1974)
5. Zadeh, L.: A Fuzzy Set-Theoretic Interpretation of Linguistic Hedges. Journal of Cybernetics 3(2), 4–34 (1972)
6. Dubois, D., Prade, H.: What are Fuzzy Rules and How to Use Them. Fuzzy Sets and Systems 84(2), 169–189 (1996)
7. Bojadziew, G., Bojadziew, M.: Fuzzy Logic for Business, Finance, and Management Modeling, 2nd edn. World Scientific Press, Singapore (1997)
8. Foster, I., Kesselman, C., Tuecke, S.: The Anatomy of The Grid: Enabling Scalable Virtual Organizations. Int. Journal of Supercomputer Applications 15(3) (2001)
9. Foster, I.: What is the Grid? A three point checklist, GRIDtoday (article in Gridtoday), vol. 1(6), (Retrieved October 26th, 2007) from http://www.gridtoday.com/02/0722/100136.html
10. Pantry, S., Griffiths, P.: The Complete Guide to Preparing and Implementary Service Level Agreements, 1st edn. Library Association Publishing (1997)
11. Epema, D.H.J., Livny, M., van Dantzig, R., Evers, X., Pruyne, J.: A Worldwide Flock of Condors: Load Sharing Among Workstation Clusters. Future Generation Computer Systems 12, 53–65 (1996)
12. Grimshaw, A.S., Wulf, W.A., French, J.C., Weaver, A.C., Reynolds Jr., P.F.: Legion: The Next Step Toward a Nationwide Virtual Computer. Technical report, No. CS-94-21, Computer Science Department, University of Virginia (June 1994)
13. Appleby, K., Gong, L., Goldszmidt, G., Kalantar, M.H.: Oceano. SLA Based Management of a Computing Utility. In: Seventh IFIP/IEEE Int. Symposium on Integrated Network Management, IM 2001 (2001)
14. Meerschsert, M.M.: Mathematic Modeling, 2nd edn. Academic Press, London (1999)

15. Vasilakos, A., Ricudis, C., Anagnostakis, K., Pedrycz, W., Pitsillides, A., Gao, X.Z.: Evolutionary-Fuzzy Prediction for Strategic ID-QoS Routing in Broadband Networks. Int. Journal of Parallel and Distributed Systems and Networks 4(4), 176–182 (2001)
16. Karl, C., Foster, I., Kesselman, C., Sander, V., Tuecke, S.: SNAP: A Protocol for Negotiating Service Level Agreements and Coordinating Resource Management in Distributed Systems. In: Feitelson, D.G., Rudolph, L., Schwiegelshohn, U. (eds.) JSSPP 2002. LNCS, vol. 2537, pp. 153–183. Springer, Heidelberg (2002)
17. Diao, Y., Hellerstein, J., Parekh, S.: Using Fuzzy Control to Maximize Profits in Service Level Management. IBM Systems Journal 41(3), 403–420 (2002)
18. Knightly, E., Shroff, N.: Admission Control for Statistical QoS: Theory and Practice. IEEE Network 13(2), 20–29 (1999)
19. Allenotor, D., Thulasiram, R.K.: G-FRoM: Grid Resources Pricing-A Fuzzy Real Option Model. In: The 3rd IEEE Int. Conference on e-Science and Grid Computing (e Science 2007) (2007)
20. Allenotor, D., Thulasiram, R.K.: A Grid Resources Valuation Model Using Fuzzy Real Option. In: Stojmenovic, I., Thulasiram, R.K., Yang, L.T., Jia, W., Guo, M., de Mello, R.F. (eds.) ISPA 2007. LNCS, vol. 4742, pp. 622–632. Springer, Heidelberg (2007)
21. Lorenz, D.H., Orda, A.: QoS Routing in Networks with Uncertain Parameters. IEEE ACM Transactions on Networking 6(6), 768–778 (1998)
22. Arnold, K.: An Introduction to The Theory of Fuzzy Subsets, vol. 1. Academic Press, London (1975)
23. Tsaur, S.-H., Chang, T.-Y., Yen, C.-H.: The Evaluation of Airline Service Quality by Fuzzy MCDM. Tourism Management 23(3), 107–115 (2002)

Guarantee the Victorious Probability of Grid Resources in the Competition for Finite Tasks

Lei Yao, Guanzhong Dai, Huixiang Zhang, and Shuai Ren

College of Automatic, Northwestern Polytechnical University, Xi'an, China
morningyao@gmail.com

Abstract. This paper establishes a resource-rich environment of the grid computing at first, and then put forward a new type of grid resource competition algorithm in the environment. There are plenty of idle resources that can complete the similar task in the resources-rich grid computing environment, hence how these resources can gain the maximum benefits are discussed here. This paper presents a Guarantee of Victorious Probability algorithm (GVP), which can predict the action of an adversary through historical information, and determine its action based on the forecast. This is the essence of the game theory and this algorithm. The results of experiments show that the resource using GVP can be close to their expectations of victorious probability compare with the other resource using the random algorithm. The game of two resources using GVP is also discussed and the final victorious probability remain at 0.5. In this paper, a more in-depth analysis of the phenomenon is made, and the Nash Equilibrium of two-resource game is also discussed.

1 Introduction

In a Grid Computing environment, all service providers set up a Grid network of services for different applications and provide highly efficient and low-cost services. The Grid resources include the computing and storage capacity provided by service providers. In order to make full use of Grid resources, the research of Grid resources management and task scheduling become a hot issue int recent years.

Grid Computing environment is quite different from the general computing environment. First, Grid Computing resources do not belong to a same organization in general. The Grid resources will be distributed in different organizations, so a unified management strategy dose not exists. Second, Grid resources can be dynamically joining and leaving. Therefore, there is not a resource that can be controlled completely over a period of time. For this reason, a task may be running in two or more resources at the same time to avoid failure of resources. And at last, the states of Grid resources are different in the structure of the system, performance, resource load, and so on. Therefore, efficient and fair resource management and task scheduling algorithm is vital to Grid Computing.

Grid task scheduling methods focus on the following points. One is based on genetic algorithm. [2] comes up with a prediction model of task completion time based on genetic algorithm. Another is based on ants algorithm. [5] designs a Grid task scheduling algorithm based on ants algorithm. The above two methods are heuristic task scheduling. There is also a method based on economics. [6] establishes an auction model between the resources and users, and discusses the grid task scheduling in terms of time and budget constraint.

Grid resources management and task scheduling based on the Game Theory and Nash equilibrium is also a hotspot for researchers. [7] investigates a divisible auction that is proportionally fair. The author proves that the auction has a unique Nash Equilibrium, and develops a decentralized negotiation strategy. [8] proposes a hierarchical Grid model based on the selfishness of resources. The selfishness of resources means resources will implement the tasks within the organization to meet its own computing needs at first. Such selfishness affects the entire Grid system performance. [9] studies the resource allocation strategies by using mobile agent technology in term of budget constraint. A agent carries a certain budget and series of tasks, and forms a Game problem that many tasks compete for one Grid resource. From the above literature it can be seen that Game Theory is a feasible and effective method to research on the Grid resource management and task scheduling.

In this paper, a novel distributed Grid task scheduling algorithm (Guarantee of Victorious Probability, GVP) based on the Game Theory is presented. Assume that the Grid environment is rich in resources. So, there are a lot of resources in the environment compete for a task that can not be decomposed. Victor of competition implements the task, and gets revenue from user. Therefore, the resources wish they can acquire the tasks as more as possible within their own ability to obtain more benefits. The GVP algorithm is not a hierarchical schedule algorithm. The resource can adjust its behavior itself to gain a great benefit. Therefore, the Gird resources have strong adaptability, and do not need intervention. The resource users choose a suitable resource to complete the task, spending less time in judging.

The remainder of the paper is structured as follows. In the next section, a resource-rich environment of Grid computing is established in detail. Then, the Guarantee of Victorious Probability (GVP) is put forward based on it. In section 4, the effectiveness of the GVP algorithm is verified through simulations. Finally, there is a conclusion in Section 5.

2 A Resource-Rich Environment

If a Grid Computing environment in which many idle resources compete for finite tasks, it is a resource-rich Grid Computing environment. Every resource wants to implement the task to gain benefit. The action of a resource in a competition is the computing capacity offered by the resource. In the view of a user, the more powerful computing offered by resource, the less time it need to complete the task. Therefore, whether this task is in a time-bound or not, the user will choose the strongest resource to implement its task. That is, the strongest computing capacity provider wins the game. But in a resource's view, to provide stronger computing capacity means to provide more CPU time and more memory space. This will inevitably lead to pay a greater cost to win the task. Therefore, the best strategy to the resources is minimizing the cost of a larger victorious probability. Such a Grid Computing environment can be described as follows:

1. Assume only one user U exists in this environment. U provides a task queue $T = \{t_0, t_1, \ldots, t_m\}$. A task can not be implemented until the previous have been completed. There is no dependency between any two tasks. U provides the tasks need be implementation, and does not participate in the Game.
2. There are n idle resources in the Grid: $R = \{R_1, R_2, \ldots, R_n\}$. All of these resources can complete the tasks in T.
3. $maxC = \{maxC_1, maxC_2, \ldots, maxC_n\}$ denotes the most computing capacity offered by the resources. The resource i can not provide more capacity than $maxC_i$ in each Game.
4. $a_i^j, i \in [1, n], j \in [0, m]$ denotes the action of resource i compete for task j, and the set of actions of resource i is $[0, maxC_i]$. $a^j = \{a_1^j, a_2^j, \ldots, a_n^j\}$ denotes the all actions of the resources compete for the task j.
5. $A^k = \{a^0, a^1, \ldots, a^{k-1}\}$ denotes the all historical information of actions when the resources compete for the task k (Perfect Recall), and so $A^0 = \emptyset$.
6. As some uncertainties exist in network, the capacity provided by resource is not equal to the action of the resource a_i^j in the user's view. The random noise of network is denoted by ε_i^j, $\varepsilon_i^j < 0$ so the actual capacity of the resource is $c_i^j = a_i^j + \varepsilon_i^j$. The network between resources and users can be seen as stable, the random noise is also stable. Let ε_i be a $N(\mu_i, \sigma_i^2)$ random variable. Because the resources are not interrelated, the random noises of the resource are independent of each other.
7. $c^j = \{c_1^j, c_2^j, \ldots, c_n^j\}$ denotes the all actual capacity provided by resources in the Game that compete for task j. $h^k = \{c^0, c^1, \ldots, c^{k-1}\}$ denotes the all actual capacity in the past Games when the resources competed for task k, and so $h^0 = \emptyset$.

Game Theory is a multiperson decision theory. The player of a Game is a subject that makes decision. The player participates in the game in order to get maximum benefits by selecting reasonable action strategy. Thus the elements of a Game including Game players, information, set of actions and payoff functions. In the above established Grid Computing environment, the competition of task k is a Game among n resources. The players of the Game are all the idle resources, and the information of the Game is A^k and h^k. The set of actions of resource R_i is $[0, maxC_i]$.

The same Game repeats $k + 1$ times from 0 to k task. These $k + 1$ Games have the same structure. They have the same players, if the dynamic joining and leaving of resources are not considered. So the competition for the whole task queue can be seen as Repeated Games, and the competition for one task is a Stage Game.

3 Algorithm and Analysis

A novel algorithm to guarantee the victorious probability of a resource in the Repeated Games is proposed in this paper. The algorithm is Guarantee of Victorious Probability algorithm (GVP). In the next subsections the algorithm is described at first, and 3.3 derive formula that to calculate the action of a resource in a two-resource Game in detail. 3.4 discuss the way to calculate the action of a resource in a multi-resource Game.

3.1 Algorithm of Users

The user's algorithm is for users to choose an appropriate resource to complete tasks. This algorithm is simply, and described as follows:

1. Put forward task j to all idle resources to launch a Game.
2. Waiting for the computing capacity return from all the resources to form c^j.
3. Find the most powerful resource, and send the task to this resource to be implemented.
4. Send c^j to all resources, and finish this Game.

This is a reasonable choice for user, because the more powerful resource is, the less time the user needs to spend on a task. For users, of course, it better to complete the task earlier when the same expense for a task is paid.

3.2 Algorithm of Resources

The resource's algorithm is running in resources. The core of the algorithm is to choose a suitable action in every round of the competition to ensure that resources can achieve its expected probability of victory in competition. This algorithm is described as follows:

1. Receives the information of the user's task, and participates in the Game of the task.
2. By A^j, h^j and expected victorious probability P_{win}, resource can calculate its action a_i^j in the Game, $a_i^j \in [0, maxC_i]$.
3. Send a_i^j to user and the other participators to form a^j.
4. The winner implements the task and gains the benefit. Because of the resource-rich environment, the losers in the competition can only wait for the next competition.

The core of the algorithm is the step 2. In this step, resources calculate the minimum a_i^j that can ensure the expected probability of victory P_{win}. In the next subsection, we will discuss how to calculate a_i^j in detail.

3.3 The Two-Player Game

The first situation considered is the Grid Computing environment has two idle resources R_1 and R_2. We discuss how to calculate the a_1^j to ensure the P_{win} of R_1 when R_1 and R_2 compete for task j.

According to A^j and h^j, we can calculate the normal distribution parameters of the network random noise:

$$\varepsilon_1 \sim N(\mu_1, \sigma_1^2) \qquad (1)$$

$$\varepsilon_2 \sim N(\mu_2, \sigma_2^2) \qquad (2)$$

By A^j, we can calculate the mean of computing capacity provided by R_2 in the past Games:

$$\bar{a}_2^j = \frac{1}{j-1} \sum_{1}^{j-1} a_2^j \qquad (3)$$

By the equality (3), the computing capacity provided by R_2 in the competition for task j can be estimated. Since the equalities (2) and (3) are known, we have the distribution of c_2^j:

$$c_2^j \sim N(\mu_2 + \bar{a}_2^j, \sigma_2^2) \tag{4}$$

Set a_1^j is the minimum computing capacity provided by R_1 to win the competition in probability P_{win}. And by equality (1), we have the distribution of c_1^j:

$$c_1^j \sim N(\mu_1 + a_1^j, \sigma_1^2) \tag{5}$$

To ensure R_1 win the competition in probability P_{win}, c_1^j must meet the following inequality:

$$P\{c_1^j \geq c_2^j\} \geq P_{win} \tag{6}$$

Set $y = c_2^j - c_1^j$, we see that:

$$P\{y \leq 0\} \geq P_{win} \tag{7}$$

According to the properties of normal distribution. Random variable y is also follow a normal distribution. Assume $y \sim N(\mu_y, \sigma_y^2)$, we have:

$$\mu_y = (\mu_2 + \bar{a}_2^j) - (\mu_1 + a_1^j), \sigma_y^2 = \sigma_2^2 + \sigma_1^2 \tag{8}$$

Thus:

$$P\{y \leq 0\} = \int_{-\infty}^{0} \frac{1}{\sqrt{2\pi}\sigma_y} e^{-\frac{(y-\mu_y)^2}{2\sigma_y^2}} dy \tag{9}$$

Set $\frac{y-\mu_y}{\sigma_y} = t$, we get:

$$P\{y \leq 0\} = \int_{-\infty}^{-\frac{\mu_y}{\sigma_y}} e^{-t^2/2} dt = \Phi(-\frac{\mu_y}{\sigma_y}) \tag{10}$$

Because Φ is a nondecreasing function, we have:

$$-\frac{\mu_y}{\sigma_y} \geq \Phi^{-1}(P_{win}) \tag{11}$$

Put (8) into the inequality (11), then the formula for calculate the action of R_1 is obtained:

$$a_1^j \geq (\mu_2 - \mu_1) + \bar{a}_2^j + (\sigma_2^2 + \sigma_1^2)^{1/2} \Phi^{-1}(P_{win}) \tag{12}$$

If a_1^j meet the inequality (12), R_1 can win the game in probability P_{win}. But with a_1^j increase, R_1 has to pay a higher cost. Hence, the value of a_1^j is minimum when a_1^j make the equality occurs. Thus, R_1 can ensure its victorious probability in Game pay the minimum cost. Subsequent experimental results also show that the algorithm can satisfy the expected victorious probability of resource better.

3.4 The Multi-player Game

The second situation considered is the Grid Computing environment has more than two idle resources. If R_1 wants to achieve its expected victorious probability P_{win}, its action must meet the following inequality:

$$P\{c_1^j \geq c_2^j\} P\{c_1^j \geq c_3^j\} \cdots P\{c_1^j \geq c_n^j\} \geq P_{win} \qquad (13)$$

Thus, the action of R_1 must be the greatest action among all in probability P_{win}. Only in this way, R_1 can achieve its expected victorious probability. By symmetry, any resource who wants to win the game in probability P_{win}, its action must be greater than any other's action in probability P_{win}.

4 Experiments and Discussion

The Grid entities involved in the experiment of this paper include Grid resources, Grid users, historical information and etc. Two Grid resources which are included in simulations are described in Table 1.

The average length of tasks is 100MI, and the deviate degree is 20 %. So the length of task is a random variable which follows a uniform distribution between 80MI and 120MI. The number of tasks is 500.

Because of the network noise follows a normal distribution $\varepsilon \sim N(\mu, \sigma^2)$, we can get $P\{|\varepsilon - \mu| \leq 3\sigma\} = 0.9974$ according to the properties of normal distribution. Therefore, the random variable always locates in a range of $(\mu - 3\sigma, \mu + 3\sigma)$. Because the noise is entirely caused by network instability, it has side effects on the capacity provided by resources. Thus, the value of μ is negative. We have the following inequality:

$$\mu + 3\sigma \leq 0, \mu < 0, \sigma > 0 \qquad (14)$$

According to the inequality we choose five sets parameters of ε, which are described in table 2. For simplicity, the noises of all resources follow a normal distribution with same parameters.

Table 1. Two Grid resources in the Simulation

Resource Name	OS	$maxC$
R_1	UNIX	200MIPS
R_2	Windows	300MIPS

Table 2. The five groups parameters of ε

μ	-3	-6	-9	-12	-15
σ^2	1	4	9	16	25

4.1 GVP Adopted by One

Compare to R_1 which uses GVP, R_2 uses a random strategy. We simulate the Game between the two resources. Because we have 500 tasks in one simulation, the same Game repeats 500 times. This is a finite Repeated Games.

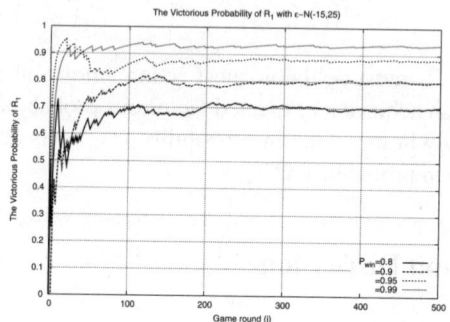

Fig. 1. Actual Victorious Probability VS Expected Victorious Probability

Table 3. Actual Victorious Probability VS Expected Victorious Probability

P_{win}	0.8	0.9	0.95	0.99
Actual Victorious Probability	0.70	0.80	0.88	0.93
Deviate (%)		12.50	11.11	7.37	6.06

The actual victorious probability of R_1 when the network noise ε is a $N(-15, 25)$ random variable is described in Figure 1. The actual victorious probability of R_1 oscillates before the 100 Game, and it does not exceed the expected victorious probability P_{win}. However, after the 100 Game, the actual victorious probability goes to stable. This is because in the initial stage of Repeated Games, R_1 lacks understanding of its competitor, so it can not forecast its competitor's action precisely enough. That is why the actual victorious probability of R_1 is not stabilizing in the initial stage of Repeated Games. After many Stage Games, historical information enriches, so R_1 can predict its competitor's action more accurately and can maintain its actual victorious probability at a stable level.

Form Fig.1, we also can find that the steady actual victorious probability of R_1 is not the same as P_{win}. The differences between actual victorious probability and expected victorious probability are listed in Table 3. From the table can be seen, no matter what the value of P_{win}, the steady actual victorious probability of R_1 is less than P_{win}. From previous discussion we know that the essence of Game is a participant predicts the other's actions in a Game, and then decides its own action based on the prediction. So the prediction of the adversary's action plays an important role in the Game. The algorithm in GVP predicts the adversary's actions based on formula (4). This method only considers the history of the opponent, and does not take into consideration of other factors. It's simple, but logical. Because in an actual Grid Computing environment, each

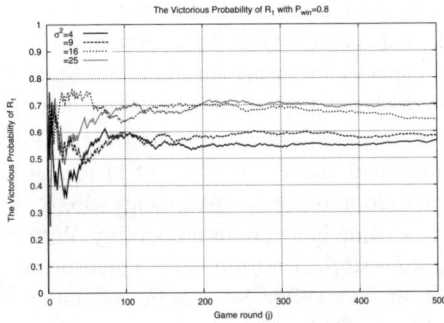

Fig. 2. Actual Victorious Probability changes with σ^2

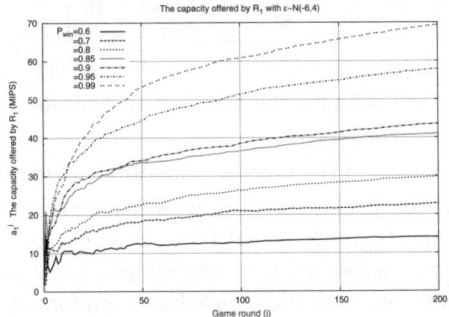

Fig. 3. a_1^j changes with P_{win}

resource's actions can be acquired conveniently after each Game. Predicting algorithm will become more complex if using other information, and the source of other information may exist dubious factor. Then the algorithm is likely to be more complex in time and space, and the accuracy of prediction can not be prominently improved.

In the case of P_{win} is equal to 0.8, the changes of R_1's actual victorious probability while disturbing by different network noise are described in Figure 2. When network noise is large, namely σ^2 is large, the actual victorious probability of R_1 is larger, and are close to P_{win}. This shows that using GVP R_1 can judge network situation in a Repeated Games, and improve its own actions in each Game against the network noise. In reverse, R_2 decides its action in each Game by using a random strategy, and network noise doesn't influence the strategy. R_2 only chooses a computing capacity randomly within the scope of its ability in each Game, and it does not have anti-jamming capability. Thus, along with the increase of network noise, the victorious probability of R_1 becomes larger and the victorious probability of R_2 becomes smaller at the same time.

4.2 GVP Adopted by All

The GVP adopted by all resources will be considered in this subsection. From Figure 3 we can see that, with the number of repetitive Game, the computing capacity provided by R_1 in each Game is rising for different P_{win}. This is because R_1 can learn from the previous Games that the capacity provided by opponent grow sustained. So, R_1 must provide more powerful capacity to ensure its P_{win} in a Stage Game. From Figure 3, we also can see that the increment speed of a_1^j is faster before the 50 Game, and the increment speed of a_1^j become a linear increase after the 50 Game. This is due to that in the initial stage of Repeated Games, shortage of historical information lead to the prediction of competitor's action is not precise enough. So, R_1 must choose a larger a_1^j to ensue its victory of this game in a certain probability. With the repetition of Game, R_1 has accumulated more historical information, which means that R_1 has gained a deeper understanding of the competitor. So, a more accurately prediction of opponent action can be made by R_1 in a Game. Therefore, after the 50 Game, the growth rate of a_1^j is slower than before the 50 Game.

From Figure 3 we also can see that the larger value of P_{win}, the larger value of a_1^j in the same round of Game. That means the curve with $P_{win} = 0.6$ is at bottom of figure compare with the curve with $P_{win} = 0.99$ is at top of figure. If R_1 wishes win the Game in a high probability, its action a_1^j must larger than a_2^j in a high probability. a_2^j is a random variable follows a normal distribution. Thus the larger value of $P\{a_1^j \geq a_2^j\}$ means a larger a_1^j.

The value of a_1^j changes with Game round with different σ^2 is described in Figure 4. From this figure we can see that, a_1^j increases with Game round with a certain σ^2. This shows that the two resources which use GVP enhance their own competitiveness constantly to ensure their expected victorious probabilities. a_1^j increases faster with a larger σ^2. A larger σ^2 means the network more unstable. Therefore, the actual capacity provided by resource c_1^j has a larger difference from a_1^j which is the actual capacity from the user's view. R_1 must provider a larger a_1^j to ensure c_1^j is also larger than c_2^j in a high probability when it understands this difference through learning. In Figure 4, the value of a_1^j is larger and increases faster with a larger σ^2 after the same numbers of Game.

Based on the above analysis of the experimental data, we can get that it is necessary for resources to pay a higher cost in order to achieve its expected victorious probability. With a higher expected victorious probability, the cost to be paid is also higher, and this

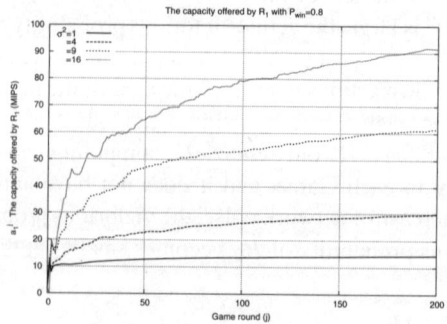

Fig. 4. a_1^j changes with σ^2

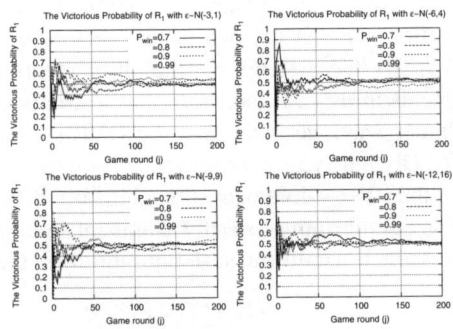

Fig. 5. Actual Victorious Probability of R_1 with different situation of network

cost increases rapidly as the network becomes more unstable. But can resource which adopts GVP strategy guarantee its own expected victorious probability when such a cost is paid? With different network noise and different P_{win}, the actual victorious probabilities of R_1 are described in Figure 5. It is clear see from this figure, whatever the situation of networks and whatever the value of P_{win} takes, the actual victorious probability of R_1 always is close to 0.5 finally. Thus, it can be concluded that regardless of what value P_{win} takes the actual victorious probability of R_1 will close to 0.5 in a Grid Computing environment, in which the GVP adopted by the both two resources.

The reason of such situation is due to that a resource acts as a Game participant can only affect the outcome of the Game, and has no ability to control the outcome of the Game.It's like the classic Beach Occupation Problem in Game Theory [10]. Each game participants want to enlarge its gains, but the result is that the Game participants sharing the proceeds. In this paper is the actual victorious probabilities of the two resources maintain a constant.

4.3 Nash Equilibrium of Two-Resource Game

Learning from the above experiments, the victorious probabilities of two resources can only achieve 0.5 when the GVP adopted by the both two resources. But if one of the resources does not use the GVP, its actual victorious probability will less than 0.5. The resource using GVP can achieve the expected victorious probability in a certain extent if the other resource uses the random strategy. Assume that the resource with a higher victorious probability can gain the higher benefit, we have the theoretical payoff matrix of the two-resource Game in Figure 6.

		R_2	
		GVP	Random Strategy
R_1	GVP	0.5, 0.5	P_{win}, $1-P_{win}$
	Random Strategy	$1-P_{win}$, P_{win}	0.5, 0.5

Fig. 6. Two-Resource Game

Set $P_{win} > 0.5$ in the two-resource Game is reasonable. Thus, $0.5 > 1 - P_{win}$. Take R_1 into consideration, we can get two payoff vectors $u_{1,1} = (0.5, P_{win})$ and $u_{1,2} = (1 - P_{win}, 0.5)$. By the assumption, the all elements in $u_{1,1}$ is larger than the corresponding elements in $u_{1,2}$. It means R_1 has a strictly dominant strategy, the GVP strategy. In a similar way, we know that the GVP strategy is also the strictly dominant strategy of R_2. Obviously, a Game player can not give up the strictly dominant strategy if it has. All of the strictly dominant strategies form the equilibrium of strictly dominant strategies. The equilibrium of strictly dominant strategies must be the Nash Equilibrium. Therefore, there is a uniform Nash Equilibrium in the two-resource Game:

$$s^* = (GVP, GVP) \qquad (15)$$

According to the above analysis we know that resource can ensure its victorious probability is equal or greater than 0.5 by using the GVP strategy. However, the victorious probability of resource which use random strategy is equal or less than 0.5. Therefore, the resource will choose GVP strategy as a rational Game player.

5 Conclusion

In this paper, we discuss the behavior of resources compete for tasks in a resource-rich Grid Computing environment using Game Theory. The behavior of resources under the different conditions is analyzed in deeply, and a novel strategy to guarantee the victorious probability of resource is presented. Via analysis of historical information, resources determine their own actions in a Stage Game. The results of experiments show that this method can increase the victorious probability of resources, and it has strong anti-jamming capability for the instability of network. Finally, we analyze the Nash Equilibrium of the two-resource Repeated Games.

This paper mainly discusses the Game of the two resources, and the situation with the number of resources more than two is discussed less. In addition, we should consider how to forecast an adversary's actions more accurately in further study. Only in this way, the resource can determine its own action based on the opponents actions to ensure its benefits. These two points mentioned above can be used as the focus of the further research.

References

1. Andronikos, T., Koziris, N.: Optimal Scheduling for UET-UCT Grids Into Fixed Number of Processors. In: Proceedings of 8th Euromicro Workshop on Parallel and Distributed Processing, pp. 237–243. IEEE Press, Los Alamitos (2000)
2. Gao, Y., Rong, H., Huang, J.Z.: Adaptive grid job scheduling with genetic algorithms. Future Generation Computer Systems 21, 151–161 (2005)
3. Yao, W., Li, B., You, J.: Genetic Scheduling on Minimal Processing Elements in the Grid. In: McKay, B., Slaney, J.K. (eds.) Canadian AI 2002. LNCS (LNAI), vol. 2557, pp. 465–476. Springer, Heidelberg (2002)
4. DiMartino, V., et al.: Scheduling in A Grid Computing Environment Using Genetic Algorithms. In: Parallel and Distributed Processing Symposium, Proceedings International IPDPS, pp. 235–239 (2002)

5. Xu, Z., Hou, X., Sun, J.: Ant Algorithm-based Task Scheduling in Grid Computing. Electrical and Computer Engineering (IEEE CCECE 2003) 2, 1107–1110 (2003)
6. Buyya, R., Abramson, D., Giddy, J., Stockinger, H.: Economic models for resource management and scheduling in grid computing. J. Concurrency Computation: Practice Experience 24, 1507–1542 (2002)
7. Maheswaran, R.T., Başar, T.: Nash equilibrium and decentralized negotiation in auctioning divisible resources. Group Decision and Negotiation 12, 361–395 (2003)
8. Kwok, Y.K., Song, S.S., Hwang, K.: Selfish grid computing: Game-Theoretic modeling and NAS performance results. In: Proceedings of CCGrid 2005, pp. 349–356 (2005)
9. Bredin, J., Kotz, D., Rus, D., Maheswaran, R.T., Imer, C., Basar, T.: Computational markets to regulate mobile-agent systems. Autonomous Agents and Multi-Agent Systems 6, 235–263 (2003)
10. Gibbons, R.: A Primer in Game Theory. Harvester Wheatsheaf, New York (1992)

Co-allocation in Data Grids: A Global, Multi-user Perspective

Adam H. Villa and Elizabeth Varki

University of New Hampshire, Durham, NH 03824 USA
{ahvilla,varki}@cs.unh.edu

Abstract. Several recent studies suggest that co-allocation techniques can improve user performance for distributed data retrieval in replicated grid systems. These studies demonstrate that co-allocation techniques can improve network bandwidth and network transfer times by concurrently utilizing as many data grid replicas as possible. However, these prior studies evaluate their techniques from a single user's perspective and overlook evaluations of system wide performance when multiple users are using co-allocation techniques. In our study, we provide multi-user evaluations of a co-allocation technique for replicated data in a controlled grid environment. We find that co-allocation works well under low-load conditions when there are only a few users using co-allocation. However, co-allocation works very poorly for medium and high-load conditions since the response time for co-allocating users grows rapidly as the number of grid users increases. The decreased performance for co-allocating users can be directly attributed to the increased workload that their greedy retrieval technique places on the replicas in the grid. Overall, we determine that uninformed, blind utilization of greedy co-allocation techniques by multiple users is detrimental to global system performance.

1 Introduction

Research communities around the world are creating massive amounts of data that need to be accessible to users in various locations. A major creator of such scientific data is the particle physics community. The Large Hadron Collider (LHC), a high energy particle accelerator at CERN, is expected to produce tens of petabytes of raw data annually in 2008 [1,2]. Geographically dispersed researchers are eagerly anticipating access to these datasets. The task of providing fast and efficient data access to these users is a major undertaking for many grid computing research groups.

Replication is used in data grids to help improve users' access to such large and high-demand datasets, by reducing access latency and bandwidth consumption [3]. Replication also helps in load balancing and can improve reliability by creating multiple copies of the same data [4]. There are several replication strategies used in data grids. These strategies can be separated into two categories: static and dynamic. In static replication systems, replicas are specifically created on storage components and remain in place. In contrast, dynamic replication automatically creates and deletes replicas in order to follow continually changing system parameters and user access patterns, which keep the performance high and resource usage in reasonable limits [4,5]. For example, CERN's replication strategy for the LHC experimental data utilizes a tiered replica structure. Raw data obtained from their instruments is immediately written to the center Tier-0 and is then replicated in a controlled fashion to multiple Tier-1 storage sites [2]. There are several Tier-2 replicas associated with each Tier-1 site that automatically receive copies of the replicated data. End users have the ability to access these Tier-2 replicas that are distributed around the world.

Replicas created by either static or dynamic strategies are managed by a replica management service, a component of Grid middleware. A replica management service is responsible for managing the replication of complete and partial copies of data sets. The service provides several functions: registers new copies in a catalog, allows users to query this catalog to find all existing copies of a particular file or collection of files, and selects the "best" replica for access based on storage and network performance predictions provided by a Grid information service [6,7]. Selecting the appropriate replica to service a user's request is a complicated and crucial task, in order to minimize a user's response time.

Even with replication and sophisticated replica management services, retrieving these large data files can be extremely time-consuming, especially for users with limited or congested network access. Network latency is a problem experienced by many users. Researchers find that the long latency of data transfer on the Internet often makes it difficult to ensure high-performance access to data and that download speeds are often limited by bandwidth traffic congestion [8].

In order to increase the performance of accessing replicated data, researchers developed the co-allocation technique, which allows a single user to simultaneously utilize multiple resources to service requests. Normally, when users want to retrieve a data file from a remote grid resource, they contact the replica management service to receive a listing of available replicas that contain the specified data. The users would then select a single replica from the listing that would best service their request. Using co-allocation, however, the users could instead utilize many or all of the available replicas. The users would then issue requests for portions of data file from these replicas. The requests would be serviced in parallel and therefore the longest response time that any user would experience would be determined by the slowest replica to service any one of the partial data requests.

Several recent studies, presented in Section 2, develop different co-allocation techniques. Some of these techniques utilize information services, like the Network Weather Service [9], to determine how to split a given request amongst available replicas in order to maximize throughput and decrease network transfer times. Other techniques use past request histories or heuristics to determine a replica's workload. Since network performance can vary greatly, some co-allocation techniques dynamically adjust the amount of data requested from each replica, as data retrieval progresses.

These recent studies compare the efficiency of their new co-allocation technique with previous work and evaluate the performance of their techniques from a single user's perspective. They do not address situations where multiple users in different locations are simultaneously utilizing their techniques, nor do they discuss the effects that these additional users would have on overall grid performance.

These overall performance effects are significant, since co-allocation increases the workload at the replicas in the system, especially as the number of users utilizing these strategies increases. Instead of a single user issuing a request to a single server, the user could be issuing tens or even hundreds of requests to various servers during the course of file retrieval. This increased workload has a negative effect on the replicas receiving the requests. The impact is even more dramatic for other users in the system that are not using any co-allocation techniques, since co-allocation increases the workload at all of the servers, even though the number of users remains the same.

We find that these recent studies overlook some important issues related to the evaluations of their co-allocation techniques. Firstly, they evaluate their techniques in terms of network transfer time and network throughput. These performance values provide only a limited view of the impact of their techniques. They neglect to examine response times experienced by users. Response time is an important performance value since it includes wait times, which are key indicators of queue lengths at resources in the grid. Without this information, it is difficult to ascertain the conditions of the resources in their experiments. In addition, they do not provide information about replica workloads or the number of users in the grid when their experiments were conducted. This information is important in order to understand and evaluate their results.

The impact of these techniques on the internal systems of the replicas is also not presented in these studies. Prefetching and caching are used by operating systems and storage systems in an effort to decrease costly disk service times. As the number of incoming user requests increases, caches throughout the system will quickly be flushed and any prefetched data will be lost. This will greatly affect disk service times and therefore impact user response times. Disk service time is becoming increasingly important in grid data retrieval, since the network resources involved in transferring the data are becoming increasingly faster and more efficient. The electromechanical nature of storage devices limits their performance at orders of magnitude lower than microprocessor and memory devices and, thereby, creates I/O bottlenecks [10]. In [11], the authors found that disk I/O, using high-end RAID servers, can account for up to 30% of the service time in grid requests and the effect of disk I/O would be even more significant in lower-end disk systems. Additionally, trends in disk storage and networking suggest that disk I/O will be of great importance in the future. Disk capacity has improved 1,000 fold in the last fifteen years, but the transfer rate has improved only 40 fold in the same time period [12]. The ratio between disk capacity and disk accesses per second is increasing more than 10 times per decade, which implies that disk accesses will become even more important [12]. In contrast, network bandwidth continues to grow. Gilder [13] predicted that network bandwidth would triple every year for the next 25 years and his prediction has been accurate so far [12]. Network speed and bandwidth will continue to grow at a much faster rate than disk throughput, and thus disk I/O is a critical component of service time for data grid requests.

In addition to examining the impact on the internal systems of a replica, a system-wide evaluation of multiple users utilizing co-allocation techniques has yet to be presented by the grid research community. To the best of our knowledge, we provide the first global, multi-user evaluations of a co-allocation technique for replicated data in a controlled, simulated environment. Our study evaluates the performance effects of multiple users utilizing a co-allocating strategy to retrieve replicated data in a grid environment. We evaluate grid user response times for both co-allocating and normal data retrieval techniques under varying user workloads. We find that there is a significant difference between the response times of both data retrieval techniques. We find that co-allocation works well under low-load conditions when there are only a few users using co-allocation. However, co-allocation works very poorly for medium and high-load conditions since the response time for co-allocating users increases greatly as the number of grid users increases. For example, when there are 85 grid users all utilizing a co-allocating technique, the average response time is 72% larger than the response times would have been if the users simply requested data from a single server. Overall, we determine that the system-wide use of co-allocation techniques for data retrieval can lead to overloading replicated data servers and can be detrimental to global grid performance.

The paper is organized as follows. Related work is presented in Section 2. Our evaluations are detailed in Section 3 and we present our conclusions in Section 4.

2 Related Work

In many research communities, extremely large data sets with gigabytes or terabytes of data are shared between geographically distributed users. Data grids have been adopted as the next generation platform by many communities that need to share, access, transport, process and manage large data collections distributed worldwide [14,15]. Data grids provide a unified interface for all data repositories in an organization and allows data to be queried, managed, synchronized, and secured [16,1].

Grid researchers examine methods for increasing the performance of accessing remote, replicated data. One of these methods is co-allocation, where a single user simultaneously utilizes several resources. There are several recent studies on the topic of co-allocation in grid computing. We present a selection of these studies focusing on the co-allocation of user data requests.

Vazhkudai presents an architecture for co-allocating grid data transfers across multiple connections [17,18]. He illustrates several techniques for downloading data in parallel. The simplest technique is brute force co-allocation, where each replica is assigned an equal portion to service. The author found this method constraining and therefore devised other techniques, including the dynamic load balancing method, which is subdivided into conservative and aggressive load balancing techniques. The conservative technique monitors the transfer rates of the replicas and automatically adjusts the load for each replica. The aggressive technique progressively increases the amount of data requested from faster replicas and reduces the amount data requested from slower replicas. Overall, the author found that the dynamic methods out performed the static methods. The author's experiments consisted of a single resource requesting data from a small number of servers over the course of several weeks. The results of the experiments were presented as changes in bandwidth (MB/s). The author neglects to mention the workloads of the replicas and overlooks other performance values, such as response time or wait times.

In [19], the authors believe that when several available replicas have almost the same network and disk throughput, choosing a single replica and disregarding the rest is unreasonable and unfair. They therefore developed algorithms that utilize multiple replicas simultaneously. Their workload placement algorithms utilize existing Grid components, such as the replica location service (RLS) [20], the network weather service (NWS) [9] and GridFTP[21]. They developed five algorithms that decide when and which replica should transfer portions of a data file. Their Baseline algorithm simply divides the whole file evenly among all available replicas, while two of their algorithms utilize the NWS to analyze the network throughput of the replicas to make informed scheduling decisions. The final algorithm presented by the authors is NoObserve, which simply uses a fixed-size segment as the basic scheduling unit and each replica is assigned an initial portion to service. When a replica finishes, it is assigned an outstanding portion to service. The authors find that their NoObserve method is characterized by superior performance and simplicity, since it is without infrastructure requirements. In their experiments, the authors have a single resource retrieving data from four servers on a grid system. The results of their experiments are presented as the aggregated bandwidth (KB/s) achieved and the duration (in seconds) of each experiments. The authors do not specify if this duration is only network transfer time or if it includes queue or storage service times, thus its meaning is unclear.

Another co-allocation technique called ReCon (Replica Convoy) is presented in [22]. ReCon simultaneously transfers portions of a source file from several replicas by utilizing several co-allocation algorithms. ReCon's greedy algorithm is similar to the NoObserve [19] algorithm. When a server completes a portion, it is immediately assigned another portion to service. The authors also present a probe-based algorithm for ReCon that uses mechanisms, such as NWS, to test current network performance. In their experiments, they find that the probe-based algorithm provides the best performance. Their experiments consisted of a single machine requesting data from five servers on the PlanetLab grid system. The authors analyze only the transfer times of their algorithms and never specify the workload of the replicas used in their experiments.

The authors of [23,24] attempt to reduce the idle time spent waiting for the slowest replica to service a request by developing a dynamic co-allocation algorithm called Anticipitative Recursive-Adjustment. The algorithm initially assigns a portion to each replica and then continuously adjusts the workload of each replica by analyzing transfer rates. The algorithm assigns smaller portions of the data file to replicas with slower network connections. In their experiments, the authors examined the bandwidth used by their algorithms and analyzed the differences in transmission times.

In all of the studies presented in this section, we find that the authors developed co-allocation techniques that are inherently selfish and greedy since they utilize as many replicas as possible without consideration for other users. Each user request generates multiple sub-requests and in some cases, the number of secondary requests could be in the hundreds. In addition, these authors analyze their techniques from a single user's perspective and neglect to examine their algorithms from a global, system wide perspective when they are utilized by multiple users. The effects their algorithms have on other users in the grid are also omitted from these studies.

Most of these recent studies examine the results of their experiments in terms of network bandwidth or network transfer times. They focus on changes in network performance values and neglect to examine the effects their algorithms have on service or queue times at the replicas that receive their requests. Many studies also focus on throughput as the most important performance value. However, throughput does not give an accurate representation of overall system performance since throughput can be quite high when a system is overloaded. Response time is a better indicator for user performance.

Co-allocation retrieval mechanisms have yet to be examined from a global, multi-user perspective. Our study provides the first global, multi-user evaluations of a co-allocation technique for replicated data in a controlled grid environment. Our study evaluates the performance effects of multiple users utilizing a co-allocating strategy to retrieve replicated data. We evaluate grid user response times for both co-allocating and normal data retrieval techniques under varying user workloads.

3 Evaluations

In our evaluations we utilize a grid simulator, GridSim [25], in order to conduct repeatable and controlled experiments. The Gridsim simulator also allows us to model realistic network environments [26], including packet schedulers, and components of real data grid systems, such as a replica management service [27]. GridSim also allows us to examine disk I/O overheads, which is an important factor of service time for user requests.

In our experiments, all users and data servers are connected via a high performance router that allows up to 1 GB/s data transfer rates from the data servers and provides users with 100 MB/s data connections. In addition, the only users in the system are those stated in our experiments. Using GridSim, we create an experimental grid environment where ten data servers contain replicated data files. The same files are present on each server and users have the ability to access any of these servers. Each replicated data server has the same storage hardware, with a fixed average seek time of 9ms.

We design experiments that evaluate a simple, straightforward co-allocation technique, similar to the brute force technique in [17] and the baseline algorithm in [19]. Since all of the users and servers in our evaluations have the same network access rates, our co-allocation technique does not have to adjust for fluctuating network conditions. There is also a fixed number of servers that contain the same data accessible for all users, which allows our technique to utilize all servers in the grid. Additionally, our evaluations are conducted in a controlled environment where no outside users are accessing the system, so our technique need not adjust for other users' workloads.

In order to evaluate our co-allocation technique, we create two users groups called *co-allocated* and *whole_file*. Both user groups have different strategies for accessing the replicated data files. The *whole_file* user group attempts to retrieve a desired data file from a single server. The *co-allocated* user group instead attempts to retrieve an equal portion of the data file from all servers. For both user groups, when a user submits a request to server, it is processed in a FCFS manner and priority is not given to any user. When our experiments start, all servers are idle, all network connections are free of traffic and all users starting submitting their requests at the same time.

Retrieving Large Data Files (1 GB)

We begin our evaluations by creating a series of experiments where the number of users in the grid increases from 1 to 140. We limit the number of users to 140, since in many grid environments dynamic replica creation occurs when traffic on a replica is greatly increased. Each user attempts to retrieve a unique 1 GB data file from the replicas or servers according to their retrieval strategy. A user in the *whole_file* group, selects a replica with the fewest number of outstanding requests and then submits a request for the entire 1 GB file from the selected replica. A user in the *co-allocated* group requests a 100 MB portion of the data file from each replica in the system. When any user receives its entire file, the user's overall response time is calculated and then the user is disconnected from the grid. We examine both user groups under these conditions.

We begin our examination by evaluating the average response time experienced by any given user. The response time for a user's request can be computed by the combination of the network service time and the replica service time. The network service time includes the time spent during transmission and communication between resources, whereas the replica service time includes the time spent performing disk I/O and internal communication. Both of these service times include the time elapsed while waiting to use various resources. These wait times depend on the number of outstanding requests and therefore a larger number of outstanding requests will result in longer wait times. The response time gives an accurate view into the current state of the system.

We calculate the average user response time for both user groups as the number of users in the system increases from 1 to 140 and the results are shown in

Figure 1a. We observe that the average response time for the *co-allocated* user group increases at much faster rate than the *whole_file* user group, as the number of grid users increases. When then number of grid users is less than the number of servers, the *co-allocated* group provides a smaller average user response time. When there are a large number of users however, the *whole_file* group provides the lowest average response times. In Figure 1b, we illustrate the percentage increase in user response times for the *co-allocated* group. For example, when there are 135 users, the average user response time for the *co-allocated* group is 78% larger than the *whole_file* group.

We also evaluate the maximum response times experienced by any given user. In Figure 1c, we show the maximum user response times for both user groups, which are similar. When there are fewer users in the system, the *co-allocated* group provides slightly decreased maximum response times. The difference between the two groups decreases however, as the number of grid users increases. When there are 75 users in the system, the maximum response time for the *co-allocated* group is only 2% lower than the *whole_file* group. In fact, there are several occasions where the *whole_file* group provides smaller maximum response times.

In order to gain further insight into the response time differences between the two groups, we analyze the response time distribution for a specific number of users. In Figure 1d, we illustrate the difference between the response time distributions for both user groups when there are 89 users present in the system. We see that the majority of users in the *co-allocated* group have higher user response times than the *whole_file* users. In fact, 93% of *co-allocated* users have response times greater than 50,000ms. Whereas, 78% of the *whole_file* users have response times less than 50,000ms. The *whole_file* user group also has 23% of users with response times less than 20,000ms.

We can attribute the decrease in user response time performance for *co-allocated* users to the increased workload their retrieval mechanism places on the servers in the grid. For every user request, ten user requests are created and one request is sent to all ten servers in the grid. Figure 1e illustrates the dramatic difference in the workload presented to the servers between the *co-allocated* and *whole_file* users. This increased workload directly relates to the decrease in user response time performance that we notice in our evaluations. Even though the co-allocated requests are for smaller file sizes, the shear number of requests waiting at the servers decreases their performance. The queue time for the co-allocated requests grows as the number of grid users increases.

Retrieving Smaller Data Files (100 MB)

We continue our evaluations by examining the user groups when we decrease the size of the entire data files requested by all users to 100 MB. An evaluation of decreased file size is relevant, since in many instances a user may only require a portion of larger data sets for their computations. We conduct experiments to see how the trends observed with 1 GB data files compare to requesting smaller data files. In this set of experiments all variables are the same except for the

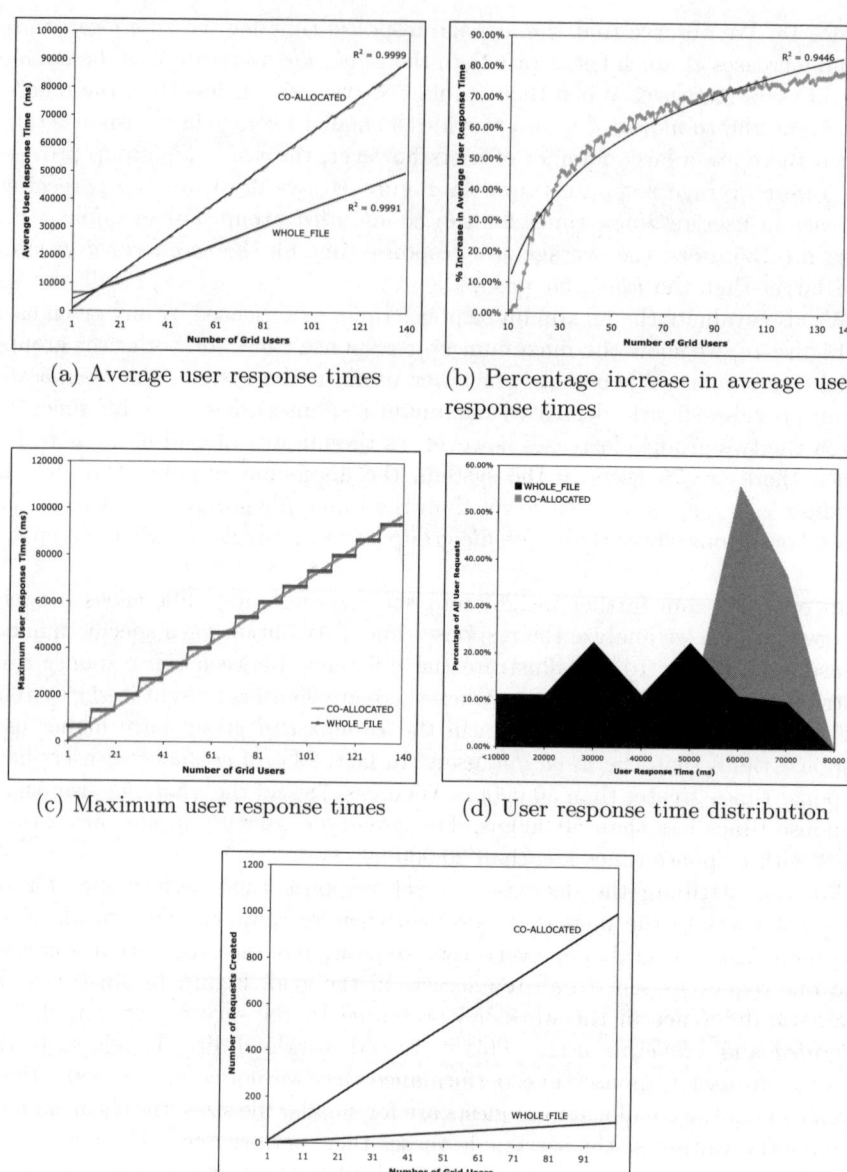

Fig. 1. Average response times for both user groups as the number of grid users increases are shown with a tight-fitting, R^2 close to 1, linear trend line (a). The percentage increase for the *co-allocated* users in response time is shown for the number of grid users with an exponential trend line, in black (b). The maximum response times experienced by any grid user (c). The response time distributions for both user groups when there are 89 grid users submitting requests (d). The number of requests generated by each user group, as the number of users increases for both groups (e).

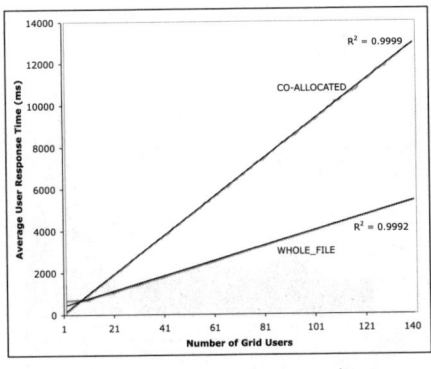 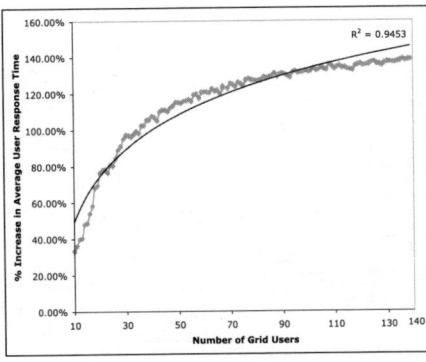

(a) Average user response times (b) Percentage increase in average user response times

Fig. 2. Average response times for both user groups as the number of grid users increases (a). The users are retrieving a 100 MB data file. Each user group's curve is shown with a tight-fitting, R^2 close to 1, linear trend line. The percentage increase in response time for the *co-allocated* users when they are retrieving a 100MB data file is shown for the number of grid users (b). The curve is shown with an exponential trend line, in black.

requested data file size. A user in the *whole_file* group, selects a replica with the fewest number of outstanding requests and then submits a request for the entire 100 MB file from the selected replica. A user in the *co-allocated* requests a 10 MB portion of the data file from each replica in the system.

We begin by analyzing the average user response times for both groups in Figure 2a. We observe a similar trend in average response time as we did with the larger file size. As the number of grid users increases, the average response time for the *co-allocated* users increases much faster than for the *whole_file* users. There is an even greater difference with the decreased file size, since the transfer time is minimized. For example, when there are 135 grid users, the average *co-allocated* user response time is 138% larger than the average *whole_file* user response time. This greater increase in average user response time is also evident in Figure 2b, which shows the percentage increase in average *co-allocated* user response time over average *whole_file* user response time.

We also find a significant change in the maximum user response times. With larger file size, we find that both user groups have relatively the same maximum user response times. With smaller file size however, we find that there is a noticeable difference between the maximum user response times for both setups as the number of grid users increases. This is illustrated in Figure 3a. We notice that the maximum response time for 130 grid users is 42% larger for the *co-allocated* user group.

To further illustrate the remarkable difference between the two user groups when they are requesting decreased file sizes, we analyze the response time distribution when there are 89 grid users in the system. The response time distributions for both groups are shown in Figure 3b, which demonstrates that 90%

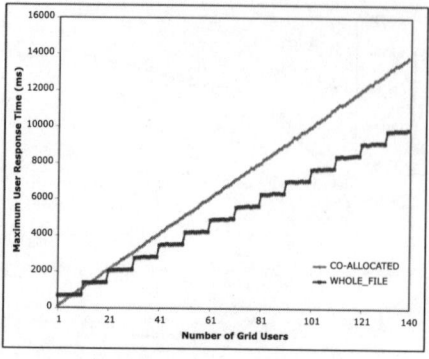
(a) Maximum user response times

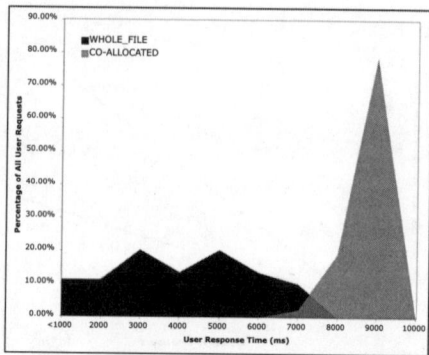
(b) User response time distribution

Fig. 3. The maximum response times experienced by any grid user, requesting a 100MB file (a). The response time distributions for both user groups when there are 89 grid users submitting requests for 100 MB data files (b).

of *whole_file* user's have response times that are less than any of the *co-allocated* users. In fact, 98% of *co-allocated* users have larger response times than any of the *whole_file* users.

Summary of Evaluations

Overall, we find in our evaluations that the *co-allocated* user group has higher average user response times as the number of grid users increases. The *co-allocated* user group also has response time distributions where a greater percentage of requests have large response times in comparison to the *whole_file* user group. The difference between the two groups is even more distinct when the entire requested data file size is decreased to 100 MB. We find that the maximum and average user response times for *co-allocated* users is drastically larger than the *whole_file* user group. The performance decrease for the *co-allocated* users can be attributed to the increased workload their retrieval mechanism places on the servers in the grid. The increased workload that they generate directly relates to the decrease in user response time performance that we notice in our evaluations.

Our evaluations in GridSim also allow us to examine disk service time as an integral component of overall request service time. Since disk I/O is becoming increasingly important as network technologies improve, it is valuable to have these evaluations where disk service time is computed. The GridSim simulator uses fixed, average values that are based on real disk I/O performance in order to calculate disk service time, such as the seek and rotation times. Since these disk service parameters are static, it is difficult to examine the intricate effects that caching and pre-fetching have on user performance when co-allocation techniques are utilized. We expect that the performance difference between the *co-allocated* and *whole_file* data retrieval techniques would be even more noticeable in real grid systems where disk service time is dynamic, with costly seek and rotation times. The request service time would also be notably affected by caching and pre-fetching mechanisms at many resources throughout the grid.

4 Conclusions

Research communities are generating massive amounts of data that need to be readily accessible to users around the world. The task of providing fast and efficient access to this data is a primary focus for many grid computing research groups. Even with replication and sophisticated replica management services, users still experience delays when accessing large data files from remote servers. Researchers attempt to find new techniques to reduce the amount of time a user must wait to retrieve large data files. The co-allocation technique was developed to serve this purpose.

Current co-allocation techniques for data retrieval from remote, replicated sources have only been evaluated from a single user's perspective. Situations where multiple users in different locations are simultaneously utilizing these techniques have yet to be evaluated. The effects that these additional users would have on overall grid performance are also unknown. For example, the internal systems of data grid replicas would be affected by these additional co-allocating users. Since prefetching and caching are used by a replica's operating systems and storage systems, the increased number of user requests would quickly flush caches throughout the system and any time saving, prefetched data would be lost. This loss will greatly affect disk service times and therefore greatly impact user response times.

Since co-allocation retrieval mechanisms have yet to be examined from a global, multi-user perspective, we develop experiments where we compare users that utilize a straightforward co-allocation technique with users that employ normal data retrieval methods. We evaluate the performance of the co-allocating technique as the number of users in the grid increases, up to 140 users. We find that there is a significant and negative change in performance for the co-allocating users as the number of grid users grows. We find that co-allocation works well under low-load conditions when there are only a few users utilizing the technique. However, we determine that under medium and high workload conditions, co-allocating users have higher average user response times and have response time distributions where a greater percentage of requests have large response times in comparison to normal data retrieval users. When there are 135 grid users all utilizing a co-allocating technique, the average response time is 78% larger than the response times would have been if the users simply requested data from a single server. This decreased performance for co-allocating users can be directly attributed to the increased workload their retrieval mechanism places on the replicas in the grid.

Overall, we find that the global use of co-allocating techniques for replicated data retrieval when done in a greedy or selfish manner is detrimental to user performance in a data grid. Replica workload must be considered when making co-allocated requests in a multi-user environment, in order to prevent overload situations. Only under low utilization conditions should co-allocation be used unchecked.

Clearly, more work is needed to fully understand the specific conditions when co-allocation is beneficial to all grid users. Co-allocation in prior work has been shown to be very beneficial for single users in isolation. We believe that co-allocation could also be advantageous for multiple grid users, however it must be used cautiously and wisely. More information should be required before users decide which resources they are going to allocate, in order to make knowledgeable and conscientious decisions. There are several possible ways that this task could be accomplished and individual grids might require different techniques. One possible solution could be the creation of a co-allocation management service that monitors the workloads present at each of the replicas in the grid. A user would then have to either contact this service for replica status or receive allocation suggestions from the service before the user could start issuing requests. Another possible solution could be to simply allow a user to make a best guess decision based on existing replica information. These suggested techniques and any other mechanisms for controlling user co-allocation need to be closely examined in order to see how they would intricately affect global grid performance. Since data sets will continue to grow at incredible rates, new co-allocation mechanisms need to be carefully developed and closely evaluated from all perspectives in order to provide users with fast and efficient data access.

Acknowledgements

This work was supported by the US National Science Foundation under grant CCR-0093111.

References

1. Minoli, D.: A Networking Approach to Grid Computing. Wiley Press, Chichester (2005)
2. Nicholson, C., Cameron, D.G., Doyle, A.T., Millar, A.P., Stockinger, K.: Dynamic data replication in lcg 2008. In: UK e-Science All Hands Conference, Nottingham (2006)
3. Lamehamedi, H., Szymanski, B., Shentu, Z., Deelman, E.: Data replication strategies in grid environments. In: ICA3PP (2002)
4. Ranganathan, K., Foster, I.T.: Identifying dynamic replication strategies for a high-performance data grid. In: GRID, pp. 75–86 (2001)
5. Slota, R., Nikolow, D., Skital, L., Kitowski, J.: Implementation of replication methods in the grid environment. Advances in Grid Computing, 474–484 (2005)
6. Allcock, W., Bester, J., Bresnahan, J., Chervenak, A., Foster, I., Kesselman, C., Meder, S., Nefedova, V., Quesnel, D., Tuecke, S.: Secure, efficient data transport and replica management for high-performance data-intensive computing. In: IEEE Mass Storage (2001)
7. Allcock, W., Bester, J., Bresnahan, J., Chervenak, A., Foster, I., Kesselman, C., Meder, S., Nefedova, V., Quesnel, D., Tuecke, S.: Data management and transfer in high performance computational grid environments. Parallel Computing Journal 28, 749–771 (2002)
8. Yang, C.T., Yang, I.H., Chen, C.H., Wang, S.Y.: Implementation of a dynamic adjustment mechanism with efficient replica selection in data grid environments. In: SAC (2006)

9. Wolski, R., Spring, N.T., Hayes, J.: The network weather service. Future Gener. Comput. Syst. 15, 757–768 (1999)
10. Farley, M.: Storage Networking Fundamentals: An Introduction to Storage Devices, Subsystems, Applications, Management, and Filing Systems. Cisco Press (2004)
11. Vazhkudai, S., Schopf, J.M.: Using disk throughput data in predictions of end-to-end grid data transfers. In: GRID, pp. 291–304 (2002)
12. Gray, J., Shenoy, P.: Rules of thumb in data engineering. In: IEEE International Conference on Data Engineering, April 2000, pp. 3–12 (2000)
13. Gilder, G.: Fiber keeps its promise. Forbes (April 7, 1997)
14. Chervenak, A., Foster, I., Kesselman, C., Salisbury, C., Tuecke, S.: The data grid: Towards an architecture for the distributed management and analysis of large scientific datasets. Journal of Network and Computer Applications, 187–200 (2001)
15. Venugopal, S., Buyya, R., Ramamohanarao, K.: A taxonomy of data grids. ACM Comput. Surv. 38, 3 (2006)
16. DiStefano, M.: Distributed Data Management for Grid Computing. John Wiley and Sons, Inc., Chichester (2005)
17. Vazhkudai, S.: Enabling the co-allocation of grid data transfers. In: GRID (2003)
18. Vazhkudai, S.: Distributed downloads of bulk, replicated grid data. Journal of Grid Computing 2, 31–42 (2004)
19. Feng, J., Humphrey, M.: Eliminating replica selection - using multiple replicas to accelerate data transfer on grids. In: ICPADS, p. 359 (2004)
20. Chervenak, A., Deelman, E., Foster, I., Guy, L., Hoschek, W., Iamnitchi, A., Kesselman, C., Kunszt, P., Ripeanu, M., Schwartzkopf, B., Stockinger, H., Stockinger, K., Tierney, B.: Giggle: a framework for constructing scalable replica location services. Supercomputing, 1–17 (2002)
21. Bresnahan, J., Link, M., Khanna, G., Imani, Z., Kettimuthu, R., Foster, I.: Globus gridftp: What's new in 2007. In: GridNets (2007)
22. Zhou, X., Kim, E., Kim, J.W., Yeom, H.Y.: Recon: A fast and reliable replica retrieval service for the data grid. In: CCGRID, pp. 446–453 (2006)
23. Yang, C.T., Chi, Y.C., Fu, C.P.: Redundant parallel file transfer with anticipative adjustment mechanism in data grids. Journal of Information Technology and Applications (2007)
24. Yang, C.T., Yang, I.H., Li, K.C., Wang, S.Y.: Improvements on dynamic adjustment mechanism in co-allocation data grid environments. The Journal of Supercomputing (2007)
25. Buyya, R., Murshed, M.: Gridsim: A toolkit for the modeling and simulation of scheduling for grid computing. In: CCPE (2002)
26. Sulistio, A., Poduval, G., Buyya, R., Tham, C.K.: On incorporating differentiated levels of network service into gridsim. Future Gen. Computer Systems (2007)
27. Sulistio, A., Cibej, U., Robic, B., Buyya, R.: A tool for modelling and simulation of data grids. Technical Report GRIDS-TR-2005-13, Grid Computing Laboratory, University of Melbourne (2005)

Scheduling for Atomic Broadcast Operation in Heterogeneous Networks with One Port Model

Ching-Hsien Hsu[1,*], Tai-Lung Chen[2], Bing-Ru Tsai[1], and Kuan-Ching Li[3]

[1] Department of Computer Science and Information Engineering,
Chung Hua University, Hsinchu 300 Taiwan
chh@chu.edu.tw
[2] Institute of Engineering and Science,
Chung Hua University, Hsinchu 300 Taiwan
ctl@sclab.csie.chu.edu.tw
[3] Department of Computer Science and Information Engineering
Providence University, Taichung, Taiwan
kuancli@pu.edu.tw

Abstract. With the emergence of the network technologies, heterogeneous computing has become a wide accept paradigm for distributed and network computing. In this paper, we present different algorithms and evaluate their performance on performing atomic one-to-all broadcast in heterogeneous network with one port model. Based on general graph model, two scheduling algorithms, the *Nearest Neighbor First* and the *Maximum Degree Neighbor First* are firstly illustrated. The pre-scheduling strategy with constructing *message forwarding table* for avoiding redundant transmissions is applied as runtime support. By extending graph-based approaches, five tree-based heuris-tic algorithms, the *Nearest Neighbor First*, the *Maximum Degree Neighbor First*, the *Maximum Height Sub-tree First*, the *Maximum Sub-Tree First* and the *Maximum Weighted Sub-tree First*, are developed based on different network characteristics. The performance analysis shows that the *Maximum Weighted Sub-tree First* performs best in high degree heterogeneous environments. Overall speaking, contribution of this study relies on informing significant suggestions for adapting proper broadcasting mechanism in different hetero-geneous platforms.

1 Introduction

One-to-all broadcast is the most primary collective communication pattern. Initially, only the source processor has the data that needs to be broadcast; at the end, there is a copy of the original data residing at each processor. The one-to-all broadcast is widely used in parallel algorithm design to send identical data to all other processors, in order to disseminate global information, such as the problem size or application parameters. Therefore, numerous broadcast algorithms have been implemented for different MPP architectures, such as mesh, hypercube or systolic array.

Because of the new paradigm of heterogeneous computing, the traditional one-to-all broadcasting method in homogeneous systems, such as parallel machines or PC

---
[*] Corresponding author.

clusters, can not be properly applied in heterogeneous systems. Therefore, it terms into great important to develop efficient one-to-all broadcast techniques that adaptive in heterogeneous networks. In general, there are three different types of one-to-all broadcast operation. 1. atomic broadcast: a single message is sent by one source processor to all other processors that reside in the same network through the communication links; 2. pipelined broadcast: the source message can be split into arbitrary number of packets, which may be routed in a pipelined fashion; 3. series of broadcasts: the same source processor sends a series of atomic broadcasts, involving messages of the same size. Objective of the first and the second types is to minimize makespan while the third type is to maximize throughput.

In this paper, we present variety heuristic algorithms aim to efficient perform one-to-all atomic broadcast in heterogeneous network. The proposed algorithms are classified into two categories, tree-based scheduling algorithms and graph-based methods. The main idea of tree-based scheduling algorithms is first to establish a minimal cost spanning tree from an ordinary network which is usually represented as an undirected graph. Base on the minimal cost spanning tree, different broadcasting heuristics are implemented according to network characteristics. The main advantage of tree-based scheduling methods is the avoidance of duplicated messaging which may occurred in communication cycle.

2 Related Work

Collective communication optimization problem has been extensively studied in both homogeneous computing paradigms and heterogeneous platforms. The former includes variety interconnection networks within traditional parallel machines, cluster systems and network of workstations (NOWs); while the later covers wide range of computing paradigms, such as distributed systems, heterogeneous network of workstations (HNOWs), Ethernet based cluster systems, grid systems and P2P systems.

Collective communication in homogeneous systems and tightly coupled parallel systems has been thoroughly researched over the years. In [6], Faraj *et al.* proposed techniques for bandwidth efficient all-to-all broadcasting on switched clusters. Moreover, because Network of Workstation (NOW) is a cost-effective alternative to massively parallel super-computers, Lin *et al.* [8] discussed single-node broadcast in switched-based Network of Workstations with network partitioning. Lin *et al.* [9] proposed three contention-free algorithms, EBS, VBBS and VBBSWF for atomic broadcasting on Heterogeneous Networks of Workstations. Simulation results showed that improvement over broadcast with minimal communication steps has been demonstrated.

Recent research efforts have investigated the problem of efficient broadcast and multicast in heterogeneous cluster systems. Both node heterogeneity and network heterogeneity were taken into account in their analytical model and scheduling algorithm design. The research done by S. Khuller and Y. Kim [7], they proposed Largest Cluster First (LCF) scheduling algorithm for collective communications in the same environment. Research literatures focused on theoretical results, such as NP-completeness and approximation algorithms, for the problem of broadcasting a message in heterogeneous cluster systems have been also developed [10, 11, 12].

Yet another model in pipelining consecutive broadcasts to maximize system throughput was first proposed in [13]. As the computational grid becomes a widely accept paradigm for large-scale parallel systems, collective communications have been paid attention recently. Angelo *et al.* [1] focused on the development of scheduling techniques to minimize makespan of a broadcast operation on a grid environment. Different to the above focus, Beaumont *et al.* [2, 3, 4] concentrated upon the problem of broadcasting in heterogeneous platforms with one port model. They also extended the broadcasting problem in multi-port model with STA (Single Tree Atomic), STP (Single Tree Pipelined) and MTP (Multiple Tree Pipelined) approaches [5].

3 Preliminaries

A Heterogeneous Network (HN) combines one or more different types of computers and/or network devices with different processing speeds. To investigate the atomic broadcast operation in heterogeneous network environment with one port communication model, we have the following assumptions.

1. Network topology is known as global information for all processors within the same network.
2. Communications over HN are point-to-point blocking send operation.
3. Each processor within HN has unique ID.
4. Message startup costs of processors are the same.

Since the communication time is an important factor to overall performance of broadcasting in heterogeneous network, efficient methods for scheduling transmissions among senders and receivers are of great importance in developing broadcasting techniques in heterogeneous networks. With one port model, a processor can perform *send* and *receive* operation simultaneously. However, there still have two general limitations of the communications between senders and receivers.

1. A sender can not send message to two or more receivers simultaneously.
2. A receiver can not receive multiple messages from two or more senders simultaneously.

To simplify the presentation, we first define notation and terminologies used in this paper as following definitions.

Definition 1: Given a graph $G = (V, E)$ and $v_i \in V$, *Neighbor* of node v_i denoted by *Neighbor*(v_i) is the set of nodes v_j, where edge e_{ij} is exist. If G is a tree, parent of node v_i will be excluded from *Neighbor*(v_i), i.e., *Neighbor*(v_i) = *Child*(v_i).

Definition 2: Given a graph $G = (V, E)$ and $v_i \in V$, the *Nearest Neighbor* of node v_i denoted by $NN(v_i)$ is the node v_j with $e_{ij} = \min\{e_{ik}\}$, for all $v_k \in Neighbor(v_i)$.

Definition 3: Given a graph $G = (V, E)$ and $v_i \in V$, the *Maximum Degree Neighbor* of node v_i denoted by $MDN(v_i)$ is the node v_j with $degree(v_j) = \max\{degree(v_k)\}$, for all $v_k \in Neighbor(v_i)$.

Definition 4: Given a graph $T = (V, E)$ is a tree and internal node $v_i \in V$, the *Maximum Height Subtree* of node v_i denoted by $T_{ij}^{\max\_depth}$, is the subtree with $height(T_{ij}) = \max\{\ height\ (T_{i1}),\ height\ (T_{i2}),\ ...,\ height\ (T_{im})\}$, where $T_{i1}, T_{i2}, ..., T_{im}$, $m = degree(v_i)$ are subtrees of v_i.

Definition 5: Given a graph $T = (V, E)$ is a tree and internal node $v_i \in V$, the *Maximum Node Subtree* of node v_i denoted by $T_{ij}^{\max\_node}$, is the subtree with $|V_{ij}| = \max\{|V_{i1}|, |V_{i2}|, ..., |V_{im}|\}$, where $T_{i1}=(V_{i1}, E_{i1})$, $T_{i2}=(V_{i2}, E_{i2})$, ..., $T_{im}=(V_{im}, E_{im})$, $m=degree(v_i)$ are subtrees of v_i and $|V_{ij}|$ is the total number of nodes in tree T_{ij}.

Definition 6: Given a graph $T = (V, E)$ is a tree, the *weight* of tree T denoted by $weight(T)$, is defined as $weight(T) = \sum |e_{ij}|$, for all $e_{ij} \in E$ and $|e_{ij}|$ is the weight of edge e_{ij}.

Definition 7: Given a graph $T = (V, E)$ s a tree and internal node $v_i \in V$, the *Maximum Weight Subtree* of node v_i denoted by $T_{ij}^{\max\_weight}$, is the subtree with $weight(T_{ij}) = \max\{weight(T_{i1}),\ weight\ (T_{i2}),\ ...,\ weight\ (T_{im})\}$, where $T_{i1}, T_{i2}, ..., T_{im}$, $m=degree(v_i)$ are subtrees of v_i.

4 Scheduling of Atomic Broadcast Operation

According to the above definitions, both graph-based and tree-based heuristic algorithms will be discussed in this section. To simplify the presentation, we use $<v_i, v_j>$ to represent the communication between node v_i and v_j, where v_i is the sender and v_j is the receiver.

4.1 Graph Based Approaches

Because of the possible existence of cycle in a general undirected graph, a pre-scheduling strategy with constructing *Message Forwarding Table* (*MFT*) to avoid redundant transmissions is applied for runtime support. Each entry of *MFT* is with the form $<\alpha, d_1, d_2,...>$, where α is the number of destination nodes to send message, d_1 is the first destination, d_2 is the second and so on. If there is no message to be forwarded, the corresponding entry will be remained empty. An example of the *MFT* for node 0 is illustrated in Table 1. The first entry <2, 1, 3> represents that if the broadcasting message is originally held by itself (i.e. node 0), it will need to forward this message to the two destinations by the order of nodes 1, then node 3; the second entry with empty means if message source is node 1, it needs not to forward this message to any of other nodes. Similarly, when message source is node 2, it will forward the message to node 4 and node 5 in sequence. In the following subsections, the *MFT* will be applied in graph based scheduling approaches.

Table 1. An example of Message Forwarding Table

Source Node \ Node ID	Node 0
Node 0	<2,1,3>
Node 1	-
Node 2	<2,4,5>
...	
Node n	<1,3>

4.1.1 Nearest Neighbor First Algorithm

NNF, short for *Nearest Neighbor First*, is performed according to the following principles.

1. Given a node v_i, it forwards message to its nearest neighbor v_j (if exist) as soon as it completely received the message from its sending source, i.e., $NN(v_i) = v_j$.

2. If cost(v_x, v_j) = cost (v_x, v_k) and node ID $j < k$, where v_j and v_k are neighbors of v_i, then <v_x, v_j> has higher priority than <v_x, v_k>.

Due to one-port communication model, there are two exception handling principles in constructing a message forwarding table.

1. If there are two or more sending sources select the same target node to send data, e.g., v_i and v_j are two sending sources select the same target v_k simultaneously, then <v_i, v_k> will be executed and <v_j, v_k> be discarded, if e_{ik} has smaller cost than e_{jk}.

2. Because of the nature of one-port communication model, one can not receive multiple messages from two or more senders simultaneously. If node v_i selects a target v_j to send data while v_j is receiving the same message from another sender v_k, then v_i will discard the transmission <v_i, v_j> and select next target to send data.

4.1.2 Maximum Degree Neighbor First (*MDNF*)

MDNF, short for *Maximum Degree Neighbor First*, is performed according to the following principles.

1. For node v_i, it forwards message to its neighbor with maximum node degree among its neighbors.
2. For nodes v_j and v_k are neighbors of node v_i, if $degree(v_j) = degree(v_j)$, node v_i prioritizes the transmissions of its neighbors according to *NNF* policies.

With one-port communication model, the following are two exception handlings applied in *MDNF* algorithm.

1. If there are two or more sending sources select the same target node to send data simultaneously, only one of them will be proceed. E.g., v_i and v_j are two sending sources select the same target v_k, then $<v_i, v_k>$ will be proceed, if e_{ik} presents smaller cost than e_{jk}.
2. Upon the restriction of one-port communication model, a processor can not receive multiple messages from two or more sending sources at a same time. E.g., if node v_i selects a target v_j to send data while v_j is receiving the same message from another source node v_k, then v_i will discard the transmission $<v_i, v_j>$ and select next target to send data.

4.2 Tree Based Approaches

As a Heterogeneous Network (*HN*) combines one or more local area networks, with different geographical distribution properties, different types of computers and network devices with different processing speeds, it is usually difficult to derive an efficient scheduling method that constitutes properties of the real network from an origin network topology. Moreover, there is additional cost to perform pre-scheduling in a general undirected graph. To address these issues, we introduce different tree based scheduling strategies to satisfy variety of heterogeneous networks' properties and demands.

First, the *Tree-based Nearest Neighbor First* scheduling method, termed as *T-NNF* is designed. Given a minimal cost spanning tree that reduced from an origin *HN*, node v_i forwards message to its nearest neighbor as soon as it completely received the message. Since *T-NNF* is analogous to the *NNF* technique that described in section 4.1, scheduling policies are mostly constituted by those of *NNF*.

Second, the *Tree-Based Maximum Degree Neighbor First* scheduling algorithm, termed as *T-MDNF*. Given a minimal cost spanning tree that reduced from an origin *HN*, node v_i forwards message to its neighbor with maximum node degree as soon as it completely received the message. Because *T-MDNF* is analogous to the *MDNF* technique, scheduling policies are also constituted by those of *MDNF*.

Third, we present the *Tree-Based Maximum Height Subtree First* scheduling algorithm, termed as *MHSF*. Given a minimal cost spanning tree that reduced from an origin *HN*, node v_i forwards message to its immediate child who is the root of the highest subtree of node v_i as soon as it received the message.

Fourth, we demonstrate the *Maximum Subtree First* scheduling method, termed as *MSF*. In *MSF*, node v_i forwards message to its immediate child who is the root of the subtree having maximum amount of tree nodes.

Finally, we examine the tree-based *Maximum Weight Subtree First* scheduling method, termed as *MWSF*. Similar to *MSF* method, *MWSF* prioritizes subtrees into a list for arranging the communication order. Instead of comparing the amount of subtree nodes, the *MWSF* method adopts total weight of a subtree as the comparison criteria.

5 Performance Evaluation

In order to evaluate performance of the proposed algorithms, we have implemented a random graph generator that contains a parametric graph simulator for generating network graphs with various characteristics. Parameters used in the simulation and comparison metrics are described as follows.

- $G = (V, E, W)$, V is the set of vertices, E is the set of edges and W represents weight of edges, in our experiments, $V = \{10, 20, 30, 40, 50\}$.
- h: Degree of heterogeneity.

$$h = \log_3(\frac{Max\{w(i,j)\} - Min\{w(i,j)\}}{Min\{w(i,j)\}}), i \neq j, \forall i, j \in V \tag{1}$$

- *S3P*: Abbreviation for *Single Source Shortest Path* algorithm. In *S3P*, the atomic broadcast operation is performed by the single source node sends message to all other nodes through the shortest path corresponding to each receiver.
- *Speedup* is defined as

$$Speedup = \frac{makespan(S3P)}{makespan(NNF / MDF / DSF / MSF / WSF)} \tag{2}$$

- *ABS*: Short for *Amount of Best Schedule*, indicating the number of best schedule achieved by single algorithm.
- *makespan()*: the completion time of an atomic broadcast operation.

Fig. 1 shows the performance results of the proposed algorithms with different number of nodes under $h = 0.1$ and $h = 5$; $h = 0.1$ implies that the simulated environment is a homogeneous-like system while $h = 5$ indicates the simulated environment is heterogeneous ones. To simplify the presentation, *G-NNF* and *T-NNF* are used to represent the graph-based *Nearest Neighbor First* and tree-based *Nearest Neighbor First*, respectively; *G-MDNF* and *T-MDNF* are used to represent the graph-based *Maximum Degree Neighbor First* and tree-based *Maximum Degree Neighbor First*, respectively; *MHSF* is for *Maximum Height Subtree First*; *MSF* is for *Maximum Subtree First* and *MWSF* is for *Maximum Weighted Subtree First*.

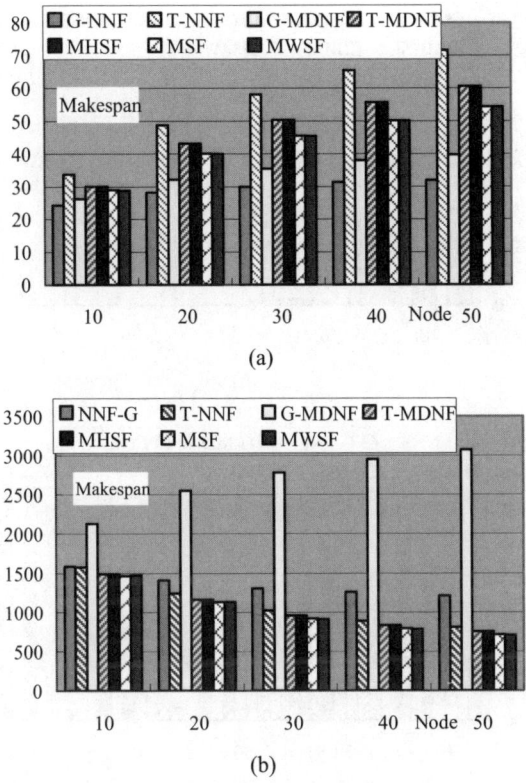

Fig. 1. Makespan comparisons with different number of nodes (a) $h = 0.1$ (b) $h = 5$

Fig. 2 gives the comparisons of *ABS* for both homogeneous-like and heterogeneous environments. From Fig. 2(a), it is quite obvious that *G-NNF* has the best performance since it presents highest *ABS*. For other approaches, they could not have best schedule in homogeneous-like environments with larger number of nodes. Reason for this result is similar to the explanation described in Fig. 1(a). We observe that *MWSF* outperforms other tree-based approaches in heterogeneous environments, especially for those cases with larger number of nodes. Because the *MWSF* can advance communications within heavy weighted subtrees, when number of node becomes numerous, it can balance the communication overheads by schedule message-forwarding into parallel transmissions. Therefore, *MWSF* achieves best *ABS* in heterogeneous environments.

Fig. 3 reports the performance results of speedup comparisons in both homogeneous-like and heterogeneous environments. The calculation of speedup is defined in (2). From Fig. 3(a), graph-based algorithms outperform tree-based one. The *G-NNF* has best speedup for all test cases in homogeneous-like environments. In Fig. 3(b), we have similar observations as those described in Fig. 1(b). Tree-based approaches outperform graph-based ones in heterogeneous environments. Because the reasons are similar to those demonstrated in Fig. 1(b), we do not describe it again.

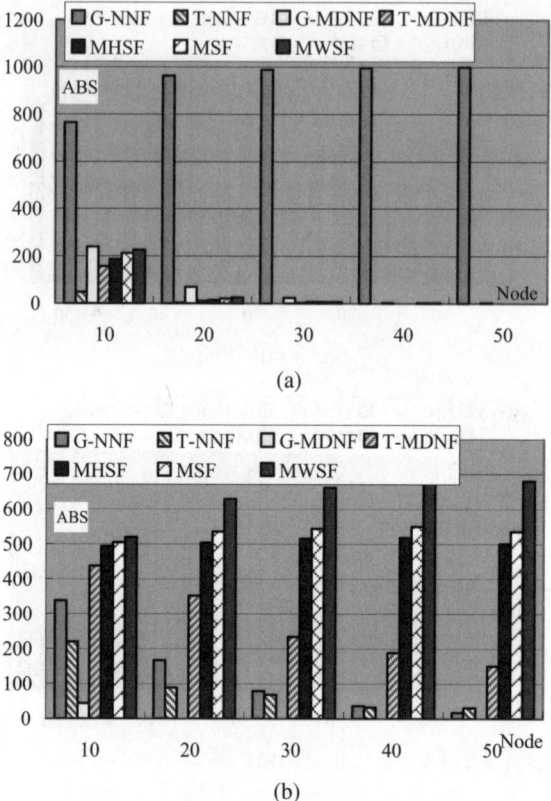

Fig. 2. *ABS* comparisons with different number of nodes (a) $h = 0.1$ (b) $h = 5$

From the above experimental results and performance analysis, we have the following remarks.

- Network heterogeneity plays as an important factor to select suitable scheduling policies in heterogeneous computing environments.
- Graph-based scheduling approaches are better used in homogeneous-like systems.
- Tree-based scheduling approaches are better used in heterogeneous systems.
- *G-NNF* outperforms other graph-based approach and has the best schedule in most test cases in low degree heterogeneous environments.
- *MWSF* outperforms other tree-based approaches and has the best schedule in most test cases in high degree heterogeneous environments. Table 2 summarizes these observations.

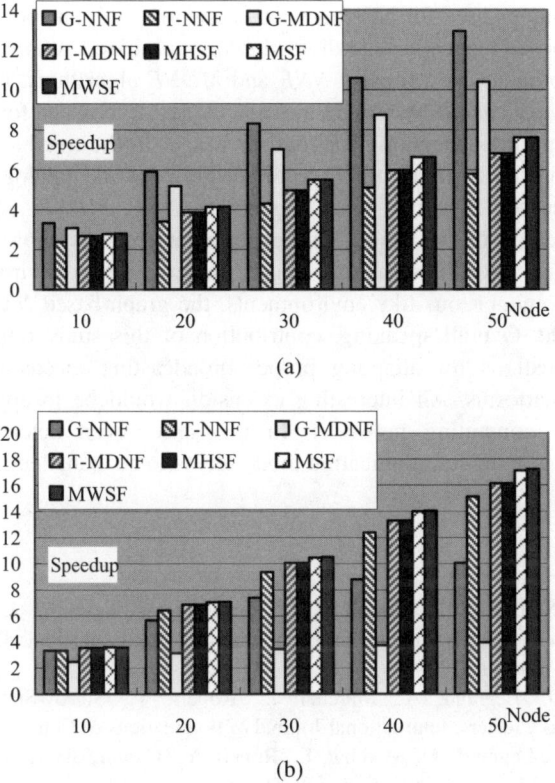

Fig. 3. Speedup comparisons with different number of nodes (a) $h = 0.1$ (b) $h = 5$

Table 2. Summary of Performance Comparisons

Network Size \ Network Heterogeneity	high	low
Small	G-NNF	MWSF
Large	G-NNF	MWSF

6 Conclusions and Future Work

Atomic broadcast operation is widely used to resolve many network problems in computer networks. It is not only an important communication pattern in many distributed computing applications, but also a fundamental operation in many on-demand routing protocols. In this paper, we have proposed different atomic broadcasts techniques used for heterogeneous networks with one port communication model. The proposed techniques are divided into graph-based and tree-based ones. In graph based approaches, we present *NNF* and *MDNF* algorithms. In order to avoid redundant messages caused by communication cycles, a message forwarding table is constructed during pre-scheduling for runtime usage. In the tree based algorithms, a minimal spanning tree is first built from the origin network topology for scheduling one-to-all broadcasts. Five tree-based algorithms *NNF*, *MDNF*, *MHSF*, *MSF* and *MWSF* are presented in this study. The experimental results show that the *MWSF* outperforms other algorithms in high degree heterogeneous environments. On the contrary, with homogeneous-like environments, the graph-based *NNF* algorithm has the best schedule. Overall speaking, contribution of this study relies on providing significant suggestions for adapting proper broadcasting mechanism in different heterogeneous platforms. An interesting extension would be to apply this work to wireless mobile computing networks. In this case, even determining the best makespan with one-port communication mode seems to be a challenging problem.

References

1. Angelo, L., Steffenel, B., Mounié, G.: Scheduling Heuristics for Efficient Broadcast Operations on Grid Environments. In: Proceedings of International Parallel and Distributed Processing Symposium (2006)
2. Beaumont, O., Legrand, A., Marchal, L., Robert, Y.: Steady-State Scheduling on Heterogeneous Clusters. International Journal of Foundations of Computer Science (2005)
3. Beaumont, O., Legrand, A., Marchal, L., Robert, Y.: Complexity Results and Heuristics for Pipelined Multicast Operations on Heterogeneous Platforms. In: Proceedings of International Conference on Parallel Processing, pp. 267–274 (2004)
4. Beaumont, O., Legrand, A., Marchal, L., Robert, Y.: Pipelining Broadcasts on Heterogeneous Platforms. IEEE Transactions on Parallel and Distributed Systems 16(4), 300–313 (2005)
5. Beaumont, O., Marchal, L., Robert, Y.: Broadcast Trees for Heterogeneous Platforms. In: Proceedings of 19th IEEE International Parallel and Distributed Processing Symposium (2005)
6. Faraj, A., Patarasuk, P., Yuan, X.: Bandwidth Efficient All-to-all Broadcast on Switched Clusters. In: Proceedings of IEEE International Conference on Cluster Computing (2005)
7. Khuller, S., Kim, Y.: On broadcasting in heterogeneous networks. In: Proceedings of the 16th Annual ACM Symposium on Parallel Architectures and Algorithms (2004)
8. Lin, C.: Efficient contention-free broadcast in heterogeneous network of workstation with multiple send and receive speeds. In: Proceedings Eighth IEEE International Symposium on Computers and Communication, vol. 2, pp. 1277–1284 (2003)
9. Lin, C.: Efficient broadcast in a heterogeneous network of workstations using two sub-networks. In: Proceedings of 7th International Symposium on Parallel Architectures, Algorithms and Networks, pp. 273–279 (2004)
10. Liu, P.: Broadcast scheduling optimization for heterogeneous cluster systems. Journal of Algorithms 42(1), 135–152 (2002)
11. Ooshita, F., Matsumae, S., Masuzawa, T., Tokura, N.: Scheduling for broadcast operation in heterogeneous parallel computing environments. Systems and Computers in Japan 35(5), 44–54 (2004)

12. Ooshita, F., Matsumae, S., Masuzawa, T.: Efficient gather operation in heterogeneous cluster systems. In: Proceedings of 16th Annual International Symposium on High Performance Computing Systems and Applications, pp. 196–204 (2002)
13. Patarasuk, P., Faraj, A., Yuan, X.: Pipelined Broadcast on Ethernet Switched Clusters. In: Proceedings of International Parallel and Distributed Processing Symposium, p. 10 (2006)

A Resource Discovery Algorithm with Probe Feedback Mechanism in Multi-domain Grid Environment*

Libing Wu[1,2], Yanxiang He[1], Jianqun Cui[3], Simeng Wang[2], Laurence T. Yang[4], and Naixue Xiong[1]

[1] School of Computer, Wuhan University, Wuhan, 430072, China
[2] National Engineering Research Center of Multimedia Software, Wuhan, 430072, China
[3] Department of Computer Science, Huazhong Normal University, Wuhan, 430079, China
[4] Department of Computer Science, St. Francis Xavier University, Canada
{wu,yxhe}@whu.edu.cn, jqcui@126.com, oncemoresisi@hotmail.com,
ltyang@stfx.ca, naixue@jaist.ac.jp

Abstract. We have presented a resource discovery algorithm with probe feedback mechanism (RDPF) in grid computing formerly. The algorithm chooses different path to send request messages and corresponding response messages. A feedback mechanism is added in response message to rediscovery requested resource if the resource can't be found in forwarding path. The experiment indicates that the algorithm can improve the success ratio of resources discovery and need not to increase the extra system cost. But the algorithm treats the grid as a full-distributed environment where every node has the same level. In fact, the real grid is composed of many different Autonomous Systems. We can use the layer character to optimize the performance. The paper presents a resource discovery algorithm with probe feedback mechanism in multi-domain grid (RDPF_MG) as an alternative to the existing resource discovery algorithm with probe feedback mechanism in order to be compatible with different grid environments.

1 Introduction

Grid resource discovery algorithm is the pivotal part of grid resource discovery mechanism, and it determines the form of grid resource service, the structure of the overlay grid, the manner of resource registration and naming, and the means of resource searching. In the meantime, it relates to the performance of grid resources discovery directly. Nowadays, the research on the grid resource discovery algorithm is the crucial problem in grid resource management area. According to different inquiry request processing modes, the grid resource discovery algorithms are mainly divided into centralized and decentralized resource discovery algorithms. In the centralized environment, the index of the shared resources which can be retrieved is reserved on the center server, all the information about the available systems is also congregated on it. Conceptually speaking this kind of discovery dispatch pattern is

---

* Support by National Natural Science Foundation of China (Grant No. 60773008, 60642006).

extremely useful, however, it comes into being a bottleneck for baffling the size of computing grid easily expands, so the research emphases shift to the decentralized grid resource discovery algorithms.

At present, there are many research productions in the area of the decentralized grid resource discovery algorithms [1-5]. In order to improve the success ratio of resources discovery algorithm on the condition of not increasing the extra system cost, we propose a novel grid resource discovery algorithm with feedback mechanism. In this algorithm, positive search and feedback message may choose different path to reach the destination node. If the resource can't be found in forwarding path, the response message will not only be sent back to resource requester but also choose a different path to rediscover the requested resource. In this way, we just increase a little system cost to achieve higher success ratio of resource discovery. However, the later research shows that the discovery algorithm with feedback mechanism regards the whole grid topology as a full-distributed system where every node is indistinctive, and it is not suitable for the common multi-domain grid environment nowadays. In this paper, we improve the resource discovery algorithm in multi-domain grid. So it is more compatible with the real grid environment.

2 Theory of Grid Resource Discovery Algorithm with Probe Feedback Mechanism

The prime innovation of the grid resource discovery algorithm with feedback mechanism can be divided into two steps: normal phase and rediscovery phase [6]. The resource request can identify the place of desired resource during normal phase if resource can be found right now. Otherwise a rediscovery phase will be started to search the proper resource again or advance reservation resource which may be idle in the near future in back way. The detail of the algorithm is introduced in ref [6], and here we just give a simple example to illuminate it briefly.

We assume the value of TTL equals to 3. Node A sends a resource request to the neighbor B based on the value of f. Node B adopts the same policy to choose D as the forwarding node. When the request is received by node F, there are some resources in local computer which can satisfy the request. So node F is the matching node. As some other algorithms, node F will reserve the resource, create a successful feedback message and send it directly to the request node A. Here directly means the path F chooses may be different from the primary way. Which path to be selected is decided by system's routing algorithm. This phase is named as normal phase and shown in Fig. 1 (a).

If node F has not any local available resources to match the request, the request will not be forwarded any more for the value of TTL has counted down to 0. When node F realizes that it is the last node, it will generate a probe feedback message which will be sent back to the request node directly. The path of probe feedback message may be similar to that of the successful feedback message. But the most different character is that the probe feedback message will inquire of every node whether there are some matching resources which can serve right now or as advance reservation resource. If there are not matching resources but some advance

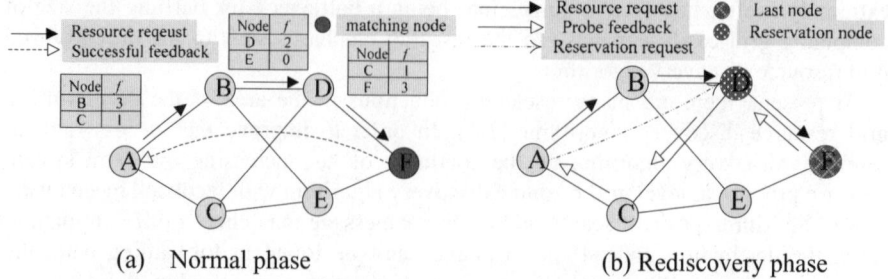

Fig. 1. Grid resource discovery algorithm with feedback mechanism

reservation resources, the message will record or update the node information and the reservation time. The update policy we use is that the recorded node can serve first. We suppose node D is the advance reservation node when the probe message is received by node A. If node A can accept the start serve time of node D, it will send an advance reservation request to node D and then send the job to node D at the reservation start time. This phase is called as rediscovery phase and shown in Fig.1 (b).

3 Algorithm Improved in Multi-domain Grid Environment

The experiment indicates that grid resource discovery algorithm with feedback mechanism can improve the success ratio of resources discovery significantly and need not to increase the extra system cost. But the algorithm treats the grid as a full-distributed environment where every node has the same level. In fact, the real grid is composed of many different Autonomous Systems. Moreover, there are usually many nodes in grid. In order to reduce the extra traffic generated by resource discovery, the algorithm with feedback mechanism adopts the policy that each resource node only transmits resource request to one neighbor node. However, the policy may slower the diffusion speed of resource request in grid. Besides, it isn't able to perform multi-path search at the same time when forwarding resource request.

Considering the above questions, this paper presents the resource discovery algorithm with probe feedback mechanism in multi-domain grid (RDPF_MG) as an alternative to the existing resource discovery algorithm with probe feedback mechanism (RDPF) in order to suit different grid environments.

3.1 Principle of the Algorithm

1. Related Definition

Definition 1 Domain: Each AS(Autonomous System) is called a independent domain.

Definition 2 BRP(Border Resource Provider): Each domain has a border resource node which is responsible to collect the information of resources distribution in this domain, record them into the resources distribution table and transmit it to other domains.

Definition 3 RDT(Resource Distribution Table): It is used for recording the informa-tion of resources distribution, every item in the table is a quadruple (v, $\{R_t\}$, $\{R_p\}$, $R_s\}$) , v represents a certain resource node in domain, $\{R_t\}$ represents all resources types belongs to that node, $\{R_p\}$ depicts resources performance corresponding to resources types in $\{R_t\}$, $\{R_s\}$ shows the status of each resource types belongs to that node, 1 means it is on using now, 0 means it has not been used.

2. Topology of the grid

RDPF_MG algorithm is built on the normal two-layer grid topology, and the whole grid is divided into many relatively independent domain which is composed of many end nodes. These nodes have two sorts, one is normal nodes in the domain, may be resources requester or provider, the other one is boundary resources provider (BRP), as it is shown in Fig. 2.

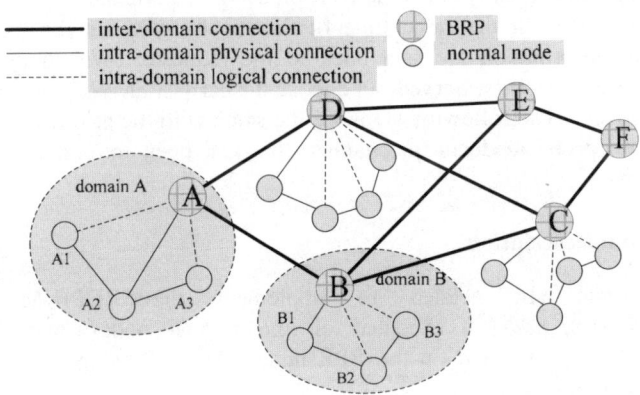

Fig. 2. Topology of multi-domain grid

As is shown in Fig. 2, there are 6 domains A, B, C, D, E, F, each domain contains one BPR node and several normal nodes (the normal nodes in E, F are elided). When system initialized, normal nodes provide BPR node with its own available resources information and record the copy of that information locally. BPR will note it on resource distributing table of its own. When the resources information provided by normal nodes are not consistent with the information that it reserves and sends to BPR, normal nodes will send update message to BPR in order to ensure the coherence of the information.

RDPF_MG based on this topology can be divided into intra-domain discovery and inter-domain discovery.

(1) Intra-domain discovery

The resources requester node (e.g. node A1) firstly sends the resources discovery request to node BPR (node A) which is in the same domain, node BPR checks within the domain whether there are suitable resources nodes, if there are, the request will be transmit to the closest suitable node(e.g. node A3), and node A3 decides whether to provide A1 the resource needed. If node A3 transmits the response message 'success' to node A1, node A1 could transmit the task which is needed to be dealt with to A3. After receiving the task, A3 needs to send resources update message to node BPR to make sure that the resources information in RDT table of node BPR is correct.

(2) Inter-domain discovery

If node BPR (node A) has not found the resources that node A1 needed in RDT, it starts algorithm of inter-domain resources discovery. In this process, we adopt the algorithm based on probe feedback mechanism. In order to accelerate the request diffusivity, when choosing adjacent node inter-domain as the receiver to the request, we will transmit the request to the nodes which had respond to this kind of resources in the past instead of just choosing the node which has the highest response frequency to the resource in the adjacency list. Although it increases the quantity of the nodes transmit at the same time to speed up search velocity, the traffic will not increase sharply because there is only one node BPR on using in a domain.

Due to multi-path at the same time fit the requirement, maybe more than one resource node information are sent back to the requester. We adopt principle of FRFS(First Response First Served) to choose the earliest arriver as the result of that resource discovery. The following steps are the same with the grid resource discovery algorithm with probe feedback mechanism that had been introduced already, here omit the details.

3.2 Algorithm Description

Two algorithms are needed to implement the RDPF_MG. One is RDPF_MG_normal_node( ) executed on the normal nodes, and the other is RDPF_MG_BRP( ) executed on the BPR nodes. The following is pseudo code of these two algorithms.

```
Algorithm 1: RDPF_MG_normal_node( )
1 send resource information message to BRP when
initialization;
2 send resource request message req·id, u, R) to BRP;
3 msg = receive_msg();   //receive_msg() will be blocked
till a message is received
4 If (isResponse_msg(msg))
5   Case t_start(msg)
6   0: send_job(Job,v); break;   //find the matching node
7    T_MAX: wait for a certain time then goto 2; break;
8    otherwise: t_end = estimate(Job,t_start);
9    send_advance_reserve_req(u,v,R,t_start,t_end);
10   If (advance reservation request is successful)
11       schedule(Job,v,t_start); //the job will be send
to v when it is time to t_start
12    Else //can not find the matching node and advance
reservation node
13       wait for a certain time then goto 2;
14    Endif
```

```
15 EndCase
16 Else
17   If (isRequest_msg(msg))  // the message is a request
message from BRP
18     reserve(R); //reserve R for the request
19     send(response_msg,u);
20   Else
21     If (isJobExeReq(msg))  //the message is a job
execution request
22       send update_msg(u, {R_t}, {R_p}, {R_s}) to BRP
23     Endif
24   Endif
25 Endif
```

Algorithm 2: RDPF_MG_BRP( )
```
1 build RDT based on resource information message of
normal nodes;
2 msg = receive_msg();   //receive_msg() will be blocked
till a message is received
3 If (isIntraRequest_msg(msg)) //the message is a
intra-domain request
4    v = lookup(RDT, R);
5    If (v is not null) //v is the match node
6      send(msg, v);
7    Else //there is not match node in the domain
8      req_msg = req(id,u,R,TTL) ;
9      If (is_ no_null({n} = node(R, f) in RAT))
10       send_ neighbor (req_message,{n});
11     Else
12       send_ neighbor (req_msg, random(n));
13     Endif
14   Endif
15 Else //the message is a inter-domain request
16   RDPF_Responser_exec_modify(msg);//it is the same
with RDPF_Responser_exec except for using send_
neighbor (req_message,{n}) instead of send_ neighbor
(req_message,{n})
17 Endif
```

4 Evaluation

4.1 Simulation Environment

In order to evaluate the performance of the algorithm above, we generate a 500-node network topology by using the Tiers network generator [9]. Then we divide these 500 nodes into 50 domains keeping to the average distribution principle. The average distance of intra-domain nodes is 100 m, while the average distance of inter-domain nodes is 10 km. All links are Full-duplex. For the sake of simplicity, we suppose every resource requester request only a single type resource, such as CPU time, memory or bandwidth. If the volume of resources of a certain node is equal to or greater than the volume of resources of a request in the course of resource discovery, we deem it able to respond to the request [10-11]. In the course of simulation, every node may submit its own resource request, and it keeps to the Poisson distribution. The experiment context is the same to the one proposed in reference [6] except the multi-domain and the much more nodes.

Because RDPF_MG in multi-domain is the improved algorithm based on RDPF including probe feedback mechanism in reference [6], we compare the two algorithms by simulation. In the course of the experiment, we choose diverse TTL values to repeat the simulation scheme and measure the same parameters as [6]-Success Ratio and Average RTT. Their meanings are following:

$$\text{Success Ratio} = \frac{Succ\_Request}{All\_Request} \times 100\% \qquad (1)$$

$$\text{Average RTT} = (\sum_{i=1}^{n} RTT(S\_Ri))/n \qquad (2)$$

Hereinto, *Succ_Request* represents the number of successfully requested resources, *All_Request* represents the total number of requested resources, *RTT(S_Ri)* represents the RTT of successful request i, n represents the returning successful requests. If a resource request gets its matching resource through several searches, we take *RTT(S_Ri)* as the sum of search time.

4.2 Results and Analysis

According to context above, we attain simulation results as Fig.3

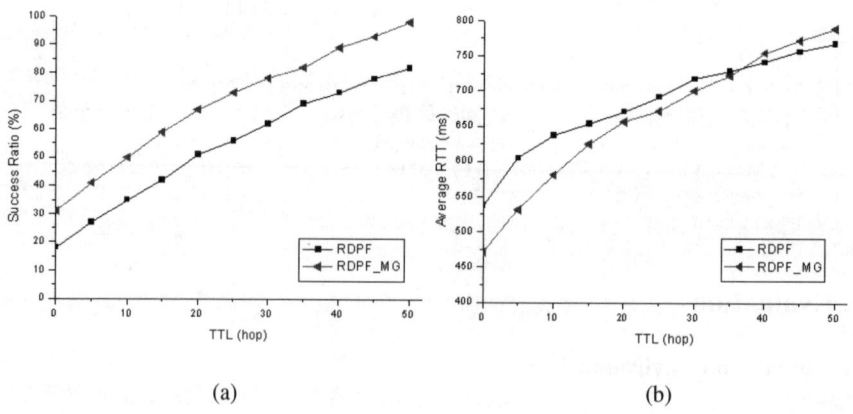

Fig. 3. Simulation results

Fig.3(a) shows that RDPF_MG algorithm has higher success ratio of resource request than RDPF with the same TTL value. Especially, when TTL value increases to 45-50, the success ratio of RDPF_MG will reach 95%+. It is because that when TTL value is big, RDPF_MG can search resources in more domains as possible while

RDPF with the same TTL value can only access the limited resource nodes, which are probably in the same domain.

Fig.3(b) shows that the RTT of RDPF_MG algorithm is shorter than that of RDPF when the TTL value is small. It is because that it makes use of centralized algorithm to search resources in the same domain, then need only enquire BRP nodes to find out whether exists required resources in this domain. That is to say, if there are request resources in this domain, it only spent a RTT in finding it successfully. Otherwise, it need make use of resource request with TTL value, and RTT will increase with TTL value. Generally, only when the requested resources are far from the resource requester, the average RTT of RDPF_MG will be bigger than that of RDPF (e.g. TTL=40 in fig.3(a)).

Based on the above analyses, it is clear that RDPF_MG algorithm can improve observably Success Ratio of resource request and save the average RTT in contrast with RDPF when the grid is multi-domain topology.

5 Conclusion and Future Work

This paper argues about an improvement scheme of the resource discovery algorithm in multi-domain grid based on the existing resource discovery algorithm including probe feedback mechanism in order to fit the multi-domain better. According to the performance analyses, the maximal number of messages generated by the algorithm is mainly related to the RTT value, while independent of the number of nodes. It shows that the algorithm has good scalability. In addition, the algorithm can afford the same Success Ratio of resource discovery in the case of holding down the TTL value by increasing resource density and average number of nodes in the domain. The simulation results show that the improved algorithm can get higher Success Ratio of resource request and shorter average RTT. The future work is put up evaluation and modification of this algorithm in the real grid environment.

References

1. Vanthournout, K., Deconinck, G., Belmans, R.: A Taxonomy for Resource Discovery. In: Müller-Schloer, C., Ungerer, T., Bauer, B. (eds.) ARCS 2004. LNCS, vol. 2981, pp. 78–91. Springer, Heidelberg (2004)
2. Gupta, A., Agrawal, D., Abbadi, A.E.: Distributed Resource Discovery in Large Scale Computing Systems. In: Proceedings of Symposium on Applications and the Internet (SAINT), pp. 320–326 (2005)
3. Iamnitchi, A., Foster, I., Nurmi, D.: A peer-to-peer approach to resource discovery in Grid environments. In: Proceedings of High Performance Distributed Computing, IEEE, Los Alamitos (2002)
4. Tangpongprasit, S., Katagiri, T., Kise, K., Honda, H., Yuba, T.: A time-to-live based reservation algorithm on fully decentralized resource discovery in Grid computing. Parallel Computing 31(6), 529–543 (2005)
5. Iamnitchi, A., Foster, I.: On fully decentralized resource discovery in Grid environments. In: Proceedings of International Workshop on Grid Computing, Denver, Colorado, pp. 51–62 (2001)

6. Cui, J., He, Y., Wu, L., Li, F.: A Novel Resource Discovery Algorithm with Feedback Mechanism in Grid Computing. In: Proceedings of the Fifth International Conference on Grid and Cooperative Computing (GCC 2006), pp. 368–376. IEEE Computer Society Press, Los Alamitos (2006)
7. Faloutsos, M., Faloutsos, P., Faloutsos, C.: On power-law relationships of the internet topology. In: SIGCOMM, pp. 251–262 (1999)
8. Jovanovic, M., Annexstein, F.S., Berman, K.A.: Modeling Peer-to-Peer Network Topologies through Small-World Models and Power Laws. In: TELFOR, Belgrade, Yugoslavia (2001)
9. Doar, M.: A better model for generating test networks. In: Proceedings of IEEE Global Telecommunications Conference, GLOBECOM 1996, London, UK, pp. 83–96 (1996)
10. Maheswaran, M., Krauter, K.: A Parameter-based approach to resource discovery in Grid computing systems. In: 1st IEEE/ACM International Workshop on Grid Computing, pp. 181–190 (2000)
11. Li, W., Xu, Z.W., Dong, F., Zhang, J.: Grid Resource Discovery Based on a Routing-Transferring Model, [EB/OL] (2004), http://www.chinagrid.net/grid/talksanddocs.htm

Middleware Integration and Deployment Strategies for Cyberinfrastructures

Sebastien Goasguen[1], Krishna Madhavan[1], David Wolinsky[2], Renato Figueiredo[2], Jaime Frey[3], Alain Roy[3], Paul Ruth[4], and Dongyan Xu[5]

[1] Clemson University, Clemson, SC 29634, USA
{sebgoa,cm}@clemson.edu
[2] University of Florida, Gainesville, FL 32601, USA
{davidiw,renato}@acis.ufl.edu
[3] University of Wisconsin-Madison, Madison, WI, USA
{jfrey,roy}@cs.wisc.edu
[4] University of Mississippi, MI, 53703, USA
ruth@olemiss.edu
[5] Purdue University, West-Lafayette, IN 47906, USA
dxu@cs.purdue.edu

Abstract. Virtual Organizations require infrastructure that meets their scientific needs. Traditionally, a VO can require access to computational backends that are suited for interactive applications, various levels of parallelism or highly distributed systems where users can contribute their own cycles. In this paper, we present a middleware integration and deployment strategy that builds a VO architecture which offers various computational tiers. The architecture offers interactive, real-time backends, batch operated small scale computational clusters, batch operated large scale remote supercomputers, and a wide area peer-to-peer network. All these middleware components are integrated into a cohesive system that accesses production resources and serves the nanotechnology community. We also present a middleware integration that meets the educational needs of the VO by integrating a course management system into the VO's portal.

1 Introduction

Virtual Organizations (VOs) [1] are at the core of grid computing. They come in various sizes and have various goals and capabilities, but they all need access to services to achieve their goals. While the infrastructures of long-standing VOs like the Compact Muon Solenoid (CMS) VO and the National Virtual Observatory (NVO) VO have evolved over several years, new VOs face the challenge of designing and building their infrastructure in a timely fashion while avoiding the reinvention of solutions and the construction of silos. LEAD has built an advanced infrastructure [2] and nanoHUB has been previously described [3]. These infrastructures exhibit a common architecture based on the concept of service orientation [4] and grid resources. Building distributed infrastructures for science has long been a primary motivation of grid computing. Service-oriented science [5] is now a well accepted concept. Simplifying the creation of a service-oriented architecture for a VO is key to easing the creation of grid architecture for scientific communities, also known as cyberinfrastructures. However, current Cyberinfrastructures still focus on integration efforts, connecting various pieces of middleware together to access the resources needed by the VO.

In this paper we present the various middleware components used in the nanoHUB (http://www.nanohub.org) to provide access to computational resources and also support the educational needs of the nanotechnology community. Due to the large number of applications provided by the nanoHUB, the computational needs are quite diverse. Other middleware needs are present due to the highly educational role of the nanoHUB. Learning objects offering training in the nanotechnology area and served by the nanoHUB must be managed as digital assets that follow the Shareable Content Object Reference Model 1.2 (SCORM). The learning objects and associated assessments can be managed through SAKAI, the open source course management system.

The paper is organized as follows; Section 2 gives an overview of the integrated architecture hat uses all the middleware components. Section 3 describes all the components in more details, section 4 highlights some security aspects and finally usage data and interesting usage patterns of that data are presented in section 5.

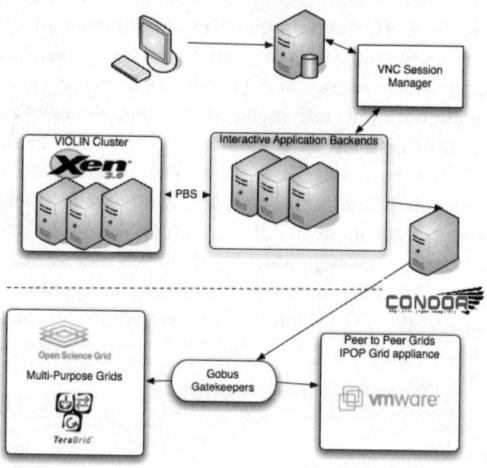

Fig. 1. Integration of interactive backends, VIOLIN, Condor and the Grid appliance to support four types of computational jobs for one VO

2 Integrated Architecture

The nanoHUB Cyberinfrastructure was originally supported by PUNCH, [6] a system that laid the foundation for the use of virtual machines to isolate the VO infrastructure from the underlying service provider hosting the VO's servers. The current iteration of this system is described in [3]. This paper describes the components comprising the core capabilities of this Cyberinfrastructure: VIOLIN, Condor, IPOP and SAKAI.

Cohesively integrating all these components is done through the deployment of a local infrastructure based on virtual machines and the use of web service interfaces. The high level architecture is depicted in Figure 1. First, the VO maintains its own user database in an LDAP and offers local file systems through a NFS server. A set of virtual machines are deployed using Xen 3.0 to ensure that authentication uses the LDAP server and that the home directories are NFS mounted. Because each virtual backend is setup as a remote PBS submit node and as a remote Condor submit node, access to the virtual machine gives direct access to the VIOLIN clusters and to all remote resources accessible via Condor, including the Peer to Peer network deployed via IPOP. Indeed, the grid appliances form a Condor pool that is accessible via a globus gatekeeper or directly from a grid appliance. The remote resources on national grid infrastructures are accessed by the community using a community credentials. VO users do not need individual certificates on these remote grids; instead, the VO accesses the resources and multiplexes the users on a single credential. Security is preserved through the use of attributes embedded in the grid proxy. Figure 6 shows the overall architecture that integrates all of the computational systems.

While users can access the architecture via standard shell access, a portal access can also be enabled via standard processes such as in OGCE. A more interactive access can be setup using VNC sessions running on the virtual backends and by embedding these VNC sessions into webpages. Single sign on for this type of access was demonstrated in [7].

3 Middleware Components

3.1 VIOLIN

VIOLIN [8] or Virtual Internetworking on OverLay Infrastructure is a novel alternative to application-level overlays. The goal of VIOLIN is to create mutually isolated autonomic VIOLIN environments that can be created for users and user groups as their "own" private distributed computation environment with the configurations of customized physical environments with administrative privileges (e.g., their own private cluster). Within VIOLIN, the user can execute and interact with unmodified parallel/distributed applications, and can expect strong confinement of potentially untrustworthy applications. Virtualised resources also address issues of security; a case for using virtual machines on grids is detailed in [9].

VIOLIN is inserted as a layer of indirection between the infrastructure and virtual machines running atop it. This layer provides users with the familiar look-and-feel of a private LAN environment while allowing sharing of the cyberinfrastructure. Infrastructure sharing is achieved by manipulating the scale and location of each virtual environment's resource allocation.

Entities in a VIOLIN virtual environment include virtual routers, switches, and end-hosts, all of which are implemented in software (many virtual machine platforms can be used by VIOLIN including Xen, VMware, and User-Mode Linux). VIOLIN network overlays connect virtual machines in a virtual environment. These environments have their own IP address spaces that completely confine all communication within the VIOLIN and maintain the appearance of standard machines connected to standard Ethernet. Because all entities of a VIOLIN environment are software, the system is extremely dynamic; entities can be created, destroyed, and migrate on-demand. Functionally, VIOLIN provides isolated virtual environments for deploying standard or non-standard distributed applications across a shared cyberinfrastructure.

Figure 2 shows how a VO user can use VIOLIN. A client connects to the VO webserver and accesses an application. The application is started on an interactive backend that redirects the application interface on the client through a VNC connection. The interactive backend is setup as a PBS frontend to the VIOLIN cluster. The VIOLIN cluster is deployed on op of a physical cluster that has installed with the Xen virtual machine software [10]. VIOLIN creates individual virtual clusters that can be mutually isolated and span various administrative domains.

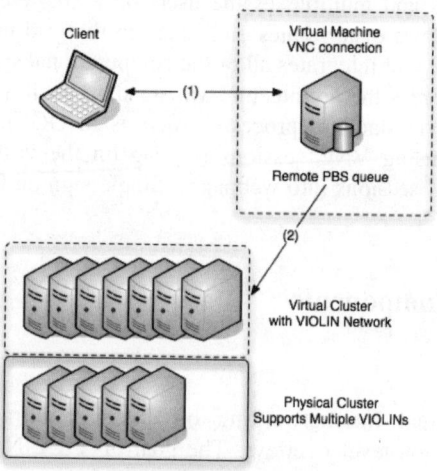

Fig. 2. VIOLIN Integration

It is also possible to create VIOLIN environments that are integrated, autonomic entities that dynamically adapt and relocate themselves to enhance the performance of the applications within [11]. This all-software virtualization of environments presents a unique opportunity to advance the performance and efficiency of a VO. Two factors drive the adaptation of virtual environments: (1) the dynamic availability of infrastructure resources and (2) the dynamic resource needs of the applications within VIOLIN environments. Dynamic resource availability may cause the VIOLIN environment to relocate its virtual machines to new physical hosts when current physical hosts experience increased workloads. At the same time, dynamic applications may require different amounts of resources throughout their execution.

The changing requirements can cause the VIOLIN environment to adapt its resource capacity in response to the needs of the application. Furthermore, the autonomic adaptation (including relocation) of the virtual computation environment is transparent to both application and user, giving users the perception of a well-provisioned, private, networked run-time environment.

3.2 Condor

As part of the nanoHUB architecture, we used the pre-existing Condor [12] software to manage jobs run on grid sites around the US. Condor's derivation, known as Condor-G [13] is an aggregate of both the Condor and Globus projects. As such, it is well suited as a meta-scheduler for any VO.

The Condor High Throughput Computing system (Condor) is a specialized workload management system for compute intensive jobs. Like other full-featured batch systems, Condor provides a job queuing mechanism, scheduling policy, priority scheme, resource monitoring, and resource management. Users submit their serial or parallel jobs to Condor. Condor queues these jobs, chooses when and where to run the jobs based upon an established policy, carefully monitors their progress, and ultimately informs the user upon completion.

Originally, the Condor job submission agent could launch jobs only upon Condor-managed resources. Condor-G is an enhanced submission agent that can launch and supervise jobs upon resources controlled by a growing list of management systems, permitting computing environments that cross administrative boundaries – a primary requirement for grid computing. Condor-G can also seamlessly utilize resources accessible by Globus Toolkit's GRAM protocol, as well as other grid interfaces. Used as a front-end to a computational grid, Condor-G can manage thousands of jobs destined to run at distributed sites. Condor-G provides job monitoring, logging, notification, policy enforcement, fault tolerance, credential management, and it can handle complex job interdependencies.

Matchmaking has been implemented to allow a job to be run on any one of the available sites. The matchmaking accounts for the need to run applications differently at different sites. The reliability of file transfer to a site has been improved. Many of the sites that are used for job submission use Globus GRAM and the native file transfer interface occasionally fails. To overcome this problem, each job is run as a workflow implemented with DAGMan: Select site, marshal data, stage data to site, submit job to site and run, stage data from site, unmarshal data.

Stork and GridFTP are used to stage the job's data back and forth, as the data may be quite large for some applications. Condor-G and GRAM are used to submit the job to the execute site. If any of these steps fail, the workflow is restarted from the beginning, preferring to select a different site. Condor is used for matchmaking to select the execution site. Currently, a random site is selected from the list of compatible sites (correct architecture, sufficient memory). All of the sites are tested every 6 hours and removed from the selection site if any of them fail. Finally, this framework is application-agnostic. For each application, a short script is written that describes what files need to be transferred and how the application needs to be invoked.

Figure 3 shows the integration with the client. The interactive backends, on which the applications interfaces are running, are setup as remote Condor queues. A Condor *schedd* runs on a virtual machines setup with a public IP address. Every application can then submit a job from an interactive backend that is on the private network and get out of the local infrastructure through the Condor submission process. In the case of Condor-G, the grid resources need a credential. The VO manages a single community credential that is refreshed on a regular basis on the Condor gateway machine.

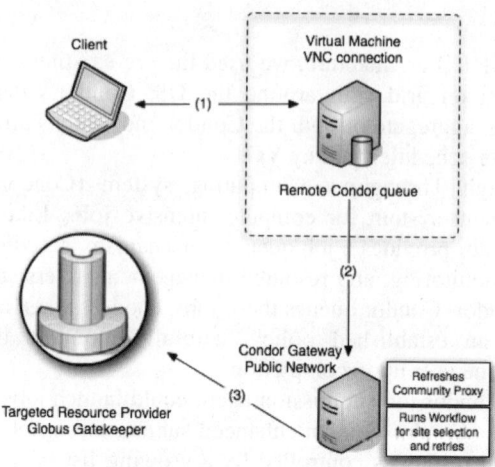

Fig. 3. Condor Integration

3.3 The Grid Appliance

The use of machine and network virtualization techniques is beneficial to provide applications with their native execution environment which is isolated from physical resources. Albeit virtual, virtual machines and networks are resources that must be managed, which is especially challenging in wide-area environments. Manual establishment and maintenance of virtual network tunnels and routing tables across multiple network domains behind different NATs and firewalls by system administrators is time-consuming, error-prone and expensive. This motivates the use of self-configuring techniques for facilitating the management of inter-networked VMs to reduce the management burdens of a large-scale virtualized WAN environment. To address this problem, we use a combination of packaging using virtual machine appliances and self-configuring virtual networks, which are integrated into easy to deploy, easy to use Grid appliances [14].

Grid appliances integrate a full-fledged self-configuring Grid middleware stack in a virtual machine image that runs unmodified on a variety of contemporary VM technologies. In the current implementation, the Grid appliance middleware is based on Condor. In addition, the Grid appliance packages the IP-over-P2P (IPOP) overlay [14], which enables self-organizing wide-area virtual private networks.

The combination of virtual appliances, IPOP and Condor allows the creation of scalable wide-area networks of virtual workstations (WOWs [16]) with little management effort that provides bi-directional TCP/IP connectivity among VMs even when nodes are behind firewalls and/or NATs. The Grid appliance allows for customization of additional per-VO software with the use of UnionFS file system "stacks." It also has provisions for facilitating transfer of data from/to its host by exporting user files through a host-only Samba file system.

Surveys from our Grid appliance users show that adding a VM guest hosted by a typical Linux, Windows, or MacOS x86-based platform to an already-running WOW involves a simple one-time setup that takes 15-30 minutes, even for entry-level users who have not used virtualization or Grid computing tools previously. By lowering the barrier of entry for users to deploy Grid middleware, the appliance helps non-expert users to learn how to use Grid computing infrastructure with a hands-on environment and without a substantial investment of time. It also enables a VO to tap into resources that would otherwise be difficult to reach (e.g. multi-domain desktop Grids) to establish pools of opportunistic resources. The Grid appliance is available for download from http://wow.acis.ufl.edu.

Figure 4 shows how the grid appliances are accessible from the Condor gateway. One of the appliances is a Globus gatekeeper that has a Condor jobmanager. In this way, resources contributed by the VO members themselves can be used.

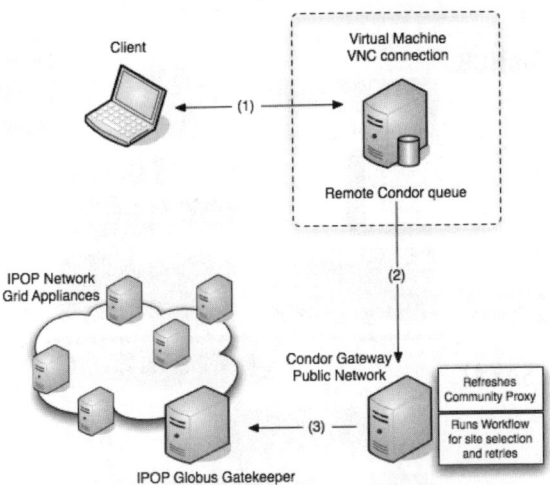

Fig. 4. Grid Appliance Integration

3.4 SAKAI

The Sakai Project is a community source software development effort to design, build and deploy a new Collaboration and Learning Environment (CLE) for higher education. Sakai is a Java-based web application, developed as an open source effort [17].

In order to integrate Sakai with the nanoHUB, the first area of consideration is user authentication. Since the VO authenticates users through a LDAP server, the Sakai login procedure was modified and used to authenticate and authorize users through the same LDAP mechanism as the VO's portal. Sakai can be configured to authenticate users against an LDAP compliant directory using the *UserDirectoryProvider* interface. This Java class makes use of Novell's JLDAP free, open-source library for communicating with LDAP servers. However, providing LDAP access alone is not sufficient to ensure SSO between Sakai and the nanoHUB. Next is the implementation of SSO (Single Sign On) between the Web server and Sakai. SSO makes it possible for already authenticated users to access Sakai without re-entering their login name and password. The Sakai web service interface allows us to easily integrate various components. The architecture utilized for this integration is shown in Figure 5.

The integration layer that is used on the nanoHUB works as follows. Once the users have been authenticated, the system automatically identifies the appropriate content context that they need to join. Once this identification is complete, the user is transparently taken to the appropriate quiz within the learning context. A learning context usually contains multiple quizzes. Therefore, the system automatically identifies and tracks users' previous visits to determine if they have already completed the quiz.

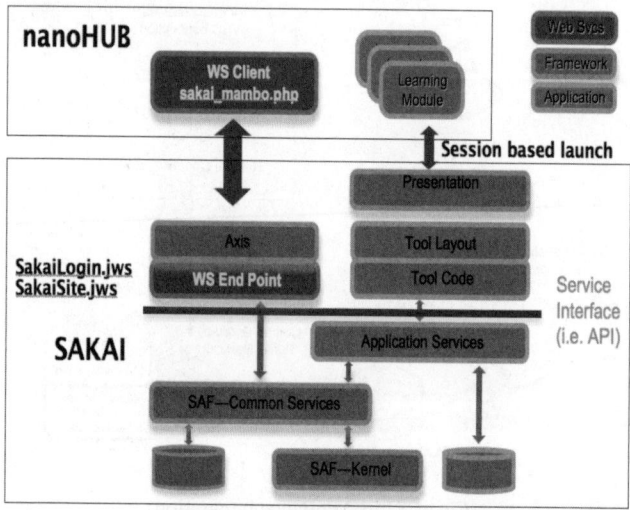

Fig. 5. NanoHUB – Sakai Integration Architecture

4 Security

One final aspect of the integration which has not been discussed in depth is security. In our case, users do not own accounts on the target resource, they do not even have a valid grid certificate. Therefore, there is no distinguished name (DN) mapped to a VO account. Indeed, a key philosophy of the architecture has been to support users that create accounts on the portal that are not aware of the underlying computational resources. In the case of the nanoHUB, the VO obtained a community allocation on the TeraGrid and formed an official VO on the Open Science Grid. While VO accounts are the norm on OSG, TeraGrid requires that some auditing trace be in place in order to run jobs under a single account on the resources.

In order to provide additional information to the targeted resource provider and information for auditing, we investigated the use of Gridshib, specifically the use of the SAML issuer. We deployed the Gridshib SAML issuer tool to embed user attributes onto the community credential used to access the TG resources. We deployed an Identity Provider tied to the LDAP server so that for each job submitted, a single proxy can be created for a particular job with the attributes of the user initiating the request.. These issues of attribute based authentication and authorization and grid security are discussed in detail in [18]. This system has been deployed and tested but is not currently used in production. Figure 6 shows the workflow, starting with a user's request, the retrieval of attributes from the identity provider, the pushing of attributes to the resource provider and the potential pulling of attributes by the resource provider.

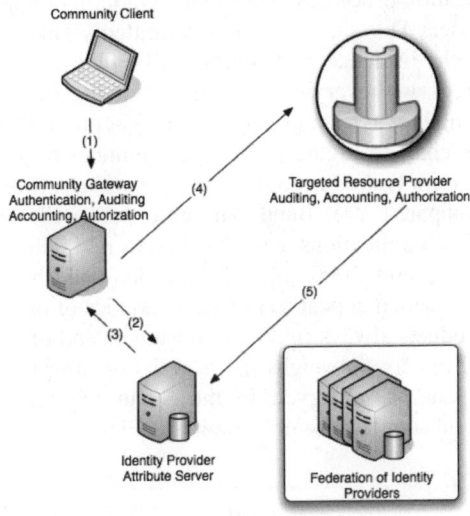

Fig. 6. Attribute based infrastructure for VO

5 Results and Usage Patterns

This last section, in which we present some usage statistics of the nanoHUB. The VIOLIN system, which has been in production since April 2006, has been one of the reliable local facilities for production nanoHUB job execution. Between July 2006 and July 2007, VIOLIN served a total of 527 simulation users and logged a total of 46,860,689 CPU seconds.

VIOLIN executed most of the nanowire simulation jobs between April 2006 and June 2007. Today, VIOLIN is still executing jobs from other nanoHUB simulations. More specifically, the Nanowire calculates current flow through a nanotube; the I-V characteristics of which require that several bias points be calculated. This type of application can be implemented either through parallel MPI algorithms which establishes a parameter sweep or through several Condor jobs.

Nanowire, which has been running on OSG and TeraGrid since June 2007, uses the reliable submission framework described in Section 3. While completed results are not yet available, initial testing shows that only 713 nanowire jobs failed of a total of 15658 jobs run. While this represents an impressive 96% rate of success for jobs going to eight different sites, those jobs that failed did so at the beginning of testing, which means that *corrected success rate* is now closer to 100%. Support for additional OSG and TeraGrid sites are being added.

While grid sites with significant computing capability are now available, most of the current applications remain interactive and are run locally on the interactive backends or the VIOLIN cluster. Consequently, because users simply wait for the results to return to their browser they have yet to adopt a batch oriented mindset that is traditional to supercomputing. CPU consumption of users running nanowire applications on the VIOLIN cluster has a peak usage period that indicates that 90 users employed application processes 2000 hours a month, or approximately 22 hours of computation per user. This number, while admittedly small, represents the truly great potential of such e-science technologies. By placing both applications and computational resources with varying capabilities in the hands of users, VIOLIN democratises computing in ways not previously thought possible.

The semi-log scale chart in Figure 8 shows the number of jobs run by users. The x-axis represents the users ranked according to the number of jobs each has run. The four applications compared are Band Structure Lab, CNTbands, FETtoy and MOSFET. Of these four applications, each has between 100 and 150 users with each user running between 8 and 1000 jobs. This chart also shows some power law behavior and long tails, which appear to be characteristics of new web offerings. New web based Internet products always find new consumers and the integrated benefits of finding these new consumers outweighs the benefits of offering just a few products. Similar power law patterns, observed in the Sloan Digital Sky Survey (SDSS) e-science portal [19], substantiate the information in Figure 7.

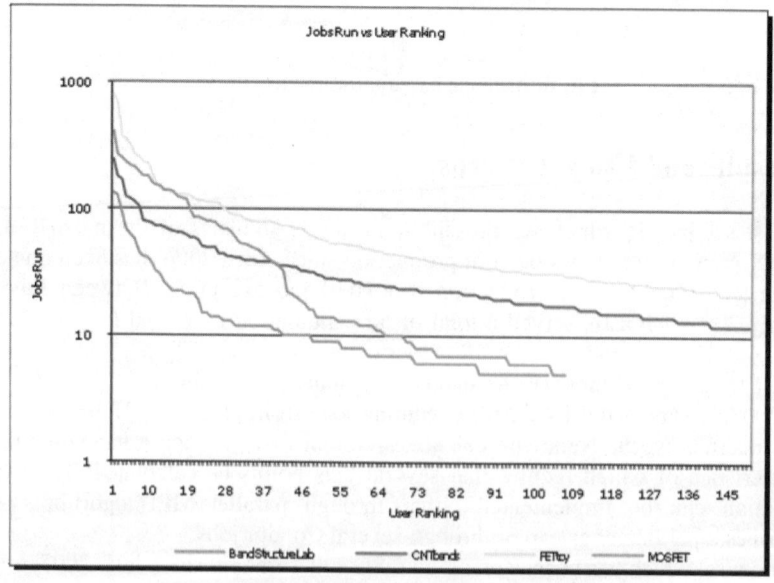

Fig. 7. Number of jobs per top users for four applications

6 Conclusions

In this paper we presented a strategy to integrate several middleware components that meet the diverse needs of a Virtual Organization (VO). For our purposes, we utilized the nanoHUB VO for the computational nanotechnology community as a case study. However, our emphasis is to show that the strategies and technologies presented in this paper are VO agnostic and can be re-used in other Cyberinfrastructures. Here we have VIOLIN, Condor and the Grid appliance which provide access to three types of computational resources: small local clusters, large scale remote clusters and HPC resources and widely distributed peer resources. We have also presented the use of an attribute based authentication and authorization system which helps shield users from the complexity of using certificates to access grid resources. Finally, we also presented an atypical type of middleware integration with SAKAI. Further work in studying these e-science usage patterns will be conducted to elucidate user behaviors, user needs, and the relevance of offering a large number of services.

Acknowledgement

This work was made possible by the National Science Foundation award SCI-0438246; the strategies explained in this paper were applied to the nanohub, http://www.nanohub.org. The authors also wish to thank the many people involved in the nanoHUB project.

References

1. Foster, I., Kesselman, C., Tuecke, S.: The Anatomy of the Grid: Enabling Scalable Virtual Organizations. International Journal of High Performance Computing Applications 15(3), 200–222 (2001)
2. Droegemeier, K.K., et al.: Service-Oriented Environments for Dynamically Interacting with Mesoscale Weather. Computing in Science & Engineering [see also IEEE Computational Science and Engineering] 7(6), 12–29 (2005)
3. Fortes, A.B., Figueiredo, J., Lundstrom, M.S.: Virtual computing infrastructures for nanoelectronics simulation. Proceedings of the IEEE 93(10), 1839–1847 (2005)
4. Papazoglou, M., Georgakopoulos, D.: Service-oriented computing: Introduction. Commun. ACM 46(10) (2003)
5. Foster, I.: Service-Oriented Science. Science 308(5723), 814–817 (2005)
6. Kapadia, N.H., Figueiredo, R.J., Fortes, J.A.B.: Punch: web portal for running tools. Micro, IEEE 20(3), 38–47 (2000)
7. Matsunaga, A., et al.: Science gateways made easy: the In-VIGO approach. In: Concurrency and Computation: Practice and Experience, Wiley Press, Chichester (2006)
8. Ruth, P., et al.: Virtual distributed environments in a shared infrastructure. Computer 38(5), 63–69 (2005)
9. Figueiredo, R.J., Dinda, P.A., Fortes, J.A.B.: A case for grid computing on virtual machines. In: Proceedings. 23rd International Conference on Distributed Computing Systems, pp. 550–559 (2003)

10. Barham, P., et al.: Xen and the art of virtualization. In: Proceedings of the nineteenth ACM symposium on Operating systems principles, pp. 164–177 (2003)
11. Ruth, P., et al.: Autonomic Live Adaptation of Virtual Computational Environments in a Multi-Domain Infrastructure. In: IEEE International Conference on in Autonomic Computing, 2006. ICAC 2006 (2006)
12. Litzkow, M.J., Livny, M., Mutka, M.W.: Condor-a hunter of idle workstations. In: 8th International Conference on Distributed Computing Systems, pp. 104–111 (1988)
13. Frey, J., et al.: Condor-G: A Computation Management Agent for Multi-Institutional Grids. Cluster Computing 5(3), 237–246 (2002)
14. David, W., Agrawal, A., Oscar Boykin, P., Davis, J., Ganguly, A., Paramygin, V., Sheng, P., Figueiredo, R.: On the Design of Virtual Machine Sandboxes for Distributed Computing in Wide Area Overlays of Virtual Workstations. In: Proc. First Workshop on Virtualization Technologies in Distributed Computing (VTDC), with Supercomputing (2006)
15. Arijit, G., Aagrawal, A., Boykin, P.O., Figueiredo, R.: IP over P2P: Enabling Self-configuring Virtual IP Networks for Grid Computing. In: Proc. 20th IEEE International Parallel and Distributed Processing Symposium (IPDPS)
16. Arijit, G., Agrawal, A., Oscar Boykin, P., Figueiredo, R.: WOW: Self-Organizing Wide Area Overlay Networks of Virtual Workstations. In: Proc. High Performance Distributed Computing (HPDC) (2006)
17. Sakai Collaboration and Learning Environment, Available at http://www.sakaiproject.org
18. Barton, T., et al.: Identity Federation and Attribute-based Authorization through the Globus Toolkit, Shibboleth, GridShib, and MyProxy. In: 5th Annual PKI R&D Workshop (April 2006)
19. http://research.microsoft.com/research/pubs/view.aspx?type=Technical%20Report&id=1236

A Multi-site Resource Allocation Strategy in Computational Grids*

Chao-Tung Yang** and Sung-Yi Chen

High-Performance Computing Laboratory
Department of Computer Science and Information Engineering
Tunghai University, Taichung, 40704, Taiwan, ROC
ctyang@thu.edu.tw

Abstract. This work presents a multi-site resource allocation (MSRA) strategy for grid resource broker to dispatch jobs to appropriate resources across multiple different administrative domains on a computational grid. The experimental result shows that MSRA can obtain better performance than other strategies. We use the Ganglia and NWS tools to monitor resource status and network-related information, respectively. The proposed grid resource broker provided secure, updated information about available resources and served as a link to the diverse systems available in the Grid.

1 Introduction

The Grid computing technology plays a role like a pharos to scientists for solving large-scale problems by providing users with a virtual supercomputer that contains distributed heterogeneous resources, which are geographically distributed and governed by different administrative domains over a network using open standards [2, 3, 4, 5, 6, 7] The Globus Toolkit® (GT), is an open source project developed by the Globus Alliance® for building grids, not only provides users with an implementation of the necessary services of a middleware to build grid infrastructures, but also able to be employed to implement immense applications on grid infrastructures. However, the GT lacks some features, such as a queuing system, a friendly interface, and a proper resource broking manager to respectively process, accept and broke jobs or workloads submitted by users. In addition, a monitoring mechanism that can monitor the status of user jobs is also expected.

In a grid environment, applications make use of shared grid resources to improve performance. The target function usually depends on many parameters, e.g., the scheduling strategies, the configurations of machines and links, the workloads in a Grid, the degree of data replication, etc. In this work, we examine how those parameters may affect performance. We choose an application's overall response time as an object function and focus on dynamically scheduling independent tasks. We

---

* This paper is supported in part by National Science Council, Taiwan, under grants no. NSC 96-2221-E-029-019-MY3 and NSC 96-2218-E-007-007.
** Corresponding author.

define the job, scheduler, and performance model of a Grid site and conduct experiments on TigerGrid platform. We use the Ganglia [10, 14, 24] and NWS [16, 27] tools to monitor resource status and network-related information, respectively. Understanding influence of each parameter is not only crucial for an application to achieve good performance, but would also help to develop effective schedule heuristics and design high quality Grids.

This work enhances the features of a grid resource broker with the capabilities provided by a network information service from a domain-based network model. Here, we will take a deeper look at what constitutes the scheduling discipline and its components. Scheduling is generally not well understood because scheduling products often integrate multiple functions into one package called a scheduler. So we are going to deconstruct scheduling into its constituent parts. The innovative contribution of the presented integration is the possibility to design and implement new mapping/scheduling mechanisms to take into account both network and computational resources.

Our previous works constructed a grid computing environment and conducted a grid resource broker on it, then worked out a network information model with an efficient bandwidth measurement and made resource broker can handle workflows [17, 18, 19, 20, 21, 22, 23, 29]. Our grid the resource broker allocates resources by sorting a particular metric without considers the multi-site situation, it brings up some problems such as allocating resource dispersedly, taking all nodes in grid into a list of resources not sets of resources, dispatching jobs by a blind measurement at risk, and sorting resource by a particular metric. The previous works lacks a viewpoint of multi-site resources when resource allocation and dispatching jobs. This work proposed a multi-site resource allocation strategy, called MSRA, which can revise the point of view in previous work and improve the performance of Resource Broker. The experimental result shows that MSRA exhibits a better performance than other strategies.

2 Backgrounds

There are many studies amid the resource management and related topics, [1] described the Grid Resource Broker portal, an advanced Web front-end for computational Grids in use at the Lecce University. The portal allows trusted users seamless access to computational resources and Grid services, providing a friendly manipulation environment that takes advantage of the underlying GT middleware, enhancing its basic services and capabilities.

In [8], authors described a resource management system which is the central component of a distributed network computing system. There have been many projects focusing on network computing that have designed and implemented resource management systems with a variety of architectures and services. In this paper, an abstract model and a comprehensive taxonomy for describing resource management architectures is developed. The paper presents taxonomy for Grid resource management systems. Requirements for resource management systems are described and an abstract functional model has been developed. The requirements and model have been used to develop a taxonomy focusing on types of Grid system, machine organization, resource model characterization, and scheduling characterization. Representative Grid resource management systems are surveyed and placed into their various categories. A software layer that interacts with Grid environments is needed to achieve these goals, i.e., middleware and its services. It is also necessary to offer resource management system to hide the underlying Grid resources complexity from Grid users [15].

In [13], authors presented design and implementation of an OGSI-compliant Grid Resource Broker compatible with both GT2 and GT3. It focuses on resource discovery and management, and dynamic policy management for job scheduling and resource selection. The presented Resource Broker is designed in an extensible and modular way using standard protocols and schemas to become compatible with new middleware versions. The paper also gave experimental results to demonstrate the Resource Broker behavior.

In [17, 19], the authors designed and implemented a resource broking system called Resource Broker. In [18, 22, 23], authors proposed a domain-based network information model for solving the overhead of bandwidth measurement among Grid nodes and attempted to make a prediction of bandwidth of a link not performed in the network information model, it solved the problem for lack of network information. In [21], authors proffered a workflow-based Resource Broker that can handle workflows that are described by using XML. Applications represented by workflow can be further decomposed into grid jobs. The main task of resource management is resource brokering that is able to optimize a global schedule for all requesting Grid jobs and all requested resources. Consequently, a global optimizing Resource Broker with network bandwidth-aware is proposed in [23]. It is embedded in applications and a resource management system. The performance of the optimization method is demonstrated by an example.

3 Multi-Site Resource Allocation Strategy

3.1 Grid Resource Broker

Resource broker discovers and evaluates grid resources, and makes job submission decisions by comparing the requirements of a job with grid resources. The system architecture of resource broker and the relation of each component were shown in Fig. 1. Each rectangular represents a unique component of our system. Users could easily make use of our resource broker through a common grid portal [3, 11, 12, 17, 20]. The primary task of resource broker is to compare requests of users and resource information provided by information service. After choosing the appropriate job assignment scheme, grid resources are assigned and the scheduler is responsible to submit the job. The results are collected and returned to resource broker. Then, resource broker records results of execution in the database of information center through the agent of information service. The user can query the results from grid portal.

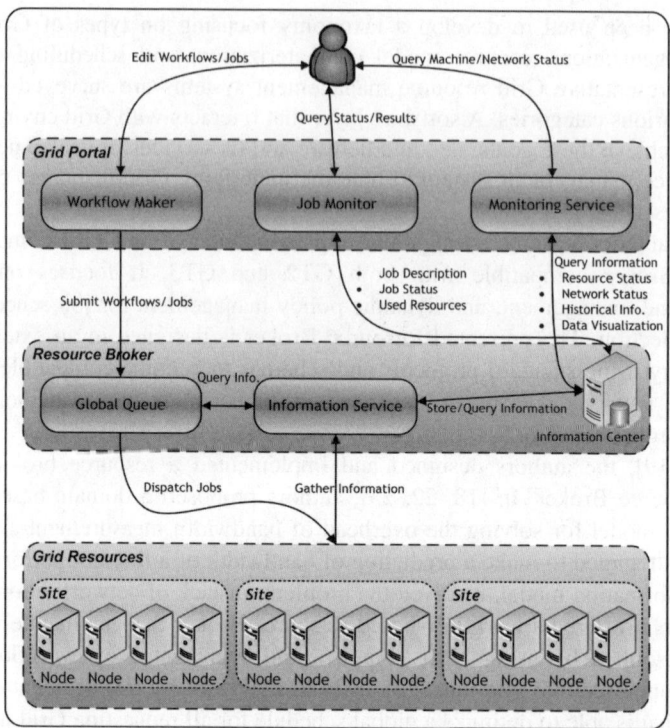

Fig. 1. System architecture

3.2 The Parameters

In this subsection, the parameters used in the algorithm are listed and explained in the following:

- job_i: The ith job dequeued from the global queue, where $i = 1 \sim n$. The job contains some information such as job name, program name, program arguments, input data, and number of processors to run on. The program is usually a parallel program written by MPI library and compiled by MPICH-G2 that is a Grid-enabled implementation of the MPI standard [7, 9, 26]. The resource broker will allocate resources according to the information provided by the job.
- NP_{req}: The number of processors used for executing job_i, if the Resource Broker dispatches the job_i successfully, the resources distributed over several Nodes or Sites used for job_i will be locked for a while until the job_i finishes.
- NP_{Grid}: The total number of processors in the Grid, if the NP_{req} is larger than the NP_{Grid}, the job will be dropped.
- $Size()$: Return the number of elements in the set, the value must be zero or positive.
- S_{cand}: A set contains Sites which is qualified to the request content of job_i, where Site is a set including available Nodes.

- *SitePair*: It is a composite set including available Sites and links between each Site, where links are constituted by the dynamic domain-based network information model [28].
- SP_{cand}: A set contains SitePairs which are qualified to the request content of job_i.
- S_{max}: The Site that has the maximum value of rank.
- SP_{max}: The SitePair that has the maximum value of rank. In this case, the factor Resource Broker considers is which SitePair has the maximum total performance power according to the expression described as below. This situation should consider the performance power value of Sites in the SitePair with the links produced by the dynamic domain-based network information model synthetically.
- $Load_i$: It is a sum of the $load^1$, $load^5$, and $load^{15}$ of $Node_i$, where $Node_i$ is the ith Node in Site and available for allocation, the expression of $Load_i$ is shown as follows:

$$Load_i = \frac{load_i^1 \times 15 + load_i^5 \times 5 + load_i^{15}}{21} \quad (1)$$

- *CP*: The computing performance power of the Site or SitePair, the expression is shown below, Where *HPL* is the benchmarking value of Site obtained by the HPL benchmarking [25], Num_{cpu} is the total number of processors of Site. Finally, the summation of available Nodes is the computing performance power of the Site.

$$CP = \sum \left(\frac{HPL}{Num_{cpu}} \times \frac{100 - Load_i}{100} \right) \quad (2)$$

- *DC*: The discount used to deduct the average bandwidth. The expression of *DC* is shown as follows, Where $X_1, \ldots, X_n$ is the bandwidth of links, σ_X is the one standard deviation of $X_1, \ldots, X_n$.

$$DC = \begin{cases} 1, \text{ if } -\sigma_X < X_1, \ldots, X_n < \sigma_X \\ 0.8, \text{ if } X_i < -\sigma_X \end{cases} \quad (3)$$

- *NP*: The network performance power of a set of links that among Sites in a SitePair. In this situation the Resource Broker should consider the comprehensive estimation of the set of links, the expression is shown as fellows:

$$NP = Avg_{ij} \times DC \quad (4)$$

Where Avg_{ij} is the average bandwidth of links that produced by the network information model. The essence of *NP* is taking into account a comprehensive estimation of the performance power of links, if the bandwidth of links are all located in one standard deviation, that means the bandwidth between any two Sites are an average, and the parallel program running on this set will perform a smooth result. If one or more bandwidth of links is smaller than a minus standard deviation, the average of bandwidth should be discounted by a value; it means one or more links will be a bottleneck of this set of links.

- *TP*: Total performance power of the Site or SitePair, the expression is shown as fellows:

$$TP = \beta \times \sum CP + (1-\beta) \times NP \qquad (5)$$

Where β is the effect ratio used to regulate the percentage of CP and NP.

3.3 The MSRA Algorithm and Flowchart

The essence part of multi-site resource allocation (MSRA) algorithm is properly deal with the situation that single Site resource cannot satisfy the request of the job. In this situation, the Resource Broker should allocate multi-site resources to satisfy the job with MSRA. There are two main factors that should be considered, such as NP_{req}, S_{max}, and SP_{max}. The first factor is used to decide which Site or SitePair can qualify to the request number of processors of the job, and the second factor is the value of rank of Site or SitePair which is used to decide which Site or SitePair has the maximum performance power to deal with the job, resulting in that the execution time can be reduced well. The procedure of MSRA is listed as follows:

```
1   MSRA(job_i) {
2       NP_Grid = getFreshInfoFromGanglia()
3       if (NP_req < NP_Grid) then
4           S_cand = chooseSiteCandidates()
5           if (Size(S_cand) > 0) then
6               S_max = getMaxRankCandidate(S_cand)
7               dispatchJob(job_i, S_max)
8           else
9               SP_cand = chooseSitePairCandidates()
10              if (Size(SP_cand) > 0) then
11                  SP_max = getMaxRankCandidate(SP_cand)
12                  dispatchJob(job_i, SP_max)
13              else
14                  enqueueJob(job_i)
15              fi
16          fi
17      fi
18  }
```

Fig. 2. The multi-site resource allocation algorithm

The functions used in the algorithm are listed and explained as follows:

- *getFreshInfoFromGanglia()*: This function used to retrieve the fresh machines information from Ganglia, and determine the total number of processors in the Grid. It is also used for later job dispatching.
- *chooseSiteCandidates()* and *chooseSitePairCandidates()*: This function used to choose candidates of Sites or SitePairs. If the Site or SitePairs can qualify the request content of job, it will be added into the candidate set.
- *getMaxRankCandidate()* and *getMaxRankCandidate()*: This function returns the Site or SitePair that has the maximum value of rank.
- *enqueueJob()*: This function used to enqueue the job into the global queue when the Resource Broker cannot allocate enough resources to the job.

The main phases of Resource Broker are Resource Discovery, Application Modeling, Information Gathering, System Selection, and Job Execution [23]. The subject matter of System Selection phase is filtering the most appropriate resources that satisfy the requirements of job and generating the machine list that selected by the resource allocation strategy. For above purposes, this work devises a strategy called Multi-Site Resource Allocation Strategy, it caused a revolution of the core of Resource Broker that devised before in [21], and the flowchart of Multi-Site Resource Allocation Strategy was shown in Fig. 3.

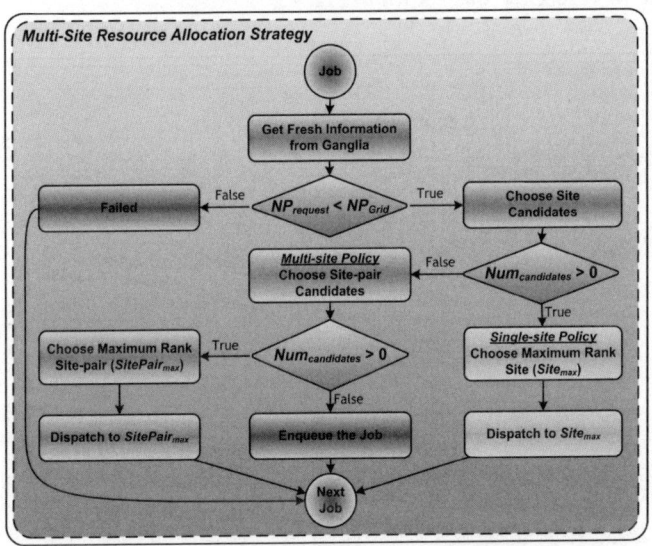

Fig. 3. Multi-Site resource allocation strategy flowchart

At beginning state, a job is dequeued from the Global Queue for scheduling. First of all is getting the fresh information from Ganglia for determining if the number of processors of request is smaller than the total number of processors of Grid. If false, the state changes to "Failed" and the system then process the next job; if true, the state changes to choose Site candidates that satisfy the condition of applications, such as the number of processors. If the number of candidates is larger than zero, it means that there are several Sites that can qualify the job Then the state changes to Single-site Policy, if equals to zero, it means that there are no candidates for the job. Then the state changes to Multi-site Policy. For the Single-site Policy, the process chooses a Site that has the maximum rank, dispatches the job, and then changes the state to process the next job. For the Multi-site Policy, the process chooses the Site-pair candidates that satisfy the condition of applications. If the number of Site-pair candidates is larger than zero, the state changes to choose a Site-pair that has a maximum rank, dispatches the job, and then changes the state to process the next job. If the number equals to zero, it means there are no enough resource for the job at present. Then the state changes to enqueue the job in the Global Queue, and the system then processes the next job.

4 Experimental Environment and Results

In this work, the experiment was conducted and evaluated on TigerGrid which consists of 101 processors distributed over 12 clusters located at 7 education organizations, such as Tunghai University (THU), National Changhua University of Education (NCUE), National Taichung University (NTCU), Hsiuping Institute of Technology (HIT), National Dali Senior High School (DALI), Lizen High School (LZSH), and Long Fong Elementary School (LFPS). The logical diagram of network environment in TigerGrid was shown in Fig. 4.

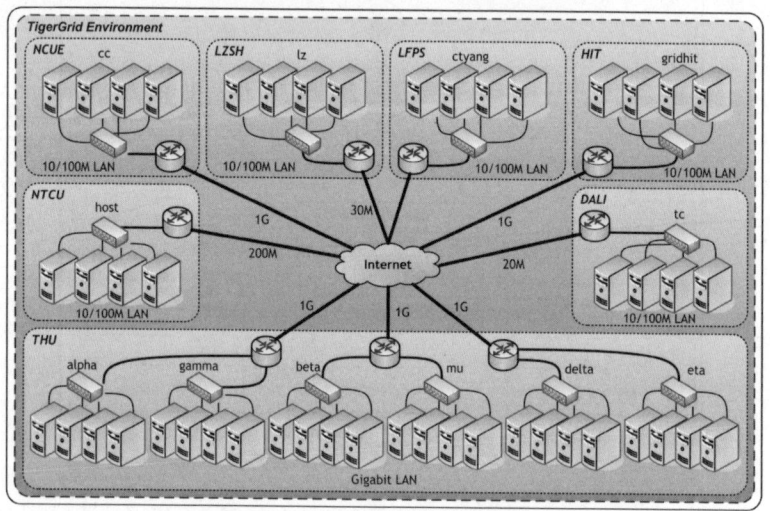

Fig. 4. The logical diagram of network environment in TigerGrid

The machine information of all clusters and network information between any two Sites among them are listed in Table 1 and Table 2, respectively. We compare the multi-site resource allocation algorithm and other resource allocation strategies addressed in previous works. The details of strategies are shown as fellows:

- Speed-only: In this strategy, resources are allocated according to clock of processors. If the Resource Broker allocates and distributes a job received to a Site whose summation of available processors is the largest. When performing the job, this scheduling scheme presents a fine result if the bandwidth between two Sites is not a bottleneck.
- Network-only: Using this strategy, the network information will be the sorted key of resources. The Resource Broker will dispatch the job to a SitePair that has the largest bandwidth measurement between two Sites. In general, this scheduling scheme usually results in a poor allocation when the SitePair has a poor computing performance power.

Table 1. The machine information of test-bed

Site	Number of CPU/Core	Total Speed (MHz)	Total Memory (MB)	HPL (GFLOPS)
alpha	8	14,264	4,096	12.5683
beta	8	22,504	4,096	20.1322
gamma	4	11,224	4,096	5.8089
delta	4	12,004	4,096	10.6146
eta	32	73,600	8,192	42.3439
mu	4	6,384	2,048	13.0716
NCUE	12	23,892	12,288	21.5136
NTCU	5	4,215	1,024	1.0285
HIT	4	11,204	2,048	7.0615
DALI	4	7,454	512	2.8229
LZSH	4	3,290	1,024	0.8562
LFPS	1	3,002	1,024	3.0390

Table 2. The network information of testbed (unit: Mb/s)

Site	alpha	beta	gamma	delta	eta	mu	NCUE	NTCU	HIT	DALI	LZSH	LFPS
alpha	613	62	612	55	55	57	6	48	44	10	25	9
beta		756	50	50	41	663	6	41	52	10	22	9
gamma			716	37	36	34	4	31	37	9	23	8
delta				766	563	37	3	43	41	10	23	6
eta					813	38	4	6	7	6	15	8
mu						468	6	38	44	9	22	9
NCUE							82	5	4	11	19	3
NTCU								33	40	9	14	5
HIT									52	9	23	3
DALI										92	9	9
LZSH											83	9
LFPS												N/A

There are two main metrics used to evaluate the performance of resource allocation strategies, including:

- The average waiting time in queue: This metric shows that the resource allocation strategy can dispatch the jobs quickly or enqueue the jobs again when there are no suitable resources for the jobs.
- The average turnaround time of a job: This metric, used to evaluate the decision made by our resource allocation strategy is more intelligent and result in a shorter Round-Trip Time (RTT) of the job compared with other scheduling strategies.

This experimentation used several parallel programs, including bucketsort_mpi, quicksort_mpi, jacobi_mpi, mm_mpi, nbody_mpi, nqueen_mpi, sat3_mpi, bw_mpi, sieve5_mpi, and pi_mpi. As shown in Fig. 5, MSRA is better than the other two strategies, the average total of execution time of a job is the summation of its queuing time and execution time. Fig. 6 shows that the increase of a job's waiting time is stable and lower than the speed-only strategy. Fig. 7 shows the variety of job execution time in a time sequence, and network-only strategy exhibits non-uniform pulses at 3rd and 16th timestamp, but MSRA performs normally.

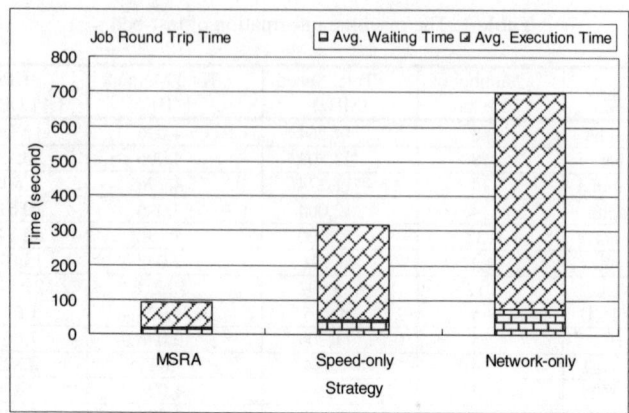

Fig. 5. The comparison of three policies of the average total time

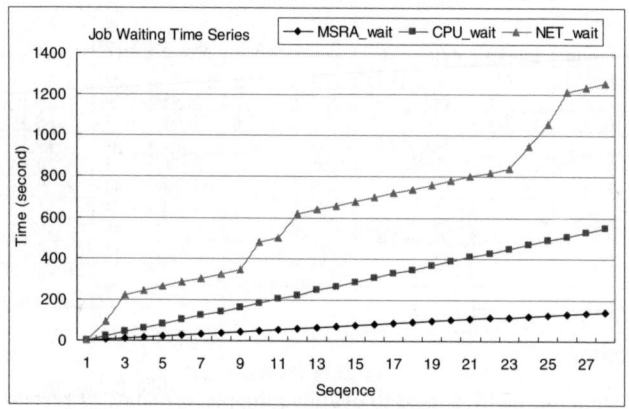

Fig. 6. The variety of job waiting time in a time sequence

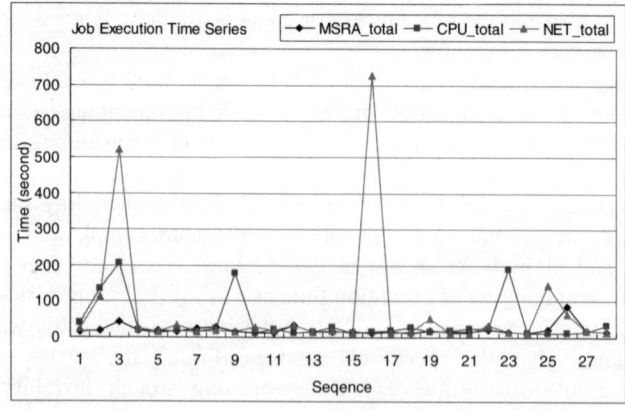

Fig. 7. The variety of job execution time in a time sequence

5 Conclusions and Future Work

This work presents the design and development of a grid resource broker which deploys multi-site resource allocation strategy. First of all, this work modifies the viewpoints of previous resource allocation strategies and improves the performance of Resource Broker. Second, this work develops a monitoring service based on open standard message exchange technique by using Ganglia, and provides an advanced Web front-end for users. Finally, Our Grid resource brokerage system is able to discover and evaluate Grid resources, and make informed job submission decisions by matching a job's requirements with an appropriate Grid resource to meet budget and deadline requirements. The innovative contribution of the presented integration is the possibility of designing and implementing new mapping/scheduling mechanisms to take into account both network and computational resources. Our future work will be enhancing the resource allocation strategy can be enhanced by historical analyze of scheduling with neural network, and analyzing the characteristics of applications so as to adjust the scheduling scheme dynamically in order to obtain improved performance in computational Grids.

References

1. Aloisio, G., Cafaro, M.: Web-based access to the Grid using the Grid Resource Broker portal. Concurrency Computation: Practice and Experience 14, 1145–1160 (2002)
2. Czajkowski, K., Fitzgerald, S., Foster, I., Kesselman, C.: Grid Information Services for Distributed Resource Sharing. In: Proceedings of the Tenth IEEE International Symposium on High-Performance Distributed Computing, IEEE press, Los Alamitos (2001)
3. Ferreira, L., Berstis, V., Armstrong, L., Kendzierski, M., Neukoetter, A., Takagi, M., Bing-Wo, R., Amir, A., Murakawa, R., Hernandez, O., Magowan, J., Bieberstein, N.: Introduction to Grid Computing with Globus. IBM Press (2003), http://www.ibm.com/redbooks
4. Foster, I., Kesselman, C.: The Grid 2: Blueprint for a New Computing Infrastructure, 2nd edn. Morgan Kaufmann, San Francisco (2003)
5. Foster, I.: The Grid: A New Infrastructure for 21st Century Science. Physics Today 55, 42–47 (2002)
6. Foster, I., Kesselman, C.: Globus: A Metacomputing Infrastructure Toolkit. International Journal of Supercomputer Applications 11, 115–128 (1997)
7. Foster, I., Karonis, N.: A Grid-Enabled MPI: Message Passing in Heterogeneous Distributed Computing Systems. In: Proceedings of 1998 Supercomputing Conference (1998)
8. Krauter, K., Buyya, R., Maheswaran, M.: A taxonomy and survey of grid resource management systems for distributed computing. Software Practice and Experience 32, 135–164 (2002)
9. Laszewski, V., Foster, I., Gawor, J., Lane, P.: A Java commodity grid kit. Concurrency and Computation: Practice and Experience 13, 645–662 (2001)
10. Massie, M.L., Chun, B.N., Culler, D.E.: The Ganglia Distributed Monitoring System: Design, Implementation, and Experience. Parallel Computing 30, 817–840 (2004)
11. Nabrzyski, J., Schopf, J.M., Weglarz, J.: Grid Resource Management. Kluwer Academic Publishers, Dordrecht (2005)

12. Park, S.M., Kim, J.H.: Chameleon: A Resource Scheduler in a Data Grid Environment. In: Proceedings of the 3rd IEEE/ACM International Symposium on Cluster Computing and the Grid, pp. 258–265. IEEE CS Press, Los Alamitos (2003)
13. Rodero, I., Corbalan, J., Badia, R.M., Labarta, J.: eNANOS Grid Resource Broker. In: Sloot, P.M.A., Hoekstra, A.G., Priol, T., Reinefeld, A., Bubak, M. (eds.) EGC 2005. LNCS, vol. 3470, pp. 111–121. Springer, Heidelberg (2005)
14. Sacerdoti, F.D., Katz, M.J., Massie, M.L., Culler, D.E.: Wide Area Cluster Monitoring with Ganglia. In: Proceedings of the IEEE Cluster Computing Conference, Hong Kong, pp. 289–298 (2003)
15. Venugopal, S., Buyya, R., Winton, L.: A Grid service broker for scheduling e-Science applications on global data Grids. Concurrency Computation: Practice and Experience 18, 685–699 (2006)
16. Wolski, R., Spring, N., Hayes, J.: The Network Weather Service: A Distributed Resource Performance Forecasting Service for Metacomputing. Journal of Future Generation Computing Systems 15, 757–768 (1999)
17. Yang, C.T., Lai, C.L., Shih, P.C., Li, K.C.: A Resource Broker for Computing Nodes Selection in Grid Computing Environments. In: Jin, H., Pan, Y., Xiao, N., Sun, J. (eds.) GCC 2004. LNCS, vol. 3251, pp. 931–934. Springer, Heidelberg (2004)
18. Yang, C.T., Shih, P.C., Chen, S.Y., Shih, W.C.: An Efficient Network Information Modeling using NWS for Grid Computing Environments. In: Zhuge, H., Fox, G.C. (eds.) GCC 2005. LNCS, vol. 3795, pp. 287–299. Springer, Heidelberg (2005)
19. Yang, C.T., Shih, P.C., Li, K.C.: A High-Performance Computational Resource Broker for Grid Computing Environments. In: Proceedings of the International Conference on AINA 2005, vol. 2, pp. 333–336 (2005)
20. Yang, C.T., Li, K.C., Chiang, W.C., Shih, P.C.: Design and Implementation of TIGER Grid: an Integrated Metropolitan-Scale Grid Environment. In: Proceedings of the 6th IEEE International Conference on PDCAT 2005, pp. 518–520 (2005)
21. Yang, C.T., Lin, C.F., Chen, S.Y.: A Workflow-based Computational Resource Broker with Information Monitoring in Grids. In: Proceedings of the 5th International Conference on Grid and Cooperative Computing (GCC 2006), pp. 199–206. IEEE CS Press, Los Alamitos (2006)
22. Yang, C.T., Shih, P.C., Chen, S.Y.: A Domain-Based Model for Efficient Measurement of Network Information on Grid Computing Environments. IEICE Trans. Information and Systems E89-D, 738–742 (2006)
23. Yang, C.T., Shih, P.C., Lin, C.F., Chen, S.Y.: A Resource Broker with an Efficient Network Information Model on Grid Environments. The Journal of Supercomputing 40, 249–267 (2007)
24. Ganglia, http://ganglia.sourceforge.net/
25. HPL, http://www.netlib.org/benchmark/hpl/
26. MPICH-G2, http://www3.niu.edu/mpi/
27. Network Weather Service, http://nws.cs.ucsb.edu/ewiki/
28. Yang, C.T., Chen, T.T., Tung, H.Y.: A Dynamic Domain-based Network Information Model for Computational Grids. In: Proceedings of 2007 International Conference on Future Generation Communication and Networking – FGCN 2007, pp. 575–578 (2007)
29. Yang, C.T., Chen, T.T., Tung, H.Y.: A Grid Resource Broker with Network Bandwidth-Aware Job Scheduling for Computational Grids. In: Cérin, C., Li, K.-C. (eds.) GPC 2007. LNCS, vol. 4459, pp. 1–12. Springer, Heidelberg (2007)

A Clustering Model for Multicast on Hypercube Network

Song Lu and XiaoDong Yang

College of Computer Science, National University of Defense Technology,
Changsha, Hunan 410073, People's Republic of China
lusong@nudt.edu.cn

Abstract. Multicast communication is one of the general patterns of collective communication in multiprocessors. On hypercube network, the optimal multicast tree problem is NP-hard and all existing multicast algorithms are heuristic. We find that the existing works are far away from optimal. Aiming to reduce the communication traffic, we propose a general clustering model for multicast on hypercube networks. Based on the model, we can construct more optimal or approximately optimal multicast algorithm for hypercube interconnection networks. And the model is also universal for existed works.

1 Introduction

Multicast is one of general collective communication operations [1,2] for interconnection networks. Multicast is the communication between a source node and some destination nodes (or one-to-k communication). The special case of multicast is broadcast (or one-to-all communication). The multicast algorithm determines the path on which the message routing to the destination nodes. There are many researches on multicast to reduce the communication traffic.

The multicast communication can be formulated as three different graph problems [3]. They are the Steiner tree (ST) problem, the multicast tree (MT) problem, and the multicast path (MP) problem based on the different underlying switching technology. However, the optimization of all these three multicast problems on hypercube networks has been proved to be NP-hard [4,5,6]. Lan, Esfahanian and Ni proposed a heuristic algorithm (LEN's MT algorithm) [7] for multicast tree problem on hypercube networks. Another heuristic algorithm for multicast tree problem was proposed by Sheu [8].

The ideas of both algorithms can be outlined as three steps. Firstly, split the destination nodes into small partitions (or clusters). Secondly, route all the partitions. Then, take the previous steps recursively. In this paper, we propose a general clustering model which is suitable for both LEN's MT algorithm and Sheu's MT algorithm. Based on the model, we can construct more optimal or approximately optimal multicast algorithm for hypercube interconnection networks.

In section 2, the definitions for multicast tree and optimal multicast tree [3,9] are presented. We also introduce the graph definition of hypercube and some related properties. In section 3, we propose the definition for *locality*. Based on the idea of locality, a general clustering model is presented. In section 4, we analyze the clustering model thoroughly and present clustering algorithms for LEN's and Sheu's algorithm and construct a new clustering algorithms. Then we propose a universal routing algorithm for clusters. Section 5 presents the performance analysis. The final section is about the conclusions.

2 Related Work

Multicast (one-to-k communication) can natively be split into many one-to-one communications. This primeval method is called unicast-based multicast [10,11]. In this method, system resources are wasted due to the unnecessary blocking caused by nondeterminism and asynchrony. Even without blocking, multicast may reduce communication traffic and latency considerably [9,12,13]. Therefore, many researches have been carried on multicast for different network topology, different underlying switching technology, software optimization and hardware acceleration [14,15]. In this section, we state the multicast tree problem and introduce some properties of hypercube interconnection topology.

2.1 Multicast Tree

Multicast tree problem is formulated as a graph problem by Lin and Ni [3,9]. The optimal multicast problem is originally defined by [16]. All these definitions are based on the graph theory [17,18].

Definition 1 (Multicast Tree). *Given a graph $G = (V, E)$, a source node u_0, and a multicast set $M \subseteq V$, a multicast tree is a subtree $G_T = (V_T, E_T)$ of G such that $M \subseteq V_T$ and for each $u \in M$, the path length from u_0 to u is equal to length on G.*

Definition 2 (Optimal Multicast Tree). *Given a graph $G = (V, E)$, the optimal multicast tree (OMT) $G_{OMT} = (V_{OMT}, E_{OMT})$ from source vertex u_0 to destination set $M = \{u_1, u_2, \cdots, u_k\}$ is a multicast tree of G such that $\|E_{OMT}\|$ is as small as possible.*

2.2 Hypercube

Hypercube is one of the most popular, versatile and efficient topological structures of interconnection networks. It has many excellent features, and, thus becomes the first choice for the topological structure of parallel processing and computing systems [19,20,21,22]. Here we define the hypercube using binary sequences.

Definition 3 (Hypercube). *A hypercube is defined as a graph $Q_n = (V, E)$. The vertex set V of Q_n consists of all binary sequence of length n on the set $\{0, 1\}$, $V = \{x_1 x_2 \cdots x_n | x_i \in \{0, 1\}, i = 1, 2, \cdots, n\}$. Two vertices $u = u_1 u_2 \cdots u_n$ and $v = v_1 v_2 \cdots v_n$ are linked by an edge if and only if u and v differ exactly in one coordinate, $E = \{(u, v) | \sum_{i=1}^{n} |u_i - v_i| = 1\}$.*

Based on the definition 3, we get the definition of subcube, relative address and distance on hypercube.

Definition 4 (Subcube of Q_n). *A subcube H_k of Q_n is a binary sequence $b_1b_2\cdots b_{n-k}$ of length $(n-k)$ which presents a subgraph containing 2^k vertices and $k\cdot 2^{k-1}$ edges. H_k can be denoted as $b_1b_2\cdots b_{n-k}\star\star\star$ inside of which the vertex has a form like $b_1b_2\cdots b_{n-k}x_{n-k+1}\cdots x_n(x_j \in \{0,1\}, n-k+1 \leqslant j \leqslant n)$* [23].

Definition 5 (Distance). *The distance between vertices is defined as the Hamming distance, $H(u,v) = \sum_{i=1}^{n}|u_i - v_i|(u = u_1u_2\cdots u_n, v = v_1v_2\cdots v_n)$. The distance between vertex sets is defined as $H(U,V) = \min_{u_i \in U, v_j \in V}(H(u_i, v_j))$.*

Definition 6 (Relative address). *The relative address of vertex u to vertex v is a binary sequence $R(u,v) \triangleq r_1r_2\cdots r_n$, where $r_i = u_i \oplus v_i (u = u_1u_2\cdots u_n, v = v_1v_2\cdots v_n)$.*

3 General Clustering Model

In this section, we study the features of multicast destination set on hypercube. We get two most essential properties for the destination set, *global-info* and *locality*. They both can be used for message routing. Based on the idea of *locality*, we propose a general clustering model with a universal routing algorithm. Both LEN's algorithm and Sheu's algorithm are both special instances of our general clustering model.

3.1 Global-Info and Locality

Multicast communication depends on a source node and some destination nodes. A multicast destination set is composed of all the corresponding vertices on the hypercube graph. Here we use *global-info* to describe the distribution of the destination vertices on hypercube.

Definition 7 (Global-info). *The global-info consists of (1) the number of destination vertices $\|M\|$, (2) the counter of relative address (see definition 6) of all destination vertices on each dimension, $t \triangleq t_1t_2\cdots t_n$, $t = \sum_{i=1}^{k}(bitxor(u_i, u_0))$.*

One metric of multicast algorithm is the total communication traffic. A multicast tree algorithm is better with fewer traffic (or with less nodes in the multicast tree). For a 1-to-k multicast, at least $k+1$ nodes are needed to form a multicast tree. For a multicast destination set only with two adjacent nodes u and v, the multicast trees with u and v on the same path which has the minimal additional traffic have less traffic than the one with u and v on different paths. Similarly, it is also true for the neighboring nodes u,v ($H(u, u_0) \gg H(u,v), H(v, u_0) \gg H(u,v)$). The nearness between nodes is called *locality*.

Definition 8 (Locality). *The locality is the extent of nearness between vertices inside destination set, which can be denoted as Loc(destinations).*

There is no locality between deferent destination subsets. And locality is no sense for only one node, so we suppose that there is no locality for a node to itself.

$$Loc(destinations) = \begin{bmatrix} \infty & H(u_1, u_2) & \cdots & H(u_1, u_k) \\ H(u_2, u_1) & \infty & \cdots & H(u_2, u_k) \\ \cdots & \cdots & \cdots & \cdots \\ H(u_k, u_1) & H(u_k, u_2) & \cdots & \infty \end{bmatrix}.$$

3.2 Clustering Model

Based on the idea of locality, the general clustering model can split the multicast destination set into clusters.

Definition 9 (Cluster). *Cluster is a set of destination nodes that are near each other. Given a graph $G = (V, E)$ and a multicast set $M \subseteq V$, a cluster is a subgraph c of G and C is the cluster set where $V(c) \subseteq M$ and $\forall c_i, c_j \in C (i \neq j), V(c_i) \cap V(c_j) = \emptyset$ and $\bigcup_{c_i \in C} V(c_i) = M$.*

Naturally, there are two metrics of a cluster c on hypercube, *weight* and *degree*. (1)*Weight*. Weight is defined by the number of nodes in the cluster. $W(c) = \|c\|$. (2)*Degree*. Degree is defined as the dimension of the expansion subcube (definition 10) of cluster c. $D(c) = k(H_k = Expan(c))$.

Definition 10 (Expansion subcube). *A expansion subcube of destination set M denoted as $Expan(M)$ is the minimal subcube containing M. $Expan(M) = \{H_k | k \leqslant i (\forall i, M \subseteq H_i)\}$.*

4 Model Analysis

Actually, considering each node or each tree as a cluster, both LEN's algorithm and Sheu's algorithm are special conditions of the general clustering model. The cluster degree for LEN's algorithm is zero. It means that LEN's algorithm doesn't use the locality between destination nodes. As mentioned above, the result from LEN's algorithm is far away from optimal. The cluster degree for Sheu's algorithm is less than the height of the tree which causes Sheu's algorithm to be little grain.

4.1 Clustering Algorithm for LEN's MT

In LEN's algorithm [7], when an intermediate node w receives the message and the destination set M, it has to check if it is a destination node itself. If so, it accepts the message locally and deletes itself from M. Then, it has to compute the relative address of all the destination nodes. For a destination u, the ith bit of u's relative address is 1 if u is different from w on dimension i. Hence, for each dimension $i(1 \leqslant i \leqslant n)$, LEN's algorithm counts how many destination nodes whose ith bit of the relative address is 1. After that, it always chooses a particular dimension j with the maximum count value. All destination nodes whose jth bit of the relative address is 1 are sent to the neighbor of w on jth dimension. Then, these nodes are deleted from destination set M. This procedure is repeated until the multicast set M becomes empty.

Treating each node as a cluster, we get a clustering algorithm (algorithm 1) for LEN's MT.

Algorithm 1. Clustering algorithm for LEN's MT on Q_n

Input : source node u_0, multicast set $M = \{u_1, u_2, \cdots, u_k\}$
Output: cluster set C

step 1: **for** $i \in [1, k]$ **do**
  | $c_i \leftarrow \{u_i\}$
  end
step 2: $C \leftarrow \{c_i | 1 \leqslant i \leqslant k\}$

LEN's MT algorithm votes for the paths to route the message depending on the global-info, without considering the locality between the destination nodes. It means that the locality of every two destination vertices is ∞.

$$Loc_{LEN}(destinations) = \begin{bmatrix} \boxed{\infty} & \infty & \cdots & \infty \\ \infty & \boxed{\infty} & \cdots & \infty \\ \cdots & \cdots & \cdots & \cdots \\ \infty & \infty & \cdots & \boxed{\infty} \end{bmatrix}. \quad (1)$$

Hence, the result from LEN's algorithm is far from optimal. Let us give an example. Consider Q_{10}, suppose the source node is 0000000000(0) and the multicast destination set $M = \{0000000001(1), 0000000011(3), 0000001000(8), 0000001111(15) 0000110000(48), 0001110000(112), 0011000000(192), 0011110000(240), 0011100000(224), 0111000000(448), 1100000000(768), 1110000000(896), 1111000000(960)\}$.

The result from LEN's algorithm is shown in figure 1, where the gray nodes are destination nodes and the nodes with dashed line are intermediate nodes. The total communication traffic is 18.

4.2 Clustering Algorithm for Sheu's MT

Sheu's algorithm [8] consists of two phases, the neighbors linking phase and the message routing phase. The neighbors linking phase is executed only on the source node. It links the destination nodes in the multicast set M which are adjacent. After this phase, the multicast set becomes a neighboring forest F in which each element is a root of tree. Taking tree as the unit, the routing

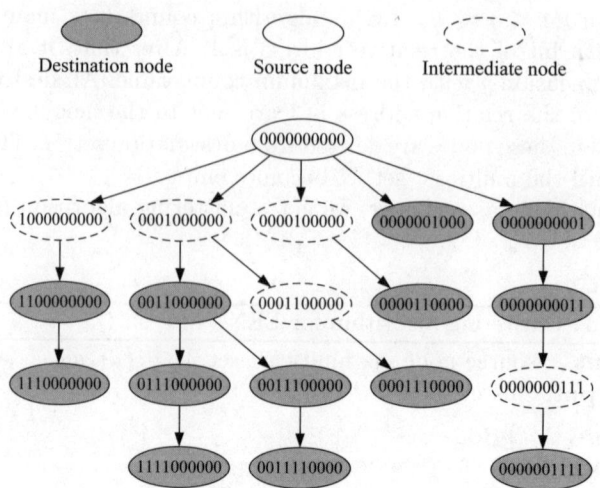

Fig. 1. The results from LEN's MT algorithm

phase votes for the paths to transfer the message which is similar to LEN's MT algorithm. The routing phase is executed on each intermediate nodes in the multicast tree. If a node is the root of a tree, the routing phase can transfer the message directly to it's children on the tree.

Treating each tree as a cluster, we get a clustering algorithm (algorithm 2) for Sheu's MT.

Algorithm 2. Clustering algorithm for Sheu's MT on Q_n

Input : source node u_0, multicast set $M = \{u_1, u_2, \cdots, u_k\}$
Output: cluster set C

step 1: $M_0 \leftarrow \{u_0\}, M_1 \leftarrow M_2 \leftarrow \cdots \leftarrow M_n \leftarrow \emptyset$
for $i \in [1, n]$ do
 | $M_i \leftarrow \{u_j | H(u_j, u_0) = i\}$
end

step 2: $\forall i \in [1, n]$; for $u \in M_i$ do
 if $\exists v \in M_{i-1}$ && $H(u, v) == 1$ then
  | $M_{i-1} \leftarrow M_{i-1} \cup \{u\}$
  | $M_i \leftarrow M_i - \{u\}$
 end
end

step 3: $C \leftarrow M_1 \cup M_2 \cup \cdots \cup M_n$

Sheu's algorithm votes for the paths depending on both the locality and the global-info of the destination nodes. However, Sheu's algorithm only use the locality that the distance of vertices is equal to 1.

Consider the previous example multicast destination set M on Q_{10}. After the neighbor linking phase, we get

$$Loc_{Sheu}(M) = \begin{bmatrix} \infty & 1 & \infty \\ 1 & \infty & 1 & & \infty & & \infty & & \infty & \infty & \infty \\ \infty & 1 & \infty \\ & & & \infty & 1 & 1 \\ & \infty & & 1 & \infty & \infty & \infty & & \infty & & \infty & \infty \\ & & & 1 & \infty & \infty \\ & & & & & & \infty & 1 & \infty \\ & \infty & & \infty & & 1 & \infty & 1 & \infty & \infty & \infty \\ & & & & & & \infty & 1 & \infty \\ & & & & & & & & \infty & 1 \\ & \infty & & \infty & & \infty & & 1 & \infty & \infty & \infty \\ & \infty & & \infty & & \infty & & \infty & & \boxed{\infty} & \infty \\ & \infty & & \infty & & \infty & & \infty & & \infty & \boxed{\infty} \end{bmatrix}. \quad (2)$$

The result from Sheu's algorithm is shown in figure 2. The total communication traffic is 18.

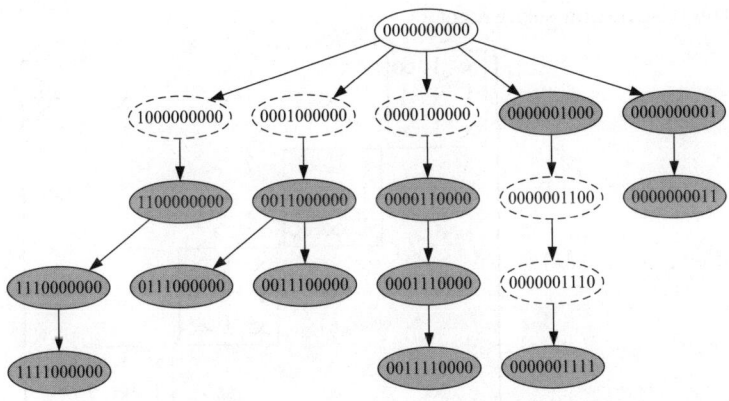

Fig. 2. The results from Sheu's MT algorithm

4.3 Our Clustering Algorithm

In our clustering algorithm (algorithm 3), we classify all the destination nodes with their distances to the source node and find out the trees which are composed of adjacent nodes in hypercube. If the expansion subcube of one tree contains the expansion subcube of other trees, we can combine these trees to form a cluster. So the output of our clustering algorithm is a cluster set.

Algorithm 3. Our Clustering algorithm on Q_n

Input : source node u_0, multicast set $M = \{u_1, u_2, \cdots, u_k\}$
Output: cluster set C

step 1: $M_0 \leftarrow \{u_0\}, M_1 \leftarrow M_2 \leftarrow \cdots \leftarrow M_n \leftarrow \emptyset$
for $i \in [1, n]$ do
$\quad | \quad M_i \leftarrow \{u_j | H(u_j, u_0) = i\}$
end

step 2: $\forall i \in [1, n]$; for $u \in M_i$ do
$\quad$ if $\exists v \in M_{i-1}$ && $H(u, v) == 1$ then
$\quad\quad | \quad M_{i-1} \leftarrow M_{i-1} \cup \{u\}$
$\quad\quad | \quad M_i \leftarrow M_i - \{u\}$
$\quad$ end
end

step 3: $C \leftarrow M_1 \cup M_2 \cup \cdots \cup M_n$
$\forall i, j \in [1, n]$; if $Expan(c_i) \subseteq Expan(c_j)$ then
$\quad | \quad c_j \leftarrow c_j \cup c_i$
$\quad | \quad c_i \leftarrow \emptyset$
end

Consider the previous example multicast destination set M on Q_{10}. By clustering the destination set, we get

$$Loc_{clustering}(M) = \begin{bmatrix} \begin{array}{|ccc|} \hline \infty & 1 & \infty \\ 1 & \infty & 1 \\ \infty & 1 & \infty \\ \hline \end{array} & \infty & \infty & \infty & \infty \\ \infty & \begin{array}{|ccc|} \hline \infty & 1 & 1 \\ 1 & \infty & \infty \\ 1 & \infty & \infty \\ \hline \end{array} & \infty & \infty & \infty \\ \infty & \infty & \begin{array}{|ccc|} \hline \infty & 1 & \infty \\ 1 & \infty & 1 \\ \infty & 1 & \infty \\ \hline \end{array} & \infty & \infty \\ \infty & \infty & \infty & \begin{array}{|ccc|} \hline \infty & 1 & 3 \\ 1 & \infty & 2 \\ 3 & 2 & \infty \\ \hline \end{array} & \infty \\ \infty & \infty & \infty & \infty & \boxed{\infty} \end{bmatrix}. \quad (3)$$

Compared with equation 1 and 2, equation 3 shows not only the locality between clusters, but also the locality inside clusters. On the diagonal line of the array in equation 3, each square denotes a $Loc(destinations)$ for a cluster. The square containing none-∞ numbers means that the distance of two destination vertices inside of a cluster containing more than one multicast destination vertex. A square containing only ∞ means that the corresponding cluster contains only one multicast destination vertex which is an isolated point on the graph of hypercube. The ∞ outside of squares shows the locality between the clusters. As mentioned before, no locality exists between the different clusters.

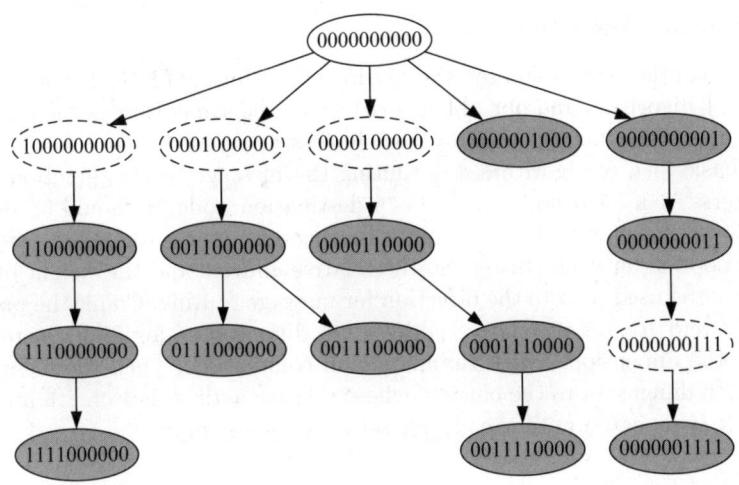

Fig. 3. The results from our clustering MT algorithm

The result from our algorithm is shown in figure 3. The total communication traffic is 17 which is better than LEN's MT and Sheu's MT algorithm.

Algorithm 4. Universal message routing algorithm for clusters

        Input   : Local node address w, cluster set C
        Output: None

step 1: **if** $\exists c \in C, w \in c$ **then**
    | send the message to local processor
    | delete w from c
    end

step 2: **foreach** $c_i \in C$ **do**
    | $u_i \leftarrow min(H(u_j, w)); (u_j \in c_i)$
    | $u_i \leftarrow$ bitxor(u_i, w)
    | $w_i \leftarrow \|c_i\|$
    end

step 3: **while** $C \neq \emptyset$ **do**
    | $t \leftarrow u_i * w_i; (t \triangleq t_1 t_2 \cdots t_n)$
    | $t_j \leftarrow \max_{1 \leq i \leq n}(t_i)$
    | $C' \leftarrow \{c_i | c_i \in C, u_i$ and w diff on dimension j $\}$
    | **if** $\exists c \in C, H(\{w\}, c) \geqslant H(c, C')$ **then**
    | | $C' \leftarrow C' \cup \{c\}$
    | | $C \leftarrow C - c$
    | **end**
    | Transmit C' and the message to node $(w \oplus 2^j)$
    | $C \leftarrow C - C'$
    end

4.4 Routing Algorithm

By clustering the destination set, the routing algorithms of LEN's MT algorithm, Sheu's MT algorithm and our MT algorithm are the same. Here is the universal routing algorithm (algorithm 4) for the clusters.

The basic idea of algorithm 4 is routing the message to the direction voted by clusters. At a local node w, if w is a destination node, it should be deleted from the multicast set. Then compute the nearest node with relative address to local node w for each cluster. So the relative address and the weight of each cluster can be used to vote the direction for message routing. Count the product of weight and ith bit of relative address On dimension i for each cluster and find out the dimension j with the maximum count value. Then the message is sent on jth dimension to the clusters whose relative address is 1 on jth bit. This procedure is repeated until the cluster set C becomes empty.

5 Performance Analysis

Consider the 1-to-k multicast on Q_n. The complexity comparison of LEN's MT, Sheu's MT and our MT algorithms is show in table 1.

Table 1. Complexities comparison

	LEN's MT	Sheu's MT	our MT
Clustering	$O(k)$	$O(n+k)$	$O(n+k)$
Routing	$O(nk)$	$O(nk)$	$O(nk)$
Total	$O(nk)$	$O(nk)$	$O(nk)$

Since the complexities of the three algorithms are approximately equal, then the multicast latency of the three algorithms are approximately equal too.

6 Conclusions

In this paper, we propose a general clustering mode for multicast on hypercube interconnection networks. This model is also suitable for the previous works. Based on the model we can construct more efficient algorithm by achieving a better balance between the global-info and locality.

References

1. Bhat, P., Raghavendra, C., Prasanna, V.: Efficient collective communication in distributed heterogeneous systems. In: Proceedings of the International Conference on Distributed Computing Systems (ICDCS) (1999)
2. Kielmann, T., Hofman, R.F.H., Bal, H.E., Plaat, A., Bhoedjang, R.A.F.: Magpie: Mpi's collective communication operations for clustered wide area systems. In: Proceedings of the 7th ACM SIGPLAN symposium on Principles and practice of parallel programming (1999)

3. Lin, X., Ni, L.M.: Multicast communication in multicomputer networks. IEEE Transactions on Parallel and Distributed Systems 4(10), 1105–1117 (1993)
4. Graham, R.L., Foulds, L.R.: Unlikelihood that minimal phylogenies for realistic biological study can be constructed in reasonable computational time. Math. Biosci. 60, 133–142 (1982)
5. Ahuja, R.K., Magnanti, T.L., Orlin, J.B.: Network Flows: Theory, Algorithms, and Applications. Prentice-Hall, Englewood Cliffs (1993)
6. Cormen, T.H., Leiserson, C.E., Rivest, R.L., Stein, C.: Introduction to Algorithms, 2nd edn. MIT Press, Cambridge (2001)
7. Lan, Y., Esfahanian, A.H., Ni, L.M.: Multicast in hypercube multiprocessors. Journal of Parallel and Distributed Computing 8(1), 30–41 (1990)
8. Sheu, S.H., Yang, C.B.: Multicast algorithms for hypercube multiprocessors. Journal of Parallel and Distributed Computing 61(1), 137–149 (2001)
9. Duato, J., Yalamanchili, S., Ni, L.M.: Interconnection Networks: An Engineering Approach. Morgan Kaufmann Publishers, San Francisco (2002)
10. Wu, J.: Distributed System Design. CRC Press, Boca Raton (1998)
11. Coulouris, G., Dollimore, J., Kindberg, T.: Distributed Systems: Concepts and Design, 4th edn. Addison-Wesley, Reading (2005)
12. Choi, Y., Esfahanian, A.H., Ni, L.M.: One-to-k communication in distributed-memory multiprocessors. In: Proceedings of 25th Annual Allerton Conference on Communication, Control, and Computing (1987)
13. Dally, W.J., Towles, B.P.: Principles and Practices of Interconnection Networks. Morgan Kaufmann Publishers, San Francisco (2003)
14. The BlueGene/L Team: An overview of the BlueGene/L supercomputer. In: ACM/IEEE conference on Supercomputing (2002)
15. Lu, S., Fan, B., Dou, Y., Yang, X.: Clustering Multicast on Hypercube Network. In: Gerndt, M., Kranzlmüller, D. (eds.) HPCC 2006. LNCS, vol. 4208, pp. 61–70. Springer, Heidelberg (2006)
16. Lan, Y., Li, L.M., Esfahanian, A.H.: Distributed multi-destination routing in hypercube multiprocessors. In: Proceedings of the third conference on Hypercube concurrent computers and applications, pp. 631–639. ACM Press, New York (1988)
17. Bondy, J.A., Murty, U.S.R.: Graph Theory With Applications. Elsevier Science Ltd., Amsterdam (1976)
18. Diestel, R.: Graph Theory, 2nd edn. Springer, Heidelberg (2000)
19. Saad, Y., Schultz, M.H.: Topological properties of hypercubes. IEEE Transactions on Computers 7, 867–872 (1988)
20. Andre, F., Verjus, J.P.: Hypercubes and Distributed computers. Horth-Halland (1989)
21. Leighton, F.T.: Introduction to Parallel Algorithms and Architectures: Arrays, Trees, Hypercubes. Morgan Kaufmann Publishers, San Francisco (1992)
22. Xu, J.: Topological Structure and Analysis of Interconnection Networks. Kluwer Academic Publishers, Dordrecht (2001)
23. Chen, J., Wang, G., Chen, S.: Locally subcube-connected hypercube networks: theoretical analysis and experimental results. IEEE Transactions on Computers 5, 530–540 (2002)

Performance Evaluation of End-to-End Path Capacity Measurement Tools in a Controlled Environment[*]

Wenwei Li[1], Bin Zeng[2], Dafang Zhang[1], and Jinmin Yang[1]

[1] School of Software, Hunan University, Changsha 410082, China
liww@hnu.cn
[2] College of Computer and Communication, Hunan University, Changsha 410082, China
{zenbing,dfzhang,rj_jmyang}@hnu.cn

Abstract. In this paper we present results of a series of end-to-end path capacity measurement experiments conducted on a fully controllable IP network built in the lab. We test and evaluate several typical path capacity measurement tools: pathchar, clink, and pathrate. The cross traffic is generated in a reproducible manner, and has similar spatial and temporal characteristics of real Internet traffics. We evaluate the measurement error and other operational characteristics of the tools and analyze factors impacting their performance. Such work is useful for tools selection and further improvement of capacity measurement tools.

1 Introduction

Active bandwidth measurement tools can not only provide network operators with useful information on network characteristics and performance, but also can enable end users (and user applications) to perform independent network auditing, load balancing, and server selection tasks, among many others, without requiring access to network elements or administrative resources. Estimating the capacity of an Internet path is a fundamental problem in bandwidth measurement that has received considerable attention in the last few years. Knowledge of the capacity of a path can be put to good use in various scenarios. Using such information, multimedia servers can determine appropriate streaming rates while ISPs can keep track of the characteristics of their own links. Further, recent research in overlay networks and application layer multicast can also benefit from such capacity information in better structuring their overlays and trees.

Guaranteeing accuracy of the measurement is a basic requirement for a practical end-to-end path capacity measurement tool. Furthermore, to decrease the impact of measurement on the network, and get meaningful results, it still requires the tool to keep minor probe costs and have minor probe time. Finally, for the complexity of networks, it also needs the tools can achieve consistent results under different network environments and different cross traffic conditions.

---

[*] This work was financial supported by National Natural Science Foundation of China under grants 60703097 and 60673155.

Starting with fulfilling all or partially of these requirements, a lot of path capacity measurement techniques and methods have been developed and evaluated primary in the community. For example, Lai and Baker [1] proposed nettimer, and compare it with pathchar [8], clink [9], and pchar [11], under a short network path and a long path, to evaluate the probe costs and measurement accuracy of these tools. However, under different cross traffic conditions, the performance characteristics of measurement tools are not the same, previous works have not took the variation of cross traffic into account. There is a lack of comprehensive experiments and evaluations of tools performance under a full controllable, repeatable network environment. Such work is important for users and network managers to select appropriate measurement tools, and to reasonable assess measurement results. Some researchers measured and analyzed bandwidth distribution characteristics of the Internet [5, 6]. Without knowledges on measurement tools, the results of these researches are not compellent.

In this paper, we focus on evaluating the performance of several typical capacity measurement tools via experiments on a controllable network. After defining a metrics set for evaluating the performance of tools according to the measurement requirements, we build a testbed IP network and inject packets into it to simulate real network traffic conditions. The selected tools are experimented and evaluated on the IP network. In experiments, we find that all the selected tools are inaccurate, and have large probe costs and long probe time, if the cross traffic is large. This finding reveals the limitations of these tools, i.e. they cannot be applied in a heavy loaded network. And it also gives the direction for further improvement of these tools.

The remainder of this paper is organized as follows. In section 2, we review the capacity measurement methods and discuss the selection of tools for experiment. In section 3, the metrics set for evaluating tools performance is defined. Section 4 describes the IP network built by ourselves, and the method to generate cross traffic. Section 5 discusses the experiment results and analyzes the causes. Finally, we conclude this paper in section 6.

2 Tools Selection

2.1 Capacity Definition

In general, an end-to-end path from the sender to the receiver consists of some packet transmitting links. For a specific end-to-end path, the path capacity is defined as the maximum IP-layer throughput that the path can provide to a flow, when there is no competing traffic load (cross traffic). The link with the minimum transmission rate determines the capacity of the path; usually, such a link is termed as narrow link. Formally, if H is the number of hops in a path, C_i is the transmission rate or capacity of link, then the path's capacity C is:

$$C = \min_{i=1...H} C_i \tag{1}$$

There is a hidden assumption in the definition described above, i.e. the path is fixed and exclusive. It means that, when measuring path capacity, the path must have no route change or route flap. However, there is a great diversity in Internet route dynamic characteristics [7]. Consequently, to avoid influence of route dynamics, the capacity measurement process must complete as soon as possible.

2.2 Measurement Techniques Review

There are mainly two kinds of techniques to measurement path capacity: variable packet size (VPS) method and packet pair/train dispersion (PPTD) method. They are based on different packet delay models. The VPS method is based on single packet delay model; it can measure the capacity of each hop along a path. The typical tools that deploy VPS technique include pathchar, clink, pchar, etc. The key element of VPS technique is to measure the minimum RTT from the source to each hop of the path as a function of the probing packet size. Specifically, the minimum RTT $T_i(L)$ for a given packet size L up to hop i is expected to be

$$T_i(L) = \alpha + \sum_{k=1}^{i} \frac{L}{C_k} = \alpha + \beta_i L \tag{2}$$

Where C_k is the capacity of the kth hop, α is the packet delays up to hop i that do not depend on the probing packet size L, and β_i is the slope of minimum RTT up to hop i against probing packet size L, given by

$$\beta_i = \sum_{k=1}^{i} \frac{1}{C_k} \tag{3}$$

Repeating the minimum RTT measurement for each hop $i = 1, ..., H$, and by linear interpolation, the capacity estimate at each hop i along the forward path is

$$C_i = \frac{1}{\beta_i - \beta_{i-1}} \tag{4}$$

The PPTD method is based on packet pair delay model, it can only measure path capacity. The typical tools that deploy PPTD technique include bprobe [6], nettimer [1,10], pathrate [3,4], etc.

When measuring path capacity, the source sends multiple packet pairs to the receiver. Each packet pair consists of two packets of the same size sent back to back. The dispersion of a packet pair at a specific link of the path is the time distance between the last bit of each packet. In general, if the dispersion prior to a link of capacity C_i is Δ_{in}, the dispersion after the link will be

$$\Delta_{out} = \max\{\Delta_{in}, \frac{L}{C_i}\} \tag{5}$$

Where C_i is the capacity of link i, L is the size of probing packet. After a packet pair goes through each link along an otherwise empty path, the dispersion Δ_R the receiver will measure is

$$\Delta_R = \max_{i=1,...,H}\{\frac{L}{C_i}\} = \frac{L}{\min_{i=1,...,H}(C_i)} = \frac{L}{C} \tag{6}$$

Where C is the end-to-end capacity of the path. Thus, the receiver can estimate the path capacity from $C = L/\Delta_R$.

2.3 Tools Selection

When selecting typical tools for evaluation, we found that, pchar cannot be built on our PC, as they cannot be built on newer Linux systems. In addition, bprobe works only on SGI Irix. Finally, Lai and Baker have concluded that nettimer has the same measurement accuracy as pathchar and clink have. Thus we choose three tools in our evaluation experiments; they are pathchar, clink and pathrate. Such a selection also covers the two measurement techniques aforementioned, VPS and PPTD.

3 Evaluation Metrics Set Definition

To evaluate the tools and techniques objectively and comprehensively, several evaluation metrics have been defined. These metrics are used to analyze and evaluate the results get from the experiments discussed in the next section, to find out the performance characteristics of different tools, and analyze the causes.

Measurement Error: If the capacity of a specific path is C, and one certain tool measured it as C_m, then the measurement error of such tool is:

$$e_m = \left|(C^m - C)/C\right| \times 100\% \qquad (7)$$

Smaller the measurement error is, more accurate the tool be. As the delay models that tools depend on are affected by cross traffic condition, it is obviously that, under different cross traffic loads, the measurement error of a certain tool is also different. But under the same cross traffic load, the measurement errors of different tools reflect their capability to estimate capacity accurately.

Measurement consistency: For a specific path, if someone measures the path capacity n times using a certain tool, and get measured results $C_1, C_2, ..., C_n$, the average of them is $\overline{C}$, then measurement consistency is:

$$S_m = \left[1 - \sum_{i=1}^{n}\left|C^i - \overline{C}\right| / (n \times \overline{C})\right] \times 100\% \qquad (8)$$

Bigger S_m means repeated measurements of a certain tool have basically the same result, indicates that the measurement of such tool is repeatable, although it may be inaccurate. A capacity measurement tool is faith worthy, only when it has both little measurement error and large measurement consistency.

Measurement probing cost: the probing cost is defined as the byte number of all the packets sent by a certain tool for running a capacity measurement.

A tool has small measurement probing cost, means that it has high efficiency and it can get a measurement with less costs. Furthermore, if the probing cost is small, then the tool has less effect on the network, and then it is adaptive to be deployed large-scale in the network.

Measurement duration: The time cost a certain tool needed to complete a capacity measurement.

In general, users and managers expect the measurement can be completed quickly. Short measurement duration means tools can give a measurement of capacity in real time.

4 Experiments Design

4.1 Testbed Network

To evaluate the performance of all tools in a controllable environment, a testbed IP network is built; the topology of it is shown in Fig. 1. The network consists of four routers from two vendors: Quidway and Cisco. To investigate whether the 2-layer store and forward devices such as switches have effect on measurement, the two centered Cisco routers are connected with a switch. All the end hosts are also connected to the network with switches. In Fig. 1, there are seven forward nodes from source to sink, but the end-to-end path has only four hops. The rate of all links is 100 Mbps, i.e. the path capacity is 100 Mbps. Many tools assume that there is only one narrow link in the network. As limited by hardware conditions, the testbed network has multiple narrow links. However, such network may be more realistic. Capacity measurement tools run on two designated end hosts: source and sink, each equipped with a 1.7 GHz Pentium IV processor, 256 MB memory, and a 3COM 100 Mbps NIC card, the operating system is RedHat Linux 7.2.

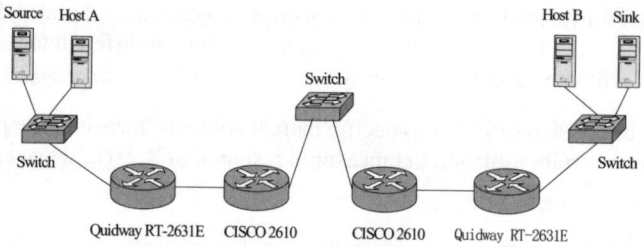

Fig. 1. Topology of the testbed IP network

4.2 Methods of Generating Cross Traffic

Host A and host B in Fig. 1 are used to generate and receive cross traffic. The algorithms used by capacity estimating tools make some assumptions about characteristics of the underlying cross-traffic. When these assumptions do not apply, tools cannot perform correctly. Therefore, test traffic must be as realistic as possible with respect to its packet inter arrival time (IAT) and size distributions. Furthermore, as many experiments must be run at every cross traffic condition, it also need the generated cross traffic is reproducible.

One way to generate cross traffic is to capture real network traffic trace and replay it in the testbed network [15, 16]. This method of cross-traffic generation reproduces actual IAT and packet size distributions but is not congestion-aware. Some other tools such as TG [20], Surge [19] can generate traffic according to the traffic parameters designated by users. However, these tools can only generate period or Poisson traffic, they do not agree with the self-similar characteristic of real network [17, 18].

Some researches discussed the problem of generating self-similar traffic [12, 13, 14]. In experiments, we choose the Harpoon tool developed by Sommers etc. to generate cross traffic. Harpoon is a self-configure cross traffic generation tool; it uses a set of distributional parameters that can be automatically extracted from Netflow [21] traces to generate flows that exhibit the same statistical qualities present in measured Internet traces, including temporal and spatial characteristics. Consequently, it is an idea cross traffic tool for our evaluation experiments.

4.3 Date Collection

The Harpoon tool operated on two additional end hosts, host A and B, and injected the cross-traffic into the main end-to-end path of the testbed network via switches. In our experiments we varied cross traffic load level from 0 to 90 Mb/s in 10 Mbps steps, which corresponds to 0-90% of the narrow link capacity. We tested one tool at a time. To avoid any edge effects, we delayed starting the tool for three minutes after initiating cross-traffic. At each load level, every selected tools runs twenty times and their measured results are recorded for analyzing and evaluating.

Table 1. Measured capacity of different tools (Mbps)

tools	Cross traffic load level									
	0%	10%	20%	30%	40%	50%	60%	70%	80%	90%
pathchar	47.8	45.3	43.5	41.7	38.4	32.8	31.7	30.4	31.2	29.8
clink	48.2	46.7	44.1	43.5	41.2	35.4	33.6	32.5	32.1	31.7
pathrate	99.5	98.8	98.4	97.7	94.3	90.6	88.5	87.3	88.3	85.4

5 Tool Evaluation Results

5.1 Comparison of Tool Measurement Error

Table 1 lists the average of measured capacity of tools. Results of tools which is based on VPS technique such as pathchar and clink are about half of the nominal path capacity 100 Mbps. The cause is that, 2-layer store and forward devices in the path break down the delay model of VPS technique [22]. To evaluation the measurement error of pathchar and clink in measuring capacity of links that have no 2-layer store and forward devices, table 2 lists the 2nd link capacity measured by pathchar and clink. The measurement accuracy is improved at large compared with table 1.

Table 2. The 2nd link capacity measured by pathchar and clink (Mbps)

tools	Cross traffic load level									
	0%	10%	20%	30%	40%	50%	60%	70%	80%	90%
pathchar	95.8	92.3	90.2	89.6	83.6	80.7	77.4	78.6	76.1	74.5
clink	97.2	93.4	91.6	89.3	85.4	81.5	76.3	75.7	73.8	72.1

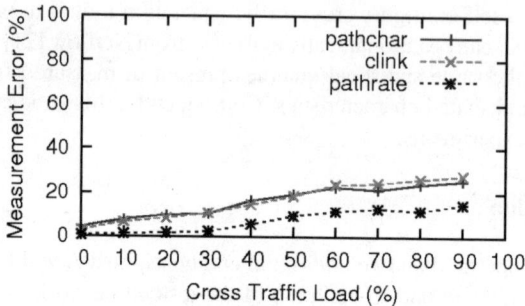

Fig. 2. The measurement errors of different tools

The measurement errors of tools under different cross traffic load levels are shown in Fig. 2. The measurement errors of pathchar and clink are calculated using table 2. When the cross traffic load level reaches 20%, the measurement error of pathchar and clink is about 10%. However, when the cross traffic load is higher, for example, 50%, which are not uncommon in the Internet [2], the measurement error of them is higher than 20%, which is not acceptable for a meaningful measurement. Obviously, the accuracy of VPS-based tools depends on cross traffic level largely. There are two causes for this. Firstly, VPS technique calculates link capacity by per-hop regression analyzing, which induces large accumulated errors, and such errors increase with the rise of cross traffic. Secondly, the user level timestamping method of pathchar and clink takes the time spent by system kernel to process packets as a part of packet delay, which also induces errors.

Relatively, pathrate is more accurate than pathchar and clink. When the cross traffic load level is lower than 30%, the measurement error of pathrate is less than 5%; even as cross traffic load level reaches 50%, pathrate still has an measurement error which is about 10%. It shows that, compared with VPS technique, PPTD technique is more adaptive to cross traffic variation. Moreover, the complex data filtering method and kernel level timstamping also give some contributions to the accuracy of pathrate [24]. However, in the circumstance of large cross traffic load level, for example, 90%, the measurement error of pathrate is also non-negligible, it reaches 15%. Finally, it can be seen from Fig. 2, although pathrate has relatively higher accuracy, but as rising of cross traffic load, the measurement error of all selected tools is increased, and these tools become unacceptable for meaningful capacity measurements. Any improvements of current tools must take this problem into account.

Another possible cause for the difference of measurement errors lies in tools implementation, especially the protocols adopted. Although stated in [23] that, for a same basic measuring algorithm, measurement tools implemented with different network protocols (ICMP or TCP) may lead to different measurement results, however, the difference is minor, and has less effect on our experiments.

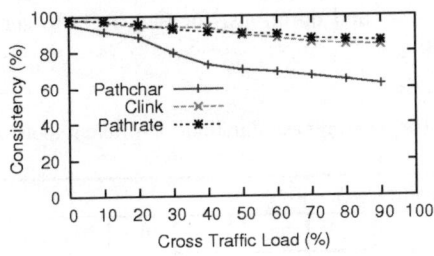

Fig. 3. The measurement consistency of different tools

5.2 Comparison of Tools Measurement Consistency

The measurement consistency of different tools is shown in Fig. 3. Pathchar is poor in measurement consistency, even at low cross traffic load levels, for exmaple, 30%. This means that, when measuring path capacity repeatedly with pathchar, it's hard to get consistent results even though the measurements are running at not very large intervals. However, the consistency of both clink and pathrate are improved significantly, for they adopt some adaptive samples collecting and filtering mechanisms to make the measurement process to be convergence. The measurements of clink and pathrate may be more reliable than that of pathchar, but as it can be seen from Fig. 3, the consistency of all tools are decreased when the cross traffic load rising. Consequently, furthere convergence mechanisms have to be proposed to improve the consistency of capacity measurement.

Table 3. The measurement probing costs of different tools

tools	Cross traffic load level									
	0%	10%	20%	30%	40%	50%	60%	70%	80%	90%
Pathchar(KB)	500.5	500.5	500.5	500.5	500.5	500.5	500.5	500.5	500.5	500.5
Clink(KB)	266	266	266	266	266	266	266	266	266	266
Pathrate(MB)	1.9	2.2	3.7	4.5	5.8	7.3	8.6	10.1	12.6	14.1

5.3 Measurement Probing Cost and Duration

The measurement probing costs and durations of different tools are listed in table 3 and table 4. The probing costs and durations of pathchar and clink are determined by running parameters, we choose their costs and durations from experiments running at 50% cross traffic load level to evaluation. So, in table 3 and 4, the probing costs and durations of pathchar and clink under different cross traffic load levels are the same. The probing costs of pathrate are large than that of pathchar and clink with one magnitude, the measurement duration of it is also longer than that of pathchar and clink. The cause is that, pathrate deployed a packet train based mechanism, which will send a large amount of packets into the path, to filter out errors and keep the measurement process convergent. Although pathrate is accurate relatively, it will induce large overheads to the network. Finally, pathchar and clink also have comparatively high measurement probing costs and durations, for they have to send probing packets to every hop along the path.

Table 4. The measurement durations of different tools(min:sec)

tools	Cross traffic load level									
	0%	10%	20%	30%	40%	50%	60%	70%	80%	90%
pathchar	3:43	3:26	3:45	3:52	3:36	3:41	3:29	3:42	3:47	3:38
clink	4:23	4:10	4:02	4:34	4:08	4:12	4:21	4:05	4:14	4:27
pathrate	2:58	3:10	3:48	3:57	4:13	4:37	5:01	5:49	7:04	8:10

6 Conclusions

Our work is the first comprehensive evaluation of typical tools for path capacity measurement on controllable and repeatable networks. We defined several metrics for evaluating tools performance. The testbed network is built by us in the lab. We found that pathrate is the most accurate tools under conditions of small cross traffic load level (less than 30%). Oppositely, pathchar and clink are inaccurate even the cross traffic load is not very high, for the defect of delay model their based. By adopting mechanisms of convergence, clink and pathrate improved their measurement consistency. However, pathrate induced large probing costs and long durations for measurement, as it has to send so many packets to filter out errors and keep the measurement process convergent. In the end, pathchar and clink also have comparatively high measurement probing costs and durations which may be improper for wide deployment in the Internet.

We demonstrated how our testbed can be used to evaluate and compare end-to-end path capacity measurement tools against reproducible cross-traffic in a fully controlled environment. We plan to use what we have learned from our experiments to further improve the path capacity measurement tools.

References

1. Lai, K., Baker, M.: Measuring Link Bandwidths Using a Deterministic Model of Packet Delay. In: Proceedings of SIGCOMM 2000 (2000)
2. Thompson, K., Miller, G.J., Wilder, R.: Wide-area Internet Traffic Patterns and Characteristics. IEEE Network 6(6), 10–23 (1997)

3. Dovrolis, C., Ramanathan, P., Moore, D.: What do packet dispersion techniques measure? In: Proceedings of IEEE INFOCOM 2001 (2001)
4. Dovrolis, C., Ramanathan, P., Moore, D.: Packet-Dispersion Techniques and a Capacity measurement Methodology. IEEE/ACM Transaction on Network 12(6), 963–977 (2004)
5. Lee, S., Sharma, P., Banerjee, S.: Measuring Bandwidth between PlanetLab Nodes. In: Proceedings of Passive & Active Measurement Workshop (2005)
6. Carter, R., Crovella, M.: Measuring Bottleneck Link Speed in Packet-Switched Networks. Performance Evaluation 27(8), 297–318 (1996)
7. Paxson, V.: End-to-End Routing Behavior in the Internet. IEEE/ACM Transactions on Networking 5(5), 601–615 (1997)
8. Jacobson, V.: Pathchar: A Tool to Infer Characteristics of Internet Paths. available at ftp://ftp.ee.lbl.gov/pathchar/
9. Downey, A.B.: Using Pathchar to Estimate Internet Link Characteristics. In: Proceedings of SIGCOMM 1999 (1999)
10. Lai, K., Baker, M.: Measuring Bandwidth. In: Proceedings of IEEE INFOCOM 1999 (1999)
11. Mah Bruce, A.: pchar: A Tool for Measuring Internet Path Characteristic, available at: http://www.kitchenlab.org/www/bmah/Software/pchar/
12. Sommers, J., Kim, H., Barford, P.: Harpoon: A Flow-level Traffic Generator for Router and Network Tests. In: Proceedings of SIGMETRICS 2004 (2004)
13. Sommers, J., Barford, P.: Self-configuring Network Traffic Generation. In: Proceedings of IMC 2004 (2004)
14. Kamath, P., Lan, K., Heidemann, J.: Generation of High Bandwidth Network Traffic Traces. In: Proceedings of IEEE MASCOTS 2002 (2002)
15. Cheng, Y., Cardwell, N., Savage, S.: Monkey see, monkey do: A Tool for TCP Tracing and Replaying. In: Proceedings of the USENIX 2004 (2004)
16. A. Turner. tcpreplay. available at: http://tcpreplay.sourceforge.net/
17. Leland, W., Taqqu, M., Willinger, W., Wilson, D.: On the Self-similar Nature of Ethernet Traffic. IEEE/ACM Transactions on Networking 2(1), 1–15 (1994)
18. Paxson, V., Floyd, S.: Wide-area traffic: The Failure of Poisson Modeling. IEEE/ACM Transactions on Networking 3(3), 226–244 (1995)
19. Barford, P.: Modeling, Measurement and Performance of World Wide Web Transactions. PhD thesis (December 2000)
20. McKenney, P.E., Lee, D.Y., Denny, B.A.: Traffic Generator Software Release Notes. SRI International and USC/ISI Postel Center for Experimental Networking (January 2002)
21. CISCO IOS NetFlow, http://www.cisco.com/warp/public/732/Tech/netflow/
22. Prasad, R.S., Dovrolis, C., Mah, B.A.: The Effect of Layer-2 Store-and-Forward Devices on Per-Hop Capacity Measurement. In: Proceedings of IEEE INFOCOM 2003 (2003)
23. Li, W.-w., Zhang, D.-f., Yang, J.-m., Xie, G.-g.: On Evaluating the Differences of TCP and ICMP in Network Measurement. Computer Communications 30(2), 428–439 (2007)
24. Li, W.-w., Tang, J.-l., Zhang, D.-f., Xie, G.-g.: Improved Sample filtering Method for Measuring End-to-End Path Capacity. Journal of Central South University of Technology 14(3), 399–403 (2007)

Protein Sequence Motif Discovery on Distributed Supercomputer

Santan Challa and Parimala Thulasiraman*

Department of Computer Science,
University of Manitoba,
Winnipeg, MB, Canada R3T 2N2
{santan,thulasir}@cs.umanitoba.ca

Abstract. The motif discovery problem has gained lot of significance in biological science over the past decade. Recently, various approaches have been used successfully to discover motifs. Some of them are based on probabilistic approach and others on combinatorial approach. We follow a graph-based approach to solve this problem, in particular, using the idea of de Bruijn graphs. The de Bruijn graph has been successfully adopted in the past to solve problems such as local multiple alignment and DNA fragment assembly. The proposed algorithm harnesses the power of the de Bruijn graph to discover the conserved regions such as motifs in a protein sequence. The sequential algorithm has 70% matches of the motifs with the MEME and 65% pattern matches with the Gibbs motif sampler. The motif discovery problem is data intensive requiring substantial computational resources and cannot be solved on a single system. In this paper, we use the distributed supercomputers available on the Western Canada Research Grid (WestGrid) to implement the distributed graph based approach to the motif discovery problem and study its performance analysis. We use the available resources efficiently to distribute data among the multicore nodes in the machine and redesign the algorithm to suit the architecture. We show that a pure distributed implementation is not efficient for this problem. We develop a hybrid algorithm that uses fine grain parallelism within the nodes and coarse grain parallelism across the nodes. Experiments show that this hybrid algorithm runs 3 times faster than the pure distributed memory implementation.

1 Introduction

Motif is a repeating pattern in a biological sequence that is conserved during the process of evolution. Motif is a very important problem in Biology. It finds applications in DNA or protein sequence analysis, comprehending disease susceptibility and disease cure. Numerous motif discovery algorithms have been

---

* Author for Correspondence:thulasir@cs.umanitoba.ca. The authors acknowledge partial financial support from the Natural Sciences and Engineering Research Council (NSERC) Canada. Our sincere thanks to the management of WestGrid for allowing us to work on their systems.

proposed till date. Motif finding algorithms can be divided into probabilistic and combinatorial approaches. Gibbs sampling [1] and Expected Maximization (EM) [2] are the two statistical computing algorithms that use the probabilistic models. Software packages such as Gibbs motif sampler [3], AlignACE [4], PhyloGibbs [5] and BioProspector [6] use Gibbs sampling strategy to find the transcription factor binding sites. MEME [7] is a popular motif searching software that uses the EM algorithm. The underlying procedure for algorithms such as TEIRESIAS [8], the Random Projections [9], SP-STAR [10], MULTIPROFILER [11], and WINNOWER [10] are combinatorial approaches. The more common WINNOWER algorithm divides each sequence into subsequences. It builds a multipartite graph using the subsequences. Two "similar" subsequences in different sequences have an edge. The motif finding problem is reduced to finding cliques in the graph. The cliques represent motifs. Therefore, motif discovery is clique discovery in the multipartite graph.

Graph theory is playing an important role in computational biology [12]. Graph-based algorithms provide a simpler and quicker solution to computationally intensive problems such as DNA fragment assembly [7] and motif discovery. However, the amount of literature available on motif discovery using graph algorithms is not proportional to the potential of the graph-based algorithms.

Motif is like an encrypted message in a large array of characters. Motif searching would have been easier if all the motif patterns were exactly the same. However, all motifs are not exact replicas of each other. They differ by at least two positions. The motifs patterns change because they undergo mutations.

Motif discovery/finding is computationally intensive. In the literature, very few attempts have been made in designing parallel or distributed algorithms for this problem. We have developed a motif discovery algorithm based on de Bruijn graph and implemented this algorithm on a distributed supercomputer. The algorithm has two phases: graph construction and graph traversal. In the graph construction phase, as the name implies, a de Bruijn graph is constructed. The graph traversal phase, identifies the motifs. Both these phases are parallelized. Besides an efficient parallel algorithm, the architecture on which the algorithm is parallelized is crucial to the performance of the algorithm. The graph construction phase requires shared address space while the graph traversal phase requires distributed access space. Therefore, we have parallelized the algorithm on a hybrid architecture which harnesses the power of the shared and distributed access space. We exploit fine grain parallelism within the nodes and coarse grain parallelism across nodes of the machine.

We have found that our parallel algorithm is successful in mining signals for larger number of sequences and at a faster rate when compared to some popular motif searching tools such as MEME [14]. We have tested the accuracy of our sequential algorithm [15] to MEME. The paper is organized as follows. The next section briefly explains the construction of de Bruijn graph. Section 3 discusses the current literature on parallelization of motif discovery problem. Section 4 describes the graph based parallel algorithm. Experimental results are provided in section 5. Section 6 concludes the paper.

2 Construction of a *de Bruijn* Graph

A de Bruijn graph is a graph whose vertices are subsequences of a given sequence and whose edges indicate the overlapping subsequences. Consider the following sequence ACCGTCT. The sequence can be resolved into the following fragments of length 4: ACCG, CCGT, CGTC, and GTCT. Each fragment is called an l-tuple. An $l-1$ tuple is obtained by further fragmenting each l-tuple. For example, ACC and CCG are $l-1$ tuples of ACCG. The $l-1$ tuples form the nodes of the de Bruijn graph. An edge exits between any two $l-1$ tuples and the edges represent the l-tuples. Figure 1 illustrates the 3-tuple de Bruijn graph construction for the sequence ACCGTCT. The multiplicity of each edge is represented by an edge with a weight. Initially every edge gets a weight 1. In case two consecutive vertices (vertices with the specified overlap) repeat, then the edge multiplicity is increased (in this case an increment in weight of the edge by 1). Similar to the strategy employed by Pevzner et al. [7], we glue the repeating edges, thereby increasing the multiplicity of one single edge as shown in Figure 2. The conserved regions are most likely to reside on the most repeated edges, i.e., edges with greater multiplicity (which have greater weight attached to them).

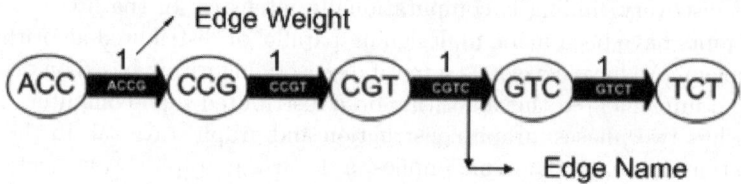

Fig. 1. Construction of a de Brujn Graph

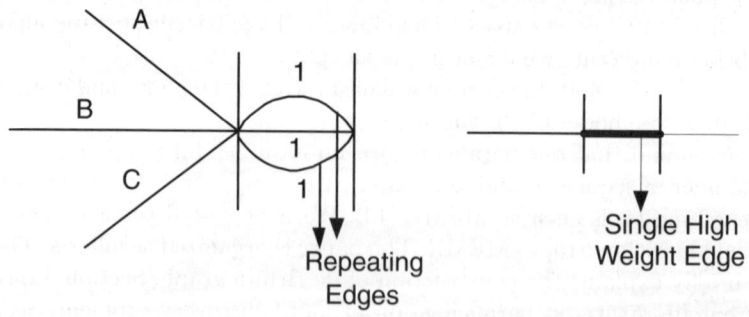

Fig. 2. Gluing of Repeating Edges

3 Related Work on Parallelization of Motif Discovery Problem

In this section, we describe the literature and previous research efforts that adopt parallel computing techniques for the motif finding problem. Software tools have been developed that apply parallelization to graph-based approach.

ParaMEME is a parallel program for the MEME software. As we have mentioned earlier, MEME is based on a probabilistic approach that uses the Expected Maximization (EM) algorithm. MEME was ported over to the 400-node Intel Paragon XP/S platform using a parallel programming language called MP++. The ParaMEME is scalable for up to 64 processors. Every job submitted by the user is assigned to 8 nodes of the cluster. Grundy et al. [16] state that ParaMEME shows an efficiency of over 70% even for large sequence datasets.

Sutou et al. [17] proposed a parallelization of a motif discovery method called the Modified PrefixSpan method. PrefixSpan is a data mining technique used to extract frequent patterns from a database. Modified PrefixSpan is a variation of the original method designed for faster pattern extraction. To reduce the computational time taken, the Modified PrefixSpan method is parallelized on 8 processors. Sutou et al. state that the parallel version of the Modified PrefixSpan is 6 times faster in comparison to the serial version.

Baldwin et al. [18], developed a motif discovery tool called *Motif Discovery Toolkit*. The toolkit uses graph algorithm to predict the gene regulation sites. Owing to the speed and efficiency of the graph algorithms when compared to other motif finding algorithms, the developers of the toolkit choose to make extensive use of techniques applied in state-of-the art graph algorithms. To discover the binding sites (motifs) in a larger sample of data (the complete genomic sequence, not just fixed length sequences), the toolkit implements the graph algorithm on a cluster of homogeneous nodes.

Qin et al. developed a parallel motif searching tool based on a serial motif finding tool called *ParSeq* [19]. ParSeq is not a graph-based motif finding algorithm. It uses an approximate search algorithm that returns the best character strings based on a query. The search is parallelized on client-server based architecture. The parallel version of ParSeq is tested on a homogeneous network of 32 processors.

Our work involves parallelization of a graph algorithm. We use protein sequences with variable length as test data. Both WINNOWER algorithm and the motif discovery toolkit developed by Baldwin et al. [18] do not consider a weighted graph. Also, they consider a clique or a vertex cover to represent motifs. We used a directed weighted de Bruijn graph instead, and in our algorithm, the edges represent potential motifs, not the complex interconnected structures.

4 Parallel Graph Based Algorithm

The algorithm works in two stages. In the first stage the de Bruijn graph is constructed. The second stage is the graph traversal stage. We use fine grain parallelism within the node in the graph construction phase and coarse grain parallelism in the graph traversal phase. We make efficient use of the shared and distributed address space provided on the grid.

4.1 Graph Construction

A de Bruijn graph is a graph whose vertices are subsequences of a given sequence and whose edges indicate the overlapping subsequences. Initially, a protein sequence is broken into a set of l-tuples. Each l-tuple is again broken into a $l-1$ tuple. An edge joins two overlapping $l-1$ tuples. The multiplicity of the corresponding directed edge increases when successive $l-1$ tuples within the same sequence or in a different sequence repeat. This corresponds to an edge gaining a higher weight. The advantage with such an arrangement as stated by Pevzner et al. [7] is that it is quite easy to identify different regions of similarity among a set of sequences. These high weight edges form potential sites for conserved regions. Note that all the sequences are not part of one graph but made of many subgraphs. Every sequence has it own sub-graph. However, whenever there are similar regions in two different sequences, the sub-graphs overlap. Thus, the de Bruijn graph is a set of overlapping sub-graphs as shown in Figure 3. Every line in Figure 3 represents a separate sequence.

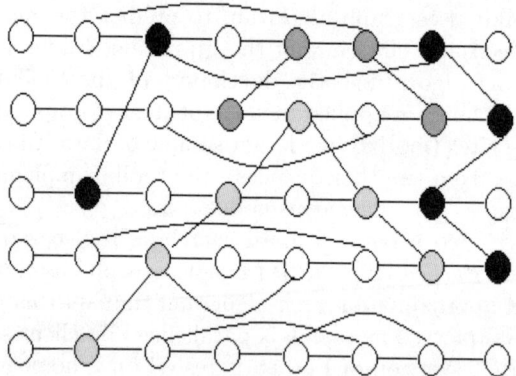

Fig. 3. Sub-graph Overlap in Sequences

Parallelization of Graph Construction: Every node in a cluster constructs its own graph. The data is distributed among the independent nodes. Within the nodes, data is shared. The adjacency list used to store the graph node information is used as a shared data structure. The construction is parallelized using multiple threads. Each thread updates the shared data structure individually. In such an arrangement, the time taken to construct the whole adjacency list is equally shared among the threads, thereby exhibiting fine grain parallelism. Once the adjacency list is constructed, the graph traversal is performed.

4.2 Graph Traversal

The next stage is graph traversal. A hash table contains all the nodes as its keys. The nodes are arranhed in an adjacency list. The set of graphs obtained from the graph construction procedure followed above are highly cyclic connected graph. The aim is to identify the dense regions of the graph where the edges have a high edge weight. Since there is no single path that covers all the nodes or edges, the best way is to individually traverse each sub-graph. For every sequence the first node that has an indegree zero, becomes the starting point of the traversal. Hence, we maintain a queue of nodes that have an indegree zero. We use a recursive Depth First Search (DFS) for performing the traversal. In order to avoid falling into an infinite loop when cycles are encountered, the algorithm visits each node exactly once. The corresponding nodes connected to a given node and the weights of the edges connecting the nodes are extracted from the hash table. After obtaining the high weight edges, the algorithm first tries to locate the entire repeated region called as the "active region". An active region is high weight region where a lot of sequences coincide upon a particular consecutive edge set. In other words, an active region is a region that contains consecutive edges that have repeated themselves. All the high weight edges need not represent motifs because there is a fair chance for them being repeats. Therefore, the search is for more prominent edges. The algorithm tries to identify edges that have more weight in an active region in comparison to the other edges. Figure 4 represents the active regions with some edges having higher weights than other. From the figure one can observe that BC and CD have a greater edge weight in comparison to edges AB and DE in the active region, ABCDE. This concept has actually worked in mining desirable motifs from the sequences. However, our algorithm failed to recognize motifs that do not exactly match with each other, for example MNPPPQF and MCPPPQF (with the second position differing). Therefore, we decided to change the way the comparison of $l - 1$ tuples is made in the initial stages. Our initial strategy was to look for straight $l - 1$ tuple matches. We modified the algorithm to find motifs with slight mismatches by introducing a parameter called distance, d. Two $l - 1$ tuples with hamming distance 1 is considered as one single $l - 1$ tuple. The nodes that follows connects to the given $l - 1$ tuple depending on the hamming distance from the already connected nodes. This allowed us to unearth subtle or weak motifs. The hamming distance depends on the amount of overlap of the $l - 1$ tuples which in turn depends on the initial motif length chosen. Therefore, a longer $l - 1$ tuple (> 7) has the distance parameter set to 2 so that the hamming distance between any two $l - 1$ tuples is 2. Hence, two nodes with a hamming distance $<= 2$ is considered as similar nodes.

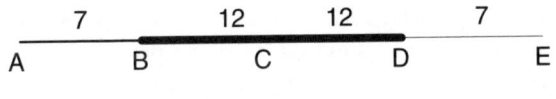

Fig. 4. Active Region

Parallelization of Graph Traversal: As explained above, graph traversal mainly involves tracing edges with higher than certain threshold weight. This is a completely independent process which does not have any dependencies. Therefore, the whole traversal operation can be performed individually on different processors. The graph is extremely large owing to the huge amount of test data. The graph traversal consumes significant amount of time when performed on a single processor. During graph traversal, edges may be shared by processors requiring constant synchronization which is costly. In the distributed memory machine, the data is distributed among the processors and each processor performs the traversal independently and through message passing for sharing of information. In the graph traversal, coarse-grained parallelism is exploited.

We adopt a dynamic "manager-worker" framework to perform the graph traversal. Every node builds its own graph as discussed in the previous section. Once the graph is constructed, the manager builds the zero indegree queue. The size of the indegree queue depends on the number of sequences. Since the indegree queue contains the starting points for the traversal, they form the work units for the worker processors. Therefore, whenever the worker needs work, the manager sends a chunk of zero indegree nodes. The worker processor performs the depth first search, traces the high weight edges and identifies the potential sites. Upon completion, the worker sends the results back to the manager and requests for more work. The whole process is an on-demand process, thus making it entirely dynamic. The manager filters the repeated potential sites and maintains a final vector containing all the potential motifs. The manager-worker communication continues as long as the zero indegree queue is not empty. When there is not enough work, the manager sends a termination signal to all the worker processors.

5 Experimental Results

We first tested the sequential algorithm against the popular MEME and Gibbs Sampler for correctness. The parallel algorithm is implemented on a cluster available on WestGrid [13]. WestGrid is a resource provider which adopts a grid-enabled system to facilitate high performance computing.

5.1 Sequential Results

The sequential algorithm is implemented using Java and C++ running on a Linux platform. Initially, the algorithm was tested on the DNA sequences that belong to the prokaryotic family. The advantage with these sequences is that they have very low or negligible number of repeats. In addition to that, the common repeating patterns in the prokaryotic sequences (the "TATA" patterns) are already known. Upon successful initial testing we tested the algorithm on the protein sequences. We chose to start off with the protein responsible for redox (oxidation and reduction) reactions called "Cytochrome" [20]. The initial testing began on just twenty sequences, with the longest sequence being 577 nucleotides. However, we ended up testing the algorithm successfully on 15000 sequences. In

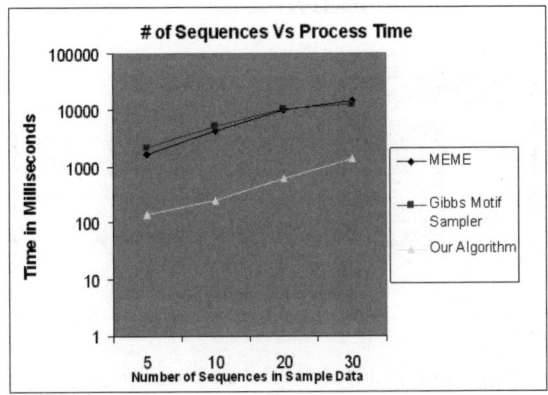

Fig. 5. Sequences Vs Process Time

this section, we will make a comparison of our algorithm with popular motif searching tools namely "MEME" and the "Gibbs sampler". Though many tools for searching motifs are available, we have chosen MEME and Gibbs sampler because they provide for testing both DNA and protein sequences. The only parameter that we ask the user to enter apart from the sequence set is the expected width of each motif.

Figure 5 shows the comparison among the three algorithms. Both MEME and Gibbs sampler have a character limit. Therefore, we could not test them for more than 30 protein sequences each averaging 200bp. Clearly our algorithm has a speed advantage over the other motif discovery tools. This comparison just gives an approximate picture of the speed levels. The next step is testing the accuracy of the results. The graph algorithm had 70% matches of the motifs with the MEME and 65% pattern matches with the Gibbs motif sampler. Out of the first 10 motifs ($length = 8$) returned by MEME, it had 7 straight matches and two partial matches (differing by one character). Analysis shows that motif length and allowed hamming distance are the primary factors that affect the performance of the algorithm. A small change in the expected length of a tuple (motif) will bring drastic change in the total time consumed. This is due to the overlap of the subsequences in the graph. Hence, changing the length of the motif will affect the length of the $l - 1$ tuple. Therefore, smaller l-tuples result in greater number of nodes in the graph. Second, the hamming distance also has a great impact on the performance because it is just an additional level of comparison which takes up a lot of processing time. However, the correct selection of hamming distance based on the overlap of subsequences will ensure the retrieval of weaker motifs which are otherwise neglected.

5.2 Performance Analysis of the Parallel Algorithm

The sequential version stands as a benchmark for all further tests on the parallel machine. We compared the parallel algorithm to a pure distributed machine

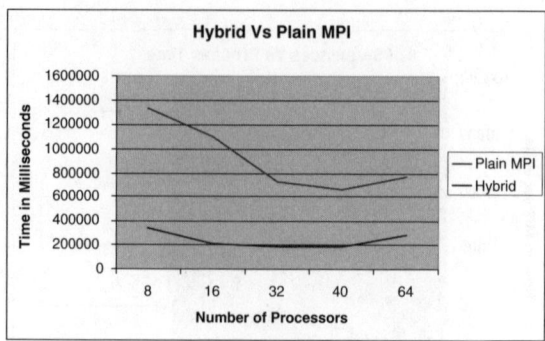

Fig. 6. Comparison of hybrid and distributed memory machines

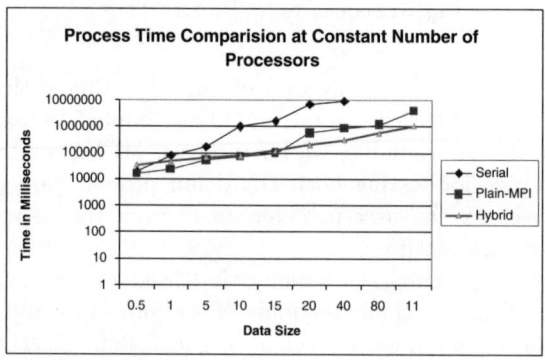

Fig. 7. Process times of serial, hybrid and pure MPI

using MPI and on a cluster that provides shared address space in every node and message passing across nodes (which we call the hybrid model). Proteins such as Cytochrome, Basigin, and Neurothelin were taken as test data. However, this time we tried to extract sequences at the genomic level. The whole cytochrome is about 110 Mega Bytes. In the hybrid model we provide a provision to read multiple protein sequence files. Each of these files is converted into a binary file which excludes the sequence headers and contains just the sequences.

Figure 6 is a comparison of the time taken by hybrid and plain MPI methods on varying number of processors with constant data size (40MB). As it is evident from the graph, the hybrid parallel algorithm runs almost 3 times as fast as the plain MPI. Figure 7 is a comparison of the serial, MPI and the hybrid implementations. From the graph it can be observed that parallel algorithm on the hybrid architecture does not perform well when the data size is small. In fact MPI and the serial algorithm show better performance until the data size is about 15MB. This is because the parallel algorithm consumes considerable amount of time in the graph construction phase where synchronization among the threads is required. However, this deficiency is compensated as the data

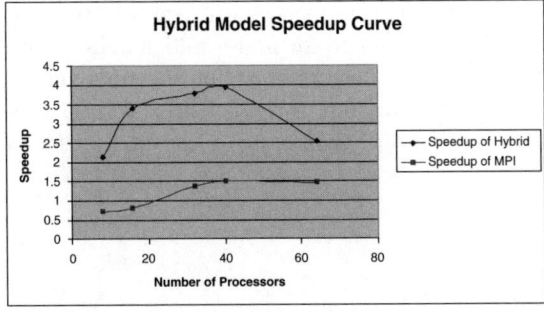

Fig. 8. Speedup of Hybrid

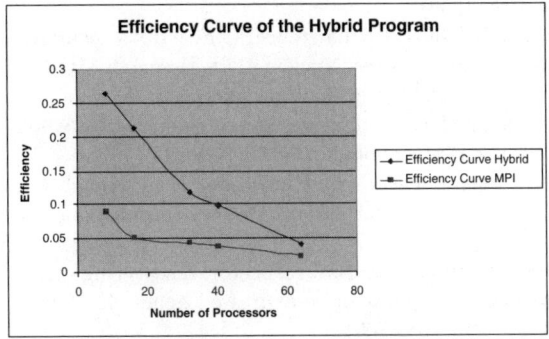

Fig. 9. Efficiency Curves

size increases. Though the synchronization time remains constant, more data is shared among the threads, thereby reducing the processing time. The speedup and efficiency curves for both hybrid and MPI implementations are illustrated in Figures 8 and 9. Its quite clear that the hybrid implementation has shown better performance than plain MPI. Motif length and hamming distance still have the same effect on the run time as described above. In addition, the performance of the parallel algorithm depends on the following factors: size of the indegree vector, the number of worker processors, and the size of the input file. The parallel algorithm is scalable for 32 processors. As seen in Figure 8 the hybrid implementation shows a steep drop in speedup when 64 processors were used.

Apparently, increasing the number of slave processors brings about more communication overhead. Repeated tests have shown that better speedup can be achieved when the algorithm is run on 16 nodes (32 processors) using optimum chunk size (number of nodes with indegree zero) for each slave processor.

6 Conclusions

In this paper we show that the de Bruijn graph can accelerate the rate of discovering motifs by more than 10 times. The graph based approach is so powerful that even minute repetitions in sequences are traced. Upon optimization, we were able to scale the algorithm to 20 nodes and handle about 1GB of input data with ease. We successfully used the distributed supercomputer available on WestGrid to speedup the algorithm. We efficiently utilized resources available on the machine redesigning the algorithm to use fine grain and coarse grain parallelism.

References

1. Geman, S., Geman, D.: Stochastic relaxation, Gibbs distributions, and the Bayesian restoration of images. Readings in uncertain reasoning, 452–472 (1990)
2. Hartley, H.O.: Maximum likelihood estimation from incomplete data. Biometrics 14(2), 174–194 (1958)
3. Thompson, W., Rouchka, E.C., Lawrence, C.E.: Gibbs recursive sampler: finding transcription factor binding sites. Nucleic Acids Research 31(13), 3580–3585 (2003)
4. Roth, F.P., Hughes, J.D., Estep, P.W., Church, G.M.: Finding DNA regulatory motifs within unaligned noncoding sequences clustered by whole-genome mRNA quantitation. Nature Biotechnology 16(10), 939–945 (1998)
5. Siddharthan, R., Siggia, E.D., van Nimwegen, E.: Phylogibbs: A gibbs sampler incorporating phylogenetic information. PLoS Computational Biology 1(7), 534–556 (2005)
6. Liu, X., Liu, J.S., Brutlag, D.L.: BioProspector: discovering conserved DNA motifs in upstream regulatory regions of co-expressed genes. In: Pacific Symposium on Biocomputing, pp. 127–138 (2001)
7. Pevzner, P.A., Tang, H., Waterman, M.S.: An Eulerian path approach to DNA fragment assembly. Proceedings of the National Academy of Sciences of the United States 98(17), 9748–9753 (2001)
8. Rigoutsos, I., Floratos, A.: Combinatorial pattern discovery in biological sequences: The TEIRESIAS algorithm. Bioinformatics 14(1), 56–57 (1998)
9. Buhler, J., Tompa, M.: Finding motifs using random projections. In: RECOMB 2001: Proceedings of the fifth annual international conference on Computational biology, pp. 69–76. ACM Press, New York (2001)
10. Pevzner, P.A., Sze, S.H.: Combinatorial approaches to finding subtle signals in DNA sequences. In: Proceedings of the Eighth International Conference on Intelligent Systems for Molecular Biology, La Jolla, CA, USA, pp. 269–278. AAAI Press, Menlo Park (2000)
11. Keich, U., Pevzner, P.A.: Finding motifs in the twilight zone. Bioinformatics 18(10), 1374–1381 (2002)
12. Setubal, J.C., Meidanis, J.: Introduction to Computational Molecular Biology. PWS Publishing Company, Boston (1997)
13. Westgrid Canada Research Grid, http://www.westgrid.ca/home.html
14. Bailey, T.L., Elkan, C.: Fitting a mixture model by expectation maximization to discover motifs in biopolymers. In: The Second International Conference on Intelligent Systems for Molecular Biology, Stanford, CA, USA, pp. 28–36. AAAI Press, Menlo Park (1994)
15. Challa, S., Thulasiraman, P.: A graph based approach to discover conserved regions in DNA and protein sequences. In: Symposium on Bioinformatics and Life Science Computing, pp. 672–677 (2007)

16. Grundy, W.N., Bailey, T.L., Elkan, C.P.: ParaMEME: a parallel implementation and a web interface for a DNA and protein motif discovery tool. Bioinformatics 12(4), 303–310 (1996)
17. Sutou, T., Tamura, K., Mori, Y., Kitakami, H.: Design and implementation of parallel modified prefixspan method. In: International Symposium on High Performance Computing, pp. 412–422 (2003)
18. Baldwin, N.E., Collins, R.L., Langston, M.A., Symons, C.T., Leuze, M.R., Voy, B.H.: High performance computational tools for motif discovery. In: Proceedings of the 18th IPDPS, Eldorado Hotel, Santa Fe, NM, USA, April 2004, IEEE, Los Alamitos (2004)
19. ParSeq: A Software Tool for Searching Motifs with Structural and Biochemical Properties in Biological Sequences (September 2005), http://www-pr.informatik.uni-tuebingen.de/parseq/
20. Cytochrome P450 cysteine heme-iron ligand signature, http://www.expasy.org/cgi-bin/nicedoc.pl?PDOC00081

Parallel and Distributed Particle Collision Simulation with Decentralized Control

Ruipeng Li[1], Hai Jiang[1], Hung-Chi Su[1], Bin Zhang[2], and Jeff Jenness[1]

[1] Department of Computer Science, Arkansas State University,
Jonesboro, Arkansas 72467, USA
{li.ruipeng,hjiang,suh,jeffj}@csm.astate.edu
[2] Department of Chemistry and Physics, Arkansas State University,
Jonesboro, Arkansas 72467, USA
bzhang@astate.edu

Abstract. Scientific computing applications with highly demanding data capacity and computation power drive a computing platform migration from shared memory machines to multi-core/multiprocessor computer clusters. However, overheads in coordinating operations across computing nodes could counteract the benefit of having extra machines. Furthermore, the hidden dependency in applications slows down the simulation over non-shared memory machines. This paper proposed a framework to utilize multi-core/multiprocessor clusters for distributed simulation. Among several coordination schemes, decentralized control approach has demonstrated its effectiveness in reducing the communication overheads. A speculative execution strategy is applied to exploit parallelism thoroughly and overcome strong data dependency. Performance analysis and experiments are provided to demonstrate the performance gains.

1 Introduction

Time and event-driven simulations have been widely used to study interactions among moving particles in atomic physics [1], molecular dynamics [2,3,4], and many other research fields [5,6,7]. However, realistic simulation process is memory-consuming and computationally intensive. Recent improvements in multi-core computers and networks have provided an opportunity to support high performance parallel applications within an everyday computing infrastructure. Memory units from different computers can be aggregated into a virtually global memory for larger data sets. Networked multi-core computers can work together as a virtual supercomputer for required computational power. To satisfy the requirements of scalability and effectiveness, parallel and distributed simulation becomes popular in scientific computing field.

However, the infrastructure of distributed systems does not fit common application's data structure naturally. When tasks and data are partitioned and dispatched onto different machines, resource sharing becomes difficult since the access patterns are changed dramatically. Moreover, communication overheads slow down the overall execution and could even counteract the performance gain acquired from the extra computing powers of new machines. New strategies in distributed simulations are on demand.

In this paper, we will focus on the dynamical simulation of a system of partons (quarks and gluons) in the Quark-Gluon Plasma produced in relativistic heavy ion collisions. Since this system contains strong data dependency, the incorrect out-of-order event simulation in distributed systems cannot be modified back by prediction-adjustment (time parallelization) [8] or recovered back by prediction-rollback (time warp) [9] approaches due to the complete invalidation and high storage cost. Demonstration of handling this kind of problem effectively will benefit many other scientific applications in distributed systems.

This paper makes the following contributions: First, a framework of parallel and distributed simulation is deployed to utilize multi-core clusters. Second, a distributed speculative execution strategy and several event coordination schemes are proposed to reduce communications. Third, performance analysis and experimental results are provided to demonstrate the performance gains.

The remainder of this paper is organized as follows: Section 2 describes the background and strategies of sequential simulation. In Section 3, a parallel simulation strategy is introduced. Section 4 discusses the proposed event coordination schemes and some optimizations in distributed simulation. Some performance analysis and experimental results are given in Sections 5 and 6, respectively. Our conclusions are presented in Section 7.

2 Sequential Simulation

When computers are used to simulate particle collision systems, time-driven and event-driven simulations are the major approaches. The former one displaces all particles synchronously over a small discrete time period whereas the latter one displaces them over a serial of predicted events. In the event-driven approach, simulation time can advance to the next event time instead of crawling through all time periods in between [1,2,4,5]. This is more efficient and widely adopted.

A discrete-event simulation needs to find out all events and simulate them one-by-one. To improve the efficiency of selecting the next collision event, cell structure [10] is brought into the simulation system based on the observation that a near future collision for a particle will most likely occur in the neighborhood of this particle. Consequently, a new kind of event (boundary crossing event) is introduced to detect if particles move into or out of neighboring cells. The sequential simulation algorithm consists of three steps:

1. Local event queue maintenance: to order all possible events for each particle and determine its next earliest one
2. Global event queue maintenance: to order the earliest events from all local event queues and select the earliest global event (overall)
3. Event simulation: to execute the earliest events (with the minimum time stamp) and update the states of involving particles

When a simulation starts, all particles participate in Step 1. Each particle checks all particles in its neighboring cells for possible collision events. Also, next boundary crossing time is estimated. All these two types of events can be put into local event queues. For efficiency, normally simulation systems keep only the earliest event in each particle's local event queue [1].

Step 2 is to find out the overall earliest event for the whole simulation system. All particles' earliest events are maintained and ordered in a global event queue which is mapped onto certain data structures, such as heaps and trees. The idea is to obtain the globally earliest event quickly.

In Step 3, the current earliest global events are verified for validity because some events might be invalidated by lazy collision determination scheme [10]. Those invalid events will be eliminated in this step. Otherwise, this step updates involving particles' states, including formation time, position, and momentum, etc. Once an event simulation is done, the system will loop back to Step 1 for next event and only the local event queues of the affected particles need updates.

3 Parallel Simulation

The most time-consuming part in the sequential algorithm is Step 1, *Local Queue Update* (LQU) due to high volume of particles involved in the systems. Thus, the parallelization of LQU will shorten the whole simulation time.

After each event, the participating particles' LQUs are recalculated for the possible collisions with particles in their 27 neighboring cells which form a 3-D cube. If multithreading is used, an Updating Thread Pool (UTP) is specified/created, and the 3-D cube is partitioned and mapped onto the threads [10].

Steps 2 and 3 in sequential algorithm do not exhibit rich parallelism. Therefore, most parallelization work focuses on Step 1 [10].

4 Parallel and Distributed Simulation

In distributed simulation systems, all steps in sequential and parallel algorithms will still be gone through. The software components are split and mapped onto multiple networked computers. Then coordination schemes of data, data structure and dynamically generated events are required.

4.1 Data Coordination

In distributed simulation, data might be partitioned and mapped onto different machines. Data sharing coordination scheme is required in such non-shared memory computer clusters. For regular problems such as molecular dynamics and relativistic particle transport simulations, non-shared programming model will be better, and data coordination is directly handled by programmers at application level since communication patterns for data consistency is predictable.

The space is partitioned into disjoint blocks and then assigned to the participating machines. A block contains a number of cells, each of which maintains a linked list for its residing particles. Machines are called neighbors if the blocks they are hosting are neighbors in the original simulation box. They introduce block and cell boundary crossing events, called BBC and CBC, respectively. A BBC event happens between two machines is also a CBC event.

4.2 Data Structure Partitioning and Coordination

In Step 2 of sequential algorithm, a global event queue is maintained by collecting the earliest events of all particles. Popular ways to implement it include min-heap and tree-like data structures. In distributed simulations, its implementation needs to be reconsidered because of the non-shared memory nature.

Thus, a block event queue, which is implemented as a block min-heap, is proposed to maintain all local events in a block. Then, the earliest events (the roots) of the block min-heaps from all blocks can be piled up to build the global min-heap which is much smaller than the original one. Therefore, the original global event queue is re-organized into a two-level structure. The storage location of new global min-heap will be determined by event coordination schemes.

4.3 Event Coordination Scheme

In simulation systems, particles move around independently. With limited number of computers, the earlier events of particles should be simulated first since such events might change some particles' states and prevent future events from happening. Because of this strong dependency among events, a scheduler has to apply certain coordination scheme to keep events in order.

Centralized Control Scheme. In Centralized Control Scheme (CCS), the new global min-heap is controlled by a light-weighted scheduler in one dedicated server. On each of other machines, called workers, a process is run to maintain partitioned data blocks and corresponding block min-heaps for real simulations. Its infrastructure is shown in Figure 1. Workload is spread among multiple workers. No collective communication calls are involved. The server and all workers talk in point-to-point communications. The root of the global min-heap indicates the block that has the earliest event. A message is sent from the server to that worker and its block min-heap is updated. As shown in Figure 1, once an event simulation is done and the global min-heap has been adjusted accordingly, the process will be repeated for the next event simulation. With this scheme, all blocks on different machines have to wait for the execution command from the centralized server which becomes the bottleneck.

Decentralized Control Scheme. Since CCS sends two messages in each step, MPI communication costs most of the running time. Hence, Decentralized Control Scheme (DCS) is proposed to reduce the number and size of MPI Send/Receive operations for better performance. DCS keeps one copy of global event queue (global min-heap) on each worker instead of server, and removes the server. Once the worker with the globally earliest event finishes its events, including all local events

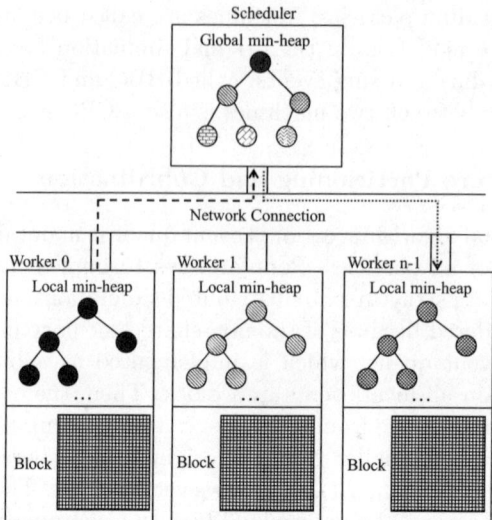

Fig. 1. Message passing in Centralized Control Scheme

earlier than events in all other blocks, it will update its local copy of global event queue. Then, it can send a message directly to that worker, which has the next earliest event, without the server's intervention. Only one message, instead of two in CCS, is sent before next event is simulated. However, it is essential to keep consistent copies of global event queue across multiple machines. Two types of global event queue maintenance protocols are proposed: Global-queue Updating Protocol (GUP) and Global-queue Overwriting Protocol (GOP).

With GUP, when one worker finishes its event handling and refreshes its local copy of global event queue, it broadcasts the differences/updates so that all other workers can refresh their copies as well. However, the overall performance of GUP depends on the broadcast primitive. If broadcast operation is supported at network level (by hardware), not many messages will be generated. Both message delivery and updating of global event queue copies can be overlapped. Thus, simulation is effective for small networks with few workers. On the other hand, if the broadcast primitive is not supported, messages will be delivered one-by-one and a large amount of messages might be generated. When they cause network traffic jams, simulation performance will deteriorate dramatically.

With GOP, new information about global event queue is only sent to the next event handling worker. Message amount is reduced to one, but its contents are the whole current global event queue. It might take a fairly long time to send and receive the global event queue, especially when many workers are involved.

The trade-offs between GUP and GOP are message amount and size. With hardware-supported broadcast primitive, GUP can generate few small messages. Simulation performance will be the best since most operations are conducted simultaneously. Without hardware support, as the number of workers increases, GUP will generate many small messages whereas GOP will produce a few large messages. As the overhead of many but small-sized messages is much higher than that of few but large-sized messages, GOP is a better choice for scalable simulation. For simulations over community computer clusters, GOP is the selection.

4.4 Non-blocking Communication

In GOP, one worker has to receive a message of new global event queue from the previous worker, and then handle the first event in block event queue. When global event queue is long, the operation of receiving a message could delay the simulation of the first local event. To avoid such kind of delay, we can overlap the communication and simulation by using *MPI_Irecv*, a non-blocking receive primitive. The pseudocode of such optimization is given in Figure 2. First, the function *MPI_Irecv* is issued to indicate that the application intends to receive a message. While the hardware components and other processors help receive the message, the current CPU can move ahead to do simulation, *EventHandling*. After the simulation is done, the completion of the message receiving is checked by issuing *MPI_Wait*. The further calculation such as *MaintainHeap* can proceed afterward. For large messages, such overlapping of communication and computation operations can speed up simulation obviously.

```
/* receive new block heap */
MPI_Irecv(...); /* non-blocking primitive */
EventHandling();
MPI_Wait(...);  /* complete message receiving */
MaintainHeap();
```

Fig. 2. Pseudocode for non-blocking communication

4.5 Speculative Simulation Infrastructure

The strategy of traditional simulation algorithms is to simulate the first event, and then the second one, and so on. The reason is that simulation events exhibit strong serialization characteristic, i.e., even if more computers are available in distributed simulation, only the worker hosting the currently earliest global event can conduct simulation. Other workers have to wait for permission to proceed. Such conservative distributed simulation can only take advantage of the aggregated memory capacity from multiple machines, not their computing powers.

An aggressive strategy, Distributed Speculative Simulation (DSS), intends to ignore dependency temporarily so that multiple events can be simulated speculatively and simultaneously. Each worker's default thread is reserved for actual simulation with its Updating Thread Pool (UTP). When one worker is dealing with real simulation, other workers' default threads and UTPs have to be blocked. Colliding particles' states will be updated with the help from the threads in UTP. If some neighboring cells are located in other workers, remote default threads and UTPs will help the update. At the same time, each worker maintains a Speculative Thread Pool (STP) for speculative simulation. While default threads and UTPs are busy or blocked for the real simulation, the threads in STPs can still conduct proper amount of speculative computation.

Once another worker is selected as the next event executor, it will scan its local block event queue. If some events have been speculatively simulated and they still stay valid, the speculation results can be adopted directly. Such Speculative Results Adoption (SRA) overhead is much smaller than the real simulation time. For a long run, it can save a tremendous amount of time. If speculative events have been invalidated, their speculative results will be abandoned and these events will be re-simulated as in the sequential and parallel algorithms.

In DSS, multiple computation operations are overlapped in a certain degree. However, the size of thread pool and the aggressiveness of speculative threads depend on the number of cores/processors on each worker and the scheduling policy of thread package. When more cores/processors are available, the sizes of UTP and STP will be larger. If threads are scheduled independently as kernel-level threads, they can simulate more events in advance. Otherwise, their aggressiveness should be adjusted dynamically [11]. All simulation parameters can be set based on cluster configuration.

5 Performance Analysis

The overall performance of parallel and distributed simulation depends on its computer nodes and network architecture. For a certain system setting, event coordination schemes may affect its behavior dramatically. Decentralized Control Scheme (DCS) with Global-queue Overwriting Protocol (GOP) is expected to perform well. Further performance gain can be obtained from Distributed Speculation Simulation (DSS). We denote the running time of GOP by t_{gop}, which can be divided into simulation computation time (t_{gop}^{comp}) and communication time (t_{gop}^{comm}), $t_{gop} = t_{gop}^{comp} + t_{gop}^{comm}$. Simulation computation time (t_{gop}^{comp}) can be given by

$$t_{gop}^{comp} = m \times t^{eh} + t_{gop}^{heap} \qquad (1)$$

where t^{eh} is average event handling time, m is total event number, and t_{gop}^{heap} is the overhead of other work including maintaining heap. Hence, t_{gop} will be

$$t_{gop} = t_{gop}^{comp} + t_{gop}^{comm} = m \times t^{eh} + t_{gop}^{heap} + t_{gop}^{comm}. \qquad (2)$$

In the same way, the running time of Distributed Speculative Simulation (t_{dss}) can be defined as

$$t_{dss} = t_{dss}^{comp} + t_{dss}^{comm} = t_{dss}^{eh} + t_{dss}^{heap} + t_{dss}^{comm}. \qquad (3)$$

According to our speculative strategy, distributed speculative event handling time (t_{dss}^{eh}) equals Speculative Results Adoption (SRA) time (t_{SRA}^{total}) plus Real Event Handling time (t_{REH}^{total}). If P_{SRA} is defined as the percentage of SRA, the speculative event handling time (t_{dss}^{eh}) can be expressed as

$$t_{dss}^{eh} = t_{REH}^{total} + t_{SRA}^{total} \approx m \times [P_{SRA} \times t_{SRA} + (1 - P_{SRA}) \times t^{eh}]. \qquad (4)$$

So,
$$t_{dss} = m \times [P_{SRA} \times t_{SRA} + (1 - P_{SRA}) \times t^{eh}] + t_{dss}^{heap} + t_{dss}^{comm}. \quad (5)$$

Since our speculation scheme does not conduct any communication operation, the communication time in DSS is equal to the one in GOP, that is, $t^{comm} = t_{dss}^{comm} = t_{gop}^{comm}$. And so does the heap maintaining time, $t^{heap} = t_{gop}^{heap} = t_{dss}^{heap}$. Furthermore, speedup of DSS over GOP can be given by,

$$\begin{aligned} speedup &= \frac{t_{gop}}{t_{dss}} = \frac{m \times t^{eh} + t^{heap} + t^{comm}}{m \times [P_{SRA} \times t_{SRA} + (1 - P_{SRA}) \times t^{eh}] + t^{heap} + t^{comm}} \\ &= \frac{1 + \frac{t^{heap}}{m \times t^{eh}} + \frac{t^{comm}}{m \times t^{eh}}}{1 - P_{SRA} \times (1 - \frac{t_{SRA}}{t^{eh}}) + \frac{t^{heap}}{m \times t^{eh}} + \frac{t^{comm}}{m \times t^{eh}}} \\ &= 1 + \frac{P_{SRA} \times (1 - \frac{t_{SRA}}{t^{eh}})}{1 - P_{SRA} \times (1 - \frac{t_{SRA}}{t^{eh}}) + \frac{t^{heap}}{m \times t^{eh}} + \frac{t^{comm}}{m \times t^{eh}}}. \quad (6) \end{aligned}$$

When particle number is given, the value of $\frac{t^{eh}}{t_{SRA}}$ is nearly a constant, defined as average speedup of speculative simulation. This value should be larger than one, which is the fundamental of speedup in the speculative scheme. And the value of $\frac{t^{heap}}{m \times t^{eh}}$ is approximately a constant, denoted by C_1. If we denote the value of $(1 - \frac{t_{SRA}}{t^{eh}})$ by C_2, finally, speedup will be

$$speedup = 1 + \frac{P_{SRA} \times C_2}{1 - P_{SRA} \times C_2 + C_1 + \frac{t^{comm}}{m \times t^{eh}}} = 1 + \frac{1}{\frac{1 + C_1 + \frac{t^{comm}}{m \times t^{eh}}}{P_{SRA} \times C_2} - 1}. \quad (7)$$

When more workers are used, more speculative computation is conducted and then P_{SRA} value is expected to rise. However, as the number of processes increases, communication time (t^{comm}) increases since simulation space is partitioned into more blocks. The increase of communication time (t^{comm}) could also be implied by the increase of t_{gop} since $t_{gop} = t^{comm} + t^{comp}$ and t^{comp} do not change as the number of workers increases. According to Eq. (7), the value of speedup would like to drop. Because of the above two factors, speedup might fluctuate as the number of workers changes.

6 Experiment Results

Our tests were conducted on Seaborg, the NERSC IBM RS/6000, a distributed memory system with 380 SMP nodes connected with IBM Colony-II switch at Lawrence Berkeley National Laboratory (LBNL). Each node consists of sixteen 375MHz Power3-II processors with peak performance of 1.5GFlops/s. The simulation space is a 3D wraparound box, i.e., when a particle moves out of the box, it will enter the box from the opposite side of the box. Since parallel and distributed systems are always helpful for larger simulations, our test focused on event coordination and speculation. To illustrate their influence, sizes of UTP

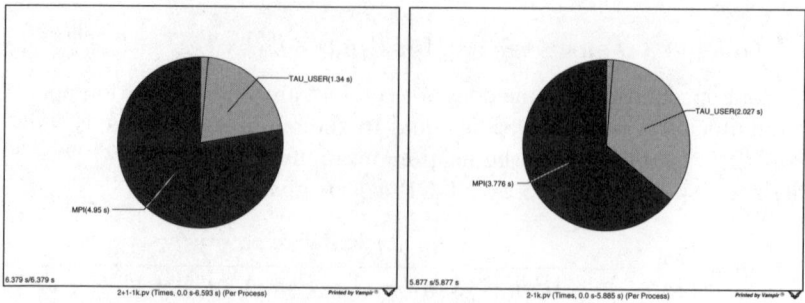

Fig. 3. Overall communication overheads in CCS (left) and DCS (right)

and STP are set to zero and one, respectively, i.e., only default thread is used to update local event queue and one speculative thread is employed on each worker.

In distributed simulation, communication operations affect the overall system performance since other costs remain almost the same. Figure 3 illustrates the overall MPI communication operation percentage in the total simulation time for CCS and DCS. The left portion is the result from CCS with one server and two workers whereas the right one comes from DCS-GOP with only two workers. As we expected, MPI operation rate drops in DCS case and the communication overhead is reduced. Thus, the performance gain of DCS-GOP is expected.

The actual simulation performances with different coordination schemes and optimizations are shown in Figure 4. Each process represents a worker on one machine. Roughly speaking, DCS variants, except DCS-GUP in large cases, are better than CCS. With non-blocking communication calls, DSS achieves the best performance. As the process number increases, simulation time rises due to the unavoidable communication cost. However, such distributed simulation system can support much bigger applications so that previously unsolvable problems are turned into doable ones.

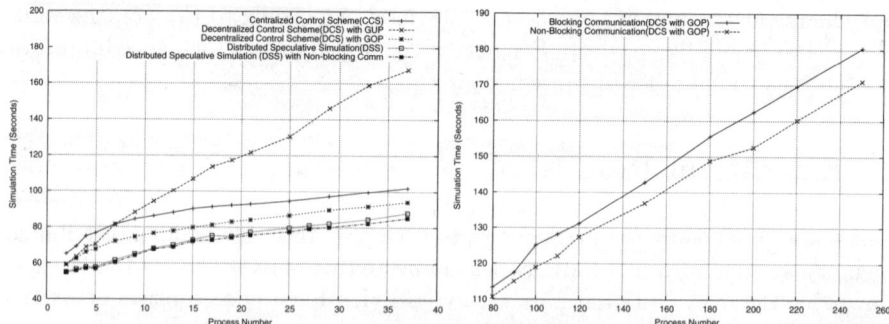

Fig. 4. Simulation performance of different coordination schemes and optimizations

Fig. 5. Blocking vs. non-blocking communications

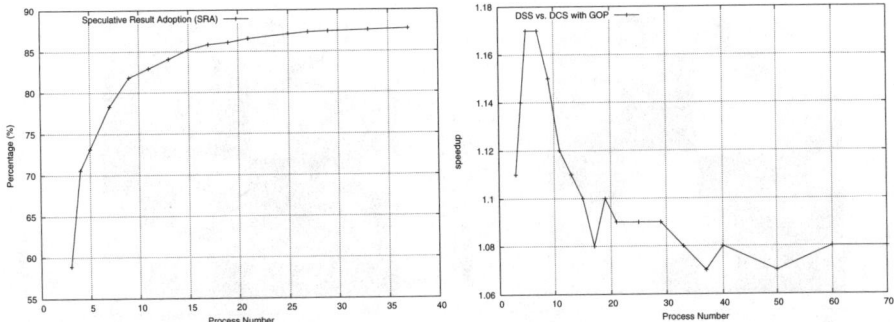

Fig. 6. Percentage of SRA in DSS   **Fig. 7.** Speedup of DSS over DCS-GOP

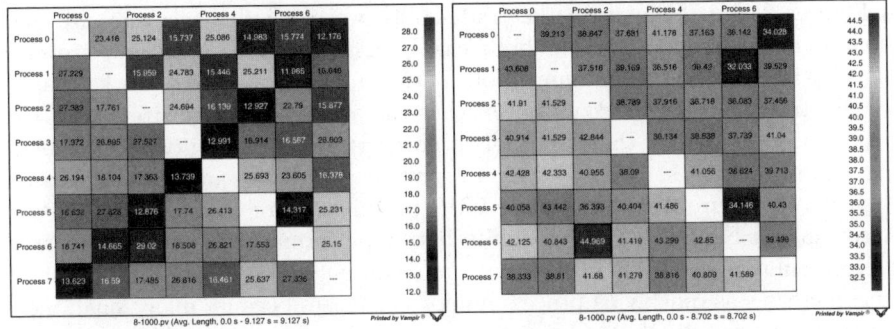

Fig. 8. Average message sizes of GUP (left) and GOP (right)

As DCS outperforms CCS, our focus will be on DCS. In Figure 4, DSS does acquire further performance gain. However, non-blocking communication can only provide minor improvement. The reason is that the message size is small when process (worker) number is small. Figure 5 shows its effectiveness in cases with much more processes (workers). Since the message contains the whole global event queue, the overhead of receiving such message is not ignorable anymore. Thus, the non-blocking communication primitive shows its benefit by overlapping communication and computation operations.

DSS-GOP wins the overall battle by ignoring event dependency and simulating future events in advance. The more events have been speculatively executed, the more simulation time will be saved. According to Eq. (7), it can help increase the speedup. Figure 6 supports this expectation: percentage of SRA (P_{SRA}) grows as process number increases. It grows fast first, but then slows down progressively since the communication overhead will occupy larger portion in the total cost chart. For speedup of DSS over DCS-GOP, as discussed in Section 5, it might fluctuate as the number of workers changes. Figure 7 shows that it approaches a relatively stable level as the number of processors increases. Certain performance gain is guaranteed.

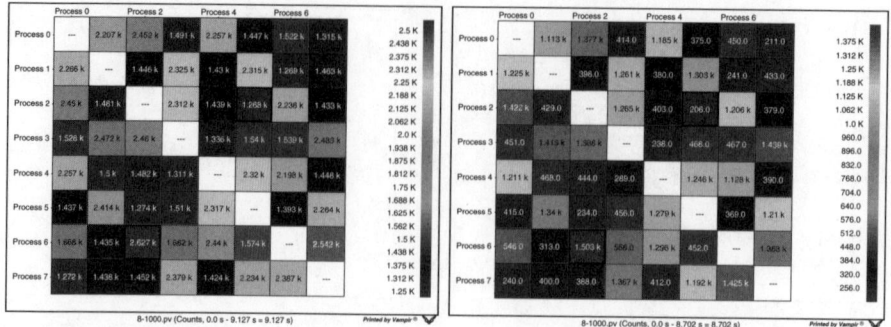

Fig. 9. Message counts of GUP (left) and GOP (right)

Figures 8 and 9 illustrate the trade-off between average message size and amount in GUP and GOP. In both cases, eight processes (workers) are employed with no server. Communications between all process-pairs (worker-pairs) are illustrated. In Figure 8, we notice that the average message size with GUP (left portion) is smaller than GOP (right portion) by comparing two corresponding grid slots in these two matrices. In same way, message amount comparison is shown in Figure 9 and this time GUP produces more messages than GOP. According to Figure 4, GOP exhibits better performance, especially in large process number cases. GUP is not bad in small networks. Then, its simulation time increases as quickly as process number increases because many small messages are generated. Obviously, there is no broadcast support at network layer. Messages can easily cause network traffic jams which delay the global event queue update on remote machines. Such overhead rises near-linearly and makes GUP even worse than CCS for large problems. These figures indicate that the message amount deteriorates performance more than the message size factor.

According to the infrastructure of parallel and distributed simulation, UTP and STP are able to improve actual and speculative simulations. However, performance gains will depend on thread schedulers [11]. Current system can adjust parameters dynamically. The thread package on our testing platform, Seaborg, causes no performance gain whereas some achievements on a local Sunfire sever are obvious. Therefore, eventual performance highly depends on the platform. This framework enables simulation systems to exploit parallelism thoroughly.

7 Conclusion

This paper proposed a framework for parallel and distributed particle collision simulation to take advantage of multi-core/multiprocessor clusters. Most configuration parameters can be set dynamically to fit the computing environment.

Several coordination schemes are compared in reducing communication cost. DCS outperforms others since few messages are required. To maintain consistent copies of global event queue in DCS, two protocols, GUP and GOP, are proposed. In cases with few nodes or hardware-supported broadcast primitive,

GUP's producing small-sized messages results in good simulation performance. Otherwise, scalability problem will be its major issue. Overall, DCS with GOP delivers better performances in general cases since it produces fewer messages. Furthermore, non-blocking communication primitives can help overlap computations and communications for performance improvement. Finally, DSS is adopted to exploit parallelism by handling events aggressively. By putting all the above together, better performance is expected.

The future work includes fault tolerant distributed simulation and load balancing across multiple machines.

Acknowledgments

This research was supported in part by the U.S. National Science Foundation under grant No. PHY-0554930. The authors would like to thank the National Energy Research Scientific Computing Center (NERSC), supported by the Office of Science of the U.S. Department of Energy under Contract No. DE-AC02-05CH11231, for providing system resources.

References

1. Zhang, B.: ZPC 1.0.1: a parton cascade for ultrarelativistic heavy ion collisions. Computer Physics Communications 109, 193–206 (1998)
2. Isobe, M.: Simple and efficient algorithm for large scale molecular dynamics simulation in hard disk system. International Journal of Modern Physics C(10), 1281–1293 (1999)
3. Donev, A., Torquato, S., Stillinger, F.: Neighbor list collision-driven molecular dynamics simulation for nonspherical hard particles. I. algorithmic details. Journal of Computational Physics 202(2), 737–764 (2005)
4. Miller, S., Luding, S.: Event-driven molecular dynamics in parallel. Journal of Computational Physics 193(1), 306–316 (2004)
5. Lubachevsky, B.D.: How to simulate billiards and similar systems. Journal of Computational Physics 94(2), 255–283 (1991)
6. Mu, M.: A multiple-heaps algorithm for parallel simulation of collision systems. Journal of Computational Physics 179(2), 539–556 (2002)
7. Sigurgeirsson, H., Stuart, A., Wan, W.L.: Algorithms for particle-field simulations with collisions. Journal of Computational Physics 172(2), 766–807 (2002)
8. Yu, Y., Srinivasan, A., Chandra, N.: Scalable time-parallelization of molecular dynamics simulations in nano mechanics. In: Proceedings of the International Conference on Parallel Processing, pp. 119–126 (2006)
9. Fujimoto, R.: Parallel discrete event simulation. Communications of the ACM 33(10), 30–53 (1990)
10. Li, R., Jiang, H., Su, H.C., Jenness, J., Zhang, B.: Speculative parallelization of many-particle collision simulations. In: Proceedings of the 2007 International Conference on Parallel and Distributed Processing Techniques and Applications, pp. 128–136 (2007)
11. Li, R., Jiang, H., Su, H.C., Zhang, B., Jenness, J.: Speculative and distributed simulation of many-particle collision simulations. In: Proceedings of the 13th International Conference on Parallel and Distributed Systems (2007)

Modeling and Simulation of Self-similar Storage I/O

Zhaobin Liu, Bo Jiang, Zixiang Zhao, and Yunhan Jiang

School of Computer Science and Technology, Dalian Maritime University,
Dalian, Liaoning, 116026, P.R. China
zhbliu@gmail.com

Abstract. Storage I/O has become a performance bottleneck for large-scale computation and storage systems. Characterization of I/O network traffic has been the observed self-similarity nowadays. In this paper, basing on the reviews of the origins of this self-similarity, we study how Stochastic Petri Net (SPN) models can be exploited for self-similar I/O behaviors of virtual storage systems. We then present the SPN models and simplifying processes of file I/O and multimedia I/O for origination node, destination node and communication link. Finally, we propose the self-similarity simulation methodologies. Analysis results show that without self-similar I/O scenario outperforms self-similar I/O scenario both for file I/O and multimedia I/O, and show how the ratio of multimedia/file I/O and the queue capability can affect the observed storage I/O self-similarity.

1 Introduction

Conventionally, most storage I/O performance theory is based on Markovian assumptions of traffic arrival processes and of service time distributions. Some researchers use many simplifying assumptions (e.g., Poisson model) for performance evaluation of storage subsystems. However, by rapid development of network storage systems, these traditional models were found to be unrealistic, and lead to wrong predictions that often have later been shown to be incorrect. A new looks on these models shows that the actual network storage systems traffic is long-range dependent and self-similar [1].

Typically, the study of the self-similarity processes was applied to network traffic, as far as we know, this methodology has not been applied to storage I/O traffic. In this paper, we are interested in the Petri nets modeling methodology of self-similar storage I/O and its simulation in our virtual storage system [2].

Petri nets are a very well established family of formal description techniques, well suited for modeling concurrent, asynchronous and non-deterministic systems. Many authors have shown the large use of Petri nets in several areas, such as computer science, electronic engineering, chemistry and business management [3]. In this paper we show how Non-Markovian Stochastic Petri Nets (SPN) models can be exploited for performance analysis of both multimedia and file I/O.

The paper is organized as follows. In incoming section, the basic concept and generation processes of self-similarity will be introduced. In Section 3, we give the

SPN modeling methodologies which are capable of describing the self-similar behavior of file I/O multimedia I/O traffics. Section 4 describes the simulation results and analysis with emphasis on I/O loss rate of self-similarity. Finally, in section 5 we give the conclusions.

2 Related Works

Self-similar processes were first introduced by Mandelbrot and his co-workers in 1968 [4-6]. These processes were thereafter found applications to many fields, such as astronomy, chemistry, economics, engineering, mathematics, physics, statistics, and etc.

The generation processes of self-Similarity are the fundament of modeling, analysis and simulation. So next, we describe the most commonly used self-similar processes: Fractional Brownian motion, F-ARIMA, chaotic maps, M/G/1 model, and ON/OFF source.

Fractional Brownian motion
Fractional Brownian motion is a self-similar Gaussian process with stationary increments [1]. For any $s \geq 0$ and $t > 0$, the increment $X=B(t)-B(s)$ is normally distributed with mean 0 and variance $(t)2H$, thus, its density function is given by:

$$p(X < x) = P((B(t) - B(s)) < x) = \frac{1}{\sqrt{2\pi(t-s)^{2H}}} \int_{-\infty}^{x} \exp\left[\frac{-u^2}{2(t-s)^{2H}}\right] du$$

Fractional ARIMA Processes
Fractional autoregressive integrated moving average (F-ARIMA) processes [7] are an attractive approach to statistical modeling and forecasting of complex temporal I/O behaviors. Typically, ARIMA models are created offline by examining all available data, then constructing and, finally, validating the models. It allows us to model SRD and LRD independently [8]. However, this offline approach often produces models and forecasts that cannot adapt to time-varying changes in I/O arrival patterns [9].

Chaotic maps
[10] presents one promising approach based on chaotic maps to capture and model the dynamics of TCP-type feedback control in such networks. Not only can appropriately chosen chaotic map models capture a range of realistic source characteristics, but by coupling these to network state equations, one can study the effects of network dynamics on the observed scaling behavior.

M/G/1 model
Another interesting self-similar process is the occupancy process of an M/G/1 queuing model, referred to as an M/G/1 process [8]. The M/G/1 model is essential in queuing analysis. Such a renewal process is analyzed and used to predict, e.g., the first and second moments of the waiting time, the busy period of a system, the distribution of queue length, etc [1].

ON/OFF source

Conventionally, the length of ON or OFF source is characterized by finite-variance distribution, such as exponential. It is demonstrated in [11] that superposition of infinitely many Pareto-distributed ON/OFF sources results in a self-similar traffic with Hurst parameter: $H = (3-\alpha)/2$. This analytical relation between α and H was, to some extent, confirmed by observations on Ethernet traffic in [12].

ON/OFF source is one of the most popular modes used nowadays, it not only can generate suitable self-similar traffic, but also has better burstiness characteristics. Our self-similarity SPN modeling is based on ON/OFF source model.

3 SPN Modeling Methodology

Petri Nets were introduced in 1962 by Carl Adam Petri. Petri nets [13, 14] are a graphical and mathematical formalism for modeling, simulation, and formal analysis of discrete event systems [15]. Other frequently used modeling formalisms like finite state machines (FSM) and marked graphs are specializations of Petri nets [16].

An ordinary Petri Net (also called Place-Transition Net) is a bipartite directed graph composed of places (drawn as ellipses), transitions (drawn as rectangles), arcs (connecting places and transitions), and inscriptions (text strings associated with places, transitions, or arcs). Places are used to model the state in a system. When a transition is enabled, it may occur and thereby remove tokens from the input places as specified by the expressions on the input arcs, and add the tokens to the output places as specified by the expressions on the output arcs.

The storage I/O processes can be classified into three parts: origination node, destination node and communication link. As for origination node modeling, the I/O pattern is original Pareto distribution, which shows many smaller files, few larger ones file size distribution. Thus, in this paper we mainly focus on the self-similar modeling of file I/O and multimedia I/O. In SPN model, the places, transitions and arcs are fixed, in other words, the dynamic characteristic of SPN merely depends on the token's flow between them.

3.1 Origination Node of Single File I/O

The typical single file I/O SPN model of origination node can be depicted in Figure 1(a). Model description is described as follows:

- Pon : represents that the file I/O origination node is ON state while it holds token.
- Poff : represents that the file I/O origination node is OFF state while it holds token.
- Ton : Transition from ON state to OFF state. Its distribution is Pareto model.
- Toff : Transition from OFF state to ON state. Its distribution is Pareto model.

Petri nets are a well suited formalism for the system modeling, however, the state space is generally too large to be analyzed for most complex systems. So we simplified the above model as showed in Figure 1(b). We assumed that each origination node send only one I/O at every time.

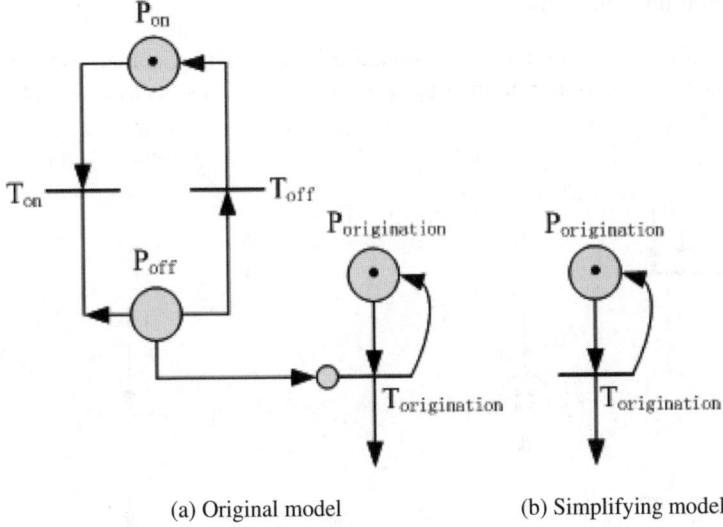

Fig. 1. Petri Nets model of origination node for single file I/O

3.2 Origination Node of Single Multimedia I/O

The single multimedia I/O model is depicted in Figure 2(a). Unlike the single file I/O model, the multimedia I/O model has m (m>1) tokens in place Pon. In other words, multimedia has multiple video or audio origination nodes□their states can be alternated between ON and OFF state asynchronously.

With the same methods of file I/O model simplification, we can simplify the multimedia model as showed in Figure 2(b).

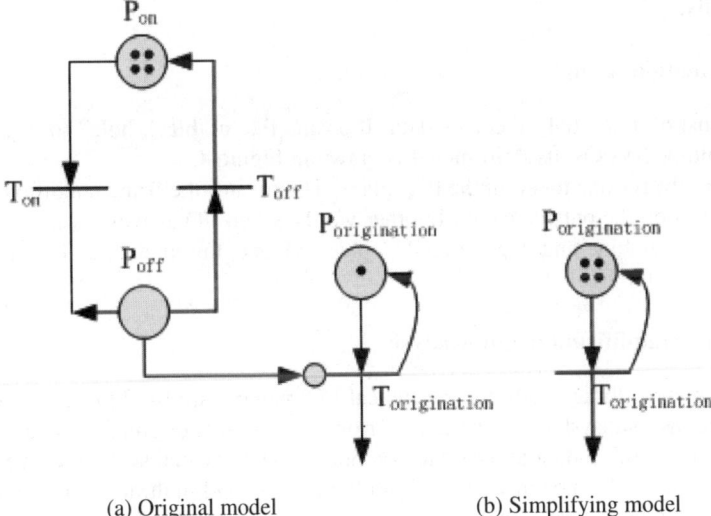

Fig. 2. Petri Nets model of origination node for single multimedia I/O

3.3 Communication Link

All origination nodes and destination nodes are connected by storage communication link. It plays an important role in large scale storage systems. Its SPN model is drawn in Figure 3.

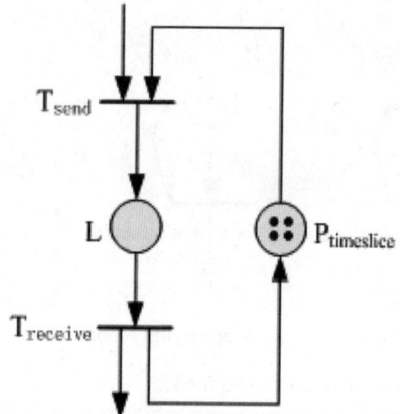

Fig. 3. SPN model of communication link

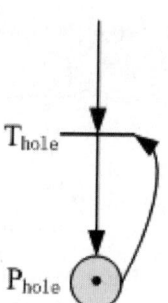

Fig. 4. SPN model of destination node

L is the place of queuing. When $P_{timeslice}$ contains token, T_{send} transition is enabled from T_{send} state to L state. Then, $T_{receive}$ transition is enabled from L state to $P_{timeslice}$ state. T_{send} firing denotes that it sends an I/O by removing a token from $P_{timeslice}$ place. $T_{receive}$ firing denotes that it not only removes an I/O from L place but also deposits two tokens, one as I/O to be outputted to destination node, the other returns $P_{timeslice}$ place. Therefore, the whole storage communication link can transmit I/Os periodically.

3.4 Destination Node

The destination node only receives data. It seems like a "black hole" to capture the file or multimedia I/Os. Its Petri model is drawn in Figure 4.

There is always one token in the P_{hole} place. That means the firing condition of T_{hole} only depends on the outside event. In other words, when I/O arrives, T_{hole} occurs, two input tokens combine and deposit to P_{hole} place. Hence, the model can effectively be used to signify the I/O behavior.

3.5 Model Simplification and Analysis

In most network storage systems, the typical I/O patterns are file I/O and multimedia I/O in storage subsystems. Therefore, from the above origination node model, communication link model and destination node model, we can synthesize the typical network storage SPN model. Because both the file I/O and multimedia I/O model are similar, the whole system model can be simplified as depicted in Figure 5.

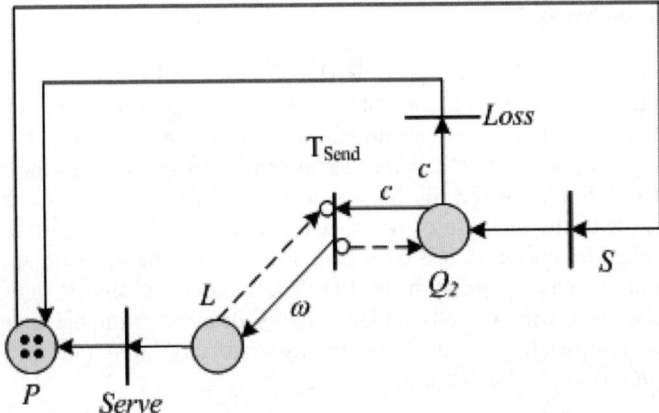

Fig. 5. Simplification SPN model (the file I/O and multimedia I/O model are folded together)

4 Simulation and Performance Evaluation

4.1 Simulation Methodology

The Stochastic Petri Net Package (SPNP) is a versatile modeling tool for performance, dependability and performability analysis of complex systems. Input models based on the theory of stochastic reward nets are solved by efficient and numerically stable algorithms. The most powerful feature of SPNP is the ability to assign reward rates at the net level and subsequently compute the desired measures of the system being modeled. The modeling description language of SPNP is CSPL, a C-like language. In the latest version (V6.0), the user can specify non-Markovian SPNs [17].

To simulate the complex, irregular self-similar I/O patterns in network storage systems, we mainly focus on the file I/O and multimedia I/O respectively. The different parameters that can be adjusted in model are described below:

- c_1: capacity of file I/O queues
- c_2: capacity of multimedia I/O queues
- T_1: throughput of file I/O
- T_2: throughput of multimedia I/O
- q_1: loss rate of file I/O
- q_2: loss rate of multimedia I/O
- λ_1: Transition rate of file I/O
- λ_2: Transition rate of multimedia I/O
- λ_3: storage service rate
- ω: factor of storage network bandwidth
- n: the ratio of multimedia and file I/O

4.2 Simulation Analysis

Let $\lambda 1=1$, $\lambda 2=2$, $\lambda 3=3$, $\lambda=R$ (Loss1) =R (Loss2) =100, c1=12, c2=5, $\omega=5$, M0 (P) =18, the relations between n and loss rate are shown in Figure 6 and Figure 7, and the relations between queue and loss rate are plotted in Figure 8 and Figure 9.

In Figure 6, we plotted two separate bar graphs corresponding to the self-similar and without self-similar of the file I/O, respectively. We can see that although both them increase with the increase of n, the without self-similar circumstance is better than self-similar circumstance. It is clear from Figure7 that the self-similar also results in the loss rate increase for multimedia I/O than without self-similar, however, both the self-similar and without self-similar patterns decrease with the increase of n. according to these results, we can adjust the loss rate and throughput of file I/O and multimedia I/O based on the factor n.

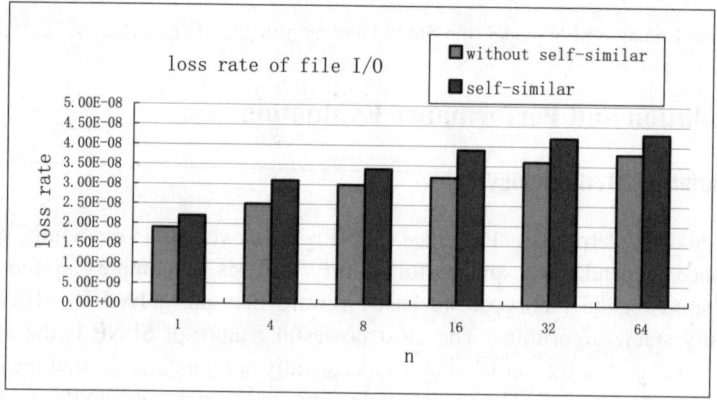

Fig. 6. The file I/O loss rate of self-similar and without self-similar

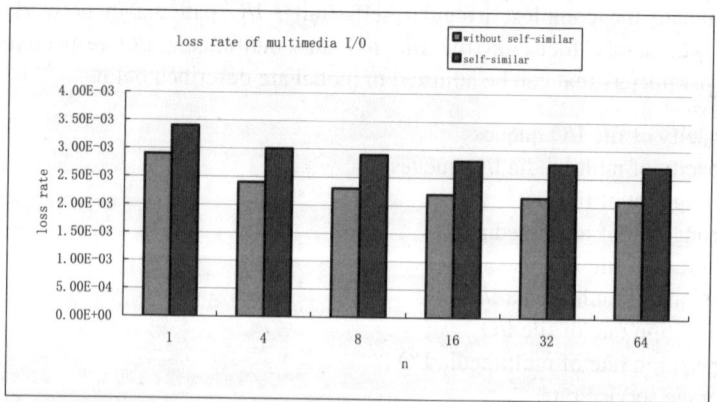

Fig. 7. The multimedia I/O loss rate of self-similar and without self-similar

Above results reflect the relation between loss rate and ratio of multimedia and file I/O. the relations between queue capacity and loss rate are shown in Figure 8 and Figure 9. We observe both the self-similar and without self-similar decrease with the increase of queue capacity for multimedia I/O and file I/O. When the queue capacity is improved, the loss rate of file I/O decreases smoothly, yet for the multimedia I/O, the loss rate decreases dramatically. In other words, multimedia I/O is more sensitive than file I/O under the effects of queue capacity.

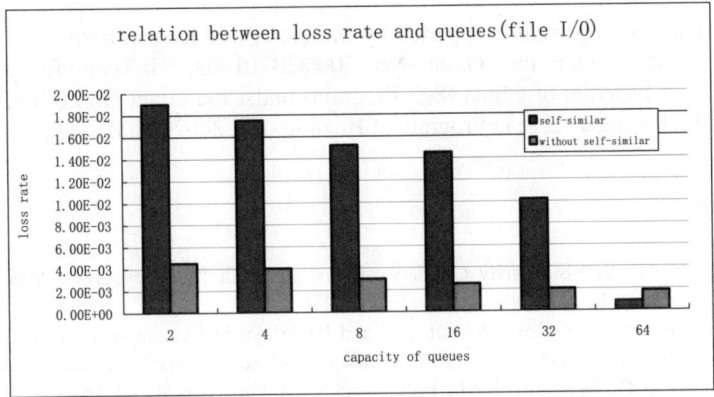

Fig. 8. The relation between queue capacity and loss rate of file I/O

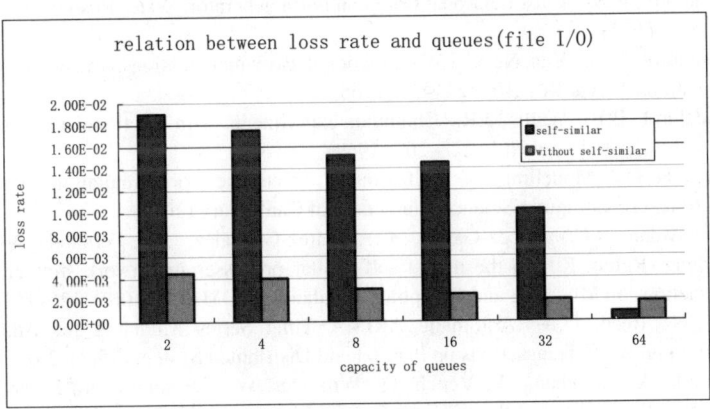

Fig. 9. The relation between queue capacity and loss rate of multimedia I/O

5 Conclusions

SPN provides a useful specification mechanism for the analysis of the large-scale distributed systems. In this paper we have shown how SPN models can be exploited for storage I/O performance analysis of virtual storage system. The SPN modeling methodology we have introduced relies on the self-similarity under both the file I/O and multimedia I/O. Furthermore, we have given the self-similarity simulation based on SNPN tool. We measured the performance of self-similar circumstance as compared to without self-similar circumstance. Results have shown that without self-similar I/O outperforms self-similar I/O both for file I/O and multimedia I/O.

Acknowledgement

This work has been partially supported by National Basic Research Program of China (973 Program) under the Grant No 2006CB701303, Hi-Tech Research and Development Program of China (863 Program) under the Grant No 2007AA12Z151 and Key Technologies R & D Program of Huzhou (No. 2007GS03).

References

1. Wang, H.-H.: Self-Similarity On network systems with finite resources. Master thesis, National Chiao Tung University, Twiwan (2003)
2. Liu, Z.: Research on Key Technologies and Performance Evaluation of Virtual Network Storage System. PhD thesis, Huazhong University of Science and Technology (2004)
3. Machado, A.P., Maciel, P.R.M., Filho, A.G.S.: A Petri Net Based Method for Storage Units Estimation. In: IEEE International Conference on Systems, Man and Cybernetics, vol. 2, pp. 1025–1031 (2003)
4. Mandelbrot, B.B.: A fast fractional Gaussian noise generator. Water Resources Research 7, 543–553 (1971)
5. Mandelbrot, B.B., Van Ness, J.W.: Fractional Brownian motions, fractional noises and applications. SIAM Rev. 10, 422–437 (1968)
6. Mandelbrot, B.B., Wallis, J.R.: Computer experiments with fractional Gaussian noises. Water Resources Research 5, 228–267 (1969)
7. Jeong, H.-D.: Modelling of Self-Similar Teletraffic for Simulation. PhD thesis, Department of Computer Science, University of Canterbury (2002)
8. López-Ardao, J.C., López-García, C., Suárez-González, A., Fernández-Veiga, M., Rodríguez-Rubio, R.: On the use of self-similar processes in network simulation. ACM Transactions on Modeling and Computer Simulation (TOMACS) 10(2), 125–151 (2000)
9. Tran, N., Reed, D.A.: Automatic ARIMA Time Series Modeling for Adaptive I/O Prefetching. IEEE Transactions on Parallel and Distributed Systems 15(4), 362–377 (2004)
10. Erramilli, A., Roughan, M., Veitch, D., Willinger, W.: Self-similar traffic and network dynamics. Proceedings of the IEEE 90(5), 800–819 (2002)
11. Willinger, W., Taqqu, M.S., Sherman, R., Wilson, D.V.: Self-similarity through high-variability: statistical analysis of Ethernet LAN trafficc at the source level. IEEE/ACM Trans. Networking 5(1), 71–86 (1997)
12. Stallings, W.: High-Speed Networks and Internets: Performance and Quality of Service, 2nd edn. Prentice-Hall, Englewood Cliffs (2002)
13. Murata, T.: Petri nets: Properties, analysis, and applications. Proceedings of the IEEE 77(4), 541–580 (1989)
14. Peterson, J.L.: Petri Net Theory and the Modeling of Systems. Prentice-Hall, Englewood Cliffs (1981)

15. Zurawski, R., Zhou, M.-C.: Petri nets and industrial applications: A tutorial. IEEE Transactions on Industrial Electronics 41(6), 567–583 (1994)
16. Naedele, M., Janneck, J.W.: Design Patterns in Petri Net System Modeling. In: Fourth IEEE International Conference on Engineering Complex Computer Systems (1998)
17. Trivedi, K.S.: SPNP User's Manual Version 6.0, http://www.ee.duke.edu/~kst/software_packages.html

PCOW: Pipelining-Based COW Snapshot Method to Decrease First Write Penalty

Zhikun Wang, Dan Feng, Ke Zhou, and Fang Wang

College of Computer, Huazhong University of Science and Technology
Division of Data Storage System, Wuhan National Laboratory for Optoelectronics, China
zkwang@smail.hust.edu.cn, {dfeng,k.zhou}@hust.edu.cn,
fangwang@smail.hust.edu.cn

Abstract. While Copy-On-Write (COW) snapshot is the popular technique for online data protection, its first write request suffers from severe performance penalty because 3 I/Os are needed for each data block after creating snapshot. This paper proposes Pipelining-based COW (PCOW) method to minimize the snapshot impact on the first write request. When origin data is read from origin volume to a buffer queue, pending host write request can be serviced immediately. Origin data will be deferred to write to the snapshot volume in a background asynchronous thread. In order to demonstrate PCOW feasibility and efficiency, we have implemented both COW and PCOW in a standard iSCSI target as independent modules. We use popular benchmarks to quantitatively compare PCOW and COW techniques. Numerical results show that PCOW can effectively decrease first write penalty and improve performance.

1 Introduction

Most of the today's storage systems provide some kinds of snapshot facility to capture data as it appears at some point of time and use it for backup, recovery and other purposes like data mining and data cloning. A snapshot can be defined as a consistent point-in-time image of data [1]. Depending on the way snapshots are created, there are mainly three kinds of snapshots: Split-Mirroring, Copy-On-Write (COW) and Redirect-On-Write (ROW).

Since COW snapshot technique has the merits of least space occupation and fast creation speed, it has been widely used in various snapshot products such as EMC TimeFinder [3] and Microsoft VSS [4] etc. COW snapshot technique does not need to preserve any data at the time of the snapshot creation. Data blocks are copied from the origin data place to the snapshot data place as they are first written. Thus, only those data blocks which are changed after the creation of the snapshot need to be copied to the snapshot volume. This incremental data protection method will minimize the capacity consumption at the most.

For the first write to a data block in the origin volume, the COW snapshot technique generates 3 IO operations for the first write block [2] as shown in Figure 1: ① read the origin data block from the origin volume, ② write the origin data block to

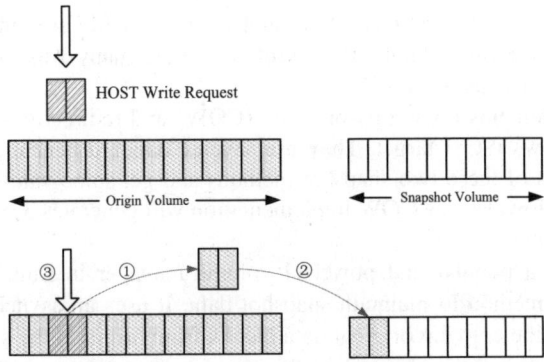

Fig. 1. Copy-On-Write Snapshot Procedure

the snapshot volume, and ③ write the host data in the origin volume. This strictly sequential "read-write-write" procedure will severely impact host write performance because of additional data copy cost.

By carefully analyzing the COW "read-write-write" procedure, we find that origin data and host data are written to different volumes and they have no data dependency. In order to minimize first write performance penalty, we propose a Pipelining-based COW (PCOW) snapshot method. When origin data is read from the origin volume to a buffer queue, pending host write request can be serviced immediately. Origin data would be deferred to be written to the snapshot volume in a background asynchronous thread.

In order to demonstrate PCOW feasibility and efficiency, we have designed and implemented both COW and PCOW in a standard iSCSI target software. Numerical results using popular benchmarks show that PCOW can substantially reduce host write response time and improve write throughput when compared to the COW snapshot approach.

The rest of this paper is organized as follows. In the next section, we describe background and related work. PCOW design and implementation issues are presented in section 3. Then we discuss performance evaluation in section 4. Section 5 summarizes our conclusions and presents future work.

2 Background and Related Work

Snapshot is a popular technique for online data protection and recovery. A good summary of various snapshot techniques could be found in [1]. A snapshot can be implemented at file system level or block device level and it has their own advantages and disadvantages.

At block device level, COW snapshot function is transparent to front-end application. There are many storage products such as EMC's TimeFinder [3], Microsoft's

VSS [4] and HDS's ShadowImage Snapshot [5] etc. At file system level, Snapshot function could have fine granularity control. There are many versioning file systems such as Elephant [6], and CVFS [7] etc.

Xiao [8] implements both copy-on-write (COW) and redirect-on-write (ROW) on their own windows iSCSI target. They use several standard benchmarks to compare the performances of these two snapshot methods and get some valuable performance characteristics. However, its COW implementation will generates 3 sequential I/Os on the first write request.

LVM2 [9] is a popular and powerful volume manager in Linux. It also adopts Copy-On-Write method to maintain snapshot data. It uses an asynchronous copying daemon handles the copying original data blocks from origin to the snapshot volume. Then the write request is performed on the origin volume. However, one major problem of LVM2 is that before a write is performed on the origin volume, origin data has to be copied to the snapshot volumes.

UNH iSCSI [10] is a widely used open source iSCSI software. It has both initiator and target packages. In order to demonstrate our proposed PCOW snapshot technique efficiency, we implement COW and PCOW snapshot methods as independent modules embedded in its target package.

3 PCOW Design and Implementation

This section presents PCOW design principles and implementation issues.

3.1 PCOW Design Principles

For the COW snapshot technique, first write request will wait until the origin data written to the snapshot volume. This will severely affect first write performance. The problem with COW algorithm is that it can not overlap writes of the host with writes of the origin data to the snapshot volume. Since these two writes have no dependency, we can service host write prior to snapshot data write to minimize host write request response time. When origin data is read from origin volume to a snapshot buffer queue, pending write requests can be written to the origin volume without waiting for origin data being written to the snapshot volume. We use an asynchronous low-priority snapshot write thread to write data in the snapshot buffer queue to the snapshot volume. The PCOW snapshot procedure is depicted in Table 1. PCOW does not eliminate writing origin data to snapshot volume but defers it to a later time.

3.2 PCOW Implementation Issues

COW snapshot procedure has been described in Fig.1. Based on the above PCOW design principles, we have implemented both COW and PCOW in UNH iSCSI target [10] as an independent module as shown in Fig.2. At the time when the snapshot is created, a small volume is allocated as a snapshot volume. The snapshot volume size can be configurable by user and the default size is 20% of the whole storage capacity.

Table 1. PCOW Snapshot Procedure

Host write thread	Snapshot Write thread
For each host write request to the origin volume 1. Determine whether or not the host request has been preserved before, if "yes" go to step 3; 2. Read origin data from the origin volume to a snapshot buffer queue; 3. Submit host write data to the origin volume; 4. Wait for the host write to complete. End	Repeat 1. Get a snapshot write request from the snapshot buffer queue head; 2. Submit the snapshot write request to the snapshot volume; 3. Wait for the snapshot write to complete. Until (the snapshot buffer queue is empty)

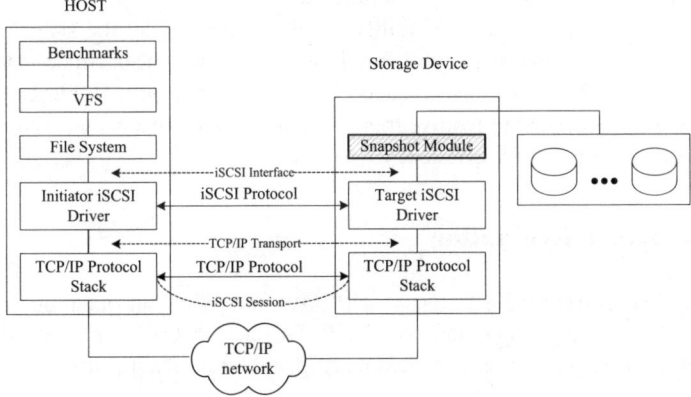

Fig. 2. Software Stack of Snapshot Implementation

For both COW and PCOW implementations, when there is a host write request, it should determine whether or not the data blocks have been preserved after creating the snapshot. We adopt hash table lookup method to facilitate this process. In order to simplify our implementation, the snapshot volume is managed using fixed data chunks referred as *snap_chunk*. Thus, all accesses to the data in the snapshot volume are done at the granularity of snap_chunk. The snap_chunk size is also a user configurable parameter and is sensitive to actual host write IO request size.

Depending on the snap_chunk size and the host write request start LBA and size, LBA alignment and data fragmentation may need to be done [8]. First, the write request is decomposed into several chunks at the granularity of the snap_chunk size. Then, for every small snap_chunk, we use its LBA as the key to look up the hash table. If the LBA cannot be found in the hash table, this indicates that this snap_chunk has not been preserved before. The origin data blocks should be read from the origin volume to the snapshot buffer queue. In addition, a new hash entry with this LBA as the key is inserted into the hash table. On the other hand, if the LBA is found in the hash table, this shows that this snap_chunk data has been preserved before and nothing needs to be done for it. After handling all chunks belonging to the host write request, the host write request can be written to the origin volume. Eventually, we can wakeup the low-priority snapshot write thread to eventually write snapshot data to the snapshot volume.

Since read requests will not change data blocks, COW and PCOW snapshot methods will not take any effect on reads operations. Our snapshot module will forward read requests directly to the origin volume.

In the COW algorithm, the storage controller never needs to buffer more than one request chunks per snapshot procedure. In the PCOW algorithm, however, the origin data must be buffered until it can be written to the snapshot volume in the background thread. The amount of memory needed for PCOW snapshot can be bounded by enforcing a limit on the number of buffers employed. In our implementation, the buffer number is 32. If no buffers are available, new snapshot process will be suspended until a buffer is freed by other snapshot process.

Another concern issue is the reliability problem. Because all the snapshot data are stored in the buffer queue, it is more fragile to the system crash. Since many storage products adopt NVRAM to ensure cache data consistent, we can allocate snapshot buffer pool from NVRAM to resolve this problem. In our experiment, we only use the RAM to demonstrate PCOW efficiency.

4 Performance Evaluation

In order to demonstrate the efficiency of PCOW, we carry out quantitative performance evaluations and comparisons of the COW and PCOW using popular benchmarks. This section presents experimental setup and numerical results.

4.1 Experimental Setup

Using our implementation described in the last section, we construct an initiator-target iSCSI prototype as shown in Fig.2. The hardware components are shown in Table 2. Two machines are interconnected using the Netcore 7016DNS Gigabit switch.

Table 2. The Platform for Performance Evaluation

Component	Description
CPU	Intel Pentium4 3GHz
Memory	512MB DDR
Mainboard	Supermicro X6DH8-XB
SATA HBA	HighPoint RocketRAID 1640
SATA Disk	Seagate ST3250823AS
NIC	Dual Broadcom BCM5721

We install Fedora 4 (Linux kernel 2.6.11) on the two machines. On the host server, the UNH iSCSI initiator [10] is installed without any modification. On the target storage machine, the modified UNH iSCSI target including snapshot function is installed. In order to void single disk bottleneck, we use linux software RAID to construct 8 SATA disk RAID0. Its chunk size is set to 64K which is the default chunk size of the software RAID. The snapshot volume size is the 20% of the whole RAID capacity.

4.2 Numerical Results and Discussions

Using our implementations and the experimental settings described in the previous sections, we use two popular benchmarks PostMark [11] and IoMeter [12] to quantitatively compare the write performance of NONE (no snapshot), COW and PCOW. In order to ensure that file system state does not affect the results, a new file system is created with mke2fs before each experiment.

PostMark was designed to measure the performance of a file system used for electronic mail, network news, and web based services [11]. It creates a large number of small files (message folders) that are constantly updated (as new mail messages arrive). PostMark can be configured in two ways [11]; the number of files to create and the total number of transactions to perform on this set of files. In our experiments we uses input 50K/50K, 50K/100K, 100K/100K and 100K/200K. Other parameters are using their default values. Snap_chunk size is 8K which is the average size of postmark requests.

Table 3. Running Time for Postmark Benchmark (second)

Input Size (#files / #transactions)	COW	PCOW	NONE
50K/50K	246	232	193
50K/100K	456	425	360
100K/100K	1246	1213	1190
100K/200K	2297	2289	2263

Table 3 shows the running time for postmark benchmark. We can find that the running time difference between NONE, COW and PCOW is not obvious. There are two major reasons for this phenomenon. First, postmark benchmark mainly tests metadata and small file requests which the write requests are not intensive. Secondly, the "write-back" buffer of UNH iSCSI target software will also alleviate snapshot impact on the write requests. COW and PCOW will only be executed when the write request data are flushed from write-back buffer to the origin volume.

In order to evaluate PCOW characteristic under write-intensive workload, we use IoMeter [12] benchmark. IoMeter is another popular benchmark that has been used extensively for basic evaluation of I/O subsystems. IoMeter has a configurable workload generator. The parameters are access pattern, mix of read and write operations, number of outstanding requests, and block size etc. Since we mainly concern the first write performance of COW and PCOW, we run IoMeter for two types of extreme workload: 100% sequential and 100% random write request.

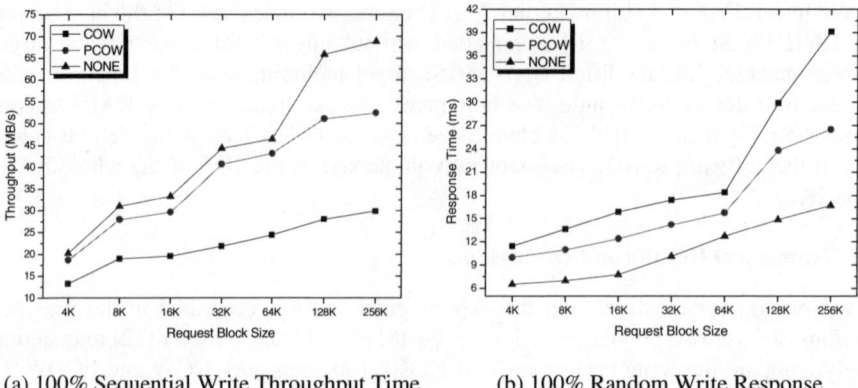

(a) 100% Sequential Write Throughput Time   (b) 100% Random Write Response

Fig. 3. IoMeter Write Performance with 16KB Snap_chunk Size

Fig.3 shows IoMeter write performance for NONE, COW and PCOW with 16KB snap_chunk size. The write request block size is from 4KB to 256KB, doubling it each time. The results reveal that PCOW can effectively decrease write response time and improve throughput, because it defers the snapshot data writes to a background thread. With the increase of the request block size, the performance gap between NONE with COW and PCOW is increasing. This is because the snap_chunk size is 16KB, when the request block size is larger than 16KB, COW and PCOW will decompose more snapshot chunks and increase snapshot overheads.

To further clarify the impact of different snap_chunk size on the snapshot performance, we use IoMeter to test 16KB sequential and 8KB random write performance with the snap_chunk size from 4KB to 64KB. The performance of snapshot is sensitive to its snap_chunk size and workload characteristics. For sequential write requests shown in Fig.4 (a), increasing snap_chunk size can improve both COW and PCOW

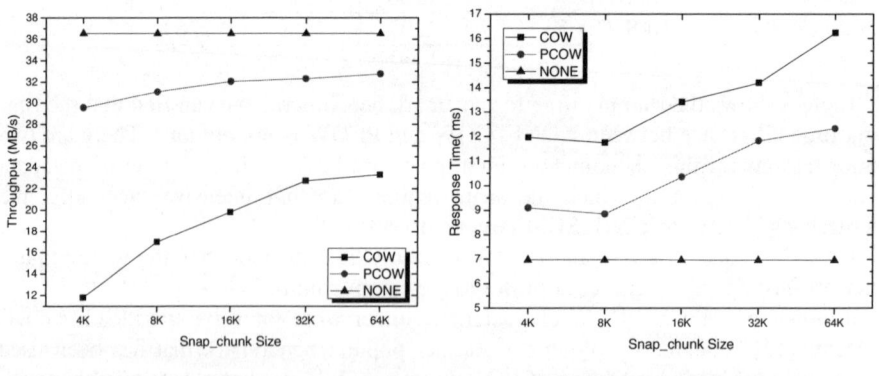

(a) 16KB Sequential Write Throughput Time   (b) 8KB Random Write Response

Fig. 4. IoMeter Write Performance with Different Snap_chunk Size

write throughput. Larger snap_chunk size can prefetch useful snapshot data to the snapshot volume and increase disk bandwidth utilization. COW will benefit more than PCOW from larger snap_chunk size. This is because COW snapshot data write is in the production time and larger snap_chunk size can avoid small snapshot data copy overhead.

But for random write requests shown in the Fig.4 (b), when the snap_chunk size is 8KB, which is equal to the random write request size, COW and PCOW will have the minimum response time. The reason is that smaller snap_chunk size will incur more snapshot data fragmentation and larger snap_chunk size will prefetch useless data, which increase disk request service time and reduce snapshot volume utilization. Therefore, it is better to set snap_chunk size to the average request size for the random writes.

5 Conclusions and Future Work

Snapshot is an important technique for the online data protection. While Copy-On-Write (COW) Snapshot is a popular technique because of its merits, it sustains bad first write performance for the additional data copy costs. In this paper, we propose a Pipelining-based COW (PCOW) snapshot technique to minimize the COW first write penalty. PCOW would defer the snapshot writes to a later time, thus it can decrease first write response time effectively. In order to demonstrate PCOW feasibility and efficiency, we have implemented both COW and PCOW as independent modules embedded in a standard iSCSI target. Extensive experiments have been carried out to quantitatively compare COW and PCOW performance. Numerical results show that PCOW can effectively decrease first write penalty and improve write performance.

In the continuing work, we are investigating using logging method to further enhance COW first write performance and reliability. Another possible optimization is using faster lookup methods such as radix-tree [13] or bloomfilter [14] to quickly determine whether the data chunk has been preserved before.

Acknowledgements

We would like to thank the anonymous reviewers for their helpful comments in reviewing this paper. This work is sponsored by the National Basic Research Program of China (973 Program) under Grant No.2004CB318201, National Science Foundation of China under Grant No.60503059, Wuhan Project under Grant No.200750730307 and Program for New Century Excellent Talents in University (NCET-04-0693).

References

1. Azagury, A., Factor, M.E., Satran, J., Micka, W.: Point-in-time copy: Yesterday, today and tomorrow. In: Proceedings of the 10th NASA Goddard, 19th IEEE Conference on Mass Storage Systems and Technologies (2002)
2. Duzy, G.: Match snaps to apps, Storage, Special Issue on Managing the information that drives the enterprise, pp. 46–52 (2005)

3. EMC Corp.: EMC TimeFinder Family,
   http://www.emc.com/products/software/timefinder.jsp
4. Sankaran, A., Guinn, K., Nguyen, D.: Volume Shadow Copy Service (2004),
   http://www.microsoft.com
5. Hitachi Ltd.: Hitachi ShadowImage implementation service (2001),
   http://www.hds.com/copy_on_write_snapshot_467_02.pdf
6. Santry, D.S., Feeley, M.J., Hutchinson, N.C., Veitch, A.C., Carton, R.W., Ofir, J.: Deciding when to forget in the Elephant file system. In: Proceedings of 17th ACM Symposium on Operating System Principles, Charleston, SC, pp. 110–123 (1999)
7. Soules, C.A.N., Goodson, G.R., Strunk, J.D., Ganger, G.R.: Metadata efficieny in versioning file systems. In: Proceedings of the 2nd USENIX Conference on File and Storage Technologies, San Francisco, CA, pp. 43–58 (2003)
8. Xiao, W., Liu, Y., Yang, Q., Ren, J., Xie, C.: Implementation and Performance Evaluation of Two Snapshot Methods on iSCSI Target Storages. In: Proceedings of NASA/IEEE Conference on Mass Storage Systems and Technologies, College Park, Maryland (2006)
9. Mauelshagen, H.: Logical Volume Manager (LVM2) (2004)
10. UNH-iSCSI Initiator and Target for Linux, http://unh-iscsi.sourceforge.net
11. Katcher, J.: PostMark: a new file system benchmark. Technical report TR3022. Network Appliance (1997)
12. IoMeter benchmark (version 2006.07.27), http://sourceforge.net/projects/Iometer/
13. Warfield, A., Ross, R., Fraser, K., Limpach, C., Steven, H.: Parallax: Managing Storage for a Million Machines. In: Proceedings of the 10th USENIX Workshop on Hot Topics in Operating Systems, Santa Fe, NM, pp. 1–11 (2005)
14. Bloom, B.: Space/time trade-offs in hashing coding with allowable errors. Communication of the ACM 13(7), 422–426 (1970)

A Component-Based Analytical Performance Model of IP-Based SAN

Min Wang[1,2], Wei Xu[1,2], and Lu Xu[1]

[1] Institute of Computing Technology, Chinese Academy of Sciences, Beijing 100080
[2] Graduate School of the Chinese Academy of Science, Beijing 100039
{wangmin,xuwei,xulu}@ict.ac.cn

Abstract. In this paper we propose a component-based analytical performance model for IP-based SAN. This model evaluates and analyzes the behavior of IP network, cache, RAID and disks under multiple synchronous I/O workloads by using closed queueing networks. The theoretical results are compared with the results from a real IP-based SAN using a variety of synthetic workloads. These experiments prove that the component-based method is an appropriate way to build performance model for a complex storage system. Using the model, we can find out that the bottleneck of SAN performance is network or storage node under different workloads or applications. We also identify areas for future research in the performance analysis of real IP-based SAN.

1 Introduction

In recent years there have been more and more companies whose important data are stored at shared storage environment such as storage area network (SAN). Fiber Channel SAN is the high-speed storage option at a top dollar price. Another SAN topology, called an IP-based SAN, becomes an appropriate solution for business critical IT environments. The IP-based SAN runs on a TCP/IP network through iSCSI or ENBD or NBD protocol. Widespread experience and familiarity with IP networks facilitate easy deployment of such technology, IP-based SAN is also more cost-effective than FC SAN. It therefore becomes an interesting issue to investigate IP-based SAN.

On the other hand, Enterprise-scale storage systems such as IP-based SAN are extremely difficult to manage due to the size of these systems and uncertain workload behaviors. Especially, IP-based SAN has more enormous amount of streams because it has more potential internet users. As a result, many automatic storage management systems such as Minerva [1] and Hippodrome [2] have appeared. In order to perform automatic management and capacity planning for IP-based SAN, it is necessary to develop performance models of IP-based SAN and predict its performance under variety workloads. However, efforts to analyze the total system performance of an IP-based SAN are still limited [3]. Since performance prediction is required to be on-line or quick in complex automatic storage management systems, we develop an analytic performance model for IP-based SAN because analytic performance models are less expensive and faster than simulation models [5].

We use a component-based method to build the entire IP-based SAN analytical performance model. We model these key components within IP-based SAN individually and validate these component models and composing them to give an entire IP-based SAN performance model. We also validate the entire IP-based SAN performance model against a real IP-based SAN system. The method has some advantages: (1) the accuracy of each component model is easy to be controlled and a single component model is easy to be modified and improved. Thus the accuracy of the entire IP-based SAN model can be guaranteed, (2) modifying and replacing a component model does not impact the other component models. Therefore our IP-based SAN model can adapt to a broader SAN structure and configuration. We can model the relatively simple components for the first step and model the more complex components in the future.

We consider our models based on the context of commodity IP-based SAN. We use commodity PCs with several disks as storage nodes and a Gigabit Ethernet network as the storage network. On the application server side we use a variety of synthetic workloads to simulate multiple synchronous I/O streams. Extensive measurements of different UNIX systems show that synchronous requests account for 51-74% of the total I/O workload on a system [14]. Other applications that generate synchronous requests are multimedia applications, large-scale scientific computations and database management systems. The key components within IP-based SAN that we extract are IP network, memory cache, RAID and disks. The other components are implicitly captured in those key component models. All models describe the behavior of the corresponding component under multiple synchronous I/O streams. For the length limitations of this paper, we just list the validation results of the entire IP-based SAN model against a real systems. As an application example, we analyzed the bottleneck of IP-based SAN under different workloads by using the entire IP-based SAN performance model.

The rest of the paper is organized as follows: Section 2 presents related work. Section 3 describes the architecture of our simplified IP-based SAN and the entire IP-based SAN model. Section 4 presents the key component models. Section 5 shows the entire model validation results. Section 6 shows the bottleneck of IP-based SAN under different workloads. The conclusion and potential future research are presented in section 7.

2 Related Work

There are few performance models for entire SAN. Zhu [3] provides a simple FC (Fiber Channel) SAN analytical model under Poisson streams using open queueing network. They do not provide detailed and adequate result data for validation. Chao [9] presents a MMQ model for SAN performance analyzing but does not have enough experiment for validation either. Nava [11] presents a component-based simulation performance model for SAN.

Most other related analytical models developed are for disk array or for IP-based SAN network connection. Shriver [4] has developed an analytic model for modern disk drives that do readahead and request reordering. Lee and katz [8] present a queueing model of a non-redundant array of disks. Merchant and Yu [12,13] present a number of queueing models for RAIDs. Varki and Merchant [5,10] have developed a performance model for a real disk array in detail. Gauger [7] presents an analytical model for iSCSI protocol.

Since our goal is to build the entire IP-based SAN model, we adopt relatively concise and feasible method to build component models in order to reduce complexity in comparison to [5,10]. For example, our analysis focus for RAID is on modeling striping and the model can be used for linux software RAID configuration. Comparing with the method in [8], we do not limit that an array request is less than the size of one stripe and the disk request size is equal to the stripe unit. Our cache model appears to be more concise and easier to validate. To our knowledge, this is the first analytical model for IP-based SAN.

3 IP-Based SAN Performance Model

We use a simple configuration of multiple hosts sharing a single storage system through an IP network. There are numerous IP-based SAN architectures designed for different applications, but it is essential that the shared storage is accessed over a network interconnecting the hosts to the shared storage node. Even so, a real IP-based SAN system is still a very complex system made up of hosts that produce IO requests, storage network connection equipment, and storage system that consists of memory cache, RAID device, disks and buses. If an analytical IP-based SAN system performance model explicitly models all these components, it would also be very complex. Hence, we model IP-based SAN by identifying the key components and explicitly modeling them firstly. The effects of all other components are implicitly captured in the service times of the explicitly modeled components. For example, the effect of network connection equipment is incorporated in the network service time, and the bus transfer time and disk caching effect is incorporated in the disk service time. The key components that we extract are network, cache, RAID and disks. The four components have different behaviors and important effect on an IP-based SAN system.

We assume that the jobs accessing the IP-based SAN generate synchronous I/O requests. Then we use a closed queueing network model to analyze the performance of the IP-based SAN system with multiple synchronous I/O streams. Each stream issues an I/O request, once the request is completed, a new request is generated and issued to the IP-based SAN immediately.

The key characteristics of an I/O stream are the request size (*reqsize*), the ratio of read account for the total requests (*rw*), and the spatial distribution of request address. The spatial distribution of request address of a workload stream is defined by P_r, which is the ratio of random requests account for the total requests, and P_s, which is the ratio of sequential requests account for the total requests, and P_l, which is the ratio of locality requests account for the total requests. A locality request begins at some short distance away from the previous request's starting address. The mean number of sequential requests in a run is defined by *run_count*, and the number of bytes between two requests accessing to the same block is defined by *res_dis*. The sequentiality describes the spatial locality of workload and the locality captures the temporal locality of workload.

Table 1. Workload Characterization

Parameters	Description
m	Number of I/O workload streams
rw	Percent of reads in all requests
reqsize	Mean request size
P_r	Percent of random requests in all requests
P_s	Percent of sequential requests in all requests
P_l	Percent of locality requests in all requests
Run_count	Mean number of sequential requests per run
Res_dis	Mean distance between locality requests

As shows in figure 1, m application servers send IO request to storage server (or storage node) through IP network. The components of storage node are memory cache, RAID controller and n disks.

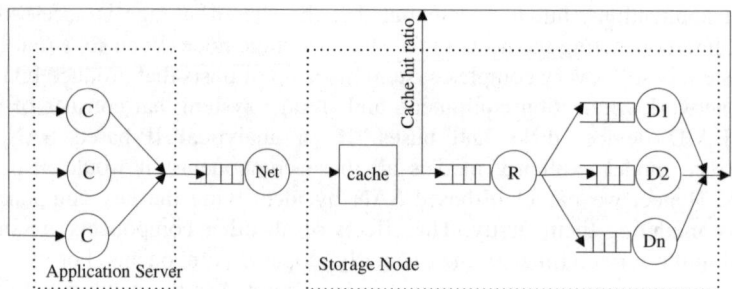

Fig. 1. Closed queueing network model of IP-based SAN

We analyze the behavior of IP-based SAN when the m synchronous I/O requests cycle among hosts, network, cache, RAID and disks. The network is modeled by a single queueing server. After a request is transmitted by the network, it is submitted to the cache. If data that the request accesses are found in the cache (cache hit), the storage system signals service completion. Otherwise, the request is forwarded to the RAID controller with probability P_{cmiss} (cache miss probability). The RAID controller and the disks are modeled by a fork-join queue network. The disks are represented by service centers of this fork-join queue. Table 2 shows the important configuration parameters of the four components of the IP-based SAN. We can derive the total response time of a request accessing the IP-based SAN R_{SAN} by using MVA technique. The MVA technique is the standard technique used to evaluate mean performance measures of closed parallel queueing networks. The total throughput (MBPS) is

$$TH_{SAN} = m \cdot reqsize / R_{SAN} \qquad (1)$$

Our IP-based SAN model is validated by comparing with a real IP-based SAN system. A limitation of this work is that the model is validated only for read workloads.

Table 2. The system parameters for IP-based SAN

Parameter	Description
RTT	Round-trip time of IP network
B	The bandwidth of IP network
T_{think}	Mean time spent by a job at its application server
Cache size	Size of memory cache
Cache line size	The unit of cache space allocation/replacement
Ra_count	Cache read ahead count
RAID controller time	The mean service time of RAID controller
SU	Size of a stripe unit
N	Number of disks in RAID
T_{pos}	Disk position time
B_{tr}	Disk transfer time per size unit

4 Component Model

In this section, we present the key component models: network model, Cache model, RAID model and disk model.

4.1 Network Model

In IP-based SAN environment hosts get access to storage node through IP network storage protocol (for example iSCSI, HyperSCSI, ENBD, NBD). Though IDC views iSCSI as the fastest-growing area of the storage market for the last year, NBD (Network Block Device) is still a convenient choice to build a IP-based SAN within local network.. We model the NBD protocol in the similar way that the iSCSI protocol has been modeled in [7]. We validate the model against real systems.

NBD is a block-level storage protocol that makes a remote storage device on a different machine act as though it were a local disk on local machine. There are two parts: NBD client and NBD server. After a data transmission connection has built from the client to the server, NBD requests can begin to send. The service time is the sum of RTT (round-trip time), the time for data transmit T_{trans}, the time for processing the request in the server T_{proc}, and the system delay T_{think}

$$T_{NBD} = RTT + T_{tran} + T_{proc} + T_{think} = RTT + \frac{reqsize}{B} + T_{proc} + T_{think} \quad (2)$$

where B is the bandwidth of the IP network. We validate the model against gibabit network and the relative error is within 13.6%.

4.2 Cache Model

When a request arrives at the cache, there are three cache behaviors: (1) cache miss. Data accessed by the request is not in cache and the request will be transmitted to storage device. (2) reference hit. The request had been referenced in the past and the request's data are still in the cache. (3) read ahead hit. The request's data are in the cache because of read ahead. We consider the LRU replacement policy because it is one of the most commonly used replacement policy.

We assume that the number of requests is N_{req} and the number of requests missed is N_{miss}. N_r, N_l, N_s is respectively the number of random requests, sequential requests and locality requests. The cache miss probability can be deduced as

$$P_{cmiss} = \frac{N_{miss}}{N_{req}} = \frac{N_r + N_l \cdot P_{l\_miss} + N_s \cdot P_{s\_miss}}{N_{req}} = P_r + P_l \times P_{l\_miss} + P_s \times P_{s\_miss} \quad (3)$$

Here, P_{l_miss} is the probability that the locality request is missed, and P_{s_miss} is the probability that the sequential request is missed.

Due to LRU replacement policy, a cache reference miss on a locality request occurs when *ref_dis* is greater than the amount of the cache line, that is

$$p_{l\_miss} = P\left\{ref\_dis > \frac{cache\_size}{line\_size}\right\} \quad (4)$$

The number of requests read-ahead, *ra_count*, is equal to the amount of data read-ahead divided by request size. A sequential run length is represented as *run_count*. Then the probability that the sequential request is missed can be written as

$$P_{s\_miss} = \frac{1}{\min\{run\_count, ra\_count\}} \quad (5)$$

We validated cache reference hit and cache read ahead hit respectively by simulation experiments. The relative errors for cache reference hit are less than 1.5%, while the relative errors for cache read ahead hit are within 0.4%.

4.3 RAID Model

RAID provides improved I/O performance by striping data across multiple disks in parallel. We primarily focus on modeling striping. Redundancy (e.g. mirroring and parity) that protects data from losing due to RAID failure is not taken into consideration in this paper because some articles have already discussed it specifically. Similar to [8], our analytic model for RAID can also be used to model RAID0 and reads for RAID5 using the left-symmetric parity placement. However, our model does not have the assumption that an array request size should be less than or equal to the full stripe size and disk sub-request size needs be a multiple of stripe units.

The fork-join model is used to analyze the RAID performance of parallel disks. The response time of a RAID request begins at the time that the first sub-request accessing to a disk is serviced and ends at the time that the last sub-request is completed, that is, it is equal to the time of a single service node and multiple disk synchronization. We use the same approximate method as [8] to analyze the closed fork-join model for multiple synchronous I/O streams.

Two important RAID configuration parameters are the stripe unit size (SU) and the number of disks (N). We assume that the RAID controller service time is close to 0 and the assumption can be used for linux software RAID configuration. We represent the probability of an array request accessing a given disk, then

$$p = \min(\lceil \frac{reqsize}{SU} \rceil, N)/N \qquad (6)$$

Here, the symbol $\lceil a \rceil$ represents the minimal integer that is greater than a. Then the expected array response time can be expressed as

$$E(R_{array}) = [(m'-1)p+1]E(s) \qquad (7)$$

Here, $E(s)$ is the disk service time, m' is the number of array requests. The RAID model could be replaced by the more accurate RAID model that incorporates other RAID features such as controller optimizations.

4.4 Disk Service Time

The disk service time consists of seek time, rotational latency and transfer time. The sum of seek time and rotational latency is the disk positioning time. Disk transfer time is equal to the disk sub-request size divided by the disk transfer rate. We analyze the disk request size and the disk positioning time.

To compute the disk transfer time, the disk request size should be calculated. When array request size is greater than the full stripe size, some disks will be accessed by disk request that is greater than one stripe unit. The maximum disk request can be calculated by a ladder function

$$diskreq_{max} = \begin{cases} size + k(1-N) \bullet SU & kN \bullet SU \leq size < (kN+1) \bullet SU \\ (k+1) \bullet SU & (kN+1) \bullet SU \leq size \leq (k+1)N \bullet SU \end{cases} \qquad (8)$$

Here, size is RAID request size , k=0,1,2...

By tracing in our experiments, we have found in our experiments that the performance is affected by the fact that the start address of the array request is not aligned with stripe unit boundary. Not aligned will add the number of the involved disk and reduce the mean disk request size. We introduce an amendatory coefficient C_a. Due to the length limitation, the computation of C_a will be presented in another paper separately.

We model disk positioning time according to the method in [5] for the disk scheduling policies such as SCAN. Here the effect of on-board caches in disk drivers for sequential I/O streams is assumed to be neglectable because there are quite a number of I/O streams while the cache is relatively small. We derive the equation for the disk positioning time as

$$T_{pos} = a + b/\sqrt{1 + m \times p} \qquad (9)$$

where a and b are two parameters related to the disk. $m' \times p$ is the disk queue length. m' is the number of requests in the disk array. We use the MVA technique to calculate the m'.

The disk service time can be represented as

$$E(s) = T_{pos} + C_a \cdot diskreq_{max} / B_{tr} \tag{10}$$

Where B_{tr} is the disk transfer rate.

5 Empirical Validation

We validated the accuracy of our analytical model by comparing the predicted throughput (MBPS) with measured values for a variety of workloads running against an real IP-based SAN. The IP-based SAN used in our experiments has 4 disks (Maxtor diamond max_plus_9, each 160GB in size), linux software RAID (raid 0, kernel 2.6.18), 512M memory cache, and Gigabit Ethernet and NBD 2.9.6. The RAID stripe unit size is 64KB and the cache line size is 4KB. The hosts accessing the SAN was running linux kernel 2.6.18 as its operating system.

In our validation experiments, we used synthetic workloads to simulate multiple synchronous streams. These streams have the same characteristics. Request sizes of these streams range from 4KB to 1024 KB and the degree of randomness includes 0.0, 0.2, 0.5, 0.8 and 1.0. The other requests are sequential and locality ones and P_l is

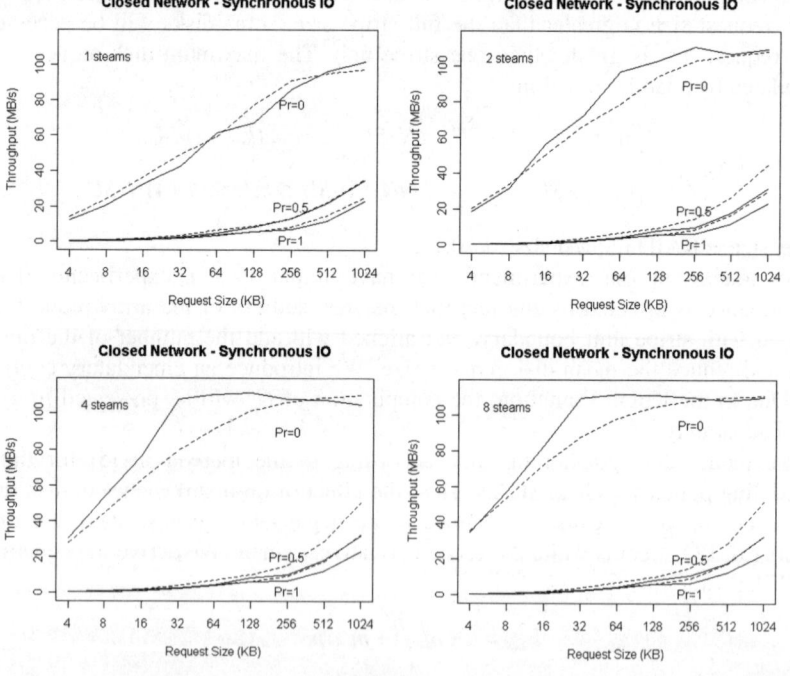

Fig. 2. Results from validating the SAN throughput model for the real IP-based SAN configuration. In the legend, solid lines denote the measured throughput and dashed lines denote the throughput from our model.

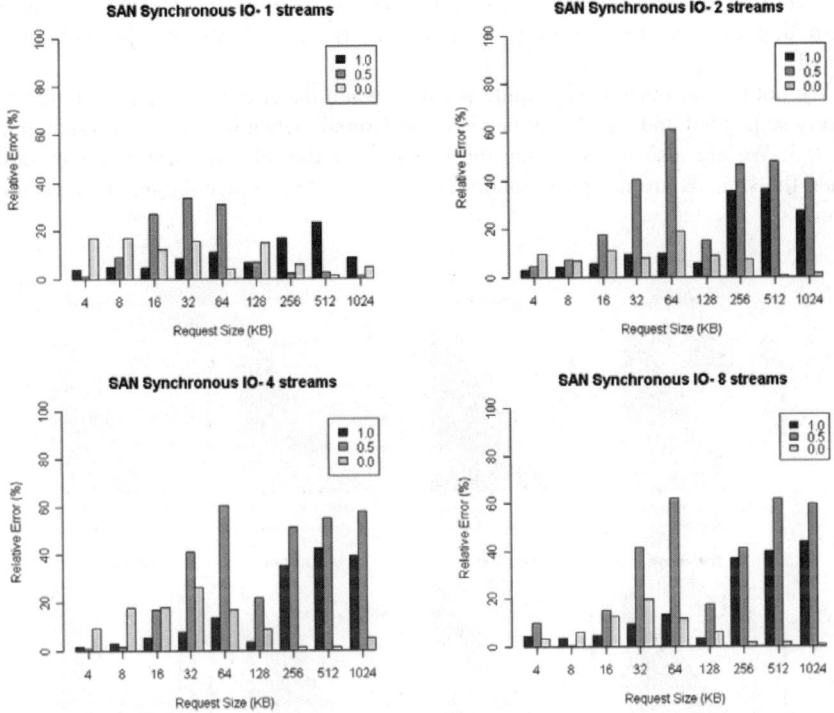

Fig. 3. Relative error in the model for the IP-based SAN with 1, 2, 4, 8 synchronous streams and Pr is equal to 1.0, 0.5, 0.0 respectively

always equal to P_s. The number of streams is 1, 2, 4, and 8. we collected the traces of all workload execution at the device driver level and analyzed the trace to compute the performance.

Table 3 contains the parameters of system configuration for our model of the IP-based SAN. Figure 2 presents the measured throughput from the IP-based SAN and the predicted throughput from the model for 1, 2, 4, and 8 synchronous read workloads for a variety of request sizes and degree of randomness. Figure 3 presents the relative error. Our results indicate that the average accruacies of our model are 10.8%, 18%, 20.8%, 19.6% for 1, 2, 4, 8 synchronous read workloads respectively. Although the maximum relative error was higher, up to 60% for multiple synchronous workloads on several points, most of the model predictions were within 40% of the

Table 3. The system configuration for our IP-based SAN

Parameter	value	Parameter	value	Parameter	value
$B(10^6 bits/s)$	935	T_{think} (ms)	0.03	Raid disk num	4
RTT (ms)	0.21	Ra_count	3	a (Disk)	5.432
Cache size(MB)	512	Raid control time	0	b (Disk)	3.773
Line size (KB)	4	Raid SU (KB)	64	B_{tr} (MB/s)	57.109

measured throughput. We believe that this is an encouraging and acceptable result for predicting the performance of so complicated IP-based SAN by our prelimimary model.

We notice that our model is quite accurate when the streams are purely random or purely sequential and our model becomes pessimistic when the degree of randomness are 0.5. We are also investigating the reason why the relative error becomes larger when the streams are not purly random or sequential to reduce the maximal relaitive error.

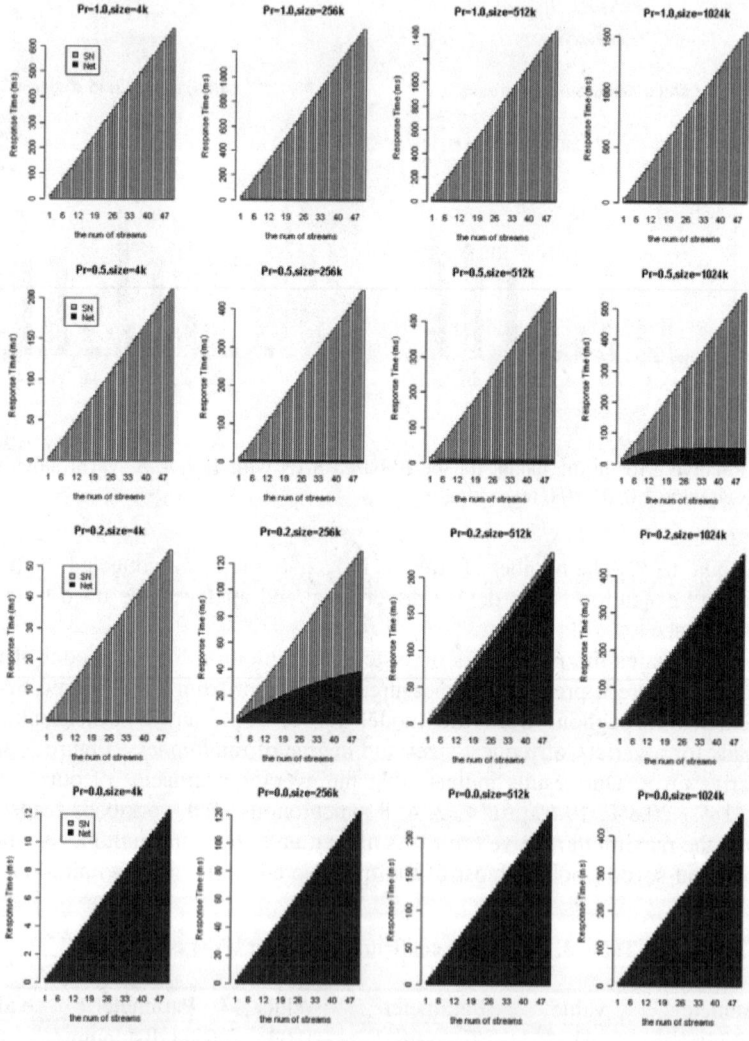

Fig. 4. Analyzing the bottleneck of IP-based SAN by comparing the response time of network and storage node under different workloads

6 The Bottleneck of IP-Based SAN

We can find out the bottleneck of IP-based SAN under different workloads by using our analytical model. As an example, we have analyzed which of the network and storage node becomes the bottleneck of the IP-based SAN under a variety of workloads. Other components such as cache or RAID can alos be considered to be the potential fine-grained bottleneck.

As shows in figure 4, we presernt that the response time of the network and storage node (SN) respectively under 1 to 50 synchronous streams with request size ranging from 4k to 1M, and P_r ranging from 1.0 to 0.0. The gray part bar reprents the response time of SN and the black one reprents the response time of network. The whole bar denotes the response time of the IP-based SAN. If the response time of one component is much bigger than the one of another, the component could be believed to be the bottleneck of the IP-based SAN under that kind of workload because an request will spend most time in the component.

Our model inputs are the same to the previous validation experiments. We can draw some conclusions by observe from these legends:

1. Under purely random I/O streams, storage node must be the bottleneck in the IP-based SAN.
2. Under purely sequetial I/O streams, network will be the bottleneck.
3. When $0< P_r <1$, storage node will become the bottleneck under I/O streams with request sizes are small, while network will be the bottleneck under streams with big I/O requests. The bottleneck transfers from storage node to network as request size is increasing.

7 Conclusions

We have presented an analytical performance model of IP-based SAN under mutiple synchronous workloads by using closed queueing network model and MVA analyzing technique, and compared the model's predictions with measurements taken on a real IP-based SAN. To our knowledge, this is the first analytical model for IP-based SAN validated against a real system. We use component-based method to build the key components of the IP-based SAN, and the key components include network, cache, RAID and disks. The accurary for the model are quite encouraging and acceptable for such an complicated storage system: although there were corner cases where the relative error is up to 60%, the most relative error were within 40% and 20% on the average. We have analyzed the bottleneck in the IP-based SAN under different workloads and drawn some useful conclusions for storage system designers and administrators.

We found that the accurary for the model are better under purely random or purely sequential workloads than under mixed workloads. We are investigating the reasons. We have not analyzed the behavior of IP-based SAN under write workloads. This is our another further work.

References

1. Alvarez, G.A., Borowsky, E., Go, S., Romer, T.H., BecherSzendy, R., Golding, R., Merchant, A., Spasojevic, M., Veitch, A., Wilkes, J.: MINERVA: an automated resource provisioning tool for large-scale storage systems. ACM Transcations on Computer Systems 19, 483–518 (2001)
2. Anderson, E., Hobbs, M., Keeton, K., Spence, S., Uysal, M., Veitch, A.: Hippodrome: running circles around storage administration. In: USENIX Conference on File and Storage Technology (FAST 2002), Berkeley, California, pp. 175–188 (2002)
3. Zhu, Y.L., Zhu, S.Y., Xiong, H.: Performance Analysis and Testing of the Storage Area Network. In: Proceedings of 10th NASA Goddard Conference on Mass Storage Systems and Technologies, Maryland, pp. 108–120 (2002)
4. Shriver, E., Merchant, A., Wilkes, J.: An analytic behavior model for disk drives with readahead caches and request reordering. In: Proceedings of ACM SIGMETRICS Conference on Measurement and Modeling of Computer Systems, Ontario, Canada, pp. 182–191 (1998)
5. Varki, E., Merchant, A., Xu, J., Qiu, X.: Issues and challenges in the performance analysis of real disk arrays. IEEE Transactions on Parallel and Distributed Systems 15, 559–574 (2004)
6. Uysal, M., Alvarez, G.A., Merchant, A.: A modular, analytical throughput model for modern disk arrays. In: The 9th International Workshop on Modeling, Analysis and Simulation of Computer and Telecommunication Systems, Cincinnati Ohio, pp. 183–192 (2001)
7. Gauger, C.M., Kohn, M., Gunreben, S., Sass, D., Perez, S.G.: Modeling and performance evaluation of iSCSI storage area networks over TCP/IP-based MAN and WAN networks. In: 2nd international conference on broadband networks, Boston, USA, pp. 850–858 (2005)
8. Lee, E.K., Katz, R.H.: An analytic performance model of disk arrays. In: Proceedings of the ACM SIGMETRICS conference on measurement and modeling of computer systems, Santa Clara California, pp. 98–109 (1993)
9. Li, C., Zhou, L.-z., Xing, C.-x.: Using MMQ model for performance simulation of storage area network. In: 21st international conference on data engineering, Tokyo, Japan, pp. 1269-1272 (2005)
10. Varki, E., Merchant, A., Xu, J., Qiu, X.: An integrated performance model of disk arrays. In: The 11th International Workshop on Modeling, Analysis and Simulation of Computer Telecommunications Systems, Orlando, Florida, pp. 296–305 (2003)
11. Aizikowitz, N., Glikson, A., Landau, A., Mendelson, B., Sandbank, T.: Component-based performance modeling of a storage area network. In: Proceedings of the 2005 winter simulation conference, Florida, USA, pp. 2417–2427 (2005)
12. Merchant, A., Yu, P.S.: Analytic modeling and comparisons of striping strategies for replicated disk arrays. IEEE transaction on computers 144, 419–433 (1995)
13. Merchant, A., Yu, P.S.: Analytic modeling of clustered RAID with Mapping based on nearly random permutation. IEEE transaction on computers 45, 367–373 (1996)
14. Ruemmler, C., Wilkes, J.: UNIX disk access patterns. In: Winter USENIX Conference, San Diego, California, pp. 405–420 (1993)

QCast: A QoS-Aware Peer-to-Peer Streaming System with DHT-Based Multicast[*]

Zhinuan Cai[1] and Xiaola Lin[1,2]

[1] School of Information Science and Technology, Sun Yat-sen University
Guangzhou 510275, China
caizhn@mail2.sysu.edu.cn, linxl@mail.sysu.edu.cn
[2] Key Laboratory of Digital Life (Sun Yat-sen University), Ministry of Eduction
Guangzhou 510275, China

Abstract. In this paper, we propose QCast, a DHT-based QoS-aware P2P streaming system. Nodes first self-organize into a DHT overlay. A simple and effective method is used to accommodate as many nodes into the distribution trees as possible. Also, we use an ID assignment method based on the QoS requirements of nodes and a buffering technology to provide QoS support. We show on the example of Pastry how to implement such a QoS-aware P2P streaming system. Simulation shows that most of the end-to-end paths in the multicast trees fulfill the bandwidth QoS requirements in this system, and the average packet loss rate is reduced effectively, both of which are usually not the cases for traditional P2P streaming systems.

1 Introduction

Peer-to-Peer (P2P) systems have emerged as a popular paradigm for providing large-scale multimedia streaming dissemination over the Internet. Usually there are two basic approaches to organizing multicast groups in P2P streaming systems. One is to make all members self-organize into a group according to some kind of topology (e.g., tree or mesh), the other is based on distributed hash table (DHT) infrastructure. In the first approach, all members need to locate upstream nodes and assume links maintenance [8] [16]. While in the second approach, these are done by the DHT and all end-to-end paths from receiving nodes to the source nodes automatically form a tree topology. Compared to the first approach, the main advantage of the DHT-based approach is that it can easily organize the multicast group relying on the DHT's routing and failure recovery functions, and does not need to handle network dynamics and maintain neighbor sets. Now developing multicast based on DHTs are popular solutions for large-scale peer-to-peer streaming.

DHT has become an appealing scheme for multicast, a number of projects have been or are being using this technique (e.g., Scribe [2], SplitStream [11], MOOD

---

[*] This work was supported in part by NSFC under Projects 60773199, U0735001, and 985 II fund under Project 3171310.

[18]). Some of them consider the network locality; some of them consider peers' capacities. However, they are insufficient in considering how to accommodate as many nodes into the p2p streaming system as possible while providing Quality of Service (QoS) support.

In this paper, we propose QCast, a DHT-based QoS-aware P2P steaming system. Nodes self-organized into a DHT overlay. We use a simple and effective method to accommodate as many nodes into the distribution trees as possible. We also use an ID assignment method based on the QoS requirements of nodes and a buffering technology to enable QoS multicast in our P2P streaming system. We show on the example of Pastry how to implement such a QoS aware P2P streaming system.

The rest of this paper is organized as follows. First we review the related work in Section 2. Then we detail our design of QCast in Section 3 and evaluate its improvements by comparing Scribe in section 4. We conclude the whole paper with Section 5.

2 Related Work

Many P2P architectures [1], [5], [6], [7] and overlay multicast systems [2], [9], [10], [11] have been proposed in recent years. Also mechanisms on how to support QoS for specific P2P networks have been proposed in [12], [13], [14], [15]. Pastry [1] is a scalable distributed object location and routing substrate for P2P applications, and we will build QCast on top of it. Scribe [2] is an overlay group communication infrastructure, which also builds on top of Pastry. Scribe is fault-tolerant and decentralized, it supports large groups, but only provides best-effort reliability guarantees. We will evaluate QCast's improvements by comparing Scribe. Pastry and Scribe will be introduced in section 2.1 and section 2.2, respectively. In section 2.3, we will introduce a QoS enabled multicast for structured P2P networks [3], which is proposed by Marc Brogle et al. We will improve this method for providing QoS support in QCast.

2.1 Pastry

Pastry [1] is a generic P2P object location and routing substrate. It is decentralized, fault-resilient, and scalable. In Pastry, each node is assigned a 128-bit identifier. This nodeId is assigned randomly to nodes when joining the system. The nodeIds are uniformly distributed in the 128-bit nodeId space. As a consequence, the QoS requirements are not taken into account for the choices of the nodeIds.

In Pastry, each node maintains a routing table, which is composed of a number of rows. Each row contains several entries. The entries of row i point to other nodes which share the same i initial digits of the nodeId with the local node. Of all the possible nodes for each entry, the one closest to the current node is chosen, according to some metric such as IP routing hops. Additionally, each node maintains two lists known as the leaf set and the neighborhood set of that node. Both the leaf set and the neighborhood set contain numerically closest nodes currently present in the Pastry network. The leaf set consists of $L/2$ entries for the larger and $L/2$ entries for the lower nodeIds, while the neighborhood set contains M entries for the closest nodes. L and M might be, for instance, 2^b. In each routing step, the locality is taken into account by choosing the closest node among all the candidates for an entry in the routing table. When a node receives a message, it sends the message to the node whose ID has a longer shared prefix with the destination ID than itself. If such node does not exist (that means such a node can not be determined from the sender's routing table), the message would be sent to a node whose ID is numerically closer to the destination ID. This node can be found in the leaf set of the current node. Totally speaking, the average steps of routing $Z < \lceil \log_{2^b} N \rceil$, where N is the amount of nodes in the Pastry network and b is typically a parameter with the value 4.

2.2 Scribe

Scribe [2], which is a system for multicasting messages to a group of Pastry nodes, is close in scope and capabilities to our desired system QCast. Both of them build on top of Pastry. Scribe uses the publish/subscribe approach, where any node can create a multicast group and any other node can later join that group. In each multicast group, there exists a topic and a root node. The root node, whose ID is numerically closest to the topic's ID, is designated to disseminate multicast data of that topic. The multicast tree of scribe is built using a scheme similar to reverse-path-forwarding. A scribe node that wishes to join a group sends a join message for the group's topic-ID. As this is routed by Scribe, each node it passes records the previous node in the route in its child table for that group, thus becoming a forwarder of the group. If this forwarder is not a member of that group, it will also send a join message to the same topic. This process is repeated until a node which has already joined the topic or the root node of the topic is reached. Then the multicast data is disseminated from the root node towards all the leave nodes by following all reverse-paths. Scribe is fault-tolerant, it supports large groups, but only provides best-effort reliability guarantees for the multicast data.

2.3 Overlay Multicast Quality of Service

Brogle et al. propose OM-QoS (Overlay Multicast Quality of Service), a method that aims to build a framework for introducing QoS to ALMs in structured P2P networks. The basic idea of OM-QoS are (1) The root of the multicast tree must be the node with the highest QoS requirement, and (2) Each child node can only have a smaller or equal QoS requirement than its parent node. In other words, each end-to-end path from the root node to a leaf node in the multicast tree has to have a monotonically decreasing QoS requirement [3].

However, Brogle's scheme is designed for a single source and therefore not suitable for any source multicast applications. In this paper, we will improve this method to build a multi source multicast p2p streaming application with QoS guarantee.

3 QCast Architecture

In our design, nodes in QCast first self-organize into a DHT overlay, we will build it on top of Pastry. In order to accommodate as many nodes into QCast as possible while providing QoS support, a simple and effective joining algorithm is used. At the same time, we use an ID assignment method based on the QoS requirements of nodes to enforce QoS-aware multicast tree construction. We also use a buffering technology to reduce package loss rate.

3.1 Joining

One important thing of a P2P streaming system is being able to accommodate as many nodes into the multicast trees as possible. Also, in a P2P streaming system, the joining algorithm should not put the source node under unnecessarily high network load. It should be able to handle joins which laugh from any node, not exclusively the source node. To facilitate this, we exploit Pastry's joining and routing functions in QCast. But before joining, some factors should be considered, such as a node's willingness to accept a new child, latency, etc.

In a peer-to-peer system based on DHT, nodes will accumulate knowledge about the layout of the overlay. For example, in Pastry, each node maintains a list of numerically closest nodes (IDs and IP addresses) with 1/2 entries for the larger and 1/2 entries for the lower IDs. Thus the node that wishes to join the multicast group can find more nodes when given a starting node. Then the joining node selects on its own which node it will join to among the nodes which are willing to accept a new child. The willingness to accept a new child is mainly determined by the node's capacity. Each node has resources limitation in terms of CPU power, memory, total outgoing bandwidth, which determine how many children the node can support.

In order to reduce latency, a bandwidth test is done in QCast before joining under a node. Unlike many other ways which will overload the network and possibly consume other connections' bandwidth during the bandwidth test, QCast uses a light solution to avoid such a problem. First, a special packet of 16 bytes size is constructed. Then QCast sends two such packets consecutively, and detects the delay between them. If the delay is t, the capacity of the estimated channel is $16/t$. QCast will do such bandwidth test for 3 times and get the average estimated channel as the result. This testing is simple, but it is effective. Experiment has shown that it can get the capacity of a full probe within 20%.

This bandwidth test is very important, as its result can provide topologically-aware construction of the multicast overlay. If the test passes, it means that the node in the Pastry network is willing to accept the potential joiner and becomes one of the candidates. Then from this candidate's neighborhood list and leaf list, the joiner can get a selection of nodes to test against, and out of this selection, it finds several nodes with the lowest RTT among the nodes which are willing to accept it. This process is repeated until the smallest RTT is selected or a default value of test times is reached. Thus we can get a better set among all candidate nodes, which can be used as a candidate set for a multi-sender algorithm. However, in QCast, the selection of nodes should consider nodes' QoS requirements, which we will discuss in section 3.2. If the node's QoS capacity does not meet the requirement, it won't be selected.

3.2 QoS Guarantee

In most DHT, each peer is identified by a unique ID which is chosen randomly when joining the P2P network. For example, in Pastry, the peer is identified by a random 128 bit long ID. If we analyze Scribe's multicast tree construction, we can see that the end-to-end path from a leaf to the root is more or less randomly chosen, due to using Pastry's random ID assignment. As Pastry's default ID assignment does not take QoS requirements of peers into account, the multicast trees constructed by Scribe are only by chance holding the property that each child node can only have a smaller or equal QoS requirement than its parent node. To enforce the construction of a QoS aware multicast tree using Scribe, Brogle et al. propose an ID assignment method based on the QoS requirements of nodes [3]. However, their method requires each multicast group has a dedicated Pastry P2P network, and the Pastry network exists only one topic. This is not suitable for P2P streaming system, in which peer usually receives streaming from several parents. We improve Brogle's method in QCast for building a multi source QoS-aware P2P streaming system. We focus on extending Pastry for such a service, but the principles and techniques developed in this paper should be easily applied to other structured P2P networks as well.

To provide QoS guarantee in the construction of multicast trees in QCast, we propose the following:

1. Nodes are partitioned into different levels, which correspond to different QoS classes. According to the OM-QoS method, the QoS requirement of each child node should not be bigger than its parent node. So we mark nodes in order to partition them into different QoS classes. Nodes who receive streaming from the streaming server directly will be marked as 0 level, which are named as root nodes and will correspond to the root class. Nodes who receive streaming from root nodes will be marked as 1 level, which will correspond to the QoS class 1, and so on. Of course, the level should not be so deep, as we should minimize the latencies from root nodes to leaf nodes. In QCast, we have 5 different QoS classes: root class, QoS class 1, QoS class 2, QoS class 3 and best effort class. We do not consider QoS requirements of nodes which belonging to the best effort class, as they are all leaf nodes in QCast and they do not carry any streaming to other nodes.
2. A multi-sender algorithm (e.g., PROMISE [17]) is employed to choose the best set among all candidate senders. This multi-sender algorithm should consider the availability of nodes and their upload bandwidths, in addition to their QoS requirements. If one node receives streaming from two parents or more simultaneously, the node will be correspond to one level lower than the smallest QoS class of its parents.
3. The ID space of Pastry is also partitioned into different segments, each segment correspond to one QoS class. The order of the QoS classes decides the

order of segments: The best-effort QoS class is located in the min ID segment and the root class is located in the max ID segment. When a node joins, its ID is chosen randomly within the corresponding segment of the ID space based on its QoS requirement [3]. Fig. 1 shows how we partition the ID space in QCast.

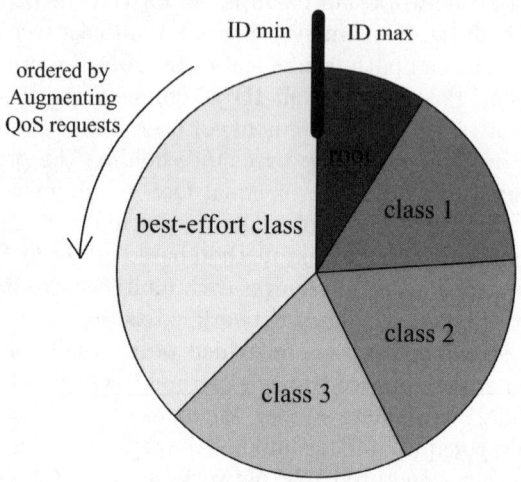

Fig. 1. ID space partition in QCast based on Pastry

There is still a problem about how large the segments should be. Should they be all of the same size or decrease in size towards the root class? As the number of nodes increase during the construction of the multicast tree, the size of each segment should decrease from the best-effort class to the root class. However, how to find the best partitioning strategy is still a problem, which has an impact on how well and evenly the overall traffic load will be distributed among the participating peers [3].

3.3 Buffering

Under some conditions, some multicast data will be missed, such as rejoining into the multicast tree. These operations can take some time and make interruptions during the streaming dissemination. In order to combat this and improve the QoS of the streaming dissemination, each node in QCast stores a buffer of the last 6 seconds of data that flows through the multicast tree. Of course, this requires the streaming server to split up streaming data into MTU-sized blobs, and each blob should be assigned a sequence number, as we can see in TCP protocol. In QCast, there is a build-in FIFO queue for this purpose. When a data packet arrives, a node will store it into the queue, along with the sequence number. If the queue is full, the first data packet at the front of the queue will be delivered to the player and the new data packet will be stored at the end of the queue. If a node rejoins into the multicast tree, it will ask its new parent for data packets with sequence numbers greater than the largest sequence number in its FIFO queue. As a consequence, it makes the streaming dissemination seems more smoothly.

This buffering technology is very important for today's network conditions, as it provides a decent guarantee of data delivery. The guarantee is not as strong as it is with TCP, but it is simple and effective.

4 Evaluation

We evaluate the properties of the multicast tree created by QCast by comparing it to Scribe. Our experiment is conducted on FreePastry [4]. FreePastry is an open-source implementation of the Pastry protocol in Java. It includes an implementation of the Scribe group communication infrastructure and a discreet event simulator. We build our prototype of QCast on top of FreePastry and use FreePastry's simulator to construct multicast trees. FreePastry emulates a network with a user-defined number of Pastry nodes. In our experiment, the number of hosts in Pastry network is varied from 100 to 1000 in steps of 100. For each group hosts, the basic network topology is a Euclidean space model, which is available in FreePastry. A Euclidean model is a hyper-cubic in a D-dimensional Euclidean space. Nodes are randomly located in the hyper-cubic. The distance metric corresponds to the Euclidean distance metric between the nodes. The settings of the simulator parameters are done by providing the values in the command line upon starting the local simulators.

In our experiment, we calculate how many percent of the end-to-end paths can hold the QoS requirement property. If one node can not hold the QoS requirement property, we would not be able to guarantee the QoS requirement for this node

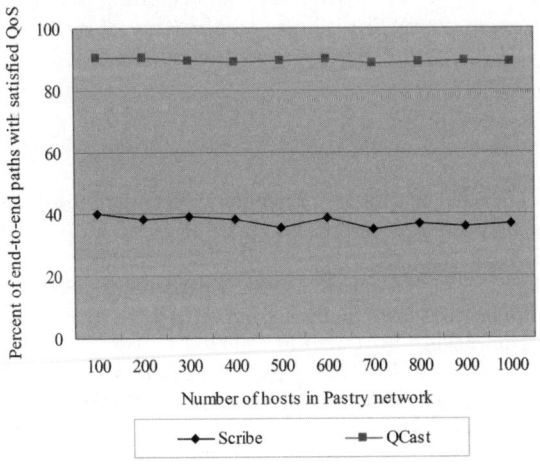

Fig. 2. End-to-end paths comparison with satisfied QoS

and all other nodes below it. Also, we will calculate packet loss rate when the number of hosts are 200, 400, 600, 800 and 1000.

As we can see in Fig. 2, about 90% of the end-to-end paths in QCast's multicast trees can hold bandwidth QoS requirement, which is an average of 30%-40% in Scribe. Obviously, QCast performs better in respect of building QoS-aware multicast trees than Scribe by using our new ID assignment method.

Table 1. Packet Loss Rate of Qcast/Scribe

	200	400	600	800	1000	Avg.
QCast	1.85	1.74	1.68	1.75	1.87	1.778
Scribe	3.50	3.98	3.74	4.21	3.96	3.878

According to Table 1, average packet loss rate of QCast is 1.778%, while average packet loss rate of Scribe is 3.878%. This indicates that the average packet loss rate of QCast is less than 46% of that in Scribe for using our joining and buffering methods.

5 Conclusion and Future Work

In this paper, we propose QCast, a Peer-to-Peer steaming system which enable QoS multicast. We modified the joining and ID assignment method in Pastry to provide QoS guarantee in the construction of multicast trees. According to our simulation, most of the end-to-end paths in the multicast trees can hold bandwidth QoS requirement by using the new ID assignment method. Also, the average packet loss rate of QCast is less than 46% of that in Scribe for our joining and buffering methods. As our future work, we plan to find a multi-sender algorithm that achieves better quality for the streaming dissemination. Also, we will focus on how to make QCast adapts to a variety of network conditions and how to design a better packet delivery strategy.

References

1. Rowstron, A., Druschel, P.: Pastry: Scalable, distributed object location and routing for large-scale peer-to-peer systems. In: Guerraoui, R. (ed.) Middleware 2001. LNCS, vol. 2218, pp. 329–350. Springer, Heidelberg (2001)
2. Castro, M., Druschel, P., Kermarrec, A.-M., Rowstron, A.: Scribe: Alarge-scale and decentralized application-level multicast infrastructure. IEEE Journal on Selected Areas in Communication (JSAC) 20(8) (2002)
3. Brogle, M., Milic, D., Braun, T.: QoS Enabled Multicast for Structured P2P Networks. In: Proceedings of workshop on Peer-to-Peer Multicasting 2007 (2007)
4. FreePastry, http://freepastry.org/
5. Zhao, B.Y., Kubiatowicz, J.D., Joseph, A.D.: Tapestry: An infrastructure for fault-tolerant wide-area location and routing. Technical Report, Berkeley, CA, USA (2001)

6. Ratnasamy, S., Francis, P., Handley, M., Karp, R., Schenker, S.: A scalable content-addressable network. In: Proceedings of the 2001 conference on Applications, technologies, architectures, and protocols for computer communications, pp. 161–172. ACM Press, New York (2001)
7. Stoica, I., Morris, R., Karger, D., Kaashoek, M.F., Balakrishnan, H.: Chord: A scalable peer-to-peer lookup service for internet applications. In: Proceedings of the 2001 conference on Applications, technologies, architectures, and protocols for computer communications, pp. 149–160. ACM Press, New York (2001)
8. Padmanabhan, V.N., Wang, H.J., Chou, P.A.: Resilient Peer-to-Peer Streaming. In: Proceedings of the 11th international conference on Network Protocols, Atlanta, Georgia, USA, pp. 16–27. IEEE Computer Society, Los Alamitos (2003)
9. Zhang, R., Hu, Y.C.: Borg: A hybrid protocol for scalable application-level multicast in peer-to-peer networks. In: Proceedings of the 13th international workshop on Network and operating systems support for digital audio and video, pp. 172–179. ACM Press, New York (2003)
10. Zhuang, S.Q., Zhao, B.Y., Joseph, A.D., Katz, R.H., Kubiatowicz, J.D.: Bayeux: an architecture for scalable and fault-tolerant wide-area data dissemination. In: Proceedings of the 11th international workshop on Network and operating systems support for digital audio and video, pp. 11–20. ACM Press, New York (2001)
11. Castro, M., Druschel, P., Kermarrec, A.-M., Nandi, A., Rowstron, A., Singh, A.: Splitstream: High-bandwidth multicast in a cooperative environment. In: 19th ACM Symposium on Operating Systems Principles, Lake Bolton, New York, USA (2003)
12. Li, Z., Mohapatra, P.: QoS-aware routing in overlay networks. IEEE Journal on Selected Areas in Communications 22(1), 29–40 (2004)
13. Rocha, B.G., Almeida, V., Guedes, D.: Increasing QoS in selfish overlay networks. IEEE IC 10(3), 24–31 (2006)
14. Li, Z.: Resiliency and quality-of-service (qos) support in multicasting and overlay networks. Ph.D. dissertation. Davis, CA, USA (2005)
15. Zhang, J., Liu, L., Pu, C., Ammar, M.: Reliable peer-to-peer end system multicasting through replication. In: Proceedings of the Fourth International Conference on Peer-to-Peer Computing, Washington, DC, USA, pp. 235–242. IEEE Computer Society Press, Los Alamitos (2004)
16. Chu, Y., Ganjam, A., Ng, T.S.E., Rao, S.G., Sripanidkulchai, K., Zhan, J., Zhang, H.: Early Experience with an Internet Broadcast System Based on Overlay Multicast. In: Proceedings of the USENIX Annual Technical Conference 2004. USENIX Association, Boston, MA, USA, pp. 12–12 (2004)
17. Hefeeda, M., Habib, A., Botev, B., Xu, D., Bhargava, B.: PROMISE: Peer-to-Peer Media Streaming Using CollectCast. In: Proceedings of the eleventh ACM international conference on Multimedia (2003)
18. Bamboo DHT project, http://bamboo-dht.org/

A Construction of Peer-to-Peer Streaming System Based on Flexible Locality-Aware Overlay Networks

Chih-Han Lai[1], Yu-Wei Chan[2], and Yeh-Ching Chung[1]

[1] Department of Computer Science, National Tsing Hua University
Hsinchu, Taiwan 30013, R.O.C
chl@sslab.cs.nthu.edu.tw, ychung@cs.nthu.edu.tw
[2] Department of Information Management, ChungChou Institute of Technology
Yuanlin, Taiwan 510, R.O.C
ywchan@dragon.ccut.edu.tw

Abstract. In the peer-to-peer multicast system, participants as peers are organized to construct overlay topology over physical infrastructures. In this manner, peers can easily disseminate data and gather from others by running multicast application. However, the negative impacts such as non-guaranteed transmission efficiency, heterogeneity of peers, dynamic of peers, which were related to the topology of overlay and directly affect the performance metrics, for example, the delivery efficiency and perceived quality. In this paper, we propose flexible locality-aware overlay to get better performance metrics. In the system, a peer can simply establish a streaming session and also as a source without the need of dedicated servers. The overlay is constructed with 2-layered structure to match the underlying topology and shorten the delivery paths. From the simulation results, our system has been demonstrated it had better transmission efficiency, shorter delivery delay, and higher reliability compared with those systems which have been developed.

1 Introduction

The success of peer-to-peer technology motivates the advance of peer-to-peer multicast [2] [4]. When applying streaming applications over peer-to-peer overlay network, the peer-to-peer streaming systems [5] [6] [8] [14] [16] [18] employ the neighbors of peers in an overlay as the streaming suppliers. These suppliers are chose by the topology of overlay, and directly affect the performance metrics, such as delivery efficiency and perceived quality. Due to the negative impacts such as non-guaranteed communication efficiency, limited upload capacity, dynamic of suppliers, etc.., these metrics may not been satisfied. As a result, how to form an overlay to properly combat these impacts is thus the challenge issues. A well-designed overlay for peer-to-peer streaming can keep stable suppliers, shorten transmission delays, and also balance the load of peers.

In this paper, we propose a flexible 2-layered locality-aware overlay by using the group concept to construct a peer-to-peer streaming system. By exploiting the surrounding neighbors of peers with low communication delay, the delivery efficiency and perceived quality can be enhanced in our system. In the proposed 2-layered overlay, peers are clustered into locality groups based on the communication delay. These locality groups form the top layer of the overlay and interconnected as a tree rooted by the streaming source. In each locality group, peers form an overlay mesh for streaming. These overlay meshes form the bottom layer of the overlay. In order to construct the 2-layered overlay efficiently, some schemes are proposed to let peers of the system locate themselves into proper groups well are as follows:

1. The peer locating scheme: it is proposed to aid peers group locating.
2. The membership management scheme: it is used to help peers with organizing the membership of peers in locality groups.
3. The split and merge schemes: they are designed to let the overlay adjust itself with the dynamics of peers.
4. The backup group probing scheme: it is used to enhance the performance of the constructed peer-to-peer streaming system.

Applying the group concepts to the constructed system will enhance the delivery efficiency and perceived quality. For example, peers can not only obtain streaming suppliers easily from others which are in the same locality group, but also shorten the delivery latency from suppliers of other groups. Since the number of peers in a locality group has upper and lower-bounded limitation, the overlay mesh helps peers gather sufficient bandwidth and retain perceived quality more easily. In a streaming session, data disseminated from a streaming source to every end-host through locality groups which has been connected. By the locality groups, the communication latency of two peers in the same locality group will be decreased. Since the delivery paths of the source-to-end are composed of the delivery links of peers, the shorter delay of every links will result in shorter delay totally.

In order to evaluate the proposed architecture, we have implemented the system with proposed scheme on the simulator with varied physical topologies, different streaming data rates, and availabilities of peers. The results of the system are compared with AnySee [8]. The simulation results show that our work can achieve better source-to-end delivery latency with different physical topologies and data rates. The perceived quality still retained high within acceptable delay while AnySee can not. Besides, the reliability of source-to-end delivery path is higher than AnySee.

The remainder of this paper is organized as follows. Session 2 reviews the related work. Session 3 describes our proposed streaming system and its schemes. Session 4 represents the simulation setup of our system. Session 5 proposes some experimental results. Session 6 concludes the paper.

2 Related Work

Many schemes have been proposed for efficient peer-to-peer streaming. The goal of these schemes is to assure that the delivery efficiency and perceived quality metrics can be constantly satisfied. They can be classified into tree-based peer-to-peer overlays [3, 6, 19, 21, 28] and mesh-based peer-to-peer overlays [9, 12, 14, 30, 34].

Most peer-to-peer multicast systems are based on tree-based overlays. CoopNet [11] is the pioneering peer-to-peer streaming system. A centralized approach is employed to efficiently maintain the distribution tree, but may lead to the overload of the streaming source due to the huge connections. Scribe [4] was built upon the structured peer-to-peer overlay. It leverages the dedicated overlays with its native multicast routing schemes. In [13], the authors proposed some schemes based on the topology-awareness of underlying CAN [12] to improve the delivery efficiency. NICE [2] and Zigzag [14] adopt the hierarchical clustering and split/merge heuristics to minimize the transmission length. They were sensitive to node dynamics and needed to adjust the topology frequently that may cause worse streaming quality. Due to the streaming of high bit rate, the tree-based structure is not suitable properly because it does not take the heterogeneity of peers into account.

The mesh-based overlay is a novel model for peer-to-peer multicast since it takes the heterogeneity of upload of peers into account. Bullet [6] is a scalable and distributed algorithm used for constructing high-bandwidth streaming overlay. In Bullet, nodes can self-organize into an overlay tree to transmit the disjoint data sets and retrieve the missed parts simultaneously. Xiang et al. [16] builds a framework for media distribution service on top of mOverlay [19], a group-based locality-aware overlay. In [16], the proposed distributed heuristic replication strategies can leverage locality groups to efficiently disseminate media content. CollectCast [5] is the multi-supplier streaming service built on top of peer-to-peer lookup substrate. The specially constructed topology and selection algorithm are used to yield an active streaming sender set from a candidate peer set. DONet [18] is a data-driven overlay network for live media streaming. By employing a gossiping protocol, peers can periodically exchanges the availabilities of data blocks for retrieving yet unavailable data and supplying available data. However, the streaming quality of DONet can not be guaranteed. AnySee [8] is a peer-to-peer live streaming system built on top of Gnutella [1]. The location-aware topology matching (LTM) [9] scheme and the adaptive connection establishment (ACE) [17] scheme are proposed to optimize the connections of neighbor peers to tackle the power-law effects [2, 24]. In AnySee, by the usage of LTM and the proposed inter-overlay optimization scheme, a peer can retain efficient and available streaming paths on the mesh-based overlay.

3 System Overview

Fig. 1 shows the proposed 2-layered overlay structure. In Fig. 1, peers are clustered into groups with bounded size. The communication delays of peers in a locality group are below a pre-defined threshold. The top layer of the overlay consists of locality groups which are interconnected as a multicast tree rooted by the streaming source. Each locality group holds a derive level that represents the level in the multicast tree. The change of the derive level of a locality group indicates that the split or merge of the locality group. If the derive level is smaller, a peer joins this locality group would experience less relay time for gathering data from streaming source. In each locality group, peers form an overlay mesh for streaming and these overlay meshes form the bottom layer of the overlay. Due to the constructed structure, streaming data can be rapidly distributed. Thus, the efficiency of streaming delivery can be enhanced for the peers located in diverse locations.

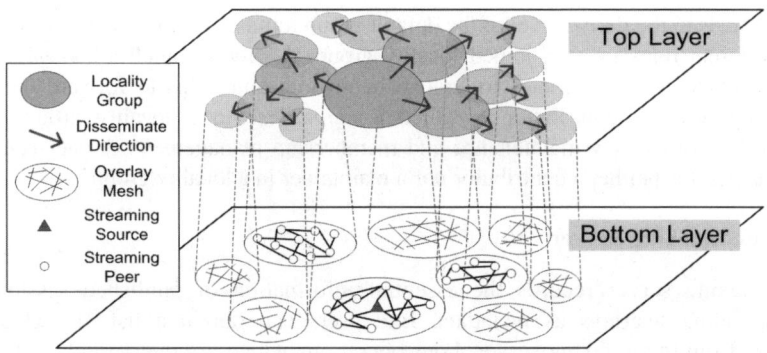

Fig. 1. Proposed flexible locality-group based peer-to-peer overlay network architecture

In this paper, we propose some schemes which have been constructed to make the system more efficiently. An *indexing server* is used to keep the information of streaming sessions with the correspondingly constructed overlay. The new peers join the proper locality group of the overlay by using the *peer locating scheme*. Streaming data from the streaming source are disseminated along with the multicast tree by continuous requests and relays. The clustered peers in a locality group are managed by the *membership management scheme*. To keep sufficient and stable suppliers, the *split/merge scheme* for overlay maintenance would be performed on locality groups. The scheme makes the overlay flexible and scalable because of the ability to grow or shrink the number of groups in an overlay. For those peers that cannot satisfy the performance metrics, the *backup peer probing scheme* is used to improve the satisfaction of peers. In the following, we will describe these schemes in detail.

3.1 The Locality Group

A locality group consists of a set of peers. In this paper, we assume that peers in a locality group are classified into two disjoint subsets, *candidate* and *separate* subsets. For peers in the candidate subset, network delays among peers are less than or equal to a predefined value according to the rate of a streaming session. In this paper, the predefined value was set between $l/2$ and l based on [16, 19], where l is the tolerable delivery latency. The delays of peers between the candidate subset and the separate subset are greater than the predefined value. The size of a locality group is bounded by $[k, (3k - 1)]$ according to [2, 14], where $k \geq 1$. If the size of a locality group is equal to $3k - 1$, it represents that the locality group is full. When a peer joins the full group, it will cause the locality group spilt into 2 groups. If the size of a group except for the streaming source is less than k due to some peers leave, the locality group will be merged with other groups resulting a size under $3k$. If no such locality group available, the merge will be delayed until such a locality group is available; or be aborted when the size of the locality group is greater than or equal to k again.

In the system, each peer will join the *default group* initially. Certain peers may act as gateway-like peers by joining another locality group which is the *source group* to handle the relays among groups. They gather streaming data from the source group and disseminate them to members which are in default group. The derive level of the source group equals to the derive level of the default group minus 1. In this situation, peers may play different roles in each joined locality group. A peer is called a *contributor* in a locality group if it contributes its upload bandwidth and helps to forward the stored streaming data. A contributor is called a *maintainer* in a locality group if it is responsible for overlay maintenance and membership management. A peer is called a *free-rider* if it is neither a contributor nor a maintainer in a locality group.

3.2 The Indexing Server

The indexing server records the essential information of published sessions and corresponding overlays as metadata. End users can obtain a list of metadata of sessions from the indexing server. Four operations which are query, add, update, and remove, are provided to access the indexing server for overlay construction and maintenance. The metadata format stored in the indexing server is divided into two parts which are named as SSPR and LGR. The SSPR represents the specification of an established streaming session. It consists of two fields, session ID and rate. The session ID field is used to recognize each streaming session. The rate field is used to specify the streaming data rate of this session. The LGR stores the information of locality groups in the corresponding overlay. It consists of three fields, group ID, derive level, and maintainer which used to record the ID, the derive level, and the maintainer of a locality group.

3.3 The Peer Locating Scheme

To establish a peer-to-peer streaming session, the streaming source acts as the maintainer of the initial locality group. It first publishes the properties of streaming session by inserting values of the rate field of SSPR and the maintainer field of LGR to the indexing server. After receiving the information, the indexing server then constructs the metadata of the session by assigning values to the session ID field of SSPR and the group ID field of LGR and setting the value of the field of derive level of LGR to be zero. Finally, the group ID is sent back to the streaming source.

When an end host p_i decides to participate a published streaming session s_j, it will call the peer locating scheme to join a locality group according to the LGR records of the session. The peer locating scheme is performed as follows:

Step 1. If no entry of LGR of s_j is stored in the group cache of p_i, then p_i gets one entry from the indexing server and inserts this entry with measured network delay of p_i.

Step 2. For the first m entries in the group cache of p_i, the maintainer in each entry sends all entries to p_i, where m is the system defined *probe number*. After received all entries from maintainers, p_i inserts these entries with measured network delays of p_i. This step is performed n times, where n is the *group probing threshold*.

Step 3. In the group cache of p_i let S_1 be a set of LGR entries whose network delays are under the predefined value according to the rate of s_j. If there is an LGR entry whose derive level is the smallest one, the locality group in this entry is the one for p_i to join. If two or more locality groups satisfy the condition, the one with the smallest network delay will be selected. If no LGR entry can be selected in S_1, the selection with the same policy is applied to S_2.

Step 4.   If all locality groups of LGR entries in the group cache are full, if S_1 is not empty, the locality group of the entry with the smallest derive level will be selected. Otherwise, the locality group of the entry with the smallest derive level in S_2 will be selected.

In the peer locating scheme, the group cache of each peer is used to store the LGR entries with measured network delay. The maintainers act as *dynamic landmark* for positioning in the overlay. The indexing server randomly selects an LGR entry as a bootstrap for the peer locating scheme to distribute the probe requests of peers among all locality groups. If some peers can not be located to a candidate subset of a locality group, this scheme accommodates them into proper group to reduce the times of adjustments.

3.4 The Membership Management Scheme

The membership management scheme is used to organize the membership in a locality group. Based on structure of the super-peer network, the maintainer of a locality group in the system acts as the super-peer to handle the join and leave operations of peers, monitor the status of peers, manage contributors, and broadcast the information of contributors.

In this system, a *member cache* is used to store the information of members in a locality group. For each joined group, a peer maintains the corresponding member cache. The information stored in the member cache consists of four fields, *type*, *network address*, *contributor rank*, and *subset*. The type field specifies the role of a member. The network address field is used to record the network address of a member. The contributor rank field is used to record the rank among all contributors. The rank is used to recover the failure of the maintainer and for the split scheme. The subset field specifies the subset (candidate or separate) of a member belongs. For monitoring the status of peers, a maintainer receives the "keep alive" messages from its members constantly to assure that they are alive. If a peer is available to be a contributor, it informs the maintainer of the default group. When a contributor lacks of the streaming data in its data cache, it will inform the maintainer. The maintainer will set the contributor as the free-rider. Based on the management of contributors, a maintainer periodically updates the information of contributors to each member. Besides, the LGR entries of the source group of the maintainer would be broadcasted periodically to organize contributors and recover failures of the maintainer.

3.5 The Overlay Maintenance Scheme

To keep sufficient and stable suppliers for streaming and ensure the loading of a maintainer, the split and merge schemes will be performed on locality groups if the number of peers in a locality group is over its bounded size or less than a threshold, respectively. In this system, a maintainer periodically checks the size of its locality group and performs the split/merge schemes if needed.

3.5.1 The Split Scheme
When the size of a locality group is larger than $3k - 1$, the following procedure is performed to split this locality group into two locality groups.

Step 1. The maintainer m_i of a locality group g_i chooses the contributor c_j with the lowest rank in its member cache as the maintainer of a new locality group.

Step 2. The contributor c_j claims itself as the maintainer m_j of a new locality group g_j by adding an LGR entry to the indexing server and acknowledges m_i the new group ID g_j.

Step 3. To decide what members should be located in the new locality group, m_i uses the following criteria to select k candidates. m_i will first select those members that fit the following criterion 1. If the number of members selected is less than k, then it will select those members that fit criterion 2, and so on, until k members are selected.

Step 4. The maintainer m_i creates a *split list* that stores the information of these k candidates, broadcasts the split list along with the LGR entry of g_j to all members in g_i, and alters the status of the contributors in the split list and c_j to free-rider in its member cache.

Step 5. When a member received the split list, it refers Table 1 to locate itself to proper group(s). When m_j changes its source group later by the split scheme, this member should follow this change as well.

Step 6. If the derive level of the source group of a maintainer changes, the derive level should be modified correspondingly. The maintainer would update the field of derive level of the LGR entry and inform this change to its members.

Table 1. Guidance of m_i when received the split list

Condition of m_i (C_1: gather streaming bandwidth from the contributors in the split list)	Decision
not in the split list and C_1 is not met	stays in g_i
not a contributor in the split list or C_1 is met	migrates from g_i to g_j
a contributor in the split list and C_1 is not met	joins g_i and g_j to relay data streams

3.5.2 The Merge Scheme

To keep moderate resources in each locality group, a locality group would perform the merge scheme when the size of the locality group is under the predefined threshold k. Assume that the size of a locality group g_i is under the predefined threshold k. The maintainer m_i of g_i first queries the maintainer, m_s of its source group g_s to obtain the size of g_s. The procedures of the scheme are that if the size of g_s is less than $3k$ after merging with g_i, all members in g_i would join g_s and m_i would act as a contributor in g_s. The corresponding LGR entry of g_i would be removed from the indexing server by m_i. For those peers that are free-riders in g_i, they need to change their derive levels.

3.6 The Backup Group Probing Scheme

When a peer is in the separate subset of a locality group, the perceived streaming quality of this peer cannot be constantly satisfied. As long as this peer acts as a contributor, it cuts down the streaming delivery performance. To tackle those negative effects, the backup group probing scheme is proposed to optimize our overlay based on the size of the locality group. The following is the procedure of the scheme.

Step 1. A maintainer of a locality group g_i periodically checks whether its size exceeds $2k$. If yes, it selects k members from the separate subset based on the time order they joined g_i for backup group probing.

Step 2. If a member p_a selected is in the candidate subset, p_a will try to find a locality group g_j in S_1 of its group cache such that the measured network delay of p_a and the maintainer of g_j is less than or equal to $l/2$ and the size of g_j is less than $3k$.

Step 3. If a member p_a selected is in the separate subset, p_a will try to find a locality group g_j in S_1 of its group cache such that the measured network delay of p_a and the maintainer of g_j is less than or equal to l and the size of g_j is less than $3k$.

4 Simulation Setup

In this section, we present the simulation setup for the evaluation. In our simulation, we generate two types of topologies, physical and logical. The physical topology represents the real network topology based on the Internet characteristics. The logical topology is composed of a number of hosts which act as peers to form the peer-to-peer overlay upon the physical topology. We adopt the Hierarchical Top-down model with GLP model [3] on AS/router layer on BRITE [10] and the pure router model on Inet-3.0 [15] to generate 5000 nodes graphs of physical topology with varied settings to yield different network delays. The detail parameters we applied on BRITE and Inet-3.0 are described in [7].

We simulate our system by running an experimental application framework on each end host. In the framework, the implemented protocol formulates the 2-layered overlay. The way we simulate the AnySee [8] system is to construct the underlying mesh-based (Gnutella-type) overlay. We observe that the dynamics of streaming paths of AnySee and evaluate its efficiency. In all simulations, we assume that the first joining peer in an overlay will act as the streaming source and will never fail. The details of the parameters we used are described in [7].

5 Performance Evaluations

In this section, we evaluate our proposed work and AnySee. Based on different aspects, we take the measurements to compare the performance of these both systems by analyzing the behavior of the corresponding overlays.

We evaluate the performance based on two major parts. Firstly, we evaluate the average of maximum delivery latency of a data block from the streaming source to each participant. The related queuing delays and processing delays are ignored. Secondly, we evaluate the average communication delays between participants and its upstream peers.

5.1 Results for Different Physical Topologies

Here we compare the proposed overlay with AnySee based on four different topologies. Fig. 2 and 3 depict the measured source-to-end delays and the average

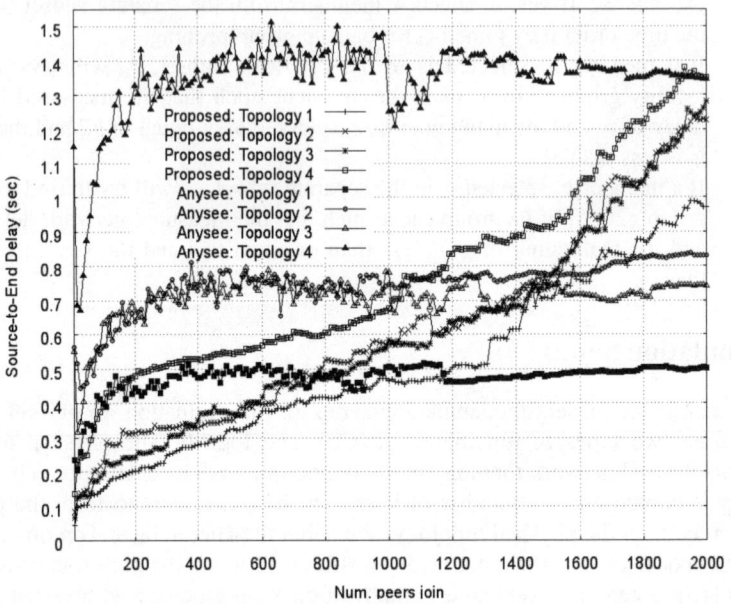

Fig. 2. Source-to-end delay under different topologies

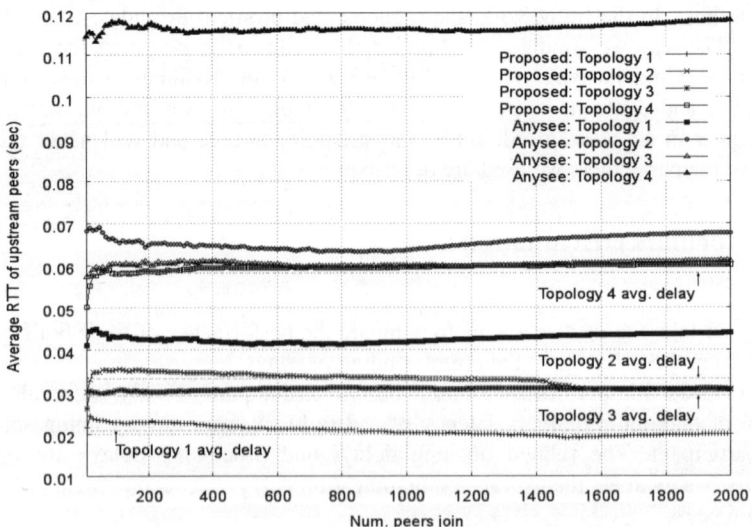

Fig. 3. Communication delay under different topologies

communication delays with increasing overlay size. In Fig. 2, the results show that the delivery latency increases because of the growing number of relay hops/groups with the increasing participants. In contrast, a peer in AnySee must actively examine the available streaming paths. According to the Fig. 2, we can realize that when the average delay of nodes increases (from Topology 1 to Topology 4), our system scales better. Also, from the Fig. 3, we can show that our system works better than Anysee that is shorter link delays and better streaming quality.

5.2 Results for Peers Failure

In the section, we investigate the behavior of two overlays by considering the failure of peers. We schedule failure "trials" in every 7 seconds throughout a stream session. Upon each trial, a peer in an overlay is selected randomly. If a randomly generated number between 0 and 1 is greater than the availability of this peer, it would fail. Otherwise, this peer keeps joining and the session continues normally until the next trial. In our simulations, the mean availability of participants is varied from 0.6 to 1.0.

We compare the proposed work with AnySee. The results are shown in Fig. 4 and 5. Fig. 4 points out the population are less than 1000, the source-to-end delivery delay decreases as the mean availability of peer decreases. This phenomenon reflects the flexibility of our system which can adjust the topology to shorten the delivery latency while AnySee cannot. It is shown in Fig. 5.

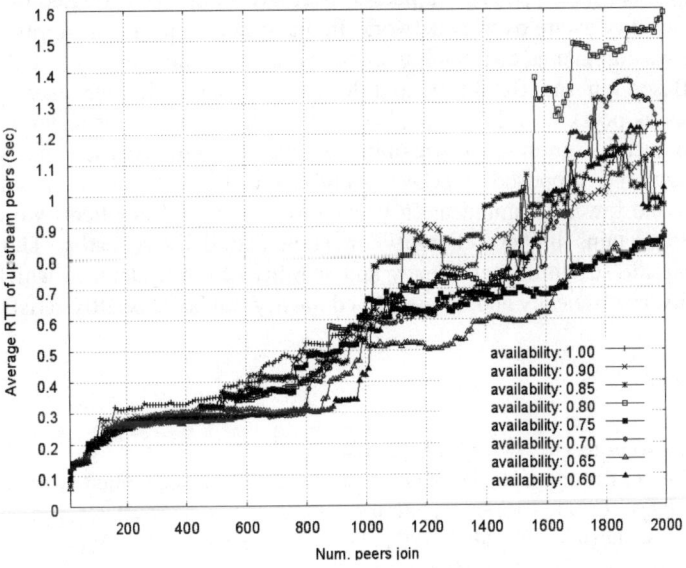

Fig. 4. Source-to-end delay of our system with peer failures

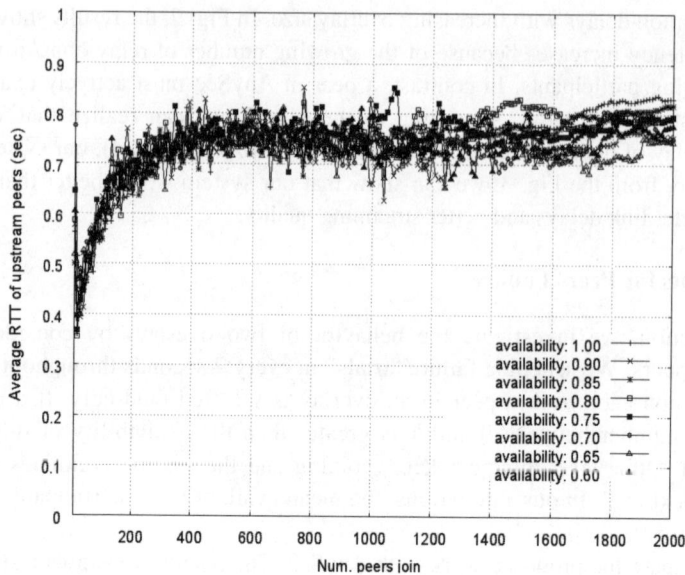

Fig. 5. Source-to-end delay of AnySee with peer failures

6 Conclusions

In this paper, we have presented a peer-to-peer streaming system based on a flexible 2-layered locality-aware overlay network. In our system, a peer can simply establish a streaming session and as a streaming source without the help by dedicated streaming servers. Based on the flexibility and locality-awareness in our overlay, session participants as peers would benefit from sufficient, stable, and efficient suppliers in the joined locality groups for streaming. Compared with AnySee, the simulation results show the proposed overlay exhibits a degree of source-to-end delivery efficiency, and lower communication latencies of streaming suppliers. Moreover, our system also retains higher reliability on streaming delivery paths. Those results demonstrate the scalability, efficiency and stability of our system, in which the data stream delivery efficiency and the perceived quality can be constantly satisfied.

References

1. Gnutella Website, http://www.gnutella.com
2. Banerjee, S., Bhattacharjee, B., Kommareddy, C.: Scalable application layer multicast. In: Proceedings of conference on Applications, technologies, architectures, and protocols for computer communications SIGCOMM 2002, Pittsburgh, PA, USA (August 2002)
3. Bu, T., Towsley, D.: On distinguishing between Internet power law topology generators. In: Proc. INFOCOM 2002, New York City, NY, USA (June 2002)

4. Castro, M., Druschel, P., Kermarrec, A.-M., Rowstron, A.I.T.: Scribe: a large-scale and decentralized application-level multicast infrastructure. IEEE J. Select. Areas in Comm. 20(8) (October 2002)
5. Hefeeda, M., Habib, A., Xu, D., Bhargava, B., Botev, B.: CollectCast: A peer-to-peer service for media streaming. ACM/Springer Multimedia Systems Journal 11(1) (November 2005)
6. Kostic, D., Rodriguez, A., Albrecht, J., Vahdat, A.: Bullet: high bandwidth data dissemination using an overlay mesh. In: Proc. ACM SOSP 2003, NY, USA (October 2003)
7. Lai, C.H., Chung, Y.C.: A Construction of Peer-to-Peer Streaming System Based on Flexible Locality-Aware Overlay Networks, M.S. Thesis, National Tsing-Hua University, Hsin-Chu, Taiwan (2007)
8. Liao, X., Jin, H., Liu, Y., Ni, L.M., Deng, D.: AnySee: Peer-to-peer live streaming. In: Proc. INFOCOM 2006, Barcelona, Catalunya, Spain (April 2006)
9. Liu, Y., Xiao, L., Liu, X., Ni, L.M., Zhang, X.: Location awareness in unstructured peer-to-peer systems. IEEE Transactions on Parallel and Distributed Systems 16(2) (February 2005)
10. Medina, A., Lakhina, A., Matta, I., Byers, J.: BRITE: an approach to universal topology generation. In: Proc. MASCOTS 2001, Cincinnati, OH (August 2001)
11. Padmanabhan, V.N., Wang, H.J., Chou, P.A., Sripanidkulchai, K.: Distributing streaming media content using cooperative networking. In: Proc. NOSSDAV 2002, Miami, FL, USA (May 2002)
12. Ratnasamy, S., Francis, P., Handley, M., Karp, R., Shenker, S.: A scalable content addressable network. In: Proc. ACM SIGCOMM 2001, San Diego, CA, USA (August 2001)
13. Ratnasamy, S., Handley, M., Karp, R., Shenker, S.: Topologically-aware overlay construction and server selection. In: Proc. INFOCOM 2002, New York, NY (June 2002)
14. Tran, D.A., Hua, K.A., Do, T.T.: A peer-to-peer architecture for media streaming. IEEE J. Select. Areas in Comm. 22(1) (January 2004)
15. Winick, J., Jamin, S.: Inet-3.0: Internet topology generator, Technical Report, CSE-TR-456-02, Department of EECS, University of Michigan (2002)
16. Xiang, Z., Zhang, Q., Zhu, W., Zhang, Z., Zhang, Y.-Q.: Peer-to-peer based multimedia distribution service. IEEE Transactions on Multimedia 6(2) (April 2004)
17. Xiao, L., Liu, Y., Ni, L.M.: Improving unstructured peer-to-peer systems by adaptive connection establishment. IEEE Transactions on Computers 54(9) (September 2005)
18. Zhang, X., Liu, J.-C., Li, B., Yum, T.-S.P.: Coolstreaming/DONet: a data-driven overlay network for peer-to-peer live media streaming. In: Proc. INFOCOM 2005, Miami, FL, USA (March 2005)
19. Zhang, X.Y., Zhang, Q., Zhang, Z., Song, G., Zhu, W.: A construction of locality-aware overlay network: mOverlay and its performance. IEEE J. Select. Areas in Comm. 22(1) (January)

Managing Data for Evaluating Trust in Unstructured Peer-to-Peer Networks*

Zhitang Li[1], Huaiqing Lin[1,2], Chuiwei Lu[1,3], and Yejiang Zhang[1]

[1] Huazhong University of Science and Technology, 1037 Luoyu Road, Wuhan, P.R. China
Postcode: 430074
{leeying,lhyzyh,lcwzm,zyj}@mail.hust.edu.cn
[2] Naval University of Engineering, 717 Jiefang Road, Wuhan, P.R.China
Postcode: 430033
[3] HuangShi Institute of Technology, 16 GuiLin Road, HuangShi, P.R. China,
Postcode: 435003

Abstract. Managing data is a problem of particular importance in trust model of peer-to-peer environments where one frequently encounters unknown agents. Existing methods for data management, which are based on DHT or Random Selection, can not apply well in the unstructured Peer-to-Peer system. They do not scale as they either require additional overhead on maintaining DHT or rely on a central database. In this paper we present an approach that manages trust data through constructing Trust Relationship Network. We quantify performance in terms of number of hits, network overhead, and response time. We use locally maintained network information and former interactions with other peers to improve the performance of searching. We present extensive experimental evaluations to demonstrate the performance of our proposed solution.

Keywords: peer-to-peer, managing data, trust, reputation.

1 Introduction

In the recent years, Peer-to-Peer system research has grown significantly. A peer-to-peer (P2P) network consists of numerous peer nodes that share data and resources with other peers on an equal basis. Unlike traditional client-server models, no central coordination exists in a P2P system, thus there is no central point of failure. P2P network are scalable, fault tolerant, and dynamic, and nodes can join and depart the network with ease. The most compelling applications on P2P systems to date have been file sharing and retrieval. For example, P2P systems such as Napster, Gnutella, KaZaA and Freenet are principally known for their file sharing capabilities, e.g., the sharing of songs, music, and so on. Furthermore, researchers have been interested in extending sophisticated IR techniques such as keyword search and relevance retrieval to P2P databases.

---

* This work was supported by the project 60573120. Project 60573120 supported by National Natural Science Foundation of China.

Peer-to-peer networks have many benefits over standard client-server approaches to data distribution, including increased robustness, scalability, and diversity of available data. However, the open and anonymous nature of these networks raises some issues. The first is a complete lack of accountability for the content a peer puts on the network, opening the doors to abuse of these networks by malicious and irresponsible peers. The other is that P2P communities are often established dynamically by peers that are unrelated and unknown to one another.

Trust model is an effective way for addressing the above-mentioned issues. In trust model, peers need aggregate the historical interaction data to evaluate the trust index of target. Then how to manage data is an important issue in the trust model. Most existing trust model [1], [2], [3] used DHT to store data. Another method, random selection, was used in [4]. However, these methods can not work well in the unstructured P2P networks. DHT can effectively locate the node that stores a desired data items. It is a very good idea that uses DHT to store trust data in DHT P2P networks. But in the unstructured P2P network, we must pay additional overhead to maintain DHT structure. The problem of random selection method is that who is responsible for selecting trust holding peers for one peer.

Flooding is the predominant search technique in unstructured P2P networks. It is natural that use flooding technique to manage trust data in unstructured P2P network. However, flooding generates huge redundant message and has poor granularity. In this paper, we proposed a new approach: Trust Relationship Network protocol that can search trust data quickly with lower network overhead.

2 Related Work

There has been a lot of research and applications recently on Peer-to-Peer network trust and reputation management.

Karl Aberer divided the architecture for trust management into three parts: network, storage and trust computation [5]. The key of trust computation is how to evaluate the trust index accurately based on the peer's historical interaction data. There are many scheme proposed to address this issue, for example, the methods of [1], [2], [3] were based on Power iteration, the method of [6] was based on the con firmation theory, the method of [7] was based on the bayesian network, the method of [8] was based on the neural network, the method of [9], [10], [11] were based on the fuzzy theory, etc.

However, only few papers discussed the issue of network and storage of trust model. [1] used Two-dimensional CAN hash space to store trust data. [2] used Terrace, which is a tree structure Distributed Hash Table, to store trust data. P-Grid is another DHT storage structure that used in [5]. Apart from DHT, random selection was an alternative method [4].

Besides the above-mentioned technology, there are many other content distribution technologies. Content distribution is an important peer-to-peer application on the Internet that has received considerable research attention. For example, FreeNet [12] uses probabilistic routing to preserve the anonymity of its users, data publishers, and data hosts. Cooperative File System (CFS) [13] is a peer-to-peer read only storage system developed at MIT with the following design goals: provable guarantee for efficiency, robustness, load balancing and scalability. PAST [14] is a large scale P2P persistent storage management system. IVY [15] is a read/write peer-to-peer file system that is distributed and decentralized and able to support multiple users concurrently. It provides an NFS-like file system view to the users, while at the same time; it can detect conflicting modifications and recover from network failure.

3 Design Considerations

Most of the trust model uses DHT to store trust data. DHT is a scheme for distributed storage, which can achieve the efficient location of the node that stores a desired data item. But in the unstructured P2P network, constructing and maintaining DHT structure will bring additional overhead.

Another scheme, random selection, was used in TrustMe [4]. TrustMe is a secure and anonymous underlying protocol for trust management It was the bootstrap server' responsibility for selecting THA-peers (peers which hold the trust value for a particular peer). This kind of approach suffers from following shortcomings:

- How to choose the bootstrap server is a very difficult task to complete.
- The security of system relied on the bootstrap server.
- No discussing data synchronization between multiple THA-peers.

All the above-mentioned schemes want to centralize the trust data to a peer or a set of peers. We thought no need to centralize trust data in unstructured P2P network. Each peer maintains its trust data. When a peer wants to evaluate other peers, it just sends a search request to network for aggregating trust data. As the inherent defects of flooding algorithm, the researchers have proposed many schemes to improve it. A hybrid search scheme was proposed in [16]. The scheme has been showed to improve performance in terms of number of hits, network overhead, and response time. We use this scheme in initial phase of our protocol.

To aggregate the trust data, a trust search message would visit many peers that no needed data. Through the interactive experience of the past, a peer can know which peers held the data he wanted. Then, the search message can be send to these peers directly. In this paper, we constructed a trust relationship network for each peer. A search message of trust data would be propagated within trust relationship network. It can decrease the number and hops of search message observably.

4 Trust Relationship Network: A Protocol for Trust Data Management

It is important for trust model that the calculation of trust index should complete quickly. So, the trust data query that is pivotal phase before trust calculation should complete within short time. Most of current work propagated query message to entire network. But relative to entire network, there are just only few peers who held someone's trust data. If the query messages are restricted within these peers, the performance of search would be improved in terms of network overhead and respond time.

4.1 Hybrid Search Scheme

Hybrid search schemes [16] which can be viewed as a random walk of substantially shorter length (and hence smaller response time) combined with very shallow flooding on every step of the random walk. Hybrid search scheme was used to search peers who held desired trust data in the first phase of our protocol.

4.2 Protocol Details

This section describes the *TRN* protocol, which specifies how to find the locations of trust data, how new nodes join the *TRN*, and how to recover from the failure of existing nodes.

The *TRN* protocol is packet_oriented and uses self_contained messages. Each message includes a source peer ID, a transaction ID, a message descriptor and payload. The message is of the form:

| Source Peer ID | Transaction ID | Message Descriptor | Payload |

The protocol consists of a set of message descriptor: Searching Neighbor, Responding Neighbor, Searching Trust Data and Responding Trust Data.

The following notations are used: *TRN(i)* stands for the trust relationship network of Peer *i*, *SN* stands for the descriptor: Searching Neighbor, *RN* stands for the descriptor: Responding Neighbor, *CN* stands for the descriptor: Confirming Neighbor, *STD* stands for the descriptor: Searching Trust Data and *RTD* stands for the descriptor: Responding Trust Data.

There are three parts in the protocol: Constructing *TRN*, Searching trust data, Maintaining *TRN*.

4.2.1 Constructing TRN

Any peer, say Peer *i*, intending to query for the trust data of Peer *j* first check if any trust neighbor about peer *j* exist in local. If the trust relationship network has not been constructed, Peer *i* make use of the hybrid search scheme to search the peers who held the trust data about Peer *j*. The query message looks like:

| Peer i ID | Transaction ID | SN | Peer j ID |

On receiving the message, the peers (Peer *k*) who held the trust data about Peer *j* can generate a reply of trust data firstly. And then if Peer *k* has the ability to accept new neighbor, a *RN* message would be send to the Peer *i*. After Peer *i* add Peer *k* to his neighbor list, Peer *k* will receive *CN* message from Peer *i* and add Peer *i* to its neighbor list. The reply and confirm message look like:

Responding Neighbor message

| Peer k ID | Transaction ID | RN | Peer j ID |

Confirming Neighbor message

| Peer i ID | Transaction ID | CN | Peer j ID |

At last, Peer *k* forward the search message for search more peers.

In process of searching trust neighbor, the protocol completes the trust data retrieval task at same time. Due to no need to send *STD* message, we can reduce costs and improve response time of protocol.

4.2.2 Searching Trust Data

When the trust relationship network has been established, any peer in this network, say Peer i, can broadcast *STD* message into *TRN*. Each peer received *STD* message will reply the *RTD* message to the source peer of message.

4.2.3 Maintaining TNR

In practice, *TRN* needs to deal with nodes that fail or leave voluntarily. This section describes how *TRN* handles these situations.

The trust neighbor list may be modified when following event occurred.

- Receiving a *RN* message. It means that someone else have accepted its join request. So he adds the peer who responded message to his trust neighbor list.
- Receiving a *CN* message. It means that someone else, say peer i, has added itself to his neighbor list. Then the peer i will be added to trust neighbor list.
- Failing or leaving voluntarily. If forwarding a message to a trust neighbor failed, this neighbor will be removed from trust neighbor list.
- Receiving a *STD* message from a peer who is not in the trust neighbor list. Because of the congestion of the underlay network, some peers removed from trust neighbor network do not forward message in time. These peers don't know that he has been removed from *TRN* and search trust data by sending message through *TRN* still. The peers that receive *STD* message from removed peers will add these peers to its trust neighbor list again. Because the peers can join the *TRN* again without issuing the *SN* message, we can decrease the overhead of the protocol.
- Each *TRN* have a timeout. If timeout expired and there no trust search message in the timeout period, the trust neighbor list would be delete, namely, *TRN* would be destroyed.

4.3 The Scheme for Searching Trust Data in TRN

There is a difference between searching in *TRN* and normal P2P network. Searching trust data in *TRN* should visit all peers in the *TRN*. The random walk is not optimized for us. The flooding scheme can address this issue. But we must address the problems, redundant messages and no scalability, brought by flooding.

We propose a new broadcast approach that can efficiently reduce broadcast redundancy in *TRN*. The approach is executed in a distributed manner. It utilizes only local topology information to avoid unnecessary rebroadcasts. It retains the merits of flooding, while introducing little control overhead.

The main idea of our broadcast algorithm is that a node need not rebroadcast a message if all its neighbors have received message from previous sending node. To reduce redundant message further, we still judge that whether the intersection of neighbors of sending node's all neighbors exists. The peer belong to the intersection should be send message only once. To achieve this, a node should gather the local topology knowledge.

Before making broadcast decision, broadcast algorithm performs two judgments: local neighbors' discovery within 1 hop of sender, local neighbors' discovery within 2 hops of sender. The first judgment can help sender know which neighbors have received message from previous sender. And second judgment can help sender know which neighbors may receive redundant message in the following broadcast. Then we can avoid it by some mechanism. In this paper the peer whose ID is smaller will rebroadcast priority.

A broadcast message's sender, say peer i, is either the source or a node that performs rebroadcast. When a node, peer j, receives a broadcast message, it can learn which peers have been covered by this transmission by checking the neighbor list of the peer i. Then these nodes are added into the broadcast cover set of the message. The broadcast send set of the message should be the difference of neighbors and broadcast cover set. Moreover, the peer that performs rebroadcast checks whether same neighbors exist in the broadcast send set and the neighbors of neighbors of peer i. Then these same peers should be removed from broadcast send set.

When making rebroadcast decision, the node checks the broadcast send set of the message. If the set is empty, then the rebroadcast operation is unnecessary and can be canceled.

For peer u, we denote its neighbor set as $N(u)$. $S(u)$ stands for the send set of peer u. The data broadcasting procedure is illustrated as follows.

1) For source s, it just broadcasts messages to all its neighbors and ignores duplicate messages received later.

2) For any other node, say u, when it receives a broadcast message m from node v, it performs the following operations:

    a) If the message has received, then it will be dropped.

    b) Or else,

$$S(u)=N(u)-N(v)-\{v\} . \qquad (1)$$

if $S(u)$ is empty, then no rebroadcast need be performed and the duplications received later will be dropped.

    c) Or else, for every $w \in N(v)$, if $u>w$, then calculate the intersection

$$P=S(u) \cap N(w) . \qquad (2)$$

and

$$S(u)=S(u)-P . \qquad (3)$$

    d) At last, peer u will rebroadcast message to every peer in the $S(u)$.

Simulation is conducted to compare the performance of the proposed approach and flooding. The simulation results show that broadcast redundancy can be reduced greatly by our approach.

5 Experiments

In this section we study the performance of searching using flooding, random walks, random walk with flooding, hybrid search scheme and *TRN*, and compare the five methods to each other. We measure the performance in terms of the average number of distinct peers visited per searching, response time of search algorithm and the number of messages that the searching algorithm uses. We show experimentally that searching by *TRN* is better than others.

5.1 Experiment Setting

Our initial simulated community consists of N peers. There are 100K peers in our experiment environment. We set the replication ratio to be 0.01. Since there are 100K peers in the topology, we uniformly place just about 1000 copies of the searched item in the network. Because the main purpose of simulation is to evaluate the algorithm performance, there are no peers join or leave P2P network.

In order to perform a fair comparison of the different searching algorithms we require that they use the same number of messages. Since it is difficult to configure the parameters of each algorithm to guarantee the exact same number of messages, we require that the expected number of messages used in each experiment is approximately the same for all algorithms.

Recent work has shown the prevalence of small-world phenomena in many networks. Small-world graphs exhibit a high degree of clustering, yet have typically short path lengths between arbitrary vertices. The topology generation algorithms GLP(Generalized Linear Preference)[18] was used in this paper to generate small-world graphs.

5.2 Number and Ratio of Hits

The performance of searching in terms of number of peers discovered is showed in table 1. The TTL column indicates that the searching schemes are using the same number of messages as if performing flooding with that TTL. The table shows that the performance of flooding, random walk, random walk with flooding and hybrid search in terms of discovering peers are similar. There are two phases: constructing and stabilization in the *TRN* protocol. Within constructing *TRN* phase, the performance of *TRN* in terms of discovering peers is similar to the hybrid search, which guarantees that the protocol search sufficient peers for constructing *TRN*. While the number of discovered peers decreased remarkably within *TRN* stabilization phase. The decrease was occurred not because the bad performance of protocol but because the search horizon was limited to trust relationship network.

The figure 1 shows the performance in terms of number of hitting peers. The X axis, TTL, indicates that the searching schemes are using the same number of messages as if performing flooding with that TTL. The figure 1 shows that the other searching schemes show the similar performance except the *TRN* protocol. In the constructing *TRN* phase, the *TRN* protocol has a good performance even using small number of messages because searching messages only propagate in *TRN*. When the *TRN* had been stabilized, our protocol can find any peer in the *TRN*.

Table 1. Performance in terms of Average Number of Discovered Peers

TTL	Flooding	Random Walk	Random Walk with Flooding	Hybrid Search	Constructing TRN	Constructed TRN
3	6075.35	5425.89	5488.41	5485.15	6208.68	999.00
4	41833.22	37441.36	36571.69	37086.76	36918.06	999.00
5	82484.85	71327.98	68801.32	61376.29	60936.16	999.00
6	96367.07	85516.65	83250.84	76719.74	76315.31	999.00
7	99195.90	90362.55	88961.43	80826.57	80299.89	999.00

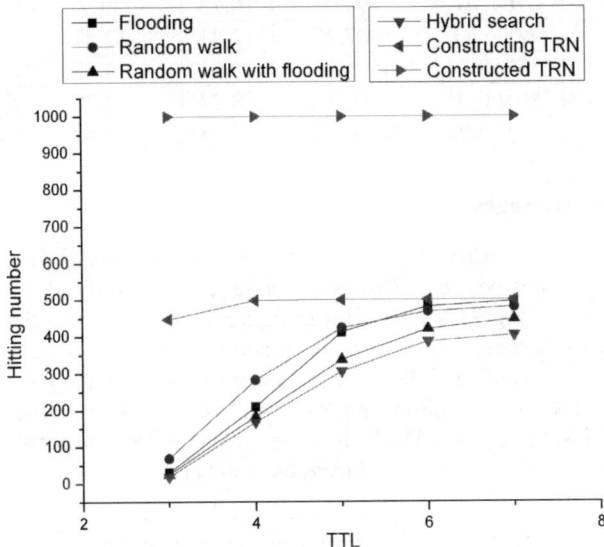

Fig. 1. Average hitting number versus TTL

5.3 Response of Time

We also measure the maximum running time of each algorithm. In this study we assume a very simple discrete time model. Each node receives queries from its neighbors and at the same time processes them and forwards copies of the queries, if necessary, to its neighbors. The latter queries will be received at the next unit of time. The hops of message are equal to the simulation time in our system. For all our schemes it is easy to compute the hops of the message, or an upper bound of it. For example, the searching time for flooding with TTL=t is t. Despite the fact that we do not model many important parameters that affect the searching time, like for example propagation and queuing delays, we believe that our definition of running time can be used to judge the relative performance of the different algorithms.

The table 2 shows the performance in terms of average hops of the message. The TTL column indicates that the searching schemes are using the same number of messages as if performing flooding with that TTL. From the table 2, we can easy conclude that the flooding has lowest hops; hybrid search and *TRN* have similar performance. The *TRN* protocol can achieve shorter running time under various conditions. In the constructing *TRN* phase, the protocol has faster response speed due to using hybrid search scheme. While in the stable phase, we can still achieve faster response speed because the searching was limited in the smaller horizon: *TRN*.

Table 2. Performance in terms of average hops

TTL	Flooding	Random Walk	Random Walk with Flooding	Hybrid Search	Constructing TRN	Constructed TRN
3	3	6764.16	194.9	10.73	11.2	12.41
4	4	66036.73	2007.25	12.41	12.51	11.05
5	5	213352.74	6596.53	14.01	14.08	13.04
6	6	386360.04	11947.67	13.23	13.28	12.57
7	7	522173.91	16147.92	13.38	13.43	13.04

5.4 Number of Messages

Good searching schemes strive to minimize the number of messages used to discover as much information as possible. *TRN* protocol has lowest overhead in terms of messages in the constructing *TRN* phase. From figure 1, we can know that the average hitting number of flooding, random walk, random walk with flooding and hybrid search increase remarkably as TTL increase 3 from 7, whereas the increment of *TRN* is not obvious. The average hitting number of *TRN* as TTL=3 almost equal to the number of other schemes as TTL=7. It means that the *TRN* protocol can hit more peers with lowest overhead in terms of message number.

Table 3. The performance of improved flooding

Searching scheme	Number of message	Efficiency of searching
Flooding	8963.00	0.11
Improved flooding	4949.05	0.20

When the *TRN* is stable, the searching message will propagate within *TRN*. The flooding can be used in this phase. But flooding will bring mass redundant message. To further enhance performance we propose a new broadcast approach that can efficiently reduce broadcast redundancy in *TRN*.

The number of messages used by improved flooding significantly decreased compared to flooding (Table 3). The main reason is that new searching scheme reduced redundant messages through utilizes only local topology information and statistical information of duplicate messages to avoid unnecessary rebroadcasts. The number of messages used by improved flooding is less than flooding by approximately 45%. We define the efficiency of searching by the flowing expressions:

$$efficiency = \frac{least\ number\ of\ message}{number\ of\ message\ used} . \qquad (4)$$

From table 3 we can see that the new flooding scheme improved efficiency through reducing redundant messages.

6 Conclusions

In this paper we have presented a trust data management protocol: Trust Relationship Network. We quantify performance in terms of number of distinct nodes discovered, the number of propagated messages (network overhead), and the maximum response time. The simulations show that the protocol can provide the trust data retrieval services with small overhead.

References

1. Kamvar, S.D., Schlosser, M.T., Garcia-Molina, H.: EigenRep: Reputation management in P2P networks. In: Proceedings of the 12th international conference on World Wide Web, vol. 1, pp. 123–134 (2003)
2. Dou, W., Wang, H.-M., Jia, Y., Zou, P.: A recommendation-based peer-to-peer trust model. Journal of Software 15, 571–583 (2004)
3. Zhang, Q., Zhang, X., Wen, X.-Z. (eds.): Construction of peer-to-peer multiple-grain trust model. Journal of Software 17, 96–107 (2006)
4. Singh, A., Liu, L.: TrustMe: Anonymous management of trust relationships in decentralized p2p systems. In: Proceedings of IEEE International Conference on P2P Computing, vol. 1, pp. 142–149 (2003)
5. Aberer, K., Despotovic, Z.: Managing Trust in a Peer-2-Peer Information System. In: Proceedings of the 10th International Conference on Information and Knowledge Management, vol. 1, pp. 310–317 (2001)
6. Hou, M.-s., Lu, X.-l., Zhou, X. (eds.): A trust model of p2p system based on confirmation theory. Operating Systems Review 39, 56–62 (2005)
7. Wang, Y., Vassileva, J.: Trust and Reputation Model in Peer-to-Peer Networks. In: Proceedings of the Third IEEE International Conference on Peer-to-Peer Computing, vol. 1, pp. 150–158 (2003)
8. Song, W.-h., Vir Phoha, V.: Neural network-based reputation model in a distributed system. In: Proceedings of IEEE 2004 CEC, vol. 1, pp. 321–324 (2004)
9. Song, S.-s., Hwang, K., Kwok, Y.-K.: Trusted Grid Computing with Security Binding and Trust Integration. Journal of Grid Computing 3, 53–73 (2005)
10. Song, S.-s., Hwang, K., Zhou, R. (eds.): Trusted P2P Transactions with Fuzzy Reputation Aggregation. IEEE Internet Computing 9, 24–34 (2005)
11. Griffiths, N., Chao, K.-M., Younas, M.: Fuzzy Trust for Peer-to-Peer Systems. In: Proceedings of the 26th IEEE International ConferenceWorkshops on Distributed Computing Systems, vol. 1, pp. 73–73 (2006)
12. Clarke, I., Sandberg, O., Wiley, B.: Freenet: A distributed anonymous information storage and retrieval system. In: Proceedings of the Workshop on Design Issues in Anonymity and Unobservability, Berkeley, California, United States, pp. 46–66 (2000)
13. Dabek, F., Kaashoek, M., Karger, D., Morris, R., Stoica, I.: Wide-area cooperative storage with CFS. In: Proceedings of the ACM Symposium on Operating Systems Principles, Banff, Canada, pp. 202–215 (2001)

14. Druschel, P., Rowstron, A.: Past: A largescale, persistent peer-to-peer storage utility. In: Proceedings of the Eighth Workshop on Hot Topics in Operating Systems, Schloss Elmau, Germany, pp. 75–80 (2001)
15. Muthitacharoen, A., Morris, R., Gil, T.M., et al.: Ivy: A read/write peer-to-peer file system. In: The 5th Symposium on Operating Systems Design and Implementation, Boston, Massachusetts (2002)
16. Gkantsidis, C., Mihail, M., Saberi, A.: Hybrid Search Schemes for Unstructured Peer-to-Peer Networks. In: INFOCOM 2005. 24th Annual Joint Conference of the IEEE Computer and Communications Societies. Proceedings IEEE, vol. 3, pp. 1526–1537 (2005)
17. Peng, W., Lu, X.-C.: On the Reduction of Broadcast Redundancy in Mobile Ad Hoc Networks. In: Proceedings of the MobiHoc Conf., pp. 129–130. IEEE, Boston (2000)
18. Bu, T., Towsley, D.: On distinguishing between Internet power law topology generators. In: Proceedings of the IEEE INFOCOM 2002, vol. 2, pp. 638–647. IEEE, New York (2002)

A Gossip-Based Protocol to Reach Consensus Via Uninorm Aggregation Operator

Qiaoli Huang, Shiqun Yin, and Zhixing Huang*

Faculty of Computer and Information Science
Southwest University, Chongqing 400715, China
{qlhuang,qiongyin,huangzx}@swu.edu.cn

Abstract. Gossip-based protocols for group communication have attractive scalability and reliability properties. This study presents a gossip-based protocol based on an *uninorm aggregation operator*, which enables agents to reach a consensus. The convergence, speed and randomness characteristics of this protocol are theoretically analyzed. The experimental results showed that this protocol is efficient, scalable and resilient against the failures under various network topologies. It indicated that this model can be used to interpret the uncertainty and the fast convergence characteristics of collective decision dynamics.

1 Introduction

Gossip-based protocols for group communication have attractive scalability and reliability properties. They have been widely used in the applications, including failure detection [1], reputation management [2, 3], data aggregation [4, 5] and consensus problem [6, 7, 8], etc.

Consensus problems can be considered as a group of agents which intend to find a common agreement about some issues which are regarded and communicated as real numbers. In traditional gossip-based consensus protocols [6, 9], each agent is usually required to know the other agents' initial opinions before he makes a decision. It becomes a major obstacle for the gossiping protocols to reach scalability and efficiency, since the agents must either know the values or identify the failures of the nodes in the system. However, it is an intuition that we needn't know all the other's initial values when we archive an agreement in a large group. Moreover, they often assume that each agent has a fixed local value, and then iteratively disseminate this value in a distributed manner. In fact, the agent may change his value(opinion) when he gets aware of the opinions of others. Thus in gossip-based consensus problems, the final result should not only take the initial values, but also the gossiping progress (e.g. the encounter sequence) into consideration. In addition, the importance of the node should be

---

* Corresponding author. This work is supported in part by National Basic Research Program of China (973 project no. 2003CB317001), the Young Scientist Foundation of Southwest University (project no. SWUQ2006015), and Southwest University Grants (project no. 140250-20710907).

considered as well. The key point of this problem is not what the agents agree on but the fact that they must all come to the same conclusion, since reaching consensus is a good in itself [8].

In this paper, we present a gossip-based protocol to reach a consensus based on an *uninorm aggregation operator* [10]. The operator to aggregate positive ratings will produce an even more positive overall rating; the operator to aggregate negative ratings will produce an even more negative overall rating; and the operator to aggregate the conflict ratings will generate a neutral rating [11]. This protocol has the following desirable properties: 1) The protocol reaches a consensus with low computation cost and with small message length. 2) It converges to a consensus within a relatively fixed round, and the convergence time does not increase exponentially with the network size increases. 3) The convergence result of this protocol not only depends on the distribution patten of initial values, but also depends on the gossiping process itself. The randomness property of the convergence result can be used to interpret the uncertainty of collective decision dynamics. 4) It is resilient against the failure of nodes and communications. The protocol also performs well in various topologies such as random networks and scale-free networks.

The rest of the paper was organized in Section 2-5. In Section 2, a basic aggregation protocol is presented and its properties are analyzed. The experimental results are showed in Section 3 and the related work is briefly discussed in Section 4. In Section 5, conclusions are drawn and our future work is pointed out.

2 Gossip-Based Aggregation

2.1 Uninorm Aggregation Operator

To clearly present a protocol, normally some operators are used. In this paper, we use a uninorm aggregation operator to describe the gossip-based aggregation protocol that we proposed. Before the description of the aggregation protocol, the concepts of the uninorm aggregation operator are briefly introduced.

Aggregation operation has been widely used in decision making processes, e.g. in distributed expert systems; such operators have been exploited to synthesize different expert systems' ratings for a particular conclusion. In most cases, the aggregation operation is some form of weighted arithmetic mean. However, arithmetic mean can work well only in the situation in which any difference is viewed as being in conflict. To overcome this shortcoming, some alternative aggregation operators have been proposed. The type of exiting aggregation operators that we consider are uninorm aggregation operators [10, 11].

Definition 1. *A binary uninorm operator* $\mathbf{U} : [0,1] \times [0,1]$ *is a uninorm operator if:*

- *monotonicity:* $\forall a_1, a_1', a_2, a_2' \in [0,1]$, $a_1 \leqslant a_1'$, $a_2 \leqslant a_2' \Rightarrow \mathbf{U}(a_1, a_2) \leqslant \mathbf{U}(a_1', a_2')$;
- *associativity:* $\forall a_1, a_2, a_3 \in [0,1]$, $\mathbf{U}(a_1, \mathbf{U}(a_2, a_3)) = \mathbf{U}(\mathbf{U}(a_1, a_2), a_3)$;

- *commutativity:* $\forall a_1, a_2 \in [0,1], \mathbf{U}(a_1, a_2) = \mathbf{U}(a_2, a_1)$; and
- *neutral element*[1]: $\exists \tau \in [0,1], \forall a \in [0,1], \mathbf{U}(a, \tau) = a$.

The uninorm-like operator is different from the averaging-like operator for the former has a neutral element τ. In particular, when the neutral element τ is 1, 0, and between 1 and 0, the uniform operator is called a *t-norm*, a *t-conorm*, and a *uninorm* aggregation operator, respectively. [10]. Here shows a special case of uninorm operators:

Example 1. The following is a uninorm aggregation operator:

$$\mathbf{U}_\tau(a_1, a_2) = \frac{(1-\tau)a_1 a_2}{(1-\tau)a_1 a_2 + \tau(1-a_1)(1-a_2)}, \quad (1)$$

where $\tau \in (0,1)$ is its neutral element.

Lemma 1. *The aggregation operator $U_\tau(a_1, a_2)$ has the following properties [11]:*

$$\forall a_1^+, a_2^+ \in (\tau, 1], U_\tau(a_1^+, a_2^+) \geqslant \max\{a_1^+, a_2^+\}; \quad (2)$$
$$\forall a_1^-, a_2^- \in [0, \tau), U_\tau(a_1^-, a_2^-) \leqslant \min\{a_1^-, a_2^-\}; \quad (3)$$
$$\forall a_1^- \in [0, \tau), a_2^+ \in (\tau, 1], a_1^- \leqslant \mathbf{U}_\tau(a_1^-, a_2^+) \leqslant a_2^+; \quad (4)$$

According to Lemma 1, we can regard the neutral element of a uninorm aggregation operator as a threshold. If a rating is greater than the threshold it is regarded as positive; otherwise it is regarded as negative. Thus, in Lemma 1, property (2) reflects the intuition that two ratings enhance the effect of each other in aggregations when they are both positive; property (3) reflects the intuition that two ratings weaken each other in aggregation when they are both negative ; and property (4) reflects the intuition that an aggregation result of aggregation is obtained when two ratings are in conflict[11]. Moreover, some special cases are worth noting.

Lemma 2. *Assume $\mathbf{U}_\tau$ is a uninorm with neutral element τ, then (1) $\mathbf{U}_\tau(a_i, 0) = 0$ for all $a_i \in [0,1)$, (2) $\mathbf{U}_\tau(a_i, 1) = 1$ for all $a_i \in (0,1]$, (3) $\mathbf{U}_\tau(\tau, \tau) = \tau$.*

Lemma 2 is immediate if we substitute 0, 1 and τ into aggregator $\mathbf{U}_\tau$. In addition, note that if (a_1, a_2) is $(1,0)$ or $(0,1)$, the denominator of aggregator $\mathbf{U}_\tau$ is zero. In this case, we use average operator instead, that is $\mathbf{U}_\tau(a_1, a_2) = \tau$.

2.2 The Basic Aggregation Protocol

Now, we describe our gossiping protocol based on the aforementioned aggregator. Suppose we are given an initial vector $A = (a_1, a_2, \cdots, a_n)$, where $a_i \in [0,1]$, $i \in \{1, \cdots, n\}$. The elements of this vector correspond to the initial values (opinions) at the nodes. We model this vector by assuming that a_i is independent on random variables with identical distribution.

---
[1] τ has also been called as *identity* in other references, such as in [10].

Algorithm 1. Skeleton of the gossiping protocol

> for $k = 1$ to n do
> $\quad (i, j) = GetPair()$
> $\quad$ if $a_i a_j + (1 - a_i)(1 - a_j) \neq 0$ and $(a_i, a_j) \neq (\tau, \tau)$ then
> $\quad\quad a_i = a_j = U_\tau(a_i, a_j)$
> $\quad$ else
> $\quad\quad a_i = \tau + \epsilon, a_j = \tau + \epsilon'$
> $\quad$ end if
> end for
> return a

The detailed protocol is shown in Algorithm 1, and it is based on the *push-pull gossiping* scheme [4]. Procedure *GetPair* plays an important role in the gossiping process. The implementation of pair selection will return random pairs such that in each execution of Algorithm 1(that is, in each cycle), each node is guaranteed to be a member of at least one pair. In Algorithm 1, for any pair (i, j), we aggregate their opinions based on U_τ. If the denominator of $U_\tau(a_i, a_j)$ is not equal to 0, we update i and j's values corresponding to the aggregated one. If the aggregated value is τ, we make a_i and a_j slightly deviate the neutral element, e.g. $|\epsilon| \leq 0.0001$. In a practical setting, the value of ϵ can be generated randomly or simply be a relatively small constant.

We continue our discussion based on the assumption that any two nodes can communicate without failures, and there is no malicious node in the system.

Theorem 1. *If the pairs are randomly and uniformly selected from n nodes, then initial vector $A = (a_1, \cdots, a_n)$ will converge to $(1, \cdots, 1)$ or $(0, \cdots, 0)$ according to the gossip protocol as described in Algorithm 1.*

Proof. We define that a_i^t is the value of a_i in round t, where $t > 0$. We also define $E(a_i^t)$ as the expected mean value of a_i^t. Suppose that $E(a_i^t) = \tau + c$, where $c \in [-\tau, 1 - \tau]$. The expected mean value of a_i in round $t + 1$ can be calculated as:

$$E(a_i^{t+1}) = E\left(\frac{(1 - \tau)a_i^t a_j^t}{(1 - \tau)a_i^t a_j^t + \tau(1 - a_i^t)(1 - a_j^t)} \right)$$

and since the pairs are randomly and uniformly generated from n nodes, and a_i^t, a_j^t are independent, and with identical distribution, $E(a_i^t) = E(a_j^t)$. Thus, the above equation can be rewritten as:

$$E(a_i^{t+1}) = \frac{(1 - \tau)E(a_i^t)^2}{(1 - \tau)E(a_i^t)^2 + \tau\bigl(1 - E(a_i^t)\bigr)^2} \quad (5)$$

For the sake of simplicity, we define $\varphi(t)$ to be the denominator of Equation (5), i.e. $\varphi(t) = (1-\tau)E(a_i^t)^2 + \tau\bigl(1 - E(a_i^t)\bigr)^2$, obviously $\varphi(t) \geq 0$. The convergence of Algorithm 1 is shown in Fig. 1. In the following, we will consider three different cases according to the value of c.

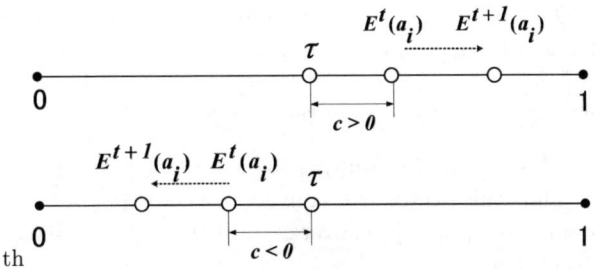

Fig. 1. Convergence of Algorithm 1: the upper shows the case when $c > 0$, the lower shows $c < 0$

(1) If $c > 0$ and $\varphi(t) \neq 0$, which means that the value of $E(a_i^t)$ is greater than the neutral element τ. Recall that $a_i \in [0,1]$, thus $\tau + c \in [0,1]$. Substitute $E(a_i^t) = \tau + c$ into the following equation, and do analyses,

$$E(a_i^{t+1}) - E(a_i^t) = \frac{(1-\tau)E(a_i^t)^2}{\varphi(t)} - E(a_i^t) = \frac{c(\tau+c)(1-\tau-c)}{\varphi(t)} \geq 0.$$

The above analyses indicate that the value $E(a_i^{t+1})$ is increased after one round, and the equator holds when $E(a_i^t) = 1$, i.e. $\forall_i a_i^t = 1$. In another word, $E(a_i^{t+1})$ is more closer to 1 than $E(a_i^t)$ except when $\forall_i a_i = 1$.

(2) If $c < 0$ and $\varphi(t) \neq 0$, similarly we have:

$$E(a_i^{t+1}) - E(a_i^t) = \frac{c(\tau+c)(1-\tau-c)}{\varphi(t)} \leq 0$$

which means $E(a_i^{t+1})$ is decreased and approached to 0 after each round.

(3) When $c = 0^2$ or $\varphi(t) = 0$, since we introduce a vibration variable ϵ to make the mean, the value of a_i slightly deviate the identity τ. Therefore, this case can be converted to the other two cases.

Therefore, we conclude that the initial vector $a - (a_1, \cdots, u_n)$ will converge to $(0, \cdots, 0)$ or $(1, \cdots, 1)$ when $t \to \infty$ in Algorithm 1.

Corollary 1. *(1) For the initial vector $a = \{a_1, \cdots, a_n\}$, if all $a_i \in [0, \tau)$, vector a will converge to $(0, \cdots, 0)$; (2) if all $a_i \in (\tau, 1]$, vector a will converge to $(1, \cdots, 1)$;*

Proof. (1) From Lemma 1 we know that $U_\tau(a_1^-, a_2^-) \geqslant \min\{a_1^-, a_2^-\}$, thus the mean value $c < 0$ in all the rounds. Combine the result of Theorem 1, a will converge to $(0, \cdots, 0)$ for certain. (2) Similarly, a will converge to $(1, \cdots, 1)$ when $\forall a_i > \tau$.

---

[2] Only when all $a_i = \tau$, c will keep to be 0 in each successive round. This makes the algorithm can't converge to 1 or 0 (it dose converge to τ). Thus, we make a small vibration when $(a_i, a_j) = (\tau, \tau)$ since in distributed environment we have no global knowledge that whether or not all the $a_i = \tau$.

Corollary 2. *(1) For any (a_1^-, a_2^-, a_3^+), where $a_1^-, a_2^- \in [0, \tau)$, $a_3^+ \in (\tau, 1]$, if $\mathbf{U}_\tau(a_1^-, a_3^+) < \tau$ and $\mathbf{U}_\tau(a_2^-, a_3^+) < \tau$, then (a_1^-, a_2^-, a_3^+) will converge to $(0, 0, 0)$; (2) For any (a_1^+, a_2^+, a_3^-), $a_1^+, a_2^+ \in (\tau, 1]$, $a_3^- \in (0, \tau]$, if $\mathbf{U}_\tau(a_1^+, a_3^-) > \tau$ and $\mathbf{U}_\tau(a_2^+, a_3^-) > \tau$, (a_1^-, a_2^-, a_3^+) will converge to $(1, 1, 1)$.*

Proof. (1) Since $\mathbf{U}_\tau(a_1^-, a_2^-) < \min\{a_1^-, a_2^-\}$, and for any $a \leq \min\{a_1^-, a_2^-\}$, $\mathbf{U}_\tau(a, a_3^+) < \tau$. Thus this vector will convert to vector (a'_1^-, a'_2^-, a'_3^-), $\forall_i a'_i < \tau$, based on theorem 2, (a_1^-, a_2^-, a_3^+) converge to $(0, 0, 0)$; (2) Similarly, (a_1^+, a_2^+, a_3^-) will converge to $(1, 1, 1)$.

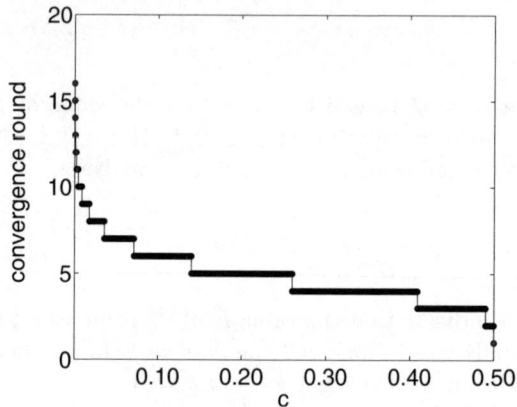

Fig. 2. The expected mean convergence round with respect to initial value c, supposing that we ignore the vibration influence when $\varphi(t) = 0$, and the precision of the values is $\epsilon = 1 \times 10^{-4}$

From Theorem 2, we know that the convergence speed of Algorithm 1 is dependent on the initial mean value of c. If we ignore the vibration cases, when $\varphi(t) = 0$, we could figure out the expected mean convergence round based on Equation (5). Fig. 2 shows the expected mean convergence round with respect to the initial value c, supposing that we ignore the vibration influence when $\varphi(t) = 0$, and we assume that the precision of each value is $\epsilon = 1 \times 10^{-4}$, and c is increased by ϵ. In addition, if $1 - E(a_i^t) < \epsilon$ then $E(a_i^t) = 1$, and if $E(a_i^t) < \epsilon$ then $E(a_i^t) = 0$. As we shall see in the later, k will be relatively stable even with the increment of n.

2.3 Randomness of the Result

Although the protocol is guaranteed to converge, the convergence result is not always unique. The convergence result is not only dependent on the pair sequence, but also dependent on the distribution pattern of the initial values. See the following example.

Example 2. Suppose there are three nodes in the system, the initial value is $a = (0.4, 0.4, 0.7)$. According to the pair sequences $S_1 = \{(1, 2), (1, 3), (2, 3), \cdots\}$

Table 1. different pair sequences $S_1 = \{(1,2),(1,3),(2,3),\cdots\}$ and $S_2 = \{(1,3),(2,3),(1,2),\cdots\}$

t	S_1	S_2
0	(0.4000 0.4000 0.7000)	(0.4000 0.4000 0.7000)
1	(0.5091 0.3155 0.3155)	(0.5091 0.5091 0.6087)
2	(0.1805 0.0953 0.0953)	(0.6259 0.6259 0.6173)
3	(0.0024 0.0000 0.0000)	(0.8187 0.8187 0.7296)
4	(0.0000 0.0000 0.0000)	(0.9821 0.9821 0.9241)
5	-	(1.0000 1.0000 0.9985)
6	-	(1.0000 1.0000 1.0000)

and $S_2 = \{(1,3),(2,3),(1,2),\cdots\}$, the initial vector a converges to $(0,0,0)$ and $(1,1,1)$, respectively. We assume that $\tau = 0.5$ and $\epsilon = 0.0001$[3].

The detailed progress of the convergence of those two sequences are demonstrated in Table 1, in the table, each row presents one round. From Table 1, we can see that the convergence results are different with respect to S_1 and S_2. The values converge to 0 after 4 aggregation rounds in $S1$ while converge to 1 after 6 rounds in S_2. It shows that the convergence result of this gossiping protocol is sensitive to pair sequence.

Lemma 3. *(1) For any (a_1^-, a_2^-, a_3^+), where $a_1^-, a_2^- \in (0,\tau)$, $a_3^+ \in (\tau,1)$, if $\mathbf{U}_\tau(a_1^-, a_3^+) > \tau$ or $\mathbf{U}_\tau(a_2^-, a_3^+) > \tau$, then (a_1^-, a_2^-, a_3^+) will converge to $(0,0,0)$ or $(1,1,1)$; (2) For any (a_1^+, a_2^+, a_3^-), $a_1^+, a_2^+ \in (\tau,1]$, $a_3^- \in (0,\tau]$, if $\mathbf{U}_\tau(a_1^+, a_3^-) < \tau$ or $\mathbf{U}_\tau(a_2^+, a_3^-) < \tau$, (a_1^-, a_2^-, a_3^+) will converge to $(0,0,0)$ or $(1,1,1)$.*

Proof. (1)Without loss of generality, we suppose that $\mathbf{U}_\tau(a_1^-, a_3^+) > \tau$. Then (a_1^-, a_2^-, a_3^+) can be converted to (a'^+_1, a_2^-, a'^+_3), $a_1^+ > \tau$ after operation $\mathbf{U}_\tau(a_1^-, a_3^+)$. If we iteratively aggregate pair $(1,3)$ until $\mathbf{U}_\tau(a'^+_1, a_2^-) > \tau$, then (a'^+_1, a_2^-, a'^+_3) will convert to $(a''^+_1, a'^+_2, a'^+_3)$, $a'^+_2 > \tau$. From the result of Corollary 1, it will converge to $(1,1,1)$. On the contrary, if we iteratively aggregate pair $(1,2)$ until $\mathbf{U}_\tau(a'^+_1, a_3^+) < \tau$, (a'^+_1, a_2^-, a'^+_3) will be converted to $(0,0,0)$ (2) Similarly, (a_1^-, a_2^-, a_3^+) will converge to $(0,0,0)$ or $(1,1,1)$.

Theorem 2. *If there exist pairs (i,j), (i',j') which satisfy that $\mathbf{U}_\tau(a_i, a_j) > \tau$ and $\mathbf{U}_\tau(a_{i'}, a_{j'}) < \tau$ at the same time, the convergence result of Algorithm 1 is not always unique; it could be $(1,\cdots,1)$ or $(0,\cdots,0)$ according to the pair sequence.*

Proof. This conclusion is immediate from the result of Example 2 and Lemma 3.

The randomness of the convergence result also depends on the distribution pattern of the initial values. See the following example.

Example 3. The initial values of all the nodes are demonstrated in the first column in Table 2. The mean values of those initial values are the same and

---
[3] Unless stated otherwise, we make the same assumption in all the examples.

Table 2. All initial vector's mean value $\bar{a}$ is equal to 0.5, $\bar{r}$ represents the average convergence round

initial value	1	0	$\bar{r}$
(0.25 0.25 1.00)	99%	1%	4.6
(0.30 0.30 0.90)	70%	30%	8.4
(0.40 0.40 0.70)	67%	33%	9.8
(0.50 0.50 0.50)	50%	50%	19.6
(0.60 0.60 0.30)	33%	67%	9.8
(0.70 0.70 0.10)	30%	70%	8.2
(0.75 0.75 0.00)	1%	99%	4.6
(1.00 0.50 0.00)	50%	50%	9.8

equal to $\tau = 0.5$. The probabilities of the result converging to 1, 0 are indicated in column 2 and 3.[4]

Although the mean values of the initial values are all the same in Table 2, however the percentages that the initial values converge to 0 and 1 are quite different. There are probably some rules between the data, but predicting the concrete percentage of the result for a given vector is a non-trivial task.

3 Empirical Results for Convergence of Aggregation

We examine Algorithm 1 using *GetPairRand* [4] for several network sizes and different network topologies, the failures of nodes and communications are also examined. In our simulation, the initial opinion is random and uniformly distributed in [0,1]. For each parameter setting, at least 100 independent experiments were performed. We set $\tau = 0.5$ and $\epsilon = 0.0001$.

3.1 Scalability

To examine the scalability of our uninorm-based gossiping protocol, we select a network size ranging from 10 to 10^5, we assume the network is a complete graph here. Fig. 3 illustrates the statistic plot of the experimental results. It shows that the mean value of convergence rounds increases slowly, it stays at round 16 as the size increases to 10^5, In that time, the mean value of the opinions approaches to τ and c is around 10^{-4}. Our theoretical results in Section 2 are consistent with the empirical results.

We can conclude that the performance of the protocol is weakly dependent on the network size, while it will be relatively stable as the number of nodes increases. This phenomenon can be used to interpret why a large-scale society reaches an agreement within a relatively short time.

---
[4] Since the search space is quite large, it is not possible to enumerate all the pair sequences. So we only demonstrate the simulation result here.

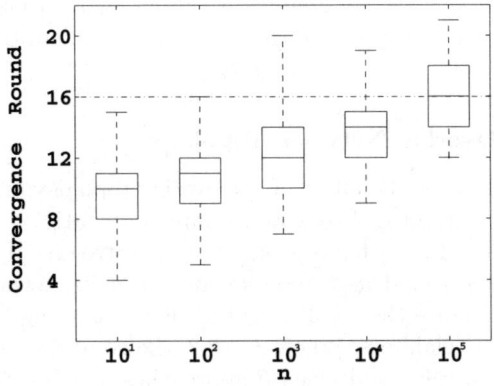

Fig. 3. Scalability

3.2 Failures and Malicious Nodes

In practical implementations, we must consider the failures of nodes and communications. We model the crashing node errors as the aggregation operation failed on both sides and the communication failure as the aggregated result will be accepted by only one side. We simulate each node with β failure probability. We also assume that the nodes are in a complete graph. Fig. 4 shows the graph with 100 nodes in the network, in which the protocol still perform well, even that the failures of nodes come up to more than 50%.

We also simulated the malicious behaviors in the system. In the experiments, we modeled two types of malicious behaviors: arbitrary action (generating value randomly) and reverse action (reversing the aggregated value, e.g.1 minus the aggregated value). The gossiping process terminated if it exceeded the predetermined bound(e.g. 40 round). In such cases, the original protocol is hard to converge; it is resilient to 10% nodes with arbitrary action or to 5% nodes with

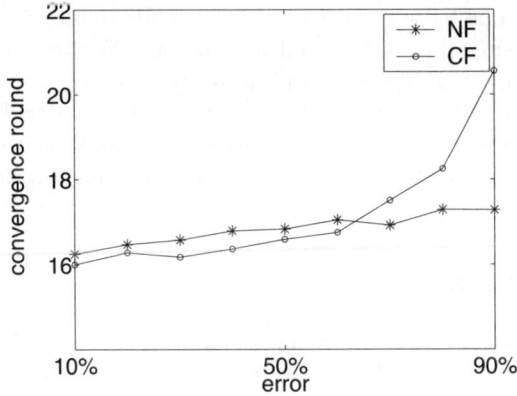

Fig. 4. Failures

reverse action. However, we can adapt a weighted aggregation method to overcome those destructive effects since the gossip-based reputation system [2] can identify these malicious nodes with high accuracy.

3.3 Impact of Overlay Network Topology

This subsection examines the effect of the overlay topology on the performance of aggregation. All of the topologies we examine are static, i.e. the neighbor set of each node is fixed. Fig. 5 focuses on the Watt-Strogatz [12] model showing that the convergence round as a function of β ranging form 0.1 to 1. In the experiments, we generate the small world for a regular ring lattice where each node has $m = 4, 6, 8$ neighbors. When $\beta > 0.2$, the convergence round is slightly above the theoretical value and when β approaches to 1 (random network), the convergence round approaches to 16.

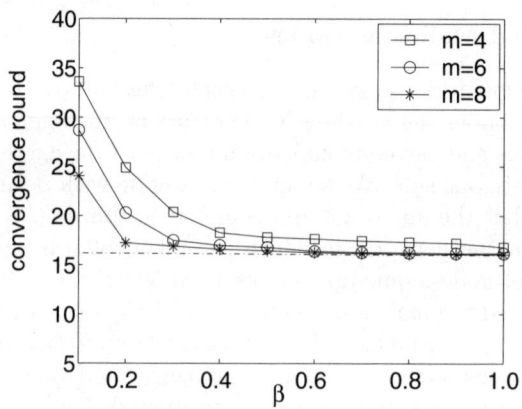

Fig. 5. Aggregation in Smallworld

We also test our protocol over scale-free graphs [13], we build the graph by adding new nodes one-by-one and wire the new node to an existing node already in the network using the preferential attachment. We test different neighbor number of the scale-free network. In short, the average convergence speed is slightly above 16 round. The more neighbors the nodes have (still far less than n), the more closer the convergence round approaches to 16. From those experiments, we can see that the protocol performs well in the small world, scale-free and random networks.

4 Related Work

Gossip-based Aggregation protocol has been studied by [2, 4, 5, 6, 7, 14, 15], etc. Kampe et al. [5] proposed a gossip-based algorithm, Push-Sum, to compute the average of values at the nodes in a network. They showed that the result approximates to the average within the relative error at most ε, and with probability at least $1-\delta$ at time $O(\log n + \log\frac{1}{\varepsilon} + \log\frac{1}{\delta})$. Procaccia [2] presented a decentralized reputation management schema which was built on Push-Sum. He pointed out the fragile of the gossiping-based aggregation, the aggregation result can be manipulated by a malicious node if Push-Sum run a large number of turns. Jelasity [4] proposed a Push-Pull gossiping schema with the similar features to Push-Sum. To reach a determinate consensus, Chlebus and Kowalski [6] designed gossiping algorithms that were efficient with respect to both time and communication by partitioning the processors into m groups, where $m = \min\{n, 2t\}$, and $t < n$ are the numbers of failures. Georgiou et al. [7] developed a deterministic gossip algorithm for synchronous, crash-prone and massage-passing processors. However, the computation time or the communication cost of the determinate algorithms increase quickly as the number of nodes increases. Conversely, in this paper we study a gossip-based protocol reaching a randomized agreement with the fast convergence speed even the number of node increases exponentially.

In a similar work, Jan Lorenz [8] proposed a multidimensional opinion dynamics model to foster consensus. In that model, agents adjust their opinions by building averages of the other's opinions, but have bounded confidence. In addition, he demonstrated the clustering dynamics and bifurcation dynamics with respect to the evolution of time and the bounded confidence. Compared to his work using a traditional average operator, our aggregation operator is more powerful and flexible.

5 Conclusion and Future Work

In this paper we presented a gossip-based consensus reaching protocol based on a uninorm aggregation operator. We analyze the convergence, the speed and the randomness of this protocol. This model can be used to demonstrate the uncertainty characteristic and the fast convergence speed of collective decision dynamics. The theoretical and experimental results show that this model is scalable and robust under various network size and topologies.

Our future work includes exploring the consensus aggregation process combined with the reputation management. That is to find an efficient method to reach consensus while identifying the malicious nodes in efficient weighted aggregation processes with the consideration of underlying network topologies. Moreover, it is also an interesting task to investigate the performance of the protocol in the context of multi-dimensional opinions and the bounded compromise.

Acknowledgements. We are grateful to Prof. Shigeo Matsubara, Prof. Xudong Luo and Dr. Yichuan Jiang for their insightful comments.

References

[1] Renesse, R.V., Minsky, Y., Hayden, M.: A gossip-style failure detection service. In: Proc. of Middleware 1998, IFIP, The Lake District, UK, September 1998, pp. 55–70 (1998)
[2] Procaccia, A.D., Bachrach, Y., Rosenschein, J.S.: Gossip-based aggregation of trust in decentralized reputation systems. In: The Twentieth International Joint Conference on Artificial Intelligence (IJCAI 2007), Hyderabad, India, pp. 1470–1475 (2007)
[3] Zhou, R., Hwang, K.: Powertrust: A robust and scalable reputation system for trusted p2p computing. IEEE Trans. on Parallel and Distributed Systems 18(5), 460–473 (2007)
[4] Jelasity, M., Montresor, A., Babaoglu, O.: Gossip-based aggregation in large dynamic networks. ACM Trans. Comput. Syst. 23(3), 219–252 (2005)
[5] Kempe, D., Dobra, A., Gehrke, J.: Gossip-based computation of aggregate information. In: FOCS 2003: Proceedings of the 44th Annual IEEE Symposium on Foundations of Computer Science, Washington, DC, USA, p. 482. IEEE Computer Society, Los Alamitos (2003)
[6] Chlebus, B.S., Kowalski, D.R.: Robust gossiping with an application to consensus. Journal of Computer and System Sciences 72(8), 1262–1281 (2006)
[7] Georgiou, C., Kowalski, D.R., Shvartsman, A.A.: Efficient gossip and robust distributed computation. Theor. Comput. Sci. 347(1-2), 130–166 (2005)
[8] Lorenz, J.: Fostering consensus in multidimensional continuous opinion dynamics under bounded confidence. In: Proceedings of Potentials of Complexity Science for Business, Governments, and the Media 2006, Budapest, August 3-5 (2006)
[9] Lamport, L., Shostak, R., Pease, M.: The byzantine generals problem. ACM Transactions on Programming Languages and Systems 4(3), 382–401 (1982)
[10] Yager, R.R., Rybalov, A.: Uninorm aggregation operators. Fuzzy Sets and Systems (80), 111–120 (1996)
[11] Luo, X., Jennings, N.R.: A spectrum of compromise aggregation operators for multi-attribute decision making. Artif. Intell. 171(2-3), 161–184 (2007)
[12] Watts, D.J., Strogatz, S.H.: Collective dynamics of 'small-world' networks. Nature 393(4), 440–442 (1998)
[13] Barabási, A.L.: Linked: The new science of networks. American Journal of Physics 4(71), 409–410 (2003)
[14] Ganesh, A.J., Kermarrec, A.M., Massoulié, L.: Peer-to-peer membership management for gossip-based protocols. IEEE Trans. Computers 52(2), 139–149 (2003)
[15] Kermarrec, A.M., Massoulié, L., Ganesh, A.J.: Probabilistic reliable dissemination in large-scale systems. IEEE Trans. Parallel Distrib. Syst. 14(3), 248–258 (2003)

HilbertChord: A P2P Framework for Service Resources Management*

Derong Shen[1], Yichuan Shao[2], Tiezheng Nie[1], Yue Kou[1], Zhenhua Wang[1], and Ge Yu[1]

[1] Dept. of Computer Sci. and Eng., Northeastern University, Shenyang, 110004, China
{Shenderong,nietiezheng,kouyue,wangzhenhua,yuge}@ise.neu.edu.cn
[2] Dept. of Computer Sci. and Eng., Shenyang University, Shenyang, 110036, China
cyc---1@sohu.com

Abstract. Aiming at the deficiency of Chord algorithm supporting single-keyword query only, a P2P framework-HilbertChord combining Hilbert and Chord is proposed for managing service resources, which supports DHT-based multi-keyword query and approximate query by means of Hilbert index to improve resources searching ability. Experiments show that HilbertChord has better efficiency and scalability for managing service resources under large scale P2P environment with higher density of services.

1 Introduction

Nowadays, resource management model on peer-to-peer infrastructure has become a popular trend, in which, three searching ways, namely centralized index, broadcasting and dynamic hash table(DHT), are used to locate service resources, where DHT method has been concerned by researchers since its key techniques aim at distributed object management mechanisms. The resource management model owns better scalability and resources load balancing as well as avoids the performance bottleneck caused by centralized server. However, DHT-based method suffers from following deficiencies: (1) It does not support multi-keyword query, since attribute keywords of a service resource are mapped to a list of hash values as indexes published across nodes, similarly, multi-step searching is needed to find the service. (2) It does not support approximate query because DHT-based query can only realize the precise matching, either matching or not matching, when there are no matching services, it is very difficult to relax the query to match the similar services or provide some similar services for compensating the query.

Chord algorithm with its simplicity and provable correctness makes it widely used, and Hilbert space filling curve [1,2] is a good way to present the spatial relationship among the space objects, so HilbertChord infrastructure is proposed by considering Chord algorithm and Hilbert space filling curve together, which not only has the characteristics of Chord, but also supports the multi-keyword query and approximate query.

---

* This research is supported by the National Natural Science Foundation of China under Grant No. 60673139, 60573090.

2 Related Work

With Chord not considering the actual network topology, lower efficiency and higher latency are its typical features, so some improved Chord structures [3,4,5] for meeting different applications have been represented to enhance the efficiency of searching services, but they can not meet multi-keyword query and approximate query.

Mainly related work for multi-keyword query can be divided into two kinds, on the one hand (e.g. [6,7]), a query was split into some sub-queries, each of which corresponded to a keyword, and the final result was the intersection of results from sub-queries or by gradually reducing the scope of services for realizing multi-keyword query. On the other hand (e.g. [8]), range query mechanism was proposed, which constructed a DHT overlay in the lower level, and each attribute dimension corresponded to a specified tier tree whose root node covered all the hash values of the description attribute.

The related applications by using Hilbert space filling curve are as follows: Andrzejak [9] used reverse SFC(Space Filling Curve) mapping, from 1-dimensional space to d-dimensional Cartesian space of CAN to support range query. Schmidt [10] was similar to the work of the paper, and supported DHT-based multi-attribute query, its idea was to map the d-dimensional attribute values to a 1-dimensional index space by means of Hilbert SFC, further map to an arbitrary P2P overlay on Internet, but it did not support approximate query. HilbertChord proposed in the paper can support both of multi-attribute query and approximate query by adding some meta-data in nodes. The main contributions of this paper are as follows:

(1) A HilbertChord infrastructure for services management is proposed by combining Hilbert and Chord.
(2) HilbertChord supports DHT-based multi-keyword query and approximate query by adopting Hilbert index.
(3) Experiments show the availability of HilbertChord as well as its limitations.

3 The Overview of HilbertChord

3.1 Related Concepts

Definition 1. Service Index Space (SISpace). Given an n-dimensional (n is the number of attribute keywords of a service) Cartesian service indexes space with fixed-space size, in which, a number of service indexes are distributed in a certain density. This space is defined as Service Index Space.

Definition 2. Service Description Array (SDArray). By using a consistent hashing, a series of attribute keywords $K_1, K_2, ..., K_n$ for describing a service are mapped to an array of $W[w_1, w_2, ..., w_n]$, where $w_1=hash(K_1)$, $w_2=hash(K_2)$, etc, which are described as a Service Description Array and each service is mapped to a point in a SISpace by means of its $W[w_1, w_2, ..., w_n]$. The Service Description Array of service S is denoted as SDArray(S).

Definition 3. Services Similarity Degree. Suppose existing SDArray(S_1) and SDArray(S_2), then Services Similarity Degree between S_1 and S_2 (Sim (S_1, S_2)) is denoted as the number of the same numerical values between S_1 and S_2. For example, if S_1=<00010,10100,10001> and S_2=<00010,11111,10100>, then Sim(S_1,S_2)=2.

Definition 4. Services Similarity Matrix. Services Similarity Matrix is composed of Services Similarity Degrees among all the service indexes in a physical node under the P2P distributed environment.

Definition 5. HilberttLength. Let $W[w_1,w_2,...,w_n]$ be Service Description Array of service S, Hilbert(W) translate the W into a Hilbert code, let HilbertLength = Hilbert(W), and HilbertLength of service S is denoted as HL(S).

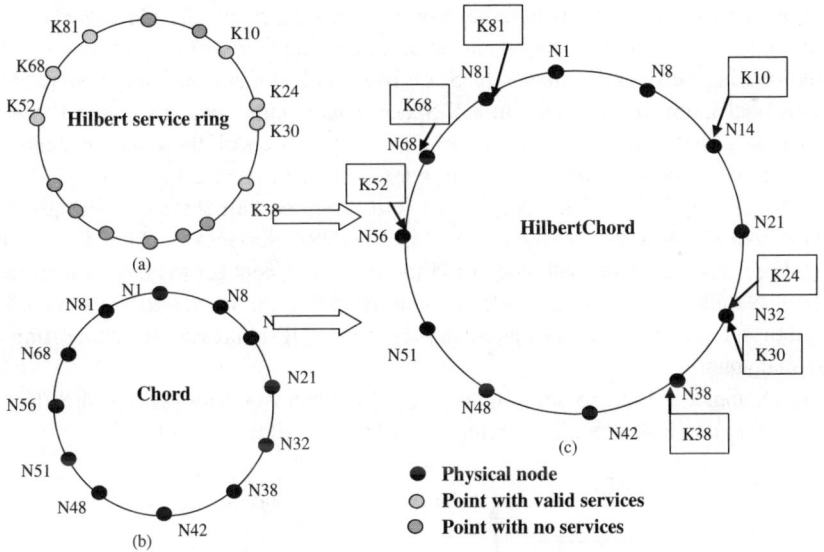

Fig. 1. The forming process of Hilbert Chord

3.2 HilbertChord Construction

HilbertChord is a Chord system by combing Hilbert SFC to support multi-keyword query and approximate query, in which, all the service index points mapped from attribute keywords of services are connected based on Hilbert SFC to form a ring named as Hilbert service ring. Hilbert service ring is mapped to a Chord as HilbertChord. While, Chord is constructed from the physical nodes on the network linked up through Chord algorithm, each of nodes has been given m bits as unique identifier generated by calculating the hash value of its IP address with equal length to HilbertLength. Fig.1 shows the forming process, where, all the service index points on Hilbert service ring(Fig.1(a)) are mapped to the nodes on Chord(Fig.1(b)), and nodes on Chord are the ones on HilbertChord. For example, in Fig.1(c), both of the service index points (K24 and K30) are mapped to node N32 on Chord, and N32 is also as a node of HilbertChord.

Thereby, HilbertChord has the following characteristics: (1) Service indexes are mapped to corresponding points in a SISpace, and their positions are not going to change even if these service indexes are copied to other physical nodes. (2) Attribute keywords of a service are mapped into a Hilbert index to support multi-keyword query. (3) Spatial relationship of service index points is maintained according to Hilbert SFC to support approximate query by means of the relationship between neighbor index points in the SISpace.

3.3 HilbertChord Supporting Approximate Query

For two services, if their attribute keywords are lexicographically close or they have common keywords, we can map their indexes to the same node or nodes that are close in the overlay network by means of SFC from multi-dimensional index space to 1-dimensional index space. Thus, in a SISpace, space points with the same keywords are bound to the same coordinates point, that is, services with the same attribute keywords are corresponding to one service index point, and service index points of similar services may be neighbor points each other. So we call services with adjoining service index points in a Hilbert space as Neighbor Services or named as Hilbert Neighbors. Therefore, on each node of HilbertChord, except for the basic finger table, Hilbert Neighbors (see Fig.4) are maintained for each of services to record its neighbor service indexes and their mapping node's IP addresses for supporting approximate query.

For example, in Fig.2, S and $\{S_1, S_2, S_3, S_4\}$ are Neighbor Services, $Sim(S, \{S_1, S_2, S_3, S_4\})=1$, and $\{S_1, S_2, S_3, S_4\}$ are registered in the SM(see Section 5.2) of service S.

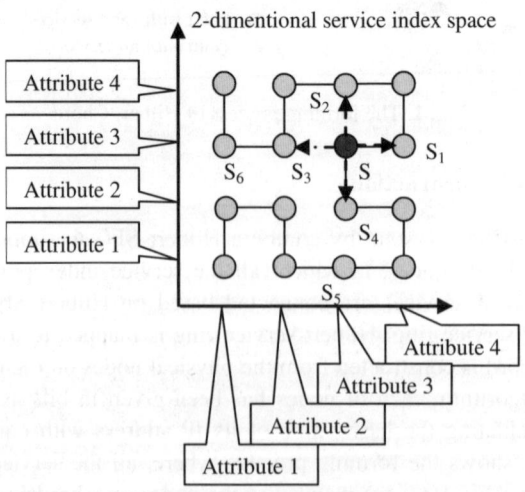

Fig. 2. Hilbert neighbors sketch

When service S is found, S_1, S_2, S_3, S_4 similar to S are found easily based on S's neighbor information, and S_5 is found easily through S_4's Hilbert Neighbors, S_6 through S_3, and so on, all the services similar to service S can be found.

4 SOA-Based Service Management on HilbertChord

4.1 Idea of SOA-Based Service Management

In HilbertChord, SOA based service management mechanism is adopted, which is shown in Fig.3, where QNode, MNode and RNode are query nodes, storage nodes and resource nodes respectively, QNodesare used to send queries and receive results, MNodes are used to store metadata of service resources, and RNodes are the location of the service resources. First, HilbertLength of service S and some metadata describing the service are registered in its corresponding MNode following the HilbertChord looking up rules. Then to discover services, which is similar to publishing services, based on the metadata of the service found via a MNode, the metadata of the service and its similar services can be obtained easily, including their URI. Finally, these services are bound to their URI and their services are shared.

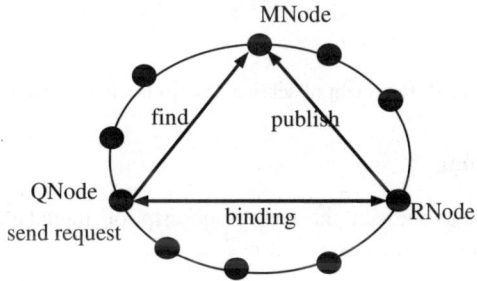

Fig. 3. SOA Service Management based on HilbertChord

4.2 Service Description Model

This paper proposes a service description model (SM) by referring to WSDL and the idea of service management above, which is denoted as follows:

$$SM(S_i) = (K_i, HL, HN, wsdlurl)$$

where, S_i is a service, K_i is a list of keywords for describing service S_i, HL is HilbertLength calculated based on K_i of service S_i, HN for Hilbert Neighbors and their corresponding IP addresses, wsdlurl for wsdl file's url. For example, Fig.4 represents the description fragment of a service, whose information includes: three keywords as key_1, key_2 and key_3, HilbertLength as 01001, six Neighbor Services and their corresponding IP addresses, where 01110, 01101 are indirect neighbors of S_i, and "http://www.neu.edu.cn:8080/axis/services/CreateStringService?wsdl" is the url of service "01001".

```xml
<?xml version="1.0" encoding="UTF-8">
<service>
 <information>
  <data1>key₁</data1>
  <data2> key₂ </data2>
  <data3> key₃</data3>
 </information>
 <HilbertLength>01001</HilbertLength>
 <HilbertNeighbor1>01010, 01001<HilbertNeighbor1>
 <Neighbor1IP>202.118.19.12, 202.118.19.112</Neighbor1IP>
 <HilbertNeighbor2>01001, 11001</HilbertNeighbor2>
 <Neighbor2IP>202.118.19.11, 202.118.19.233<Neighbor1IP>
 <HilbertNeighbor3>01110, 01101</HilbertNeighbor3>
 <Neighbor3IP>202.118.1.12, 202.118.1.12<Neighbor3IP>
 <wsdlurl>http://www.neu.edu.cn:8080/axis/services/CreateStringService?wsdl</wsdlurl>
</service>
```

Fig. 4. Fragment of service description information

4.3 Service Publishing

Service publishing is to register the service description metadata into a MNode on HilbertChord, the detail process is as follows:

(1) Use a hashing to map the sorted attribute keywords $K_1, K_2, ..., K_n$ of a service S into a sequence of hash values as SDArray(S) represented by W $[w_1, w, ... ,w_n]$ (n is the number of keywords).
(2) Transform SDArray(S) to HilbertLength of service S as the service's identifier.
(3) Publish service S at node n, firstly match the HilbertLength of service S with all HilbertLength items in the "finger table" of node n, if the matched HilbertLength is found, directly register the metadata of service S to its corresponding node, otherwise, find one with less than the nearest HilbertLength of S, and transmit the publishing request to the node.
(4) Repeat these steps above until the successor node the metadata of service S registered is found.
(5) Write S's Hilbert Neighbors information, the process of registering Hilbert Neighbors is shown in the following.
(6) Finally, renew Service Similarity Matrix on the node where the metadata of service S is in, and calculate the similarity degrees between the existed services on the node and service S, and then the publishing process is terminated.

Maintenance of Hilbert Neighbors. In a SISpace, the adjacent service index points along an attribute dimensional direction are named as neighbor services or called Hilbert Neighbors, shown in Fig.5, S_1, S_2, S_3, S_4 are all the neighbors of service S, whose number is the double of attribute keywords. The registering process is as follows:

(1) First, according to SDArray(S), get the HilbertLength of a neighbor service of S on one attribute dimensional direction, such as S_1.

(2) According to Hilbert Neighbors information of service S_1, all the Hilbert Neighbors on the attribute dimension are found, for example, in Fig.6, S_{i1}, S_{i2},..., S_{im} are Hilbert Neighbors of S_1 on the i-dimensional attribute, then compare L(S) with each of services L[S_{i1}, S_{i2},..., S_{im}] to select S_a and S_b with HL[S_a] <HL[S]<HL[S_b], then S should be inserted between S_a and S_b, in this way, Hilbert Neighbors information of {S_a,S,S_b} are needed to be maintained.

(3) If there are no services on the nearest neighbor point, then the next indirect neighbor point will be searched along the attribute dimension until the node with services is found, and then Hilbert Neighbors information of these services will be maintained on the node. If no services are found within a certain convergence time or so it is not in the SISpace, null is assigned to Hilbert Neighbors of service S.

(4) After all the steps above for each of attribute dimensions are finished, the maintenance of Hilbert Neighbors information in the SISpace is over.

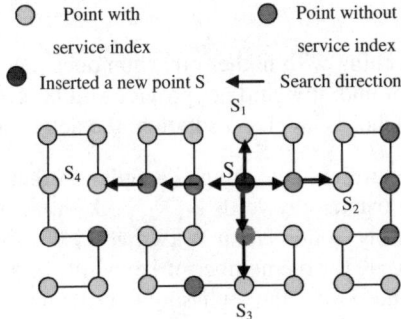

Fig. 5. Process of registering Hilbert Neighbors of the service S in 2-dimensional index space

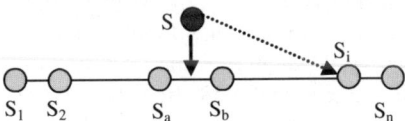

Fig. 6. The registering process of service S's Hilbert Neighbors

Maintaining Services Similarity Matrix. According to the feature of Hilbert filling curve, the points closed to each other in a SISpace may also be closed to each other on its corresponding Hilbert filling curve. Therefore, these similar service points are not far from each other in some degree, even most of them are on the same node. So if you want to search for the similar service points, first you'd better search for them on the 'local'. Services Similarity Matrix is used to find out the most similar service on the same node. Since it represents the similarity degree or the difference among the service indexes registered on the same node of HilbertChord. After a service is published and the maintenance of Hilbert Neighbors information is over, Services Similarity Matrixes on the nodes with Hilbert Neighbors information changed are maintained. For example, Fig.7 shows the Services Similarity Matrix of Fig.5 on node n, it is easy to find the similar services of S, where, $Sim(S,S_1)$ is 1, and $Sim(S,S_2)$ is 1, etc.

$$\begin{array}{c} & S & S_1 & S_2 & S_3 & S_4 \\ S & \begin{pmatrix} 0 & 1 & 1 & 1 & 1 \\ S_1 & 1 & 0 & 2 & 2 & 2 \\ S_2 & 1 & 2 & 0 & 2 & 2 \\ S_3 & 1 & 2 & 2 & 0 & 2 \\ S_4 & 1 & 2 & 2 & 2 & 0 \end{pmatrix} \end{array}$$

Fig. 7. Services Similarity Matrix

4.4 Service Searching

DHT-based services searching with higher precision does not support similar services query, if no services are found, it would not provide similar services for compensating the query. While HilbertChord can give a solution, the details are as follows:

(1) The process of services searching is similar to that of services publishing, firstly sort the attribute keywords $k_1, k_2, ..., k_n$ in keywords list, then hash K_i to generate an array of numerical W $[w_1, w_2 ... w_n]$, $W_n = hash(K_n)$. If NumberK<n, (NumberK for the number of keywords of a query), 0 is assigned to the hash values of the missing attributes, then calculate HilbertLength=Hilbert(W).
(2) Suppose a query is sent from a physical node n, firstly search the matched HilbertLength in the finger table of node n, if matched services are found, send the request directly to the corresponding node and meanwhile get all related services on each of attribute dimensional directions as the approximate results of the query. Then all or some ranking results are sent to the user.
(3) If no matched services arefound, find the nearest node with HilbertLength less than that of the node in its finger table, and transmit the request to the node as a query node. Further it looks for its successor node as the same as Chord by recurring above steps to find the matched services.

(4) If no matched services are found, e.g., the service index point does not exist, services similarity matrix can help to find similar services S_i, further according to HilbertNeighbor information of S_i, other indirect neighbors can also be found as similar services and be returned to users.

5 Experiments

The experiments consist of two parts: one is to compare the performance of HilbertChord with that of Chord, the other one is to test the principle of HilbertChord.

5.1 Comparison between HilbertChord and Chord

Let n be the number of attribute dimensions of a SISpaces, V be the size of the SISpace, p be the density of services and N be the total number of nodes. Experiments are conducted under the cases with four variable parameters, the testing results are shown in Fig.8,9,10,11, where n is horizontal coordinates, and the number of hops as vertical coordinates. Experiments show that when the number of attribute dimensions exceeds 3 or the density of services in a service index pace is lower, the cost of HilbertChord on either publishing or searching services is expensive.

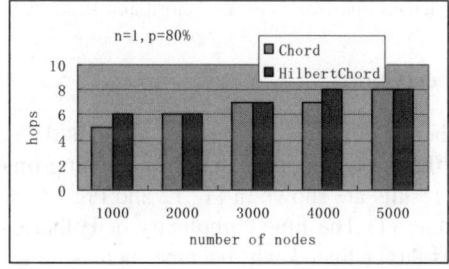

Fig. 8. Performance comparison between Chord and HilbertChord (n=1,p=80%)

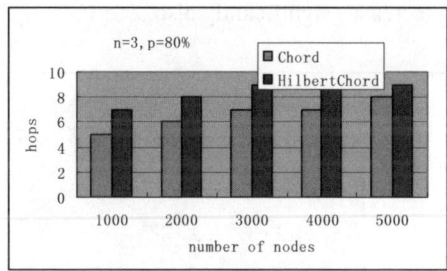

Fig. 9. Performance comparison between Chord and HilbertChord (n=3,p=80%)

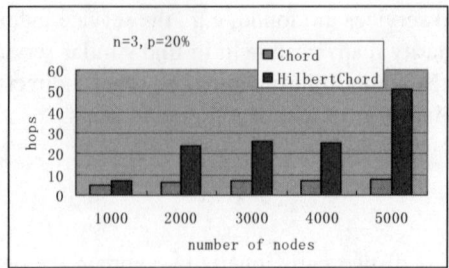

Fig. 10. Performance comparison between Chord and HilbertChord (n=3,p=20%)

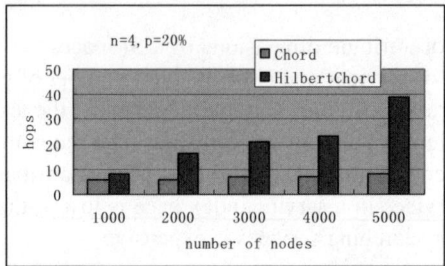

Fig. 11. Performance comparison between Chord and HilbertChord (n=4,p=80%)

5.2 Principle of HilbertChord

Suppose n is the number of attribute dimensions, and p is the density of services in a SISpace, then we test the publishing time and the searching time with variable values of n and p, the testing results are shown in Fig.12 and Fig.13. According to the testing results, we can conclude: (1) The time complexity of HilbertChord with the number of attribute dimensions larger than 3 will become increasing since the cost of Hilbert function with larger than 3-dimensions space is expensive and result in higher time complexity either for services publishing or services searching; (2) When the density of services in a SISpace is less than 80%, the time complexity of services publishing and services searching increases significantly also.

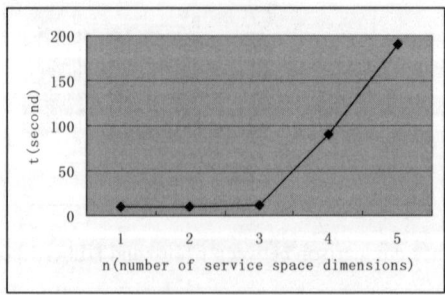

Fig. 12. The service publishing time with different service space dimensions

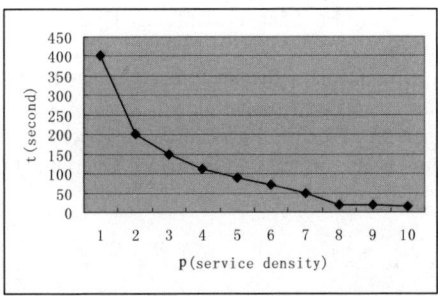

Fig. 13. The service publishing time with different service density

6 Conclusions

This paper focuses on building flexible, scalable infrastructure for managing service resources and a service resources management framework-HilbertChord is proposed by combing Hilbert and Chord for supporting DHT-based multi-keyword query and approximate query by means of Hilbert index to improve the efficiency of resources searching and the completeness of results obtained.

Experiments show that HilbertChord is adoptable to large-scale service index space with higher density of services and has presented its high efficiency, good scalability for service resources management. But for SISpace with lower density of services or with higher dimensional space, the efficiency of publishing and searching services will become lower, which will be focused on further to improve its limitations.

References

1. Moon, B., Jagadish, H.V., Faloutsos, C., Saltz, J.H.: Analysis of the clustering properties of the Hilbert space-filling curve. IEEE Transactions on Knowledge and Data Engineering 13(1), 124–141 (2001)
2. Lawder, J.K., King, P.J.H.: Using space filling curves for multi-dimensional indexing. In: 17th British National Conference on Databases, Exeter, UK (2000)
3. Chen, D., Yang, S., Peng, X.: TaChord: a Chord System Using Topology-Aware Routing and Super Peers. Journal of Southeast University (English Edition) 20(3), 273–278 (2004)
4. Mesaros, V.A., Carton, B., Roy, P.V.: S-Chord: Using Symmetry to Improve Lookup Efficiency in Chord. Technical Report 2002-08, UC-Louvain (2002)
5. Liu, J.: Study and Implementation on P2P Structure and Meta-information Management Supporting Data Grid. A Master Thesis of Northeastern University (2006)
6. Cai, M., Frank, M., Chen, J., Szekely, P.: MAAN: A Multi-Attribute Addressable Network for Grid Information Services. In: Proceedings of 4th Int. Workshop on Grid Computing, pp. 184–191 (2003)
7. Oppenheimer, D., Albrecht, J., Patterson, D., Vahdat, A.: Distributed Resource Discovery on Planetlab with SWORD. In Proceedings of the First Workshop on Real, Large Distributed Systems (2004)

8. Ratnasamy, S., Hellerstein, J.M., Shenker, S.: Range Queries over DHTs. IRB-TR-03-009, Intel Corporation (2003)
9. Andrzejak, A., Xu, Z.: Scalable. Efficient Range Queries for Grid Information Services. In: 2nd Int. Conf. on Peer-to-Peer Computing, pp. 33–40 (2002)
10. Schmidt, C., Parashar, M.: Flexible Information Discovery in Decentralized Distributed Systems. In: 12th Int. Symp. on High-Performance Distributed Computing, pp. 226–235 (2003)

A Peer-to-Peer Assisting Scheme for Live Streaming Services

Jian Wan, Liangjin Lu, Xianghua Xu, and Xueping Ren

Institute of Software and Intelligent Technology, Hangzhou Dianzi University,
Hangzhou 310018, China
wanjian@hdu.edu.cn, xuxhcs@zju.edu.cn

Abstract. Recently, peer-to-peer approach has emerged as an effective solution for live streaming services. However, some channels may not provide good streaming services due to their less audience, and some peers may receive bad services owning to their relatively narrower bandwidth. To address these issues, we introduce a peer-to-peer inter-channel assisting scheme for live streaming services. In the scheme, the social network theory is employed to construct the inter-channel overlay network. The scope of cooperation is scaled from intra-channel to inter-channel through active assistance and passive assistance. Besides, the relationship in social network works as the incentive mechanism to stimulate the assisting behaviors among peers. Simulations demonstrate that our scheme can promote the cooperation effectively and consequently improve the streaming qualities significantly.

1 Introduction

Large-scale live streaming services over Internet have been a quite challenging problem for many years. The traditional Client/Server architecture turns out to be incapable due to server-side bottleneck and single point failure problems along with the growth of clients. In recent years, peer-to-peer computing has been employed for efficient live streaming distribution. In a peer-to-peer overlay network, every peer works in a relay mode to download data from the nearest peers and upload to others. Through sufficiently utilizing the bandwidth and computation resources possessed by peers, workload placed on the media source servers is reduced and hence the overall scalability is greatly increased.

The main idea of peer-to-peer data distribution is the cooperation of massive peers generated formidable aggregate service ability. The more peers online, the better the streaming quality will be in general. However, most of existing media distribution models only share data in the same channel. The cooperative scope is very limited to the unpopular programs and the peers far from their neighbors. In this paper we thus propose an inter-channel assisting scheme that organizes all peers into a global overlay on the basis of social network. Our design allows peers to invite other members, including the idle peers who do not join any channels and peers in other channels who have ability to help others, to provide active and passive assistances when the streaming quality degrades. Moreover, a social relationship based incentive mechanism is adopted to avoid the free-riding phenomena.

The rest of this paper is organized as follows: Section 2 describes works related to peer-to-peer live streaming and assisting scheme. The detail of social network and assisting distribution scheme is presented in Section 3. Section 4 discusses performance evaluation. We conclude this paper in Section 5.

2 Related Works

Most previous models focused on the intra-channel cooperation can be summarized to three categories:

1) Tree based sender driven push models [1][2][3];
2) Mesh based receiver driven pull models [4];
3) Push and pull combined models [5].

The push models are one-to-many distribution models that have the least end-to-end delay. But they are not resilient to network churns and underutilize the resources of leaves. To improve the robustness of services, pull models have been proposed to exchange delay and storage for stability and scalability through many-to-many downloading strategy. The push and pull combined models inherit the low-latency and stability merits of previous two models. Nevertheless, the intra-channel cooperation models haven't fully exhibited the potential power of global overlay network.

Wong introduced the idea of download with helpers for the first time in [6]. Peers join the swarm of BitTorrent [7] to contribute their bandwidth. When and how many helpers should be introduced into the swarm are decided by the content providers according to the network conditions. The model is not sensitive to the degradation of streaming quality of minority peers owing to central management. Furthermore, the lack of suitable incentive mechanism makes it impractical in real-world. More recently, Pouwelse proposed a social-based P2P file-sharing paradigm to exploit social group phenomena in content discovering and downloading [8]. However, problems in live streaming area have to be further studied. As in [9], we build a social network with distributed relationship memory to tackle various attacks in our assisting scheme.

AnySee [10] adopts an inter-overlay optimization scheme to find the nearest neighbors, and improves global resource utilization to achieve better service quality. However, AnySee neglects the resources of idle peers who are not in any channel. The idle peers will be willing to contribute their resources by an effective incentive mechanism.

3 System Design

The typical scenario of our model is as follows. A peer joins the social network to construct friend relationship circle. It will join a channel if it wants to view a program. In the course of playback, the peer will invite its friends in the social network, known as assistants, to download some media data blocks when the streaming quality degrades. The streaming quality of the weak peer will be improved with the help of the assistants. The overlay network and data distribution mechanism are two key issues of P2P live systems. We introduce the construction and evolution of social network and assisting distribution mechanism in this section.

3.1 Social Network

To support assisting distribution, the overlay network must meet the following requirements:

1) A peer should know where to find assistants.
2) A peer should be able to distinguish between friend and foe.

The intra-channel cooperation models cannot meet these requirements. The reason lies in the independent data distribution overlays of different channels. The peer in one overlay has no knowledge of peers in other overlays. This brings difficulty for the weak peers to search for assistants inter-channel. Another problem is raised for the insufficiency of IPv4 address space. Many a NATs [11] are deployed between intranet and Internet. The same peer will be treated as a different peer after it re-joins the overlay because a new IP address is assigned by NAT. Hence, the re-construction of overlay will lead to the loss of relationship between peers.

Relationship in peer-to-peer network, in some aspect, is similar to the human relationship in real society where people incline to interact with familiar and trusted friends. The "Six Degree of Separation" phenomenon [12] demonstrates that social network contributes to information spread and relationship maintenance. Consequently, we propose the idea of social network to tackle problems encountered in assisting scheme. The outline of our scheme is shown in Figure 1.

The whole overlay includes two layers: the channel overlay and the inter-channel overlay. The outer circle represents the inter-channel overlay based on social network. The solid line means neighbor relationship of the same channel and the dotted line means friend relationship in the social network. As shown in Figure 1, the social

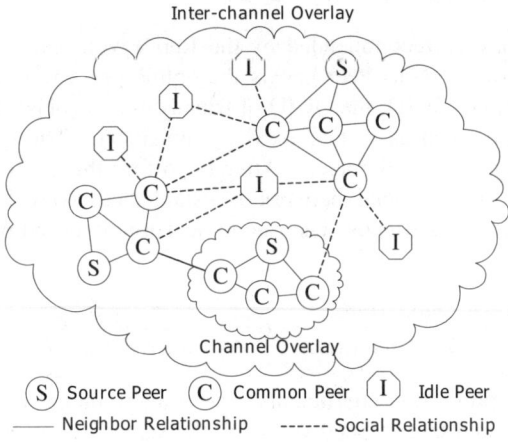

Fig. 1. Outline of system

network is the bridge that connects each channel overlay. Since the topology of channel overlay varies in different models, we thus focus on the construction and evolution of social network.

The diagram of a peer is given in Figure 2. The buffer collects intra-channel data from neighbors and inter-channel data from friends, and sends them to the media player.

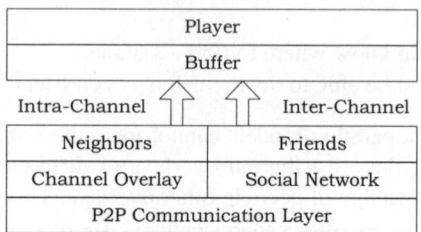

Fig. 2. Diagram of a peer

In the social network, each peer is assigned a global unique identifier (GUID). When the peers join the social network, they will notify their friends the GUID and their new IP addresses through the Rendezvous Peer and the online friends who have persistent IP, and keep in touch with them by periodical heartbeat messages. As interaction only occurs between friends occasionally and no flooding method is used in social network, the overhead is acceptable.

The peer-to-peer network is highly dynamic: peers join and leave freely. Therefore, peers always need to discover new friends. We introduce three ways to discover new friends.

1) The friends in real society.
2) Recommended by the Rendezvous Peer.
3) Recommended by existing friends.

Most friends may be recommended by the Rendezvous Peer at the beginning of revolution as the Rendezvous Peer knows the online peers who join recently. Since each peer has a unique GUID, the GUID of friends in real society can be obtained by out-of-band method, such as instant message, email, etc. The new friends may be relatives or colleagues in real society. After importing the GUID into the software, friendship in the virtual social network is established. New friends can also be recommended by existing friends. The rule to accept new friend by peer i to peer j is given in formula 1.

$$FC_{ij} = \alpha * \frac{Bandwidth_{ij}}{Max(Bandwidth)} + \beta * \left(1 - \frac{FriendCount_i}{Max(FriendCount)}\right) \quad (1)$$

α and β are the proportion coefficients. The strategy makes peer i to select a new friend with higher end-to-end bandwidth. At the same time peer i has more urgent desire to accept new friends when it has fewer friends.

Just like people in real society, peers in social network will strengthen the relationship with those who always provide assistances to them, and weaken the relationship with malicious peers and free-riders. Here we assume every peer is rational and tries to maximum its own interest. Rational Peers will refuse to provide assistances to others without incentives because the assistances will consume their resources and degrade their performance. In social network, the friend relationship works as an incentive to encourage contribution. A virtual money mechanism is employed to measure the strength of relationship between friends. The assistants will be rewarded certain amount of virtual money for the assistance behavior. The virtual money earned by peer i from peer j (M_{ij}) is proportional to the assisted data quantity that peer i provides to peer j and the time peer i takes in assistances.

$$M_{ij} = \sum AssistedDataQuantity * \mu + \sum AssistedTime * v \qquad (2)$$

In formula 2, μ and v are the conversion factors from the data quantity and the time to virtual money. The formula to calculate relationship strength is given as follows.

$$R_{ij} = \frac{M_{ji}}{M_{ij} + M_{ji}} \qquad R_{ij} \in [0,1] \qquad (3)$$

As shown in formula 3, R_{ij}=0.5 means two peers help each other to the same degree, R_{ij}>0.5 means peer j is generous in giving assistances and a good friend to peer i. The threshold of relationship strength is set to recognize the free-riders who rarely offer assistances to others. The virtual money of a new friend is set an initial value. The relationship strength is updated after each assistance procedure and stored in both sides. The free-riders will be kicked out by their friends with less contribution.

The social relationship incentive mechanism is similar to Tit-for-Tat mechanism of BitTorrent [7] protocol. The more assistances one peer provides to its friends, the stronger the relationship will be, and also the more assistances the peer can obtain from its friends.

3.2 Assisting Distribution Scheme

Statistics show that channel popularity follows a Zipf distribution [13]. It means the minority of hot channels absorbed most of audience, while the majority of channels have only the less audience in most of the time. For this reason, the unpopular channel cannot make full use of the advantages of peer-to-peer to provide high streaming quality. In the mean time, some peers may have less bandwidth and locate far away from other members in network owing to the heterogeneity of peers and overlay topology. This brings about bad user experience to the weak peers. We put forward two ways of assistances to settle these two challenges: active assistance and passive assistance.

(1) Active assistance

Active assistance is sponsored by the idle peers to increase the population of unpopular programs. The active assistance aims to improve the overall performance of the target channels by expanding the choice of data suppliers.

Active assistance is relatively easy to implement. The idle peer sends idle notification to its online friends. The friends will relay the notification to its Tracker

Server who is the neighbor manager of specified channel. If the number of online peers is less than a threshold, the idle peer will join the channel to run as a regular neighbor to other members. In order to punish the free-riders, only peers having relationship strength value is above the lowest threshold is allowed to get active assistance from the idle peers. The active assistance will be withdrawn when the audience goes beyond the threshold and switch to other channels.

(2) Passive assistance

Passive assistance is sponsored by the weak peers who need help. The only goal of passive assistance is to improve the streaming quality of the weak peers. Here we need to make quantitative analysis to following two problems:

1) What situation calls for passive assistance?
2) How to determine whether to provide passive assistance?

The first one is essentially a problem of service quality (QoS) evaluation. In a streaming media system, the continuity of playback is the major factor of QoS. As shown in Figure 2, the buffer of a channel is a cycle queue, and it is divided into blocks. Every block holds a second of media data with a unique sequence number. The Play Pointer points to the block which has sent to the player recently. It moves forward one block per second. If one of the media data blocks cannot arrive before the playback deadline, a vibration or pause will be appeared in the player. So we define Continuity Degree of peer i as follows:

$$CD_i = \frac{Number\ of\ On\ Time\ Blocks}{Number\ of\ Total\ Blocks} \quad (4)$$

The on time blocks are the blocks downloaded before its playback deadline.

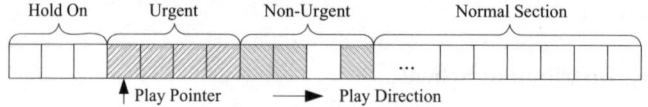

Fig. 3. Channel buffer snapshot

The passive assistance will be launched when a peer detects its Continuity Degree is less than the specified threshold. An assistance invitation will be sent to its online friends. The invitees fall into two categories: idle peers and busy peers. The busy peers are playing a program in one of the channel overlays. To the busy peers, the assistance will influence the streaming quality of them and their neighbors, so two factors should be taken into account when considering whether to accept the invitation: their unoccupied bandwidth and the social relationship strength with the inviter, while the idle invitees will only consider the latter one. As it is hard to measure the unoccupied bandwidth in the dynamic network, we use the Free Degree to estimate it.

$$FD_i = \sum_{j=1}^{k} \frac{PlaybackDeadline_j - ArriveTime_j}{BufferLength} \bigg/ k \quad (5)$$

The parameter k is the total blocks which have been finished downloading. The formula denotes that the earlier the data blocks are downloaded, the more free bandwidth the peer may has. Consequently, we define a Decision Function for the invitee i to determine whether to accept the invitation of peer j as follows.

$$D_{ij} = \begin{cases} 1 & FD_i > \phi \ \cap \ R_{ij} > \varphi \\ 0 & otherwise \end{cases} \quad (6)$$

The Free Degree of peer i (FD_i) is set to 1 when the invitee is idle. The Decision Function denotes that peer i will accept the invitation only when it has enough unoccupied bandwidth resources ($FD_i > \phi$) and strong social relationship with the inviter ($R_{ij} > \varphi$). The decision is made by the invitee according to its local information. As a result, the mechanism is robust enough to defend the malicious attacks, for a "bad guy" will not be acknowledged even if it juggled its local virtual money value. Stimulated by the Decision Function, peers will be delighted to join the social network to strengthen the relationship with their friends when they are free.

If the invitee accepts the request, it will join the same channel as the inviter. The inviter will assign a download task of some empty blocks to the assistants. As the busy peers will handle their own matters first, we employ a slowly increase algorithm to avoid the overload of assistants. At first, every assistant is assigned a fixed number of blocks. If the previous tasks can be finished on time, the assignment will increase slowly until it reaches the threshold. Otherwise, the assignment will be decreased. The inviter will download the blocks which cannot be downloaded by the assistants. Since each assistant forwards different blocks to the inviter without overlap, it seems that the bandwidth of the inviter is widened by the passive assistants.

4 Performance Evaluation

We implement the assisting scheme upon the mesh based pull model. The system has run well in the campus network for more than one month. We also implement a simulator based on Peersim[14] and made preliminary simulation to test this model.

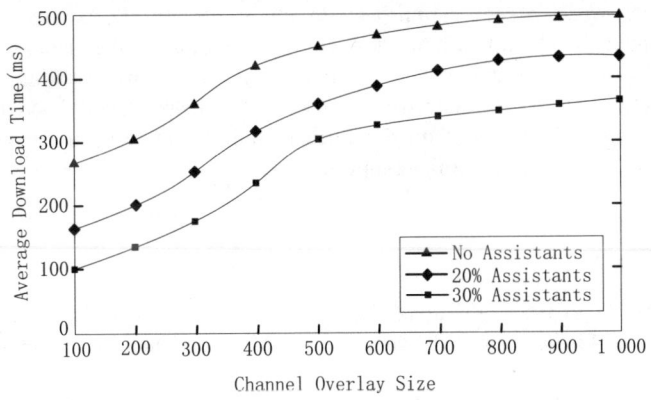

Fig. 4. Average Download Time V.S. overlay size

The bandwidth is set between 1024kbps and 3072kbps, and the ON/OFF cycle is set to 600s. The Average Download Time of introducing different amount of active assistants is compared. The result is given in Figure 4.

As shown in Figure 4, the Average Download Time is apparently decreased by fully utilizing the upload capacity of active assistants. We also compare the Continuity Degree of passive assistance and normal pull model with the same neighbor count. The result is shown in Figure 5.

The passive assistance gains more Continuity Degree because the assistants download data according to the desire of the inviters, while the neighbors of normal pull mode download data based on their own need.

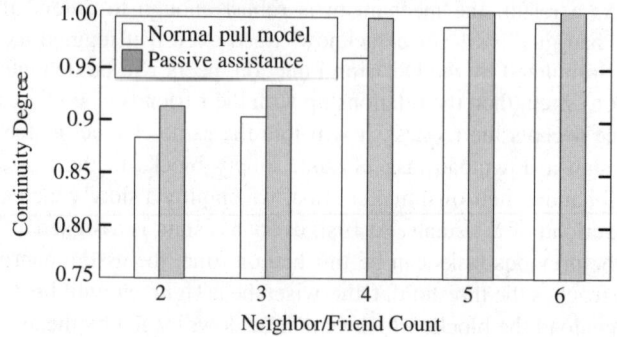

Fig. 5. Continuity degree of passive assistance and normal pull model

5 Conclusions

In this paper, we present an inter-channel assisting distribution scheme for P2P live streaming. As an effective complement to the intra-channel models, it builds the overlay network on the basis of social network to provide a robust and persistent platform for more cooperation. On this platform, some peers play the role of assistant to help other weak peers to improve streaming quality. Peers are voluntary to contribute their bandwidth when they are free owing to the social relationship incentive. However, there is much room to improve in the assisting distribution algorithm and incentive mechanism because of the heterogeneity and dynamic of peer-to-peer network. We will do the further studies and tests in the real Internet environment as well as the mobile computing area.

References

1. Castro, M., Druschel, P., Kermarrec, A., et al.: Splitstream: High-Bandwidth Multicast in Cooperative Environments. In: Proc. of ACM Symposium on Operating Systems Principles, pp. 298–313 (2003)
2. Banerjee, S., Bhattacharjee, B., Kommareddy, C.: Scalable Application Layer Multicast. In: Proc. of ACM SIGCOMM, pp. 205–217 (2002)

3. Tran, D., Hua, K., Do., T.: ZIGZAG: An Efficient Peer-to-Peer Scheme for Media Streaming. In: Proc. of IEEE Infocom, pp. 649–652 (2003)
4. Zhang, X., Liu, J., Li, B., et al.: DONet: A Data-Driven Overlay Network for Live Media Streaming. In: Proc. of IEEE Infocom, Miami, USA, pp. 2102–2111 (2005)
5. Li, Z., Jian, G., Meng, Z., et al.: Gridmedia: A Practical Peer-to-Peer based Live Video Streaming System. In: Proc. of IEEE 7th Workshop on Multimedia Signal Processing, pp. 287–290 (2005)
6. Wong, J.: Enhancing Collaborative Content Distribution with Helpers. Master's thesis, The University of British Columbia (2004)
7. Cohen, B.: Incentives Build Robustness in BitTorrent. In: Proc. of 1st Workshop on Economics of Peer-to-Peer Systems, Berkeley (2003)
8. Pouwelse, J., Garbacki, P., Wang, J., et al.: Tribler: A Social-based Peer-to-Peer System. In: Proc. of the 5th Int'l Workshop on Peer-to-peer Systems, pp. 391–394 (2006)
9. Wang, W., Zhao, L., Yuan, R.: Improving Cooperation in Peer-to-Peer Systems Using Social Networks. In: Proc. of 3rd Workshop on Hot Topic in Peer-to-Peer Systems, Greece, pp. 50–57 (2006)
10. Liao, X., Jin, H., Liu, Y., et al.: AnySee: Peer-to-Peer Live Streaming. In: Proc. of IEEE Infocom, Barcelona, Spain, pp. 23–29 (2006)
11. Huston, G.: A look inside network address translators. The Internet Protocol Journal 7(3), 2–32 (2004)
12. Watts, D., Strogatz, S.: Collective Dynamics of Small-World Networks. Nature 393(6), 440–442 (1998)
13. Zhou, X., Xu, C.: Optimal Video Replication and Placement on a Cluster of Video-on-Demand Servers. In: Proc. of the 2002 International Conference on Parallel Processing, pp. 547–555 (2002)
14. Jelasity, M., Montresor, A., Jesi, G.P.: Peersim: Peer-to-Peer simulator (2004), http://peersim.sourceforge.net

A Novel Ownership Scheme to Maintain Web Content Consistency*

Chi-Hung Chi[1], Choon-Keng Chua[2], and Weihong Song[1]

[1] School of Software, Tsinghua University
[2] National University of Singapore
chichihung@mail.tsinghua.edu.cn

Abstract. In this paper, we would like to address the consistency problem for web content presentation through explicit ownership schemes when its information is retrieved and reused through the Internet. Our previous study [4] on the real-time monitoring of web content already showed that for most content distribution networks (including Content Distribution Network (CDN), replica, web mirroring, and peer-to-peer), consistency problem often arises, which results in unpredictable caching behavior, performance loss, and content presentation errors. And as the client requester, current validation schemes are not enough due to the assumption on the equivalence of the content distribution address to content ownership. Our solution covers both protocols and supports for most of the necessary functions such as validation, delegation, presentation, ..., etc. that need to be done in the network.

Keywords: Web, Content Distribution, Performance, Consistency.

1 Introduction

Content distribution has already been proven to be a key feature in today's Internet infrastructure. Independent of the types of networks being used for content dissemination (such as CDN, web mirroring, replica, or peer-to-peer), it is always desirable to have copies of the "fresh" content located closer to the clients for faster access [17]. Furthermore, the demand for value-added services in the network and best-fit content presentation instead of the simple raw data retrieval is also increasing due to the heterogeneous pervasive Internet access [2] [11]. To support the correct execution of these functions in the network, there lies a fundamental difference between "data" and "content". Besides the raw data information, content such as a web page also encapsulates attributes to administrate various functions in content distribution and delivery.

It is observed that while most attentions have been paid to maintain the bit-by-bit equivalence between the original and replicated/cached copies of a web object, the consistency of their attributes is often overlooked. In fact, even the HTTP protocol

---

* This work is supported by the China National Science Foundation Project #90604028 and China 863 project #2007AA01-Z122.

allows attributes of a retrieved web object to be modified legally. This creates a big concern because the attribute values will determine (i) whether the network and presentation functions will work properly, and (ii) the performance efficiency of content distribution and delivery. With the increasing demand for pervasive Internet access, the traditional consistency concept of bit-by-bit equivalence requirement is getting to be too restrictive. For example, two different versions of an image can be considered as consistent if a user wants to display them on a handphone through transcoding.

In this paper, we would like to address this content consistency problem through the introduction of the ownership concept. Our solutions cover both the protocols and supports for most of the necessary delivery-related functions such as validation, delegation, presentation, ..., etc. that need to be done in the network. To make our solution more concrete, we implement our proposal in one CDN and one peer-to-peer network to study its performance overhead. All results show the feasibility and practicability of our solution.

The outline for the rest of this paper is as follows. Section 2 summarizes related work to this content consistency problem over Internet. In Section 3, the concept of content ownership is clearly defined. Section 4 gives the performance study of our content ownership solution. Finally, the paper concludes in Section 5.

2 Related Work

HTTP/1.1 [7][12] supports basic consistency management using TTL (time-to-live) mechanism. Each content is assigned a TTL value by the server. When thee TTL time has elapsed, the content is marked as invalid and clients must check with the origin server for an updated copy. This method works best if the next update time of content is known a priori (good for news website). However, this is not the case for most other contents; content providers simply do not know when contents will be updated. As a result, TTL values are usually assigned conservatively (by setting a low TTL). To overcome these limitations, two variations of TTL have been proposed. Gwertzman et al. [10] proposed the adaptive TTL which is based on the Alex file system [1]. In this approach, the validity duration of a content is the product of its age and an update threshold.

Weak consistency guarantee offered by TTL may not be sufficient for certain applications, such as websites with many dynamic or frequently changing objects. As a result, server-driven approach was proposed to offer strong consistency guarantee [14]. This mechanism requires the server to maintain states such as which client has which object leases. An important issue that determines the feasibility of this approach is its scalability.

An important parameter for the lease algorithm is the lease duration. Having short lease duration reduces the server state overhead but increases control message overhead and vice versa. Duvvuri et al. [5] proposed adaptive lease which intelligently computes the optimal duration of leases to balance these tradeoffs. Yin et al. [18] proposed volume lease as a way to further reduce the overhead associated with the leases. A problem observed in the basic lease approach is the high overhead in lease renewals. To counter this problem, the authors proposed to group related objects into volumes. And the duration of volume lease is configured to be much lower than that of object leases. This has the effect of amortizing volume lease renewal overheads over many objects in a volume.

Many web pages are dynamically generated upon request and are usually marked as non-cachable. This causes clients to retrieve them upon every request, thus increasing server and network resource usage. Challenger et al. [3] proposed the Data Update Propagation (DUP) technique, which maintains data dependence information between cached objects and the underlying data (eg. database) which affect their values in a graph. In this approach, response for dynamic web pages is cached and used to satisfy subsequent requests. When the underlying data changes, their dependent cache entries are invalidated or updated. MONARCH is proposed to offer strong consistency without having servers to maintain per-client state [15]. The approach achieves strong consistency by examining the objects composing a web page, selecting the most frequently changing object on that page and having the cache request or validate that object on every access. The goal of this approach is to offer strong consistency for non-deterministic objects (objects that change at an unpredictable rate). Traditional TTL approach forces publishers to set conservative TTL in order to achieve high consistency at the cost of high revalidation overhead. With MONARCH, these objects can be safely cached by exploiting the relationship and change pattern of page container and objects.

Caching and replication creates multiple copies of content, therefore consistency must be maintained. This problem is not limited to the web, many other distributed computing systems also cache or replicate content. Saito et al. [17] did an excellent survey of consistency management in various distributed systems. Solutions for consistency management in distributed systems share similar objective, but differ in their design and implementation. They make use of their specific system characteristics to make consistency management more efficient. For example, Ninan et al. [16] extended the lease approach for use in CDN, by introducing the cooperative lease approach. Another solution for consistency management in CDN is [6]. On the other hand, solutions available for the web or CDN are inappropriate for P2P as peers can join and leave unexpectedly. Solutions specifically designed for P2P environments include [8] [13].

3 Definition of Content Ownership

With replication and mirroring, contents are made available at multiple hosts. Even though these hosts help to distribute contents, they may not be authorized to perform other tasks such as cache revalidation on behalf of the owner. A fundamental issue we have not addressed yet for the web is the *ownership* of contents. *At this moment, it is assumed that the content distribution address has the content ownership, which is in fact not correct.*

With proper ownership defined, we can answer questions such as:

- When we obtain a content from somewhere, we can go back to the owner and ask "is my copy valid?"
- When we are doubt of integrity of a content, we can ask the owner "is my copy modified or corrupted?"

There are many other questions content owners can answer better than anyone else. The fundamental idea is that since contents are created and maintained by owners, they can precisely answer all questions regarding the contents. The focus of our ownership approach here is to use ownership for checking content consistency.

Ownership itself is a profound subject which must be thoroughly studied. In particular, we have yet to answer questions such as:

- How is ownership represented?
- Can ownership be transferred? What condition should trigger the transfer of ownership?
- Can a content have more than 1 owner (multi-ownership)? What is the relationship among owners? How do owners cooperate and work together? How does validation work in the presence of multiple owners?

In this paper, we present a single-ownership model. In our model, each content has only one owner and that ownership association is static (no transfer or change in ownership). This allows us to demonstrate the importance and value of ownership for checking content consistency, without complicating our solution.

3.1 Basic Network Entities

Firstly, we model a network for content delivery, making minimum assumptions about the underlying network.

Definition 1: Node
A node (N) is a computer system on the network, identified by a globally unique identifier, *NodeID*.

Definition 2: Content
A content (C) is a subject of interest in the network, identified by a globally unique identifier, *ContentID*.

Each content has a predefined Time-to-Live (TTL) of which the content is valid to use. ContentID should be persistent.

Definition 3: Owner
The owner (Ow) is an entity that creates (and subsequently updates) content(s), identified by a globally unique identifier, *OwnerID*.

Typically, owner refers to an organization or individual. The OwnerID should be persistent.

Definition 4: Ownership
The ownership (C, Ow) is a tuple that associates a content (C) with an owner (Ow).

The owner has full knowledge about the content and has complete control over all aspects of its delivery, such as how the content should be accessed, delivered, presented, cached, replicated etc. When implementing ownership, we have two design options:

- Tag ownership information with the content by means of its attributes, or
- Let an ownership-manager maintain all content ownership information. Users query the ownership-manager to obtain the most updated ownership information of contents.

There are pros and cons associated with each option. The tagging option is simple and makes ownership information readily available as long as a user has the content. This, however, requires that the ownership information persists over times (because we cannot modify ownership for contents that have been delivered). On the other hand, the ownership-manager option does not require the ownership information to be persistent, but incurs overhead in additional query traffic.

3.2 Supporting Ownership in HTTP/1.1

This section describes how ownership can be supported in web content delivery – HTTP/1.1.

3.2.1 Basic Entities
First, let us map the three basic entities of ownership to the web, as discussed below.

- *ContentID* of a web content is its URL.
- *NodeID* of a host is represented by its hostname or IP address.
- *OwnerID* is not currently defined in HTTP. We propose using content's official URL as its OwnerID. A content's official URL is the URL maintained by its author or the author's representative and we assume that each content has only one official URL. If the author publishes a content at more than one URLs, he needs to choose one of the URLs as the official URL (as thus the OwnerID); other URLs are regarded as mirrors. Hereafter, the term owner and official site/URL are used interchangeably.

As described in the previous section, ownership information can either be tagged with content or externally managed by an ownership-manager. We opt for the tagging option since we do not want to introduce additional round trip when accessing or validating contents. The tagging option is deemed more efficient and suitable for the web environment.

All mirrored contents must specify OwnerID. Contents at their official URLs need not specify OwnerID. A content's semantics is defined by its body and attributes. Therefore, mirrors should preserve the body and all HTTP headers of contents except transitional headers such as Via and Connection response-headers.

3.2.2 Certified Mirrors
To offload the owner, we propose to let owners elect trusted nodes as certified mirrors. Certified mirrors differ from other mirrors in that the mirrored contents (both attributes and body) are certified consistent with the official site. Hence, users can download and validate with certified mirrors without any consistency issue.

We do not propose any mechanism for owner to ensure that a certified mirror is consistent with the official site. It is the responsibility of the owner to ensure that certified mirrors are consistent with the official site. Typically, the owner and the certified mirrors will have tight collaboration and the certified mirror is committed to keep all mirrored contents consistent with the owner. Among several ways to achieve consistency, the official site can push all updates to certified mirrors or certified mirrors can run in reverse-proxy configuration.

The owner elects a node as a certified mirror by granting it a mirror certificate. The certificate is a signed XML document that indicates the identity of the certified mirror, the path of mirrored contents and the validity period of the certificate. It is signed by the owner using the owner's private key, so end users can use the owner's public key to verify the certificate. Certified mirrors add a MirrorCert header into the responses for mirrored contents.

3.2.3 Validation

Validation is an important process to ensure that content is fresh and valid to use. The validation process involves two fundamental questions. Firstly, whom should users validate with? Users should only validate with a site that can guarantee consistency of the content. In this case, this refers to the owner and certified mirrors. Uncertified mirrors should not be used for validation (as opposed to HTTP). Secondly, when should users validate? A content should be validated whenever it has expired or its validity is unknown (eg. when download from uncertified mirrors).

In ownership-based web content delivery, there are three cases of validation depending on where the content is retrieved from, as shown in Figure 1. In the first case, if content is retrieved from the owner, users must validate with the owner. Users know that a site is the official site (owner) if the site does not specify the OwnerID

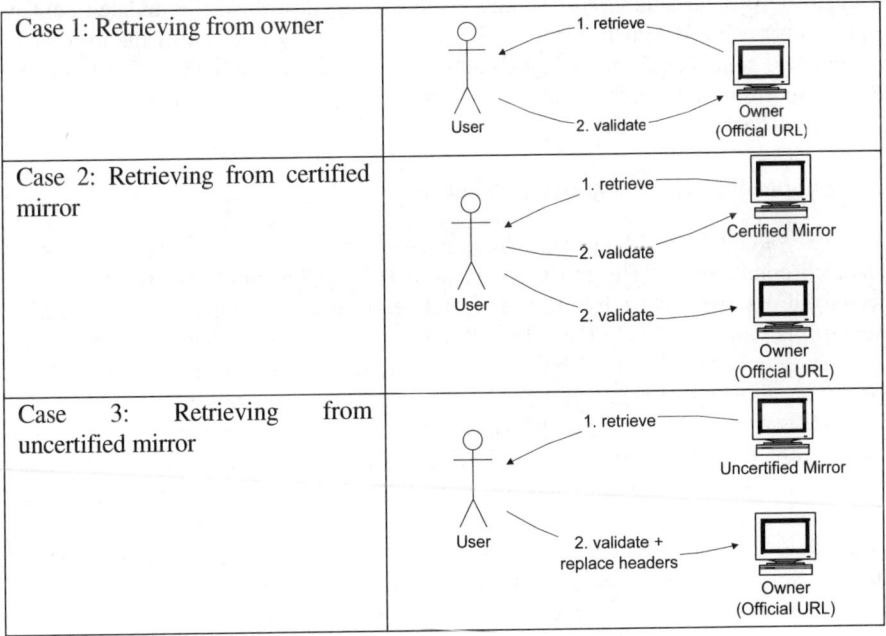

Fig. 1. Validation in Ownership-based Web Content Delivery

header in the response. Note that for mirrors that do not specify the ownership (and thus do not have the OwnerID header), we would consider them as the official sites as well.

In the second case, if users retrieve a content from a certified mirror, they can safely use the content until it expires; after which users must validate with the certified mirror if the mirror certificate is still valid, or with the owner otherwise. A certified mirror is identified when the mirror specifies the OwnerID and MirrorCert headers in the response and that the mirror certificate is valid. Content retrieved from a certified mirror is guaranteed to be consistent with the official site.

In the third case, if a content is retrieved from an uncertified mirror, validity of the content is unknown, so users should validate with the official site before using the content to ensure that the content is valid. An uncertified mirror is identified when the mirror specifies the OwnerID header in the response, but MirrorCert is absent or the mirror certificate is invalid. Validation can be done immediately after the full response-headers have been received from the uncertified mirror or after the entire content has been downloaded. Clients may postpone validation until expiry of contents, but bear the risk that the content may not be consistent with the official site. Since inconsistency of headers is a common problem, when validating with the owner, clients must replace the mirror's headers (except the OwnerID header) with those received from the owner.

An uncertified mirror should at least preserve the ETag and Last-Modified response-headers of the original content. Otherwise, using them to validate with the owner will cause validation failure and redundant transfer. When performing revalidation, the official site will send the updated content if available. In order to offload the official site, clients should always try to download the updated content from mirror using If-Match conditional request if an ETag is given. If the mirror has the updated content, then the client can abort the connection with the official site and download from some mirror instead. Otherwise, the client continues to download from an official site as usual.

3.3 Supporting Ownership in Gnutella/0.6

The P2P architecture is growing in popularity, and has caught the attention of research communities. The most widely used P2P application today is file-sharing, which allows files to be freely shared and replicated. A popular P2P file-sharing network is Gnutella [9]. In Gnutella, all contents are assumed static (never change) and have infinite lifetime. Thus, there is no mechanism to revalidate contents. However, in reality, contents do not stay static forever or have infinite lifetime.

Besides content lifetime, Gnutella also does not consider ownership, which poses more problems than in the web. It is because in P2P, contents are more widely replicated - each single file may be shared by thousands of peers. When users download a content from another peer, important questions to ask are: "is it original?", "is it up-to-date?", "is it intact (not corrupted)?" etc, but Gnutella has no mechanism to answer these questions. Therefore, the consistency and quality of contents tend to degrade as contents are passed from peer to peer. In this section, we introduce ownership and revalidation mechanisms to Gnutella/0.6.

3.3.1 Basic Entities
First, let us map the three basic entities in ownership to the Gnutella network.

- *ContentID* - each content in Gnutella is identified by a simple URI which is constructed from the peer's address, fileindex and filename (eg. http://69.23.58.41/get/556/jackson.mp3). Since peers' address may change from time to time, URI is not persistent and is not a suitable candidate for ContentID. In 2002, the Hash/URN Gnutella Extensions (HUGE) [9] was proposed as identifier for contents. An URN is generated by hashing the content's body (eg. urn:sha1:PLSTHIPQGSSZTS5FJUPAKUZWUGYQYPFB). Since our goal is to allow validation for contents that may change from time to time, HUGE is unsuitable as ContentID because it changes whenever the content changes. Since existing Gnutella specification does not offer an addressing scheme that is suitable for our use, we propose to generate ContentID by concatenating OwnerID and a local ContentID (local ContentID must be unique and should be persistent within the OwnerID's namespace). The syntax for ContentID is: OwnerID "/" Local_ContentID.
- *NodeID* of a host is represented by its hostname or IP address.
- *OwnerID* must be globally unique and should be persistent. However, in Gnutella, peers can join and leave at their wish and their addresses may change from time to time. Thus, so peer's address cannot be used as OwnerID. Since owners' availability is unpredictable, we propose that every owner elects a delegate to represent him/her in performing certain tasks. A delegate is a highly available server, with persistent NodeID (address). Each owner has only one delegate, but each delegate can represent one or more owners, each having a local owner identifier. The syntax of OwnerID is defined as: Delegate_NodeID "/" Local_OwnerID. For example, if the owner elects "delegate.com" as its delegate and the Local_OwnerID is "john", then the OwnerID will be "delegate.com/john".

3.3.2 Delegate
Having a delegate is necessary because the owner may not always be online. The owner requires a delegate to represent him in performing certain task (See Figure 2). First, let us analyze the type of tasks performed by owner when he is online:

- Validation – we propose to introduce content TTL and a mechanism to allow peers to validate the contents they retrieve.
- Alternate Locations – when responding to download requests, the owner may send a list of alternate locations for the content using the "X-Gnutella-Alternate-Location" response header. The requesting peer then decides which peer(s) he would download the content from.
- Content delivery – other peers can request to download contents directly from the owner. Contents are delivered to the requesting peer using out-of-band transfers.
- Respond to queries – owner responds to queries that match his contents. To respond to queries, the owner must participate in the Gnutella network, so that he can receive query messages.

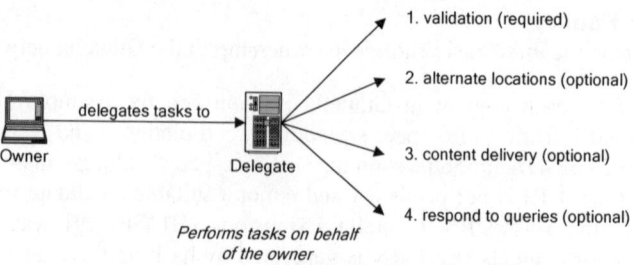

Fig. 2. Tasks Performed by Delegates

The next question is which tasks should be delegated? We suggest that owner delegates "critical" tasks so that these critical tasks can still be performed even when the owner goes offline. Among the four tasks listed, we view validation as the most critical task. Users should always be able to validate content. Therefore, we define revalidation as a compulsory task for delegate. Whenever content is updated, the owner must submit the latest headers and validators (ETag or Last-Modified) to the delegate to allow revalidation be performed on its behalf.

The owner may also delegate the other three tasks depending on the requirements of the owner. We highly recommend owners to delegate the "alternate locations" task so that users can easily locate peers to download the content by asking the delegate. The "alternate locations" can be updated through the following means:

- "Alternate locations" can be updated by peers themselves, after they have completely downloaded the content (either from the delegate or other peers), if they are willing to serve as the download locations.
- "Alternate locations" can be updated by the owner if the owner knows where the content can be downloaded from. For example, the owner may have agreements with a few peers who will serve as the seed download locations.
- The delegate can periodically query the network to search for peers that have the content.
- If the delegate also delivers the content, it can actively add peers that have downloaded the content to the list.

A delegate may internally divide alternate locations into 2 types: permanent and temporary. Permanent locations are for those explicitly marked as such by the owner, while the rest are temporary locations that will be replaced according to some replacement algorithm. The delegate may also implement some method to load-balance among the alternate locations. The owner may delegate the "content delivery" task if the owner wants users to be able to download the content even when it goes offline. The delegate may serve as a full-time download location, or only when the owner goes offline. "Respond to queries" should be delegated only when "content delivery" or "alternate locations" is delegated. Delegate should not respond to queries if it cannot deliver the content or provide alternate locations for the content.

3.3.3 Validation

The Gnutella protocol only specifies how peers join the network and how queries are sent. Actual transfer of contents, from sender to receiver, is done using a trimmed-down version of HTTP. Basic features of HTTP such as persistent connection, chunked encoding and range requests are supported. However, the HTTP expiration and validation model are not implemented due to the following reasons:

- Gnutella assumes that files are static and remain unchanged once they are created. However, this assumption is inappropriate. Not all files are static, for example, software programs are subject to update, document files are subject to editing, etc.
- HTTP specifies that validation is performed at the host the content is retrieved from. In Gnutella, peers merely serve as download locations. The peer a content is downloaded from is not the owner of the content and has no authority to perform validation. Thus, the HTTP validation model cannot be applied to Gnutella verbatim, without appropriate modifications.

We propose to implement the HTTP expiration and validation model in Gnutella. At the same time, the validation model will be extended to include delegates. All existing HTTP caching and expiration headers will be reused in Gnutella. The proposed revalidation mechanism for Gnutella is illustrated in Figure 3. When delivering content to a requesting peer, the response carries a ContentID header, which indicates the owner's delegate. Clients should validate with the owner's delegate, and replace the existing content headers with those delivered by the delegate.

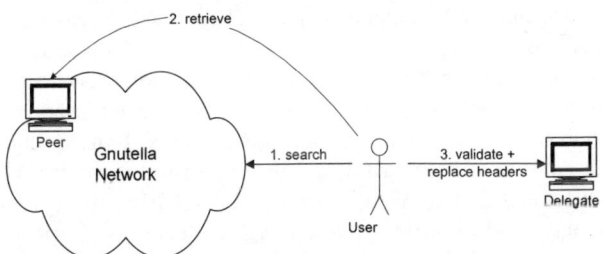

Fig. 3. Proposed Content Retrieval and Validation in Gnutella

Similar to the HTTP, validation in Gnutella is performed by sending conditional requests such as If-modified-since or If-none-match. On the web, the server will deliver the updated content if the content has changed, otherwise it will return the "304 Not Modified" status. However for Gnutella, if the content has changed, the delegate may not be able to deliver the updated content if it has not been delegated the "content delivery" task by the owner. So, we propose a new "506 Modified But Unavailable" status for this purpose.

Delegate that we propose for Gnutella is analogous to the official URL we propose for the web. However, we do not propose to have certified mirrors for Gnutella because content delivery is already offloaded to many peers so the load on one delegate should not be too much. Nevertheless, certified mirrors can be added easily, similar that we propose for the web.

4 Performance Study

To illustrate the potentials of our scheme, we implemented our solution in HTTP/1.1 and Gnutella/0.6. The performance focus of study is from two aspects: content size and latency. Firstly, we introduced two new headers: OwnerID and MirrorCert (for web mirrors) or ContentID (for P2P). We calculate the overhead of the two headers using the statistics from the NLANR trace, as shown in Table 1.

Table 1. Statistics of NLANR Traces

Input traces	NLANR Sept 21, 2004
Total URL	2,131,838
Average URL Length	62 characters or bytes
Average content headers size	280 characters or bytes
Average content body size	23,562 characters or bytes

For mirrored web contents, the OwnerID and MirrorCert headers will consume about 166 bytes if we assume both headers contain a URL. Likewise, P2P contents will need to include OwnerID and ContentID which occupy around 148 bytes. In these two cases, the content size only increases by a negligible 0.70% and 0.62% respectively.

Secondly, when mirrored contents expire, clients will revalidate with owners instead of mirror hosts. Since we only change the target of revalidation, there is no extra latency overhead incurred (assuming mirror and owner have the same network latency). Nevertheless, our solution offers an option to let users revalidate with owners immediately upon retrieval of mirrored contents. If users choose to do so, there will be an additional round trip to owner to perform revalidation. On the other hand, even though certified mirrored contents do not have to be revalidated upon retrieval, users may need to retrieve the mirror certificate for verification if only the certificate link is provided. However, a certificate is usually shared among a set of mirrored contents, so the latency in retrieving the certificate will be amortized among the mirrored contents.

5 Conclusion

In this paper, we propose a new ownership concept to maintain the consistency of content that needs to be retrieved through the Internet. Instead of the traditional assumption on the equivalence between the content distribution address and the content ownership, we argue that explicit ownership information has to be specified as part of the content attributes. Both the protocols and system supports for this ownership scheme are given. We clearly define the roles and responsibility of each entity participating in the content delivery process. This makes it easy to identify the owner of content whom users can check consistency with. Experimental results show that the performance overhead incurred by the scheme is practical enough for real deployment.

References

1. Cate, V.: Alex – a global filesystem. In: Proceedings of the 1992 USENIX File System Workshop (May 1992)
2. OPES Home Page, http://www.ietf-opes.org
3. Challenger, J., Iyengar, A., Dantzig, P.: A Scalable System for Consistently Caching Dynamic Web Data. In: Proceedings of IEEE INFOCOM 1999 (March 1999)
4. Chua, C.K., Chi, C.H.: Content Consistency for Web-Based Information Retrieval. Internal Report, School of Computing, National University of Singapore (2005)
5. Duvvuri, V., Shemoy, P., Tewari, R.: Adaptive leases: A Strong Consistency Mechanism for the World Wide Web. In: Proceedings of INFOCOM 2000 (2000)
6. Fei, Z.: A Novel Approach to Managing Consistency in Content Distribution Networks. In: Proceedings of the 6th International Web Caching and Content Delivery Workshop, Boston, MA (2001)
7. Fielding, R., Gettys, J., Mogul, J., Frystyk, H., Masinter, L., Leach, P., Berners-Lee, T.: RFC2616 Hypertext Transfer Protocol – HTTP/1.1
8. Song, G.: Dynamic Data Consistency Maintenance in Peer-to-Peer Caching System. Master's Thesis, National University of Singapore (2004)
9. Gnutella, http://www.gnutella.com
10. Gwertzman, J., Seltzer, M.: World-wide Web cache consistency. In: Proceedings of the 1996 Usenix Technical Conference (1996)
11. Internet Content Adaptation Protocols forum, http://www.i-cap.org
12. Krishnamurty, B., Rexford, J.: Web Protocols and Practice. Addison Wesley, Reading (2001)
13. Lan, J., Liu, X., Shenoy, P., Ramamritham, K.: Consistency Maintenance in Peer-to-Peer File Sharing Networks. In: Proceedings of the 3rd IEEE Workshop on Internet Applications (2003)
14. Liu, C., Cao, P.: Maintaining Strong Cache Consistency in the World-Wide Web. IEEE Transactions on Computers (1998)
15. Mikhailov, M., Wills, C.E.: Evaluating a New Approach to Strong Web Cache Consistency with Snapshots of Collected Content. In: Proceedings of WWW 2003 (May 2003)
16. Ninan, A., Kulkarni, P., Shenoy, P., Ramamritham, K., Tewari, R.: Cooperative Leases: Mechanisms for Scalable Consistency Maintenance in Content Distribution Networks. In: Proceedings of WWW 2002 (May 2002)
17. Rabinovich, M., Spatcheck, O.: Web Caching and Replication. Addison Wesley, Reading (2002)
18. Yin, J., Alvisi, L., Dahlin, M., Lin, C.: Volume Leases to Support Consistency in Large-Scale Systems. IEEE Transactions on Knowledge and Data Engineering (February 1999)

Together: A Hybrid Overlay for Application-Layer Multicast in Heterogeneous Environment

Zuo Ke, Dong-min Hu, Huai-min Wang, and Quan-yuan Wu

National University of Defense Technology, Changsha, P.R. China
{icekezuo,tigiu_niuniu}@gmail.com, {hmwang,qywu}@nudt.edu.cn

Abstract. In this paper, we present a novel hybrid overlay, named as Together, for application multicast in heterogeneous environment. We analyze the reasons to cause bandwidth bottleneck in tree-based approach and correspondingly define a special set called Spare Capacity Set. Based on this definition, we further design a bandwidth adaptive auxiliary mesh which can be reconciled with a stable multiple trees structure under a coherent framework. The hybrid approach can achieve good performance as well as maximized utilization of node bandwidth, which is essential in heterogeneous environment.

1 Introduction

Peer-to-Peer (P2P) overlays offer a promising approach to streaming live video over the Internet without any a special infrastructure support from the network [2]. This approach is generally referred as P2P Streaming. Recently a large number of mechanisms have been proposed with intention to implement P2P streaming systems. Some of these systems (e.g., www.sopcast.com) have become available for broadcasting live event such as World Cup 2006. We are certain that P2P streaming will become more popular for the people to participate in and feel the passion of the Beijing 2008 Olympic Games.

Existing approaches for P2P streaming can be generally divided into two classes: tree-based approaches and mesh-based (or known as data-driven) approaches. In tree-based approaches, nodes are organized into multiple tree-based structured overlays. An interior node in one tree is a leaf node in all the remaining trees. Each description of Multiple Description Coded (MDC) content is split into k stripes, and then pushed down through a separate tree. Tree-based approaches are perhaps the most natural way to construct overlays for live P2P streaming. However in the presence of churn, maintaining multiple trees could be very challenging. Furthermore, the interior nodes carry all burden of forwarding multicast messages while the outgoing bandwidth of leaf nodes that are majority in the structure can not be effectively utilized. In mesh-based approaches, nodes form a randomly connected mesh by maintaining a set of partners and periodically exchanging data availability information with them. Without an explicit structure support, the mesh-based overlay is robust to failures. A node can use other partners to receive data when one or more its neighbors depart. Further, potential bandwidth of a node can be fully utilized by the randomized partnerships as the mesh size grows. However, the lack of a well-ordered parent/children relation and the data pulling mechanism from neighbors make the meshed-based overlay suffer an efficiency-latency tradeoff.

Both approaches have shown their success in practical deployment, as well as potential limitations that could restrict individual development. A natural question is whether we can combine above two approaches to realize a hybrid overlay towards efficient bandwidth utilization and structure robustness in heterogeneous environment, especially a network formed by wireless and wired systems with inherent bandwidth heterogeneity. In this paper we propose a novel hybrid overlay that is referred as Together (this name implies that the overlay is not only combined by two well known approaches mentioned above, but expects more nodes to participate in P2P streaming). A series of interesting but challenged issues are addressed in Together. Firstly, we analyze the reasons of bandwidth bottleneck and identify Spare Capacity Set that will be the basis to construct mesh overlay. Furthermore, we design a set of construction and evolution mechanism, which maximize bandwidth utilization at a node with low control overhead. Such results are reaffirmed by our experiments.

The remainder of this paper is organized as follows: In Section 2, we introduce the related work and motivation. Section 3 analyzes the reasons to cause bandwidth bottleneck and give the definition of Spare Capacity Set. Details about Together are discussed in Section 4 and the performance is evaluated in Section 5. Finally, Section 6 concludes the paper.

2 Related Work and Motivation

Multicast is a classical research topic in networks. Many existing works are focused on the design of scalable multicast protocols or systems in both wired and wireless environment [5]. SplitStream [1] is proposed for the purpose to provide an application-level multicast system for data dissemination in cooperative environment. The system stripes the data across a forest of multicast tree to balance forwarding load and to tolerate faults. It is implemented using Scribe and Pastry. As mentioned before, tree-based structure suffers from two limitations: disruptive content delivery due to failures of interior nodes especially in high level, and underutilized outgoing bandwidth in leaf nodes.

More resilient structures, in particular, mesh-based thus have been introduced. CoolStreaming [8] is one of the first data-driven systems that construct a mesh out of the overlay nodes, with each node having a small set of neighbors to exchange data. CoolStreaming does not maintain an explicit overlay structure, but adaptively forwards data according to data availability and demanding information. CoolStreaming proposes a scalable membership and partnership management algorithm together with an intelligent scheduling algorithm, which enables efficient contents streaming. The most recent study in mesh-based approach is PRIME [3]. In this work, PRIME derives proper peer connectivity to minimize bandwidth bottleneck as well as an efficient pattern of swarming delivery for live content over a random mesh to minimize content bottleneck. A mesh-based system is more robust than tree-based system, but experiences longer delays and high control overhead.

An early attempt towards hybrid overlays is HON [9], which focuses on on-demanding streaming. Following this approach, ChunkySpread [6] is proposed to further construct trees by coordination with an auxiliary neighboring graph. A recently work is mTreebone [7] which puts forward an explicit definition of a single-tree structure treebone comprised by the stable nodes that can be identified by an age threshold. It also has a set of mechanism to optimize the entire system performance.

Existing systems have made good attempts to integrate two approaches under one framework, yet none of them can clearly distinguish the key characteristics of one approach from another. In [4], a valuable comparison of P2P streaming approaches has been studied and provided comprehensive contrast of representative protocols from each approach. There are two conclusions worthy to be noted. First, while these two approaches use different overlay construction algorithms, the overall shape of their resulting overlays is very similar. Second, the mesh-based approach exhibits a superior performance over the tree-based approach. The valuable results give us motivation to design Together in terms of following ideas: i) the homogeneous provides an effective way to reconcile two approaches, and ii) the superior performance of mesh-based approach inspires us to construct a mesh overlay auxiliary to a multiple trees structure in order to improve the overall system performance, together with resilient against node dynamics. Unless explicit explanations, we use multiple trees and tree-based interchangeably in following sections.

3 Analysis of Bandwidth Bottleneck

In heterogeneous environment, the key mission is to fully utilize bandwidth so as to maximize live content delivery. Next, we analyze the reasons to cause bandwidth bottleneck.

Let N be the set of nodes and k be the number of stripes that resource s originates. The four parameters $indeg_i$, $inbw_i$, $outdeg_i$ and $outbw_i$ denote indegree, inbound bandwidth, outdegree and outbound bandwidth of node i, respectively. C_i denotes the stripes that node i should additionally receive in order to accept all k stripes for optimal delivery quality. There are two conditions need to be satisfied for the feasibility of multiple trees construction.

CONDITION 1. *If multiple trees construction is feasible, the sum of the inbound bandwidth cannot exceed the sum of the outbound bandwidth:*

$$\sum_{\forall i \in N} inbw_i \leq \sum_{\forall i \in N} outbw_i. \tag{1}$$

CONDITION 2. *A sufficient condition for the feasibility of multiple trees construction is for Condition 1 to hold and for all nodes whose outbound bandwidth exceeds their inbound bandwidth to receive or originate all k stripes:*

$$\forall i : outbw_i \geq inbw_i \Rightarrow indeg_i + C_i = k. \tag{2}$$

If a set of nodes can satisfy Condition 1 and Condition 2 at the same time, the corresponding tree-based overlay can be build with every high probability provided that there is a modest amount of bandwidth underutilized. However, this goal is hard to achieve and bandwidth bottleneck still exists by reason of the mismatching problem between indegree and inbound bandwidth, along with outdegree and outbound bandwidth at a node. Furthermore, the issue of free-riding can also induce the problem which is not covered this paper. Next, we firstly introduce Spare Capacity Set, and then analyze the reasons to cause bandwidth bottleneck.

Definition 1. *Spare Capacity Set (SCS)*
A Spare Capacity Set, referred as SCS, is composed of arbitrary node i that satisfy any one of following conditions.

- Cond.1: $indeg_i$ is smaller than its desired indegree, which correspondingly underutilize $inbw_i$. We denoted Con.1 as SCS_inbw_i.
- Cond.2: $outdeg_i$ is smaller than its desired outdegree, which underutilize $outbw_i$. We denote Con.2 as SCS_outbw_i.
- Cond.3: Cond.1 and Cond.2 are satisfied simultaneously. We denote Con.3 as $SCS\_inoutbw_i$.

It is easy to observe that a node's inbound bandwidth is proportional to its indegree, which is the number of stripes the node chooses to receive. When $indeg_i$ equals to its desired indegree, it implies that $inbw_i$ has reached saturation and inbound bandwidth is fully utilized. Here are three cases need to further consider in this scenario. First, $outdeg_i$ is big enough to guarantee that $outbw_i$ would be fully utilized. Second, $outdeg_i$ is not big enough and SCS_outbw_i is satisfied. Third, $outdeg_i$ may exceed node i's $outbw_i$ if no limitation on outdegree size. Generally a tree-base overlay system has a mechanism to limit a node's outdegree for the last case.

When $indeg_i$ is smaller than its desired indegree, Cond.1 occurs. It implies $inbw_i$ has spare capacity and SCS_inbw_i is satisfied. We further introduce the concept of content bottleneck for next discussion.

Definition 2. *Content Bottleneck*
When one (or multiple) parents(s) of a child node does not have a useful data stripe to offer, the child node cannot utilize the bandwidth of the corresponding connection(s) and experiences content bottleneck.

If SCS_inbw_i is satisfied meanwhile i is experiencing content bottleneck, then $outdeg_i$ is underutilized and SCS_outbw_i is consequently satisfied.

Content Bottleneck could be happened frequently in the presence of churn which will be discussed in Section 4.5. Therefore, the key idea of Together is to minimize spare capacity of $inbw_i$ so as to alleviate the bandwidth bottleneck.

4 Together Design

4.1 A Stable Multiple Trees

We adopt the concept of stable nodes of mTreebone, and use it to construct multiple trees structure in Together. In heterogeneous environment, in particular, a network that seamlessly link wireless and wired systems, a number of stable nodes often located in the wired system. These nodes are very important to support the entire overlay for P2P streaming. All stable nodes can be identified by an age threshold, and then organized into multiple trees structure. Details can be found in [7]. Figure 1.(a) represents the organized overview of multiple trees.

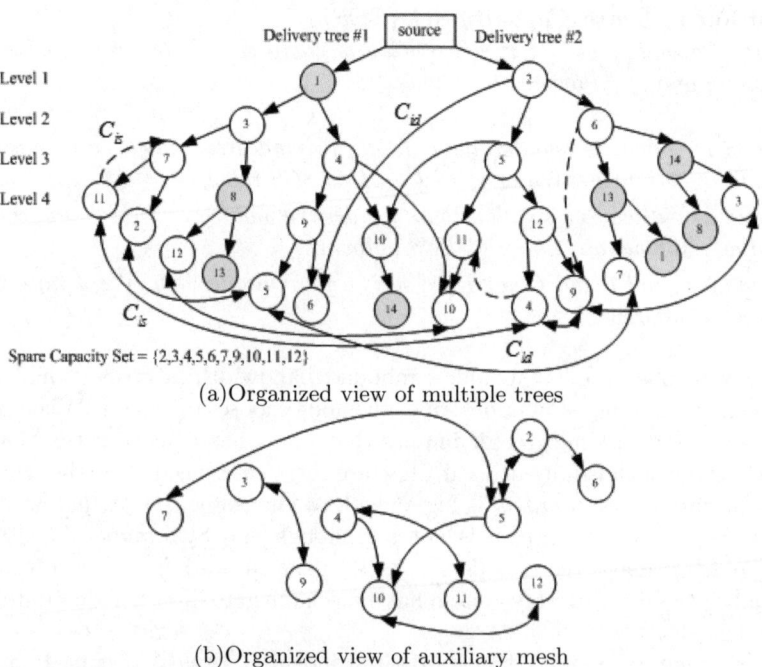

(a) Organized view of multiple trees

(b) Organized view of auxiliary mesh

Fig. 1. Organized view of Together

4.2 An Bandwidth Adaptive Auxiliary Mesh

The stable multi-tree overlay ignored the potential bandwidth between the unstable nodes. In addition, the dynamics of interior nodes especially in high lever can dramatically influence the entire performance.

To improve the utilization of nodes inbound bandwidth as analyzed in Section 3.1, we organize the nodes in SCS into a mesh overlay. Similar to CoolStreaming, each node keeps a partial list of the active overlay nodes and their status. This local list facilitates the node to locate a set of mesh neighbors to exchange available useful stripes.

The connections of two nodes in mesh overlay can be divided into the following four classes based on their locations: (a) connection between the nodes at the bottom of two different delivery trees (C_{ld}), (b) connection between the nodes at the bottom of the same delivery trees (C_{ls}), (c) connection between the nodes at the bottom of one delivery tree to an interior node on a different delivery tree (C_{id}), (d) connection between the nodes at the bottom of one delivery tree to an interior node on the same delivery tree (C_{is}). A sample connection is shown in Figure 1.(a). We identify the four classes for the design of data delivery in Together that will be discussed in Section 4.4.

4.3 Together Bootstrapping and Evolution

After given the Overview of Together, we now introduce how a node evolves into the system. We assume that initially only the source node is in the multiple trees and some nodes in SCS that forms the auxiliary mesh overlay. When a new node wants to join Together, it sends an advertisement to all nodes in SCS. One or more nodes will send back a response that is near to the new node, and then put it into their partner list for exchanging available content. The new node will correspondingly build its own list according to all received answers. It is important to notice that the responding nodes must not be an ancestor of the new node in the stable multiple trees, for the sake of avoiding a cycle. To enable this, each node maintains its path to the root of each stripe that it receives.

When inbound and outbound bandwidth have been both exhausted, the node is full enabled and no more indegree or outdegree can be increased correspondingly. It will simply quit the spare capacity group and keep exchanging stripes with its neighbors, as well as pushing to its children if it is also a stable node in the multiple trees.

When a node's age exceeds the threshold of stability, it becomes an orphaned child and tries to locate its parent in the multiple trees. In order to reduce the average depth of the forest and the play out delay, each node p periodically checks whether there are nodes closer to the source than its parent. If so and one such node q is also in SCS, node p will leave its original parent and attach itself to q as a child. The optimization will be iteratively executed until no node can be found for swapping. When it terminates, the average depth of multiple trees is eventually decreased.

4.4 Data Delivery and Duplication Reduction

In order to maximize bandwidth utility of each participating peers in heterogeneous environment, the stripes of data content can be delivered concurrently by two means. They can be pushed over the multiple trees and pulled from neighbors in auxiliary mesh as well. However, many duplicated data will be received by nodes, and even at worst case, a stripe could be rejected by nodes when received concurrently. Therefore, we introduce *tree-delivery preemption* and *neighbor selection* mechanisms to effectively reduce stripes duplication.

Tree-delivery Preemption: When a node is connected both in a separate tree and in a mesh, it could receive duplicated data stripes from pushing and pulling delivery at the same time. Due to the correspondingly stable quality of stripes delivered in multiple trees, the tree-push is always kept front to the mesh-pull so as to reduce the duplication as excessively as possible.

Neighbor Selection: In mesh overlay, a large number of duplicated stripes are generated from C_{is} shown in Figure 1. To avoid C_{is}, a node does not pick those nodes that either have a common or themselves are its ancestors as neighbor in mesh overlay. As presented in Figure 1, the dashed curly arrows will be ignored when selection neighbors by nodes.

4.5 Node Dynamics

A node may initiatively leave the overlay, or unpredictably fail to depart without any notification. In the former, the node will proactively inform its neighbors in mesh and all children in separate tree. Once neighbors or children receive the information, they will start up an iteration to find a substitute for the removed node. In either case, the node dynamics will be perceptive by Together for next handling procedure.

If the churn occurs at an interior node x in stable multiple trees, all sub-trees joint at x become disconnected and thus unable to accept any new leaf node. We denote this as a deadlock event. In the design of representative protocols for multiple trees overlay, all sub-trees periodically try to rejoin the multiple trees overlay until they succeeds. This produces a large number of time overhead and communicating consume. In Together, it is simply but effectively handled in auxiliary mesh in term of Theorem 1.

Theorem 1. *If a node i leaves the stable tree, all nodes in the sub-trees rooted at i will join Spare Capacity Set accordingly.*

Proof. When the node *i* departs, *indeg* of all direct children decrease, correspondingly the bandwidth utilization of these nodes are not fully used in terms of the proportional relationship, thereby these nodes will join SCS. For all descendants, except for direct children, they dose not receive any new stripes because the node departure. Hence they experiences *content bottleneck* and bandwidth of the corresponding connections cannot be fully utilized. All descendants will join SCS as well. Thus, Theorem 1 holds.

In such a scenario, Together employs nodes in sub-trees to check their local lists and attempts to build connections with neighbor already existing in SCS, which forms a mesh eventually.

5 Performance Evaluation

In this section, we examine the performance of content delivery mechanism over a static overlay and correspondingly the robustness against node dynamics. To evaluate the performance, we contrast Together with SplitStream. We have also implemented two state-of-the-art application layer multicast systems for comparison, namely, CoolStream and mTreebone. SplitStream is the first proposed

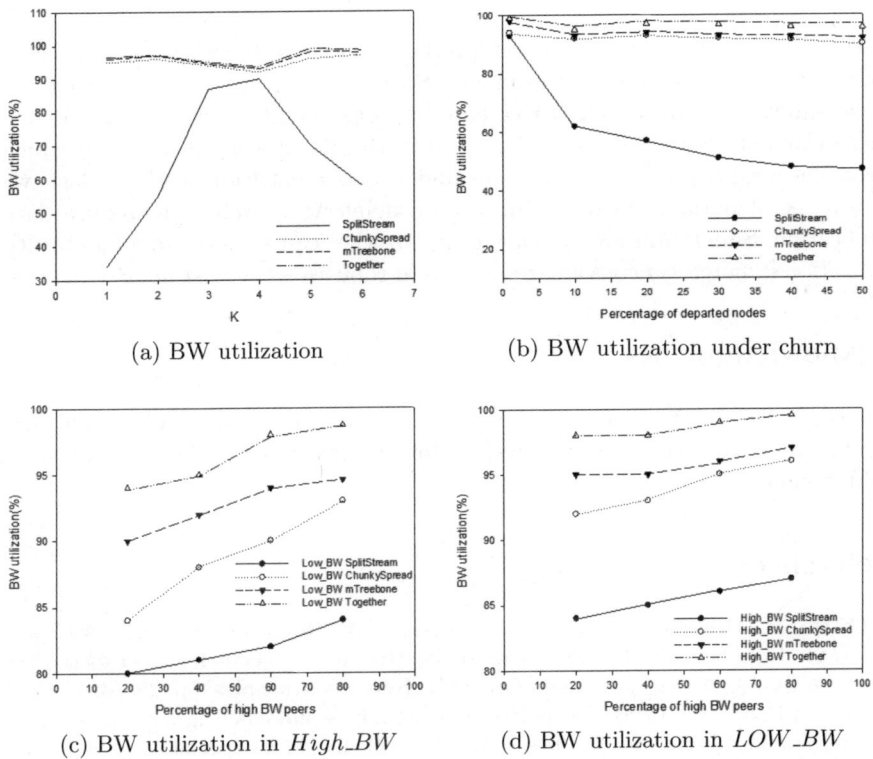

Fig. 2. Simulation Results

multiple trees system that becomes a representative of tree-based approach. CoolStream is a typical mesh system. mTreebone is proposed recently as a hybrid approach to integrate single-tree structure with mesh overlay.

We firstly examine the effect of bandwidth utilization on the system performance as shown in Figure 2(a). It is obviously that the mesh-based and both hybrid approaches achieve high bandwidth utilization ($> 90\%$). In contrast, the bandwidth utilization in the tree-based approach has a sweet spot and for other values it exhibits significantly lower bandwidth utilization.

Next we simulate the effect of bandwidth heterogeneity by setting two groups of nodes with symmetric bandwidth of 900 Kbps and 300 Kbps, and peer degree of 10 and 5. Figure 2 (c) and (d) represent the results, respectively in high bandwidth and low bandwidth. We can easily find that the BW utilization of Together is superior to other three systems in both cases, due to the novel design of bandwidth adaptive auxiliary mesh by use of SCS.

Last we evaluate the robustness against node failures of all four systems. Due to the resilience of multiple trees and mesh overlay, Together can achieve better BW utilization than other three systems even when over half part of nodes depart the network. Figure 2(b) shows the results.

6 Conclusion

In this paper, we present a hybrid overlay named as Together for live video multicast in heterogeneous environment. Specifically, we analyze the reasons to cause bandwidth bottleneck in tree-based approach and correspondingly define Spare Capacity Set. We designed a bandwidth adaptive auxiliary mesh which reconciles with a stable multiple trees under a coherent framework. At last, we gave a set of mechanism to optimize data delivery, as well as to reduce data duplication. Simulation results show that Together can achieve good bandwidth utilization in heterogeneous environment and robustness against node dynamics.

Acknowledgments

We would like to thank Cai Zhiping for the useful discussion. We would also like to thank M.Castro and A.Rowstron for providing us the simulator code for SplitStream.

References

1. Castro, M., Druschel, P., Kermarrec, A., Nandi, A., Rowstron, A., Singh, A.: Splitstream: High-bandwidth multicast in cooperative environments. In: The Proceedings of the 19th ACM Symposium on Operating Systems Principles, pp. 298–313 (2003)
2. Liu, J., Rao, S.G., Li, B., Zhang, H.: Opportunities and challenges of peer-to-peer internet video broadcast. In: The Proceedings of the IEEE, Special Issue on Recent Advances in Distributed Multimedia Communications, pp. 11–24 (2007)
3. Magharei, N., Rejaie, R.: Prime: Peer-to-peer receiver-driven mesh-based streaming. In: The Proceedings of the 26th IEEE International Conference on Computer Communications, pp. 1415–1423 (2007)
4. Magharei, N., Rejaie, R., Guo, Y.: Mesh or multiple-tree: A comparative study of live p2p streaming approaches. In: The Proceedings of the 26th IEEE International Conference on Computer Communications, pp. 1424–1432 (2007)
5. Peng, S., Li, S., Chen, L., Xiao, N., Peng, Y.: Sencast: Scalable multicast in wireless sensor networks. In: The Proceedings of the IEEE International Parallel and Distributed Processing Symposium (2008)
6. Venkataraman, J., Francis, P.: Chunkyspread: Multitree unstructured peer-to-peer multicast. In: The Proceedings of the 5th International Workshop on Peer-to-Peer Systems (2006)
7. Wang, F., Xiong, Y., Liu, J.: mTreebone: A hybrid tree/mesh overlay for application-layer live video multicast. In: The Proceedings of the 27th IEEE International Conference on Distributed Computing Systems, p. 49 (2007)
8. Zhang, X., Liu, J., Li, B., Yum, T.-S.P.: Coolstreaming/donet: A data-driven overlay network for efficient live media streaming. In: The Proceedings of the 24th IEEE International Conference on Computer Communications, pp. 2102–2111 (2005)
9. Zhou, M., Liu, J.: A hybrid overlay network for video-ondemand. In: The Proceedings of the IEEE International Conference on Communications, pp. 1309–1313 (2005)

Node Placement of Linear Wireless Multimedia Sensor Networks for Maximum Network Lifetime

Ming Cao[1], Laurence T. Yang[2], Xinmeng Chen[1], and Naixue Xiong[3]

[1] School of Computer, Wuhan University, Wuhan, China 430079
caomingwhu@yahoo.com.cn
[2] Department of Computer Science, St. Francis Xavier University, Canada
lyang@stfx.ca
[3] Department of Computer Science, Georgia State University, US
nxiong@cs.gsu.edu

Abstract. Power consumption is a fundamental concern in wireless multimedia sensor networks (WMSNs). Node placement scheme in WMSNs has considerable impact on network lifetime. In this paper, we investigate and develop an power-efficient node placement scheme (PENPS) in linear wireless multimedia sensor networks, which can minimize the average energy consumption per node and maximize the network lifetime. The analysis of PENPS and the comparison of performance with the equal-spaced placement scheme (EPS) show that PENPS scheme can significantly decrease the average energy consumption per node, which can prolong the lifetime of sensor nodes and sensor networks effectively.

1 Introduction

Wireless sensor networks [1] have drawn the attention of the research community in the last few years, driven by a wealth of theoretical and practical challenges. More recently, the availability of inexpensive hardware such as CMOS cameras and microphones that are able to ubiquitously capture multimedia content from the environment has fostered the development of Wireless Multimedia Sensor Networks (WMSNs) [2], i.e., networks of wirelessly interconnected devices that allow retrieving video and audio streams, still images, and scalar sensor data.

Wireless multimedia sensor networks will not only enhance existing sensor network applications such as tracking, home automation, and environmental monitoring, but they will also enable several new applications such as storage of potentially relevant activities, person locator services, industrial process control, especially in traffic avoidance/enforcement and control systems. And the road traffic monitor system [3, 4] based on wireless multimedia sensor networks performs well in alleviating generic problems such as highway congestion.

Wireless sensor networks are composed of a great number of sensor nodes deployed in a fashion that may revolutionize information collecting. Sensor networks are different from other wireless networks due to the limitations on battery power, node densities, and huge data volume. Power conservation is the primary concern in prolonging the lifetime of a network operation. Many applications, such as traffic monitoring, expect the network to operate for a long time period. The lifetime of a wireless sensor network could be affected by many factors, such as topology management, MAC and routing protocol design, and error control schemes.

Different methods for reducing power consumption in wireless sensor networks have been explored in the literature. Some approaches were suggested, such as shortening redundant idle listening time for each sensor to save unnecessary power consumption [5, 6, 7], increasing the density of sensor nodes to reduce transmission range, reducing standby power consumption via suitable protocol design, and advanced hardware implementation methods [8]. Some of the existing power-conservation schemes, such as those proposed in [9, 10, 11], try to identify those redundant nodes. Joint optimization of sensor placement and transmission structure was considered in [12] with specified distortion bounds. The presence of spatial correlation in in-cluster data has been exploited to minimize communication costs (and hence, energy costs) incurred during data gathering in a sensor network [13].

Load balance between nodes is one of the main factors that can influence the network lifetime [25, 26]. As in the many-to-one wireless multimedia sensor networks, data collected from all nodes is aggregated to a sink node. Data load is generally asymmetric in this case. Nodes closer to the sink node have heavier traffic load, since they not only collect data within their sensing ranges but relay data for nodes further away as well [25, 26]. Such an unbalanced data volume introduces an uneven power consumption distribution among different sensor nodes. Since traffic load and power consumption of each node are location-dependent, network lifetime can be limited by nodes with heavier data load and thus greater power consumption. Therefore, node placement scheme will have considerable impact on network lifetime.

A commonly used approach for deploying sensor networks is the equal-spaced placement in which sensor nodes are placed with equal distance in between. Such a deployment strategy is usually the easiest. Radom deployment is also commonly used for its easy implementation. Not considering their influence on the network lifetime, these two schemes can easily cause network fail for some nodes running out of energy.

In this paper, our objective is to find an effective node placement scheme such that the lifetime of a linear wireless multimedia sensor network can be maximized, assuming each node allocated with homogeneous initial energy. The first step is to find the optimized distance between nodes with given constant nodes number in the network; The second step is to find the optimal nodes number with given node distance accordingly.

The rest of the paper is organized as follows. Section 2 describes the relevant work to this paper. In Section 3, we describe the linear sensor network model. In Section 4, we present our optimal node placement scheme for linear multimedia sensor networks. Numerical results are presented in Section 5. We explore the scheme proposed and evaluate it through comparisons. Conclusion and future work are finally given in Section 6.

2 Related Work

Many of the requisite features of a sensor network such as connectivity, coverage and power efficiency are significantly affected by the deployment strategy. Hence, sensor deployment strategies play a significant role in determining the performance of static sensor networks.

In [14], Bogdanov considered the deployment of sinks in a scenario of multiple sinks. Authors of [15,16] proposed to relocate mobile sensors to some appropriate locations in response to the node failure and lost of sensing area. All these proposals, however, are developed for other purposes without considerations of the impact of the Sink routing-hole problem.

A power-aware node deployment in wireless sensor networks is proposed in [17], which is optimized to maintain a continuous connectivity-coverage instead of that for some particular snapshots of the network. The problem of energy efficient random deployment of sensor network is considered in [18]. It found the sensor node density, which results in allocating the minimum total energy source subject to constraints on the quality of monitoring and network lifetime.

There have been a couple of research results on deriving an upper bound on the service lifetime of sensor networks. The service lifetime of a sensor network has been derived in [19, 20] by multi-commodity flow non-linear programming formulation. It can be shown that the problem we state in this paper which is finding the maximum lifetime is equal to minimizing the power consumption per unit time for each node, assuming each node allocated with homogeneous initial energy.

The above mentioned works are the most relevant works to our proposed paper. There is a large body of other works that address the connectivity [21] and coverage problems [21, 22] in distributed sensing for generic applications (e.g., target tracking). Most of these works use uniform deployment strategy or a deployment scheme that minimizes the probability of detection along the exposure paths in the case of target tracking.

3 Network Model

We consider a linear sensor network, which consists of a set of sensor nodes deployed along a long and narrow area with a sink node at the end. Each node collect the sampled data within its sensing range, relaying information towards the sink node for further processing, as shown in Fig.1. Note that each node also relays data for nodes further away, i.e., node Xi also relays the data collected by nodes from X_1 to X_{i-1}.

Fig.2 models different tiers of a hierarchical linear multimedia sensor network where each sensor node within a cluster only sends data to its aggregation node and the aggregation node relays information to the sink node. For a higher tier, we need to consider how aggregation nodes build a network and relay data to a sink node. For a lower tier, we could regard each cluster as a sensor network where the aggregation node is the sink node. Here X_1 is an aggregation node, which is also the sink node for node X_{11} and X_{12}.

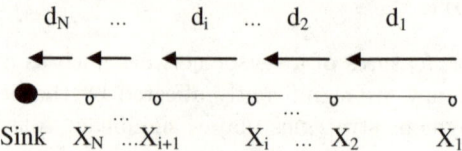

Fig. 1. Network model of linear wireless multimedia sensor networks

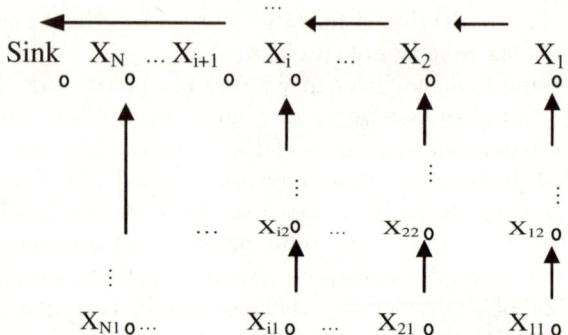

Fig. 2. Hierarchical linear wireless multimedia sensor networks model

Each node has a certain amount of initial energy E_0 and a sensing range D. Let d_i be the distance between node X_i and X_{i+1}, $i = 1, ..., n-1$, and d_N be the distance between node X_N and Sink. The linear network covers the area of length L. We have $\sum_{i=1}^{N} d_i = L$. Note we have $d_i \leq D$ for all i, which guarantees the coverage. We also have $\max\{d_i\} \leq r_{max}$, r_{max} denotes the maximal relaying range of node in the network. The relaying nodes, such as $X_2, ..., X_N$, not only monitor and collect data within its sensing range, but also relay data collected by other nodes towards the sink node. Let R_i be the sampled data sensed by the node X_i, the total data traffic relayed by the X_i for other nodes $X_1, ..., X_{i-1}$ will be $\sum_{j=1}^{i-1} R_j$, and the total data traffic to be sent to next node X_{i+1} will be $\sum_{j=1}^{i} R_j$.

Energy consumption is not only a chief issue in designing the wireless sensor network, but also an important metric to evaluate network performance. It has been observed that communication-related power is usually a significant component of the total power consumed in a sensor network [8,23,24]. We assume that the ratio of the other power consumptions to the total power consumption is only a constant factor. Thus, we only consider transmission power in this paper. Our work is to design an effective node placement scheme for network lifetime maximization, based on the metric of average energy consumption per node in the network. For each node, energy consumption consists of two parts: E_{send} denotes the energy consumed to send data, and $E_{receive}$ denotes the energy consumed to receive the data. For node X_i, its sending per bit data consumes energy: $E_{send} = ad_i^k$, where a is a constant and k denotes the path loss exponent,

$k \in [2, 4]$ depending on different channel models, in addition k is equal to 2 in free space. Let $E_{receive} = b$ be the energy consumption to receive per bit data, b is also a constant. Then we have

$$E_{ave} = \frac{1}{N} \sum_{i=1}^{N} (ad_i^k \sum_{j=1}^{i} R_j + b \sum_{j=1}^{i-1} R_j) \quad (1)$$

Eq. (1) is the average energy consumption per node, $ad_i^k \sum_{j=1}^{i} R_j$ is the energy consumption to relay data to next node from node X_i, $b \sum_{j=1}^{i-1} R_j$ is the energy consumption to receive data for node X_i.

Communication over a long link is severely penalized, because power consumption over a long link is much higher than the total power consumed over several short links, i.e.,

$$(d_1 + d_2 + ... + d_n)^k \gg d_1^k + d_2^k + ...d_n^k \quad (2)$$

4 Energy-Efficient Node Placement Scheme

The node placement scheme is to design node number placed in the linear sensor network and the node distance in between. Based on the linear sensor network shown in Fig.1, we propose an energy-efficient node placement scheme, introducing the principal of maximizing the lifetime of sensor nodes and sensor networks. In this proposed scheme, all nodes run out of energy at the same time and each node tries to take best advantage of its energy resource, prolonging the network lifetime. In this case, node X_i does not directly send data to node X_j where $j \geq i+2$, because communication over long links is not desirable. Thus, a node should only relay data to its nearest neighbor towards the sink node. According to the problem setup, maximizing the lifetime is equal to minimizing the power consumption per unit time for each node.

The scheme optimizes the placed node number N and the distance between nodes $\{d_i\}_{i=1}^{N}$. Supposing node number N is the constant, the first step is to find the optimized distance between nodes $\{d_i\}_{i=1}^{N}$ to minimize average energy consumption per node; The second step is to find the optimal nodes number N with given node distance $\{d_i\}_{i=1}^{N}$.

4.1 Node Distance Optimal Design

The design goal of node distance is as follows. Given the number of sensor nodes N (suppose N is reasonable), and the constraint $\sum_{i=1}^{N} d_i = L$, we have to get the optimal node distance $\{d_i\}_{i=1}^{N}$ to maximize the lifetime of sensor nodes and networks. That is to minimize the value of Eq. (3). Under the constraint of Eq. (5), the above objective can be transformed to the optimal problem.

Minimize:

$$E_{ave} = \frac{1}{N} \sum_{i=1}^{N} (ad_i^k \sum_{j=1}^{i} R_j + b \sum_{j=1}^{i-1} R_j) \quad (3)$$

or Maximize:

$$T_{ave} = \frac{E_0}{E_{ave}} = \frac{E_0}{\frac{1}{N}\sum_{i=1}^{N}(ad_i^k \sum_{j=1}^{i} R_j + b\sum_{j=1}^{i-1} R_j)} \qquad (4)$$

Subject to:

$$\sum_{i=1}^{N} d_i = L \qquad (5)$$

Eq. (4) is the node lifetime, E_0 is the initial energy for all nodes. Eq. (5) is the distance constraint, $\sum_{i=1}^{N} d_i$ is the distance from X_1 to the sink node.

Introducing the Lagrange multiplier method, we get the optimal solution of d_i:

$$d_i = \frac{L}{(\sum_{j=1}^{i} R_j)^{\frac{1}{k-1}} \times \sum_{i=1}^{N}(\frac{1}{\sum_{j=1}^{i} R_j})^{\frac{1}{k-1}}}, 1 \leq i \leq N \qquad (6)$$

Especially, when the data collected by each node is equal, we have an addition constraint $R_1 = R_2 = ... = R_N$, Eq. (6) can be reformulated as the following:

$$d_i = \frac{L}{i^{\frac{1}{k-1}} \sum_{i=1}^{N}(\frac{1}{i})^{\frac{1}{k-1}}}, 1 \leq i \leq N \qquad (7)$$

Eq. (6) is the node distance design to minimize the average node consumption with the given node number N. The value d_i in the scheme is only decided by the monitor area length L, path loss exponent k and the data collected by node R_i.

4.2 Node Number Optimal Design

Here we put Eq. (6) into the Eq. (4), the node lifetime is reformulated as the following:

$$T_{ave} = \frac{E_0}{\frac{aL^k}{N[\sum_{i=1}^{N}(\frac{1}{\sum_{j=1}^{i} R_j})^{\frac{1}{k-1}}]^{k-1}} + \frac{b}{N}\sum_{i=1}^{N}\sum_{j=1}^{i-1} R_j} \qquad (8)$$

See from Eq. (8), the node lifetime relates with the node number N.

In the design of optimal node number, there are two factors to be considered: i) the node distance can not exceed the node relaying range, that is, $\max\{d_i\} \leq r_{max}$; ii) the total node number can not exceed the budget, that is, $N \times C_{node} \leq C_{total}$, C_{node} denotes the single node cost, and C_{total} denotes the total cost. Under these two constraints, to get the minimal node number N_{opt}, the above objective can be transformed to the optimal problem as follows:

Maximize:

$$T_{ave} = \frac{E_0}{\frac{aL^k}{N[\sum_{i=1}^{N}(\frac{1}{\sum_{j=1}^{i} R_j})^{\frac{1}{k-1}}]^{k-1}} + \frac{b}{N}\sum_{i=1}^{N}\sum_{j=1}^{i-1} R_j} \qquad (9)$$

Subject to :

$$(i) \max \left\{ \frac{L}{(\sum_{j=1}^{i} R_j)^{\frac{1}{k-1}} \times \sum_{i=1}^{N} (\frac{1}{\sum_{j=1}^{i} R_j})^{\frac{1}{k-1}}} \right\} \leq r_{max}$$

$$(ii) \quad N \times C_{node} \leq C_{total} \quad (10)$$

We get the value range of N: $N_{min} \leq N \leq N_{max}$, N_{min} and N_{max} denotes the minimal and maximal node number placed in the network accordingly. The numerical value of N_{min} and N_{max} can be get from Eq. (10). In the value range of N, we get the optimal node number N_{opt}:

$$N_{opt} \approx \arg\max_N T_{ave} = \arg\max_N$$

$$\left\{ \frac{E_0}{\frac{aL^k}{N[\sum_{i=1}^{N}(\frac{1}{\sum_{j=1}^{i} R_j})^{\frac{1}{k-1}}]^{k-1}} + \frac{b}{N}\sum_{i=1}^{N}\sum_{j=1}^{i-1} R_j} \right\} \quad (11)$$

5 Performance Evaluation

We give the numerical value of $\{d_i\}_{i=1}^{N}$ and N_{opt} in the PENPS from the material parameters, and we have comparison of average node lifetime between PENPS and the equal-spaced placement scheme(EPS). Supposing the data collected by

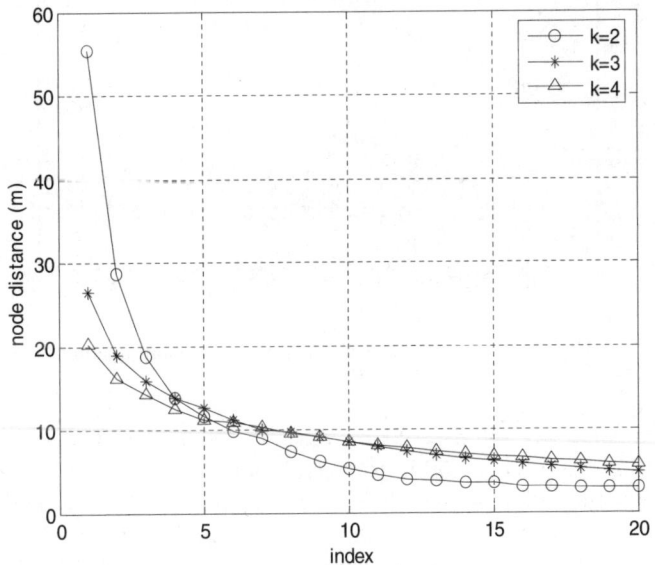

Fig. 3. Node distance of different path loss exponent

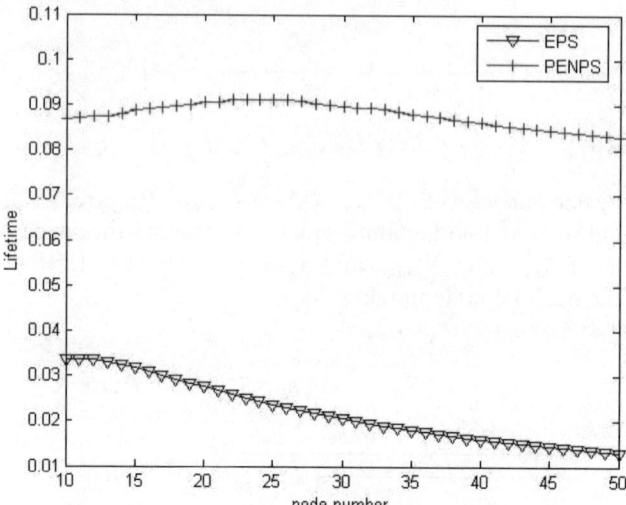

Fig. 4. Comparison of node lifetime

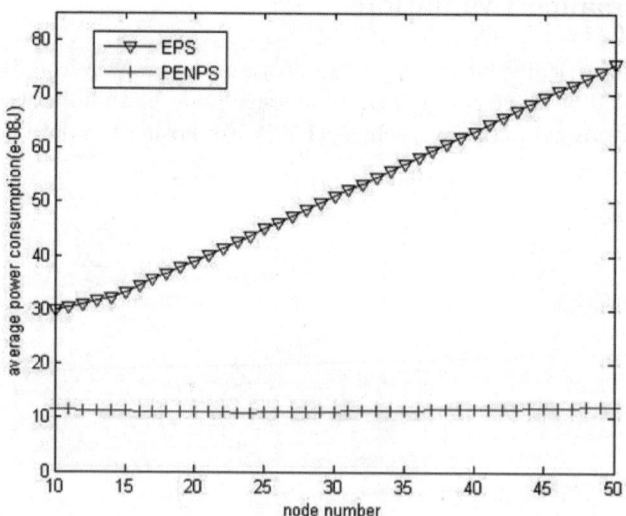

Fig. 5. Comparison of average power consumption

each node is equal, we set $L = 200m$, $r_{max} = 100m$, $a = 3.3e - 11 J/bit$, $b = 3e - 08 J/bit$, $C_{total}/C_{node} = 50$ in the simulation.

Fig.3 shows the different path loss exponent influence on the node distance with the given node number $N = 20$. The closer node is to the sink node, the smaller the node distance is. We notice that each curve can be divided into two parts at the node index 5. For those nodes with node index smaller than 5, the node distance in between is obviously larger than other nodes. For nodes closer to

Table 1. Optimal node number of different path loss exponent

k	2	3	4
N_{opt}	25	34	50

the sink carrying more relay loads, shortening its relaying distance can decrease energy consumption partly. Furthermore, when path loss exponent $k = 4$, its curve is smoother than other two. For the larger path loss exponent is, the more energy consumption is with the increased node distance. So the node distance is relatively even when the path loss exponent is larger.

Fig.4 shows the comparison of node lifetime between PENPS and EPS, given $k = 2$. We notice that when $N = 25$, the network lives much longer using PENPS than the eaual-spaced placement scheme. It's obvious that PENPS performs better than the latter, and it succeeds prolonging the node lifetime through decreasing the average energy consumption per node. Also from the curve of PENPS, we get that the node and network lifetime is relatively longer when $N = 25$.

See from Fig.5, we also have the comparison of average power consumption between PENPS and EPS. The proposed scheme can obviously decrease the average energy consumption per node with any given node numbers. When node number $N = 25$, we can get the minimal node energy consumption.

Table.1 gives the optimal node number N_{opt} with different path loss exponent. We points that when $k = 4$, the ideal value of N will be 64, which exceed the initialization of $N_{max} = 50$. So N_{opt} can only be 50.

6 Conclusions

This paper analyzes the node placement scheme influence on the network energy consumption in the linear multimedia sensor network. Based on the principle of minimal average energy consumption, the paper proposed an power-efficient node placement scheme, in which we design the optimal node number and node distance accordingly with different path loss exponent. Compared to the equal-placed scheme, PENPS obviously decreases the average energy consumption, prolongs the network lifetime effectively.

Our next plan is to investigate the node placement scheme in a more general sensor networks with non-simple topology. Another challenging future work is to explore the impact of data aggregation schemes, together with node placement, on network lifetime and power consumption in sensor networks.

Acknowledgment

This research has been supported by National Natural Science Foundation of China under Grant No.90104005, in part by the US National Science Foundation CAREER Award under Grant No. CCF-0545667.

We are indebted to many colleagues for their constructive criticism and helpful suggestions for improving the overall quality of this paper. We also would like to express our appreciation to the anonymous reviewers for their helpful comments on this paper.

References

1. Akyildiz, I.F., Weilian, S., Sankarasubramaniam, Y.: A survey on sensor networks. IEEE Communications 40, 102–114 (2002)
2. Akyildiz, T.M.I.F., Chowdhury, K.R.: A survey on wireless multimedia sensor networks. Computer Networks 4, 921–960 (2007)
3. Hsieh, T.T.: Using sensor networks for highway and traffic applications. IEEE Potentials 23, 102–114 (2004)
4. Nekovee, M.: Sensor networks on the road: the promises and challenges of vehicular adhoc networks and vehicular grids. In: Proceedings of the Workshop on Ubiquitous Computing and e-Research, Edinburgh, UK (2005)
5. Ye, W., Heidemann, J., Estrin, D.: Medium access control with coordinated adaptive sleeping for wireless sensor networks. IEEE/ACM Transaction on Networking 12, 493–506 (2004)
6. Zheng, T., Radhakrishnan, S., Sarangan, V.: Pmac: An adaptive energy-efficient mac protocol for wireless sensor networks. In: Proceedings of IEEE WMAN 2005, Denver, Colorado, USA, pp. 65–72 (2005)
7. Singh, S., Raghavendra, C.S.: Pamas: power aware multi-access protocol with signaling for ad hoc networks. ACM SIGCOM Computer Communication, 5–26 (1998)
8. Rabaey, J., et al.: Pico radios for wireless sensor sensor networks: The next challenge in ultra low power design. In: Proceedings of the ISSCC (2002)
9. Chen, B., Jamieson, K., Balakrishnan, H., Morris, R.: Span:an energy efficient coordination algorithm for topology manitenance in ad hoc wireless. In: Proceedings of mobicom (2001)
10. Cerpa, A., Estrin, D.: Ascent: Adaptive self-configuring sensor networks topologyies. In: Proceedings of infocom (2002)
11. Liu, Y., Liu, X., Xiao, L.: Location-aware topology matching in p2p systems. In: Proceedings of infocom (2004)
12. Ganesan, D., Cristescu, R., Beferull-Lozano, B.: Power efficient sensor placement and transmission structure for data gathering under distortion constraints. In: Proceedings of the third international symposium on Information processing in sensor networks, pp. 26–27 (2004)
13. Gupta, H., Navda, V., Das, S.R., Chowdhary, V.: Efficient gathering of correlated data in sensor networks. In: Proceedings of the 6th ACM internationalsymposium on Mobile ad hoc networking and computing, Urbana-Champaign, IL, USA, pp. 402–413 (2005)
14. Maneva, E., Bogdanov, A., Riesenfeld, S.: Power-aware base station positioning. In: Proceedings of Infocom (2004)
15. Wu, J., Yang, S.: Smart: a scan-based movement-assisted sensor deployment mehtod in wireless sensor networks. In: Proceedings of infocom (2005)
16. Porta, T.L., Wang, G., Cao, G., Zhang, W.: Sensor relocation in mobile sensor networks. In: Proceedings of infocom (2005)
17. Liu, Y., Ngan, H., Ni, L.M.: Power-aware node deployment in wireless sensor networks. In: Proceedings of IEEE SUTC 2006 (2006)

18. Maleki, M., Pedram, M.: Qom and lifetime-constrained random deployment of sensor networks for minimum energy consumption. In: Information Processing in Sensor Networks, pp. 293–300 (2005)
19. Chang, H., TAssiulas, L.: Energy conserving routing in wireless ad hoc networks. In: Proceedings of infocom, pp. 22–31 (2001)
20. Bhardwaj, M., Chandrakasan, A.P.: Bounding the lifetime of sensor networks via optimal role assignments. In: Proceedings of infocom, New York, pp. 1587–1596 (2002)
21. Srikant, R., Shakkottai, S., Shroff, N.: Unreliable sensor grids: Coverage, connectivity and diameter. In: Proceedings of infocom (2003)
22. Franceschetti, M., Booth, L., Bruck, J., Meester, R.: Covering algorithms, continuum percolation, and the geometry of wireless networks. Annals of Applied Probability 13 (2003)
23. Pottie, G.J.: Wireless sensor networks. In: Information theory workshop
24. Min, R., Chandrakasan, A.: Energy-efficient communication for ad-hoc wireless sensor networks. In: Conference Record of the Thirty-Fifth Asilomar Conference on Signals, Systems and Computers, vol. 1, pp. 139–143 (2001)
25. Xiong, N., Yang, L.T., Cao, J., Yang, Y., He, Y.: PIDNN: An Adaptive and Predictive Approach for Autonomic Multicast Networks. ACM Transactions on Autonomous and Adaptive Systems: Special Issue on Adaptive Learning in Autonomic Communication (2008)
26. Xiong, N., Defago, X., Jia, X., Yang, Y., He, Y.: Design and Analysis of a Self-tuning Proportional and Integral Controller for AQM Routers to Support TCP Flows. In: IEEE INFOCOM 2006, Barcelona, Spain (2006)

The Weighted Shortest Path Search in Mobile GIS Services

Min Peng[1], Naixue Xiong[2], Gang Xie[1], and Laurence T. Yang[3]

[1] Department of Computer, Wuhan University, Wuhan, China
hhdawn@sina.com
[2] School of Infor. Scie., Japan Advanced Institute of Scie. and Techn., Japan
naixue@jaist.ac.jp
[3] Department of Computer Science, St. Francis Xavier University, Antigonish, Canada
ltyang@stfx.ca

Abstract. Traditional GIS buffer inquiries focus on the length of the road path on map only. In this paper, an expanded method is proposed to support the distribution of mobile GIS services. According to the user's requirement and known buffer area radius on map, we defined the factors to calculate the optimal path from one node to the target node in a map, which considers not only the length of the road, but also traffic flow, road cost and other factors. We use the integrated cost to re-define the road path weights, and then select the optimal path among the road based on the minimum weight. The actual experimental results shown that based on the quantified traffic flow and road condition, from node to other target nodes, we can get an optimal path on map, which satisfies the condition mostly. The results can greatly assist the inquiry of the optimal path in GIS services.

1 Introduction

In the GIS network mode [1], the geographical feature has always been abstract for chain nodes and other targets during the same time to pay attention to connectivity. In GIS Network model [5], one node can contact with other nodes and network data model will be organized into a graph.

Optimal Path Search is to select the best path from known point to target nodes that meet the conditions on the map in the known circumstances and the radius of buffer area, according to the user's request. Decision support module in many cases is used to the optimum path search. For example, in the oil crisis of the value-added services, users may have several options for filling stations. Every gas station may have more than one path to reach, then, which path is the best one for them to go to a gas station? This involves the search for the best path problem, for example, the value-added services and navigation services. From one city to another city, there are multiple paths, which path is best? This is a problem for the search on the optimal path.

2 Optimal Path Search in Time Transport Network

2.1 The Time Traffic Network Graph Model

It is the simplest way for Optimal Path Search to directly comparing path length, the shortest path is selected. But this method does not take traffic congestion into account. Sometime, the shortest path is excessive with traffic jam, and takes more time [9-10]. Therefore, traffic volume, road conditions, and other facts must be considered in the best routing algorithm. So we should re-define the weight of each traffic path with the traffic state. Which is the optimal path that should be chosen can be determined according to the last weight value [2].

In network model, nodes are objects, which need to be linked. A digitization spatial network is generated as a modeling graph from the input spatial objects. The modeling graph contains three categories of graphs: the network junctions, the start/end points of a road segment, and other auxiliary points (such as speed limit change points). In order to reflect some factors in network model, such as a traffic volume, the road conditions and other real time traffic factors, the path between two nodes A and B is identified by the travel time to reflect the above factors. And the value of the path between nodes A and B will act as a weight, which will be added to original spatial model and form the new travel time network graph model [7].

2.2 Speed-Flow Relationship Model Parameters

To analyze the traffic condition in all levels roads, traffic flows, speed, and road states are considered, which are accessed as the basic data of the distance in time traffic network. Currently, the information access of freeway based on the video monitor, microcontroller and traffic monitoring systems and other means is carried out in full swing [4]. And there are a lot of mature road infrastructure and monitor technologies in the world now [3]. In the article "Highway Traffic Practical Speed-flow Model", a lot of traffic data are used in cities, highway traffic levels and the speed-flow model are established based on the traffic condition. Generic function expression is described as formula (1), where the practical traffic conditions are modeled based on defined model parameters.

$$\left. \begin{array}{l} U = \dfrac{\alpha_1 U_s}{1+(V/C)^\beta} \\ \beta = \alpha_2 + \alpha_3 \left(\dfrac{V}{C}\right)^3 \end{array} \right\} \quad (1)$$

In the above equation, U is speed, V is the number of arrived vehicles, which means vehicle flow, α_1, α_2 and α_3 are return parameters, U_s is the speed designed for the highways, C is capacity of road. All the served parameters defined in Table 1.

There are little changes in parameters α_2, α_3. In order to facilitate, we can fix $\alpha_2 = 1.88$. For a highway and a class road, we set $\alpha_3 = 4.90$. While for a general road (include B class road and C class road), we set $\alpha_3 = 7.00$.

According to the above model, we can create a highway traffic control speed-flow model (SFM). In the SFM, based on the real time monitoring of traffic flow on each

Table 1. The highways speed-flow generic model table

Highway types	$U_S(km\cdot h^{-1})$ Design speed	C (pcu·h^{-1}) Traffic Capaity	α_1	α_2	α_3
Highway	120	2200	0.93	1.88	4.85
	100	2200	0.95	1.88	4.86
	80	2000	1.00	1.88	4.90
	60	1800	1.20	1.88	4.88
A level Road	100	2100	0.93	1.88	4.93
	80	1950	0.98	1.88	4.88
	60	1650	1.10	1.88	4.85
B level Road	80	1400	0.95	1.88	6.97
	40	900	1.40	1.88	6.97
C level Road	40	600	1.00	1.88	7.00
	20	400	1.50	1.88	7.00

road in given areas, and the given parameters, the average travel time and average speed in each road section can be predicted, it is very useful to distribute the traffic network.

2.3 Incremental Euclidean Restriction (IER) Algorithm Optimize

2.3.1 IER Arithmetic

Usually, the shortest path between two points or for a moving object in traffic is always moved in the defined networks (such as roads, Railways). Therefore, for the travel between two objects, the calculation of the distance among the space network is much more appropriate than the calculation of a purely Euclidean distance. In [6], the Incremental Euclidean Restriction (IER) algorithm and Incremental Network Expansion (INE) algorithm are proposed to resolve the nearest neighborhood query problems in space network. In this paper, based on the SFM, we modify and improve the IER algorithm to solve the optimized path query problem in travel time networks.

In IER algorithm, the multi-step K-Nearest Neighbor (KNN) method [6] is used to get high dimensional data similarity. With common Incremental KNN algorithm, the nearest neighbor nodes of node Q are searched as following. Firstly, IER retrieves the nearest neighbor of Q, and marks it as n1. Based on Euclidean distance, we calculate the Euclidean distance between them, which is marked as $ED(Q, n_1)$. Secondly, we calculate the distance of Q and n1 in space network, which is marketed as $ND(Q, n_1)$. Subsequently, the IER algorithm can use Q as the center to draw two concentric circles with radii $ED(Q, n_1)$ and $ND(Q, n_1)$, respectively. Due to the Euclidean lower bound property (i.e., for any two nodes i and j, their Educlidean distance $ED(n_{i,j})$ always provides a lower bound on their network distance $ND(n_{i,j})$). Objects closer to Q than n1 in the space network must be within the circle, which is made by $ND(Q, n_1)$ as its radius. Therefore, the search space becomes the ring area between the two circles as shown in Figure 1. In the next iteration, the second closest object n_2 is retrieved (by Euclidean distance). Since in the given example $ND(Q, n_2) < ND(Q, n_1)$, n_2 becomes the current candidate for spatial network nearest neighbor and the reach upper bound becomes $ND(Q, n_2)$. This procedure is repeated until the next Euclidean nearest neighbor is located beyond the reach region (as n_3 in Figure 1).

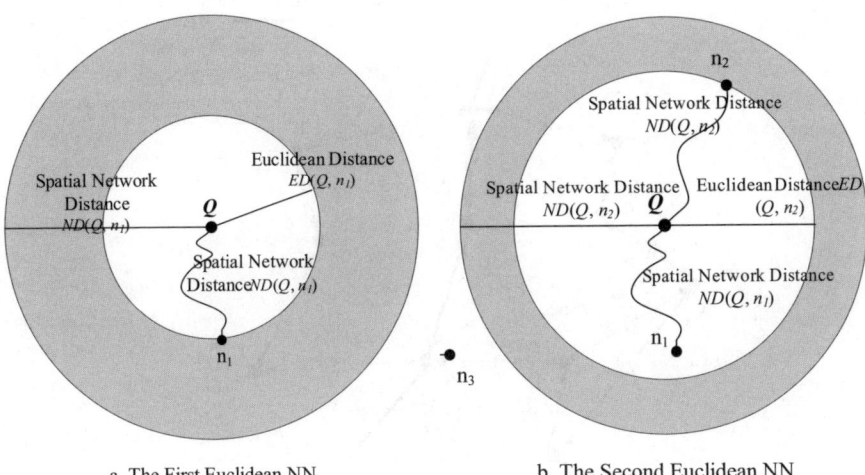

a. The First Euclidean NN　　　　　　b. The Second Euclidean NN

Fig. 1. IER Algorithm

2.3.2 Algorithm Exp-IER Expansion of the IER

In this paper, we use travel time network to replace the space network in IER algorithm and propose Exp-IER algorithm. The travel time network enables the integration of real time traffic information into a spatial representation. The spatial distance between two points of IER is replaced by the travel time, which can measure road and traffic conditions. Figures 2 and 3 illustrate the use of travel time in the path of the road map [8].

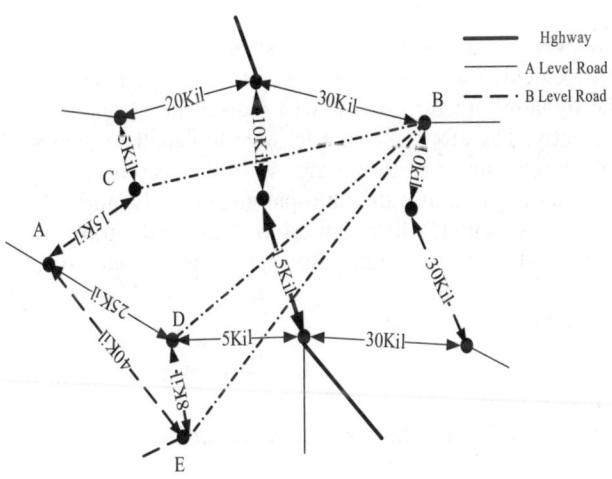

Fig. 2. Space network

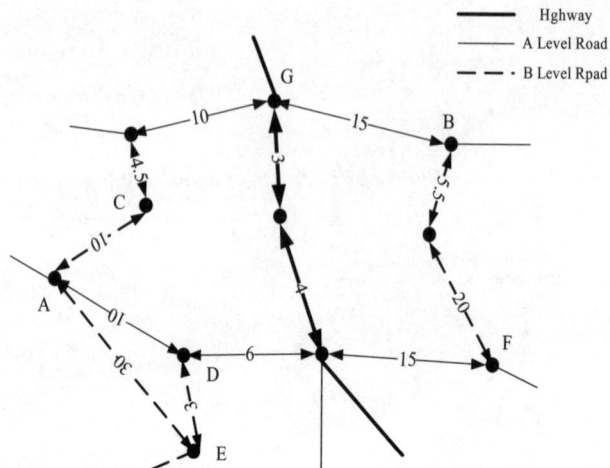

Fig. 3. Time Road Traffic Network

The travel time of node n_i to n_j along one road can be marked as the cost of the path between two nodes, and it is also shown as the weight of the path. From the speed-flow generic model, we can get (2).

$$\cos t_{n_i n_j} = \frac{Dist_N(n_i, n_j)}{U_{n_i n_j}} = \frac{Dist_N(n_i, n_j)\left(1 + (V_{n_i n_j}/C)^\beta\right)}{\alpha_1 U_s} \quad (2)$$

$$\beta = \alpha_2 + \alpha_3 \left(\frac{V_{n_i n_j}}{C}\right)^3$$

The dynamic weights of each path can be gotten from the speed-flow generic model, but in the calculation of *KNN* process, if all the distance comparison is concerned with the dynamic traffic flow, it will reduce the efficiency of the optimized path querying greatly. Therefore, it is not feasible to calculate the travel time of each path by the real-time inquiring of flow status *V*. In the searching process of the shortest path node, it's available to use the ratio parameter of dynamic changed flow $Vn_i n_j$ to road capacity *C* as a weight, which is used to evaluate the traffic status. Figure 4 is a simulation of the value of the weight information dialog interface, which describes the real-time flow of the road. According to the weights *V/C*, the traffic can be divided into the following four categories:

Category 1 – Expedite: In this path, the traffic flow is small, speed limits are reached, $0 < V/C < 0.8$.

Category 2 – Normal: Traffic flow in this road is under normal conditions, speed is little lower than designed speed, $0.8 \leq V/C < 0.95$.

Category 3 – Slow: A road segment traffic will exceed its capacity, but still can contain travel forward, the vehicle speed is below the speed designed, $0.95 \leq V/C < 1.2$.

Category 4 – Congestion : The real traffic speed of a road segment is much lower than the speed limit, and vehicles need to waiting in line, $V/C \geq 1.2$.

Category 5 – Detour : A road segment is closed and mobile host has to take a circuitous route, the actual flow of V is zero.

The weights V/C can be calculated in the system separately, so that users can choose the best path when targets are set to filter unnecessary path computation. Meanwhile, by accessing the speed-flow SFDB, traffic flow, vehicle speed and some parameters relatively with them in a given road segment, and a given time can be gained immediately. They are associated with the following algorithm. If we set out from one point in a given time, the destination (that meets the requirements on maps) and the optimal path to the destination can be gained.

2.3.3 Exp-IER Arithmetic Description

During the searching of the nearest neighbor, Exp-IER arithmetic is still based on the actual distance, which is the distance between the space road networks. But it should take the traffic flow V of each road segment into consideration. If a road segment traffic type is Class 3 or Class 4, then all corresponding destination nodes in this road segment are removed from the search area. The Exp_IER Arithmetic is shown as following.

```
Arithmetic: Exp_IER(Q, k)
   for all k nearest neighbors from R-tree
      from i = 1 to k
      if 0<V(Q, n_i) < 2
         {n_1,..., n_k} = Euclidian _ NN(Q, k);
         else  n_{k+1} = next _ Euclidean _ NN(Q, k);
               delete n_i from {n_1,..., n_k}
               insert n_{k+1} in {n_1,..., n_k}
      for each point n_i
      Dist_N(Q, n_i) = compute _ ND(Q, n_i)
      sort {n_1,..., n_k} in ascending order of Dist_N(Q, n_i)
      Dist_{E max} = Dist_N(Q, n_k)
      repeat
         if 0<V(Q, n) < 2
            (n, Dist_E(Q, n)) = next _ Euclidean _ NN(Q);
               if (Dist_N(Q, n)) < Dist_N(Q, n_k)
                  insert n in {n_1,..., n_k}
                  Dist_{E max} = Dist_N(Q, n_k)
      until Dist_E(Q, n) > Dist_{E max}
   End IER
```

2.4 Time Transport Network's Optimal Path Search

Assuming a user is in the position A, we use the improved Exp_IER method to implement A road space NN inquiries, and gained a nearest neighbor in B position. Next, we should ensure the best path to reach B from A.

In this step, the space road network is replaced by the time traffic information network. And the space road network uses the weight of the road and traffic conditions to replace the IER distance parameters between two points, to calculate the travel time of all the trails from A to B, and to find the shortest time one, which is the optimized path we wanted.

Algorithm Greedy Nearest Neighbor Graph Path: *GNN* (q, k) is shown as following.

```
Algorithm GNN(q, k)
        {n₁,...,nₖ}= Exp_IER(q, k)
        result =  {(q, n₁),...,(q, nₖ)}
        for each surrounding road segment (q, nᵢ) in the TTN do
        Dist_N(q, nᵢ) = compute _ ND(q, nᵢ)
        {α₁,α₂,α₃,C,Uₛ} = Speed-Flow(q, nᵢ)
```

$$\beta = \alpha_2 + \alpha_3 \left(\frac{V_{qn_i}}{C} \right)^3$$

$$\cos t_{qn_i} = \frac{Dist_N(q, n_i)\left(1 + (V_{qn_i} / C)^\beta\right)}{\alpha_1 U_s}$$

```
        cost_min =  min{cost_qn₁,...,cost_qnₖ}
        select the path from q to one point which
        has the minimum traffic time cost cost_min
END GNN(q, k)
```

3 Algorithm Performance Analysis

Using three types of reference data sets: highway, A level road and B level road, we simulate and test the Optimized Path searching Algorithm in time traffic network. In the simulation, it is necessary to consider not only the different road level such as highway, A level road and B level road on maps, but also the path selection among same type roads. Test parameters include the travel distance, travel time, traffic load V/C, comparison of actual time cost to the previous time cost (in space distance network, travel time is not considered), and the average driving time saving rate.

Fig. 4. Weight of road

Simulation is carried on the computer, which has Pentium IV, 2.3GHz processor and Windows NT. The road segment is $|n| = 1000$, including urban and rural highways, city A level road, urban, and rural B level roads. After the filtering of other unused map layer, a clear road linked map is used (see in Figure 4).

3.1 The Impact of Road Type on the Travel Time

In Figure 5, vehicles set out from a point, and travel in different types of road. They are with the increase of the travel distance, and the corresponding average time required. In the simulation, we assume that the designed vehicles speed limits, and the capacity and other parameters of each type of road is set as following on Table 2.

Based on the test and graph, if the traffic is in the same situation and moving the same distance, it is clear that the different types of vehicles on the road will need different time. Therefore, highway will take shortest time, and B level road will take longest time.

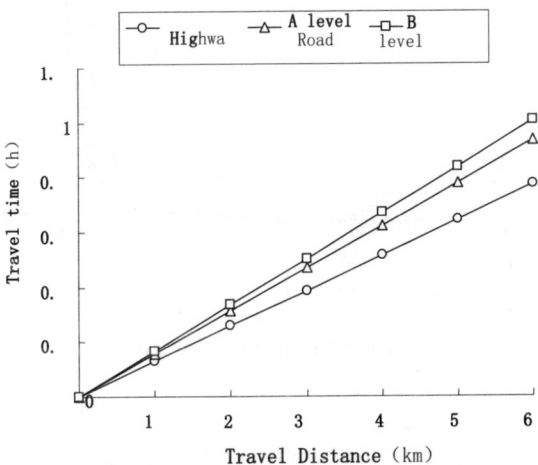

Fig. 5. Comparison of the travel time in different types of roads

Table 2. Road designed speed limit, capacity and other parameters

Highway types	$U_S(km \cdot h^{-1})$ Design speed	$C(pcu \cdot h^{-1})$ Traffic capacity	α_1	α_2	α_3	V/C
Highway	100	2200	0.95	1.88	4.86	0.6
A level road	80	1950	0.98	1.88	4.88	0.6
B level road	60	1150	1.17	1.88	6.97	0.6

In the algorithm, in the same distance traffic load conditions, the path with shortest time ($cost_{min}$) on the road will be selected. Based on the results in graph, it can be concluded that it was very necessary to replace the space network model by the travel time network model to measure the optimal path querying.

3.2 The Impact on the Travel Time of Traffic Load V/C

Traffic flow condition can be predicted by the traffic load weight V/C, so the average vehicle speed and the travel time at a certain distance can be predicted. Figure 6 and Figure 7 describe the average travel time that vehicles needed in 40 kilometers distance in different road types and traffic load.

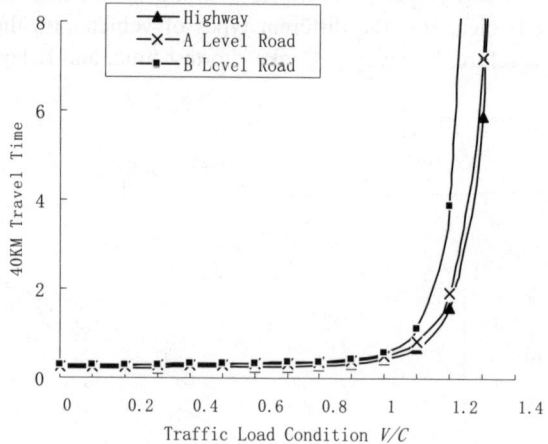

Fig. 6. 40 km distance travel time

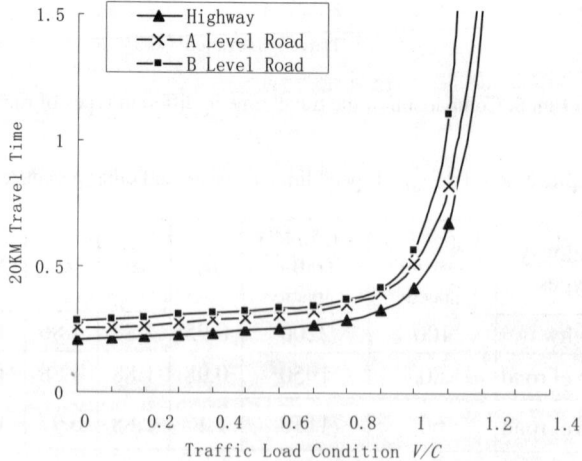

Fig. 7. 20 km distance travel time (enlarge)

From the graphs, we can see that when weight of V/C is from 0 to 0.8, vehicles can maintain normal travel and have no block. While it is with the weight value's increasing, i.e. the increasing of travel flow value. Thus, travel time will increase correspondingly. When the traffic load is from 0.8 to 0.95, vehicles can still maintain a certain speed to travel, while the cost time for vehicles is more than 1/3 normal traffic load. When weight of V/C is close to 1.2, the travel time is increased rapidly, and the traffic congestion condition is shown here. It is impossible to complete the travel in such a road segment practically.

The travel status in graph also reflects the four categories of road travel status classed based on traffic load weight V/C, which is Normal, Slow, Congestion and Detour. Meanwhile, it can also be concluded form graphs that along with the changes of traffic load in highway, A level road and B level road, the travel time are changed pro rata. In the same traffic load condition, it cost the shortest travel time in highway.

3.3 The Average Time Saving Rate of Optimal Path Search in Travel Time Network

In this paper, we use the travel time network to replace the original space network and expand the original shortest path query method in the space network. Based on the target node and buffer inquiries information, our model can choose a path adaptively from setting out node to target node, which cost the shortest time, the chosen path is the optimized path considering traffic conditions. In the experiment, three kinds of road are considered when we calculate optimal path, i.e., highway, A level road and B level road. We use the travel time saving rate to measure the performance difference between our algorithm and the shortest path querying method in space network. We define Time Savings Rate to weigh the performance, in the different traffic load condition. It is the ratio of saving travel time of the new method IER-EXP in this paper than the travel time in original method IER in space network, that is $(cost_{SN} - cost_{TTN})/cost_{SN}$. It reflects how the travel time is saved in optimized path query travel time network compared to space network, which is in the same known condition and user requirement.

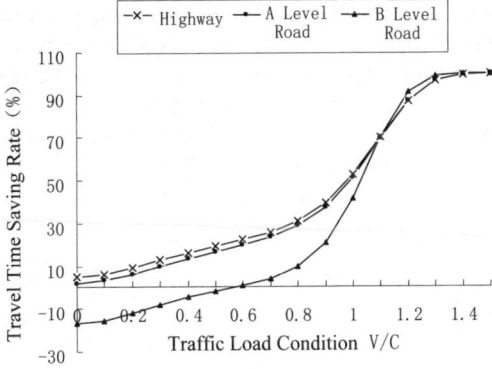

Fig. 8. Average travel time saving rate in each road type traffic load

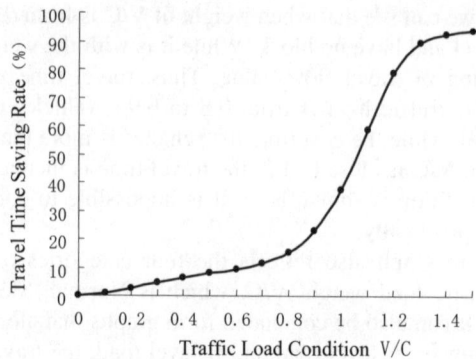

Fig. 9. Average travel time saving rate in different Traffic load

Figure 8 is the average savings rate, which only considers road type data sets. Figure 9 is the average savings rate of IER-EXP method to original IER method with the increase of traffic load condition, which considers integrated data sets with all kinds of road types. The choice of the optimal path is not limited by road type restrictions. It can be concluded from the graph that, along with the increase in traffic load condition, the consideration of road traffic conditions in our algorithm get a larger saving rate.

4 Summary

In this paper, we primarily deal with a very important issue, i.e., the optimal path query problem.

Traditional GIS buffer inquiries only focus on the length of the road path in a map. In this paper, an expanded method is proposed to support the distribution of mobile GIS services. According to the user's requirement and the known buffer area radius in a map, we defined the factors to calculate the optimal path from one node to the target node in a map. The factors consider not only the length of the road, but also traffic flow, road cost and other factors. We use the integrated cost to re-define the road path weights, and the optimal path among the roads is selected based on the minimum weight. The actual experimental results demonstrate that in the search process, based on the quantified traffic flow and road condition, from node to other target nodes, we can get an optimal path on map, which satisfies the condition mostly. The results can greatly assist the inquiry of the optimal path in GIS services.

References

1. Kharola, P.S., Gopalkrishna, B., Prakash, D.C.: Fleet Management using GPS and GIS. Bangalore Metropolitan Transport Corporation (BMTC) case study, Map India (2001)
2. Ku, W.-S., Zimmermann, R., Wang, H., Wan, C.-N.: Adaptive Nearest Neighbor Queries in Travel Time Networks. In: Proceedings of GIS 2005, Bremen, Germany, pp. 210–219 (2005)

3. Papadias, D., Zhang, J., Mamoulis, N., Tao, Y.: Query Processing in Spatial Network Databases. In: Proceedings of the International Conference on Very Large Data-bases (VLDB), pp. 790–801 (2003)
4. Yu, T., Yu, L., Wang, Z.: The Development and Application of GIS in Mobile Computing Envirepment. Bulletin of Surveying and Mapping (3) (2002)
5. Open GIS Consortium (OGC): Open GIS geography markup Language (2000), http://www.opengis.org/techno/specs
6. Wang, F.J., Jusoh, S.: Integrating Multiple Web-based Geographic Information Systems. IEEE Multimedia, 49–61 (January-March 1999)
7. Wong, S.H., Swartz, S.L.: A Middleware Architecture for Open and Interoperable GISs. In: IEEE MultiMedia, pp. 62–76 (April-June 2002)
8. Kim, K.-C., Yun, S.-W.: MR-Tree: A Cache-Conscious Main Memory Spatial index Structure for Mobile GIS. In: Kwon, Y.-J., Bouju, A., Claramunt, C. (eds.) W2GIS 2004. LNCS, vol. 3428, pp. 167–180. Springer, Heidelberg (2005)
9. Xiong, N., Yang, L.T., jiannong, C., Yang, Y., He, Y.: PIDNN: An Efficient and Distributed Flow Control Approach for Multicast Networks. ACM Transactions on Autonomous and Adaptive Systems: Special Issue on Adaptive Learning in Autonomic Communication (2008)
10. Xiong, N., Defago, X., Jia, X., Yang, Y., He, Y.: Design and Analysis of a Self-tuning Proportional and Integral Controller for Active Queue Management Routers to Support TCP Flows. In: Proc. of IEEE Infocomm 2006, Barcelona, Spain, April 23-29 (2006)

On Maximizing the Throughput of Convergecast in Wireless Sensor Networks

Nai-Luen Lai, Chung-Ta King, and Chun-Han Lin

Department of Computer Science, National Tsing Hua University,
Hsinchu, Taiwan 300
{king,chlin}@cs.nthu.edu.tw

Abstract. A primary task of wireless sensor networks is collecting environmental information. In most cases, a sink node is responsible for collecting data from all sensor nodes. The radio congestion around the sink becomes the main bottleneck to maximizing the throughput of the convergecast. A general strategy to alleviating the problem is to schedule the communications among sensors to avoid interference. In this paper, we consider both routing structures and communication schedules for optimizing the scheduling length. We show that the shortest-length conflict-free scheduling is equivalent to finding a minimal vertex coloring. To solve the schedule problem, a virtual-node expansion is proposed to handle the relay operations in convergecast, and then coloring algorithms are used to obtain the communication schedule. However, scheduling only solves part of the problem. Routing structures will also affect the scheduling quality. The disjoint-strips routing is thus proposed to leverage possible parallel transmissions in convergecast. The proposed algorithms are evaluated through simulations.

1 Introduction

Monitoring environments is one of the fundamental tasks in *wireless sensor networks* (WSNs). In these tasks, sensors may periodically report sensed data to a sink for further analysis. This data collection operation, called *convergecast*, usually causes communication congestion around the sink. The problem is critical to applications that require high sampling rate, such as acoustics, seismology, structure monitoring, and neuron technology. One possible solution is to reduce the size of data by means of compression or in-network aggregation. But designing aggregation functions on resource-limited sensors is a challenge for complicated applications. Besides, some applications have to collect raw data instead of summaries. Therefore, an efficient approach for convergecast is necessary.

Two approaches are generally used to control the efficient access to the communication media. One is contention-based, such as *carrier-sense multiple access* (CSMA), and the other is schedule-based, such as *time-division multiple access* (TDMA). If the communications are highly utilized, contention-based mechanisms are known to be inefficient due to high probability of collisions. Since the communication utilization of convergecast is proportional to the sampling rate, schedule-based mechanisms are more suitable for high sampling rate applications. Many studies have been performed on the schedule-based mechanisms in WSNs. Most of them [1][2][3][4][5] focus on prolonging the network lifetime and do not address the performance of convergecast. Funneling-MAC [6] studies the balance between data collection throughput and system flexibility by a hybrid approach that adopts TDMA in the neighborhood of the sink and CSMA elsewhere. *Node-based scheduling* (NBS) [7] reduces the length (in number of slots) of a conflict-free schedule by utilizing graph coloring techniques. Mao et al [8] formularize the communication scheduling to an optimization problem, and applied genetic algorithms and particle swarm optimization algorithms to search for solutions. Besides the communication scheduling, routing structures affect the performance of convergecast. Many existing works [9] implicitly adopt *shortest-path routing* and do not address the effects of routing structures on convergecast.

In this paper, we schedule transmissions to avoid interference and collisions to improve the convergecast. We also examine the effects of routing structures on convergecast. A routing algorithm is proposed as an alternative to existing shortest-path routing. Our solution to convergecast thus consists of two stages. First, a routing structure is constructed from the connectivity graph. Next, communications on the routing structure are scheduled to efficiently perform convergecast.

The remainder of this paper is organized as follows. Section 2 gives the system model and the problem definition in detail. Then, Algorithms for the scheduling problem are shown in section 3. Section 4 discusses the effect of routing topology and proposes the disjoint-strips algorithm. Next, section 5 shows performance evaluations through simulations. Finally, conclusions are given in section 6.

2 Problem Statement

2.1 System Model

In schedule-based WSNs, time is divided into equal-length *slots*. Transmitting one piece of data takes one slot. A *schedule* consists of many slots and a specification of which nodes to transmit at which slots. Nodes are assumed to be synchronized and homogeneous, and each node generates one data during a collecting cycle. We consider *convergecast* which is to collect all data at the sink. This model is also adopted by Funneling-MAC [6] and NBS [7]. Since sensors have to send their own data and relay data for other nodes, each sensor may be assigned more than one slot in a schedule. No aggregation or compression operations are adopted. A sensor can successfully receive data if only one transmitting node exists within its *communication range* and no other interference. The distance within which a transmission will interfere with receiving operations is called the *carrier-sense range*. The carrier-sense range is typically two to four times of the communication range. We assume that inter-node communications and conflict relationships are known. Transmissions will *conflict* with each other if any one of the following situations holds:

- A transmission targets at a sensor that is sending data.
- Two simultaneous transmissions target at the same node.

More than one sensor transmits data within the interfering range of a node that is receiving data.

2.2 Problem Definition

Our goal is to reduce the number of slots in a schedule. Since the number of slots equals a collecting cycle, the sampling rate can increase with short schedules. In this paper, a schedule will satisfy following properties:

- It accommodates transmissions of one collecting cycle.
- Transmissions arranged in same slot will not conflict with each other.

Let $V=\{v_i \mid i=1...n\}$ donate the set of all n sensors (excluding the sink) in the network, and $E=\{e_i \mid i=1...n\}$ the set of edges of a tree rooted at the sink. An edge e_i is the communication link from the node v_i to its parent in the tree. The conflict function $I(i,j)=1$ if transmission over e_i conflicts with that over e_j, where $i \neq j$, and $I(i,j)=0$ otherwise. The set $S=\{T_i \mid T_i \subset V, i=1...m\}$ is a schedule with m slots, where T_i is the set of sensors that can transmit data in the i_{th} slot. The goal is to find a schedule S with the minimal length m satisfying the constraints:

- $I(i,j) = \{0 \mid e_i \neq e_j, \{e_i, e_j\} \subset T_k\}, \forall k \in \{1...m\}$
- $|O_i|=o_i+1$ for $O_i = \{j \mid v_i \in T_j\}, \forall j \in \{1...m\}$, where o_i is the number of children of v_i in the tree.

3 Scheduling Algorithms

In this section, we describe a process to solve the scheduling problem by utilizing graph-coloring techniques. First, it is shown that the shortest conflict-free scheduling is equivalent to finding a minimal vertex coloring. Then a transformation between scheduling problem and coloring problem is given. Finally, two coloring algorithms with different performance bounds are proposed.

3.1 Graph-Coloring Technique

In Optimal conflict-free scheduling of wireless communication is shown to be NP-complete [10]. It is no easier than a graph vertex-coloring problem. Thus, a common strategy to solving the scheduling problem is through graph-coloring techniques. In the following, we illustrate how to transform a scheduling problem into a graph coloring problem, and show the correspondence between a proper coloring and a conflict-free schedule. Figure 1 shows the topology of an example network. We can construct a *conflict graph* by taking each link in the routing tree as a vertex, and connecting two vertices with an edge if transmissions through them conflict. This conflict graph is shown in figure 2. Once given a proper coloring of the conflict graph by any coloring algorithms, we can easily convert it to a conflict-free schedule. Because all conflicting transmission pairs have a link in the conflict graph and they are not assigned the same color, all transmissions in the same slot are thus conflict-free.

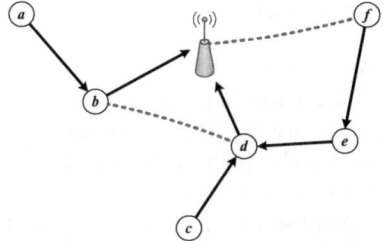

Fig. 1. A data-collecting scenario. Solid arrows are communication links of the routing tree. Node pairs within the interfering range are shown with dotted lines.

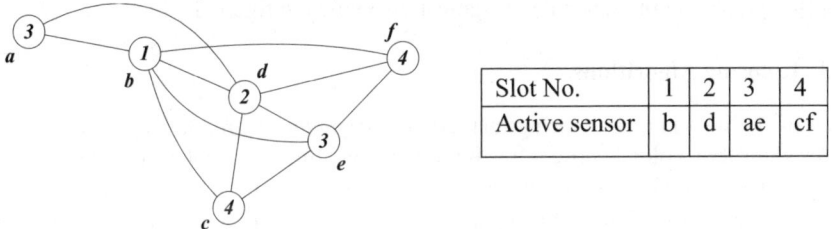

Fig. 2. The conflict graph and its schedule. The number in a node is the color assigned. Taking each color in the conflict graph as one slot in the schedule, nodes can then be scheduled to transmit in the slot of the assigned color.

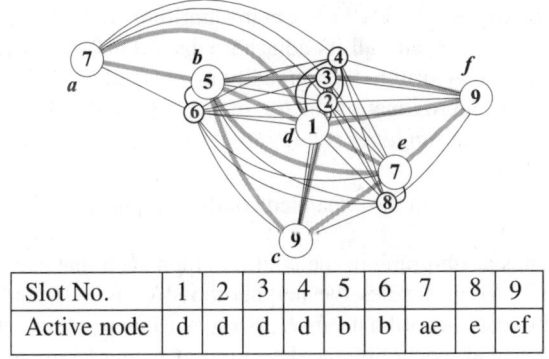

Slot No.	1	2	3	4	5	6	7	8	9
Active node	d	d	d	d	b	b	ae	e	cf

Fig. 3. The expended conflict graph and its schedule

After transformation of the problem, finding a shortest-length schedule is equivalent to finding the minimal vertex coloring. Let S be the conflict-free schedule that has the minimal length m. Then, S's corresponding graph coloring uses the minimal number of colors. Let the minimal length of a conflict-free schedule be m. Then, any schedule with a length less than m is not conflict-free. The *chromatic number* of the graph is also m.

3.2 Virtual–Node Expansion (VNE)

Some sensors have to relay data in convergecast. To accommodate these relaying transmissions, NBS [7] divides scheduling into two stages. The first stage is to schedule the routing links in a greedy fashion. The second stage then repeats the schedule—with those slots in which no node having data to send skipped—until all transmissions is satisfied. Only partial information is available in each stage. Instead of repeating the original schedules, we propose to expand the relaying transmissions into *virtual nodes* and to schedule expanded conflict graph. A virtual node conflicts with all transmission of its original node. Since a sensor and its virtual nodes also conflict with each other, they should be connected as well. VNE reveals all conflict relationships to the coloring algorithms to plan the more efficient schedules. The expanded conflict graph and the schedule of figure 1 are shown in figure 3.

3.3 Coloring Algorithms

One of the well-known coloring methods is *(maximum-degree first) greedy coloring*. This algorithm colors vertices by iteratively picking an uncolored vertex with the largest degree, and assigning it the first color not used by its neighbors. This algorithm colors a graph $G(V, E)$ using at most $\triangle(G)+1$ colors, where $\triangle(G)$ is the maximum degree in G. The time complexity is $O(|V|^2)$. Although greedy coloring provides a satisfactory result most of the time, it has no constant performance bound to the optimal solution. Let $\delta(G)$ denote the largest d such that the graph G contains a subgraph in which every vertex has a degree at least d. The work of Li et al [11] describe an approximate coloring algorithm to find $\delta(G)$ and to color G using $\delta(G)+1$ colors with a time complexity of $O(|V|+|E|)$. Their algorithm finds the vertex v_i with the least degree, and removes v_i and all its adjacent edges. This step is repeated until all nodes are removed. The algorithm then greedily assigns colors in the reverse order of removing nodes. The approximation factor of approximate coloring algorithm depends on the *carrier-sense range/receiving range ratio (CS_RX_ratio)*.

Theorems. $OPT(G) \geq \frac{2 \times \delta(G)}{k}+1$ in the expanded conflict graphs

Proof. Let H donates a sub-graph of the conflict graph such that each vertex in H has degree at least $\delta(G)$, $N_H(v)$ donates the neighborhood of v in H, and v^* donates the node with the leftmost x-coordinate in H. Since an independent set in any node's neighborhood has size at most k, by the definition of v^* and k, any independent set in $N_H(v^*)$ has size no greater than $k/2$. Thus the number of independent sets in $N_H(v^*)$ can not be smaller than $2* N_H(v^*)/k$, which means that no coloring algorithm can color $N_H(v^*)$ using less than $2* N_H(v^*)/k$ colors. So an optimal algorithm uses at least $(2* N_H(v^*)/k)+1$ colors to color v^* and $N_H(v^*)$, and $N_H(v^*) \geq \delta(G)$ by the choice of H. Thus, $OPT(G) \geq \frac{2 \times \delta(G)}{k}+1$. □

Let $OPT(G)$ and $APPR(G)$ donate the number of colors used by the optimal and approximate algorithm respectively to color a graph, k be the maximum size of an independent set in the neighborhood of a node in the graph. Marathe et al [12] have proved that $OPT(G) \geq \delta(G)/3 + 1$ in any *unit-disk graph*. Because the expanded conflict graph is not a unit-disk graph, we show that $OPT(G) \geq \frac{2 \times \delta(G)}{k} + 1$ in expanded conflict graphs. Furthermore, with $APPR(G) \leq \delta(G)+1$, we can derive $APPR(G) \leq \frac{k}{2} \times OPT(G)$.

Determining the value of k is equivalent to finding the maximum size of an induced sub-graph with a star topology. A star sub-graph is shown in figure 4. The maximum number of surrounding transmissions depends on CS_RX_ratio. Figure 5 shows the minimum θ such that the transmission αB does not interfere with transmission βC. The distance between α and C is at least the carrier-sense range, which is the same for that between β and C. We derive k as a function of CS_RX_ratio from figure 5.

$$\cos(\theta) \geq \frac{CS+Rx}{2 \times CS} \Rightarrow \cos(\theta) \geq \frac{r+1}{2 \times r}, r \text{ is } CS\_RX\_ratio \Rightarrow \theta \geq \cos^{-1}\left(\frac{r+1}{2 \times r}\right)$$

$$k = \max\left(\left\lfloor \frac{2\pi}{\theta} \right\rfloor\right) = \left\lfloor \frac{2\pi}{\theta_{\min}} \right\rfloor = \left\lfloor 2\pi / \cos^{-1}\left(\frac{r+1}{2 \times r}\right) \right\rfloor$$

We then can determine the approximation factor of approximate coloring with k.

$$APPR(G) \leq \left\lfloor \frac{\pi}{\cos^{-1}\left(\frac{r+1}{2 \times r}\right)} \right\rfloor \times OPT(G), \quad r = CS\_RX\_ratio$$

A plot of the approximation factor under various CS_RX_ratio is shown in figure 6.

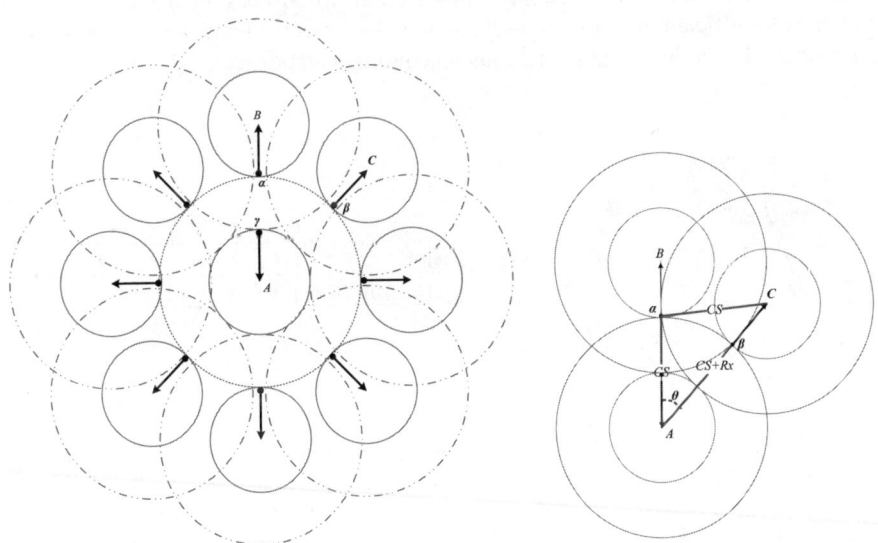

Fig. 4. The induced star sub-graph. Each arrow represents a transmission

Fig. 5. The minimum angle between two transmissions

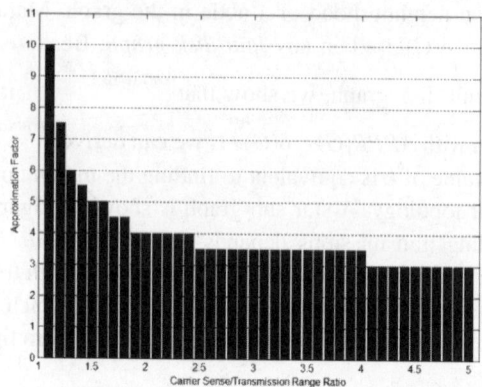

Fig. 6. Approximation factors under different *CS_RX_ratios*

4 Disjoint-Strips Routing

In previous section, we improve the throughput by arranging communications to minimize the length of the schedule. The assumption is that the routing structure is given. However, the routing structure will also affect the quality of the scheduling. This can be illustrated by an example in figure 7. From this example, we can see that in order to achieve the maximum data-gathering throughput, it is necessary to take routing topology into consideration. In this section, we discuss the design of routing structures for efficient transmission scheduling. As far as we know, the effect of routing structure is not discussed in previous scheduling methods.

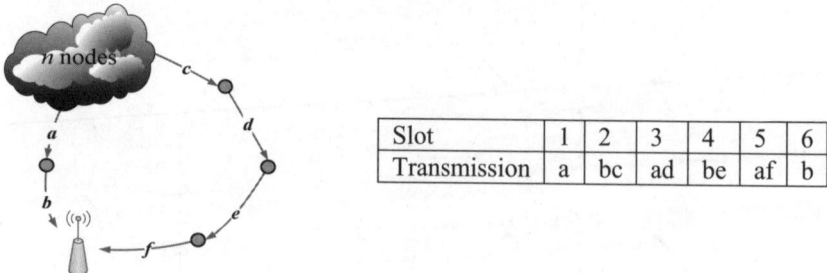

Fig. 7. Two possible routes to the sink and a schedule with $n=4$. In left network, n sensor nodes locate in a small area. There are two routes from these nodes to the sink. If all their data go through the shorter route in a and b, both links a and b will be activated at least n times in one gathering cycle. Since a and b can not be active at the same time, the schedule length will require at least $2n$ slots. On the other hand, we can find a schedule shorter than $2n$ if some nodes can route via links c, d, e, f to the sink. The schedule listed in right part can send four data back to the sink within six slots: three through a and b and one through c, d, e, and f.

Before designing a routing algorithm for fast convergecast, the metrics to evaluate a routing structure must be clarified. As in a network designed for high throughput, achievable lower bound of the schedule length is the most accurate metric to evaluate a routing method. Although it is possible to calculate the lower bound in simple examples like figure 7, it is not easy for general cases. Furthermore, Jain, et al. [13] have shown that determining a routing structure for optimal throughput is NP-hard. Thus, we resort to simple heuristics in this paper. It follows that an alternative way to evaluate a routing is to examine network properties that affect the scheduling method. Take the two coloring algorithms in the previous section as examples: their performances are bounded by $\Delta(G)$ and $\delta(G)$ respectively. By minimizing $\Delta(G)$ and $\delta(G)$, the worst-case performance of the scheduling algorithms can be improved, but this is not necessarily true for average cases. In order to collect data in the shortest time, it is intuitive to route data through the shortest paths to minimize the number of relay transmissions. In the example in figure 7, the shortest-path routing structure minimizes the number of transmissions, but it does not achieve the best performance. We can see that the shortest-path routing may cause all transmissions to follow a few paths. These paths limit the scheduling options and make the schedule length unnecessarily long. On the other hand, if data are routed along different paths which are not necessarily the shortest ones, the total number of transmissions may be increased, but data can be relayed in parallel. The schedule length may decrease by relieving the load on the critical paths. We design a routing algorithm based on this idea, which is presented in the next section.

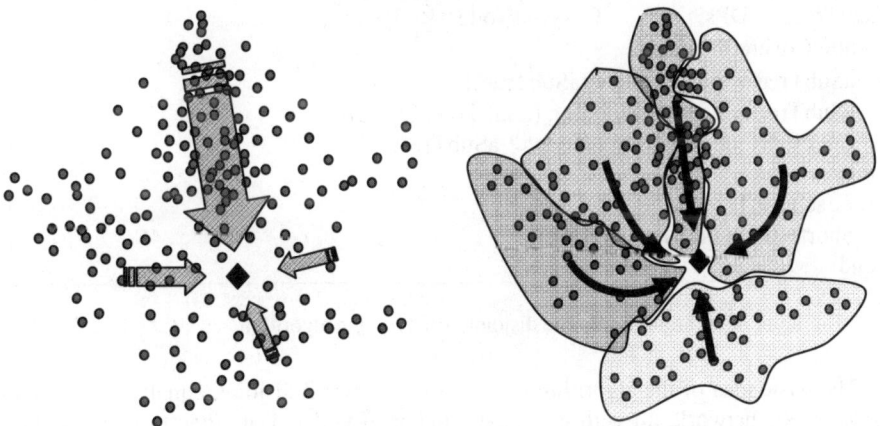

Fig. 8. An unbalanced deployment and the corresponding DS routing with five strips. In left network, many nodes reside at the north side of the sink node. If the shortest-path routing is applied, a large amount of data will flow from the north to the sink. These data form the critical paths, which force a long schedule length. Meanwhile, there are relatively few transmissions elsewhere in the network. Right graph shows our idea, in which there are five strips, all lead to the sink. Strips are disjoint, and the distance between two strips allows radio interference to alternate that makes simultaneous transmissions possible. The large amount of data to the north of the sink are thus scattered and carried by several routes.

```
INPUT: The connectivity graph, G(V, E)
OUTPUT: a list of preceding nodes in the routing tree
/*estimate number of disjoint strips*/
Do single-source shortest path from the sink.
for i=1:diameter/2
  #EstimatedDS := MIN(number of i-hop node, #EstimatedDS, 6);
end
/*find several equally spaced disjoint paths*/
pathEnd := PickFarthest(G, sink);
#DP := [];        CoveredNode := [];  subG := G;
While #DP < #EstimatedDS && CoveredNode ≠ V
  subG := subG - Coverednode;
  aDisjPath := ShortestPath(subG, pathEnd, sink);
  if aDisjPath = ∅
    CoveredNode := CoveredNode ∪ pathEnd;
    pathEnd := PickFarthest(subG);    Continue;
  else
    DPs := DPs ∪ aDisjPath;   #DP++;
  end
  DPstrip := LimitedFlooding(aDP, ExpSize);
  CoveredNode := CoveredNode ∪ DPstrip;
  pathEnd := PickFarthest (DPstrip[last]);
end
/*expand paths to equal-size strips*/
subTrees := DPs;        CoveredNode = ∅;
while CoveredNode ≠ V
  aSubTree := pickSmallest(aSubTree);
  aSubTree := LimitedFlooding (aSubTree, ExpSize);
  CoveredNode := CoveredNode ∪ aSubTree;
end
for each subTrees
  ShortestPath (subTree[i], sink);
end.
```

Fig. 9. The disjoint-strips routing algorithm

The basic idea of the algorithm is to construct several disjoint, equally spaced *node strips* in the network, all with the same number of nodes. Data then flow along these strips to reach the sink. Two distanced strips are likely to relay data simultaneously without interfering with each other. With data evenly distributed to the strips, it is unlikely that a few paths will carry the majority traffic. Figure 8 illustrates an example.

Most load-balancing routings [5][14] require location information to build spatially distributed routes. However, location information may not be available in most WSNs, and locating node position is either costly or inaccurate. In this paper, we assume physical location information is not available. Instead we use the node connectivity graph to approximate ideal disjoint strips. The algorithm of DS routing is shown in figure 9. The time complexity is $O(|V|^3)$, where $|V|$ is the number of sensors.

5 Performance Evaluation

The proposed algorithms are implemented with MATLAB to evaluate their performance. Sensors are randomly deployed and then the routing algorithms are applied. Next, scheduling algorithms are applied to generate schedules. We record the throughput of the schedule, which is defined as the ratio of the number of sensors to the length of the schedule.

5.1 Virtual-Node Expansion

Figure 10 shows the performance of the virtual-node expansion technique. The schedule of VNE outperforms that of NBS, because VNE provides relay information to the coloring algorithm. The schedules of VNE have higher throughput as the network size grows. The reason is that more nodes can be arranged to transmit simultaneously in larger networks.

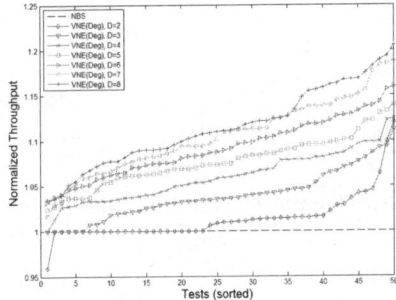

Fig. 10. Comparison between VNE and NBS. 50 experiments are sorted in ascending order.

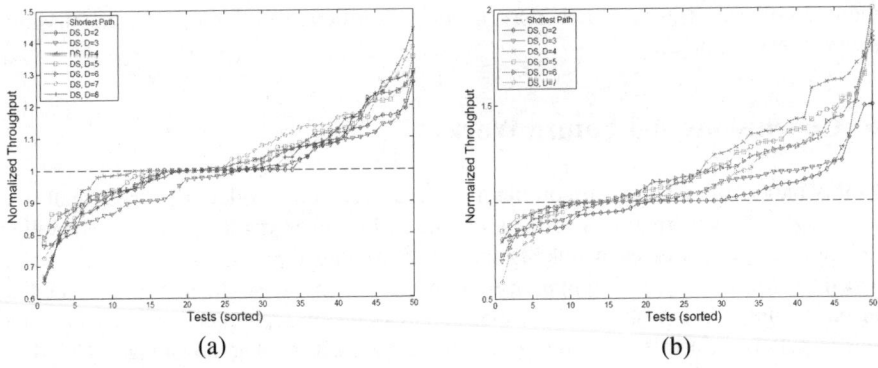

(a)   (b)

Fig. 11. Comparison between DS routing and shortest-path routing. VNE scheduling algorithm is adopted. In left graph (a), sink is located near the center of the network. In right graph (b), skewed deployment is applied.

5.2 Disjoint-Strips Routing

Figure 11 compares disjoint-strip routing and the shortest-path routing. In figure 11(a), we can observe that DS routing performs better than shortest-path routing in half of the cases, but worse in the other half. As shown in figure 11(b), in unbalanced deployment, DS routing yields better schedules in most cases. In general, shortest-path routing is suitable for balanced deployments, while DS routing is suitable for unbalanced ones. It is expected that DS routing and shortest-path routing have similar average performance.

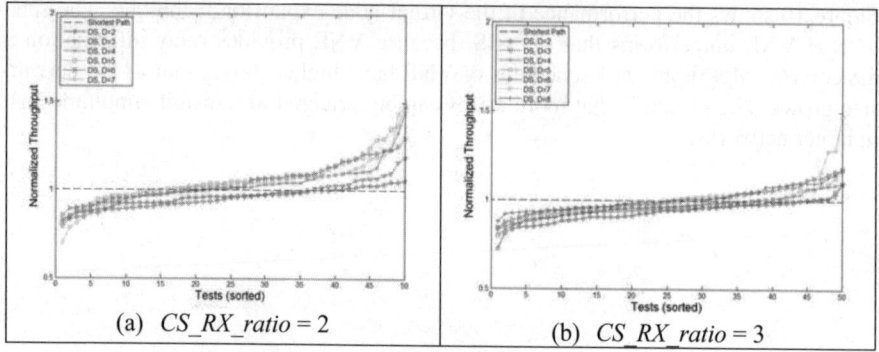

(a) $CS\_RX\_ratio = 2$ (b) $CS\_RX\_ratio = 3$

Fig. 12. Normalized throughput under DS routing in skewed deployment

5.3 Effect of CS/RX Ratio

Figure 12 shows the effect of CS_RX_ratio on DS routing. CS_RX_ratio is defined as the ratio of carrier-sense range to transmission range. We observe that the improvement becomes smaller as CS_RX_ratio increases. Since larger CS_RX_ratio introduces more conflicts, disjoint routes may become conflictive and parallel transmissions become less possible.

6 Conclusions and Future Works

In this paper, we separate the problem of optimizing data-collecting throughput into two stages: 1) constructing a routing structure on a given deployment; 2) scheduling the activation time of each link. Determining routing topology and communication schedule for optimal throughput are shown to be hard, so heuristics are applied in either stage. We propose the virtual-node expansion technique, which makes the traffic pattern information visible to a coloring algorithm. The advantage of VNE is verified through simulations. The VNE technique can be applied to any coloring algorithm, and any deterministic traffic pattern. In this paper, we show that routing structures set a limit on the capacity of scheduling techniques. There are two possible ways in routing algorithms to improve the throughput: 1) reducing the total number of transmissions during collecting; 2) transferring data in parallel. The shortest-path routing addresses the first point while the disjoint-strips routing addresses the second.

As expected, when the deployment is even and balanced, minimizing the number of transmissions is more effective than parallel transmissions. On the other hand, when the deployment is unbalanced and conflicts are not strict, parallel transmissions can improve the throughput.

Our work focuses on investigating high throughput in WSNs. There are still many issues to work on. Currently, our DS routing only approximates disjoint strips by heuristics. By supporting location information, its performance may be improved. In this work, only tree structures are considered. We believe that a multi-path routing in a mesh topology is much more flexible than trees.

Acknowledgement

This work was supported by the National Science Council of the Republic of China under Grants NSC 95-2219-E-007-008 and NSC 96-2218-E-007-009, and by the ICL of ITRI.

References

1. Madden, S.R., Franklin, M.J., Hellerstein, J.M., Hong, W.: TinyDB: An acquisitional query processing system for sensor networks. ACM Trans. on Database Systems 30 (2005)
2. Rajendran, V., Obraczka, K., Garcia-Luna-Aceves, J.J.: Energy-efficient collision-free medium access control for wireless sensor networks. In: Proc. of the International Conf. on Embedded Networked Sensor Systems (2003)
3. Hohlt, B., Doherty, L., Brewer, E.: Flexible Power Scheduling for Sensor Networks. In: Proc. of the Third International Symposium on Information Processing in Sensor Networks (2004)
4. Rhee, I., Warrier, A., Aia, M., Min, J.: Z-MAC: A hybrid MAC for wireless sensor networks. In: Proc. of the 3rd International Conf. on Embedded Networked Sensor Systems (2005)
5. Trigoni, N., Yao, Y., Demers, A., Gehrke, J., Rajaraman, R.: Wave Scheduling and Routing in Sensor Networks. ACM Trans. on Sensor Networks 3 (2007)
6. Ahn, G.-S., Hong, S.G., Miluzzo, E., Campbell, A.T., Cuomo, F.: Funneling-MAC: A localized, sink-oriented MAC for boosting fidelity in sensor networks. In: Proc. of the International Conf. on Embedded Networked Sensor Systems (2006)
7. Ergen, S.C., Varaiya, P.: TDMA Scheduling Algorithms for Sensor Networks. Technical Report, Department of EECS, University of California, Berkeley (2005)
8. Mao, J., Wu, Z., Wu, X.: A TDMA Scheduling Scheme for Many-to-one Communications in Wireless Sensor Networks. Computer Communications 30, 863–872 (2007)
9. Chen, X., Hu, X., Zhu, J.: Minimum Data Aggregation Time Problem in Wireless Sensor Networks. In: Proc. of the International Conf. on Mobile Ad-hoc and Sensor Networks (2005)
10. Ramanathan, S.: A Unified Framework and Algorithm for Channel Assignment in Wireless Networks. Wireless Networks 5, 81–94 (1999)
11. Li, X.-Y., Wang, Y.: Simple Heuristics and PTASs for Intersection Graphs in Wireless Ad Hoc Networks. In: Proc. of the International Workshop on Discrete Algorithms and Methods for Mobile Computing and Communications (2002)

12. Marathe, M.V., Breu, H., Hunt III, H.B., Ravi, S.S., Rosenkrantz, D.J.: Simple Heuristics for Unit Disk Graphs. Networks 25, 59–68 (1995)
13. Jain, K., Padhye, J., Padmanabhan, V.N., Qiu, L.: Impact of Interference on Multi-hop Wire-less Network Performance. In: Proc. of the Annual International Conf. on Mobile Computing and Networking (2003)
14. Transier, M., Füßler, H., Mauve, M., Widmer, J., Effelsberg, W.: Dynamic Load Balancing for Position-based Routing. In: Proc. of the Conf. on Emerging Network Experiment and Technology (2005)

A Self-organizing Communication Architecture for ZigBee

Seong Hoon Kim, Jeong Seok Kang, and Hong Seong Park

Department of Electronic and Telecommunication Engineering,
Kangwon National University, Chuncheon-si, Korea
shkim1980@gmail.com, sleeper82@control.kangwon.ac.kr,
hspark@kangwon.ac.kr

Abstract. This paper proposes self-organizing communication architecture for ZigBee. In our approach, we integrate application level communication facilities and network level management functions by putting all elements of gateways, ad hoc networking, network management, and plug-and-play services together. Namely, we use ad hoc networking facilities provided by ZigBee, and build ZigBee network management architecture (ZNMA) for autonomously and efficiently managing networks and ZigBee gateway by leveraging Universal Plug and Play (UPnP) as a key to interconnecting ZigBee with Internet. And then we combine all the elements together to enable the self-organizing communication architecture as a whole to provide autonomy, fault-tolerance, self-configuration, and self-organization capability. And we demonstrate our proposed architecture through implementation and evaluation.

1 Introduction

Recently updated ZigBee [1] is one of promising technologies for pervasive computing because it is designed for low cost and low power consumption. To minimize power consumption and promote long battery life (assuming battery-powered devices), ZigBee end devices can spend most of their time under sleep mode, waking up only when they need to communicate and then going immediately back to sleep mode. Furthermore, ZigBee supports addressing, multicasting, fault tolerant mesh networking at network level and grouping, group addressing, binding at application level. And ZigBee also provides several management functions like security, node, power, and binding backup and restoration facilities as well as device and service discovery facilities including proxy cache discovery for sleeping end devices.

In view of network level, ZigBee is a self-organization system [2] in a sense that ZigBee nodes themselves join a network in an ad hoc manner. Addresses are automatically allocated to the nodes. And then the nodes can communicate with any nodes on the network while providing network management functions. Additionally, ZigBee supports a native fault-tolerance mechanism in that recovery/repair procedure referred to as orphaning procedure occurs to rejoin the existing network when there are repeated communication failures in the requests for data transmissions.

Even though ZigBee has the above functions, ZigBee is not fully self-organizable. In order that ZigBee itself becomes a self-organization system applicable to actual environment, integration between ZigBee networks and Internet also should be dealt with. Besides, in case of failures like partial network destructions, restoring original states should also be appropriately performed while minimizing damages on the network. For this, all the information regarding configurations, devices and services in the ZigBee multi-hop networks should be always synchronized with Internet applications via gateways in order that Internet applications achieve knowledge of services provide by the ZigBee networks. That is, it is necessary to consider not only ZigBee-Internet gateways but also all elements of ad hoc networking, network management, and plug-and-play services together; needless to say all those operations should be performed without any user intervention.

To address the issues above, we propose SElf-organizing Communication Architecture for ZigBee (SECAZ). In our approach, we integrate application level communication facilities and network level management functions. That is, we use ad hoc networking functions at network layer and build ZigBee network management architecture (ZNMA) for autonomously and efficiently managing networks and ZigBee gateway by employing Universal Plug and Play (UPnP) [8] as a key to interconnecting ZigBee with Internet. And then we combine all elements together. In doing so, ZNMA forms hierarchical management architecture and consists of supervisors located in the gateways, local managers in routers, and agents in end devices. Based on the structure, ZNMA efficiently provides reliable self-configuration and fault tolerant functions by autonomously managing local network and having a recovery phase while supporting multiple gateways. In addition, ZNMA informs UPnP-ZigBee gateways of network changes such as join or leave of ZigBee nodes and provides service and device information of the ZigBee nodes joining the network. It leads that UPnP-ZigBee gateways are easily synchronized with an actual ZigBee network and let physical ZigBee devices represented as virtual UPnP devices playing a role of dynamic proxies according to the presence of physical ZigBee devices and services. As a result, the SECAZ dynamically and automatically integrates the ZigBee nodes with Internet and is highly available even with faults on ZigBee networks by combining the ZigBee network and UPnP-ZigBee gateways.

The remainder of this paper is organized as follows: Section 2 illustrates related studies and Section 3 describes the proposed the self-organizing communication architecture for ZigBee and its operations in detail. Implementations and evaluations are presented in Section 4, followed by conclusion in Section 5.

2 Related Work

Zero configuration networking [3] is a concept to enable networking without configured information from either a user or infrastructure in order to make networking as easy as possible. The Zeroconf WG has defined requirements for four zero configuration networking protocol areas; they are *IP interface configuration and IP multicast address allocation* at the network level, and *translation between host name and IP address* and *service discovery* at the application level. Zero configuration networking is required for environments where administration is impractical or impossible, such as in the home or small office, embedded systems as in an automobile. Even though its concept is similar to ours, it is based on IP-networking and further it is not applicable to ZigBee because ZigBee has its own protocol stack designed for small devices with low cost, low power consumption, and low bandwidth communication capability whereas Zeroconf requires the TCP/IP stack and consumes large amounts of bandwidth in comparison with ZigBee.

The Devices Profile for Web Services (DPWS) standard [4] defines a minimal set of Web service protocol and implementation constraints in order to be implemented on devices with limited resources. DPWS is partially based on the Web Service Architecture (WSA) and uses Web service technology such as WS-Addressing, WS-Discovery, WS-MetadataExchange and WS-Eventing etc. It provides secure Web service messaging, dynamic discovery, description and publish/subscribe eventing. However, no matter what DPWS is designed for devices with limited resources DPWS is too heavy to be ported to small ZigBee devices with sensors and actuators.

Atlas [5] is a service oriented sensor and actor platform. Atlas encompasses the concepts of self-integrative, programmable pervasive spaces based on the OSGi [6] framework used to handle the required service discovery and registry mechanisms. The Atlas platform allows sensors and actors to expose themselves as services to other components by combining hardware and software elements. The Atlas platform provides the programmers with a plug-and-play mechanism for integrating new sensors and actors in the house. And the Atlas support ZigBee platform together with WLAN, and Bluetooth. However, Atlas does not consider network management functions required for multi-hop communication despite its necessity.

Shaman [7] is a Java-based service gateway which can load and instantiate code during runtime. Each gateway service is a process (running in its own Java VM) that belongs to only one sensor -actuator module (SAM) and can handle multiple clients. That is, each SAM is associated with its own gateway service. Following the leasing concept, a service manager connected to each SAM boots gateway services on demand and shuts them down when they are no longer needed. Even though Shaman provides dynamic functions needed to accommodate new services without stopping existing services, it requires Shaman gateways as many as the number of sensor and actuator devices in a wireless network. Therefore, it is not suitable because ZigBee gateways basically have to be able to process a number of sensor and actuator devices.

3 A Self-organizing Communication Architecture for ZigBee (SECAZ)

In a self-organization system, interacting components continuously adapt to each other until mutually satisfactory. And this may first happen locally, but it is propagated to other components to achieve global goals. In addition, the self-organization system has to be capable of repair or correct by itself even with partial destructions. In this context, new ZigBee devices joining/leaving a network have to be recognized by local network management functions, propagated to the ZigBee gateways, and finally Internet applications or users have to perceive that new services are plugged into/out them. Along with it, when a network is partially destructed, for example, sudden breakdown of a router which incurs that all children lost their communication link, the child nodes have to not only continuously operate but be still appeared at Internet sides. That is, to be a self-organization system, ZigBee networks have to supply alternative path to Internet, detection of the failure and other related functions at network level and finally forward them to the gateways to reflect the network changes.

ZigBee basically provides addressing scheme, tree and AODV [10]-like routing at network layer. Hence, alternative path to Internet can be achieved by using the native ZigBee network functions. And also ZigBee management functions can be utilized for managing and monitoring network changes. However, as far as some information like topology changes like join, leave, and movement of nodes are concerned, using native management functions provided by ZigBee is not appropriate because all required information of all nodes within the ZigBee network has to be requested and processed in a client-server manner and the information should be periodically updated and reflected, which results in large amount burdens like bandwidth consumptions and network traffic concentration, and response impulsions problem. Hence, it is necessary for ZigBee to efficiently manage networks while reducing the overheads incurred.

To support self-organization functionalities and cope with the problems mentioned above, the proposed architecture consists of the following components: UPnP-ZigBee gateways, and ZigBee network management architecture containing network supervisors, local managers on ZigBee routers and agents on ZigBee end devices. Fig.1. shows a comprehensive view of the proposed self-organizing communication architecture for ZigBee, which consists of multiple UPnP-ZigBee gateways, wireless ZigBee mesh network, and ZigBee network management architecture (ZNMA). Due to space constraint, in the following subsection, we briefly describe the two components: UPnP-ZigBee gateway and ZNMA.

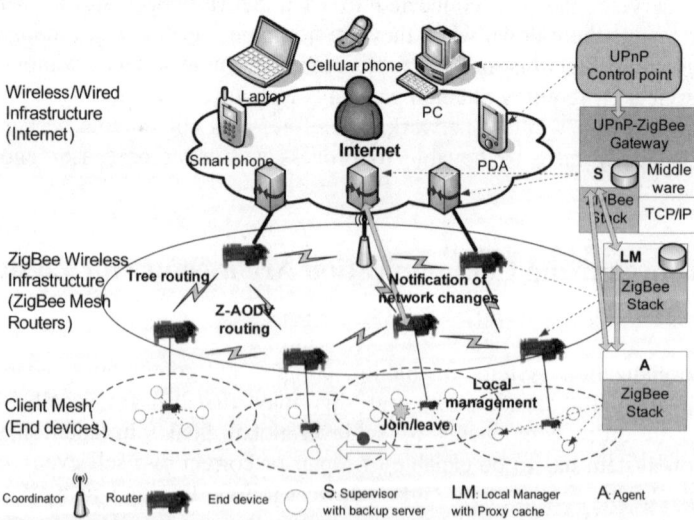

Fig. 1. A Self-organizing communication architecture consisting of ad hoc networking, network management functions, and UPnP-ZigBee gateway

3.1 Core components

- **UPnP-ZigBee Gateway**

A UPnP-ZigBee gateway is a key to interconnecting ZigBee networks with Internet and provides plug-and-play capability. The UPnP-ZigBee gateway basically translates ZigBee application messages into UPnP messages and reversely, and provides means for registering device and service information of new joining nodes. And to monitor event messages regarding join and leave of nodes on its connected ZigBee sub-network it embeds a network supervisor, which will be described later. Here, on receiving the event messages containing IEEE and short address, and capability information, a UPnP ZigBee gateway collects node's service and device information (node descriptor, power descriptor, user descriptor, active end point list, and simple descriptors corresponding to the each end point) and the collected information is translated into UPnP descriptions and used to dynamically represent the ZigBee nodes as dynamic proxies called virtual UPnP devices. Fig. 2 shows the UPnP-ZigBee gateway architecture and interaction with Internet and ZigBee network management architecture.

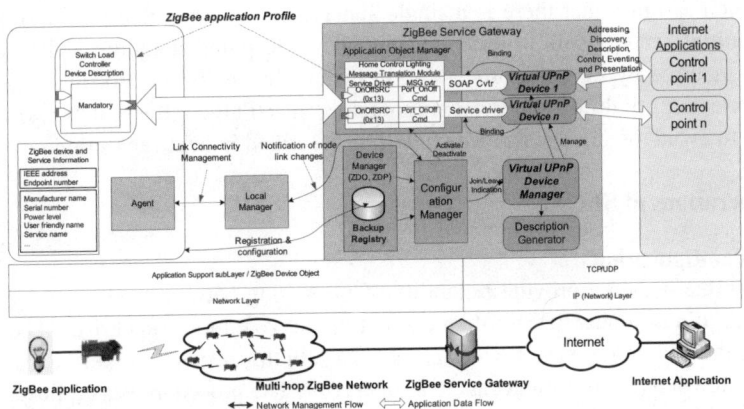

Fig. 2. A UPnP-ZigBee gateway architecture and interaction with Internet (a control point) and ZigBee network management architecture

- **ZigBee Network Management Architecture**

Regarding ZigBee Network Management Architecture, we integrate our management scheme into Guerilla network management architecture [11], but do not use its operations like mobile code technique, decision-theoretic approach for adaptive management. This is because both routers and a coordinator in all types of topologies (tree, start, and mesh) supported by ZigBee are not mobile but static and only end devices have mobility while Guerilla architecture is for managing ad hoc network with mobility of all participating nodes.

Based on the architecture, three actors are involved in network management architecture; *agent*, *local manager*, and *supervisor*. The agent located in end devices responds to requests for information from a local manager (which is may be its parent), responds to request for actions from the manager, and may asynchronously provide the manager with crucial but unsolicited information. The local managers are autonomous, which do not need attention from a supervisor. They reduce the load on the supervisor by freeing the supervisor from periodically polling other managed nodes. Local Managers are executed locally which will reduce bandwidth consumption incurred via standard-based polling mechanism (which polls all network routers to discover topology via unicast). The supervisor, serving as top level manager, contained in a UPnP ZigBee gateway is mainly responsible for monitoring changes and controlling its descendant managers on a basis of address hierarchy. The supervisor can be connected to a ZigBee coordinator or routers (base station) and provide the means for registering and backing up required descriptors (i.e. node, node power, simple descriptor for each end points and son on) of all managed ZigBee nodes, which are the descendants of the base station connected to the supervisor, in a database after extracting them from all the managed nodes. That is, the supervisor maintains at least a summary of the information maintained at each of the descendant manager in the ZigBee network.

Even though we integrate our architecture with Guerilla management architecture [11], which assumes that there is a single supervisor, we think that it is desirable to allow multiple supervisors in order to remove single point of failure and to reduce burdens incurred by message processing in the single supervisor. For that reason, in our architecture, multiple supervisors (contained in UPnP-ZigBee gateways) can be adopted to avoid the drawbacks, which will be described in next subsection.

3.2 Operations of SECAZ

- **Self-Configuration**

Since ZigBee does not provide reliability of messaging between endpoints, an event indicating join of a new device often can not be delivered to a supervisor. Therefore, ensuring the addition of new devices is necessary. In this respect, we define a protocol to make sure delivery of join events to a supervisor. The procedure is as follows.

Fig. 3(A) shows the procedure that a new router device, which can receive messages at any time, having a local manager joins a ZigBee network through the parent router device. In this case, (1) after a new node has associated with its parent, (2) the local manager of the parent device (routers or a coordinator) can know the device information through network layer management functions. Hence, (3) the local manager informs a UPnP-ZigBee gateway (playing a role of its supervisor) of addition of the new node with short and extended address, and capability information by sending a *DevRegisterReq* message. At the same time, the configurator of the new nodes itself sets a timer to expire at a specified time for waiting a *ConfigCompletion* message containing a short address of a base station node, which ensures that the configurator itself determines the completion of configuration (including registration for service and device information). Then, (4, 5, and 6) the gateway starts to collect and store all required information of the new device into a backup registry. If all the information of the new node has already registered by its gateway, the new device immediately receives the *ConfigCompletion*

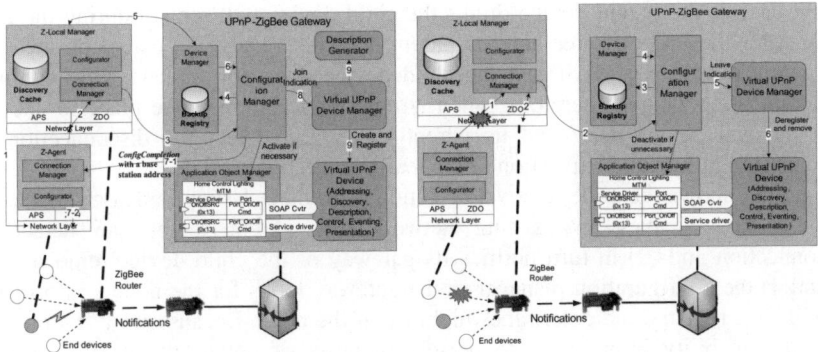

Fig. 3. (A) Self-configuration procedure. (B) Procedure for managing removal of nodes

message with status ALREADY_CONFIGED. Then, (7-1) if the configurator receives the *ConfigCompletion* before expiration of the timer, the configurator determines by itself that it is completely configured and, thus, starts to normal operation mode. (7-2) Otherwise, the local manager restarts the above procedure by sending the *DevRegisterReq* message again to its supervisor through its parent local manager until receiving the *ConfigCompletion* message. In the meanwhile, (8) the configuration manager in the UPnP-ZigBee gateway indicates join of the new node with the information collected to the VUDM. (9) The VUDM generates a corresponding UPnP description, and then creates and registers a virtual UPnP device acting as a proxy of the node join the ZigBee network.

It is worth noting that all new nodes joining the network can know the address of a base station along the network hierarchy without the need for broadcasting discovery messages for gateways. It means that not only a coordinator but routers can be the base station nodes connected to the gateways. Therefore, the proposed scheme is efficient while supporting multiple gateways.

- **Management of node removals**

As mentioned before, in ZigBee, parent nodes can not detect when its child nodes leave the local network whereas the child nodes themselves can detect loss of link connectivity. In terms of wireless mesh network [9] using ZigBee, since parent nodes can not have any knowledge of the left child nodes, the mesh routers or a coordinator with gateways functionality can not know it as well. Therefore, connectivity management is needed to allow the parents node to detect the link failure with regard to its child nodes. Typically, the connectivity management is performed via hello message using periodic broadcast or unicast polling. However, this is not suitable for ZigBee because end devices can not readily receive any message while sleeping. For that reason, we introduce lease-based link connectivity management scheme to solve the problem.

A lease is a guarantee that a child device will keep connecting to its parent device for the term of the lease. When a child device (a leaseholder) grants approval for its link connectivity by sending a lease request message containing a lease term to its parent device, the parent device thinks the child device will remain during the lease term. After the lease expires and the parent does not receive an extension message, the parent device regards it that the child device does not want to stay within its communication range. Therefore, when an end device moves one place to another, both the end device itself and its parent router can detect the disconnection via transmission failure and expiration of the lease, respectively.

Fig 3(B) shows the node removal detection procedure. Using the lease scheme, (1) when a node leaves an existing network, the parent router can detect the disconnection and (2) in turn notifies its gateway of the child device removal. And (3 and 4) the configuration manager in the gateway looks for the node's information from device registry and determines mobility of the node. Because we use a reserved field of capability information to present mobility of nodes, the mobility can be determined. If the node has mobility, configuration manager sets a timer for *HandoverTransactionPersistanceTime* to wait for rejoin of existing node. Note that the configuration manager receives end device announcement message with a changed short address incurred via movement and association with other parent before expiration of the timer, the timer is canceled. This enables Internet applications to transparently perform its tasks even with changes of the ZigBee network. (5) If the node does not have mobility or the timer is expired, it immediately notifies VUDM of the node removal with its unique identifier. Finally, (6) the VUDM deregisters and remove the corresponding VUD.

- **Fault-tolerant Operations**

When a ZigBee network starts, it first forms hierarchical management architecture as described previously and all ZigBee devices within a communication range are configured through the configuration procedure. And, finally, all the devices are represented as the corresponding virtual UPnP devices (acting as proxies of the physical ZigBee devices) via the UPnP-ZigBee gateways. From that time, all the ZigBee devices can interact with control points on the UPnP network.

When some failures happen, SECAZ can autonomously recover itself and restore original state because all gateways share all binding information on the network. When some routers on a ZigBee network partially break down, all their descendant devices have to be reconfigured. Since a local manager in the routers can force all the descendants to leave and reset, the descendant devices can rejoin the network through other parent and be configured by other UPnP-ZigBee gateways (supervisors) after being orphaned.

When a UPnP-ZigBee gateway fails, as shown in Fig. 4, because the devices, except for other base station devices having parent-child relationship, that have registered to the failed gateway and directly associated with the base station device as one of child device can detect the loss of synchronization with its parent (the base station device), they can restart themselves and re-associated with another parent through rejoin procedure defined in ZigBee specification. It is important to note that the child devices, excluding base station devices, of the failed base station device can force their all descendant devices to leave the current network and to disassociate with current parent via network leave command, where the network leave command, in ZigBee specification, can be processed by all the descendant devices by a cascaded broadcast. This is the network reconfiguration procedure where the SECAZ itself is autonomous and do not need attention from human operator.

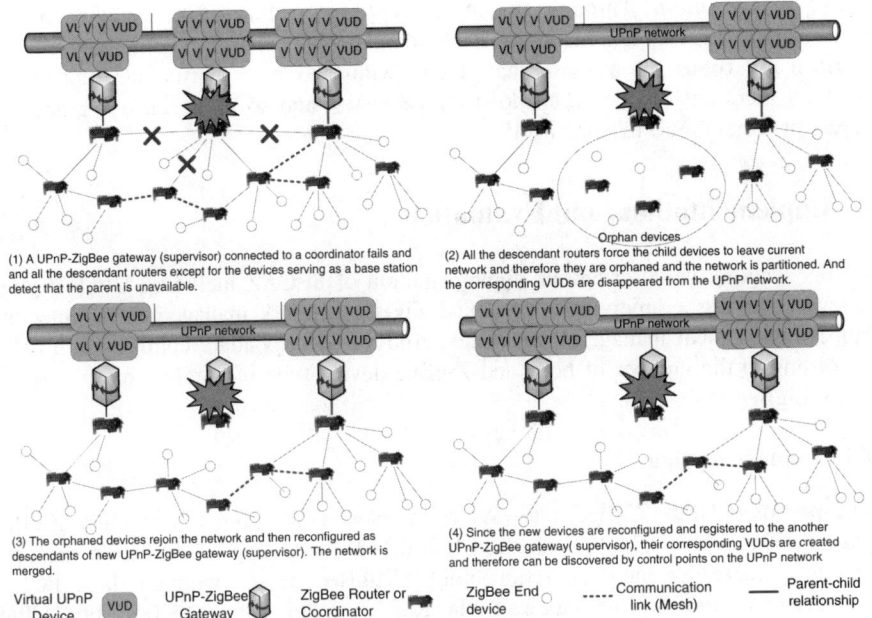

Fig. 4. Reconfiguration procedure of the proposed Self-organizing communication architecture (assuming that a wireless mesh network is used)

3.3 Summary of SECAZ

As described until now, in the proposed self-organizing communication architecture, multiple UPnP-ZigBee gateways can be placed between the ZigBee network and the UPnP network. The proposed architecture provides plug-and-play capability from the ZigBee network (over multi-hop) at a low level to the UPnP network at a high level by completely cooperating with one another. Eventually, the SECAZ as a whole organizes a hierarchically structured network of association by itself and continuously adapts to newly introduced devices and disappeared devices. In summary, the proposed architecture as a whole supports autonomy, self-healing, fault-tolerance, self-configuration, and self-organization [2].

Autonomy: While the architecture is operating there is no need for attention from network operator.

Self-healing: The architecture has a phase applied to the process of recovery in case of when some node fails, when network hierarchy is partially destructed, when sudden breakdown of gateway happens, and so on.

Fault tolerance: The architecture continues operating properly in the event of failures (presented above) since it is capable of the above self-healing. Thus, this results in that the architecture is high available.

Reliable self-(re)configuration: Every networked ZigBee device itself tries to continue (re)configuring itself until success (through the proposed configuration procedure).

Self-organization: Through the above features, a functional structure of the infrastructure appears and maintains itself spontaneously. That is, the infrastructure is intrinsically robust in a sense that it can withstand even partial destructions of network hierarchy, sudden breakdown of gateways, and so on because it gracefully repair or correct most damage itself.

4 Implementations and Evaluation

In this section, we describe our implementation of SECAZ including UPnP-ZigBee gateway playing a supervisor's role, and ZigBee network management architecture consisting of local managers and agents. And we also evaluate configuration delay according to the number of hops and ZigBee device type in wireless mesh network using ZigBee.

4.1 Implementation

The proposed UPnP-ZigBee gateway was implemented using C and C++. ZigBee base stations with CC2430 Evaluation Board [12] containing a connection manager and host controller interface (connecting a ZigBee device with the host PC) is connected to the ZigBee gateway via RS232 (baud rate: 115200). For UPnP middleware, we used open source UPnP stack provided by CyberLink [13]. As a result of it, the code sizes of UPnP-ZigBee gateway including UPnP middleware consumed 1348 Kbytes. To exemplify our gateway, we also implemented two message translation modules. The one was for an application sensing temperature and humidity level and another was for home control lightening, based on a profile provided by Texas Instruments [12], including several device description such as switch remote controller (SRC), switch load controller (SLC), and light sensor monochromatic (LSM) devices. The code sizes of the respective message translation modules were 44 Kbytes and 25 Kbytes.

The UPnP-ZigBee gateway was hosted on the desktop running windows operation system, with a 1.7 GHz Pentium 4 and 256 Mbytes RAM. As for the UPnP control point, we used Intel Device Spy [14] as a UPnP control point in order to evaluate the interoperability of the gateway and it ran on the desktop, which uses windows operation system, with a 1.6 GHz Pentium 4, and 512 Mbytes of RAM. By using this tool, we could confirm that the UPnP-ZigBee gateway provided not only interoperability between UPnP and ZigBee but also dynamicity. Fig. 5 depicts the execution of description, control and eventing by Intel Device Spy [14].

For the network management functions we implemented local manager and agent. The code size of a local manager was 23 Kbytes and that of an agent was 12 Kbytes. And since the supervisors are integrated into UPnP-ZigBee gateway, we do not measure the size of code but we observed that the code size of host controller interface code for base station was 56 Kbytes.

During all experiments, we set the network mode as mesh network and force to all end devices poll its parent to receive pending data temporarily stored every 1 second. And we made the entire devices have only one application object, therefore, one device can be seen as one service. And every measurement is performed more than 20 times.

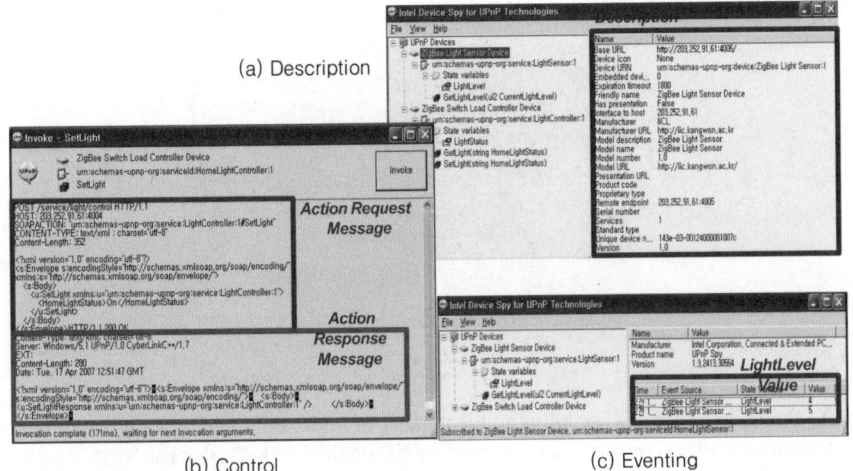

Fig. 5. Results showing each phase of description, control, and eventing of ZigBee devices by Intel Devices Spy

4.2 Performance Evaluation

In this subsection, we evaluate the configuration delay of UPnP-ZigBee gateway. The configuration delay is incurred via collection and configuration procedure plus creating a corresponding virtual UPnP device. Since delay incurred by information collection is affected by the number of hops, we measured the time taken to collect all required information by a UPnP-ZigBee gateway. Here, we define minimum and full configuration. The minimum configuration is a process whereby the supervisor only sends queries for active end points and the corresponding simple descriptors. This is because the simple descriptors are enough to determine the types of services provided by the ZigBee devices. Full configuration is to collect all information including node, power, user, and complex descriptor plus the simple descriptor for the connected application object.

To measure configuration delay over multi-hop wireless network we had to make sure that all packets pass through over multi hop. For that reason, we reduced transmission range as short as possible by minimizing transmission power and we set the maximal number of routing and neighbor entry in ZigBee stack as only one. And then we placed the nodes in a row while ensuring that every node had only one child. As a result, every node could communicate and associate with other nodes within about 20 cm and all packets were relayed along tree route. Fig. 6 shows the configuration delay as the increasing number of hops. The average minimal configuration delay of both router and end device within one hop takes less than 2 seconds. One of outstanding features is that, comparing with other cases, the configuration delay of a node in one hop was quite shorter than other cases. This is because messages from or to the one-hop device does not be relayed by any routers but directly forwarded to gateway. The configuration delays of the node within from two hops to five hops are almost same. From those results, we observed that the

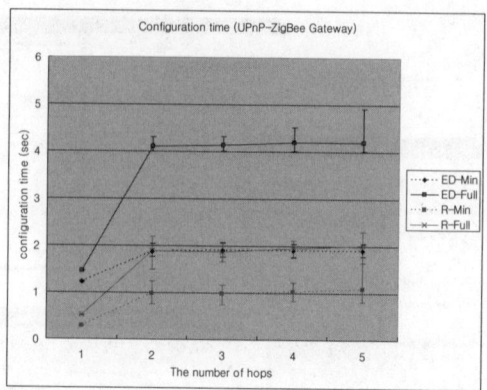

Fig. 6. Configuration delay according to the number of hops (from join of a ZigBee device in the ZigBee network to creating a corresponding VUD on the UPnP-ZigBee gateway)

number of hops except for the case of node within one hop does not significantly affect the confirmation delay. Rather, we found out that the type of nodes (end device or not) influenced the configuration delay.

5 Conclusion

Self-organization is that a structure consisting of functions appears and maintains spontaneously by controlling all participating components themselves in a distributed manner. Interacting components in a self-organization system continuously adapt to each other until mutually satisfactory.

In this context, in order that ZigBee itself becomes a self-organization system applicable to actual environment, it is necessary to put all elements of gateways, ad hoc networking, network management, and plug-and-play services together. To address this issue, we used ZigBee ad hoc networking facilities and proposed the ZigBee network management architecture (ZNMA) and the UPnP-ZigBee gateway. And then all the elements were combined together to enable the self-organizing communication architecture as a whole. As a result of it, we showed that the proposed communication architecture was self-configurable, fault tolerant, and self-organizable. From the implementation and evaluation, we demonstrated self-organizing communication architecture for ZigBee.

References

1. Alliance, Z.: ZigBee specification: ZigBee document 053474r013 Version 1.1, (December 1, 2006), http://www.zigbee.org
2. Heylighen, F., Gershenson, C.: The Meaning of Self-organization in Computing. IEEE Intelligent Systems, section Trends & Controversies - Self-organization and Information Systems (2003)

3. Williams: ZeroConf Requirements, Internet draft, Zeroconf WG, (September 19, 2002), http://files.zeroconf.org/draft-ietf-zeroconf-reqts-12.txt
4. Chan, S., Conti, D., Kaler, C., Kuehnel, T., Regnier, A., Roe, B., Sather, D., Schlimmer, J., Sekine, H., Thelin, J., Walter, D., Weast, J., Whitehead, D., Wright, D., Yarmosh, Y.: Devices Profile for Web Services, Microsoft Developers Network Library (February 2006), http://specs.xmlsoap.org/ws/2006/02/devprof/devicesprofile.pdf
5. King, J., Bose, R., Yang, H., Pickles, S., Helal, A.: Atlas – A Service-Oriented Sensor Platform. In: Proceedings of the first IEEE International Workshop on Practical Issues in Building Sensor Network Applications (2006)
6. Open Service Gateway Initiative (OSGi), http://www.osgi.org/
7. Schramm, P., Naroska, E., Resch, P., Platte, P., Linde, H., Stromberg, G., Sturm, T.: A Service Gateway for Networked Sensor Systems. IEEE Pervasive Computing, 66–74 (2004)
8. Universal Plug and Play (UPnP) Device Architecture Reference Specification Version 1.0. Microsoft Corporation (June 2000), http://www.upnp.org
9. Akyildiz, I.F., Wang, X., Wang, W.: Wireless mesh networks: a survey. Elsevier Computer Networks 47, 445–487 (2005)
10. Perkins, C., Royer, E.: Ad hoc on-demand distance vector routing. In: 2nd IEEE Workshop on Mobile Computing Systems and Applications, pp. 90–100 (1999)
11. Shen, C., Srisathapornphat, C., Jaikaeo, C.: An adaptive management architecture for ad hoc networks. IEEE Communication Magazine 41(2), 108–115 (2003)
12. Texas Instrument CC2430DBK, http://www.ti.com/
13. CyberLink UPnP, http://www.cybergarage.org/net/upnp/cc/index.html
14. Intel Device Spy, http://www.intel.com

A Semantic Service Matching Middleware for Mobile Devices Discovering Grid Services

Tao Guan, Ed Zaluska, and David De Roure

School of Electronics and Computer Science, University of Southampton,
Southampton, UK
{tg04r,ejz,dder}@ecs.soton.ac.uk

Abstract. The combination of mobile and Grid computing enables high performance Grid access through resource-limited mobile devices. Many challenges require to be addressed before vision of building the bridge between Grid and mobile computing field is realized. One of the essential challenges is that mobile devices need to locate and select appropriate Grid services in an automatic and flexible way. However, at the current stage, both Grid service description and discovery mechanisms are still at an immature stage. This paper presents research into building a service matching middleware with Semantic Web technologies. Semantic Web technologies permit an efficient discovery of various Grid services for mobile devices by adding the machine-processable explicit knowledge into the interaction between mobile devices and Grid services. The middleware has been implemented successfully and interacts correctly with other service-oriented mobile Grid middleware, thus facilitating an enhanced Grid access for mobile devices.

1 Introduction

The purpose of Grid computing is to coordinate resource sharing in dynamic and multi-institutional virtual organizations, enabling heterogeneous resources to be aggregated to facilitate new functionalities and capabilities [1]. As a service-oriented approach to Grid computing is increasingly adopted, many systems able to discover Grid resources on-the-fly and access them dynamically become possible. Mobile computing is an extension of the traditional distributed and desktop computing, seamlessly integrating various computing devices (e.g. mobile phones, PDAs) into our daily life. Although new-generation mobile devices have improved their absolute capabilities, there is no doubt that creating complex applications on them is still a challenging objective because such devices are inevitably resource-constrained.

One possible solution is for mobile devices to make use of Grid services so that mobile users are able to access distributed resources automatically on demand with appropriate quality of service delivery. Various Grid services enhance the capabilities of mobile devices, with the potential that complicated tasks can be completed through user handheld devices. However, the combination of Grid and mobile computing models has the potential to realize a very significant development in the adoption of high-performance Grid access through resource-limited mobile devices. It is quite evident that a great number of challenges must be solved before this vision of building the bridge between Grid and mobile computing is realized. In a previous paper [2], we discussed a system architecture to integrate mobile devices into the service-oriented Grid environment in an open and flexible way. Another important challenge is that at present, Grid service discovery mechanisms are still at an immature stage. Semantic web technologies, providing a very considerable degree of automatic processing, interoperation and integration, will help in the implementation of an effective Grid service matching mechanism.

With the proliferation of Grid services, semantic specifications of Grid services are gradually becoming a necessary requirement for the automatic flexible service provision and utilization necessary for Grid clients to perform various tasks. It is not straightforward for a requesting client to locate required services in order to execute a task in a service-rich Grid environment. Semantics of Grid services abstract top-level concepts and relationships between concepts so that both service discovery and automatic conversion of interaction formats between heterogeneous services can be realized. Furthermore, a semantic definition mechanism provides a comprehensive representation of a variety of Grid service aspects, building an essential foundation for possible automatic behaviors throughout the whole Grid service development lifecycle.

In this paper, we have presented a service matching mechanism by using Semantic Web technologies to support mobile devices accessing Grid services. The rest of this paper is organized as follows. Section 2 introduces related work. Section 3 presents the general methodology for semantic service description and matching. Section 4 describes the attribute definition of Grid services. Service discovery mechanism is discussed in section 5, with its implementation and experimental results in section 6. Section 7 concludes our current research work and discusses further directions.

2 Related Work

Service discovery protocols are adopted to simplify the interaction between service consumers and service providers. A number of service discovery protocols have been introduced during the past several years. In the field of mobile computing, examples of description and discovery solutions are the Bluetooth Service Discovery Protocol [3], Jini [4], and Universal Plug and Play (UPnP) [5]. In the field of Web Services, Universal Description Discovery and Integration (UDDI) is a platform-independent and XML-based registry which enables businesses to publish service listings and discover each other. However, none of these service discovery mechanisms support flexible matching between service advertisements and requests, and users therefore cannot locate services automatically on the basis of the capabilities that these services provide.

Semantic Web technologies allow web services to provide a rich semantic specification to enable flexible automation of service provision and utilization. A number of semantic-based web service matching mechanisms have been developed using Semantic Web technologies, such as [6] [7] [8]. They add a semantic layer between users and the web service WSDL description, which makes it possible to compose the web service request with high-level abstract concepts rather than syntactic level terms, addressing several limitations in the traditional web service discovery techniques. The service registry plays an important role for the service discovery. It is responsible for storing the advertisements of web services and finding a match between query requests and service advertisements. UDDI, the traditional Web Service registry protocol, only supports keyword-based search and does not meet the requirement of the capability-based service discovery. To solve this problem, [9] introduce the idea of mapping the OWL-S service profile into the UDDI web service representation and They believe OWL-S and UDDI can complement each other.

Generally speaking, Grid services are stateful Web Services, and most of current service-oriented Grid middleware techniques are based on the Web Service standards. Hence, the semantic approach in the web service discovery provides a potential direction for implementing a semantic-enhanced Grid service discovery mechanism. However, these current solutions have their limitations (e.g. no ranking in the service matching, judging concept similarity with subsumption reasoning only) and another issues are required to be considered when building a semantic framework for the service information centre middleware in the mobile Grid environment. In particular, most of semantic approach for web service discovery perform the service matching with service function attributes (e.g. inputs, outputs, preconditions, effects), and their purpose is the service discovery in the enterprise environment. Our system architecture, on the other hand, combines both Grid and mobile computing. Hence, other service characteristics except service capabilities are required to be considered for the service discovery, for example, service types, service resources and service context information.

3 Methodology for Semantic Matching

A semantic approach for service matching requires a service description complete with the ontology definition and a service search engine with reasoning mechanisms. Ontology approach is usually used to present services with abstract and high-level concepts for the service description. As long as users describe their service requirements with terms from the same ontology model used to build the service descriptions, logical reasoning mechanisms can check the semantic similarity between the service description and the user requirements, and the matching services will be discovered and returned to users.

The service provider represents all characteristics of a service in the service description. The term *description collection* indicates all possible attributes to be described for a service. These attributes may be either concepts or restrictions for existent concepts. For each individual service attribute, an ontology is usually designed to illustrate the definition of the attribute and its relationship with other service attributes. Similar to the service description, a *service request* often consists of many individual requirements, specifying the service attribute to be expected in a service. These requirements may include service outputs, effects, inputs, function, location or any possible attributes in terms of the different service request. For a specific service request, all of the requirements can be divided into two categories, a group of strict requirements and a set of general requirements. The strict requirement specifies that this kind of requirement is essential for the service request and has to be met precisely in the service matching, while the general requirement means this kind of requirement is not as important as the strict one and only an approximate matching is necessary between the requirement and the related service attribute.

Although we assume that the service request attempts to describe expected requirements with terms from the same ontology model used to build the service description, it is impractical that every service request will obtain the exact same service even though the required services have already been deployed and advertised because one service could have a number of description formats. In fact, the responsibility of the service search engine is to find all of the related services including those that deviate from the request in certain degrees. These deviation services should not be discarded but instead classified in an predefined rule (e.g. by matching degree). The service request determines which service will be selected based on the information returned from the service matching middleware. The service search engine takes a *service request* and available service *description collections* as inputs, and returns matching services as well as their matching degrees.

The service matching engine is responsible for comparing the service request against each service description and judging whether a service should be included in the list of candidate results. The evaluation of semantic similarity between concepts is fundamental for implementing the service matching engine. Most of the previous work adopts subsumption reasoning to determine the semantic distance between concepts in the request and in the description. However, this is not sufficient for building an effective service matching engine. We use the method presented in [10] to check the semantic similarity between two concepts. The attributes in a service description are categorized into three types. Type one includes attributes whose similarity can be judged using the subsumption reasoning. Type two includes attributes whose similarity can not be judged using subsumption reasoning only. These assume that the knowledge of similarities between these concepts can be acquired by using available similarity measurement approaches such as [11] and [12]. Type three means numeric attributes. The similarity between these concept types can be qualified by using the percentage deviation from the requested value or a fuzzy membership function.

4 Attribute Definition for Service Description

4.1 Attribute Definition

Inputs, outputs, preconditions and effects (IOPEs) are important functional attributes for a web/Grid service. Inputs and preconditions define the constrains required for a service invocation, and outputs and effects indicate the results or the state transformation of a service execution. As a standard web service description language, OWL-S [13] provides an comprehensive ontology definition for describing IOPEs.

Service-oriented Grid computing architecture is an extension of current Web Service technologies. In the computing architecture, applications are built on top of a set of common, standard and high-level services, which meet the definition of Open Grid Services Architecture (OGSA). One of the important requirements of OGSA is that the underlying middleware should store information about the service state because Grid application users usually need this kind of information to be maintained from one invocation to another. Because the service resource is the key parameter for the Grid service invocation, we regard it as an important functional attribute in the Grid service description.

In a service-oriented mobile Grid environment, mobile devices form the intersection between the physical world and the digital world. Users execute their tasks by using a variety of Grid services through their mobile handheld devices. Two main styles of application scenario are identified from the viewpoint of users: an information access scenario and a work assistant scenario. In the information access scenario, the main task is to collect required information or knowledge. Mobile devices act as universal operating terminals to access various available Grid services. In the work assistant scenario, users usually need to execute relatively complicated applications (such as data-deluge programs) to achieve specific tasks using their mobile devices. However, due to resource limitations, most complex programs cannot be executed on a handheld device. Users have to offload resource-demanding programs of the task to the Grid, and the Grid provides the executing environment for users to achieve their tasks.

An ontology is defined on the basis of the analysis of two application scenarios. The ontology represents a hierarchy of possible application scenarios and contains a taxonomy of service types which are usable for mobile clients. The top-level concept of the ontology is *Service*, which represents the most generic type. There are two direct subclasses of *Service*: the *InfoAccess* class represents the general service for the information access scenario; the *WorkAssistant* class represents the general service for the work assistant scenario.

Service context attributes are required when describing a Grid service. An ontology is designed to model the context of the service-oriented Grid environment. At present, we consider two context attributes in the Grid service description: the first is the service location, which corresponds to the "Place" class of the environment context ontology; the second is the service access range, based on which a service discovery restricting mechanism is implemented.

Mobile users access Grid services with their portable devices, which may expose their personal information. For example, if the service directory is so "open" that every mobile user can discover and obtain all deployed Grid services, a user location information may be exposed to other users as long as they can locate and try to invoke corresponding location-monitoring services. Protecting personal privacy thus becomes an important issue when designing a service discovery mechanism. The user personal information decides their accessing level during the authorization process, which is kept in their "User" class. The service provider defines the service range for every service in the service description. When a new mobile user sends a request to search Grid services, the service searching engine will reason and decide whether Grid services can be exposed by comparing the service access range of Grid services and the access level of the mobile user.

4.2 Service Description with Extended OWL-S

OWL-S [13] is a language for describing services, which provides a standard vocabulary that can be used together with other aspects of the OWL description language to create service descriptions. The structure of the OWL-S upper-level ontology is based on the types of knowledge of service description: the "Service Profile" provides the high-level descriptive information of a service, such as the name, input/output of the service, and additional text description; the "Service Model" and "Service Grounding" provide information on how the service is used and how to interact with the service.

We use the OWL-S language to describe Grid services. However, the "Service Profile" does not specify the Grid service attributes required in our mobile Grid computing environment and has to be extended by adding the service parameters discussed above. Figure 1 illustrates the extended service profile class and its properties.

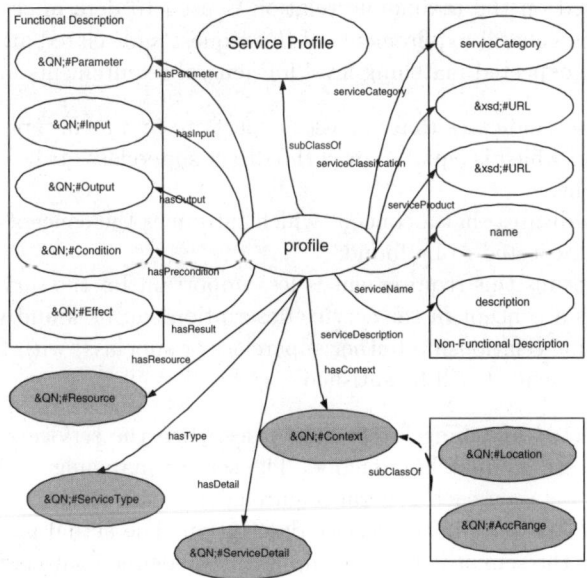

Fig. 1. Extended Service Profile

Grid services are described based on the extended service profile. For a Grid service, its description collection may include the functional attributes (e.g. inputs, outputs, preconditions, effects), the service type (an instance of *InfoAccess* class or *WorkAssistant* class), the service resource, the service detail, and the service context information (the location of the service provider and the service access range).

5 Service Discovery Algorithm

A service request is composed of a number of individual requirements, specifying various attributes to be expected in services. The service matching engine takes a service request and a group of service description collections as inputs, and is responsible for determining whether a Grid service is a matching service for this service request. The comparison between the service request and the service description collection consists of two steps. Initially, the service matching engine will check to judge whether each strict requirement can be matched precisely in the service description. If a service description does not contain the expected attributes, it will be dismissed and the service matching engine will compare the next service description to the service request. If a Grid service satisfies all of the strict requirements, the matching engine will then turn to estimate the general requirements.

As discussed in the Methodology section, the concepts are categorized into three types when checking the semantic similarity. For type one, subsumption reasoning based on the taxonomic relation is used to determine the matching degree between general requirements of the request and related attributes of the service. Three expected matching level for general requirements are defined:

- "Substitute" indicates that the user expects to find a concept in the service description which is equal to or is the direct superclass of the concept in the requirement.
- "Cover" indicates that a concept which subsumes the concept in the service request is expected to be found.
- "Fuzzy" means this requirement is less important for the service matching. As long as a concept in the service description can be found which has the subsumption relationship (either superclass or subclass) with the concept in the requirement, it will be satisfied.

These expected matching levels can be set when the service request is submitted to the service matching engine. The service matching engine will check the similarity between each general requirement in the service request and the related service attribute in the service description. The actual matching level is determined by the semantic relationship in the predefined ontology structure. If all of the expected matching levels are satisfied, this service will be a reasonable candidate for the service request.

For type two, the knowledge of similarities between concepts is assumed to be available, and the service matching engine will take the decision according to all of close degrees between user requirements and related attributes. For type three, both the attributes and the requirements are numeric. Their similarity can be checked using the percentage deviation from the requested value or a fuzzy membership function, depending on the detailed service implementation and the user requirement.

The service matching engine may find a number of candidate services for a specific service request. Although the service discovery mechanism is not responsible for the service selection, the matching degree information about each candidate service is required to be provided as a result for the service request. We use the term "MatchingScore" to show the matching degree of the candidate service. For a candidate service, its MatchingScore is calculated using the following equation:

$$MatchingScore = \sum_{i=1}^{n} Score_i / n \qquad (1)$$

The "$Score_i$" indicates the matching degree of every individual general requirement in the service request against the related service attribute in the service description, which is obtained based on the concept types categorized for checking the semantic similarity. For type one, because the subsumption relation exists between these concepts, the score can be obtained based on the semantic distance $||C_r, C_a||$ between the individual requirement (C_r) and the related service attributes (C_a) in the ontology structure. The following equations are used to calculate the individual score:

$$Score_i = \begin{cases} 1 & if\ C_a = C_r \\ \frac{1}{2} + \frac{1}{2*(||C_r,C_a||+1)} & if\ C_a\ is\ a\ superclass\ of\ C_r \\ \frac{1}{2*(||C_r,C_a||+1)} & if\ C_r\ is\ a\ superclass\ of\ C_a \end{cases} \qquad (2)$$

For type two, the score is assumed to be acquired from an available similarity measurement approach [11] [12]. For type three, similar to the similarity checking, the score can be obtained using the percentage deviation from the requested value or a fuzzy membership function.

The matching score of each candidate service is calculated based on $Score_i$, and it will determine the ranking of candidate services. The higher the score is, the higher ranking the candidate service has.

6 Implementation and Experimental Results

The ontology classes for the service description are defined with the OWL language using the Protege toolkit (an open-source ontology editor and knowledge-based framework). Protege can also be used to create OWL-S services by integrating an OWL-S editor plug-in [14].

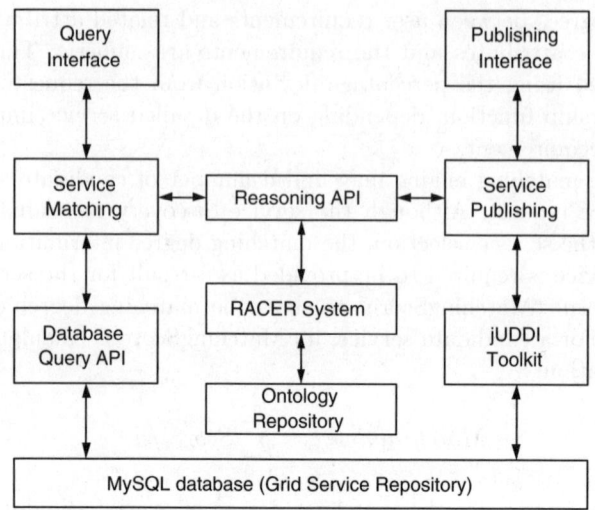

Fig. 2. Internal Components of Service Matching Middleware

The Grid service matching middleware has been implemented with the jUDDI toolkit, the Racer system [15], the MySQL database and other related techniques. Figure 2 shows its internal components. The middleware is written as both a Java Web Service for use by other middleware in the system architecture and an AJAX web application which can be accessed through a standard web interface.

We evaluated our service matching middleware in two stages. First, we integrated it into our system architecture to evaluate whether it interfaces well with the other middleware. Second, we measured the performance of our service matching middleware against a number of typical service requests.

In our system architecture, the static distributed Grid resources and mobile devices are interconnected by the Grid gateway. The Grid gateway is a small server available for nearby mobile devices within the covered range through the local wireless network, providing a relatively resource-rich, stable execution environment with enhanced network connectivity for handheld devices. Three kinds of middleware exist in the Grid gateway: the mobile deputy middleware performs a reliable task management mechanism (including task submission, execution, monitoring and result storing on behalf of mobile users) by accepting and packing tasks as the deputy object; the service-based Grid middleware provides access interfaces for Grid service invocation to execute user tasks; the service matching middleware is responsible for the implementation of Grid service registration, discovery and management so that mobile users are able to locate and select required Grid services to achieve their tasks.

In order to evaluate the system performance, we compare our semantic service matching middleware with UDDI, the traditional web service registry. We use the system response time as the performance index and focus on calculating the time required to process a query. The time of publishing a Grid service is

Table 1. Time of Querying a Service

	UDDI	Semantic Matching Middleware
Time (ms)	37.4	52.1

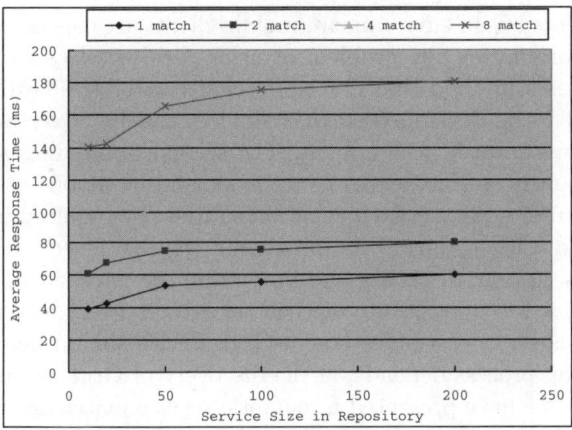

Fig. 3. Average Query Time from Service Matching Middleware

not relevant in this study because in our system architecture, mobile users are usually Grid service consumers rather than service providers.

The following experiment was designed in order to obtain the time of querying a Grid service. Both the description information of real Grid services and a large number of pseudo services are published in the service repository. Altogether, more than fifty services can be accessed by the semantic service matching middleware. A UDDI web service registry was built and a number of web services is published onto it. Table 1 shows the average time of querying a service on two different service discovery platform. The time of querying a Grid service with semantic concepts is longer, because the additional computation effort is required to determine the concept subsumption relationships in the logic reasoning system.

Although UDDI has a faster system querying performance than our semantic service matching middleware, it has several shortcomings when used in practice for the service discovery. UDDI does not provide sufficient technical details of the service, does not support any inference based on the concepts, can only support the search based on the string comparison, and cannot identify a match between functionally equivalent services that are described by different key words. Our service matching middleware overcomes these shortcomings by using the semantic service description and discovery mechanism. We believe it is worth obtaining a relatively-significant improvement in system function at the price of a small increase in the service discovery time.

In the above experiment, the time of returning one service only is measured. To test the system scalability, we used five kinds of service repository sizes (10, 20, 50, 100, and 200) and varied the number of matching services to be one, two, four or eight. Figure 3 shows the experimental results. As we expected, the system response time is within an acceptable limit and loosely proportional to the size of the service repository and the number of the matching results.

7 Conclusion

In a service-oriented Grid environment, mobile clients are concerned about three aspects when considering the problem of using Grid services to perform their tasks. The first is a method that describes what capabilities Grid services support is required to be developed so that services can be advertised to provide contributions for the task achievement. The second is building a Grid service discovery mechanism so that services can be located by mobile users. The third is the mechanism of Grid service invocation so that the required information or resources can be utilized during the process of the task execution. Essentially, Grid service description, discovery and invocation are interdependent: Grid service description is the prerequisite of Grid service discovery; the mechanism of Grid service discovery determines how a Grid service should be described; the service invocation process depends on the discovery of Grid services.

In this paper, we have presented a semantic service matching middleware for the service-oriented mobile Grid environment. A number of service attributes have been defined to represent service characteristics in the service description. Because of the centralized range of Grid service registry in the system infrastructure, a service search engine is built with the extended OWL-S semantic language and the RACER ontology reasoning system, providing query interfaces for users or other middleware systems to locate required services. The semantic service matching middleware has been integrated into our system architecture and demonstrated to interact correctly with other middleware. We have also measured its performance against a number of service request, and the results show that there is only a small increase in the service discovery time compared to the traditional service discovery mechanism in return for the significant improvement obtained.

In the future, we plan to continue the current research work to allow such a Grid service matching mechanism to be extended so that it can be more suitable for the service-oriented mobile Grid environment. OWL-S supports not only automatic service discovery, but also automatic service invocation, composition and interoperation. At present, we only use the "Profile model" to describe Grid services. In the future, we will extend the system to use both the "Process model" and the "Grounding model" to build Grid service descriptions, enabling the vision of automatic service discovery, composition, and invocation to be realized.

References

1. Foster, I., Kesselman, C., Teucke, S.: The anatomy of the grid: Enabling scalable virtual organizations. International Journal of Supercomputer Applications 15 (2001)
2. Guan, T., Zaluska, E., Roure, D.D.: Extending pervasive devices with the semantic grid: A service infrastructure approach. In: Sixth IEEE Conference on Computer and Information Technology, Seoul, Korea (2006)

3. Haartsen, J., Allen, W., Inouye, J.: Bluetooth: Vision, goals, and architecture. Mobile Computing and Communications Review 1, 1–23 (2006)
4. Waldo, J.: The Jini Specifications. Addison-Wesley Longman Publishing Co., Inc., Boston (2000)
5. Allard, J., Chinta, V., Gundala, S., Richard, G.: Jini meets upnp: an architecture for jini/upnp interoperability. In: Proceedings of Symposium on Applications and the Internet, pp. 268–275 (2003)
6. Srinivasan, N., Paolucci, M., Sycara, K.: Semantic web service discovery in the owl-s ide. In: Proceedings of the 39th Hawaii International Conference on System Sciences, Hawaii, USA, p. 109 (2006)
7. Majithia, S., Ali, A.S., Rana, O.F., Walker, D.W.: Reputation-based semantic service discovery. In: Proceedings of the 13th IEEE International Workshops on Enabling Technologies: Infrastructure for Collaborative Enterprises, Modena, Italy, pp. 297–302 (2004)
8. Li, L., Horrock, I.: A software framework for matchmaking based on semantic web technology. In: Proceedings of 12th International World Wide Web Conference Workshop on E-Service and the Semantic Web, Budapest, Hungary, pp. 331–339 (2003)
9. Martin, D., Paolucci, M., Mcilraith, S., Burstein, M.: Bringing semantics to web services: The owl-s approach. In: First International Workshop on Semantic Web Services and Web Process Composition (SWSWPC 2004), San Diego, CA, USA (2004)
10. Bandara, A., Payne, T., Roure, D.D., Lewis, T.: A semantic approach for service matching in pervasive environments. In: Technical Report in IAM group shool of ECS (2007)
11. Schwering, A.: Hybrid model for semantic similarity measurement. In: Meersman, R., Tari, Z. (eds.) OTM 2005. LNCS, vol. 3761, pp. 1449–1465. Springer, Heidelberg (2005)
12. Tverski, A.: Features of similarity. Phychological Review 8, 327–352 (1977)
13. Acuna, C., Marcos, E.: Modeling semantic web services: A case study. In: Proceedings of the 6th international conference on Web engineering, Palo Alto, California, USA, pp. 32–39 (2006)
14. Elenius, D., Denker, G., Martin, D., Gilham, F., Khouri, J., Sadaati, S., Senanayake, R.: The owl-s editor - a development tool for semantic web services. In: Gómez-Pérez, A., Euzenat, J. (eds.) ESWC 2005. LNCS, vol. 3532, pp. 78–92. Springer, Heidelberg (2005)
15. Haarslev, V., Moller, R.: Racer: a core inference engine for the semantic web. In: Proceedings of 2nd International Workshop on Evaluation of Ontology-based Tools, Sanibel Island, Florida, USA, pp. 27–36 (2003)

A Pragmatic Approach for the Semantic Description and Matching of Pervasive Resources

Ayomi Bandara[1], Terry Payne[1], David De Roure[1], Nicholas Gibbins[1], and Tim Lewis[2]

[1] University of Southampton, Southampton, UK
{hmab02r,trp,dder,nmg}@ecs.soton.ac.uk
[2] Telecommunications Research Laboratory, Toshiba Research Europe Ltd, Bristol, UK
Tim.Lewis@toshiba-trel.com

Abstract. The increasing popularity of personal wireless devices has raised new demands for the efficient discovery of heterogeneous devices and services in pervasive environments. With the advancement of the electronic world, the diversity of available services is increasing rapidly. Traditional approaches for service discovery describe services at a syntactic level and the matching mechanisms available for these approaches are limited to syntactic comparisons based on attributes or interfaces. In order to overcome these limitations, there has been an increased interest in the use of semantic description and matching techniques to support effective service discovery. In this paper, we present a semantic matching approach to facilitate the discovery of device-based services in pervasive environments. The approach includes a ranking mechanism that orders services according to their suitability and also considers priorities placed on individual requirements in a request during the matching process. The solution has been systematically evaluated for its retrieval effectiveness and the results have shown that the matcher results agree reasonably well with human judgement. Another important practical concern is the efficiency and the scalability of the semantic matching solution. Therefore, we have evaluated the scalability of the proposed solution by investigating the variation in matching time in response to increasing numbers of advertisements and increasing request sizes, and have presented the empirical results.

1 Introduction

Recent technological trends in electronics have resulted in a change in lifestyle, whereby pervasive mobile devices such as mobile phones, PDA's, GPS devices, etc. have become an integral part of everyday life. This trend, together with the advancement in wireless communications (resulting in an increasingly wireless world) have raised users' expectations about the accessibility of services in pervasive environments. This has raised challenges for service discovery in a dynamic environment, where the services accessible to a user can change continuously. Although there are several traditional approaches to service discovery such as UPnP [1], Jini [2], etc., in general these provide syntactic approaches to service description and discovery, whereby locating appropriate services rely on matching service descriptions based on keywords or interfaces. As such, they cannot detect a match in cases where the service descriptions involve different representations of conceptually equivalent content, which thus poses a serious limitation.

With the advent of the Semantic Web, there has been an increased interest in the use of semantic descriptions of services and the use of logical reasoning mechanisms to support service matching. The advantage of such frameworks include the ability to extend and adapt the vocabulary used to describe services and to harness the inferential benefits of logical reasoning over such descriptions. Recently, a number of semantic matching approaches have been developed (targeted at different domains), which try to address various limitations in the traditional discovery techniques.

Chakraborty et al. [3] and Avancha et.al. [4] have proposed Semantic Matching approaches for pervasive environments. Both use ontologies to describe the services and a Prolog-based reasoning engine to facilitate the semantic matching. They provide 'approximate' matches if no exact match exists for the given request. However, the criteria used for judging the 'closeness' between the service advertisements and the request is not clear from the literature. In both these approaches, the matching process does not perform any form of match ranking. There have also been a number of efforts that use description logic (DL) based approaches for semantically matching web services. For example the matchmaking framework presented in [5] uses a DAML-S based ontology for describing the services. A DL reasoner has been used to compute the matches for a given request, where matches are classified into one of its five "degrees of match" (namely *Exact, Plug-In, Subsume, Intersection* and *Disjoint*) by computing the subsumption relationship of the request description w.r.t. all the advertisement descriptions. No ranking is performed in the matching process, although the match class suggesting the 'degree of match' gives an indication of how 'good' a match is.

In general, these semantic matching solutions have provided important research directions in overcoming the limitations present in the traditional approaches for service matching. However, they have a number of overlooked issues and lacks certain desirable properties that must be present in an effective solution to support service discovery. Particularly, these approaches lack an appropriate criterion to approximate the available service advertisements with respect to a given request and to rank them accordingly. Furthermore, these approaches do not consider any priorities/ weights on the individual requirements of a request during the matching process.

In this paper we present a solution to facilitate the effective semantic matching of resources in pervasive environments. The proposed matching approach semantically compares the request against the available services and provides a ranked list of most suitable services. The rank will indicate the appropriateness of a service to satisfy a given request. The matching process also considers the priorities/ weights on the individual requirements of a request. The retrieval effectiveness of the proposed solution has been systematically evaluated by comparing the match results with human judgement. Furthermore, the semantic matching solution must be scalable and must demonstrate acceptable execution times for it to be used in practice. Therefore, we investigate the scalability of the proposed solution w.r.t. the number of advertisements involved in matching and the request size (i.e. the number of requirements in a request).

The remainder of this paper is organised as follows: Section 2 discusses the motivation behind the proposed matching framework and identifies the requirements of a pragmatic approach for matching pervasive resources. Section 3 describes the methodology behind the matchmaking framework and its implementation in a pervasive scenario.

Section 4 discusses the experiments carried out to evaluate the retrieval effectiveness and scalability of the proposed semantic matching solution and presents the results obtained. Section 5 presents the concluding remarks and the future directions of this work.

2 Motivation and Requirements

A pragmatic approach for semantic service matching must possess several properties and must satisfy certain requirements for it to be effective and usable in practice. In this section we discuss these along with the motivating reasons behind them.

Semantic Description and Matching: The use of reasoning mechanisms to support service discovery and matching enables logical inferencing over the service descriptions and therefore offers several benefits over the traditional syntactic approaches. It is often the case, that the service providers usually describe devices in terms of lower-level properties, and the service seekers or clients usually prefer to describe service requests using more abstract or higher level concepts. Semantic matching approaches supported by logical reasoning mechanisms will be able to identify a match between logically equivalent services that have syntactically different descriptions and therefore can offer flexibility in how the service advertisements and requests are described.

Ranking of Potential Matches: Ranking refers to the ordering of the available advertisements in the order of their suitability to satisfy the given request. In the absence of an exact match, a requester might be willing to consider other advertisements that are closer to the request and thus the ranking will be useful in gaining an understanding of the appropriateness of the advertisement. Most existing matchmaking solutions do not have an effective criterion to rank the available services according to their suitability. Providing a ranking mechanism that will rank the advertisements on the basis of how well it satisfies the properties specified in the request, is one of the main objectives behind the proposed matching approach.

Approximate Matching: Providing approximate or flexible matching, is one of the core objectives of semantic matching. i.e. services that deviate from the request in certain aspects should not be discarded but must be ranked or classified appropriately to indicate the suitability. In current Description Logic approaches for semantic matching ([5], [6], etc.), the suitability of the advertisements have been determined based on the taxonomic relation between the concepts. However, we argue that this is not sufficient in determining similarity for the purpose of resource matching in certain situations. For example, consider the concept *Processor*; assume there is a request for a computer that has a *Pentium4* processor, and advertisements of computers with processors *Pentium3* and *Pentium1*. Both *Pentium3* and *Pentium1* will be disjoint from the originally requested concept of *Pentium4*; however, a requester may consider *Pentium3* to be a better match than *Pentium1* and thus would be ranked higher. Hence, the type of attribute involved in the individual requirement of a request will have to be considered in approximating and ranking of advertisements. The different types of attributes and the approach taken in judging the similarity between them is presented in Section 3.

Consideration of Priorities on Requirements: In many practical scenarios, certain requirements/ attributes in a request will be more important than others, either due to the context involved or the subjective preferences of the user. In such cases, facilitating priority-handling in the matching process will produce match results that are more relevant and suitable for the context involved. Most existing semantic matching approaches do not consider any priorities or preferences that a user/agent may be having with respect to various attributes or properties of a service (except in [6]). Mandatory requirements or strict matching requirements have to be considered when the resource seekers requires a certain individual property requirement in a request, to be strictly met by any potential resource advertisement. I.e. resource seekers will not want to consider any advertisements that will have even a minor deviation, with respect to that property. Mandatory requirements can in fact be viewed as a specific case of priority assignments. Priorities and mandatory requirements will be taken into account in the proposed work by giving a service requester the option of placing priorities/ weights on the specified attributes of the service request. These priorities will be considered during the matching process when evaluating the suitability of the advertisements w.r.t. a given request.

Performance of the Matching Solution: The matching approach must demonstrate a reasonable level performance w.r.t. the retrieval effectiveness and efficiency. Retrieval effectiveness refers to the ability of the matcher to retrieve 'relevant' matches (as determined by a domain expert/user) in relation to a given resource request; i.e. the matcher results must agree reasonably well with human judgement. Also, the matching solution must be scalable and must demonstrate reasonable response times for it to be used in practical environments. Therefore, we have evaluated the effectiveness of the proposed solution by comparing the match results with human judgement, and have investigated the scalability (against increasing numbers of advertisements and increasing request sizes) and response times of the implemented solution.

3 The Semantic Matching Approach

3.1 Description of Requests and Advertisements

For effective semantic matching, the services must be described in a language that will facilitate logical reasoning. In the proposed approach, we use the Web Ontology Language (OWL) to describe the requests and advertisements.

A request will typically consist of several individual requirements to be satisfied. Each requirement will specify: the description of the requirement (which is the resource characteristic the resource seekers expect in a resource, for the their needs to be satisfied) and the priority or weight of that individual requirement, which will be a decimal value that indicates the relative importance of the particular requirement. The priority value can also be used to indicate if the requirement considered is a mandatory requirement; i.e. if the requirement should be strictly satisfied in an advertisement for the requester to consider it as a potential match. The description of an individual requirement will include the property or attribute the requesters are interested in and the ideal value desired. The request will take the form:

$$Request \equiv (Req_1) \sqcap (Req_2) \sqcap \ldots \sqcap (Req_n)$$

where Req_i is an individual requirement[1]. The requirement takes the form:

$$Req \sqsubseteq (= 1hasDescription.RD) \sqcap (= 1hasPriority.PriorityValue)$$

where RD is the requirement description, which can be either a named concept or an existential restriction of the form, $\exists p.C$ where p is a role and C is a named concept or a complex concept. For describing each RD, an ontology that describes the services in the domain concerned can be used. The $PriorityValue$ indicates the relative importance of the individual requirement in the request. This is a decimal value defined between 0 and 1. In addition, to indicate that the requirement is a mandatory requirement that must be strictly met in any potential match, the $PriorityValue$ is defined as 2. The resource seeker must pick the appropriate $PriorityValue$ (according to these pre-defined values) for each individual requirement, to indicate its relative importance.

The resource provider will specify all the relevant characteristics of the available resource in the resource advertisement. The advertisement can take the form:

$$Advertisement \equiv (r_1) \sqcap (r_2) \sqcap \ldots \sqcap (r_n);$$

where r_i is either a named concept or an existential restriction describing a characteristic of the resource.

3.2 Judging Semantic Similarity

We distinguish between three types of concepts or properties occurring in the individual requirements of a resource description for the purpose of approximate matching. These types and the method followed in determining similarity within each of these types during the matching process, are discussed below.

Type 1: Named Concepts having a Taxonomic Relation: When two concepts are related through a taxonomy, the subsumption or taxonomic relation between these two concepts can fall into one of five categories. Assuming C_R is the requested concept and C_A is the advertised concept; the possible taxonomic relations and the similarity scores assigned in each case are summarised in Table 1.

For cases when C_A is a super concept of C_R and when C_R and C_A intersect; the similarity between the concepts (t and r) will be a value between 1 and 0. In this case we have to judge the similarity based on the probability of satisfying the given requirement. i.e. given that what is available is C_A, we have to judge the likelihood that it is also C_R.

There have been a number of approaches for determining similarity between concepts in a taxonomy [8,9], that are based on probability. Since the exact number of instances belonging to the classes in a taxonomy are not known; these approaches take into account the fact that the number of instances of a class are inversely related to

---

[1] Although the resources are described in OWL, for the sake of readability and brevity of this discussion, we have used description logic (DL) notation. An explanation of the syntax and semantics of the DL language can be found in [7].

Table 1. Assignment of similarity scores when Subsumption Relation is considered

Taxonomic Relation Between C_R and C_A	Similarity Score
$C_A \equiv C_R$	1.0
$C_A \sqsubseteq C_R$	1.0
$C_R \sqsubseteq C_A$	t (where $t \in [0,1]$)
$\neg(C_R \sqcap C_A \sqsubseteq \bot)$	r (where $r \in [0,1]$)
$(C_R \sqcap C_A \sqsubseteq \bot)$	0.0

the depth of the class in the hierarchy; i.e. the number of its superclasses or ancestors. Based on this assumption, Skoutas et.al. [10] have provided an estimation for the similarity between two concepts C_R and C_A (the values for t and r in this case) as:

$$t \mid r = \frac{|A(C_A) \cap A(C_R)|}{|A(C_R)|} \quad (1)$$

where $A(C)$ denotes the set of superclasses of a class C. Note that in the case when $C_R \sqsubseteq C_A$; $|A(C_A) \cap A(C_R)| = |A(C_A)|$. Therefore $t = \frac{|A(C_A)|}{|A(C_R)|}$.

Hence Similarity Score for two concepts C_R and C_A can be determined as:

$$SimilarityScore(C_R, C_A) = \begin{cases} 1 & if\ C_A \equiv C_R \\ \frac{|A(C_A)|}{|A(C_R)|} & if\ C_R \sqsubseteq C_A \\ 1 & if\ C_A \sqsubseteq C_R \\ \frac{|A(C_A) \cap A(C_R)|}{|A(C_R)|} & if\ \neg(C_R \sqcap C_A \sqsubseteq \bot) \\ 0 & if\ C_R \sqcap C_A \sqsubseteq \bot \end{cases} \quad (2)$$

Type 2: Named Concepts not having a Taxonomic Relation: There may be certain classes of concepts where although no subsumption relation exists between them (disjoint concepts), some concepts can be thought of as being 'more closer or similar' to another concept than the rest. When properties involve such concepts, some other method will have to be sought to find the similarity between such concepts.

Consider the scenario when reasoning with the following concepts: Processor Type (Pentium 3, Pentium 4, Athlon etc.), Display Type (CRT, LCD, Plasma etc.) or Paper Size (A0, A1, B1 etc.). If a service requester requires a computer with a Pentium 4 processor, how can we rank service advertisements having Pentium 3, Celeron and AMD Athlon processors as their processor type? In this case we have to use some similarity measure that indicates the closeness between the concepts (the different processor types in this example) in order to assign a sub-score with respect to the processor type requirement and thereby match the request and advertisement.

Several proposals for measuring concept similarity exist; Schwering in [11] provides an overview of some of the existing approaches. For example Tversky et al. in [12] has proposed a feature-based metric of similarity, in which common features tend to increase the perceived similarity of two concepts, and where feature differences tend to diminish perceived similarity. For instance, Tomato and Cherry are similar by virtue of their common features Round, Fruit, Red and Succulent. Likewise, there are dissimilar by virtue of their differences, namely Size (Large versus Small) and Seed (Stone versus NoStone). Hence in our work, if we wanted to find similarity between different Processor Types for example, the features/properties of the Processors such as clock speed, cache size, manufacturer, etc. will have to be used in measuring the similarity.

However, measuring similarity between concepts is not within the scope of the current research and we assume that the knowledge of concept similarities between such concepts is available to the semantic matcher (either measured by using a third party approach for semantic similarity measurement or available as domain knowledge). This knowledge will then be used during the matching process by the semantic matcher, to obtain similarity values between Type 2 concepts. Hence for the purpose of matching, Similarity Score for two Type 2 concepts C_R and C_A can be determined as:

$$SimilarityScore(C_R, C_A) = ConceptSimilarity(C_R, C_A) \qquad (3)$$

Type 3: Constraints on Datatypes: When available resources fail to meet requested characteristics with respect to numeric attributes, the domain users tend to evaluate the suitability of the available resources in proportion of the violation of the requested numeric constraint. For instance, if a resource seeker requires a computer with a *memory size of 1GB*, and there are two available advertisements of computers with *memory size of 512MB* and *256MB*, these two advertisements both fail to meet the requirement set by the resource seeker. If only DL subsumption reasoning is used, both will be classified as failed matches. However, for effective approximate matching, they must be distinguished for the level of deviation from the original request and penalised accordingly during the matching process; i.e. the second advertisement (with the 256MB memory size) must be ranked lower when ranking.

Thus, when judging the similarity within individual requirements that involve numeric or datatype properties, the similarity measure has to consider the extent to which an available numeric value (in an advertisement) can satisfy the requested datatype criterion specified in a request. i.e. if a restriction '*>20*' applies, how well would values of '*21*', '*18*' and '*15*' satisfy this constraint? Assuming that is a flexible or imprecise criterion, intuitively we could say that '*21*' strongly satisfies the constraint, whereas '*18*' and '*15*' partially satisfy the constraint. Dealing with such cases of imprecision and vagueness is the principle behind fuzzy logic [13] introduced by Zadeh.

There have been many motivating scenarios in a variety of application domains, that stresses the need for dealing with fuzziness and imprecision in the Semantic Web and description logics. Straccia in [14] has presented a fuzzy description logic that combines fuzzy logic with description logics. Typically, DLs are limited to dealing with crisp concepts; an individual is either an instance of a concept or it is not. In Fuzzy description logics, the concepts can be imprecise and thus an individual can belong to a concept only 'to a certain degree'; it allows for expressions of the form $\langle C(a)n \rangle, (n \in [0, 1])$ which means 'the membership degree of individual a being an instance of the concept C is at least n'. For example, there can be a concept $Tall$ and an individual tom can belong to the concept $Tall$ to a degree of at least 0.7.

However, unlike in the domain described by [14], the knowledge base dealt with in the proposed semantic matching framework is not fuzzy. i.e. it contains precise knowledge and crisp concepts. For example concepts such as Computer, Processor, Pentium4 are all crisp concepts and an individual is either an instance of such a concept or it is not. Also, the resource requests or advertisements do not contain any fuzzy predicates such as *Large Memory*, *High Capacity Disk* etc., but specify precise concepts or data values. However, in approximate matching, when judging similarity within individual requirements of a request that involves constraints on datatypes, it is desirable to consider these as soft constraints as already emphasised. Therefore, we consider the relevant data range restrictions to be fuzzy concepts or fuzzy boundaries and follow the approach discussed in fuzzy description logic [14] when determining similarity between the required and the available property values.

Datatype constraints specified in a request can be an exact, at least, at most or a range restriction. These datatype constraints specified will be considered as fuzzy boundaries and the deviation with respect to the specified constraint can be evaluated using a fuzzy membership function. Due to space limitations, the details of the membership functions we use will not be included in this paper. However, a more detailed discussion can be found in [15]. A constraint for a datatype property in a requirement ($c_{k,l}$) can take the form of ($= k$), ($\geq k$), ($\leq k$), or ($\geq k \sqcap \leq l$) for given constants k and l. If the value for the same datatype property in the advertisement is specified as v, then the similarity score between a constraint $c_{k,l}$ and v (indicating how well v satisfies the required constraint $c_{k,l}$) can be determined as:

$$SimilarityScore\ (c_{k,l}\ ,\ v) = \mu(v; k, l) \qquad (4)$$

where μ denotes the membership function and $\mu(x) \in \{\geq_k (x),\ \leq_k (x),\ =_k(x),\ \geq_k, \leq_l (x)\}$

3.3 Matching Process and Implementation

A request will consist of a number of individual requirements along with their priority values. The presence of any mandatory requirements that must be fully satisfied by any potential match will also be indicated by using the appropriate priority value as described in Section 3.1. In the matching process, the available resource will be checked to see if each mandatory individual requirement (RD) is satisfied in the advertisement description. If the mandatory requirement(s) are met, then the advertisement will be evaluated through approximate matching.

In approximate matching, the available resources should be evaluated according to how well it satisfies each individual requirement specified in a request; i.e. the matching engine should quantify the extent to which each individual requirement description (RD) is satisfied by the resource advertisement. For this, the matching engine will check how similar the advertisement is with respect to each non-mandatory requirement (RD) specified in the request; the similarity will be determined depending on the semantic deviation of the expected value in request and the available value in advertisement for the same requirement, and a score will be assigned accordingly ($Score_i$).

Each characteristic specified in the request (RD) can be a named concept(C_R) or an existential restriction ($\exists p.C_R$). If it is a named concept, similarity will be compared between the corresponding concepts in request and advertisement ($Similarity(C_R, C_A)$); the degree of similarity between concepts will be determined depending on the type of concept or attribute involved, as discussed in Section 3.2. If it is an existential restriction, the corresponding existential restriction(s) will be found in the advertisement ($\exists p.C_A$) and the similarity will be compared between the corresponding concepts in request and advertisement. If it is a composite concept, the similarity will be judged recursively. The score ($Score_i$) for each individual characteristic in the request will be assigned depending on this similarity.

A score ($Score_i$) is assigned for each sub-requirement (RD) specified in the request. The score for the advertisement (match score) will be determined by using the weighted average of these individual scores (the weight will be the corresponding priority value of each individual requirement). $MatchScore = \sum_{i=1}^{n} w_i.Score_i \div \sum_{i=1}^{n} w_i$ where w_i and $Score_i$ is the priority value and the score of the individual requirement RD_i. The overall score for the advertisement provides an indication of how good the advertisement is in satisfying the given request. The score for an advertisement will in turn be used as the basis for ranking; the highest score will receive the highest rank and so on. The algorithm for the matching process and an example illustration can be found in [15].

The proposed semantic matching approach has been implemented in a pervasive context for matching of device based services. The advertisements and the individual requirements in a request are described using the Device Ontology presented in [16] (available at http://www.ecs.soton.ac.uk/~hmab02r/DeviceOnt/DevOntology.owl). This facilitates the description of features and functionalities of the devices and their services. The necessary ontologies were developed with the Protégé ontology editor. The matching engine was implemented in Java and the Pellet DL reasoner in combination with the Pellet-API is used to facilitate the necessary reasoning tasks during the matching process.

4 Evaluation

We evaluate the matching framework with respect to two aspects: effectiveness (i.e. how good the system is in discovering the relevant or suitable resources); and efficiency/scalability, to justify that any compromise in performance resulting from the involvement of reasoning mechanisms, is outweighed by the benefits gained from semantic matching. The solution must be scalable and must demonstrate acceptable execution/response times for matching, to be applied in practical environments.

4.1 Evaluating Retrieval Effectiveness

The proposed matching solution was evaluated for effectiveness by comparing the results of the matching system with human perception. This is done by comparing the matcher rankings with the rankings provided by domain users that rank the available resources in the same scenario[2]. We conducted several experiments to test the effectiveness of the proposed matching solution in four aspects. Specifically, the experiments

---

[2] A human participant study was conducted to obtain the human rankings for this evaluation exercise.

were devised to test the added utility of: (1) ranking (as opposed to classification) of matches, (2) using the proposed approximate matching mechanism (as opposed to using subsumption reasoning alone), (3) consideration of priorities on individual requirements during the matching process, and (4) consideration of mandatory requirements.

Due to space limitations, the detailed results of all the experiments in this evaluation exercise will not be presented in this paper. However, a more detailed discussion of the experiments: the human participant study, experimental results and their analysis, are presented in [15]. In general, the results from the effectiveness evaluation experiments demonstrated that the Semantic Matcher results are compatible with human judgement and thus is effective in retrieving the relevant matches. Specifically, through the experimental results it was observed, that each of the desirable properties present in the Semantic Matcher, namely: ranking of matches, approximate matching, consideration of priorities on individual requirements and consideration of mandatory requirements in the matching process, has caused the match results to be more effective.

4.2 Evaluating Scalability

The proposed semantic matching approach must have a reasonable level of performance (w.r.t. matching time) for its practical use in facilitating the discovery of resources. Therefore, we evaluate the performance of the solution using the prototype implementation of this system, through the use of two experiments. Specifically, we investigate the scalability of the solution in terms of the number of advertisements matched and the size of the resource request. The objective of this evaluation exercise is to investigate the variation in execution time of the matching process, when the number of advertisements matched and the size of the resource request increases. If the Semantic Matcher is scalable, the execution times must be acceptable, for reasonable numbers of advertisements and request sizes. The experiments were carried out using a 3.2GHz, Intel PentiumD PC with 2GB of memory. The execution times are averaged over 30 runs and therefore the results are significant at a 95% confidence interval.

To test the scalability of the system in terms of the number of advertisements involved in the matching process, we vary the number of advertisements available for matching between 10 and 10000 and the execution time taken for the matching process is measured in milliseconds (while keeping the size of the request constant at 4). We obtain two sets of results:

1. When the resources are described using the Printer Ontology[3] which contains 126 concepts, 67 properties and 65 restrictions.
2. When the resources are described using the Computer Ontology[4] which contains 156 concepts, 103 properties and 75 restrictions.

Figure 1(a) graphically illustrates the execution times for both ontologies. It can be observed from the two plots, that for both ontologies the execution times for the match-

---

[3] The Printer Ontology is a specialization of the generic Device Ontology ([16]) and defines additional concepts and properties necessary to describe printers (such as printer resolution, supported media types, printing speed etc.).

[4] Again, this is a specialization of the generic Device Ontology and defines additional concepts and properties necessary to describe computers.

ing process keeps increasing, with increasing numbers of advertisements. The execution time becomes noticeably high, when the number of advertisements involved is high. For example, it has taken approximately 37 seconds to match 2000 advertisements with a request; this will mean a response time of 37 seconds when 2000 advertisements are present. Although the matching times are relatively low for small numbers of advertisements, these response times may become undesirable in the presence of a large number of advertisements. To overcome this issue, load balancing solutions that will distribute the matching load between a number of nodes [17], can be used.

It can also be observed that, the execution times taken when the advertisements and requests are described using the Computer ontology (which is the larger ontology), are generally higher when compared to the execution times related to the Printer ontology. This may be due to the fact that, when the size of the ontology is larger, the knowledge base that the reasoning mechanism has to deal with becomes larger and thus this can affect the execution time.

Although the plots seems almost linear, on closer observation of the execution times, it can be seen that the gradient of the plot keeps gradually increasing (from 17.34 to 22.88 for the plot related to the Computer ontology) when the number of advertisements increases. However, the rate of the increase observed is low. The execution time taken to match reasonable numbers of advertisements[5], can be observed to be within acceptable limits. For example, when the number of advertisements is 200 and 500, the matching time taken is approximately 4.5s and 9.8s respectively (for Printer Ontology). Thus, the results indicate that, the execution time for the matching process is satisfactory, for reasonable numbers of advertisements.

To test the scalability of the system in terms of the size of the resource request (i.e. the number of individual requirements involved in the request); we vary the number of individual requirements in the resource request between 1 and 7 and measure the execution time taken by the matching process (while keeping the number of advertisements constant at 50). For this case again, we obtain two sets of results for the two ontologies: (1) When the resources are described using the Printer Ontology. (2) When the resources are described using the Computer Ontology.

Figure 1(b) graphically illustrates the execution times for both ontologies. From the graph it can be observed, that for both ontologies the execution times for the matching process keeps increasing, when the request size is increased. The matching time for a request that has 5 individual requirements specified (when described with the Computer ontology, in the presence of 50 advertisements to be matched), is approximately 1.8 seconds, which can be acceptable, given the benefits provided by semantic matching. As with the previous experiment, the same observation can be made regarding the execution times related to the two ontologies; the execution time related to the larger ontology (the Computer ontology) is higher than for the smaller ontology. The plots related to both ontologies are approximately linear. The execution times for the matching process for increasing request sizes (up to a size of 7), can be observed to be acceptable. For example, when the request size is 4, the matching time is 1.4s approximately (for Printer Ontology); when the request size is 6, the matching time is 1.7s. Thus,

---

[5] For example, we can assume that, the maximum number of devices available in an average enterprise will be typically around 500 - 1000.

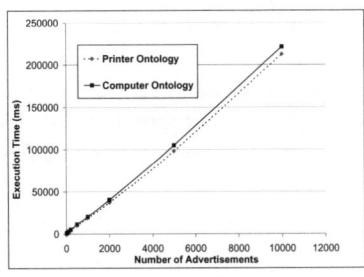 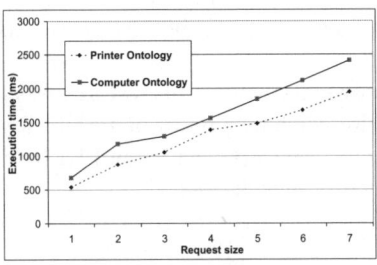

(a) Number of Advertisements Vs Execution Time

(b) Request Size Vs Execution Time

Fig. 1. Plots obtained for Scalability Experiments

from these results we can observe that, the execution time for the matching process is satisfactory for reasonable request sizes[6].

5 Conclusions and Future Work

In this paper, we have presented a semantic matching approach that can facilitate the effective discovery of pervasive resources. The approach provides an approximate matching mechanism that overcomes the limitations present in matchers which uses subsumption reasoning alone. The potential matches are ranked in the order of their suitability to satisfy the request under concern. The matching approach also incorporates priority handling in the matching process; this helps to identify the relative importance of the individual requirements in a request and also to indicate whether certain requirements are mandatory. Hence the matching system can produce results that better suit the context involved and the subjective preferences of service seekers. The involvement of match ranking and the priority handling are both important and useful additions to the existing work on service matching. The proposed solution has been implemented in a pervasive context and results have been obtained. We have used this implementation for subsequent evaluation experiments, to test the retrieval effectiveness of the solution and to investigate the scalability and matching times.

The effectiveness of the solution has been evaluated and the results demonstrates that the Semantic Matcher results agree reasonably well with human judgement, and thus is effective in retrieving the relevant matches. A further evaluation was conducted on the scalability of the Semantic Matcher with respect to: (1) the number of advertisements matched; and (2) the size of the request in terms of the number of individual requirements. Other aspects of performance also need to be investigated, which will help towards judging the usability of the Semantic Matcher in practical environments. For example, when the Semantic Matcher is deployed on a network to support service

---

[6] We also assume that, the number of requirements that can be expected in a device request in most typical pervasive environments, could range from 3-6.

discovery, the transmission times between the resource seekers/ providers and the directory service can be measured to test the communication overhead involved.

Acknowledgements. This research was funded and supported by the Telecommunications Research Laboratory of Toshiba Research Europe Ltd and partially funded by the Semantic Media project: grant EP/C010078/1 from the UK Engineering and Physical Sciences Research Council.

References

1. UPnP Forum: UPnP Device Architecture (2006), http://www.upnp.org/specs/arch/UPnP-DeviceArchitecture-v1.0.pdf
2. Arnold, K., OSullivan, B., Scheifler, R.W., Waldo, J., Wollrath, A.: The Jini Specification. Addison-Wesley, Reading (1999)
3. Chakraborty, D., Perich, F., Avancha, S., Joshi, A.: Dreggie: Semantic service discovery for m-commerce applications. In: Workshop on Reliable and Secure Applications in Mobile Environment, Symposium on Reliable Distributed Systems (2001)
4. Avancha, S., Joshi, A., Finin, T.: Enhancing the bluetooth service discovery protocol. Technical report, University of Maryland Baltimore County (2001)
5. Li, L., Horrocks, I.: A software framework for matchmaking based on semantic web technology. In: Int. World Wide Web Conference, pp. 331–339. ACM, New York (2003)
6. Paolucci, M., Kawamura, T., Payne, T., Sycara, K.: Semantic matching of web services capabilities. In: Int. Semantic Web Conference, pp. 333–347 (2002)
7. Baader, F., McGuinness, D.L., Nardi, D., Patel-Schneider, P.F.: Description Logic Handbook - Theory, Implementation and Applications. Cambridge University Press, Cambridge (2003)
8. Resnik, P.: Using information content to evaluate semantic similarity in a taxonomy. In: IJCAI, pp. 448–453 (1995)
9. Lin, D.: An information-theoretic definition of similarity. In: Proc. 15th International Conf. on Machine Learning, pp. 296–304. Morgan Kaufmann, San Francisco (1998)
10. Skoutas, D., Simitsis, A., Sellis, T.K.: A ranking mechanism for semanticweb service discovery. In: IEEE SCW, pp. 41–48 (2007)
11. Schwering, A.: Hybrid model for semantic similarity measurement. In: Meersman, R., Tari, Z. (eds.) OTM 2005. LNCS, vol. 3761, pp. 1449–1465. Springer, Heidelberg (2005)
12. Tversky, A.: Features of similarity. Psychological Review 84, 327–352 (1977)
13. Zadeh, L.: Fuzzy sets. Information and Control 8, 338–353 (1965)
14. Straccia, U.: A fuzzy description logic for the semantic web. Capturing Intelligence: Fuzzy Logic and the Semantic Web (2005)
15. Bandara, A., Payne, T., de Roure, D., Gibbins, N., Lewis, T.: Semantic resource matching for pervasive environments: The approach and its evaluation. Technical report, School of Electronics & Computer Science, University of Southampton (2008)
16. Bandara, A., Payne, T., de Roure, D., Clemo, G.: An ontological framework for semantic description of devices (poster). In: McIlraith, S.A., Plexousakis, D., van Harmelen, F. (eds.) ISWC 2004. LNCS, vol. 3298, Springer, Heidelberg (2004)
17. Kopparapu, C.: Load Balancing Servers, Firewalls, and Caches. John Wiley & Sons, Inc., New York (2002)

An Efficient Method to Measure the Semantic Similarity of Ontologies

James Z. Wang, Farha Ali, and Pradip K. Srimani

Department of Computer Science, Clemson University, Box 340974,
Clemson, SC 29634-0974, USA
{jzwang,fali,Srimani}@cs.clemson.edu

Abstract. With the recent availability of large number of bioinformatics data sources, query from such databases and rigorous annotation of experimental results often use semantic frameworks in the form of an ontology. With the growing access to heterogeneous and independent data repositories, determining the semantic similarity or difference of two ontologies is critical in information retrieval, information integration and semantic web services. In this paper, a sense refinement algorithm is proposed to construct a refined sense set (RSS) for an ontology so that the senses (synonym words) in this refined sense set represent the semantic meanings of the terms used by this ontology. In addition, a semantic set that combines the refined sense set of ontology with the relationship edges connecting the terms in this ontology is proposed to represent the semantics of this ontology. With the semantic sets, measuring the semantic similarity or difference of two ontologies is simplified as comparing the commonality or difference of two sets. The experimental studies show that the proposed method of measuring the semantic similarity or difference of two ontologies is efficient and accurate.

1 Introduction

An ontology is a formal specification of objects, concepts, entities, and their relationships, which are assumed to exist in a specific domain of interest. In past years, studies have been focused on evaluating the semantic similarity or difference of the natural language terms or concepts. Little effort [1, 2] has been made to measure the semantic similarity of two ontologies within the same scope. However, evaluating the semantic similarity of ontologies is as important as measuring the semantic similarity of the terms or concepts in natural language. Our purpose in this paper is to focus on measuring the semantic similarity of two ontologies in the same domain – the objective is to develop a rigorous model to precisely define similarity of ontologies that will be applicable to any application domain and to design efficient scalable algorithms to measure the similarities given two ontologies. We introduce the concepts and measures often using two small natural language ontologies and then present extensive experimental results showing the applicability of the results to ontologies from different application domains.

2 Semantic Similarity of Ontologies

2.1 Semantics of an Ontology

The biggest challenge is how to extract a set of features from an ontology that can accurately represent the semantics of this ontology. To achieve this, we first give a formal definition of a natural language ontology. An ontology is defined as a Directed Acyclic Graph (DAG), $O = [T, E, R]$, where $T = \{t_1, t_2, ..., t_n\}$ is a set of natural language terms (words or phrases) and $E = \{e_1, e_2, ..., e_m\}$ is a set of edges connecting these terms with relationships defined in $R = \{r_1, r_2, ..., r_k\}$. Specifically, an edge e_i is defined as a triplet $[t_{i1}, t_{i2}, r_j]$ where $t_{i1}, t_{i2} \in T$ and $r_j \in R$. In addition, two terms can only be linked by one relationship, that is,

$$\forall l \neq k, [t_i, t_j, r_k] \in E \Rightarrow [t_i, t_j, r_l] \notin E.$$

For instance, Fig. 1 depicts an ontology with T = {Building, Room, Red, Bedroom}, R = {part-of, is-a, feature-of}, and E = {[Bedroom, Room, is-a], [Room, Building, part-of], [Red, Building, feature-of]}.

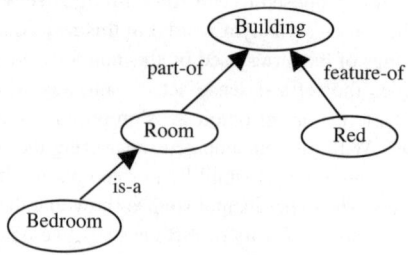

Fig. 1. An ontology example

Intuitively, one may think that the union of the set of labeling terms and the set of edges in an ontology includes all features of this ontology. However, this feature set may not represent the ontology's semantics. In the natural language domain, the meanings of terms and the understanding of concepts differ from community to community. People might use the same term for various concepts or use different terms for the same concept. Therefore, the set of conceptual terms in an ontology may not reveal the semantic meanings or concepts that the ontology is intended to represent. To reveal the semantics of an ontology, it is essential to discover the semantic meanings of the terms used in this ontology.

In natural language domain, the semantic meanings of a term are generally represented by a set of synonymous words semantically related to this term. This set is often called as the sense set of the specific term with the synonymous words being called as senses. For notational convenience, we use $SS(t)$ to represent the sense set for a term t. Similarly, given an ontology $O = [T, E, R]$, its sense set can be defined as $SS(O) = \cup_{t \in R} SS(t)$. That is, a sense set of an ontology is the union of the sense sets of all terms in the ontology. However, some synonymous words in a term's sense set may not reflect the semantic meanings of this term in the context where it is used. In particular, the semantic meanings of a term in an ontology are constrained by its relationships with other terms in this ontology. Therefore we need to refine the sense set for an ontology to include only the synonymous words that represent the semantic meanings of the conceptual terms in context of this ontology. We call the refined sense set for an ontology $O = [T, E, R]$ as $RSS(O)$. A set of features used to represent the semantics of an ontology should include the refined sense set of the ontology and the relationships among the conceptual terms of the ontology. Therefore, we define a semantic set, $SMS(O)$, for an ontology $O = [T, E, R]$ as

$$SMS(O) = RSS(O) \cup E \qquad (1)$$

where $RSS(O)$ is the refined sense set and E is the set of edges specifying the relationships among the terms in ontology O.

2.2 Semantic Similarity or Difference

Using the semantic set defined in Equation (1) to represent the semantics of an ontology, we can define the semantic similarity of two ontologies based on Tversky's similarity measurement model. Given two ontologies $O_1 = [T_1, E_1, R_1]$ and $O_2 = [T_2, E_2, R_2]$, their semantic similarity is defined as

$$Sim(O_1, O_2) = \frac{|SMS(O_1) \cap SMS(O_2)|}{|SMS(O_1) \cup SMS(O_2)|} \qquad (2).$$

The cardinality of $SMS(O_1) \cap SMS(O_2)$ represents the number of common features in ontologies O_1 and O_2, while the cardinality of $SMS(O_1) \cup SMS(O_2)$ represents the total number of distinct features in ontologies O_1 and O_2. Obviously, $0 \leq Sim(O_1, O_2) \leq 1$.

Some applications, such as semantic web applications, are also interested in the semantic difference of two ontologies. We define the semantic difference from ontology O_1 to ontology O_2 as

$$Diff(O_1, O_2) = \frac{|SMS(O_1) - SMS(O_2)|}{|SMS(O_1)|} \qquad (3)$$

The cardinality of set $SMS(O_1) - SMS(O_2)$ stands for the number of features in ontology O_1 but not in ontology O_2, while the cardinality of set $SMS(O_1)$ represents the total number of semantic features in ontology O_1. Thus, $0 \leq Diff(O_1, O_2) \leq 1$.

Equation (3) is not forced to satisfy the symmetry property which is preserved by the semantic distance based models [3]. That is, the semantic difference from ontology O_1 to ontology O_2 may not be the same as the semantic difference from ontology O_2 to ontology O_1. Employing such an asymmetric measurement is important in many applications because it ensures that this measurement is consistent with human judgments, in which cognitive properties of similarity play key roles. If $SMS(O_1) \subseteq SMS(O_2)$, then $Diff(O_1, O_2) = 0$, meaning that semantic features existing in ontology O_1 is also in ontology O_2. Conversely, $Diff(O_2, O_1) > 0$, meaning that ontology O_2 has some features that do not belong to ontology O_1. Similar asymmetric measurement approaches are also used by some studies for comparing the class entities within an ontology.

3 Sense Refinement

Based on our definitions, the real challenge in measuring the semantic similarity or difference of two ontologies is to obtain their refined sense sets. We call this process as the sense refinement. Usually, the semantic meanings of a term are associated with the specific domain in which the term is used. Since we measure the semantic similarity of natural language ontologies, our sense refinement process must consider the characteristics of the natural language domain.

3.1 Formal Definition of a Refined Sense Set

To formalize the sense refinement process, we first represent the entire natural language domain as a universal ontology $U = [T_u, E_u, R_u]$ where T_u is the set of all natural language terms, R_u includes all kinds of relationships between two natural language terms, and E_u is the set of edges linking terms in T_u with relationships in R_u. Thus, for any natural language ontology $O = [T, E, R]$, we have $T \subseteq T_u$, $E \subseteq E_u$, and $R \subseteq R_u$. Since the senses for a natural language term are also terms in the natural language domain, we must have $SS(O) \subseteq T_u$. Now we give a formal definition of the refined sense set for a natural language ontology.

Definition: Given an ontology $O = [T, E, R]$ and a universal ontology $U = [T_u, E_u, R_u]$, a refined sense set for ontology O is defined as a subset of its sense set ($RSS(O) \subseteq SS(O)$) that, $\forall s_i, s_j \in SS(O)$, $s_i, s_j \in RSS(O)$ iff $\exists t_i, t_j \in T$, $s_i \in SS(t_i)$, $s_j \in SS(t_j)$, $[t_i, t_j, r_k] \in E$ and $[s_i, s_j, r_k] \in E_u$.

For any two senses s_i and s_j in $SS(O)$, these two senses also belong to $RSS(O)$ if and only if there is an edge $[t_i, t_j, r_k]$ in ontology O ($[t_i, t_j, r_k] \in E$) and also an edge $[s_i, s_j, r_k]$ in the universal ontology U ($[s_i, s_j, r_k] \in E_u$) with the same relationship r_k, where s_i is a sense of t_i ($s_i \in SS(t_i)$) and s_j is a sense of t_j ($s_j \in SS(t_j)$). In another words, a pair of senses in $SS(O)$ also belong to $RSS(O)$ if and only if the relationship of these senses in the universal ontology U is the same as the relationship of their associated terms in ontology O.

3.2 Sense Refinement Algorithm

Based on our definitions, we present the pseudo code of our sense refinement (SR) algorithm in Fig. 2. There are three factors contributing the complexity of the sense refinement algorithm. These factors include the number of edges in ontology O and the universal ontology U respectively, the number of senses for each term in Ontology O. If we assume that the average number of senses for a term is K, the complexity of the sense refinement algorithm is $O(K^2 \cdot |E| \cdot |E_u|)$. If we replace the input universal natural language ontology U with a domain-specific universal ontology U_d, this sense refinement algorithm can be used to obtain the refine sense set for an ontology in a specific domain, such as geographic information systems (GIS) or biology.

```
Algorithm: SR

Input:
    Ontology O = [T, E, R];
    Universal Ontology U = [T_u, E_u, R_u];
Output:
    Refined Sense Set RSS(O);
procedure SR(O, U)
    begin
        RSS = {};
        for any [c, p, r] ∈ E
            S_p = SS(p);
            S_c = SS(c);
            for any s ∈ S_c
                if ( ∃ h ∈ S_p, [s, h, r] ∈ E_u)
                    RSS = RSS ∪ {s, h}
                endif
            endfor
        endfor
        return RSS;
    end
```

Fig. 2. Sense Refinement Algorithm

4 Semantic Set Construction

In past years, researchers have tried to build a merged ontology by sharing ideas from all available ontologies. The SUMO (Suggested Upper Merged Ontology) [4] project is one of such efforts. The goal of SUMO is to develop a standard upper ontology to assist information integration, information retrieval, and natural language processing. SUMO can also be used by ontology designers to design ontologies in their specific domains. Therefore, it seems to be reasonable to use SUMO as the universal ontology in our senses refinement process. However, SUMO actually maps all its terms to the concepts defined in WordNet [5], an online lexical reference system whose design is inspired by current psycholinguistic theories of human lexical memory. In WordNet, English nouns, verbs, adjectives and adverbs are organized into synonym sets, each representing one underlying lexical concept. Different relations link the synonym sets. Thus, the set of terms in WordNet is a superset of the terms in SUMO. In addition, WordNet defines all possible relationships between synonym sets. Thus, it is better to use WordNet as the universal ontology for the sense refinement in natural language domain since it contains two key components needed for the sense refinement process, the senses (synonym words) for a term and the relationships between the senses.

Many natural language applications used WordNet for information retrieval [6, 7], sense identification [8], text classification [9], internet search [10], etc. The WordNet system consists of lexicographer files, code to convert these files into a database, and search routines and interfaces that display information from the database. Information in WordNet is organized around logical groupings called synsets. Each synset consists of a list of synonymous words or collocations. Semantic relationships between two synsets include (but are not limited to) hypernymy/hyponymy ("is-a" relationship), antonymy ("opposite-to"), entailment ("inheritance"), and meronymy/holonymy ("part-of" relationship). Especially, hypernymy ("is-a") and meronymy ("part-of") relationships are two dominate relationships in an ontology. These relationships can be used to represent the edges that connect two ontology terms. Thus, it is practical to use WordNet as an alternative to the universal ontology for our senses refinement process.

In WordNet, natural language terms are grouped together based on their semantic meanings. Each group contains the terms representing a particular semantic meaning, which is also called the sense, of these terms. One term may exist in different groups representing different senses due to synonymy. In addition, these sense groups are connected by semantic relationships, such as "is-a" relationship, in WordNet. Fig. 2 depicts a general algorithm for sense refinement with a universal ontology. When WordNet is used as the universal ontology, the algorithm is slightly different. The modified algorithm is represented in

Fig. 4. This algorithm takes an ontology O= [T, E, R] and WordNet as the input and construct a refined sense set for this ontology. To assist better understanding of this algorithm, we use a simple ontology, OntoBeverage, shown in Fig. 3 to demonstrate the sense refinement process.

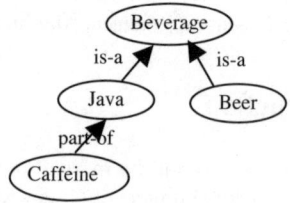

Fig. 3. OntoBeverage

OntoBeverage is a simple ontology representing two beverages, Java and Beer. Caffeine is a part of Java. Table 1 contains the terms in OntoBeverage and their associated senses and hypernyms obtained from WordNet. In WordNet, each sense is associated with a unique ID. These IDs can be used for efficient matching between the parent senses and the children hypernyms or holonyms. There are several level of hypernyms associated with each sense, in our table we only show the hypernym that is a sense of a parent term because this hypernym preserves the relationship between the parent and child terms. If there is no match between hypernyms of a child with its parent sense set, then only the conceptual term is included in the refined sense set.

To get the RSS for OntoBeverage, we examine all terms in this ontology starting from the root term "beverage". Initially, the refined sense set is empty, i.e., RSS(OntoBeverage) = { }. The root term "beverage" has only one sense in WordNet with ID = 07775114. Term "java" contains three senses having IDs 08780566, 07822148, and 06808625. Among these senses, the ID for the hypernym of the sense with ID = 07822148 is 07775114, equal to the ID of the sense for term "beverage". It means there is an edge connecting sense 07822148 and sense 07775114 with a "is-a" relation in WordNet. So we will include the synsets with ID: 07822148 and ID:

```
Algorithm SR_WN(Ontology O, Wordnet)
begin
  RSS = {};
  P = {p | p ∈ O && p is a parent in ontology O}
  for any p ∈ P
    P_flag = false;
    S_p = Sense set of p from WordNet;
    C = {c | c is a child of p in ontology O }
    for any c ∈ C
      C_flag = false;
      S_c = Senses set of c from WordNet;
      for any s ∈ S_c
        H = Hypernym/Holonym set of s;
        for any h ∈ H
          C_flag = true; P_flag = true;
          RSS = RSS ∪ {(id_s, s), (id_h, h)};
        endfor
        if (!C_flag) RSS = RSS ∪ {(c, c)};
      endfor
    endfor
    if (!P_flag) RSS = RSS ∪ {(p, p)};
  endfor
  return RSS;
end
```

Fig. 4. Sense Refinement with WordNet

Table 1. Senses and Hypernyms/Holonyms for OntoBeverage

Term Label	Senses		Hypernyms/Holonyms	
	ID	Synset	ID	Sysnet
Beverage	07775114	beverage, drink, drinkable, potable	00020429	food, nutrient
Java	08780566	java	09182497	island
	07822148	coffee, java	07775114	beverage, drink, drinkable potable
	06808625	java	06808256	object-oriented programming language, object-oriented programing language
Beer	07780090	beer	07775114	beverage, drink, drinkable, potable
Caffeine	4566829	caffeine, caffein	07822148	coffee, java

07775114 in the refined sense set. We get RSS(OntoBeverage) = {*(07775114, beverage), (07775114, drink), (07775114, drinkable), (07775114, potable), (07822148, coffee), (07822148, java)*}. The next term is "Beer". Its second level hypernym 07775114 is also the sense for term "beverage". Therefore, the sense 07780090 and its hypernym 07775114 will be included in the semantic set. We get RSS(OntoBeverage) = {*(07775114, beverage), (07775114, drink), (07775114, drinkable), (07775114, potable), (07822148, coffee), (07822148, java), (07780090, beer)*}. Finally, we check term "caffeine" which is a child of "java" with "part-of" relationship. "Caffeine" has only one sense {caffeine, caffeine} with ID = 4566829. The Holonym of the sense 4566829 is the synset 07822148, which is a sense of java. It means there is an edge connecting the sense 4566829 and the sense 07822148 with "part-of" relationship. So we have RSS(OntoBeverage) = {(07775114, beverage), (07775114, drink), (07775114, drinkable), (07775114, potable), (07822148, coffee), (07822148, java), (07780090, beer), (4566829, caffeine), (4566829, caffein) }. This refined sense set can also be represented as a two column table depicted in Table 2.

Table 2. Refined Sense Set for OntoBeverage

07775114	beverage, drink, drinkable, potable
07822148	coffee, java
07780090	Beer
14566829	caffeine, caffeine

Table 3. Semantic Set for OntoBeverage

07775114	beverage, drink, drinkable, potable
07822148	coffee, java, 07775114
07780090	beer, 07775114
14566829	caffeine, caffein, 07822148

Based on our definition in Equation 1, a semantic set of an ontology is the union of its RSS and the relationship edges in the ontology. An edge can be represented by two sense IDs it connects. To make the representation for senses and edges consistent, we store the refined senses and edges using the same two column table. For refined senses, one column is for the sense IDs while the other column contains all text strings representing the synset. For an edge, we store the starting sense ID in the first column and the ending sense ID in the second column. Since the starting sense ID of an edge must have been used by the representation of refined senses, we will simply add the ending sense ID into the corresponding second column of that refined sense. Therefore, the semantic set for OntoBeverage can be represented by Table 3.

This table contains all senses that are related to other sense(s) in the ontology and the semantic relationships between senses. Sometimes, none of the hypernyms or holonyms of a child sense matches with any of the parent senses. In this case, we simply store the term label on both column of the table. We can also represent the semantic set for OntoBeverage in traditional set format as SMS(OntoBeverage) = {(07775114, beverage), (07775114, drink), (07775114, drinkable), (07775114, portable), (07822148, coffee), (07822148, java), (07822148, 07775114), (07780090, beer), (07780090, 07775114), (14566829, caffeine), (14566829, caffein), (14566829, 07822148)}.

To measure the semantic similarity of any two ontologies, we first obtain their semantic sets using the discussed method. After that, the semantic similarity or difference can be calculated using Equation 2 or Equation 3 respectively. We use some simple ontologies to demonstrate this process. We first measure the semantic difference between OntoBeverage, depicted in Fig. 3 and ontology, OntoPL, shown in Fig. 5. OntoBeverage is a simple ontology representing two drinks and OntoPL is a

Fig. 5. OntoPL   **Fig. 6.** OntoDrink

simple ontology representing programming languages Java and FORTRAN. We assume OntoBeverage is the target ontology and OntoPL is the source ontology.

To measure the semantic difference of these two ontologies, we need to get their respective semantic sets. Since we have obtained the semantic set for ontology OntoBeverage in the previous section, we only need to get the semantic set for ontology OntoPL using the same procedure. Table 4 depicts the semantic set for OntoPL. This semantic set can also be presented as SMS(OntoPL) ={*(06805924, Programming language), (06805924, Programing language), (06808625, java), (06808625, 06805924), (06810054, FORTRAN), (06810054, 06805924)*}. Using Equation 3, we get the semantic difference from OntoBeverage to OntoPL as,

Diff(OntoBeverage, OntoPL) = 1.

This semantic difference value indicates that ontologies OntoBeverage and OntoPL are totally different, even though the same term "java" is used in both ontologies.

Now we measure the semantic difference between OntoBeverage and another simple ontology, OntoDrink, depicted in Fig. 6.

Table 4. Semantic Set for OntoPL

06805924	Programming language, programing language
06808625	Java, 06805924
06810054	FORTRAN, 06805924

Table 5. Semantic Set for OntoDrink

07775114	Beverage, drink, drinkable, potable
07822148	Coffee, Java, 07775114
07820560	Cola, dope, 07775114

Using the same procedure, we can get the semantic set for OntoDrink as shown in Table 5. This semantic set can also be presented as SMS(OntoDrink) = {*(07775114, beverage), (07775114, drink), (07775114, drinkable), (07775114, portable), (07822148, coffee), (07822148, java), (07822148, 07775114), (07820560, cola), (07820560, dope), (07820560, 07775114)*}.

Using Equation 3, we get the semantic difference from OntoBeverage to OntoDrink as *Diff*(OntoBeverage, OntoDrink) = 0.42. This result indicates that ontologies OntoBeverage and OntoDrink are somewhat similar, although different conceptual terms are used in these ontologies. Since those three ontologies are very simple, we can tell that the semantic difference values obtained by our procedure are consistent with human perspectives. These results demonstrate that our approach of measuring the semantic difference of ontologies is reasonable. We also note here that the IDs used in this paper were obtained from WordNet database. Due to the revolution or upgrade of WordNet, the same sense may have different IDs in different versions of WordNet. However, for the same version of WordNet, these IDs are unique for different senses.

5 Performance Evaluation

Because the senses refinement takes extra time, one may think using the proposed ontology difference measurement procedure may require more processing time than the approach that uses the non-refined senses set to represent the semantics of ontologies. To evaluate how quickly our algorithm returns the semantic difference of two given ontologies, we measure the differences of some simple ontologies presented in Fig. 7 using these two approaches.

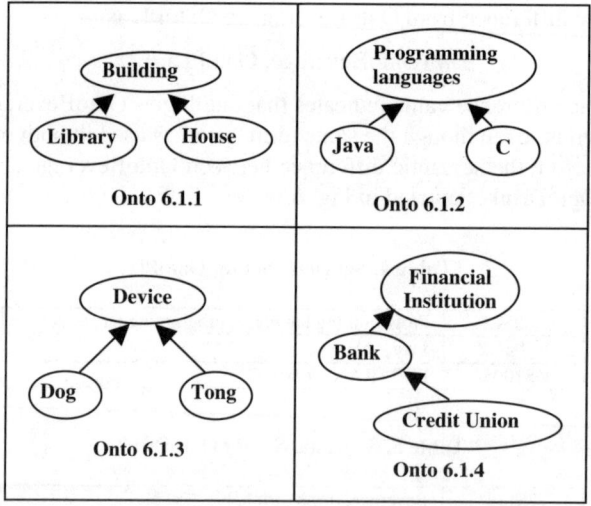

Fig. 7. Ontologies for evaluating the efficiency of different approaches

We choose these ontologies because most of their concepts have a lot of senses. Thus the time spent in the sense refinement should be noticeable. We use J2SE to implement different measurement approaches. Without the loss of generality, we measure the semantic difference of an ontology with itself using different approaches and observe the processing times. The experimental studies are conducted on a desktop computer equipped with 1.3GHz Intel Pentium M processor and 512 MB RAM. The experimental results are depicted in Table 6.

An Efficient Method to Measure the Semantic Similarity of Ontologies 457

Table 6. Processing time using different approaches

Ontology	Processing Time (milliseconds)	
	Sense refinement	Non-refined sense set
Onto 6.1.1	0.108	0.235
Onto 6.1.2	0.044	0.216
Onto 6.1.3	0.105	0.169
Onto 6.1.4	0.016	0.216

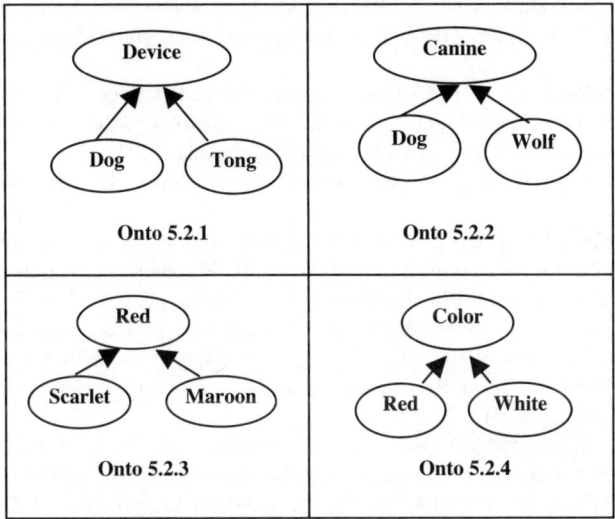

Fig. 8. Ontologies for evaluating the accuracy of different approaches

Table 7. Ontology differences under different senses set construction algorithms

Target Ontology	Source Ontology	Ontology Difference	
		Sense refinement	Non-refined sense set
Onto 5.2.1	Onto 5.2.2	1.0	0.2
Onto 5.2.2	Onto 5.2.1	1.0	0.44
Onto 5.2.3	Onto 5.2.4	0.714	0.333
Onto 5.2.4	Onto 5.2.3	0.778	0.835

To evaluate the accuracy of the proposed ontology difference measurement algorithm, we measure the semantic differences of some simple ontologies in Fig. 8 using our proposed approach and the naïve non-refined sense set approach.

We choose these ontologies because they are very simple and the semantic differences between them can be easily judged by human observation. The measurement results are depicted in Table 7. These results show that our proposed ontology difference measurement algorithm is more accurate than the naive non-refined senses set approach.

References

1. Maedche, A., Staab, S.: Comparing Ontologies— Similarity Measures and a Comparison Study, Internal Report No. 408, Institute AIFB, University of Karlsruhe, 76128 Karlsruhe, Germany (2001)
2. Wang, J.Z., Ali, F.: An Efficient Ontology Comparison Tool for Semantic Web Applications. In: IEEE/WIC/ACM International Conference on Web Intelligence (WI 2005), pp. 372–378 (2005)
3. Rada, R.H., Hili, H., Bicknell, E., Blettner, M.: Development and Application of a Metric on Semantic Nets. IEEE Transactions on System, Man, and Cybernetics 19(1), 17–30 (1989)
4. Pease, A., Niles, I., Li, J.: The Suggested Upper Merged Ontology: A Large Ontology for the Semantic Web and its Applications. In: Working Notes of the AAAI-2002 Workshop on Ontologies and the Semantic Web, Edmonton, Canada (2002)
5. Fellbaum, C. (ed.): WordNet: An Electronic Lexical Database. The MIT Press, Cambridge (1998)
6. Voorhees, E.M.: Using WordNet to disambiguate word senses for text retrieval. In: Proceedings of the 16th annual international ACM SIGIR conference on Research and development in information retrieval, Pittsburgh, Pennsylvania, pp. 171–180 (1993)
7. Liu, S., Liu, F., Yu, C., Meng, W.: An effective approach to document retrieval via utilizing WordNet and recognizing phrases. In: Proceedings of the 27th annual international ACM SIGIR conference on Research and development in information retrieval, Sheffield, United Kingdom, pp. 266–272 (2004)
8. Leacock, C., Chodorow, M., Miller, G.A.: Using Corpus Statistics and WordNet Relations for Sense Identification. Compuitational Liguistics 24(1), 147–165 (1998)
9. Scott, S., Matwin, S.: Text Classification using WordNet hypernyms. In: Usage of WordNet in Natural Language Processing Systems: Proceedings of the Workshop, pp. 45–51 (1998), http://www.ai.sri.com/~harabagi/colingacl98/acl_work/acl_work.html
10. Moldovan, D.I., Mihalcea, R.: Using WordNet and lexical operators to improve Internet searches. IEEE Internet Computing 4(1), 34–43 (2000)

A Dynamic Awareness Model for Service-Based Collaborative Grid Application in Access Grid*

Xiaowu Chen, Xiangyu Ji, and Qinping Zhao

The State Key Laboratory of Virtual Reality Technology and Systems
School of Computer Science and Engineering, Beihang University
Beijing 100083, P.R. China
chen@buaa.edu.cn

Abstract. Access Grid is an ensemble of resources that can provide an immersive, interactive, and collaborative environment for grid applications. Collaborative awareness support is a basic requirement of Access Grid, and is needed to provide adequate awareness information for collaborators to effectively cooperate with grid applications. However, most existing collaborative awareness models are unable to characterize the dynamic relationships between collaborators and their tasks with the standards of OGSA and WSRF. Therefore, this paper presents a dynamic collaborative awareness model, which characterizes above dynamic relationships for service-based collaborative grid applications in Access Grid. Based on the dynamic properties of services and the relationships between collaborators and services, this model firstly calculates the degrees of correlations between the actions of collaborators, and quantifies the intensities of each collaborator's awareness of other collaborators' actions, secondly divides awareness spaces by comparing the awareness intensities with their thresholds, thirdly selects and filters cooperation information according to the awareness spaces. Finally, the usability of this model is evaluated with the heuristic method, and an experiment is given to demonstrate that this model can increase the efficiency of cooperative work in Access Grid.

1 Introduction

Access Grid is an ensemble of resources that can provide an immersive, interactive, and collaborative environment for grid applications, and it mainly studies the way of group-to-group communication, access of grid resources and users' cooperation method in grid environment [1]. In order to support developing collaborative grid applications, Access Grid should solve the collaborative awareness problem, which means to provide a method for information exchanging among users of collaborative applications in grid environment. Hence, it is necessary for Access Grid to support collaborative awareness capability to provide adequate cooperation information, reduce the cost and conflicts, and increase the efficiency of cooperative work.

---

* This paper is supported by National Natural Science Foundation of China (60503066), National High-Tech Research and Development Program (2006AA01Z311), The National Basic Research Program (2006CB303007), Program for New Century Excellent Talents in University (NCET-05-0187), China Education and Research Grid Program (ChinaGrid).

Recently Grid Computing is converging with Web Services according to the standards of OGSA (Open Grid Service Architecture) and WSRF (WS-Resource Framework), and thus it is possible to build cross-institutional distributed computing infrastructure utilizing SOA approach[2] [3]. Along with OGSA and WSRF, a new requirement of Access Grid comes out for collaborative awareness issue, all resources in collaborative grid applications appear in the form of service. The service offering resources has dynamic properties, which are represented as the functions and permitted to be changed. That means the tasks of the grid applications are not static but dynamic, and the tasks in grid applications can not be assigned to collaborators in advance. Then all of these dynamic facts require that the collaborative awareness model could characterize these dynamic relationships between collaborators and their tasks.

However, most collaboration tools in Access Grid systems are still lack of collaborative awareness capability to meet above requirement. The representative collaboration tool is Access Grid Toolkit [3] (short for AGTK), developed by U.S. Argonne National Laboratory. It is defined as an ensemble of resources including multimedia large-format displays, presentation and interactive environments, and interfaces to Grid middleware and to visualization environments to support group-to-group interactions across the Grid [1]. And it provides the application-based collaborative awareness, which shares the information of collaborators' actions to all the collaborators in the application. But such model is short of the states of grid services and can not represent the relationships between services, and it can not select and filter out cooperation information based on each collaborator's demand, thereby it is unable to meet the collaborative awareness requirement of access grid.

Moreover, the issue of collaborative awareness has been a key topic in CSCW (Computer Supported Cooperative Work) from the early 90s. Benford proposed a spatial awareness model, which depicts the awareness intensity between two actors by the intersection and union operation of the objects in users' interest space and effect space [5]. Tom Rodden extended the spatial objects awareness model to depict the relations among cooperative applications in common applications [6], which measures the awareness intensity by information flow chart among applications. The hierarchy awareness model [7] simply uses awareness hierarchy to measure the cooperative level of different actors in collaborations. And In reference [8], the measurement of awareness intensity is more concerned in a new group-awareness model based on role and task. However, most awareness models above are based on static tasks and relationships between collaborators, which cannot represent the dynamic properties of service-based collaborative grid applications. Therefore, these models cannot precisely characterize the changing tasks, roles and actions in grid environment.

According to above analysis, most existing tools are lack of collaborative awareness capability to provide adequate information and reduce the cost and conflicts for cooperative work in Access Grid, and most existing collaborative awareness models are unable to represent the dynamic properties of collaborative grid applications. Therefore, in this paper, a new dynamic collaborative awareness model is proposed to characterize the dynamic relationships between collaborators and tasks for service-based collaborative grid applications in Access Grid. Based on the dynamic properties of services and the relationships between collaborators and services, this model firstly calculates the degrees of correlations between the actions of collaborators, and quantifies the intensities of each collaborator's awareness of other collaborators' actions, secondly divides awareness spaces by comparing the awareness intensities with their thresholds, thirdly selects and filters cooperation information according to the awareness spaces to increase the efficiency of cooperative work. A collaboration tool based on this model is implemented for an Access Grid system, and includes grid service interface, event service, space service, collaboration service and related clients.

Section 2 presents the formalization definition of this model and provides the formulas to calculate awareness intensity and awareness space. Section 3 introduces the implementation of a collaboration tool based on this model for ChinaGrid Access Grid (CGAG). And Section 4 verifies the usability of this model and its collaboration tool by heuristic method and an experiment. Finally, Section 5 ends up with conclusion.

2 Dynamic Collaborative Awareness Model

Based on the dynamic properties of services and the relationships between collaborators and services, a dynamic awareness model is presented for services-based collaborative grid applications in Access Grid. Firstly, it introduces the definitions of the basic elements and relations in this model. Secondly, an abstract Object-Method graph is defined to describe various services and the relationships. Through this graph, it calculates the intensities of each collaborator's awareness of other collaborators' actions. Then it divides awareness spaces and filters cooperation information.

2.1 Basic Elements and Relations

OBJECT is the service in collaborative grid application, each object is an instance of a service, and object set is denoted by O. METHOD is the method that is used to interact with service, method set is denoted by M. STATE is the state of service instance, includes sleeping, ready, running, suspended, failed, finished, also state set is denoted by S. USER is the collaborator in collaborative grid application, it is denoted by U. TIME is time duration which collaborator spends in cooperation, and time set is denoted by T.

OPERATION RELATION: $OPR = \{O, M, f_{opr}\}, f_{opr} : O \rightarrow 2^M$. Operation relation (OPR) represents the methods, with which collaborator can operate the object. When $f_{opr} : o \rightarrow \varnothing$, it represents that the object does not support to be operated.

OBJECT RELATION: $ROO = \{O, f_{roo}\}, f_{roo} : O \times O \rightarrow \{True, False\}$. Object relation (ROO) represents whether there is interdependence between two in Object set. And the object interdependence reflects the types of relationships of grid services, such as uses, composes delegates, refers, and extends. For Instance, if service A is running and it uses service B to finish its task, then $f_{roo} : A \times B \rightarrow True$, And vice versa.

ACTION RELATION: $ACT = \{U, T, OPR, f_{act}\}, f_{act} : U \times T \to OPR$. Action Relation (ACT) represents collaborators' actions in the process of collaboration. The action of a collaborator at t moment can be expressed as

$$ACT_{(u,t)} = \{u, t, opr, f_{act}\}, u \in U, t \in T$$

It describes that the collaborator u operated with the object at t moment by operation relation. And a subset of a collaborator's action can be expressed as

$$ACT_u = \{u, T, OPR, f_{act}\}, u \in U, ACT_u \subseteq ACT$$

It describes the dynamic relationship between user u and services in the process of collaboration.

SERVICE STATE RELATION: $ROS = \{O, T, S, f_{ros}\}, f_{ros} : O \times T \to S$. Service State Relation (ROS) represents the dynamic states of services in the process of collaborations.

According to the above definition of the elements and the relations, we present the definition of the collaborative grid application in Access Grid as follow.

$$CGA = <E, \Re>$$

Collaborative Grid Application is a two-tuple that is composed by the relations among elements, in which $E = \{O, M\}$, and $R = \{OPR, ROO\}$.

Collaboration Process is the process of cooperation on a collaborative grid application; it is also defined as a two-tuple:

$$CP = <E_1, \Re_1>$$

Where $E_1 = \{E, U, T, S\}$, and $\Re_1 = \{\Re, ACT, ROS\}$.

2.2 Object-Method Graph

According to the object set, method set and the relations in a collaborative grid application, the Object-Method graph is defined to represent the awareness character of collaborative grid application.

There are two kinds of nodes in the Object-Method graph. One is Object node, denoted by $Object(X)$. The other one is Method node, denoted by $Method(i)$. Figure 1-i shows an Object-Method graph, where Capital letters A, B, C, D, E, F, G, H, I node are object nodes and lowercase letters i, j, m node are method nodes. If operation relation exists between object node $Object(X)$ and method node $Method(i)$, there will be an edge between $Object(X)$ and $Method(i)$, called operation Edge, denoted by $pE(Object(X), Method(i))$. If Object relation exists between two object node $Object(X)$ and $Object(Y)$, there will be an edge between $Object(X)$ and $Object(Y)$, called interaction Edge, denoted by $iE(Object(X), Object(Y))$. In Figure 1-i, the edges

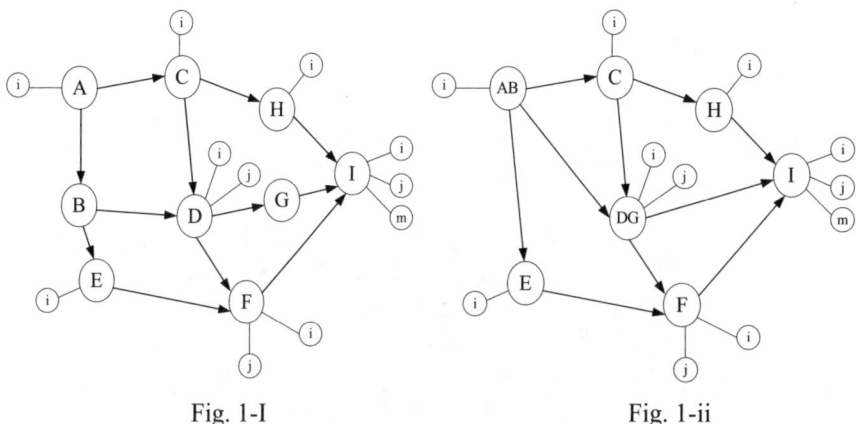

Fig. 1-I Fig. 1-ii

Fig. 1. Object-Method graph

without arrow are operation Edges, and the others are interaction Edges. The arrows represent the relationships between two nodes. For instance, the interaction edge from $Object(A)$ to $Object(B)$ means that A uses C to finish its task.

In the collaborative grid application, some object nodes in the object-method graph have no operation edge, such as node B and node G in Figure 1-i. That means the grid services that are represented by this kind of object nodes will not require collaborators' intervention in executing the tasks. Therefore, it is necessary to simplify the object-method graph to remove this kind of object nodes to make collaborators focus on the operational nodes. Analyzing the topology of these nodes, we merge these nodes and their adjacent nodes into a new object node.

For instance, as shown in Figure 1-ii, node B is merged with node A to form a new object node, called complex node. Thus, after merging the object nodes without operation edges, collaborators could focus on node A and do not need to consider the node B.

2.3 Calculating Awareness Intensity

The awareness intensity of two collaborators is inversely proportional to the shortest distance between two operation nodes which are operated by these two collaborators, we set the value of edges in the object-method graph to calculate the value of the awareness intensity. The value of each operation edge $pE(Object(X), Method(i))$ is set to zero, denoted by $Len(X,i) = 0$, as shown in figure 2. It describes that the awareness intensity is greatest when collaborators' operating the same object. The value of each inter-action edge $iE(Object(X), Object(Y))$ is set to one, denoted by $Len(X,Y) = 1$, as shown in Figure 2. It describes that the awareness intensity becomes smaller when the length between operated objects becomes further. The value of formula $Len(M,N)$ is equal to the shortest distance between two nodes, where M and N are random nodes in the graph.

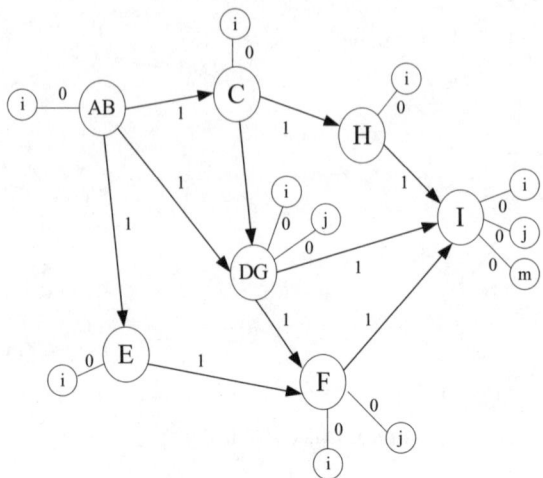

Fig. 2. Object-Method graph with values

In Figure 2, the value of each interaction edge is 1, which shows that the strength of subtasks' relationships that collaborators are executing at a moment is inversely proportional to the shortest path. The value of each operation edge is 0, which shows that the awareness intensity between them is greatest while collaborators are executing the same subtask.

The awareness intensity between collaborators is related to the relationship between subtasks which will be executed at a moment. Thus the awareness intensity, between the collaborator and other collaborator's action can be calculated as followed:

$$Aware(user_1, t1, act_2) = RA(act_1, act_2) = \frac{1}{Len(f_{act_1}, f_{act_2}) + 1}, t1 \in T$$

With above formula, it can be calculated at any time in this object-method graph that the value of the awareness intensity between any collaborator and any action.

2.4 Dividing Awareness Space

Awareness Space is the subset of Action relation, and a collaborator can be aware of others' actions in his awareness space as follow.

$$AS(user, t) = \{act | Aware(user, t, act) \geq x, x \in [0,1], t \in T, act \in ACT\}$$

Where x is the threshold of the collaborator, and the collaborator can use x to dynamically control the range of awareness space. Through this formula, the awareness space of collaborators can be dynamically calculated based on the collaborator's action rather than static collaborators' relationship. For instance, when the x was set to 0.5, figure 3 shows collaborator's dynamic awareness space.

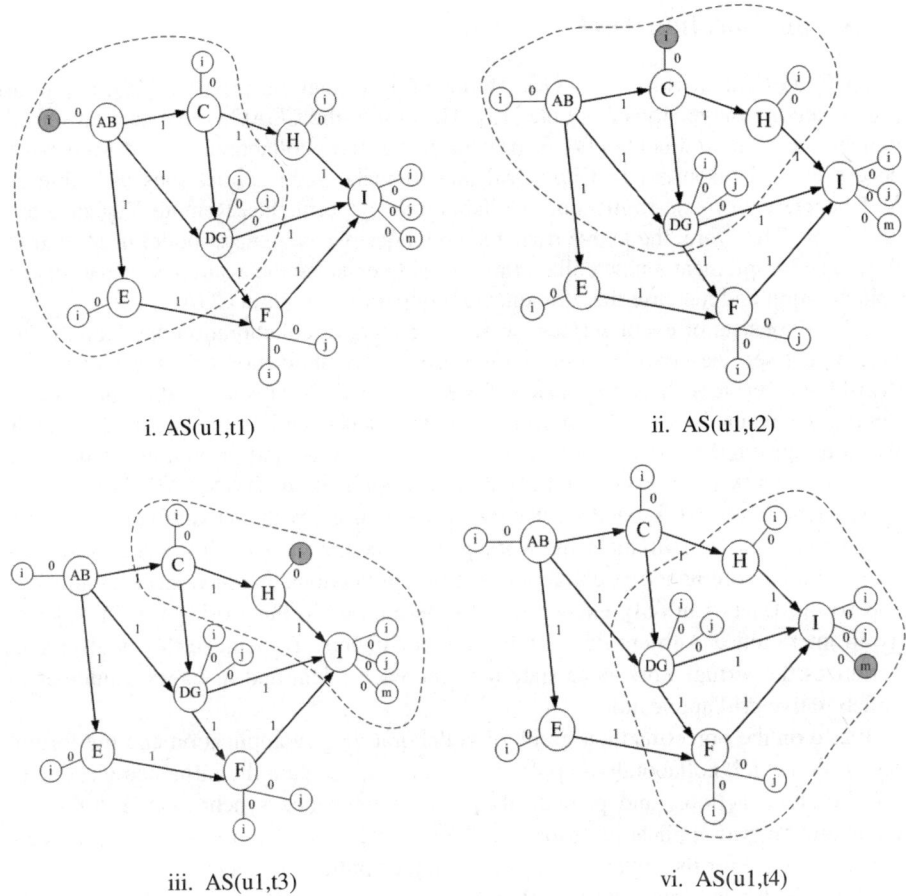

i. AS(u1,t1) 　　　　ii. AS(u1,t2)

iii. AS(u1,t3) 　　　　vi. AS(u1,t4)

Fig. 3. Shows dynamic awareness space while x is 0.5. (dashed line is the range of awareness space, gray node is the operation node where the u1 was at that moment.)

Figure 3 shows a collaborator's dynamic awareness space in the collaboration process, there are 3 subfigures and the dashed line marks the range of the collaborator's awareness space, which means that he concerns on the actions occurring on those objects. Figure 3-i shows the collaborator's awareness space while being in the operation node of node AB at t1 moment. Figure 3-ii shows the collaborator's awareness space while being in the operation node of node C at t2 moment. Figure 3-iii shows the collaborator's awareness space while being in the operation node of node H at t3 moment. Figure 3-vi shows the collaborator's awareness space while being in the operation node of node I at t4 moment.

According to the above method for dynamically dividing the awareness spaces, this collaborative awareness model can provide the awareness information for collaborators based on the objects' relationships rather than static collaborators' relationships or static subtasks' relationships.

3 A Collaboration Tool

The CGAG (ChinaGrid Access Grid) founded by ChinaGrid program [12], is a joint project among universities in China [13]. The aim of the CGAG is to create advanced collaborative environments [14] to provide interactive, collaborative, and immersive access of grid resources in ChinaGrid and to make such applications available as Videoconference, Tele-immersion, Collaborative Experiments, Remote Visualization and so on. Therefore, the above dynamic collaborative awareness model is applied to design and implement a new collaboration tool to enhance the awareness capability of collaboration and increase the efficiency of cooperative work in CGAG.

Server consists of event service, workspace service, collaboration application service. Event service provides users with a group communication-oriented receipt and distribution services. It is responsible for receiving all the events within the system, putting the events into the queue with a FIFO sequence, calling the handling methods that are registered for the events, updating system status, and providing the delivery method for workspace service and collaboration application service.

The function of workspace service is to provide users with an overall environment. It guarantees the users in the same workspace to see the same environmental information, including online users, collaborative grid applications that have been established and so on. Users can only exchange with the entities in the workspace, in order to avoid interference with entities in other establishments. To achieve this goal, it synchronizes the virtual workspace state between each client and manages a number of collaborative grid applications.

Based on the object-method graph of collaborative grid application and the formulas of the model, collaborative application services calculate the influencing scope of collaborators' actions, and provide the state maintenance synchronously for every collaborative grid application. Moreover, collaborative application services provide a consistent view for the collaborators who join the application later.

Client is divided into 4 parts including grid service interface, events client, workspace client, and collaborative application client. Firstly, collaborative collaborators land to server through client, and obtain the information (including the information that describe the collaborative application) of workspace state from the server. Then, collaborative collaborators join the collaborative application, and get the state information of application from the server, such as task that needs to be done currently, content, and the list of participants. In succession, collaborators choose relevant subtasks depending on personal interest and ability, and develop the collaborative work. Grid service interface provides the unified interfaces to invoke grid service, and receive the variational information of grid services' states. Event client provides a unified interface to dispose events for upper-level service. Workspace client is responsible for providing the graphical interface and communication tools for users, so that the users can conveniently manage their own spaces, find out collaborative grid applications or build up their own. Collaboration application client provides the unified expressive modality of collaborative tasks' state interface and methods interface, and users' action information.

4 Evaluation

4.1 Heuristic Evaluation

Heuristic method [16] is used to evaluate the usability of this model, according to the types of collaborative awareness presented by Guwin in the reference [9], five heuristics can be summarized as follows.

1) What are the tasks of applications? The operation nodes in object-method graph that should be completed by collaborators represent the tasks. 2) Has the task been completed? ROS relation represents the task's state. When all the object nodes' states are finished, the task has been completed. 3) What are the tasks being carried out by other collaborators? The object node that the collaborator was operating represents this collaborator's task. 4) What are other collaborators doing? ACT relation represents the collaborator's action. 5) What is the next step of other collaborators? If the current task has not been completed, the collaborator's next step is still at this task. If not, the next step could be deduced by the position of this collaborator in the object-method graph.

Based on the calculation method of awareness intensity, it presents that collaborative awareness model uses the interdependent relationship and the action relationship to describe the relationship between the collaborators and cooperative tasks in collaborative grid applications, and solve the former problem that it can not predetermine the accurate correspondence relationship among roles and tasks, roles and actions.

Therefore, by the analysis above, the usability of this collaboration awareness model is to provide the state of the tasks in collaborative grid applications, and the information such as tasks, actions and intentions being carried out by the other collaborators. What's more, through the interdependent relationship and the operation relationship, and based on the correlative degree among the actions of collaborators, it quantifies accurately the awareness intensity, calculates the awareness space, and filters irrelevant information to increase the efficiency of cooperative work.

4.2 Experiment

Given a collaborative grid application, we compared the CGAG collaboration tool with AGTK collaboration tool, in order to verify that the CGAG collaborative tool based-on this model can reduce the amount of information within a certain scope and increase the efficiency of cooperative work in Access Grid.

In AGTK, each collaborator acquires all of the information because of application-based collaborative awareness. For the N collaborators, each collaborator should send out own action events and receive the information of all the collaborators. Given L is the amount of action events sent by all the collaborators, the total flux of information in the collaboration process is:

$$I = L + NL = (N+1)L.$$

In CGAG, each collaborator sent own information, and meanwhile receives the information of other collaborators within the scope of his awareness space. So the total flux of information is:

$$I = L + \sum_{j=1}^{M}\sum_{i=1}^{N} AS(user_i, t_j) = L + \sum_{j=1}^{M}\sum_{i=1}^{N} \left\{ act \,\middle|\, Aware(user_i, t_j, act) \geq x_i, act \in ACT_{t_j} \right\}$$

Xi is the awareness threshold set by each collaborator. According to the formulas of calculating the amount of information, the difference of total information flux of the two tools is:

$$I_{diff} = NL - \sum_{j=1}^{M}\sum_{i=1}^{N} AS(user_i, t_j)$$

1) $I_{diff} = 0$. When the thresholds of all collaborators are set as $X = 0$, it means that all collaborators will apperceive all the actions, so $NL = \sum_{j=1}^{M}\sum_{i=1}^{N} AS(user_i, t_j)$.

2) $I_{diff} > 0$: When the thresholds $X \neq 0$, the collaborators can only receive the actions of other collaborators within their own awareness space, so $NL > \sum_{j=1}^{M}\sum_{i=1}^{N} AS(user_i, t_j)$.

Thus, CGAG collaboration tool can reduce more information amount of collaborative tasks in service-based grid applications than the AGTK. Furthermore, we developed the collaborative grid application for this experiment with Globus Toolkit 4, and the collaborative task is described as follows.

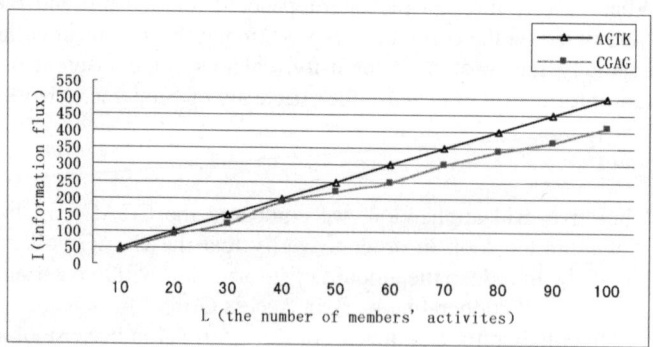

Fig. 4. Relation between L (the number of actions) and I (the information flux)

There are eight services in this application, which represent eight subtasks. Each service has two or three methods to provide the different operations, and there are ten collaborators in total. It was recorded that the total information flux produced in collaboration process of CGAG and AGTK for 10 times to verify the result of above qualitative analysis. The experimental data is shown in Figure 4, N (the number of collaborative collaborators" actions) is invariable, and I (the information flux) was recorded according to the changes of L (the number of collaborators) in 10 times measure.

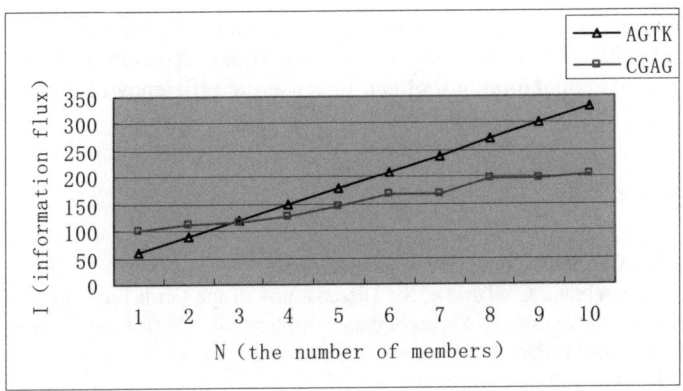

Fig. 5. Relation between N (the number of collaborators) and I (the information flux)

When the number of collaborators is invariable, it can be clearly seen that the number of information brought by CGAG is smaller than the one brought by AGTK. As shown in Figure 5, L (the total number of collaborators' actions) is invariable, and I (the information flux) was recorded according to the changes of N (the number of collaborators) in 10 times measure. As the number of collaborators increases, the numbers of information in AGTK in-creases by direct proportion. But the number of information in CGAG increases with a slow increase trend.

Therefore, through heuristic evaluation of this model and an experiment, it is verified that this model and its collaboration tool can provide adequate cooperation information, reduce the cost and conflicts, and increase the efficiency of cooperative work in Access Grid.

5 Conclusions

Collaborative awareness support is a basic requirement of Access Grid, and is needed to provide adequate awareness information for collaborators to effectively cooperate with grid applications. However, most existing collaborative awareness models are unable to characterize the dynamic relationships between collaborators and their tasks with the standards of OGSA and WSRF. In this paper, a new dynamic collaborative awareness model is proposed to characterize the dynamic relationships between collaborators and tasks for service-based collaborative grid applications in Access Grid. Based on the dynamic properties of services and the relationships between collaborators and services, this model firstly calculates the degrees of correlations between the actions of collaborators, and quantifies the intensities of each collaborator's awareness of other collaborators' actions, secondly divides awareness spaces by comparing the awareness intensities with their thresholds, thirdly selects and filters cooperation information according to the awareness spaces to increase the efficiency of cooperative work.

Based on this model, a collaboration tool is designed and implemented for an Access Grid system, and includes grid service interface, event service, space service, collaboration service and related clients. Finally, the usability of this model is evaluated with the heuristic method, and an experiment is given to demonstrate that this model and its collaboration tool can increase the efficiency of cooperative work in Access Grid.

References

1. Access Grid Web Pages, http://www.accessgrid.org
2. Foster, I., Kesselman, C., Tuecke, S.: The anatomy of the Grid: Enabling scalable virtual organizations. Int' Journal of Supercomputer Applications 15(3), 1–10 (2001)
3. GGF, Global Grid Forum, http://www.gridforum.org
4. The AG Toolkit. Software (April 2007), http://www-unix.mcs.anl.gov/fl/research/accessgrid
5. Benford, S.D., Fahlen, L.E.: A spatial model of interaction in large virtual environments. In: Proceedings of the 3rd European Conference on CSCW (ECSCW 1993), pp. 109–124. Kluwer Academic Publishers, Milan, Italy (1993)
6. Rodden, T.: Populating the application: a model of awareness for cooperative applications. In: Proceedings of the ACM CSCW 1996 Conference on Computer-Supported Cooperative Work, pp. 87–96. ACM Press, Boston (1996)
7. Daneshgar, F., Ray, P.: Awareness modeling and its application in cooperative network management. In: Proceedings of the 7th IEEE International Conference on Parallel and Distributed Systems, pp. 357–363. IEEE Press, Iwate, Japan (2000)
8. Sheng, G., Dianfu, M., Jinpeng, H.: A role-based group awareness model. Journal of Software 12(6), 864–869 (2001)
9. Gutwin, C.: Workspace awareness in real-time distributed groupware. Calgary, the University of Calgary (1997)
10. Drury, J., Williams, M.G.: A framework for role-based specification and evaluation of awareness support in synchronous collaborative applications. In: Proceedings of the Eleventh IEEE International Workshops on Enabling Technologies (WET ICE 2002), pp. 12–17. IEEE Press, Pittsburgh (2002)
11. Gutwin, C., Greenberg, S.: A descriptive framework of work space awareness for real-time groupware. Computer-Supported Cooperative Work 34, 411–446 (2002)
12. Jin, H.: ChinaGrid: Making Grid Computing a Reality. In: Chen, Z., Chen, H., Miao, Q., Fu, Y., Fox, E., Lim, E.-p. (eds.) ICADL 2004. LNCS, vol. 3334, pp. 13–24. Springer, Heidelberg (2004)
13. Chen, X., Ji, X., Jiang, K., Li, Y.: New toolkits for creating grid-based colabrative applications in CGAG. In: IEEE Swarm Intelligence Symposium, Indianapolis, Indiana, USA, pp. 191–196 (2006)
14. The Advanced Collaborative Environments (ACE) Research Group, https://forge.gridforum.org/projects/ace-rg
15. The China Education and Research Network, http://www.edu.cn
16. Molich, R., Nielsen, J.: Improving a human-computer dialog. Communications of the ACM 33(3), 338–348 (1990)

A Suggested Framework for Exploring Contextual Information to Evaluate and Recommend Services

Hao Wu[1], Fei Luo[2], Xiaomin Ning[2], and Hai Jin[2]

[1] School of Information Science and Engineering, Yunnan University,
No.2, North Green Lake Road, Kunming, P.R. China, 650091
haowu@ynu.edu.cn
[2] School of Computer, Huazhong University of Science and Technology,
1037 Luoyu Road, Wuhan, P.R. China, 430074
{luofeiren,ningxm,hjin}@hust.edu.cn

Abstract. Web services are service endpoints in Service Oriented Architecture (SOA). If the SOA paradigm succeeds there will be soon several thousand services, which can be used for composing required applications. For this, these services must first be discovered. However, the existing infrastructure for services publishing and management are built on the back of centralized registry (mostly as UDDI). They lack the flexibility to support personalized user requirements, known as services evaluation, services recommendation. In this paper, we will suggest a framework exploiting link analysis mechanism to assist web services discovery. The main idea is measuring the importance of a service within services network, and then recommending the services to end users. By pass, the user's private requirements will be considered.

1 Introduction

Service-oriented architectures (SOA) emphasize that it is the service that counts for the customer, not the specific software or hardware component that is used to implement it. SOAs will likely become a leading software paradigm quickly. However, they will not scale without significant mechanization of service discovery. At present, there are totally three kinds of approaches for discovering web service (cf. [1]). The first of which is the core web service standard UDDI (Universal Description, Discovery, and Integration). It is a standard for centralized repositories and important software vendors that run so-called UDDI Business Registries (UBR) as search points for services. The second approach depends on specific resources for locating available web services. These web services either crawl the web and aggregate the content found, or revert to databases with manually registered services. The third approach accesses standard web search engines that restrict the search to WSDL files.

However, mostly those discovery schemas are built on back of the registry infrastructures as UDDI. UDDI offers a limited set of query facilities to allow end-users to search for services. The model for discovery is that of browsing: a user may browse all services provided by a specified business, or all the services corresponding to a specified category. This type of search has some drawbacks: it may return an unmanageable number of results, and requires a high degree of human-user involvement. Another problem in searching the UDDI registry is that publishers often misinterpret the meaning of the different fields in the UDDI data structures [1]. The missing information, coupled with the highly-structured search parameters required to search a UDDI registry may be detrimental to the completeness of service discovery. Moreover, it lacks the flexibility to support personalized user requirements, known as services evaluation, services recommendation.

In this paper, we will propose a method exploiting contextual analysis mechanism to assist Web services discovery. The main idea is measuring the importance of a service within services network, and then recommending the services to end users. By pass, the user's private requirements will be considered.

The rest of paper is structured as follows. Section 2 presents the recommendation framework. We will interpret how to deploy it with existing discovery infrastructures. In section 3, we present a simple context model in which the question how the services network is will be addressed. The different elements affecting the importance of a service will be presented respectively. Next, we will design concrete computation policy and recommendation mechanism based on former context. Then, the related works are reviewed in section 5. Finally, a conclusion and future works are given.

2 Service Evaluation and Recommendation Framework

Figure 1 shows the deployment framework of evaluation and recommendation mechanism. The skeleton mainly includes the information storage infrastructure of UDDI registry and Context Knowledge Base (KB), discovery portal, evaluation sub-system and recommendation module. The user can discover services and obtain assistant services from this system.

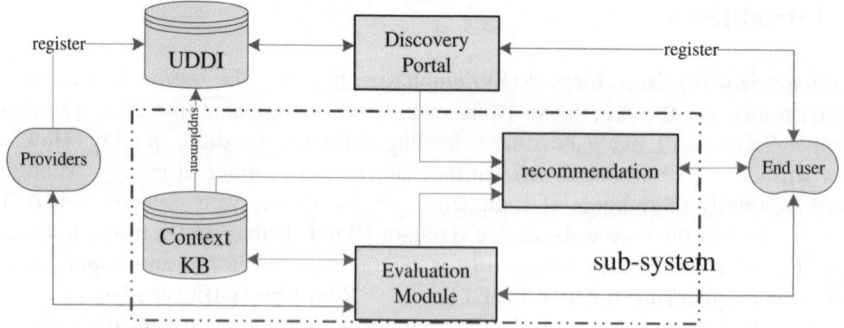

Fig. 1. The deployment framework of evaluation and recommendation mechanism

UDDI Registry is a general designation for all sites which provide public UDDI registration service. It is a logic consolidation, but is implemented by physical distributed architecture. The different registration sites are inter-connected by Peer-to-Peer architecture. Therefore, the user can access the whole UDDI registry by entering any operator site. UDDI stores the basic information about a service, such as functional description, non-functional description. By traversing the UDDI, we can obtain the link structure among services and providers, etc.

Context Knowledge Base (KB) stores the contextual information which are organized and stored in ontology (here, we use the standard RDF(S) language). The concrete composition of the context is discussed at next section.

The service discovery portal provides users the first hand discovery service. Evaluation and recommendation system are being as the supplementary module of the discovery portal. The user can enter into the online portal to organize and manage his social network. The social networks of the users are also service spreading chains, it indicates how the services transfer and exchange at consumer's groups. Such contextual data of the users' social network facilitate the social network based ranking to the services. At last, all services contextual information will be taken as the fact, and put into semantic network to infer out the services related with user's request.

The whole processing of the framework is given as followings:

a) The evaluation module periodically reads the contextual information from the context KB, and does global co-ranking for the objects of the service network, then caches the computation results.

b) An end user enters into the discovery portal to search service information, for example, he/she may input keywords and find a list of relevant services.

c) The recommendation module analyses the social context of the current user. Then for each service object inside the result collection returned by step b), it calculates the social-network-based ranking value.

d) The recommendation module interacts with the end user, and then makes final recommendation by integrating relevance ranking, global co-ranking and social-network-based ranking.

3 Modeling Simple Context Inside Services Network

Nowadays, the context plays an importance role in pervasive computing environment [2]. There are many works which focus on how to completely model application's context. To achieve our target and exploit the power of contextual information, the application context about services must be carefully considered.

The current service ontology (refer to OWL-S [3]) describes some metadata of web service, among them, some characteristics can be seen as the makeup of the special context. We go into details of the context information below.

Service Citation: Citation relations between scientific literatures or web pages play key role in measuring importance of the objects of literatures or pages, since all successful page linking analysis are based on this kind of citation meaning. Following a similar train of thought, if a service is taken as service module by other services to participate in the service composition or cooperation computing, its importance will be determined very easily. We can define the probability that a certain web service X can be reached at a certain depth, given that another web service Y has been accessed. Web services can also be considered as web resources that point to other web resources. Assume a web service Y that provides a semantic data type T as an output parameter, and a web service X that accepts data type T as its input parameter. In this case, we assume that there is a forward link between X and Y. Likewise; we can define backward links as well. This kind of relation among services constitutes the hard core of the service network. Suppose that there exists a knowledge repository which stores linking descriptions of composition services or workflows (e.g., built with BPEL), we can easily obtain the available citation graph of services.

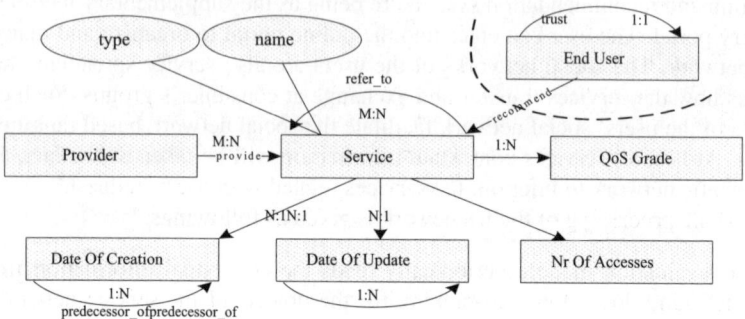

Fig. 2. A service context schema

Service Provider: Some service providers will have cooperative relations with others; the low level providers may lend the foundation service for the high level providers. This kind of phenomenon exists extensively on present Internet, for example, the network service provider (ISP) will supply a basic rental service for the contents service provider (ASP). Certainly, the social connection of the providers has already been contained into services citation, therefore it does not need consider provision relations among the service providers; however, a big service provider may offer many services series, correspondingly its influence would also be great. The importance of the provider would affect the rank of the services offered by provider itself when determining the importance of services.

End User: The end user means the person (may be agent) purely using the services. The service provider may act a dual role as a provider and a customer in the meantime, here we use "terminal" to show differentiation. The function which the end user acts probably contains two aspects: on one hand, the hobby of the customer will influence the ranking of services. The different customer has different loyalty to the different service provider, and such ingredient will cause its preference for some special services. On the other hand, the dissemination network of the end user will influence the service network creation. Just such as front say, services spreading inside social network will have a so-called civil influence. Therefore, the ranking method that can aware the customer's requirement will make sense.

Service Non-functional Aspect: Currently, the elements which can mark the service grade all concentrate at the non-functional aspect of services description. For example, the QoS grade [4] has a range of 0 to 1. When a service participates a combination, its QoS grade becomes great useful under the condition that the whole service flow need consider QoS constraints. In the meantime, service's flow will consider how much other possible paths exist, between two services. The safe degree and credibility of a single service are very crucial for insuring the whole credibility of the work flow project. Owing to this, the safe factor and the QoS grade of the service will be important context elements.

Services History Records: History records include creation date of the service, update date of the service, and access times of the service, and so on. Such history records indicate externally temporal information about a service and reflect the user activities. They can influence the ranking computation and the evaluation for a service. Obviously, a newer service with high access frequency would be more attractive for the end users. To represent how these factors influence to evaluate services, we just include these factors into our context schema and assign different weights to different context relations.

We conclude the contextual information that can affect the evaluation for a service, and propose a simple context schema shown as Fig. 2. Our contextual information graphs add additional information to the services and connect the services. This makes it possible to use link-based algorithms like PageRank[5] to enhance ranking. In next step, we will design the recommendation mechanism on the base of this context schema.

4 Designing Evaluation and Recommendation Mechanism Based on Contextual Information

Given the fact that rank computation on the service network would not be possible without the contextual information, which provides semantic links among resources, thus in section 3, a context schema has been created to describe all aspects and relationships among resources influencing the ranking. In this section, we have to specify how these aspects influence importance.

4.1 Global Co-ranking

To decide an importance or impact factor of a service network entity, we borrow the concept of authority transfer schema graphs from the work [6]. It extends database schemas by adding weights and edges in order to express how importance propagates among the entities. These weights and edges represent authority transfer annotations, which extend our context schema with the information. We need to compute ranks for all instances of the classes defined in the context schema.

Fig.3 depicts the weighted context schema for global co-ranking. The edges represent the relations between concepts are annotated with weights and these weights are suggested by domain experts with careful consideration. Every edge from the schema graph is splitted into pair-wised to indicate the forwarding and backward transferring status. This is motivated by the observation that authority potentially flows in both directions and not only in the direction that appears in the schema: if we know that a particular provider is important, we also want all services offered by this provider ranked higher; vice versa, many services offered by this provider ranked higher will highly improve its prestige. In the next, we will shortly introduce this computation.

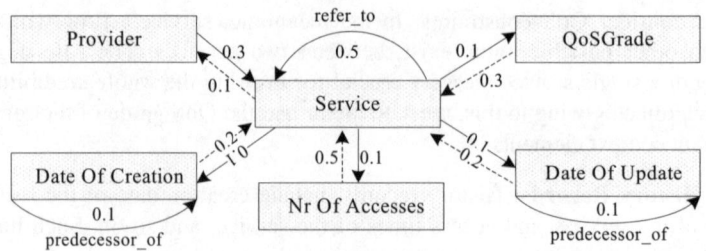

Fig. 3. Weighted context schema for global co-ranking

PageRank is an ordering nodes technique via a random surfer model in a directed graph $G = (V, E)$, where $V = \{v_1, ..., v_n\}$ is the set of nodes (web pages) and E is the set of edges (hyperlinks). The random surfer performs a Markovian walk on G. The surfer jumps from node to node following a hyperlink with uniform probability d or gets bored and jumps to a random node with probability $1-d$, where d is the dampening factor and is usually set to 0.85. The PageRank value of node v_i is the probability $p(v_i)$ that the surfer is at the given node v_i. Let p be the vector $[p(v_1), ..., p(v_i), ..., p(v_n)]^T$, then successively iterates the following ranking formulation using power method computing until convergence:

$$p^{(m)} = d \cdot A \cdot p^{(m-1)} + \frac{(1-d)}{|V|} \cdot r \qquad (1)$$

Here A is an $n \times n$ matrix with elements $A_{ij} = 1/h_j$ if there is a hyperlink from v_j to v_i, and h_j is the outgoing degree of v_j, and $A_{ij} = 0$ otherwise. The personalization vector r can bias the surfer to prefer certain kinds of node when getting bored and is set as unit vector in standard PageRank.

A data instance graph should adhere to the data schema graph. The ranking focuses on the instances level other than the schema level. In the data instance graph, given the source node v_i and the edge $e: v_i \rightarrow v_j$ with the relationship type T, the edge weight $w(e)$ is computed as follows:

$$w(e) = \begin{cases} \dfrac{w(T)}{OutDegree(v_i, T)}, & \text{if } OutDegree(v_i, T) > 0 \\ 0, & \text{otherwise} \end{cases} \qquad (2)$$

In Equation 2, $w(T)$ is the edge weigh of the relationship typed T in the data schema graph, and $OutDegree(v_i, T)$ is the number of outlinks typed T from v_i.

Based on the above information, the global co-ranking process works as follows: At every stage of the new services registration (we can set a threshold to spring the ranking computation process, for example, the proportion of newly increased services reaches 5%), the algorithm examines the UDDI and the contextual knowledge base to build a data instance graph corresponding to the context data schema graph; Then, initialize the adjacent matrix A according to equation 2, also set personalization vector r as unit vector $[1.0f, ..., 1.0f, ..., 1.0f]^T$; Finally, carry out equation 1 to get the iterative pageranks. Each pagerank value is linked to corresponding object of the data instance graph and the importance of object is decided by its pagerank value. More meaningfully, global co-ranking need not be calculated at discovery time since it is computationally demanding, and we can keep offline processing to a minimum (For more details of the computation, refer to works in [6]). The global co-ranking value (GR) of each entity can be stored in the contextual knowledge base until being updated at next time.

4.2 Social-Network-Based Ranking

Using trust and reputation mechanisms offers a promising way to solve the web service selection problem. In distributed scenario, each user may share service resources within the social network. If a user receives service information with recommendation from several members of his interest group, for which he has different levels of trust, he would like to regard more important for the service information received from his most trusted neighbors. The benefits of the web in nearly every context is that individuals have control over their own data, and that data is maintained in a distributed way. While most social networks on the web currently are within closed websites, restricted only to members, the Semantic Web provides a method by which data can be stored anywhere and integrated through a common foundation. Therefore, in our framework, we just propose a closed social network website where users can register as members to retrieval web services and exchange private preference information.

To take different trust values for different peers into account for ranking services, we present social-network-based ranking, which is computed using the trust values (direct or inferred) for the people who have rated the service (the raters). For the set of selected users N, the Social-Network-Based Ranking SR from user u to service s is the average of the service ratings from users in N weighted by the trust value t from u to each user (shown as formula 3). As a simple example, consider the following: Wu trusts Luo 0.8; Wu trusts Ning 0.5; Luo rates the service "Online Sales" with 4 stars; Ning rates the service "Online Sales" with 2 stars. Then Wu's SR for "Online Sales" is calculated as $(0.8*4+0.5*2)/((0.8+0.4)*5)=3.5$. If we normalize SR by $SR/max(SR)$, the final value would be $3.5/5=0.7$.

$$SR_{u \to s} = \sum_{i \in N} t_{u \to i} \cdot SR_{i \to s} \bigg/ \sum_{i \in N} t_{u \to i} \quad (3)$$

If the user u has directly assigned a trust rating to another user i, then the trust value $t_{u \to i}$ is known. If u has not rated i, we need to infer how much u might trust i. Trust inference systems are a growing area of interest. Here, we utilize TidalTrust [7], a breadth first search-based algorithm that outputs an inferred trust value by finding paths form u to i and composing the trust values found along those paths inside a social network. First, the system searches for raters that the source knows directly. If there are no direct connections from the user to any raters, the system moves one step out to find connections from the user to raters of path length 2. This process repeats until a path is found. Then, the trust value is calculated by TidalTrust for each rater at the given depth. Finally, the selected rater set N will be determined; their ratings for the service (maybe in number of stars) are averaged.

4.3 Recommendation

Our recommendation is designed to work with service discovery process. Here we generalize the service discovery process on the base of the service semantics. Following formula (a) represents the semantic of Service Ontology, in which QoS Profile (We proposed QoS ontology to represent the semantics of QoS layer in [8]) semantically describes quality information of a service; Others Profile meets an emergency for services. Service Query (b) and Service Advertisement (c) both are formulated by the Service Ontology. Service discovery is executed by logic-based precise matchmaking $matches(Q)=\{A \in s | \neg (A \sqcap Q \sqsubseteq \bot)\}$ or relevance-based selection between query and advertisement $matches(Q)=\{A \in s | Sim(Q,A) > threshold\}$.

$$\text{ServiceOntology} \equiv \text{ServiceProfile} \sqcup \text{QoSProfile} \sqcup \text{OthersProfile} \quad (a)$$

$$\text{ServiceQuery} \sqsubseteq \text{ServiceOntology} \quad (b)$$

$$\text{ServiceAdvertise} \sqsubseteq \text{ServiceOntology} \quad (c)$$

To recommend services, we consider two scenarios:

1. The users want to know the reputation of a services provider, or the rank level of a service instead of making discovery. Under this condition, we just tell the users how important the provider is, or the global co-ranking value and social network based ranking level corresponding to the target service. Users can make a private evaluation according to such ranking guideline.

2. The users need locate services. For this case, the users may first make a searching by inputting keyword or submitting a request formalized by services ontology. Whatever happens, the users may find many similar services. To overcome this problem, we propose such policies:

Let matching degree between query and answer $matches(Q)$, let the global co-ranking of the first matched service s as $GR(s)$, and let the Social-Network-Based Ranking of the current user with the service s as $SR(s)$. First, make an amalgamation with $matches(Q)$, $GR(s)$ and $SR(s)$, and then recommend the top-n services to the users. The recommendation metric is shown as formula 4, where λ is the coefficient to balance $GR(s)$ and $SR(s)$. If $\lambda = 1$, the social network based ranking value will not be considered; if $\lambda = 0$, the global co-ranking value will not act up. Since $GR(s)$ is usually larger than 1.0, we use $GR'(s) = \sqrt{GR(s)/max(GR)}$ to normalize it, where $max(GR)$ means the highest global co-ranking value in service network. We also call the right part of the multiply symbol as Contextual-Ranking, accordingly, $CR(s)$ is the contextual ranking value of the service s.

$$RecDegree_s = matches(Q) * [\lambda \cdot GR'(s) + (1-\lambda) \cdot SR(s)] \quad (4)$$

In addition, for the user, they can set a threshold to filter those matching results, the results larger than the threshold will be returned to the end users, and those services not very satisfy request will be discarded.

5 Case Study and Discussions

We gather a dataset about 500 services from the Web and make an analysis; however, these services lack enough contextual information. The services are most submitted by self-governed organizations or personnel, and lack interconnection. Therefore, the case study is made by simulation examples.

According to the former analysis, we can see that the service network connect among each other, and can be modeled as a collaboration network like the science collaboration network (SCN). Furthermore, Newman has already announced the public SCN is scale-free network and the node distribution obeys the power-law discipline [9]. According to this principle, we give an emulation network composed of 10 services and 4 service providers. The services are interconnected through the invocation relations and have no loop path in the connection graph. Each service randomly belongs to a service provider. In addition, each service is assigned with some topics to simulate the content matching condition.

Table 1. The contextual information of the services network

Entity	Semantic Relations	Entity
P_1	provides ↔ provided_by	S_1, S_2, S_3
P_2	same as above	S_4, S_5, S_6, S_7
P_3	same as above	S_8, S_9
P_4	same as above	S_{10}
S_3	refer_to ↔ referred_by	S_4
S_7	same as above	S_4, S_6
S_8	same as above	S_7
S_9	same as above	S_2
S_{10}	same as above	S_1, S_9

Although considering two kinds of entities, in actually, the service provider also acts as the role of the customer. The invocation times of the service can also reflect its visited frequent degree; therefore, it can also get a reasonable result. Table 1 shows the contextual information of the services network. To easily remember, we rename and mark the network entities above-mentioned, where P represents a provider and S indicates a service.

For the first recommendation scenario, we use the global co-ranking algorithm to work on the data example, then obtain the providers ranking sequence as $\{P_2 \to P_1 \to P_3 \to P_4\}$ and the services ranking sequence $\{S_4 \to S_6 \to S_7 \to S_5 \to S_2 \to S_1 \to S_3 \to S_9 \to S_{10} \to S_8\}$, respectively. From the ranking order of the provider, we can see that P_1 and P_2 both have two services to participate in service composition of the third party, however, the importance of P_1 decreases reasonably and is debased after P_2 owing to S_3 of the P_1 invocating S_4 of the P_2. P_4 lies in the last stage because its services refer to the services provided by P_3 and P_1; furthermore, its service access times are zero.

Next step, to easily analyze the rationality of the services ranking, we compute the services importance only by considering the service citation relationship (This process applies PageRank on service reference graph) and achieve such outcome

{S_4–S_2–S_7–S_6–S_1/S_9–S_3–S_8/S_{10}–S_5} where '/' means coordinate ranking. After comparing it with the former sequence, we can see that our global co-ranking can weigh the importance of services impersonally and restrain the inequality leaded by services self-invocation of the service provider. This conclusion is based on such observation, namely, S_7 of the P_2 self-invocates S_6 and S_7 is externally invocated one time. In general, S_6 must be important than S_7. However, if only ranking them by reference relation, the importance of S_6 is underestimated owing to self-invocation of the P_2; On the contrary, if the contextual information is considered, such problem can easily be alleviated and the importance of S_6 will be measured more reasonably.

For the second scenario, several queries contain specific topics are issued, and then recommendation is carried out on returned matching results. We obtain a promising conclusion that the average positive evaluation of recommendation result at top1 and top2 can reach 80%. For example, there hit four services S_2, S_6, S_7 and S_{10} when the query "online sales" is issued by the user U_1. Their matching degree $matches(Q, S)$ are 0.8, 0.8, 0.6 and 0.7; $GR(s)$ are 0.844809, 1.349823, 1.127907 and 0.315490, respectively, $max(GR)$ is 3.766379. If we do not consider $SR(s)$ ($\lambda = 1$), the recommended result list will be S_6, S_7, S_2 and S_{10}. Obviously, the most suitable service S_6 is ranked at first as our expectation. However, if we consider the $SR(s)$, the result whose match degree is not high can also be recommended at leading position. We use the example data shown as Table 2, where U_1's trust network is given and his/her friends have rated the services, to demonstrate this change. By using formula 3, we can obtain the $SR(s)$ sequence of the former result as {0.6, 0.55, 0.84, 0.6}. If we filter the result only by considering the trust network ($\lambda = 0$), the recommendation list will be S_7, S_2, S_6 and S_{10}. Suppose that λ is set as 0.5, the $CR(s)$ sequence of the former result is 0.53, 0.57, 0.70 and 0.45, and then the final list is S_6, S_2, S_7 and S_{10}. Obviously, the services that have both the higher matching degree with request and the good contextual force will rank higher.

Table 2. A simulated trust network for case study

	U_1	U_2	U_3	U_4	S_1	S_2	S_3	S_4	S_5	S_6	S_7	S_8	S_9	S_{10}
U_1	1.0	0.8	0.6	0.4	/	/	/	/	/	/	/	/	/	/
U_2	/	/	/	/	/	3	/	/	/	3	4	/	/	3
U_3	/	/	/	/	/	3	/	/	/	3	4	/	/	3
U_4	/	/	/	/	/	3	/	/	/	4	5	/	/	/

According to case study, we can learn that our service recommendation mechanism can satisfy the application requirements in a flexible manner. Each part of the recommendation expression can be solely used. GR(s) can measure the importance of the services and the service providers. SR(s) can be used to adjust the recommendation order by collaboration filter. CR(s) can indicate the service force inside the service network. They can all solely work with the existing ranked matching methods. Despite lacking the further practical verification, we also confirm it is a promising way to enhance the existing service discovery mechanisms.

6 Related Works

The services discovery research has lasted a long time and there emerge various service selection methods. [10] and [11] both are logic-based matchmaking. They rank the services by the matching degree. [12] makes service selection on the base of relevance computation. However, they both lack global evaluation capacity. They can only be used to decide whether the service satisfy the service request or not, but not evaluate how about the providers. More important, they work on the service ontology or WSDL structures instead of the contextual information. Whereas, our approach is based on the contextual information and can be a good reinforce for these mature discovery methods.

The idea of exploiting link analysis to observe service network has been also suggested in [13]. The authors use a set of heuristics derived from the connectivity structure of the service repository in order to effectively guide the composition process. The methodologies described in this paper are also inspired by research in areas of citation analyze. But we give a different research on this field and propose an adaptive link analysis method to deal with services evaluation. We also give a context schema to model the contextual information which may influence the services ranking. In addition, considering the end user's discovery requirement, we have designed the recommendation mechanism to help them.

Another relevant works are exploiting the context information to discovery services, such as [14-16]. However, these works focus on dynamic selecting and recommending service by matching contextual information inside pervasive computing environment. Compared with them, we handle the contextual information in a totally different way. Our context schema composes of the semantic relationship inside the service network and the user activity information, while their schemas usually include temporal, spatial information and non-functional information about services.

7 Conclusion and Future Works

An approach for promote service discovery based on capture the contexts inside the services network is proposed in detailed. With the deep development of the services oriented computing, the services network will shows a complicate environment, like the scientific collaboration network which shows the power-law discipline and possess the classical properties of social networks. Thus, we exploit link analysis method to observe new questions in services network, and the fact prove our idea is a promise way to evaluate and recommend service. Now, we are implementing the framework as a pluggable module. Next step we will plant it to our services search engine or a complete registry center to make realistic contributions. The realistic evaluation will also be done to improve our context model.

Acknowledgment. This work is supported by the Scientific Research Project of Yunnan University under Grant No. 2007Z006C.

References

1. Bachlechner, D., Siorpaes, K., Fensel, D., Toma, I.: Web Service Discovery – A Reality Check, Technical Report, DERI – Digital Enterprise Research Institute, January 17 (2006)
2. Satyanarayanan, M.: Pervasive Computing: Vision and Challenges. IEEE Personal Communications 8(4), 10–17 (2001)
3. McIlraith, S.A., Martin, D.L.: Bringing Semantics to Web Services. IEEE Intelligent Systems 18(1), 90–93 (2003)
4. Menasce, D.A.: Composing Web Service: A QoS View. IEEE Internet Computing 8(6), 88–90 (2004)
5. Brin, S., Page, L.: The Anatomy of A Large-Scale Hypertextual Web Search Engine. In: Proceedings of the 7th International Conference on World Wide Web, pp. 107–117 (1998)
6. Balmin, A., Hristidis, V., Papakonstantinou, Y.: ObjectRank: Authority-Based Keyword Search in Databases. In: Proceedings of the 30th International Conference on Very Large Data Bases (VLDB 2004), pp. 564–575 (2004)
7. Golbeck, J., Hendler, J.: Inferring Binary Trust Relationships in Web-Based Social Networks. ACM Transaction on Internet Technology 6(4), 497–529 (2006)
8. Jin, H., Wu, H.: Semantic-enabled Specification for Web Service Agreement. International Journal of Web Services Practices 1(1-2), 13–20 (2005)
9. Newman, J.M.E.: The Structure of Scientific Collaboration Networks. Proceedings of the National Academy of Sciences 98, 404–409 (2001)
10. Li, L., Horrocks, I.: A Software Framework for Matchmaking Based on Semantic Web Technology. In: Proceedings of the 12th International World Wide Web Conference, pp. 331–339 (2003)
11. Paolucci, M., Kawamura, T., Payne, T.R., Sycara, K.P.: Semantic Matching of Web Services Capabilities. In: Proceedings the 1st International Semantic Web Conference, Sardinia, Italy, June 2002, pp. 333–347 (2002)
12. Wang, Y., Stroulia, E.: Semantic Structure Matching for Assessing Web-Service Similarity. In: Proceedings of First International Conference on Service Oriented Computing, Trento, Italy, December 15-18 (2003)
13. Gekas, J., Fasli, M.: Automatic Web Service Composition Based on Graph Network Analysis Metrics. In: Meersman, R., Tari, Z. (eds.) OTM 2005. LNCS, vol. 3761, pp. 1571–1587. Springer, Heidelberg (2005)
14. Most'efaoui, S.K., Tafat-Bouzid, A., Hirsbrunner, B.: Using Context Information for Service Discovery and Composition. In: Proceedings of the Fifth International Conference on Information Integration and Web-based Applications and Services (IIWAS 2003), pp. 129–138 (2003)
15. Pawar, P., Tomakoff, A.: Ontology-based Context-Aware Service Discovery for Pervasive Environments. In: Proceedings of the First IEEE International Workshop on Service Integration in Pervasive Environments (2006)
16. Bottaro, A., Hall, R.S.: Dynamic Contextual Service Ranking. In: Proceedings of the 6th International Symposium on Software Composition, Braga, Portugal (March 2007)

A Model of Service Scheduling Based on Market Mechanism and Semantic

Gang Wang[1], Yuhui Qiu[1,*], and Guolin Pu[2]

[1] Semantic Grid Laboratory, Southwest University, ChongQing, 400715, P.R. China
[2] Computer Science Department, SiChuan University of Arts and Science, DaZhou, 635000, P.R. China
{wangg,yhqiu,glpu}@swu.edu.cn

Abstract. We should do service scheduling in pervasive environments. By comparing some present resource scheduling methods and discussing the importance of combining the market mechanism with semantic, we propose a model of service scheduling based on market mechanism and semantic (Market-Semantic). It includes the similarity measure between ontologies, the ascertaining of utility functions and resource price. By designing a new method to measure the similarity between ontology, and by looking on the ratio of capability and cost as the utility functions, we explore a method of service scheduling by which users not only can get the service satisfied, but also the resource can be allocated efficiently, Finally, the experiment proves that our method is better than the methods of Max-Semantic and Semantic-Cost-Max-Min.

Keywords: Market mechanism, Ontology, Similarity Measure, Service scheduling, Semantic, Grid.

1 Introduction

Ontology is used widely in knowledge express [1], context awareness computing, literature retrieval and semantic web. It can provide the common knowledge and concepts of a field, and it's a tool to share the knowledge. Also it provides reason mechanism to reason based on the relations, there are four basic relations in ontology, which are the part of, kind of, instance of and attribute of. We can show the ontology by ontology graphs.

There have already more strategies to schedule the service [2] [3]. First is the strategies based on the applications, which select the service best satisfied the task, by comparing each scheduling project. Different task may have different requirement, commonly it need the time is shorter and the cost is cheaper, however these strategies may affect the capability of the system. Second is the scheduling strategies based on the system view, it's goal is to improve the system capability of the system ,for example the ratio of input and output, the rate of the resource used, the balance of the task loading and so on. Third is the strategies based on the resource market. The main idea of this

---

* Corresponding author.

strategy is to look on the grid environment as a market environment, in which, user is buyer, the resource owner is seller, and the process of resource scheduling is the same as the goods transaction. Market mechanism is convenient to allocate the resource, it can do decision based on the price and user interest, There exists a general equilibrium in market system which is a model of resource allocation in economic area, in this model, each user get their maximum earnings, and each resource is used efficiently.

Service scheduling is important in grid, we think that we should not only consider the executing time and system capability, but also we should introduce the semantic in scheduling. The service scheduling should not only satisfy one user, but also it should make all users get the service satisfied. So we propose a model of service scheduling based on semantic and market mechanism (Market-Semantic). To measure the similarity between ontologies, we divide the ontology concept into semantic units; we use the semantic units to express the meaning of the concepts and relations of ontology. The goal of our research is to make user gain the maximum income make the resource be used efficiency. By programming the resource allocation in constraint conditions, we have the method to allocate the resource.

2 The Similarity Measure of the Ontology

2.1 The Semantic Unit and Matching

The similarity measures of ontology include the measure of concepts and the measure of relations [4] [5]. At present, the measure is mainly about the concepts by calculating the distance between the concepts; the main methods of which is to calculate the distance by the level and place where concept located in and by the term databases[6][7]. However, there are some difficulties, first is that the level and the place of concept must be assigned by expert carefully, second is that although the concept may locate in any place and any level, the distance between two concepts should be only one, this fact makes the measure of concept be more difficulty, third is that it is difficult to know the semantic[8][9], in [10], they think that the top-down relations of concepts stand for the semantic, however, this may not express the complete semantic. For example, there haven't the top-down relations between concepts snow and cold, but we can know that the weather is cold, when we meet the concept snow; the concept snow may mean that the weather is cold, so the top-down relations can't descript the semantic completely.

To overcome those problems, we propose the method to measure the similarity of concept based on semantic units. We take emphasis on the implication of the concept, and we neglect the place and level of the concept in ontology. The semantic unit we proposed is the minimum unit to express the meaning of concept. Generally the concept $C = \{ \bigcup_{i=1}^{k} e_i \}$, e_i is the semantic unit of concept C. For example, snow= {cold, winter, sweater, 0°C...}, these units express the meaning of concept snow; certainly the semantic units should be referred by expert. We can judge whether the semantic units are matching or not by following formula.

$C_1:\{e_1,e_2,e_{3...},..e_m\}; C_2\{e_1',e_2',e_3'...,..e_n'\}$,

$$\text{Sim}(e_i,e_j)=\begin{cases}0: e_i\ne e_j\\1: e_i= e_j\end{cases}$$

We can get the concept similarity by the formula:

$$\text{Sim}(c_i,c_j)=\frac{1}{m\times n}\times\sum_{\substack{i=1\\j=1}}^{\substack{i=m\\j=n}}\text{sim}(e_i,e_j)$$

m and n are the semantic unit's number of concept c_i, and c_j. We calculate the concept similarity of ontology by the formula:

$$\text{Sim-concept}(O_x,O_y)=\frac{1}{n_1\times n_2}\times\sum_{\substack{i=1\\j=1}}^{\substack{i=n_1,\\j=n_2}}\text{sim}(c_i,c_j)$$

n_1 and n_2 are the numbers of concepts in ontology.

We think that relation is tuple of the concepts and relations name, for example: $R_1=<c_1, c_2, r_1>$, c_1, c_2 are the concept and r_1 is the relation name

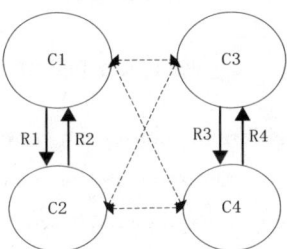

Fig. 1. Concepts and relations

Let $\text{sim}(R_i,R_j)=\text{sim}(c_i^1,c_j^1)\times\text{sim}(c_i^2,c_j^2)\times\text{sim}(r_i, r_j)$, $c_i^1, c_i^2 \in R_i$, $c_j^1, c_j^2 \in R_j$,

For example, in fig. 1, $\text{sim}(R_1,R_3)=\text{sim}(c_1,c_3)\times\text{sim}(c_2,c_4)\times\text{sim}(r_1,r_3)$

We define the similarity of relations by the formula:

$$\text{sim-relation}(O_x,O_y)=\frac{1}{h_1\times h_2}\sum_{\substack{i=1\\j=1}}^{\substack{i=h_1\\j=h_2}}\text{sim}(R_i,R_j)$$

h_1 and h_2 are the relations number of ontology O_x and O_y, $R_i\in O_x$, $R_j\in O_y$.

We define the similarity of ontology by the formula:

Sim-ontology (O_x,O_y)=sim-concept$(O_x,O_y)\times$sim-relation (O_x,O_y)

3 The General Equilibrium and the Solution [11]

3.1 The Market Mechanism and Equilibrium

We assume that there are n consumer, m factory and t resource. x is the number of resource k, p is the price of resource k.. $X=(x_1,x_2,x_3,....,x_t)$, $p=(p_1,p_2,p_3,....,p_t)$, $X\bullet P= \sum_{i=1}^{t} P_i x_i$,x_i is the resource number consumer i consumed. $x_i=(x_1^i,x_2^i,...,x_t^i)$, x_k^i is the number of resource k consumer i consumed. U_i is the utility function. Each consumer can select the resource number to maximize the utility function. That is to say we may select x_i^*, which is the optimal solution of the following programming

$$\max_{x_{ii}} u_i\, x_i \quad \text{s.t. } P\bullet X_i \le I_i$$

In economics theory, I_i is the income of consumer i, if the resource number user owned is W_i, earnings of the user is $P\bullet W_i$, the budget constraint is: $p \bullet x_i \le p \bullet w_i$. If the condition $\sum_{i=1}^{n} x_i^* + \sum_{j=1}^{m} x_j^* = \sum_{j=1}^{m} F_j(x_j^*) + \sum_{i=1}^{n} W_i$ is satisfied, the system is reach to a general equilibrium status [11]. In equilibrium status, each consumer provide their income to buy products based on the budget constraint, and each factory may decide the numbers of the products and decide their own requirement based on the goal of maximizing their benefit. The price of general equilibrium status is the general equilibrium price, General Equilibrium exists in market environment, and the equilibrium price becomes a lever.

3.2 The Optimal Solution of the Customer Requirement

Kun-Tucher's theory provides a method to get the best solution of the problem program:

$$\text{Max } (f(x))$$

$$\text{s.t } g(x)\le 0\ h(x)=0.$$

In the program, $f(x)$ is the goal function, $g(x)$ and $h(x)$ is the constraint condition.

Kun-Tucher's theory assume that $f(x)$ and $g(x)$ are derivative, if the solution x^* is optimal, and there exist variables $\lambda \ge 0$ and u, which make the following formula satisfied,

$$\frac{\partial}{\partial x_1}(f(x^*) - \lambda \frac{\partial}{\partial x_1} g(x^*) - u \frac{\partial}{\partial x_1} h(x^*) = 0$$

$$\frac{\partial}{\partial x_2}(f(x^*) - \lambda \frac{\partial}{\partial x_2} g(x^*) - u \frac{\partial}{\partial x_2} h(x^*) = 0$$

....

$$\frac{\partial}{\partial x_i}(f(x^*) - \lambda \frac{\partial}{\partial x_i} g(x^*) - u \frac{\partial}{\partial x_i} h(x^*) = 0$$

For example:

$$\max(f(x_1, x_2)) = -x_1^2 + 2x_2$$

s.t. $x_1 + x_2 \leq 10$

Let $L = f(x_1, x_2) - \lambda \times g(x_1, x_2) = -x_1^2 + 2x_2 - \lambda(x_1 + x_2 - 10)$, and we calculate the derivative based on the x_1, x_2, λ, and let the derivative be equal to zero.

$$\frac{\partial L}{\partial x_1} = -2x_1 - \lambda = 0 \tag{1}$$

$$\frac{\partial L}{\partial x_2} = 2 - \lambda = 0 \tag{2}$$

$$x_1 + x_2 - 10 = 0 \tag{3}$$

Finally, the solution is $x_1 = -1, x_2 = 11, \lambda = 2$

4 The Model of Service Scheduling Based on Market and Semantic (Market –Semantic)

There are two modules in our model, one is the module of similarity measure between service ontology and resource ontology, and other is the service scheduling module. Just as fig. 2, firstly, we calculate the ontology similarity; the result is the table of ontology similarity. Consumer psychologies tell us that customers are willing to buy the products, which have the maximum ratio about capability and price. So we use the function $u_i(x) = g_1 \frac{s_i}{c_i}(x)$ to be the utility function, g_1 is a constant, S_i is the similarity.

Because it is difficult to get the cost of service, we use the prediction time instead of the cost which is also the methods other model used. The earnings of user is defined $B_i(f) = (g_1 \frac{s_i}{c_i} - g_2 \cdot c_i) \times f$, g_1 and g_2 are constant, f is the solution we need, which can be get by the following program

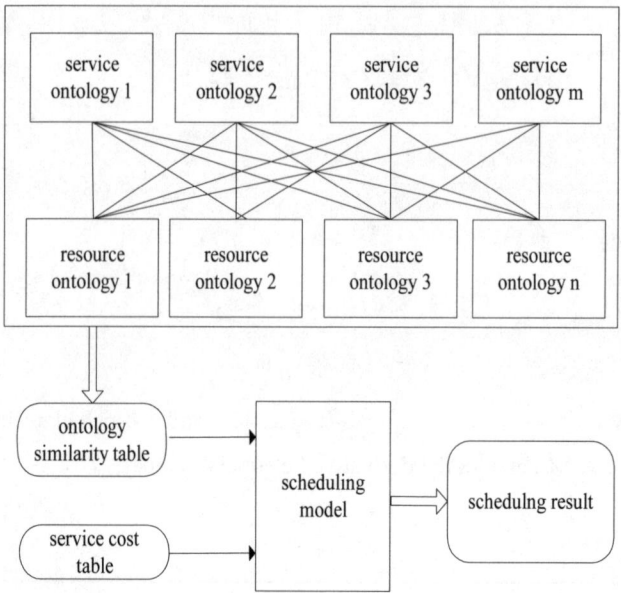

Fig. 2. The model of scheduling based on ontology similarity and service cost

$$\text{Max } (B_i(f)) \text{ s.t } \begin{cases} \sum_{i=1}^{n} f_{ij} \leq 1 \\ \sum_{j=1}^{m} f_{ij} \leq 1 \\ f_{ij} \geq 0, 1 \leq i \leq n, 1 \leq j \leq m \\ f_{ij} \leq 1 \end{cases} \quad (4)$$

We use the function linprog of matlab to calculate the solution, because $B_i(f)$ is maximum, $\sum_{i=1}^{n}(B_i(f))$ is maximum certainly, which is the total earnings of system.

5 Algorithms and Experiments

5.1 Algorithm of Max-Semantic

We compare our methods with Max-semantic and semantic-cost-max-min algorithms. Let e is the rate of resource used, $e=\frac{n}{T}$, in which n is the number of resource used, T is the number of resource. The goal of Max-semantic algorithm is to get the maximum semantic value in service scheduling. Next is the Max-semantic algorithm

(1) S_{ij} is the element of matrix s-r
(2) Length is the row number of matrix s-r
(3) *Place (i)* =*max(s (i, :))*
(4) *j* is the element number of *place(i)*
(5) Resource used rate $e=\dfrac{j}{length}$

5.2 Algorithm of Semantic-Cost-Max-Min

The goal of traditional famous MM algorithm is to look for the solution, of which the execute time is shortest, and the rate of the resource used is satisfied, MM algorithm use time matrix to allocate the resource, here, we use the matrix of the ration of capability and cost instead of the time matrix, and the goal is to make the ratio of capability and cost maximum. Next is the semantic-cost-max-min algorithm.

(1) $\{s_{i,j}\}$ is the similarity between ontology *i* and ontology *j*
(2) $\{c_{i,j}\}$ is the cost of ontology *i* and ontology *j*
(3) $\{\dfrac{c_{i,j}}{s_{i,j}}\}$ is the ratio matrix of the capability and cost
(4) Let mincost(*i*)=mct(*i,k*), mincost(*i*) is an array ,it means if service *i* have selected the resource *k*, the ratio of capability and cost would be minimum.
(5) Selecting the service t_a, of which, the ratio of capability and cost is maximum, and we allocate it to resource *b*
(6) Add the value of t_a to the other volume of matrix, and delete the row of t_a to renew the matrix.
(7) Go to (4) until there have only one service s_e to schedule
(8) Select the resource to service s_e, of which, the ratio of capability and cost is maximum
(9) Calculate the resource used rate e'

5.3 Experiments and Results

Let the matrix is $N\times N$, the value of N is {5,10,15,20}, Both of the number of service and resource are N, constant g_1=2000, g_2=1. The matrix is obtained randomly using matlab tools, for example: N =5; *s* is the similarity matrix, *c* is the service cost matrix.

$$s = \begin{bmatrix} 0.0002, 0.0005, 0.0002, 0.0001, 0.0003 \\ 0.0005, 0.0001, 0.0009, 0.0008, 0.0007 \\ 0.0007, 0.0006, 0.0001, 0.0000, 0.0003 \\ 0.0009, 0.0004, 0.0010, 0.0003, 0.0001 \\ 0.0004, 0.0002, 0.0007, 0.0005, 0.0004 \end{bmatrix}, c = \begin{bmatrix} 0.24, 0.56, 0.66, 0.31, 0.42 \\ 0.21, 0.42, 0.56, 0.35, 0.44 \\ 0.47, 0.24, 0.46, 0.56, 0.23 \\ 0.27, 0.21, 0.32, 0.44, 0.51 \\ 0.53, 0.42, 0.51, 0.44, 0.32 \end{bmatrix}.$$

Just as fig. 3 and fig. 4, we can draw a conclusion that the earnings of the Market–Semantic is maximum, the earnings of Max-semantic is more than Semantic-Cost-Max-Min, the resource used rate of the Market-Semantic is maximum, and the resource used rate of Semantic-Cost-Max-Min is more than Max-Semantic. It proves that our method is better than the traditional methods in service scheduling and selection.

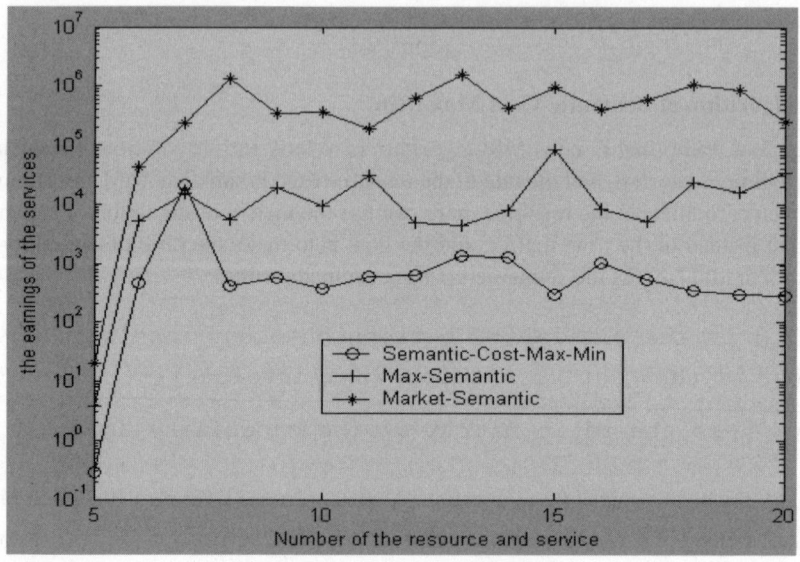

Fig. 3. The earnings of different algorithms

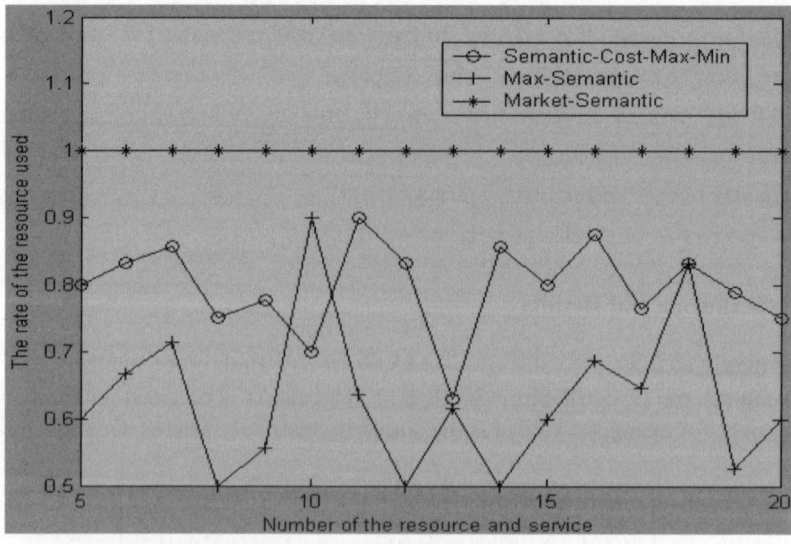

Fig. 4. The using rates of resource in different algorithm

6 Conclusions

In order to provide the service user satisfied, we propose a model of service scheduling based on market mechanism and semantic, we look on the resource and service as ontology, we have a method to measure the similarity between ontologies, and we use the general equilibrium theory and utility functions to get the solutions of resource allocation, by which user can gain service satisfied and the resource used rate is maximum. Our model provides an efficient method to do service scheduling proved by the examples. Next works are the research of how to measure the similarity efficiently based on semantic, how to select the utility functions user satisfied, and how to ascertain the cost of the service scientifically.

Acknowledgments. This work is supported by national 973 funds of China (Number: 2003cb317008) and the scientific innovation foundation of south west university of China (Number: 2006011).

References

1. Hongsuda, T., Stefan, D., Carl, K.: Ontology Based Resource Matching in the grid–The Grid Meets the Semantic Web. In: Proceedings of The Second International Semantic Web Conference, Sanibel-Captiva Islands, Florida, USA (October 2003)
2. Liu, Foster, I.: A Constraint Language Approach to Grid Resources election. In: Proceedings of the Twelfth IEEE International Symposium on High Performance Distributed Computing (HPDC-12) (June 2003)
3. Wache, H., Vogele, T., Visser, U.: Ontology-Based Integration of Information–A Survey of Existing Approaches. In: Proc. of the IJCAI-01 Workshop: Ontologies and Information Sharing, Seattle, WA, pp. 101–117 (2001)
4. Lei, L., Horrocks, I.: A Software Framework for Matchmaking Based on Semantic Web Technology. In: Proceedings of the Twelfth International World Wide Web Conference (2003)
5. Massimo, P.: Semantic Matching of Web Service Capabilities. In: Proceedings of the First International Semantic Web Conference (2002)
6. Solomon, M., Raman, R.: Matchmaking Distributed Resource Management for High Throughput Computing[C]. In: Proceedings of the Seventh IEEE International Symposium on High Performance Distributed Computing, Chicago (July 1998)
7. Solomon, M., Raman, R.: Resource Management through Multilateral Matchmaking. In: Proceedings of the Ninth IEEE Symposium on High Performance Distributed Computing (HPDC9), Pittsburgh, August 2000, pp. 290–291 (2000)
8. Devis, B., Valeria, A., Michele, M.: Hybrid Ontology Based Matchmaking for Service Discovery. In: Symposium on Applied Computing Proceedings of the 2006 ACM symposium on Applied computing, pp. 1707–1708 (2006)
9. Wu, J., Zhao, W., Ying, L.: Web Service Discovery Based on Ontology and Similarity of Words. Chinese Journal Of Computers, 595–562 (2005)
10. Weinstein, P., Birmingham, W.: Comparing concepts in differentiated ontologies. In: Proceed. of KAW 1999 (1999)
11. Yi, G., Hai, W.: Microeconomic theory, pp. 185–201. People Press of ShangHai (2003)
12. Lu, C., Yg, X.: The general Equilibrium Theory. Financial Press of shanghai (2001)

Flexible and Semantics-Based Support for Web Services Transaction Protocols

Trieu Minh, Nhut Le, and Jinli Cao

Department of Computer Science and Computer Engineering
La Trobe University, Bundoora, VIC 3086, Australia
tm4le@students.cs.latrobe.edu.au, j.cao@latrobe.edu.au

Abstract. Increasing successful rate of long running transactions is challenging in the heterogeneous environment because business processes become complex and the spanning time are unpredictable. This paper focuses on reducing the failure rate of completing transactions. A novel algorithm for flexible and semantic-based support to executing long running transactions is proposed. The algorithm is to provide a novel management for Web service transactions. The solution is to classify services based on semantics, and provide flexibility by calculation of recommendation. Furthermore, the proposed algorithm can be employed by many transaction protocols to improve the management of transactions. Tentative Hold Protocol is used and combined with the proposed solution to achieve flexibility of execution transactions.

1 Introduction

Web service Transaction Management has become more interesting due to its efficiency on business activities. Millions of organizations around the world have used Web Services to publish services, interoperate business processes, and improve business partner relationships via the Internet [1,2,3,4,5,6]. However, there many problems exist in business processing because its operations are unpredictable for participants' selection and unknown limited time for long running transaction. It is very expensive if the traditional transaction management protocol is used. It is not tolerable to abort long running transactions. Failure of long running business transactions is high in traditional execution environment. Therefore, most of solutions are focused on reducing the failure rate during the execution of process. The paper [7] proposed the solution, which supply all information of transactions and systems in a set of XML-based notation. Therefore, they can recovered, interpreted and executed during execution process so as to cope the failure of transactions or systems. Narendra and Gundugola [8] also proposed the automated determination on Web service execution adaptation using context ontology. Authors focus on Web service execution and present an algorithm for automated workflow adaptation based on context ontology. This paper will propose a new solution for management using flexible and semantic-based support for transaction protocols during the execution process. The solution makes the transaction more flexible by using the semantics. The purpose of the research is to reduce failure rate and increase the performance of Web services execution.

Organization of the paper is present as follows: Section 2 discusses previous work. Section 3 describes the architecture of Web service transaction. The next section expresses our solution for Flexible transaction Management. Section 5 presents Flexible Transaction Model with Tentative Hold Protocol. In section 6, simulation is evaluated. The last is the conclusion section.

2 Related Work

Numerous researches have proposed some solutions to processing of business transactions based on Tentative hold Protocol (THP) [9,10,11,12,13,14]. Automation is the best described for the many-to-many interaction between businesses in the complex Web environment and make network market more dynamic and lively.

In THP architecture, coordinators have created in both providers and customers, namely, Resource Coordinator (RC) and Client Coordinator (CC), so as to provide flexibility for transactions. Coordinators are responsible for communicating various messages each other such as hold requests and cancellations. The CC can exchange messages to customers for hold requests and canceling resources. The providers can also receive and send messages to RC for tentative hold resources and cancel notification.

The THP supplies not only expired time for client purchase being set by providers' policies for holding items but also canceled phase can be triggered by either sides consumers or providers. The RC can communicate with providers supporting policy and expire time for resources. Tentative reservation holds can be canceled for the following reasons. Clients cancel the tentative hold to resources for any reasons such as not purchase, expired time through notifying cancel message. Providers cancel the tentative hold when the hold expires (time out) or unavailable resource by sending notification's messages to relative clients. The canceling hold requests is set by clients and providers namely policies, which could be breached during business processes [9,10].

The Tentative reservations grant the client requesting multiple providers as a sequence services (airline, hotel and taxi) in a single coordinated purchase which could satisfy the price, composition and availability before committing the transaction. If any service is unavailable or unsuitable, another available service will be replaced without loss any prior hold of reservation. The providers can grant non-blocking reservation on their products and maintain control resources while enabling clients more flexibility in coordinating the process.

The THP is the best protocol for describing long running transaction management because CC and RC can support significantly for our solution flexible transaction algorithm by hold, cancellation or failure messages. Our algorithm can be added with the THP as a model for attaching it to any transaction protocols.

3 Architecture of Web Service Transaction

A Web service process can consists of a sequence of business activities to achieve a specific business goal. These activities are carried out as conversations such as the exchange of context-based messages between the parties getting involved in. The reliability concerns of business goals impose transactional behavior on these conversations. Within a conversation the unit of work at each service is known as a sub-transaction. The conversational transactions involve sub-transaction, which are independent and only relate to conversations through the context of business transaction.

Based on the distributed transaction processing, Web service Transaction Management can divide into three layers, namely, discovery layer, composition layer, and execution layer. The transactions will be proceed and passed through these layers from high to low. Figure 1 shows the architecture of Web service transactions management.

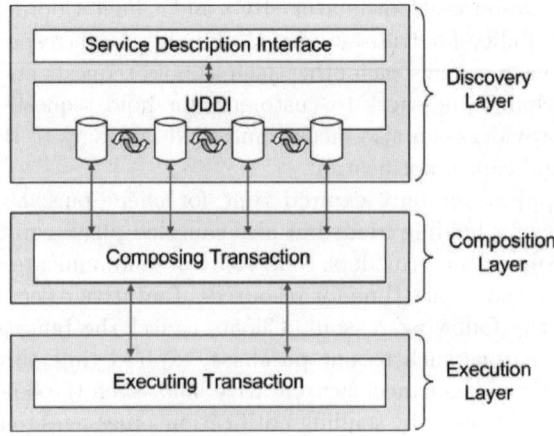

Fig. 1. Architecture of Web service transaction management

Discovery layer

There are two main functions of Discovery layers which are Web service Description and Web service Discovery. The service information is created and published on UDDI by service providers. Over the Web, consumers can ask for providing services through the interface. The discovery layer processes requester's requirements. Services are analyzed into simple requests or composed requests. The searching and matching for various types of services are preformed at this layer.

Composition layer

In this layer, Web services are composed and associated with each others into a sequence of business activities. These business activities are involved business collaborations within and across organizational boundaries. The complex requirements of services will be composed into a simple description.

Execution layer

This layer has a task to complete the rest of the business processes into real businesses. It means that after the whole process of transaction has been analyzed, scheduled and composed through above layers, the transactions will execute the whole services then give out the final result to consumers. The responsibility of this layer is to conduct the execution of composite services to be completed by the service providers.

The proposed flexible transaction model will be used in this layer. The transaction will be flexible for the completion with the recommendation based on semantics. The detailed work will be described in next section.

4 A Flexible Transaction Management (FTM)

The main idea of the proposed model is to keep all participants getting involved in completion of long running transactions. Using semantics of sub transactions, the global transaction will be evaluated for its success factor. The final result of transactions will depend on the recommendation calculated by a formula. This will reduce the failure rate of participants of transactions so as to make the transaction more flexible.

The proposed FTM will perform the following tasks:

- To classify the services based on the semantics of services.
- To design a new property called weight to emphasize service's role on the business transaction.
- To calculate the transaction's result based on the weight
- To recommend the possibility of business transaction satisfying customers' requirement.

4.1 Classify Services Using Semantics

The most important of this solution is to classify services. Each service has to identify its contribution in the whole business transaction which is defined as a global transaction.

Definition 1. *Let T_G be a global transaction which is conducted from the request of the consumers. T_G is generally a long running transaction.*

Definition 2. *Let $T_i(i \in [1..n])$ be a sub-transaction of T_G or a service. Global transaction $T_G = \{T_1, T_2, \ldots, T_n\}$ includes a sequence of sub-transactions or services which are independent. It means that the result of each transaction does not affect to the others.*

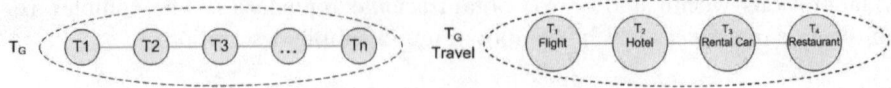

Fig. 2. Global transaction

Example: The Requirement about travel includes four services Flight, Hotel, Rental Car and Restaurant, which can perform in figure 2.

A global transaction consists of a number of sub-transactions. Each sub-transaction can play the main role or the extra role in the business activities. Therefore, the service's organizer has to use the semantics of service to categorize the services. Classification can be changed in period by Clients' feedback or the organizers' experience dynamically. In this way, table 1 illustrate the classification of travel services.

Table 1. Classification Travel Services

Services	level
Flight	Very Important
Hotel	Important
Motel	Important
Rental Car	Moderate
Taxi	Moderate
Insurance travel	Moderate
Restaurant	Moderate
Tourist guide	Moderate
Travel Guide book	Low
Map	Low

4.2 Design and Calculate the Weight Value for Business Transaction

Definition 3. *Let W_j be a property Weight in each sub-transaction T_i, and let m be a number of level which services are classified.*

Without loss of generality, sub-transactions can have the same weight property for a same dimension. There are m weight values $(W_1, W_2, \ldots, W_m)$. $W_j (j \in [i, m])$ is a value in m levels. This set of values is sorted $(W_1 > W_2 > \ldots > W_m)$. Thus, the highest level will have weight (W_1).

Assumption: If one of the important levels of sub-transactions is fail, global transaction will fail.

For each business Transaction, n services will be divided into m level. The same level will be assigned the same weight. The greater weight will illustrate more important service than the others. Each level j could have k_j different services. In other word, there are k_j services having the same Weight (W_j).

Firstly, any constant number (C) can be chosen for the highest level

$$W_1 = C \quad (C = \text{constant}). \tag{1}$$

Base on the assumption, the total weight of all services level j (W_j) is less than a service weight $j-1(W_{j-1})$. Thus, the weight of the lower level has been calculated by using formula 2

$$W_j = \frac{W_{j-1}}{k_j + 1} \qquad j = \overline{2..m}. \tag{2}$$

Example: There are four services Fight, Hotel, Rental Car, and Restaurant. Based on the Classified Table 1 of Travel service, the business transaction should be divided into three levels. We have

(1) $\Longrightarrow W_1 = $ Flight . Weight $= 10$.

(2) $\Longrightarrow W_2 = $ Hotel . Weight $= \dfrac{10}{1+1} = 5$

$\Longrightarrow W_3 = $ RentalCar . Weight $=$ Restaurant . Weight $= \dfrac{5}{2+1} = 1.66667$.

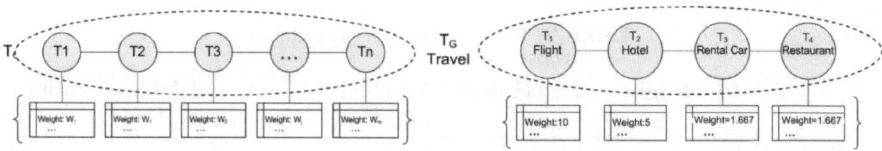

Fig. 3. Weight Property

4.3 Formulate and Evaluate the Result of Business Transaction

Definition 4. *Let $i \in \{1, \ldots, n\}$ and let R_i be a result of sub-transaction T_i. If sub-transaction T_i commits, R_i will be assigned to 1 (one). Otherwise, R_i will be assigned to 0 (zero). In addition, let R_G be a result of global transaction which is calculated by the following formula:*

$$R_G = \frac{\sum_{i=1}^{n}(W_i * R_i)}{\sum_{i=1}^{n} W_i} \qquad 0 \le R_G \le 1. \tag{3}$$

Deriving from definition 4, any global transaction may have one of the following possible results:

$R_G = 1 \quad \Longleftrightarrow \quad$ All sub-transaction are success.
$R_G = 0 \quad \Longleftrightarrow \quad$ All sub-transaction are failure.
$0 < R_G < 1 \Longleftrightarrow \quad$ Some sub-transaction are failure and the others are success.

After the global transaction has executed and given out the result of each sub-transaction, if any sub-transaction is failed, the process for evaluation of the transaction will be activated.

It is to note that a global transaction consists of a number of sub-transactions.

Definition 5. Let $l \in \{1, \ldots, m-1\}$ and let EN_l be an evaluated number for a sub-transaction. It is used to compare with the number result calculated in formula (3) in the evaluation process. We have

$$EN_l = \frac{\sum_{j=1}^{l}(k_j * W_j)}{\sum_{i=1}^{n} W_i} \quad (l < m), \qquad (4)$$

where k_j is a number of sub-transaction of level j consisting in a global transaction, m is a number of level of global transaction and n is a number of sub-transaction consisting in global transaction.

This formula is calculated and compared with resulted number in formula (3). Then, the result of the transaction will be exposed.

If $R_G \geq EN_l$, the global transaction will satisfy l levels from the highest level. Otherwise, it will fail.

Example: For the travel service global transaction with sub transactions: Flight, Hotel, Rental Car, and Restaurant, the following Table 2 can show four possible cases of results of the sub-transactions of T1, T2, T3,and T4. The fate of the global transaction will be depended on the evaluation according to the formula 4.

Table 2. Result of global transaction

	T1 (Flight)	T2 (Hotel)	T3 (RentalCar)	T2 (Restaurant)
Weight	10	5	1.6667	1.6667
Result 1	1	1	1	0
Result 2	1	0	1	0
Result 3	0	1	1	1

Before evaluating transaction, the evaluation number (EN) has to be calculated with formula (4). Then EN_1 is an evaluation number which satisfy the first important level of global transaction

$$EN_1 = \frac{1 * 10}{10 + 5 + 1.6667 + 1.6667} = 0.54545,$$

and EN_2 is an evaluation number which satisfy the first and second important level of global transaction

$$EN_2 = \frac{1 * 10 + 1 * 5}{10 + 5 + 1.6667 + 1.6667} = 0.81818.$$

Then calculate the R_G with formula (1), if the global transaction outcome is the result 1 of the table 2 then

$$R_G = \frac{10 * 1 + 5 * 1 + 1.6667 * 1 + 1.6667 * 0}{10 + 5 + 1.6667 + 1.6667} = 0.90909.$$

Notice that $R_G \geq EN_2$, we give a strongly recommended result because global transaction satisfy the first and second highest level.

If the global transaction outcome is the result 2 of the table 2 then

$$R_G = \frac{10*1 + 5*0 + 1.6667*1 + 1.6667*0}{10 + 5 + 1.6667 + 1.6667} = 0.63636.$$

Notice that $R_G \geq EN_1$, we give a recommended result because global transaction satisfy the highest level.

If the global transaction outcome is the result 3 of the table 2 then

$$R_G = \frac{10*0 + 5*1 + 1.6667*1 + 1.6667*1}{10 + 5 + 1.6667 + 1.6667} = 0.45454.$$

Notice that $R_G < EN_1$, we give the failure message for the failed global transaction.

5 Flexible Transaction Model with Tentative Hold Protocol

In this section, the improvement of FTM with THP will be illustrated more details.

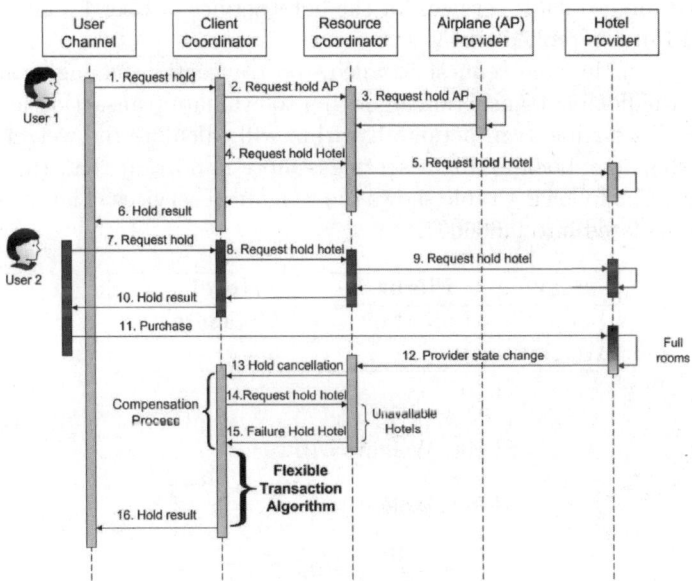

Fig. 4. THP with Flexible transaction algorithm

Figure 4 illustrates an example using the proposed FTM for transactions. The steps are described as follows.

Form step 1 to 6, User 1 requires travel service to the resources. The THP finds appropriate resources for user's request with supplying information of CC and RC.

In step 6, the CC processes all tentative holds after receiving all replies from RC. If all the requests succeed to tentative holds, the success result of request will be sent. Otherwise, any tentative request holds reply failure. Transaction management will react for each case of failure. There are two main reasons for failures. The first reason is a replying message of service which is unsuitable resource for whole transaction, and then the compensation process will be activated to find another suitable service by resending the similar tentative request hold. This process has been discussed in some papers [10,11,12,14]. The second reason is the replied message which notifies no services available with the request (for example fully booked all Airplane services). In this case, the traditional transaction managements reply failure for user request. However, the transaction is becoming more flexible when adding the flexible transaction process demonstrated in solution section. Figure 4 shows the flexible transaction process which is going to explain more detail by following steps.

The User 2 sends the request for finding a hotel service. The hold hotel of User 2 is exactly the same as User 1. Therefore, the RC routes the same resources to User 1 from step 7 to step 10.

In step 11, receiving the result, the User 2 immediately pays money for booking the hotel. From step 12 to step 15 are a compensation process for user 1. However, there are not any available services for the hotel service of User 1's request. The failure hold Hotel is replied to CC.

Step 16, when the hold request is failed, the transaction management application runs the flexible transaction algorithm to evaluate transaction for recommendation. The flexible transaction algorithm will calculate the weight of each service. In this case, booking flight service is more important than the booking hotel service. The following table shows the weights of services. The corresponding EN is calculated into 0.666667.

Service	Flight	Hotel
Level	Important	Moderate
Weight	10	5

$$\text{Flight.Weight} = 10$$
$$\text{Hotel.Weight} = \frac{10}{1+1} = 5$$
$$EN = \frac{10}{10+5} = 0.666667.$$

Services	Flight	Hotel
Weight	10	5
Result	Commit = 1	Fail = 0

$$R_G = \frac{10*1 + 5*0}{10+5} = 0.666667.$$

According to the definition, $R_G \geq EN$ then the result message is "*Recommend*". Because of $R_G = EN = 0.666667$, the highest important level is successful. After that, the RC replies the message "*Recommend*" to User 1.

6 Simulation and Evaluation

In this section, the performance of proposed solution is given to demonstrate the flexible transaction management by simulation. Table 3 shows the input information of the simulation to observe the result of executions of transactions.

Table 3. Configuration of the system in Simulation

Parameter	Value	Description
$N_{transaction}$	1,0000	Number of Transaction being executed
Level	4	all services are divided into four level (Very Important, Important, Moderate and Low)
Services	10	Max. No. of services in the system
$P_{execution}$	0.95	probability of successful execution of each sub-transaction
T_{size}	110	Size of each global transaction (No. of sub-transaction)

Assume that size (T_{size}) of global is generated randomly. The successful rate is $(P_{execteion})$ of sub-transactions is following standard distribution. The probability of successful executions of same transactions is also used $P_{execteion}$ under traditional transaction protocol. Simultaneously, the same set of transactions is executed using our FTM and existing traditional protocol. The results are illustrated with the following figure 5.

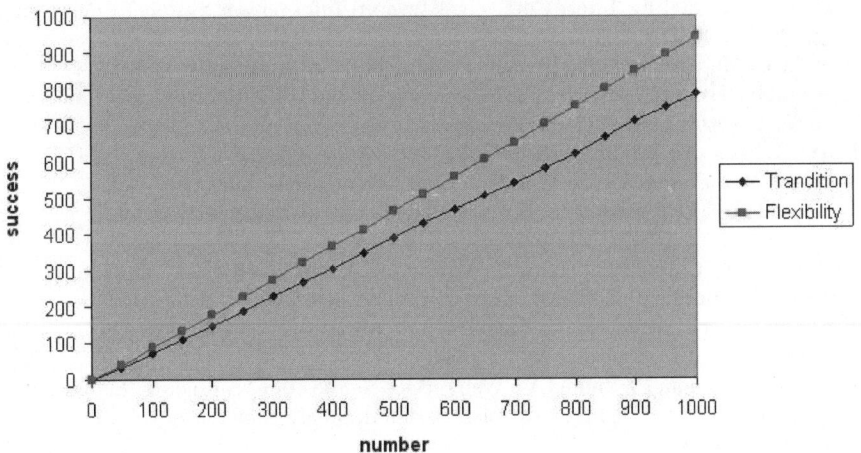

Fig. 5. Simulation

Figure 5 shows the significant improvement in increasing number of successful transactions. The flexible and semantic-based transaction protocol is outperformed than the traditional transaction protocol. Therefore, the proposed solution of this paper has brought more effective results for execution, especially, long running transactions.

7 Conclusion

In this paper, we have presented a new algorithm for flexible Web service transactions. The algorithm is based on classifying semantic of services. After that, the flexibility of transaction is performed by adding this algorithm in the THP. Consequently, this solution could provide a flexible transaction management for many transaction protocols. The experimental result shows that our approach of flexible transaction is outperformed compared with the traditional transaction protocols.

References

1. Quintero, R., Pelechano, V.: Conceptual modeling of service composition using aggregation and specialization relationships. In: ACM Southeast Regional Conference Proceedings of the 44th annual Southeast regional conference, pp. 452–457 (2006)
2. Choudry, B., Bertok, P., Cao, J.: Cost based web services transactions management. The International Journal Web and Grid Services 2, 198–220 (2006)
3. Choudry, B., Cao, J.: Towards dynamic integration of heterogeneous web services transaction partners. In: Proceedings of 9th International Conference on Information Integration and Web-based Applications and Services (2007)
4. Little, M.: Transaction and web services. Communications of the ACM 46(10), 49–54 (2003)
5. Hao, Y., Zhang, Y., Cao, J.: Wsxplorer: Searching for desired web services. In: Proceedings of 19th Interl Conf. on Advanced Information Systems Engineering, pp. 49–54 (2007)
6. Pistore, M., Traverso, P., Bertoli, P., Marconi, A.: Automated synthesis of composite bpel4ws web services. In: Proceedings of the IEEE International Conference on Web Services, pp. 293–301 (2005)
7. Ye, X.: Towards a reliable distributed web service execution engine, In: IEEE International Conference on Web Services (2006) (0-7695-2669-1)
8. Narendra, N.C., Gundugola, S.: Automated context-aware adaptation of web service executions. IEEE (244-0212-3.1-4)
9. Roberts, J., Collier, T., Malu, P., Srinivasan, K.: Tentative hold protocol part 2: Technical specification (2001), http://www.w3.org/TR/tenthold-2/
10. Srinivasan, K., Malu, P.G., Moakley, G.: Automatic multibusiness transaction. IEEE Internet Computing, 66–73 (2003)
11. Limthanmaphon, B., Zhang, Y.: Web service composition transaction management. In: Proceedings of the fifteenth Australasian database conference, vol. 27, pp. 171–179 (2004)

12. Xu, W., Yang, Z., Liu, W., Xu, L.: tathp: A transaction-aware protocol for web services transaction coordination. In: IEEE Region 10 Conference, pp. 1–4 (2006)
13. Park, J., Choi, K.-S.: Design of an efficient tentative hold protocol for automated coordination of multi-business transactions, In: Proceedings of IEEE International Conference on E-Commerce (2003) (0-7695-1969-5)
14. Roberts, J., Srinivasan, K.: Tentative hold protocol part 1: White paper, http://www.w3.org/TR/tenthold-1/

EX_QoS Driven Approach for Finding Replacement Services in Distributed Service Composition

Lei Yang, Yu Dai, and Bin Zhang

College of Information Science and Technology, Northeastern University
yanglei@mail.neu.edu.cn

Abstract. Web services can be composed together in order to carry out complex transactions or workflows. During the execution of the composite service, if one component service fails, a mechanism is needed to ensure that the failed service can be quickly and efficiently replaced. In this paper, based on the proposed dependent quality model extended QoS model (EX_QoS), we present an approach for finding replacement composite service in order to make the composite service can automatically switch to the new replacement composite services. Compared with works have been done, this paper emphasizes on find-ing the replacement composite service with global optimization in decentralized service composition and through making the backing up process begin at the failure happening time and before the service invoking time, the approach can make the replacement composite service more available and can minimize the interrupting time caused by the backing up process.

1 Introduction

Since web services operate autonomously within a highly variable environment, as a result of which their QoS may evolve relatively frequently, either because of internal changes or changes in their environment [1], such dynamic property of web services requires that composite service must adjust itself during runtime.

Although several works focusing on how to establish the QoS model in order to evaluate the quality of services and how to do the selection in order to achieve end-to-end quality constraint have been studied, they lack of the ability to adapt to changes especially occurred during the execution of composite service. A native approach to handle the problem is to re-compose from scratch every time a change occurs. However, this may not be a feasible solution due to that the time complexity of the re-composition is high which will interrupt execution of the composite service.

For such reason, researchers based on the replacement composite service idea propose approaches [2, 3] of backing up a composite service from current service to the end of the composite process in order to make the composite service automatically switch to the replacement one whenever current service becomes unavailable. However, in current approach, the backing up process usually begins before the time of composite service execution. As the interval between the backing up time and the failure happening time may be long (this situation may occur especially when there exist long transactional services), during such interval, services of the replacement one may become unavailable which makes the automatically switching impossible. Finding the replacement composite service when it is just to invoke the service, may insure the availability of the replacement one. However, this may interrupt execution of the composite service. Thus, how to improve the availability of the replacement composite service and minimize the interrupting time caused by the online backing up process is still a problem needed to solve.

Besides this, current approach for finding replacement composite service with global optimization is only suitable for centralized service composition. Currently, there exist two models for invoking composite service: centralized model [1, 4] and decentralized model [5]. For such two models, QoS for evaluating the quality of services must be computed differently. In centralized model (Fig. 1 (a)), there exists a centralized engine. According to the routing information of composite service, such engine will route data among component services. In this model, QoS information about data transmission time for the service selection will be the time of routing data between the component service and the centralized engine. The selection of one service will not influence the selection of others. In decentralized model (Fig. 1 (b)), on each component service, there exists a routing table generated from the routing information of the composite service. Such routing table is used for routing data among component services. In this model, QoS information about data transmission time for the service selection will be the time of routing data between the component services. That is to say, the selection of one service will influence the selection of others. Thus, how to find replacement composite service with global optimization in distributed service composition is still another problem needed to solve.

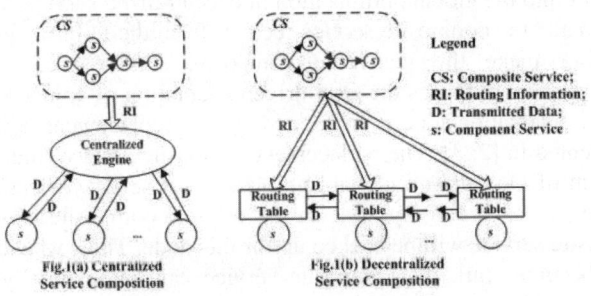

Fig. 1. Two Service Composition Models

With all these in mind, we present a solution for finding replacement composite service. Compared with current approaches which emphasize on the adaptation in centralized service composition, we propose the EX-QoS model which is an extension of the traditional QoS model to support the decentralized service composition. Meantime, based on such EX-QoS model, we provide a quality feedback mechanism in order to feedback the change of the quality of some service and if such change is prone to a failure, the process of finding the replacement composite service will be triggered. Such quality feedback mechanism can make the backing up process begin at failure happening time and before service invoking time which will make the replacement composite service more available and minimize the interrupting time caused by online backing up process. Besides these, in order to improve the runtime efficiency of finding replacement composite service, a heuristic algorithm is proposed. The experimentations show the better performance of the proposed approach.

2 Related Works

Finding a replacement composite service is to re-select the un-executed services, the process of which is similar to QoS driven service selection. QoS driven service selection includes local and global optimization polices. Currently, local policy adopts multi-object policy to score candidate services and based on such score, selects the optimal candidate service for the service class of composite service. [5, 6] support the local optimal selection of service. [1] is one of the representative approaches adopting global policy for service selection. [1] uses a graph to describe process of composite service and uses integer programming algorithm in order to optimize QoS of the composite service. [7] uses a directed acyclic graph to describe process of composite service and a dynamic programming algorithm is applied for service selection. [1, 6, 7] are for centralized service compositions which support both local and global optimization policy while [5] is for decentralized one which support local optimization policy. Compared with above works, this paper emphasizes on how to establish the dependent QoS model in order to evaluate how the selection of one service influences the QoS of others in decentralized service composition and apply such QoS model into the global optimization in decentralized service composition.

In order to make the composite service recover from the failure with minimal user intervention and make the recovered composite service meet the end-to-end constraint, researchers proposes the QoS-driven adaptation of composite service. Part of our dynamic adaptation idea is motivated by the replacement composite service algorithm presented in [2, 3]. The replacement composite service finding algorithm is as the algorithm of QoS driven global optimization of service selection. During the selection phase, for each activity node in the original composite service, a close-to optimal composite service will be backed up for this node. Thus, whenever the service for the node becomes fail, the composite service can automatically switch to the corresponding replacement composite service. Although such approaches can minimize the interrupting time caused by the backing up process, the availability of the replacement composite service can not be insured. This is because that backing up process begins before composite service execution and the QoS performance of service during the execution may not be considered. Compared above works, this paper emphasizes on improving the availability of the replacement composite service through backing up at failure happening time and before service invoking time.

3 EX_QoS Driven Approach for Finding Replacement Service

In order to improve the availability of the replacement composite service and minimize the interrupting time of execution, this paper proposes a framework for adapting to the decentralized service composition (Fig 2). In this framework, each service downloads and installs 2 agents: monitor and executing broker. The executing broker [5] has the responsibility to invoke corresponding service, according to the routing table send the result to the successor service and send the execution progress of the service to the monitor of composite service. The monitor of service takes charge of sending the EX_QoS detecting message to corresponding service according to the detecting plan and sending the EX_QoS value to the execution log. When the quality of certain service changes, the following activities will be done:

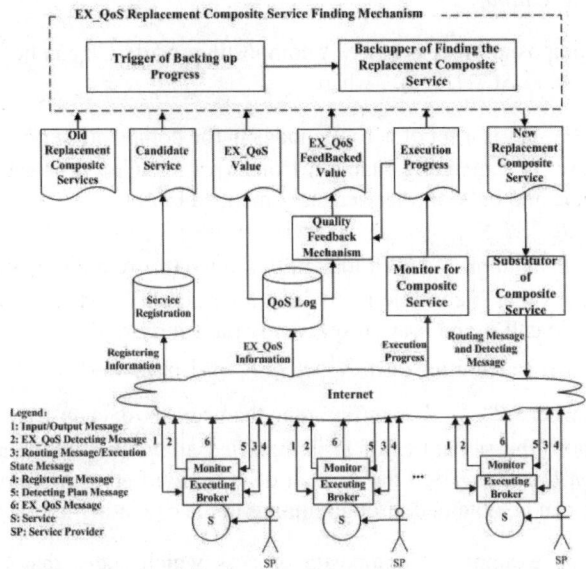

Fig. 2. EX_QoS Driven Adaptive Service Composition Framework

Firstly, the quality feedback mechanism feedbacks EX_QoS value of the service to the EX_QoS driven replacement composite service finding mechanism;

Secondly, according to the EX_QoS value provided by the quality feedback mechanism, the trigger of backing up progress will determine whether the services have been incurred a failure and whether the corresponding replacement composite service is available. And if so, the trigger will trigger the backing up process;

Thirdly, the backupper based on the heuristic replacement composite service finding algorithm, backs up the replacement one;

Finally, the substitutor substitutes the original composite service with the replacement one, modifies the routing plan and sends out the routing plan to the corresponding services.

3.1 Preliminaries

In order to make the concept of services clearly, we give a definition as follows:

Definition 1. Service (*s*). A service *s* can be defined as a 4-vector: $s=<Fc, D, C, Q>$, where *Fc* is the function class; *D* is the basic description containing service name, service provider and other textual description; *C* is the capability description containing input and output parameters; *Q* is the quality description of the service.

Definition 2. Service Class (*SC*). A service class is a set of services with the same function class and capability description which can be defined as a 3-vector: $SC=<Fc, C, ServiceSet>$, where *Fc* is the function class; *C* is the capability description; $ServiceSet=\{s_1,...,s_n\}$, for each $s_i \in ServiceSet$, $s_i.Fc=SC.Fc \wedge s_i.C.Input=SC.C.Inpu \wedge s_i.C.Output=SC.C.Output$.

Definition 3. Composite Process (*CP*). A composite process *CP* can be defined as a 5-vector: $CP=<Nset, f_1, SCset, T, f_2>$, where:

- $Nset=\{n_1, n_2,..., n_k\}$ is a set of activity nodes in the composite service;
- f_1: $Nset \rightarrow SCset$ is a mapping function from *Nset* to *SCset*. For each node in *CS*, there exists one and only one service class mapped to it;
- $SCset=\{SC_1, SC_2,..., SC_m\}$ is a set of service classes;
- $T \subseteq Nset \times Nset \times condition$ is used to signify the control relation. For each $e=(n_i, n_j, c_u) \in T$, it means that if condition c_u is true, after activity node n_i is finished, n_j will be invoked. We call n_i and n_j are respectively the source and target activity node of *e* which can also be signified as $n_i \prec_{c_u} n_j$, or $n_i=n_j-1$ or $n_j=n_i+1$;
- f_2: $T'' \rightarrow \{m\}$ where $T'' \subseteq T$, signifies that there exists data *m* transported on the control relation, the semantics of *m* is signified as *m.Sem*; the data type of *m* is signified as *m.DataType*; and the amount of *m* is signified as *m.Amount* (the value of *m.Amount* can be obtained through mining in the executing log of services).

Fig 3 gives an example of composite process which states that "UserRequest" firstly receive user requirements and then, a search for attractions is done in parallel with a flight and a hotel booking, after the searching and booking operations complete, the distance from the hotel to the restaurant is computed, either a car rental activity or bike rental activity is invoked and finally the composing result will through "UserInform" be given to the user.

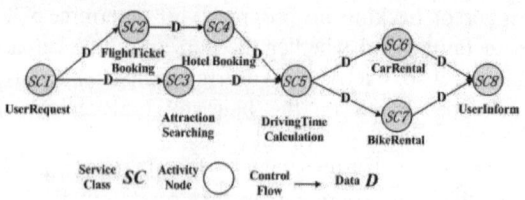

Fig. 3. Example of Composite Process

In order to simplify the problem, this paper will take the pipeline composite service [7] as the researching object, in which there only exists one path (Seen in Fig 4).

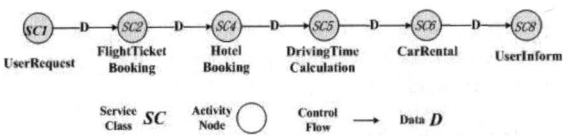

Fig. 4. An example of pipeline composite process

Definition 3. Assign (A). For composite process CP where $n \in Nset$ and $s \in f_1(Nset).ServiceSet$, we call the pair $<n, s>$ an assign of n, and s is signified as $g(n)$.

Definition 4. Part Plan and Plan. A part plan for a composite process CP is a set of assigns. For each assign $<n, s>$ in part plan, $n \in CP.Nset$ and for this n, there exist no other assign such as $<n, s>$ in the part plan. A plan for a composite process CP is a set of assigns and for each $n \in CP.Nset$, there exist one and only one assign in the plan.

For example, $\{<n_1, s_{11}>\}$ is a part plan of composite process in Fig 2 and $\{<n_1, s_{11}>, <n_2, s_{22}>, <n_3, s_{31}>, <n_4, s_{43}>, <n_5, s_{51}>, <n_6, s_{62}>, <n_7, s_{79}>, <n_8, s_{88}>\}$ is a plan.

Definition 5. Composite Service (CS) For composite process CP and its plan p, if CP will invoke services to perform its function according to p, we call under p, CP is a composite service, signified as $CS=f_p(CP)$ or $CP=f_p^{-1}(CS)$.

3.2 Dependent Quality Model Extended QoS Model

In decentralized service composition, it is needed to consider the dependent relation between services since such relation can affect quality of composite service.

Definition 6. Data Transmission Time Dependent Relation. For composite service CS and plan p, composite process $CP=f_p^{-1}(CS)$, the activity nodes $n_a, n_b \in CP.Nset$ and in p, there exist assigns $<n_a, s_a>$ and $<n_b, s_b>$. If $t=(n_a, n_b) \in CP.T$ and $\exists m<>null$, $f_2(t)=m$, we call that there exists data transmission time dependent relation ti between s_a and s_b, signified as $R_{ti}(n_a, n_b, s_a, s_b)$; else if $!\exists m<>null$, $f_2(t)=m$, we call that there exist reversed data transmission time dependent relation ti between s_a and s_b, signified as $\overline{R_{ti}}(n_a, n_b, s_a, s_b)$.

For example, in Fig 4, if s_2 and s_3 can be assigned to SC_1 and SC_2 respectively and there exists transmission data between SC_1 and SC_2, there exist data transmission time dependent relation between s_2 and s_3.

Definition 7. Dependent QoS Model for Component Service and Composite Service. For composite service CS, service s is one of the component services in CS. The dependent quality model of s in CS can be defined as a 2-vector $DQ(s)=<q^{(ti)}(s, s'), q^{(ti)}(s'', s)>$, where for n, n', n'', there exist relation $R_{ti}(n, n', s, s')$ or $R_{ti}(n'', n, s'', s)$ or $\overline{R_{ti}}(n, n', s, s')$ or $\overline{R_{ti}}(n'', n, s'', s)$. If $R_{ti}(n_1, n_2, s_1, s_2)$ is true, $q^{(ti)}(s_1, s_2)= f_2(n_1, n_2).Amount/bw(s_1, s_2)$ (where bw is the function returning the bandwidth between s_1 and s_2); else, $q^{(ti)}(s_1, s_2)=0$. For composite service CS, the dependent quality model of CS can be defined as a vector $DQ(CS)=<q^{(ti)}(CS)>$. $q^{(ti)}(CS)=\sum_{\forall n_i} \sum_{n_j \wedge (n_i,n_j) \in T} q^{(ti)}(g(n_i), g(n_j))$,

where $n_i, n_j \in f_p^{-1}(CS).Nset$.

Through adding dependent QoS model into current QoS model, the new QoS can reflect how the bandwidth between component services influences the QoS of duration time of composite service.

Definition 8. Dependent Quality Model Extended QoS Model (EX_QoS). For service s, EX_QoS model of s in CS can be defined as 3-vector: EX_QoS(s)=<$q^{(te)}(s)$, $q^{(p)}(s)$, $DQ(s)$>, where $q^{(te)}(s)$ is the request deposing time, $q^{(p)}(s)$ is the cost for invoking the service, and $DQ(s)$ is the dependent QoS of s. Since that the physical meaning of $q^{(t)}(s)=q^{(te)}(s)+q^{(ti)}(s, s')+q^{(ti)}(s'', s)$ is the duration time from invoking s to receiving the result, $q^{(t)}(s)$ can be used to evaluate the duration time of s. Thus, the EX_QoS of s can also be defined as: EX_QoS(s)=<$q^{(t)}(s)$, $q^{(p)}(s)$>. For composite service CS, EX_QoS model of CS can be defined as a 2-vector: EX_QoS(s)=<$q^{(t)}(CS)$, $q^{(p)}(CS)$>, where $q^{(p)}(CS)$ is the sum of cost for invoking all services in CS and $q^{(t)}(CS)=q^{(ti)}(CS)+\sum_{s_i} q^{(te)}(s_i)$ is duration time of execution of CS.

3.3 Problem Description

In order to determine whether a service is occurred by a failure, EX_QoS feedback information which is returned by the monitor of service and composite service will be used. EX_QoS feedback information reflects the quality of services in the composite service at some time t, which can be defined as: QoS_FB=<CS, t, QoS_S, ReferQoS_S>, where QoS_S={$qs(s_1),..., qs(s_n)$}, $qs(s_i)$ is the EX_QoS of service s_i and s_i is the unexecuted service in CS; ReferQoS_S ={$rqs(s_1),..., rqs(s_n)$}, $rqs(s_i)$= $q^{(ti)}(s_i, s)$ is the refereed QoS of s_i which can be used to determine the whether the bad QoS of data transmission time is caused by service s_i and s is the QoS detecting service which will not be failed.

Definition 10. Reliable Degree. s is one of the service in composite service CS. The refereed QoS of s before some time t is $rqs(s)$, and at t, the refereed QoS of s is $rqs'(s)$. The reliable degree of s reflects the degree of quality of s to be bad, signified as $CD(s)$.

$$CD(s) = \begin{cases} \frac{rqs'(s)}{rqs(s)}, & if\ rqs'(s) < rqs(s) \\ 1, else \end{cases} \qquad (1)$$

In order to determine whether a service is failed according to the EX_QoS feedback information, we will give the following definition of failure service.

Definition 11. Failure Service. For composite process CP, there exist a plan p of it and $CS=f_p(CP)$. There exists an activity node n_a in CP, and $s_a=g(n_a)$. At some time t, the EX_QoS feedback information of s_a (s_a will implement the activity node n_a in CS) in CS before t is <$q_1^{(te)}(s_a)$, $q_1^{(p)}(s_a)$, $q_{11}^{(ti)}(s_{a-1}, s_a)$, $q_{12}^{(ti)}(s_a, s_{a+1})$> and the EX_QoS feedback information of s_a in CS after t is <$q_1^{(te)}(s_a)$, $q_1^{(p)}(s_a)$, $q_{11}^{(ti)}(s_{a-1}, s_a)$, $q_{12}^{(ti)}(s_a, s_{a+1})$>. If one of the following conditions is true, we call service s_a the disabled service under n_a in CS, or n_a is the failure activity node affected by s_a. (in the following, <$\delta_{n_a}^{(te)}$, $\delta_{n_a}^{(p)}$, $\delta_{n_a}^{(ti)}$> is the vector of failure threshold and ς is the threshold of reliable degree)

- $\frac{q_2^{(te)}(s_a) - q_1^{(te)}(s_a)}{q_1^{(te)}(s_a)} \geq \delta_{n_a}^{(u)}$ or $\frac{q_2^{(p)}(s_a) - q_1^{(p)}(s_a)}{q_1^{(p)}(s_a)} \geq \delta_{n_a}^{(p)}$;
- $(R_{ti}(n_a, n_{a+1}, s_a, s_{a+1}) \Rightarrow \frac{q_{22}^{(ti)}(s_a, s_{a+1}) - q_{12}^{(ti)}(s_a, s_{a+1})}{q_{12}^{(ti)}(s_a, s_{a+1})} \geq \delta_{n_{a+1}}^{(u)})$ ∧ $(R_{ti}(n_{a-1}, n_a, s_{a-1}, s_a) \Rightarrow \frac{q_{21}^{(ti)}(s_{a-1}, s_a) - q_{11}^{(ti)}(s_{a-1}, s_a)}{q_{11}^{(ti)}(s_{a-1}, s_a)} \geq \delta_{n_a}^{(u)})$ ∧ the reliable degree of $s_a < \varsigma$.

Definition 12. EX_QoS Driven Replacement Composite Service Finding Problem. For part composite service *PCS* affected by disabled service, EX_QoS driven replacement composite service finding problem is to select another composite service for composite process $CP = f^{-1}{}_p(PCS)$, which can satisfy user's constraint with the optimal synthesized quality F.

$$\max_{\forall i}\{F(f_{p_i}(CP))\} \quad s.t. \quad q^{(t)}(f_{p_i}(CP)) \leq cons^{(t)} \quad (2)$$

Where, $F(x)$ is the synthesized quality of x which can be calculated as (3).

$$F(x) = w^{(p)} * V(q^{(p)}(x)) + w^{(t)} * V(q^{(t)}(x)), \quad (3)$$
$$V(q^{(z)}(x)) = \frac{q_{max}^{(z)} - q^{(z)}(x)}{q_{max}^{(z)} - q_{min}^{(z)}}, (z \in \{p,t\})$$

Such problem can be modeled as a multiple choice knapsack problem [8] which has been proved as a NP hard problem and solving this problem needs high time complexity.

4 EX_QoS Driven Adaptive Algorithm

In the proposed framework, we use the EX_QoS feedback information to determine whether a failure is occurred. If so, the backing up process will be triggered in order to finding the replacement composite service when the failure is happened and before the invoking time. Based on Definition 11, Algorithm 1 gives the algorithm for determining whether the backing up process will be triggered.

Algorithm 1. Determining the triggering time of backing up

DisabledN Backup_Identification(*CS, QoS_FB, Thold*)//*Thold*[n_i] is the set of failure thresholds; *DisabledN*[] is the nodes set affected by disabled services.
1 **Begin**
2 **for** each $n_i \in f_p^{-1}(CS)$ and n_i is not executed **do**
3 **begin**
4   $s_i = g(n_i)$; //<s_i, n_i> is an assign
5   **if** n_i is the failure activity node affected by s_i **then** //determine based on Definition 11
6   **if** $\exists s_u \in$ old replacement composite service of n_i and n_v is the failure activity node affected by s_u **then**
7   *DisabledN*[*l*++].s=s_i; *DisabledN*[*l*++].N=n_i;// n_i is failed node affected by s_i.
8 **end**
9 **return** *DisabledN*;
10 **End**

This paper proposes a heuristic algorithm (Algorithm 2). The basic idea of the algorithm is: firstly, for each activity node, keep invariable number of part plans in order to control the time complexity; then, based on the heuristic function to select the part plans which is most possible to be the optimized replacement composite service; finally, if the heuristic process cannot find the replacement composite service which satisfy user's constraint, a process of neighbor searching will be done in order to find the needed composite service through adjustment.

Definition 13. *i* level Plan. For the composite process CP, p_i is the part plan, if for each $n_u \in CP.Nset$ ($u \in [1, i]$), $\exists A=(n_u, s_u) \in p_i$, we call that p_i is the *i* level plan of CP.

Definition 14. QoS Govern. p_i^1 and p_i^2 are the *i* level plans of CP. If $q^{(z)}(p_i^1) > q^{(z)}(p_i^2)$, we call under factor z, p_i^1 governs p_i^2.

Definition 15. Ideal Plan and Nonideal Plan. p_i^* and $\overline{p_i^*}$ are two virtual *i* level plans of composite process CP. If for each $p_i^u \in i$ level plans of CP, and under each factor z, p_i^* governs p_i^u, we call p_i^* is the ideal plan. If for each $p_i^u \in i$ level plans of CP, and under each factor z, p_i^u governs $\overline{p_i^*}$, we call $\overline{p_i^*}$ is the nonideal plan. (Since that in the reality, the ideal and nonideal plans are not existed, such two plans are virtual plans). The EX_QoS of p_i^* and $\overline{p_i^*}$ can be calculated as $EX\_QoS(p_i^*) = (\min q^{(p)}(P), \min q^{(t)}(P)); EX\_QoS(\overline{p_i^*}) = (\max q^{(p)}(P), \max q^{(t)}(P))$. Since that p_i^* and $\overline{p_i^*}$ defines the quality range of all plans, they can be used as the referenced point to evaluate certain level plan. For the *i* level plan p, $h(p)$ is used to give score to p.

$$h(P) = \frac{\sqrt{(q^{(p)}(\overline{P_i^*}) - q^{(p)}(P))^2 + (q^{(t)}(\overline{P_i^*}) - q^{(t)}(P))^2 + (F(\overline{P_i^*}) - F(P))^2}}{\sqrt{(q^{(p)}(\overline{P_i^*}) - q^{(p)}(P_i^*))^2 + (q^{(t)}(\overline{P_i^*}) - q^{(t)}(P_i^*))^2 + (F(\overline{P_i^*}) - F(P_i^*))^2}} \quad (4)$$

Where $0 \leq h(p) \leq 1$, and the bigger is $h(p)$, the more closer is p to the optimal plan. This paper uses $h(p)$ as the heuristic function. During the finding process, keep the plans with bigger $h(p)$ and remove the plan with smaller $h(p)$. For that $h(p)$ evaluates the plan based on the local comparison, the heuristic process will be failed as a result of no satisfied composite service being found. For such problem, this paper uses the neighbor searching algorithm to adjust the composite service, the basic idea of which is to modify some assignments of the composite service.

Definition 16. *n*-Neighbor of Composite Service. For composite service CS, the set of composite services which have *n* different assignments as CS is called *n*-neighbor of CS.

Algorithm 2. Finding Replacement composite service

PCS Find_HEU(*PCP*, *cons*, *W*)//*PCP* is the composite process acquired through Algorithm 2.
1 **begin**
2 **for** *i*<GetLength(*PCP.Nset*) **do**
3 **begin**
4 **for** each $s_{ij} \in f_I(n_i).ServiceSet$ **do**

5 **begin**
6 **For** each $P_{i-1}^u \in P_{i-1}$ **do**
7 **begin**
8 put (n_i, s_{ij}) into P_{i-1}^u in order to form P_i^u;
9 compute QoS of P_i^u;
10 **end**
11 Get P_i^* and $\overline{P_i^*}$;
12 **for** each $P_i^u \in P_i$ **do**
13 calculate $h(P_i^u)$;
14 keep top k in P_i;
15 **end** 16 **end**
17 **if** $\exists P_i^u \in P_i$ and $P_i^u.q^{(t)} \leq cons^{(t)}$ **then**
18 **return** P_i^u;
19 **else**
20 **begin**
21 select $P_i^u \in P_i$ with maximum of QoS;
22 **return** NeighborSearch($CP, P_i^u, cons, w$);
23 **end** 24 **end**

OptimizedCS NeighborSearch($PCP, P_i^u, cons, w$)
1 **begin**
2 $n=1$;
3 **while** n<GetLength($PCP.Nset$) **do**
4 **begin**
5 construct N_{CS}^n;
6 **if** $\exists CS_i \in N_{CS}^n$ and $CS_i.q^{(t)} \leq cons^{(t)}$ **then**
7 **return** CS_i;
8 **end**
9 **return** null;
10 **end**

5 Experimentations

Experimentation 1 is used to test the performance of the replacement composite service finding heuristic algorithm. Randomly generate 200 scenarios and in each scenario, the number of activity nodes is 100, the number of services for each activity node is 50. The number k of part plans kept for each level may be 5, 10, 20, 40 or 80. Compare the hit count (hc=the number of finding the satisfied composite service during the heuristic process), distance (d=(F(the satisfied composite service found in the heuristic process)-F(the optimal composite service))/F(the optimal composite service)), missing count (mc=the number of doing not find the satisfied composite service during the heuristic process), 1-neighbor success count (1nsc-the number of find the satisfied composite service during the 1-neigbhor searching process). Table 1 gives this comparison result. Randomly generate 200 scenarios, in each of which the number of activity nodes may be 5, 10, 20 and 40 respectively, the number of services for each node is 10 and k is 20. Fig 5(a) shows the comparison of runtime. Randomly generate 200 scenarios, in each of which the number of activity nodes is 20, the number of services for each node may be 10, 20, 50 or 100 and k is 20. Fig 5(b) shows the comparison of runtime.

Table 1. Relation between the number of part plans kept in each level and effectiveness

k	HC	D	MC	1nsc
5	85	1.41%	81	40
10	104	0.87%	70	29
20	128	0.46%	43	21
40	143	0.34%	46	8
80	167	0.21%	27	5

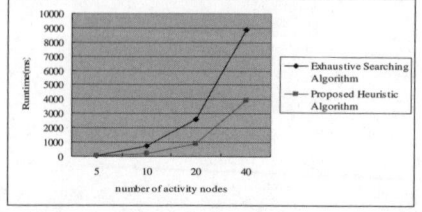
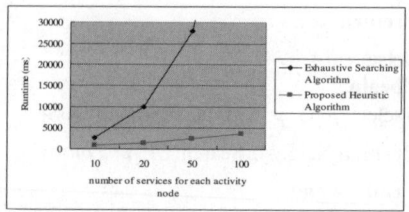

(a) Relation between runtime and num-ber of activity nodes

(b) Relation between runtime and num-ber of services for each activity node

Fig. 5. Runtime comparison between exhaustive searching algorithm and heuristic algorithm

Table 1 shows that with k growing larger, the algorithm will be more effective with the hit count bigger and the distance lower. Thus, if k is appropriate, the algorithm will be efficient. From Fig 5, the runtime of the proposed algorithm is less than the one of the exhaustive searching algorithm.

Experimentation 3 is to test the interrupting time caused by the online backing up approach, traditional pre-backing up approach and our approach. Randomly generate 10 scenarios, compare the interrupting time of these three approaches, the result of which is shown in Fig 6.

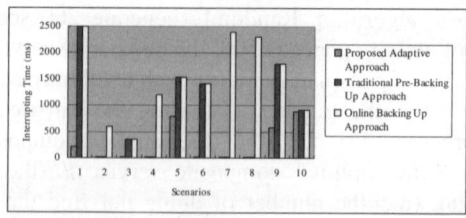

Fig. 6. Comparison of Interrupting Time Caused by Backing up process of three approaches

Fig 6 shows that the interrupting time of the proposed approach is always the least one among the three approaches. Because the proposed approach is a complementary of the traditional pre-backing up approach, which can find the replacement composite service before the invoking time of the failure service and thus, improve the availability of the replacement composite service.

Experimentation 4 is to test the effectiveness of the proposed EX_QoS model in supporting finding replacement composite service to achieve end-to-end constraint in decentralized service composition. We use satisfied degree of execution duration to evaluate the effectiveness of the proposed EX_QoS. The satisfied degree of execution duration is the degree of how the execution duration of found replacement composite service satisfies the user's constraint. Equation (6) gives how to compute the satisfied degree of execution duration. Give 200 scenarios where the average amount of data transmission between activity nodes in the composite service can be 0, 10, 50, 100 or 200 bit. Compare the satisfied degree of execution duration of the composite services backed up according to the QoS model proposed by [1] and the EX_QoS model proposed in this paper. Fig. 7 shows the experimentation result.

$$SD(CS, cons^{(t)}) = \begin{cases} \dfrac{q^{(t)}(CS)}{cons^{(t)}}, & q^{(t)}(CS) < cons^{(t)} \\ 1, else \end{cases} \tag{5}$$

Where, $q^{(t)}(CS)$ will be calculated as Definition 9 and $cons^{(t)}$ is the execution duration of the user constraint.

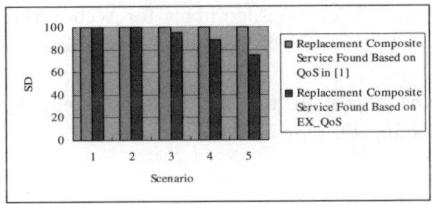

Fig. 7. Relation between the SD and the average amount of data transmission

From Fig 7, as EX_QoS considers the invoking time dependent relation between services, the execution duration can always meet the needs of users and thus, the SD of the composite service backed up based on EX_QoS is higher than the one based on the QoS in [1].

6 Conclusions

In this paper, based on the proposed EX_QoS model, we present a framework for adaptive service composition and the corresponding adaptive algorithms. The experimentations show that proposed approach can improve the availability of the replacement composite service, minimize the interrupting time caused by finding the replacement one and be effectiveness in decentralized service composition. In this paper, we only consider one of the QoS dependent relations—invoking time dependent relation. In the future, we will better our QoS dependent model. And in this paper where we only solve the problem of finding replacement composite service for pipe-line composite service, in the future, we will study on how to find replacement composite service for complex composite service. This work is supported by the National Natural Science Foundation of China under Grant No.60773218

References

1. Zeng, L.Z., Benatallah, B.: QoS-Aware Middleware for Web Services Composition. IEEE Transactions on Software Engineering 30(5), 311–327 (2004)
2. Yu, T., Lin, K.J.: Adaptive algorithms for Finding Replacement Services in Autonomic Distributed Business Processes. In: The 7th International Symposium on Autonomous Decentralized Systems, Chengdu, China, pp. 427–434 (2005)
3. Girish, C., Koustuv, D., Arun, K., Sumit, M., Biplav, S.: Adaptation in Web Service Composition and Execution. In: IEEE International Conference on Web Services, USA, pp. 549–557 (2006)
4. Casati, F., Ilnicki, S., Jin, L.J.: Adaptive and Dynamic Service Composition in eFlow. In: Wangler, B., Bergman, L.D. (eds.) CAiSE 2000. LNCS, vol. 1789, pp. 13–31. Springer, Heidelberg (2000)
5. Benatallah, B., Sheng, Q.Z., Dumas, M.: The Self-Serv Environment for Web Services Composition. IEEE Internet Computing 7(1), 40–48 (2003)
6. Zeng, L.Z., Benatallah, B., Marlon, D.: Quality Driven Web Services Composition. In: International conference on World Wide Web, Budapest, Hungary, pp. 411–421 (2003)
7. Yu, T., Lin, K.J.: Service Selection Algorithms for Web Services with End-to-end QoS Constraints. Journal of Information Systems and e-Business Management 3(2), 103–126 (2005)
8. Dyer, M.E.: An O(n) algorithm for the multiple-choice knapsack linear program. Mathematical programming 29, 57–63 (1984)

Author Index

Ali, Farha   447
Allam, Vineel   4
Allenotor, David   128

Bandara, Ayomi   434

Cai, Zhinuan   287
Cao, Haijun   48
Cao, Jinli   492
Cao, Ming   373
Challa, Santan   232
Chan, Yu-Wei   296
Chen, Shih-Chang   29
Chen, Sung-Yi   199
Chen, Tai-Lung   166
Chen, Xiaowu   459
Chen, Xinmeng   373
Chi, Chi-Hung   352
Chua, Choon-Keng   352
Chung, Yeh-Ching   116, 296
Cui, Jianqun   178

Dai, Guanzhong   140
Dai, Yu   504

Feng, Dan   266
Figueiredo, Renato   187
Frey, Jaime   187

Gibbins, Nicholas   434
Goasguen, Sebastien   187
Guan, Tao   422
Gupta, Bidyut   4

He, Yanxiang   178
Ho, Li-Yung   38
Hsu, Ching-Hsien   29, 166
Hu, Dong-min   364
Huang, Kuo-Chan   116
Huang, Qiaoli   319
Huang, Zhixing   319
Hwang, Kai   1
Hwang, San-Yih   59

Jenness, Jeff   244
Ji, Xiangyu   459

Jiang, Bo   256
Jiang, Hai   244
Jiang, Yunhan   256
Jin, Hai   48, 93, 471
Jupally, Vamshi   4

Kaashoek, M. Frans   2
Kang, Jeong Seok   409
Ke, Zuo   364
Kim, Seong Hoon   409
King, Chung-Ta   396
Kou, Yue   331

Lai, Chih-Han   296
Lai, Nai-Luen   396
Le, Nhut   492
Lewis, Tim   434
Li, Keqiu   71
Li, Kuan-Ching   166
Li, Minglu   104
Li, Ruipeng   244
Li, Wenwei   222
Li, Zhitang   308
Lin, Chun-Han   396
Lin, Hong-Yang   59
Lin, Huaiqing   308
Lin, Xiaola   287
Liu, Fangai   83
Liu, Pangfeng   38
Liu, Zhaobin   256
Lu, Chuiwei   308
Lu, Liangjin   343
Lu, Song   211
Lu, Xinda   104
Luo, Fei   471

Madhavan, Krishna   187
Minh, Trieu   492

Nie, Tiezheng   331
Ning, Xiaomin   471

Park, Hong Seong   409
Payne, Terry   434
Peng, Min   384
Pu, Guolin   483

Qi, Li   93
Qiu, Yuhui   483
Qu, Wenyu   71

Rahimi, Shahram   4
Ren, Shuai   140
Ren, Xueping   343
Roure, David De   422, 434
Roy, Alain   187
Ruth, Paul   187

Shao, Yichuan   331
Shen, Derong   331
Shi, Xuanhua   93
Shih, Po-Chi   116
Song, Fenglong   83
Song, Weihong   352
Srimani, Pradip K.   447
Su, Hung-Chi   244

Tang, Jian   59
Tao, Yongcai   48
Thulasiram, Ruppa K.   128
Thulasiraman, Parimala   232
Tsai, Bing-Ru   166

Varki, Elizabeth   152
Villa, Adam H.   152

Wan, Jian   343
Wang, Chien-Min   38
Wang, Chun-Ching   29
Wang, Fang   266
Wang, Gang   483
Wang, Huai-min   364
Wang, James Z.   447
Wang, Min   275
Wang, Simeng   178
Wang, Wen-Hann   3

Wang, Zhenhua   331
Wang, Zhikun   266
Weng, Chuliang   104
Wolinsky, David   187
Wu, Hao   471
Wu, Jan-Jan   38
Wu, Libing   178
Wu, Quan-yuan   364
Wu, Song   48

Xie, Gang   384
Xiong, Naixue   178, 373, 384
Xu, Dongyan   187
Xu, Lu   275
Xu, Wei   275
Xu, Xianghua   343

Yang, Chao-Tung   29, 199
Yang, Jinmin   222
Yang, Laurence T.   178, 373, 384
Yang, Lei   504
Yang, XiaoDong   211
Yao, Lei   140
Yin, Shiqun   319
Yu, Ge   331
Yu, Kun-Ming   18

Zaluska, Ed   422
Zeng, Bin   222
Zhang, Bin   244, 504
Zhang, Dafang   222
Zhang, Huixiang   140
Zhang, Yejiang   308
Zhang, Yong   71
Zhao, Qinping   459
Zhao, Zixiang   256
Zhou, Jiayi   18
Zhou, Ke   266
Zhu, Wei   93

Lecture Notes in Computer Science

Sublibrary 1: Theoretical Computer Science and General Issues

For information about Vols. 1– 4688
please contact your bookseller or Springer

Vol. 5036: S. Wu, L.T. Yang, T.L. Xu (Eds.), Advances in Grid and Pervasive Computing. XV, 518 pages. 2008.

Vol. 5018: M. Grohe, R. Niedermeier (Eds.), Parameterized and Exact Computation. X, 227 pages. 2008.

Vol. 5011: A.J. van der Poorten, A. Stein (Eds.), Algorithmic Number Theory. IX, 455 pages. 2008.

Vol. 5010: E.A. Hirsch, A.A. Razborov, A. Semenov, A. Slissenko (Eds.), Computer Science – Theory and Applications. XIII, 411 pages. 2008.

Vol. 5008: A. Gasteratos, M. Vincze, J.K. Tsotsos (Eds.), Computer Vision Systems. XV, 560 pages. 2008.

Vol. 5004: R. Eigenmann, B.R. de Supinski (Eds.), OpenMP in a New Era of Parallelism. X, 191 pages. 2008.

Vol. 4996: H. Kleine Büning, X. Zhao (Eds.), Theory and Applications of Satisfiability Testing – SAT 2008. X, 305 pages. 2008.

Vol. 4988: R. Berghammer, B. Möller, G. Struth (Eds.), Relations and Kleene Algebra in Computer Science. X, 397 pages. 2008.

Vol. 4981: M. Egerstedt, B. Mishra (Eds.), Hybrid Systems: Computation and Control. XV, 680 pages. 2008.

Vol. 4978: M. Agrawal, D. Du, Z. Duan, A. Li (Eds.), Theory and Applications of Models of Computation. XII, 598 pages. 2008.

Vol. 4975: F. Chen, B. Jüttler (Eds.), Advances in Geometric Modeling and Processing. XV, 606 pages. 2008.

Vol. 4974: M. Giacobini, A. Brabazon, S. Cagnoni, G.A. Di Caro, R. Drechsler, A. Ekárt, A.I. Esparcia-Alcázar, M. Farooq, A. Fink, J. McCormack, M. O'Neill, J. Romero, F. Rothlauf, G. Squillero, A.Ş. Uyar, S. Yang (Eds.), Applications of Evolutionary Computing. XXV, 701 pages. 2008.

Vol. 4973: E. Marchiori, J.H. Moore (Eds.), Evolutionary Computation, Machine Learning and Data Mining in Bioinformatics. X, 213 pages. 2008.

Vol. 4972: J. van Hemert, C. Cotta (Eds.), Evolutionary Computation in Combinatorial Optimization. XII, 289 pages. 2008.

Vol. 4971: M. O'Neill, L. Vanneschi, S. Gustafson, A.I. Esparcia Alcázar, I. De Falco, A. Della Cioppa, E. Tarantino (Eds.), Genetic Programming. XI, 375 pages. 2008.

Vol. 4963: C.R. Ramakrishnan, J. Rehof (Eds.), Tools and Algorithms for the Construction and Analysis of Systems. XVI, 518 pages. 2008.

Vol. 4962: R. Amadio (Ed.), Foundations of Software Science and Computational Structures. XV, 505 pages. 2008.

Vol. 4961: J.L. Fiadeiro, P. Inverardi (Eds.), Fundamental Approaches to Software Engineering. XIII, 430 pages. 2008.

Vol. 4960: S. Drossopoulou (Ed.), Programming Languages and Systems. XIII, 399 pages. 2008.

Vol. 4959: L. Hendren (Ed.), Compiler Construction. XII, 307 pages. 2008.

Vol. 4957: E.S. Laber, C. Bornstein, L.T. Nogueira, L. Faria (Eds.), LATIN 2008: Theoretical Informatics. XVII, 794 pages. 2008.

Vol. 4943: R. Woods, K. Compton, C. Bouganis, P.C. Diniz (Eds.), Reconfigurable Computing: Architectures, Tools and Applications. XIV, 344 pages. 2008.

Vol. 4942: E. Frachtenberg, U. Schwiegelshohn (Eds.), Job Scheduling Strategies for Parallel Processing. VII, 189 pages. 2008.

Vol. 4941: M. Miculan, I. Scagnetto, F. Honsell (Eds.), Types for Proofs and Programs. VII, 203 pages. 2008.

Vol. 4934: U. Brinkschulte, T. Ungerer, C. Hochberger, R.G. Spallek (Eds.), Architecture of Computing Systems – ARCS 2008. XI, 287 pages. 2008.

Vol. 4927: C. Kaklamanis, M. Skutella (Eds.), Approximation and Online Algorithms. X, 289 pages. 2008.

Vol. 4926: N. Monmarché, E.-G. Talbi, P. Collet, M. Schoenauer, E. Lutton (Eds.), Artificial Evolution. XIII, 327 pages. 2008.

Vol. 4921: S.-i. Nakano, M.. S. Rahman (Eds.), WALCOM: Algorithms and Computation. XII, 241 pages. 2008.

Vol. 4919: A. Gelbukh (Ed.), Computational Linguistics and Intelligent Text Processing. XVIII, 666 pages. 2008.

Vol. 4917: P. Stenström, M. Dubois, M. Katevenis, R. Gupta, T. Ungerer (Eds.), High Performance Embedded Architectures and Compilers. XIII, 400 pages. 2008.

Vol. 4915: A. King (Ed.), Logic-Based Program Synthesis and Transformation. X, 219 pages. 2008.

Vol. 4912: G. Barthe, C. Fournet (Eds.), Trustworthy Global Computing. XI, 401 pages. 2008.

Vol. 4910: V. Geffert, J. Karhumäki, A. Bertoni, B. Preneel, P. Návrat, M. Bieliková (Eds.), SOFSEM 2008: Theory and Practice of Computer Science. XV, 792 pages. 2008.

Vol. 4905: F. Logozzo, D.A. Peled, L.D. Zuck (Eds.), Verification, Model Checking, and Abstract Interpretation. X, 325 pages. 2008.

Vol. 4904: S. Rao, M. Chatterjee, P. Jayanti, C.S.R. Murthy, S.K. Saha (Eds.), Distributed Computing and Networking. XVIII, 588 pages. 2007.

Vol. 4878: E. Tovar, P. Tsigas, H. Fouchal (Eds.), Principles of Distributed Systems. XIII, 457 pages. 2007.

Vol. 4875: S.-H. Hong, T. Nishizeki, W. Quan (Eds.), Graph Drawing. XIII, 402 pages. 2008.

Vol. 4873: S. Aluru, M. Parashar, R. Badrinath, V.K. Prasanna (Eds.), High Performance Computing – HiPC 2007. XXIV, 663 pages. 2007.

Vol. 4863: A. Bonato, F.R.K. Chung (Eds.), Algorithms and Models for the Web-Graph. X, 217 pages. 2007.

Vol. 4860: G. Eleftherakis, P. Kefalas, G. Păun, G. Rozenberg, A. Salomaa (Eds.), Membrane Computing. IX, 453 pages. 2007.

Vol. 4855: V. Arvind, S. Prasad (Eds.), FSTTCS 2007: Foundations of Software Technology and Theoretical Computer Science. XIV, 558 pages. 2007.

Vol. 4854: L. Bougé, M. Forsell, J.L. Träff, A. Streit, W. Ziegler, M. Alexander, S. Childs (Eds.), Euro-Par 2007 Workshops: Parallel Processing. XVII, 236 pages. 2008.

Vol. 4851: S. Boztaş, H.-F.(F.) Lu (Eds.), Applied Algebra, Algebraic Algorithms and Error-Correcting Codes. XII, 368 pages. 2007.

Vol. 4848: M.H. Garzon, H. Yan (Eds.), DNA Computing. XI, 292 pages. 2008.

Vol. 4847: M. Xu, Y. Zhan, J. Cao, Y. Liu (Eds.), Advanced Parallel Processing Technologies. XIX, 767 pages. 2007.

Vol. 4846: I. Cervesato (Ed.), Advances in Computer Science – ASIAN 2007. XI, 313 pages. 2007.

Vol. 4838: T. Masuzawa, S. Tixeuil (Eds.), Stabilization, Safety, and Security of Distributed Systems. XIII, 409 pages. 2007.

Vol. 4835: T. Tokuyama (Ed.), Algorithms and Computation. XVII, 929 pages. 2007.

Vol. 4818: I. Lirkov, S. Margenov, J. Waśniewski (Eds.), Large-Scale Scientific Computing. XIV, 755 pages. 2008.

Vol. 4800: A. Avron, N. Dershowitz, A. Rabinovich (Eds.), Pillars of Computer Science. XXI, 683 pages. 2008.

Vol. 4783: J. Holub, J. Žďárek (Eds.), Implementation and Application of Automata. XIII, 324 pages. 2007.

Vol. 4782: R. Perrott, B.M. Chapman, J. Subhlok, R.F. de Mello, L.T. Yang (Eds.), High Performance Computing and Communications. XIX, 823 pages. 2007.

Vol. 4771: T. Bartz-Beielstein, M.J. Blesa Aguilera, C. Blum, B. Naujoks, A. Roli, G. Rudolph, M. Sampels (Eds.), Hybrid Metaheuristics. X, 202 pages. 2007.

Vol. 4770: V.G. Ganzha, E.W. Mayr, E.V. Vorozhtsov (Eds.), Computer Algebra in Scientific Computing. XIII, 460 pages. 2007.

Vol. 4769: A. Brandstädt, D. Kratsch, H. Müller (Eds.), Graph-Theoretic Concepts in Computer Science. XIII, 341 pages. 2007.

Vol. 4763: J.-F. Raskin, P.S. Thiagarajan (Eds.), Formal Modeling and Analysis of Timed Systems. X, 369 pages. 2007.

Vol. 4759: J. Labarta, K. Joe, T. Sato (Eds.), High-Performance Computing. XV, 524 pages. 2008.

Vol. 4746: A. Bondavalli, F. Brasileiro, S. Rajsbaum (Eds.), Dependable Computing. XV, 239 pages. 2007.

Vol. 4743: P. Thulasiraman, X. He, T.L. Xu, M.K. Denko, R.K. Thulasiram, L.T. Yang (Eds.), Frontiers of High Performance Computing and Networking ISPA 2007 Workshops. XXIX, 536 pages. 2007.

Vol. 4742: I. Stojmenovic, R.K. Thulasiram, L.T. Yang, W. Jia, M. Guo, R.F. de Mello (Eds.), Parallel and Distributed Processing and Applications. XX, 995 pages. 2007.

Vol. 4739: R. Moreno Díaz, F. Pichler, A. Quesada Arencibia (Eds.), Computer Aided Systems Theory – EUROCAST 2007. XIX, 1233 pages. 2007.

Vol. 4736: S. Winter, M. Duckham, L. Kulik, B. Kuipers (Eds.), Spatial Information Theory. XV, 455 pages. 2007.

Vol. 4732: K. Schneider, J. Brandt (Eds.), Theorem Proving in Higher Order Logics. IX, 401 pages. 2007.

Vol. 4731: A. Pelc (Ed.), Distributed Computing. XVI, 510 pages. 2007.

Vol. 4728: S. Bozapalidis, G. Rahonis (Eds.), Algebraic Informatics. VIII, 291 pages. 2007.

Vol. 4726: N. Ziviani, R. Baeza-Yates (Eds.), String Processing and Information Retrieval. XII, 311 pages. 2007.

Vol. 4719: R. Backhouse, J. Gibbons, R. Hinze, J. Jeuring (Eds.), Datatype-Generic Programming. XI, 369 pages. 2007.

Vol. 4711: C.B. Jones, Z. Liu, J. Woodcock (Eds.), Theoretical Aspects of Computing – ICTAC 2007. XI, 483 pages. 2007.

Vol. 4710: C.W. George, Z. Liu, J. Woodcock (Eds.), Domain Modeling and the Duration Calculus. XI, 237 pages. 2007.

Vol. 4708: L. Kučera, A. Kučera (Eds.), Mathematical Foundations of Computer Science 2007. XVIII, 764 pages. 2007.

Vol. 4707: O. Gervasi, M.L. Gavrilova (Eds.), Computational Science and Its Applications – ICCSA 2007, Part III. XXIV, 1205 pages. 2007.

Vol. 4706: O. Gervasi, M.L. Gavrilova (Eds.), Computational Science and Its Applications – ICCSA 2007, Part II. XXIII, 1129 pages. 2007.

Vol. 4705: O. Gervasi, M.L. Gavrilova (Eds.), Computational Science and Its Applications – ICCSA 2007, Part I. XLIV, 1169 pages. 2007.

Vol. 4703: L. Caires, V.T. Vasconcelos (Eds.), CONCUR 2007 – Concurrency Theory. XIII, 507 pages. 2007.

Vol. 4700: C.B. Jones, Z. Liu, J. Woodcock (Eds.), Formal Methods and Hybrid Real-Time Systems. XVI, 539 pages. 2007.

Vol. 4699: B. Kågström, E. Elmroth, J. Dongarra, J. Waśniewski (Eds.), Applied Parallel Computing. XXIX, 1192 pages. 2007.

Vol. 4698: L. Arge, M. Hoffmann, E. Welzl (Eds.), Algorithms – ESA 2007. XV, 769 pages. 2007.

Vol. 4697: L. Choi, Y. Paek, S. Cho (Eds.), Advances in Computer Systems Architecture. XIII, 400 pages. 2007.